Kant and Eighteenth-Century German Philosophy

Kant and Eighteenth-Century German Philosophy

Contexts, Influences and Controversies

Edited by
Andree Hahmann and Stefan Klingner

DE GRUYTER

ISBN 978-3-11-221421-3
e-ISBN (PDF) 978-3-11-079385-7
e-ISBN (EPUB) 978-3-11-079420-5

Library of Congress Control Number: 2023939274

Bibliographic information published by the Deutsche Nationalbibliothek
The Deutsche Nationalbibliothek lists this publication in the Deutsche Nationalbibliografie;
detailed bibliographic data are available on the internet at http://dnb.dnb.de.

© 2025 Walter de Gruyter GmbH, Berlin/Boston
This volume is text- and page-identical with the hardback published in 2023.
Cover image: StockSanta / iStock / Getty Images Plus
Printing and binding: CPI books GmbH, Leck

www.degruyter.com

Table of Contents

Andree Hahmann, Stefan Klingner
Kant in the Context of Eighteenth-Century German Philosophy: Some Preliminary Reflections —— 1

Part I: Contexts

Patricia Kitcher
Analyzing Apperception [*Gewahrnehmen*] —— 13

Udo Thiel
Between Empirical Psychology and Transcendental Philosophy: Ernst Platner on the Feeling of Self —— 47

Andree Hahmann
The Debate on the Fundamental Powers of the Soul: Crusius, Platner, Kant, and Schmid —— 69

Stefan Klingner
C. C. E. Schmid on Kant's Distinction Between Sensibility and Understanding —— 97

Achim Vesper
Between Hume and Kant: The Foundation of Morality in Feder's *Inquiries on the Human Will* —— 119

Part II: Influences

Tinca Prunea-Bretonnet
Crusius and Kant on Distinctness, Certainty, and Method in Philosophy —— 145

Marion Heinz
Johann Georg Sulzer and the Beginnings of Kant's Doctrine of Three Faculties —— 165

Paolo Pecere
Lambert, Kant and Solidity: A Matter of Method —— 185

Heiner F. Klemme
Johann Georg Sulzer's "Mixed Doctrine of Morals": A Contribution to the History of the Development of Kant's Ethics Between 1770 and 1785 —— 203

Gabriel Rivero
Dependence and Obedience: Crusius' Concept of Obligation and its Influence on Kant's Moral Philosophy —— 217

Part III: Controversies

Stefanie Buchenau
Human Dignity: The Garve-Kant Controversy —— 237

Dieter Hüning
"These Objections are Therefore Nothing but Misunderstandings": Kant's Critique of Garve in His Essay *On the Common Saying* —— 261

Gideon Stiening
The "Entire Human Being" Rather Than "Pure Reason": Feder's *Philosophische Bibliothek* **and His Review of the** *Kritik der praktischen Vernunft* —— 279

Rudolf Meer
"On this Occasion, I cannot but […] speak a few words with Mr. Kant": On the Meiners-Kant Controversy 1786 —— 305

Andreas Brandt
Meiners's Critique of Kant —— 321

Abbreviations of Kant's Works —— 345

Bibliography —— 347

Index of Names —— 371

Sources —— 375

Andree Hahmann, Stefan Klingner
Kant in the Context of Eighteenth-Century German Philosophy: Some Preliminary Reflections

1 Kant in Context?

It is almost commonplace for historians of philosophy to claim that the publication of the *Critique of Pure Reason* marks the beginning of a new philosophy that stands out decisively from the "dogmatic" approaches of its predecessors. Thus, to this day, it is natural to understand the mature systematics of Kant's critical philosophy as the product of particularly thorough thinking uninfluenced by other ideas, and furthermore as the act of a truly philosophical genius. This understanding goes back to Kant's contemporaries and immediate successors (e. g., Bouterwek 1805, 11–68; Schopenhauer 1819, 593–596) and was extended by Neo-Kantianism (e. g., Cohen 1871, VI–II; Vaihinger 1881, 3–11) and the historiography of "German" philosophy (e. g., Wundt 1945, 329, 339) to the great Kant commentaries of the twentieth century, in which, for example, the *Critique of Pure Reason* is understood as "opening up a world of altogether new ideas" (Paton 1936, I, 47) or as the "basic book [*Grundbuch*] of the newer philosophy" (Messer 1923, 3; Baumanns 1997, 10; Natterer 2003, 3).[1] And to a certain extent it continues to have an effect today in the countless contributions to Kant scholarship that attempt to reconstruct Kant's arguments without drawing on the historical context.

Despite its revolutionary novelty, however, Kant's critical philosophy was significantly shaped by the development of eighteenth-century German philosophy. Of course, Kant's philosophy is in many ways crucial to our understanding of this epoch; not least, the publication of the *Critique of Pure Reason* marks the beginning of a new philosophical epoch, a turning point in modern philosophy that probably no one would doubt today. So, if eighteenth-century German philosophy is still mainly viewed from Kant's perspective, this is not least due to this fact. However, this approach becomes problematic if one focuses exclusively on the mature

---

[1] Even authors like Husserl or Heidegger, who emphasize more strongly Kant's attachment to the philosophical tradition, nevertheless see something extraordinary in his philosophy. According to Husserl, Kant had done "as deep insights as none before him" (Husserl 1956, 356), and Heidegger claims that Kant's works "initiate the final turn of occidental metaphysics" (Heidegger 1976, 200). (All translations from German are ours).

systematics of Kant's critical philosophy and its further development by the early idealists. For Kant's thought is in many ways anchored in the philosophical discourse of his time, which is why one must also take into account the necessary conditions for the development of Kant's philosophy among his predecessors and contemporaries.

Although Kant assumed the role that is attributed to him today late in life, he had already engaged intensively with the approaches of his contemporaries and predecessors earlier on.[2] Since his first publications, Kant's thoughts had been motivated above all by questions that, in the broadest sense, originated in the circle of the Leibniz-Wolffian philosophy, even if many of the protagonists of these debates are today partly forgotten or known only through their mention by Kant. At the same time, Kant repeatedly proves to be an attentive observer of those philosophical reflections that reached the German-speaking world from England and Scotland from the middle of the eighteenth-century onwards and were received by the popular philosophers or the Göttingen empiricists.[3] In contrast to Hegel, Kant seemed to have regarded German Enlightenment philosophy as more than "insubstantial, dull chatter" (Hegel 1836, 531).

In the last three decades, interest in Kant's philosophical contemporaries has slowly but steadily increased. As a result, numerous anthologies and monographs have appeared in German and English that attempt to make Kant's philosophy intelligible on the basis of his contemporary debates (see, for example, Schwaiger 1999; Zammito 2002; Heßbrüggen-Walter 2004; Watkins 2005; Wunderlich 2005; Hahmann 2009; Watkins 2009; Kitcher 2011; Dyck 2014; Buchenau 2015; Dyck/Wunderlich 2018; Dahlstrom 2018; de Boer 2020). This approach breaks with a dogma of Kant scholarship that has dominated the last decades, especially in Anglophone research. According to this old dogma, Kant's philosophy should be understood solely from within itself (an exception is Beck 1969). This hermetic reading of Kant has also proved to be a rejection of a historicizing, hermeneutic approach to philosophy common on the European continent. In a sense, behind the Anglophone approach is the welcome and correct idea that philosophical thought and argument cannot be historicized; that is, that it cannot dissolve in its history like a lump of sugar in water. Whether this view has actually ever been held by anyone is admittedly questionable.[4] It is undisputed, however, that the so-called *Einflussforschung*,

---

[2] For an initial overview of Kant's predecessors, contemporaries, and successors, see Dyck/Wunderlich 2018, 6–9.

[3] On "German empiricism" in the second half of the eighteenth-century, see Kuehn 1987; Kuehn 1996; de Boer/Prunea-Bretonnet 2021; Thiel 2023.

[4] Indeed, numerous Kant receptions in German-language philosophy have been (and still are) committed to the idea of a revolutionary new approach to Kant's critical philosophy. See, e. g., Zoch-

which seeks to explain the author's thoughts by embedding them in historical developments and contextualizing them through direct references to predecessors and contemporaries, had gained a considerable influence on the historiography of philosophy in post-war Germany (cf. the assessment in Nagl 1981, 2–5).

How difficult it can be in detail, however, to distinguish philosophically relevant contextual research from a conceptual-historical cabinet of rarities becomes clear, for example, when one traces the meaning of the terminology used by Kant in the *Critique of Pure Reason*. It is obvious that the terms used by Kant, such as "category," "transcendental," "canon," "antinomy," etc., deserve the greatest attention for a proper understanding of the critical project. This need not mean, however, that this understanding can be gained by tracing these terms back to their use in seventeenth-century Aristotelian school philosophy in Germany. In fact, a purely concept-historical tracing back to the use and understanding of these terms in seventeenth-century school philosophy does relatively little to illuminate the critical thoughts Kant associates with these terms. Instead, such conceptual-historical accounts, however illuminating they may be for a purely historical interest, tend to have a discouraging effect on philosophically interested readers, as they give the impression that one can only understand Kant if one has previously struggled through mountains of books by insignificant and mostly forgotten thinkers.[5]

In fact, a closer look at the context of the reception of critical philosophy by Kant's contemporaries teaches us that they were in part as perplexed as modern readers in the face of the terminology used in the *Critique of Pure Reason*. Indeed, the novelty of these terms was also perceived by Kant's contemporaries, as shown, for example, by the reaction of Garve: the latter was famously tasked with reviewing the *Critique of Pure Reason* and ultimately failed miserably at this task. Horrified by the result and the reaction to his work, he turned to Kant and described in a letter the difficulties he had encountered in reading the text, partly because of

---

er 1959; Funke 1979; Kopper 1984; Schmitz 1989; Baumanns 1997; Flach 2002; Höffe 2003; Förster 2011.

5 How the concepts developed in detail, which were taken up by Kant and adapted to his philosophical project, has been treated extensively in German research in the so-called *Begriffsgeschichte*. In addition to the work of Giorgio Tonelli, Norbert Hinske deserves special mention for his groundbreaking research. Hinske has made lasting contributions to historical research, especially in working out the terminological references to the argumentative contexts and textbooks of seventeenth century Germany, many of which can hardly be found today. Hinske particularly highlights the writings of Johannes Scharff (1595–1660), whose extensive major work *Theoria transcendentalis Primae Philosophiae, quam vocant Metaphysicam* is said to play an important role in the conceptual development of the transcendental philosophical approach. Thus, in Scharff's work, "transcendental theory" and metaphysics are equated for the first time (Hinske 1968, 93). But Hinske also attributes other important Kantian achievements to Scharff's work.

the unfamiliar terminology, so that both the subject matter and Kant's approach to determining the limits of reason took him to the limits of his own capacity for understanding. However, a look at Garve also shows that Kant used these terms precisely to break with contemporary discussion, to indicate the novelty and otherness of his approach.[6]

In a contextualizing account, then, one must carefully distinguish between what can really be made more comprehensible by recourse to contemporary debates, and those points that rather satisfy a singular historical interest of experts. For of course not everything can and must be made historically comprehensible. But unfortunately, what was good and right about this approach, namely the insight that even a philosopher's tools and motivation, that is, his conceptualizations and forms of argumentation as well as the problems that stimulated his thinking, did not emerge from within himself, has been buried under the shortcomings associated with this hermeneutic approach.

Ultimately, however, it is true that Kant's ideas did not originate in a historical vacuum. Even if philosophical thoughts cannot be dissolved in history, they do have a history. While the history of their discovery and formulation is not synonymous with philosophical content, it is significant insofar as its uncovering helps to adequately grasp the philosophical thought itself. And in this respect, the effort to understand Kant in the context of the philosophy of his time is a necessary task of Kant studies.

2 The Contextualization of Philosophical Thoughts and its Usefulness

If one takes the concern of such contextualization seriously and asks about the specificity of an adequate record of the history of philosophical thought, at least three components can be distinguished:[7]
1. First of all, it is important to note that the articulation of theses and arguments takes place in specific argumentative contexts. Accordingly, they must be understood in terms of situations and discussions relevant to the philosophical

---

[6] This claim to novelty, which is already indicated by a superficial reading, is even explicitly underlined by Kant in a letter to Marcus Herz (Letter to Herz, 24/11/1776, Nr. 112; AA X 19).
[7] The concept of context is restricted here to the *philosophically* relevant content in the narrower sense, and material, social, or economic aspects are left aside. For a more differentiated concept of context and the fundamental importance of context for the interpretation of philosophical texts, see, e.g., Rescher 2007, chapters 2 and 3.

questions at hand. Their meaning is very often decisively different from that which we associate with similar terms, theses, and arguments today.
2. It is also helpful to understand the motivation that led to the development of the respective theses and arguments. Some theses are absurd from today's perspective, or some arguments seem superfluous or cumbersome. An adequate understanding often requires the identification of the contemporary positions against which the respective thesis is supposed to distinguish itself, or against which the respective argument is directed. Since, especially in a complex philosophical discussion, the relevant positions are rarely mentioned by name and a certain knowledge – of standard arguments or the latest fashions, for example – is simply assumed on the part of the reader, a lot of work usually has to be done to make the unsaid speak.
3. Finally, however, it is also important to uncover the historically contingent elements of these thoughts and to distinguish them from the philosophical content. One must detach these elements from the content in order to preserve, so to speak, the timeless or rational core of the respective philosophy. Only in this way can one finally judge the originality – or conventionality – of the thoughts of the respective author.

Such contextualization thus makes it possible to better understand the conceptions, theses and arguments, and even the choice of topics treated, against the background of contemporary discussion and to separate the original from the conventional. Especially with an author like Kant, this is of course worthwhile. Not infrequently, his reflections are seen as difficult or his argumentation as hard to follow. At the same time, he is considered a philosophical genius whose work is bursting with innovations. Considering the concrete philosophical context; that is, naming the authors to whom he refers – at least implicitly – can only be helpful in eliminating such difficulties and at the same time distinguishing more precisely between Kant's revolutionary and traditional thoughts.

From another point of view, contextualizing Kant's philosophy can also make an excellent contribution to the study of eighteenth-century German philosophy. In the course of the development of Kant's thought, almost all the central problems and discourses of Enlightenment philosophy come together – but from the perspective of a philosopher who was trained in Wolffian tradition and was not content to ground metaphysics and moral philosophy on naive empiricism, psychology, or anthropology. The study of Kant's philosophical-historical environment therefore offers the opportunity to better understand not only his own philosophy, but also the debates and problems discussed in German philosophy during the Enlightenment as a whole. Last but not least, as a result of this investigation, one or the other discovery can be made that lies beyond the traditional canon, that can complete our picture of the philosophy "between Wolff and Kant" (Gawlick 1985, 26) or that can even be stimulating for today's debates.

When the two tasks mentioned above – a better understanding of Kant's philosophy and a better understanding of the thought of less prominent authors – are combined, Kant's philosophical work can be used as a key to an adequate understanding of German philosophy in the eighteenth-century. Again, three aspects of this central function can be distinguished:

1. Kant's work reveals central themes of the philosophy of his time. One can think here of the discussions on the status of apperception, the faculties of the soul or the justification of morality.
2. A look at the reflections of predecessors and contemporaries enables us to discover their direct influences on Kant's philosophy. This concerns both the specific choice of topics Kant dealt with and individual criticisms he made of the positions of his predecessors and contemporaries. Such a view can make it understandable why Kant was interested, for example, in the very question of the method of metaphysics or the metaphysical foundations of moral philosophy and physics, and against whom his own answers were directed.
3. In the 1780s and 1790s there were numerous, often vigorous reactions to Kant's critical philosophy (see Sassen 2000 for criticism from the empiricist side). We can use these reactions to approach the philosophy of the late Enlightenment as well. This is especially true because of the attacks launched against Kant and his "new" philosophy. Their objections not only shed light on contemporary school opinions and tendencies, but are still of systematic relevance today (see recently e.g., Karampatsou 2023). Moreover, both Kant himself and his followers responded to many of these reactions, so that clarifications and changes emerged from these discussions that are crucial both for understanding the development of Kant's thought and for the further development of German philosophy "after Kant."

We propose to use these three perspectives as analytical tools to systematize recent research on the immediate historical background of Kant's philosophy. In contrast to attempts at chronological ordering (as, for example, in Dyck/Wunderlich 2018, 5–9), this procedure has the advantage of making it possible to better distinguish between different methodological and thematic approaches in current research. On this basis, we are also in a better position to determine the benefit of these distinct methodological approaches. Accordingly, under the three headings of "Contexts," "Influences," and "Controversies," we can arrange a variety of different research contributions that illuminate either the context from which Kant's thought emerged, or the influences that historical predecessors or contemporaries exerted on Kant, and finally the philosophical controversies in which Kant and his "new" philosophy were involved. All of these approaches not only have their own theme, but also start from a different idea of how to understand the emergence of Kant's own philosophical project. It is therefore useful to distinguish between these approaches in order to answer detailed questions within Kant's work or for current systematic discussions.

3 The Present Volume

Like Kant's philosophy, the present volume has its own history – though not such a long and complex one. The historical material from which it has emerged comes from the series "Werkprofile," which has been published by De Gruyter since 2011. This series is dedicated to philosophers and thinkers of the seventeenth and eighteenth centuries who stimulated innovations in the discussions of their time or created syntheses whose significance has not yet been sufficiently appreciated by researchers. The aim is to lay the foundations for research in the history of ideas and philosophy and to stimulate the study of these thinkers, some of whose approaches were fundamental to the emergence of philosophical discourse in Germany. Last but not least, it is also about "rediscovering" the representatives of this epoch in a certain sense. So far, the series has dealt with numerous authors whose conceptions and ideas shaped the intellectual-historical environment of the eighteenth-century and determined the topics of philosophical debates. Not infrequently, these are debates and questions that are unfamiliar to today's readers and occasionally even seem obscure.

Kant's thought is also rooted in these debates, and this is where Kant's philosophical development began. Kant sometimes refers explicitly to these discussions, but often without naming the protagonists. Many of his new ideas, however, must be understood as reactions and innovations with regard to these debates. It is therefore not surprising that Kant's philosophy has been a frequent topic in the series "Werkprofile." In these contributions, Kant's philosophical development is discussed in the context of the overarching debates, or central conceptualizations of Kant's philosophical project are made understandable against the background of the approaches of his predecessors.

The aim of this anthology is to bring together in one volume some of the texts published in the series "Werkprofile," which deal with Kant's relationship to his philosophical contemporaries and predecessors, and to make them accessible to a wider audience in English. Our project is thus aimed at those who have an interest in better understanding the preconditions and development of Kant's philosophy in its historical context, which exerted a not inconsiderable influence on its development and many fundamental conceptions. Kant's philosophical motivation, his commitment to answering certain questions, but also his silence on other questions can rarely be understood immanently in terms of his work, and require a further historical approach, which in this way will also be helpful in getting a better grip on the respective systematic questions. The volume thus aims to invite the reader to consider Kant's philosophy from a broader perspective by bringing numerous historical references to the fore. Although research into these references has gained momentum in recent years, it is still in its infancy. Our volume aims to build on this development and, with the contributions collected here, to complement and further expand existing research, both with regard to the authors treated and the topics dealt with.

By drawing on the previously edited material of the "Werkprofile," the contributions deal primarily with protagonists of an anti-Wolffian or empiricist character, namely Christian August Crusius (1715–1775), Johannes Nikolaus Tetens (1736–1807), Johann Georg Heinrich Feder (1740–1821), Christian Garve (1742–1798), Ernst Platner (1744–1818), and Christoph Meiners (1747–1810). This is welcome insofar as the historiography of German philosophy to this day tends to neglect the tradition of a philosophy not in the succession of Wolff, but of Christian Thomasius (1655–1728), as Crusius aspires to (see Grunert/Hahmann/Stiening 2021, 5–6), as well as the turn to psychology and anthropology in the second half of the eighteenth-century. Some of these authors were important sources of inspiration for Kant's critical philosophy (e.g., Crusius and Garve), others can serve to show how Kant's critical philosophy was perceived rather as a step backwards into "dogmatic" rationalism from an empiricist point of view (especially Feder and Meiners). However, we will also deal with philosophers who were closer to Wolff, such as Johann Georg Sulzer (1720–1779) and Johann Heinrich Lambert (1728–1777). They are also known to have had a certain influence on Kant, but the extent of this is not yet known exactly. Finally, we will also address Carl Christian Erhard Schmid (1761–1812), one of the first Kantians to strive to hold on to the Kantian "letter" against the idealistic further developments and to defend a realist reading of Kant's transcendental philosophy.

In accordance with the above three perspectives, the contributions are divided into three thematic sections relating to Kant's philosophy. The first section deals with the various thematic contexts that shaped Kant's philosophical development or for which Kant's philosophical reflections provided decisive impulses. The contributions in this section deal with three such contexts: the discussions of apperception, inner sense, and feeling of self (Patricia Kitcher and Udo Thiel), the conceptions of the various powers and faculties of the soul (Andree Hahmann and Stefan Klingner), and the foundation of morality (Achim Vesper). The second section deals with direct influences that affected Kant's choice of topics, problem definitions, or individual critical positions. In addition to Kant's early understanding of philosophical method and the doctrine of faculties (Tinca Prunea-Bretonnet and Marion Heinz), this section addresses Kant's metaphysics of nature and metaphysics of morals, more specifically his concept of matter (Paolo Pecere), the motivational power of pure reason, (Heiner F. Klemme) and the concept of obligation (Gabriel Rivero). Finally, the third complex presents controversies that Kant's philosophy triggered and in which Kant himself was sometimes involved. The contributions in this section first deal with the debates on an appropriate understanding of human dignity and on the relationship between theory and practice (Stefanie Buchenau and Dieter Hüning) and then take a look at the criticism of Kant's critical philosophy by the Göttingen empiricists (Gideon Stiening, Rudolf Meer, and Andreas Brandt).

Most of the contributions are English translations of essays from the "Werkprofile." The translations are from the authors or from Andree Hahmann, in the case of Heiner F. Klemme's contribution from John Walsh. The "Sources" section at the end of the volume provides further information.

Part I: **Contexts**

Patricia Kitcher
Analyzing Apperception [*Gewahrnehmen*]

Abstract: In his *Philosophical Essays*, J. N. Tetens investigates the faculty of apperception from two directions. He considers whether it is possible to reduce apperceptive awareness to a more basic faculty and he considers how apperception plays a role in other mental capacities, most importantly cognition. The first project ties him to the then contemporary search for the most basic faculties; the second to Kant's efforts to explain the possibility of cognition. One question for the search for basic qualities is whether an active faculty can somehow be assimilated to feeling.f Because Kant is known to have studied Tetens's essays carefully, I conclude with a discussion of how they differ in respect to the unity of apperception and the source of the I-representation.

1 The Observational Method

Although Tetens' lengthy volumes seldom employ the term "apperception," the concept is the topic of the third of his *Philosophical Essays on Human Nature and its Development* (*Philosophische Versuche über die Menschliche Natur und ihre Entwicklung*).[1] It is also discussed extensively in other sections of volume 1, especially Essay 4. His preferred expression is "*Gewahrnehmen*," (e.g., 1777/1979, 1.262) which I simply translate as "apperception." The faculty of apperception appears in the study in two guises. It is one of the faculties through which complex capacities are decomposed into their more basic sub-capacities. It is also an *analysandum*. One of Tetens' central questions is whether apperception can be reduced to an even more basic faculty.

Tetens prefaces the *Essays* with an account of his method. He describes it as having been pioneered by Locke and followed by recent psychologists. It is a matter of observing the effects of mental faculties under different conditions and of analyzing the results with a view to discovering the simplest faculties of the mind (1777/1979, 1.iii–iv). As Udo Thiel has recently noted, however, Tetens' methodological stance is more nuanced than some of his bolder pronouncements suggest (2018, 61–62). Although he characterizes the observational method and the metaphysical methods of analytic psychology and anthropology as entirely different ways of proceeding (1777/1979, 1.iv), he remarks that in studying psychology it is

---

[1] References to this work will be given in the text by volume and page number.

difficult to separate out the elements produced by reasoning from what is observed. More importantly, he explains that he will base his account on nothing other than direct observation *or* reasoning that is self-evident and confirmed by observed evidence (1777/1979, 1.xxx).

Although Tetens thinks that contemporary psychologists mainly follow Locke, he objects that some deviate from the method in two different ways. The French (later Swiss) naturalist Charles Bonnet had argued that the only way to study the soul is through its faculties and that the only way to study these faculties is through their effects (Bonnet 1755, 122). Yet, as Tetens points out, Bonnet injects metaphysical assumptions into his work (1777/1979, 1.v). First, he is concerned to explain mentality in terms of neural action and these accounts considerably outrun the observational data (1777/1979, 1.v). Second, he makes an error which is common to the work of Claude Adrien Helvetius and Étienne Bonnot de Condillac. Like Leibniz and Christian Wolff, these theorists assume that, since the soul is a simple being, then its various activities must be expressions of a single basic faculty (1777/1979, 1.4).

Tetens' critique is not so much of the assumption of a fundamental faculty as of its pernicious effects on the work of analysis. It is not enough just to abstract from differences across faculties or to try to tie them together under a single name. There must be a genuine resolution that makes obvious the inner identity of the (apparently) different activities (1777/1979, 1.5–7). Although he greatly admires Bonnet's explanations of the effects of the soul's faculties, explanations that he thinks are distinguished by their precision and practical brilliance (1777/1979, 1.291), he cannot go along with his attempt to account for consciousness and apperception in terms of feeling and sensing [*Empfinden*]. That is a bold leap of imagination that goes beyond the bounds of intelligibility (1777/1979, 1.7).

Tetens' prefatory remarks indicate his fealty to Locke's methods. He also accepts many of his theories. In particular, Tetens devotes considerable efforts to defending two of Locke's central theses: Nothing is in the mind which was not first in the senses; concepts are nothing outside the mind. As has often been noted, these doctrines are in some tension. There is no hint of anything conventional in the way in which the senses "furnish the mind with ideas." They simply convey perceptions or sensations from external objects into the mind (Locke 1690/1975, 2.1.2–5, 104–106). On the other hand, Locke is adamant that general terms are conventional,

> are creatures of our own making (Locke 1690/1975, 3.3.11, 414).

On Locke's account, humans acquire general terms; for example, "man," through forming general ideas on the basis of sensing particulars; for example, Peter, Jane, Mary, and James. He recognizes that it seems puzzling *how general Words* could be made (Locke 1690/1975, 3.3.6, 410).

The puzzle he focuses on is metaphysical: How can humans use general terms to refer to things when the world is made up of individuals? There is, however, an equally obvious puzzle in his epistemology. How can natural interactions of sensing particulars lead to the formation of conventional general words? His solution to the metaphysical problem and (*de facto* to the epistemological one) is his theory of resemblance and abstraction. The idea of "man" is formed when cognizers retain qualities that are common to the sensory representations of different humans and leave out qualities in which they differ (Locke 1690/1975, 3.3.8, 411), and when they leave out the particularity of the particulars, the time, location and fact of existence of the individual (Locke 1690/1975, 2.9.9, 159). Although Tetens does not frame his discussions in terms of reconciling Locke's Empiricism and his conventionalism, he ends up claiming that his own account of apperception provides a way of reconciling the doctrines.

Tetens parts company with Locke on the long-running disagreement over unconscious ideas. Since he takes apperception to be the *differentia* of conscious as opposed to unconscious ideas, his theory of apperception is also a significant departure from Lockean orthodoxy. Locke had been adamant that all ideas must be conscious. He began the second book of the *Essay Concerning Human Understanding* with the declaration that every man is conscious to himself that he thinks. This need not imply that whenever a man thinks, he is conscious of doing so, but shortly afterwards, he explains that

> it [is] ... hard to conceive that anything should think and not be conscious of it (Locke 1690/1975, 2.1.11).

Further, in his familiar account of what "person" stands for, he again ties thinking to consciousness:

> a thinking intelligent Being, that has reason and reflection, and can consider itself as itself, the same thinking thing, in different times and places; which it does only by that consciousness which is inseparable from thinking, and as seems to me essential to it: *It being impossible for anyone to perceive, without perceiving, that he does perceive ... this consciousness always accompanies thinking*. (Locke 1690/1975, 2.27.9, my italics)

Although Leibniz later disputes Locke's position, he seemed originally to think that the mind perceived its perceptions. He writes in an early theological writing, *The Confession of Nature against Atheists* (1669), that

> [i]f one of the actions of a being is thinking, one of its actions is immediately perceptible, without supposing any parts in it.
>
> For thought is (1) a thing that is immediately perceptible, mind being immediate to itself when it perceives itself thinking. (2) Thought is a perceptible thing without being aware of its parts. (Leibniz 1969, 113)

Somewhat later, in unpublished notes on metaphysics from April of 1676, he expresses doubts about the perceptual model.

> In our mind there is perception or a sense of itself as of a certain specific thing; this is always in us, because, as often as we use the name, we at once recognize it. As often as we will, we recognize that we perceive our thoughts, that is, that we have thought a little earlier. Therefore, intellectual memory consists not in what we sense but in that we sense – that we are those who sense. This is what we commonly call identity. (Leibniz 1969, 161–162)

Although Leibniz claims that we perceive both ourselves and our thoughts, he ends up denying that this is really a matter of sensing. Rather, we recognize that we think and perceive.

By the time of the *New Essays on Human Understanding* (1704, published 1765), Leibniz had firmly rejected the view that all thinking is self-conscious at least on the model of perceiving perceptions. He offers the now familiar criticism that such a model would involve an infinite regress.

> It is impossible that we should always reflect explicitly on all our thoughts; for if we did, the mind would reflect on each reflection, ad infinitum. (Leibniz 1765/1996, 2.1.19, 118)

He also offers a memorable example as evidence for unconscious perceptions: the sounds of individual waves that make up the roar of the ocean, but that cannot be separately differentiated (Leibniz 1765/1996, 54). The example is not entirely convincing, since people may not hear the individual waves, but only their combination. By the time that Tetens considers the issue, better examples are available. In *Vernünftige Gedancken von Gott, der Welt und der Seele des Menschen, auch allen dingen überhaupt* (1751), better known as the *German Metaphysics*, Christian Wolff also rejects the claim that nothing can be in the mind of which it is unaware (*Meta.* §193).

> I see in a faraway field something white, but do not know what I can make of it not being able to distinguish one part from the other; so the thought that I have of it is obscure. (Wolff 1751/1983, Meta. §199)

In the "Essay on the Origin of Human Knowledge" (1746/1947, 6), Condillac argues for unconscious perceptions through the example of reading. It seems as though one is only conscious of the ideas and not of the letters. On the other hand, a reader must be conscious of the letters. Without such consciousness, he could be aware of neither the words nor the ideas. As was often the case with disputants over unconscious perceptions, Condillac tries to solve the puzzle by appealing to memory: Readers are aware of all the impressions, but the awareness is so superficial that it leaves no memory trace (Condillac 1746/1947, 12). Tetens maintains that there are representations that are unconscious (1777/1979, 1.265) and offers similar examples: One cannot distinguish even the fronts of the different leaves in a tree swaying in the distance or the different sounds of the instruments in a concert, yet these visual and sound pieces must be pieces of the whole perceptions (1777/1979, 1.172–173).

Tetens' concern with unconscious representations is not so much with their existence, but with how to understand the difference between representations that are conscious and those that are not. As he observes, it is not useful to know that there are unconscious representations unless we know in what sense (1777/1979, 1.265). This problem is central to his account of apperception, because, as noted, conscious representations are those that are apperceived (1777/1979, 1.262–263). In the course of analyzing apperception, Tetens discusses a number of issues, including the status of the *cogito* and the origin of the concept of the self. But he develops his theory of apperception in response to the demands of the controversy over unconscious perceptions, the one fundamental faculty thesis, and Locke's claims for the necessary sensory basis – and conventionality – of thought. Sometimes he wonders whether these systematic concerns lead him, as well as his opponents, to outrun the data of observation (1777/1979, 1.293–294).

Tetens' *Essays* have been of great interest to Kant scholars, because he is known to have read them with some care in the crucial years just before the appearance of the first edition of the *Critique of Pure Reason*.[2] Since the "transcendental unity of apperception" lies at the heart of the *Critique*, I will conclude by briefly contrasting Tetens' account of apperception with Kant's. I will also briefly consider Kant's objection to those who confuse apperception with inner sense, since his target may well have been Tetens. Most of the chapter will, however, be devoted to laying out and evaluating Teten's theory of apperception.

---

2 The oft-recounted story from Hamann is that Tetens' book lay open on Kant's desk as he wrote the *Critique*. See Meyer (1870, 56). Kant reports his reading in a letter to Marcus Herz of April 1778: "Tetens, in his diffuse work on human nature, made some penetrating points; but it certainly looks as if for the most part he let his work be published just as he wrote it down, without corrections. ... After exhausting himself and his reader [in a discussion of freedom from the second volume] he left the matter just as he found it, advising his reader to consult his own feelings (10.232)." Carl (1989, 115) discusses additional evidence, including notes in Kant's hand in his copy of Tetens.

2 Essay Three: On Apperception and Consciousness, Sections 1–3

2.1 Locating Apperception

Like Wolff before him and Kant after him, Tetens takes the basic genus of the mental realm to be "representation." Within that class, he distinguishes the conscious from the unconscious. Consciousness has two constituents: feeling and apperception (1777/1979, 1.263). Feeling is essential to consciousness because it supplies the qualities of which the subject is conscious. He characterizes the other essential element of consciousness as "apperception," because he takes that to be the genus for a variety of more specific mental operations, including noticing, becoming conscious of something, being conscious, recognizing something and so forth (1777/1979, 1.262). His description of the genus is analogical; it also quite close to Wolff's picture of consciousness as active differentiating:

> When the soul says internally as though to itself, and where this act is especially lively, it really expresses it thusly: See; when namely it apprehends an object as a particular object, knows it among others, distinguishes it; then what is present is called coming to apperceive or apperceiving. (1777/1979, 1.262)

Further, this distinguishing includes a representation of the self:

> Consciousness is on one side a feeling, but a clear feeling, a clear impression, which is connected with distinguishing between the felt thing and the self. (1777/1979, 1.263)

After considering the relation between feeling and apperceiving, I turn to the issue of the relation between the thing distinguished and the self (see below 21).

Having analyzed consciousness into two aspects in the first section, Tetens considers in the second whether apperceiving is one and the same as the act of feeling or one and the same as the act of representing (1777/1979, 1.263). He notes that Condillac held that attending, comparing and reflecting were merely higher degrees of feeling (1777/1979, 1.264). He then turns to a result from the First Essay. A sensed object is not apperceived in the first moment when the impression is received. Apperception takes place through *"Nachempfindung"* (1777/1979, 1.264). Unfortunately, the First Essay's explanation of the notion of *"Nachempfindung"* (literally "after-impression") is unclear. It offers the analogy of a musical string. A string is bowed and it continues to vibrate (1777/1979, 1.31). Similarly, when a stream of light falls on the eye, the change persists in us for a while (1777/1979, 1.32).

> There [in the persisting modification] is the after-impression or the sensory representation of the present object or, as well, the impression itself regarded as a representation of an object. (1777/1979, 1.32)

The string analogy was very popular in speculating about the motions of the nerves, but Tetens seems to appeal to it just to illustrate what he was certain that people observed anyway: Their sensations continue after the stimulus is past (1777/1979, 1.32–33). It is unclear, however, how a *continuing* sense impression is thereby understood to represent a present object. Perhaps the connection is indirect. Continuation or memory of a sensation was widely believed to be crucial to consciousness and consciousness is necessary for object representation.

After revisiting the delay before apperceiving in Essay 3, Tetens moves from unapperceived (first) impressions to the question of the sense in which there are representations without consciousness. He thinks that the question is not answered by appeals to memory. Undifferentiated representations can also be repeated (1777/1979, 1.265). Since repetition is not the *differentia* of conscious representations, he tries to turn the debate in a more promising direction (1777/1979, 1.266). The underlying issue is whether there are representations that are sufficiently clearly and strongly represented that they could be apperceived, even though they are not yet apperceived. More briefly, are there non-apperceived but apperceptible representations?

> Are there representations in us, regarded as images and signs, which are sufficiently expressed, and strongly enough separated from others in the fantasy, that they and through them their objects can be distinguished from others? [...] Or must they perhaps receive that material clarity only through the same act, through which they are actually apperceived, and actually used as images and signs? through the act whereby they are animated with consciousness and become ideas? (1777/1979, 1.266)

This question is crucial, because if representations are fully apperceptible prior to being apperceived, then apperceiving would not alter their contents. The soul would add only consciousness to an already fully expressed representation (1777/1979, 1.271–272). Under these circumstances, two key issues would be settled. There would be unconscious representations in the sense of fully formed representations that are not conscious; the difference between sensory images and ideas would be one of degree, not kind (of content). Ideas would just be stronger, clearer images and the one faculty thesis would be vindicated.

Having cast the issue of unconscious representations in this way, Tetens considers the evidence on both sides. On the one hand, it seems probable that we could not have a visible figure present in us that we do not at the same time see; on the other it seems that we see so much in a representation when we turn our full attention to it that we do not recall noticing in the impression (1777/1979, 1.268). He then turns to two further considerations that point to a negative answer, although he does not consider them decisive.

The first is if it is relations that we apperceive in comparing the present representation of something that is [just] absent with other [previous] representations that we have, then this [extra content] is a new effect of our reflection (1777/1979, 1.268). The thinking power adds these relational thoughts to the representations; by contrast absolute properties can only be added by the fantasy or perhaps through the association of ideas. In these cases, the additions are either fictional or accidental (1777/1979, 1.271).

The second consideration is that when the thinking power expresses itself, intercedes with a representation, it must modify it (1777/1979, 1.271). If the thinking power added only consciousness to a fully complete representation and did not alter it, then the case would differ from other similar cases (1777/1979, 1.272). Tetens does not say which cases he has in mind, but the next section considers relations of sameness and difference and placing objects in spatial and temporal relations, and these species of relations involve additional content. So perhaps his two arguments against the possibility of apperceptible but unapperceived representations and so, unconscious perceptions in this specific sense, are merely two ways of making the point that an [active] mental power of apperception expresses itself by adding relational content to representations. On his Wolffian view, a feeling or representation becomes conscious or becomes an object of consciousness by being separated out from something else and that activity *ipso facto* adds relational content, of the representation to a background.

2.2 Apperception, Relations and Subjectivity

Section three elaborates the connection between apperception and thoughts of relations, and the possibility of reducing that faculty to feeling. Because apperceiving is a matter of differentiating, it must give rise to the idea of a relation between one thing and others (1777/1979, 1.273). This property of apperceiving provides a criterial difference with feeling. The proper objects of feeling are absolute qualities, not relational ones. Tetens notes that one might try to find a common genus for these two sorts of properties or predicates, the absolute and the relational (11777/1979, 1.275). This would, however, be just the sort of papering over differences with a common name that he decried in Essay 1 (above, p. 14). Although he does not claim to have fully proven that the acts of feeling and apperceiving are at bottom different, he thinks the proposition that they are has been made probable (1777/1979, 1.275).

Within the overarching project of section three, that of advancing the discussion of reducibility, Tetens raises several interesting contemporary issues. One concerns Descartes' thesis of "material falsity" (1777/1979, 1.274). Can only judgments be false or is it possible to have a false idea? The issue arises, because Tetens tries to determine whether apperceiving or differentiating is a type of judging. Insofar as judging is a matter of relating ideas, apperceiving could not be a type of judging. Such judging presupposes ideas and ideas only arise through differentiating. On the other hand, apperceiving must be considered as a kind of judging, because it produces the thought of one particular object – the object that is seen – in relation to others. Apperceiving

> consists in distinguishing and knowing that I have this thought in me, even if it is neither present in the form of a full judgment, nor signified in actual words. (1777/1979, 1.273)

Again, I consider below what Tetens might mean by "in me" (p. 23). Here my concern is with his claim that apperception alters a representation by imbuing it with a relational aspect: It is singled out in relation to some undifferentiated background.

Tetens uses his account of apperception to answer the Cartesian question about false ideas. Since apperceiving inevitably relates a representation/object to a background, it can be considered a kind of judging. In that case, all errors would be errors of judgment. If these are removed, then nothing would remain of our cognition except mere images. And however unnatural, unsuitable to their objects and full of mistakes they might be, they could not amount to error, because there would be no act of the thinking faculty (1777/1979, 1.274). Here it seems clear that Tetens considers apperceiving to be a source of error and a kind of judging, because it is an act of the thinking faculty.

Apperceiving introduces relational properties into representations, so those properties are its special province as opposed to the absolute properties that are the objects of feeling. The relational properties produced by apperceiving belong to what Tetens characterizes as the "first species" of relations, relations of sameness and difference. He thinks that, in this first species, we can see very clearly the difference between the absolute qualities of things, their sizes, shapes, weights and colors, which are objective and objects of the faculty of feeling, and relative or relational properties. The similarity of two things cannot be located in the objects; the relations must be subjective, produced by the thinking faculty:

> The thought of a relation is produced by the thinking power, and is nothing outside of the understanding ... a concoction of that power, with which we compare those present representations of things in us as objects, and then so to speak impress them with a seal of our comparing activity. (1777/1979, 1.276)

Although the metaphor of a seal is quite striking, Tetens goes on note that the "seal" is an example of a broader phenomenon:

> When the thought of the relation is once produced, then the power of the soul has expressed its activity, and this action is a change in the soul, which, like every other, leaves traces behind, which in a similar manner as other representations, can be reawakened without it being the case that the first or original act of thinking itself is repeated. (1777/1979, 1.276)

Under these circumstances, when an apperceived representation, say of a linden tree, is reawakened, it will not be a bare tree image, but a representation of a tree-image as singled out.

Tetens tries to avoid a possible misunderstanding of the view that a mental act of relating leaves its seal on the singled-out representation. The act of relating may be reawakened as part of the content of the enhanced representation – tree or tree image as singled out – but that should not lead to a false view of the concept of relation.

> One complains about the subtlety; I have no objections. But it is still so; one must look on all sides. It is one thing, first to elucidate things as the same or to distinguish them; and it is another to imagine these thoughts again, to abstract from them, to separate out the commonality in many relational thoughts and from that draw out a universal concept of relational thought and of relations themselves. (1777/1979, 1.276–277)

His point is that although we cannot single out things without identifying them or differentiating them and cannot form the concept of relation without comparing cases and abstracting from their differences, the two sorts of activities have different effects. Apperceiving produces relations of singled out to background that cannot be understood in terms of comparing ideas, because it is the source of ideas. He proceeds to offer examples of other relations that do not involve comparison, *viz.*, spatial, temporal and causal relations among real objects. In Essay 4, he presents another important counter-example to the thesis that all relations include the idea of comparison: How could the reference of a representation to an object be a matter of comparison? (1777/1979, 1.364)

The theory about mental action and content that Tetens offers in these passages does involve a subtle distinction. Apperceiving a tree produces a representation of a tree representation/object as singled out in relation to a background; the act imbues the image with relational content by means of a trace of the action (but see below, p. 23). This enhanced representation is not the concept of relation, however, any more than a judging is the idea of judging (1777/1979, 1.339). When subjects form the concept of relation, they must compare different cases of relational representations; although comparing and abstracting are necessary for forming the concept of relation, that concept does not include the idea of comparing. We can see this, because some relations; for example, singling out, being next to or ahead of or behind, reference to an object, do not involve a comparing of ideas.

Tetens does not spell out why some mental actions leave their seal on representations where others do not, but the two cases involve a crucial difference in level. Concept formation requires conscious representations. What it means for a representation to be conscious is that it is singled out. Hence the materials from which concepts are abstracted are singled out representations. By contrast, comparing is an operation carried out on conscious representations. If that action also added content to the compared representations, then the process would never terminate, since the representations would need to be compared in respect of that additional content on *infinitum*.[3] Yet it seems obvious to Tetens and his contemporaries that subjects are able to form concepts by engaging in activities of comparing and abstracting. Further, since those activities were widely thought to be necessary to form any concept, then if the concept of "relation" includes the concept of comparing, so should the content of; for example, the concept of a "tree." On the other hand, if all concepts are produced through abstracting and comparing, then the concept of "concept" should include the idea of comparing. And that seems to be Tetens' point. Those who think the idea of relation must include that of comparison are confusing the contents that fall under the concept "relation" with the process by which the universal concept "relation" is formed.

Although Tetens is not explicit that the relational content introduced into representations by apperception is subjective until Essay 4 (1777/1979, 1.303), the earlier discussions contain ample hints of that view. These relational contents belong to the species of relations of sameness and difference that is the parade case of content that does not reside in objects but is created by the subject. At this point we can begin see the shape of a possible Tetensian reconciliation of Empiricism and the conventionality of thought. Apperceived representations or ideas, and concepts and judgments are of a piece in being subjective and so nothing but creatures of the mind.

Lockean Empiricism explains the needed fit between sensory representations and concepts by having sensory representations lead the way. Concepts are made by comparing and abstracting from similar representations, representations that are copies of sensory representations, so there is no mystery how concepts can

---

[3] This seems inconsistent with Tetens' claim at 1.276 (above p. 21–22) that apperceiving is a matter of comparing and that comparing leaves its seal on the representation. In other places, however, Tetens is clear that apperceiving cannot be a matter of comparing, although it is like it in some respects. Since he is discussing apperceiving in this passage, I read this passage as using "comparing" in the looser sense in which apperceiving is a kind of comparing.

be applied on the basis of sensory perceptions. Locke sees a world of individuals and the absence of an epistemic route to real essences; he notes the divergences across concepts in different language communities and so takes concepts to be conventional. He can remain true to Empiricism by explaining concept formation in terms of (objective) agreement or resemblance across representations (1690/1975, 3.3.7, p. 411, 3.3.9, p. 412) and the comparing and abstracting of various properties. As J. L. Mackie, among others, noted, resemblance and abstraction are not sufficient to resolve the issue of conventionality. Locke must also appeal to something like selective attention and assume that there is an oversupply of "agreeing" qualities, so that members of one language community could selectively attend to qualities a,b,e, and f and so use those as the "nominal essence" of "man" and another selectively attend to qualities a,c,d (1976, 136).

Tetens does not rest his claims for the subjectivity of thought on linguistic differences. On his account subjectivity enters cognition at the ground floor of conscious representations. Representations are made conscious by the active faculty of apperception. It is a basic capacity of the mind that underlies judging, concept formation and clarifying the parts of concepts (1777/1979, 1.310, 311, 299). Representations and their constituents become available for the formation of concepts through comparison and abstraction only because they have been made conscious or singled out. For example, I can form the concept of a tree only because I have apperceived representations of the trunks, leaves, and branches of linden trees, spruces, willows, etc., and can compare those representations with respect to similarity and difference. For Tetens, these comparisons do not reflect objective similarities, but create subjective relations of sameness and difference across representations.[4]

Before comparing can take place, apperceiving has already introduced two sorts of subjectivity into the process. The first sort is causal: The singling out is an activity of the thinking power, so that what is singled out is a product of that power which expresses its nature. The second sort is representational: The representations that I use to form the concept of a tree are all stamped with the seal of being singled out (perhaps by me, see below, p. 32). Because Tetens maintains that representations are not merely accompanied by consciousness, but must be made conscious through acts of apperceiving, his understanding of the relation between percepts and concepts differs from Locke's in two crucial respects. First, conscious representations are like concepts in being creatures of the mind; since they are creatures of the same active thinking faculty, there is no tension either between

---

[4] Locke also thinks that relations are not contained in the real existence of things, but are extraneous, super-induced (1690/1975, 2.25.7, 122).

natural perceptions and artificial concepts, or between subjective representations of different faculties. Singling out cannot be exactly the same operation as comparing representations, because prior to the singling out there are no representations available to compare. Still, Tetens thinks that the operations are analogous and that they are different expressions of the same basic power. Second, the harmony of percepts and concepts is thus due to the active involvement of the thinking power at all levels of conscious representation.

Although Tetens takes himself to be providing a robust defense Locke's view that concepts are mind-dependent, he concedes in Essay 4 that he might be charged with betraying his Empiricism. His observations about relational representations seem to imply counter-examples to the universal rule that all ideas and concepts arise from impressions. (1777/1979, 1.336) He replies to the anticipated objection by arguing that his position is just the refinement of Empiricism that Locke had pioneered. The objection errs in assuming an Aristotelian version of the doctrine that nothing is in the mind which is not first in the senses. Locke, on the other hand, explained quite clearly that he also counted self-feelings among impressions (1777/1979, 1.338). If we look back at how relational thoughts arise, then we see that the *prima facie* doubtful case is no such thing. Relational thoughts are brought about through an activity that expresses the thinking power (1777/1979, 1.338). This activity must have lasting effects that are felt and sensed; a felt modification must have its after-impression and its left behind trace. Those re-awakeable impressions of the singled out, apperceived and distinguished are then the basis for the relational thought or idea of the singled out (and part of the material for forming the universal concept of relation). In this case as in all others, it is impossible for anyone to have an idea – here a relational idea – without first having an impression of the activity of relating as well as (previous) impressions of the materials related (1777/1979, 1.339). Given Locke's refinement, Tetens faults Leibniz for holding that his version of the Empiricist *credo*, "nothing is in the mind which is not first in the senses, except the mind itself," represents a new insight (1777/1979, 1.337). Locke had already dealt with the activities of the faculties in producing representations when he introduced the notion of an "inner sense."

Despite Tetens' eagerness to align his theories with those of his predecessor, his understanding of the role that Locke assigns to inner sense in this discussion is tendentious. Locke does not posit a faculty of inner sense to explain how human representations of things have subjective elements. As Tetens understands (see below, p. 28), he introduces the faculty to explain how humans have ideas of mental activities such as perceiving, thinking, believing, reasoning and willing (1690/1975, 2.1.4, 105). More, importantly, Tetens can honor the Empiricist *credo* only by sliding between two candidates for the relational content added by apperceiving.

What content is to be traced back to the impression of the act of apperceiving? At the beginning of the discussion, the claim is that through apperceiving

there arises in us a thought of a relation of one thing against [gegen] others (p. 273).

This account fits with Tetens' earlier claim that the relation produced by apperceiving belongs to the first species of sameness and difference. The trace that is re-awakened, however, is not the after-impression of the relation of one thing to a background, but the after-impression of the act of relating one thing to a background. The difference between the two contents is evident when we ask about the *relata:* Are they the object or image singled out and a background, or the object and the act of "seeing" that object?[5] If they are the former, then the Empiricist *credo* has been violated, because there is no impression of such a relation. If they are the latter, then there is no thought (content) of a thing against others.[6] Further, the point of tracing concepts back to representations of sense is to guarantee that they have application to some actual objects. By tracing relational properties back to impressions of mental activities, Tetens would have shown that they are nothing outside the mind. Under these circumstances, why assume that they can be employed to make true judgments about objects?

Further still, if the content of the thought or idea is a relation between an object or image and an act of apperceiving/"seeing," then Tetens has offered an account of how apperceiving leads cognitive subjects to recognize representations as products of their cognitive activities and so, perhaps, as representations. In that case, however, he would be explaining the origin of the metacognitive idea of a representation, and not the origin of the relational contents of particular representations. That is a useful thing to explain, but it is not what he is trying to explain in defending the Empiricist credentials of his theory of relational content.

Tetens realizes that tracing representational contents back to the activities of the thinking faculty does not explain their objectivity, though he does not discuss the problem until Essay 7. Thoughts of sameness and difference are clearly subjective. That may or may not be the case for other relations; for example, those of coexistence and causation. (In Essay 3, he noted that Leibniz, Mendelssohn, and Kant

---

[5] In the case of the representation and idea of space, Tetens is clear that although acts of relating are required to produce the representation of space that is apperceived and so the idea of space, the actual material for the idea of space is the unified image and not the acts of unifying (1777/1979, 1.360). On the other hand, Essay 3 suggests that with apperceiving, the reawakened trace is of an object or image as singled out (by an act). See above, p. 10.

[6] It does not help to suggest that the impression is of an act of relating an object to a background, since that is still an impression of an act, not that of two items standing in a relation.

had all maintained different versions of the thesis that spatial and temporal relations were subjective (1777/1979, 1.277.)) Even if all relational thought were subjective, however, what would that mean? (1777/1979, 1.538–539) If the relations that we encounter in our impressions were bound to our sort of impression, then they would have to be considered merely subjective. If, however, the relations were independent of our kind of impression, and were the same for every other thinking being, then they would be objective (1777/1979, 1.538). It is impossible to press the question further, because then one would have to ask whether there were relations that could be apperceived by creatures with a different thinking power. Although there is no way to eliminate this possibility, there is also nothing to be done with it. Since we can think at all only by thinking in terms of, e. g., sameness and difference, we could never understand the mind of a god or angel who did not think as our mind thinks (1777/1979, 1.538). Tetens does not advocate completely abandoning any distinction between appearance and reality (1777/1979, 1.536), but rather giving up the terms "objective" and "subjective" and using the expressions "inalterably subjective" and "alterably subjective" instead (1777/1979, 1.540). It is, however, unclear how he proposes to establish that some feature of our representations is "inalterably subjective."

I will not try to evaluate Tetens' proposal for "reforming" the concept of objectivity. It rests on the familiar move that humans must take the "laws" that govern their own thinking to be privileged in some way, because they are incapable even of entertaining, no less evaluating, other allegedly possible modes of thought; it is also not particularly developed and would take us too far from the topic of apperception. By contrast, Tetens' spends considerable effort in supporting and developing his claim that the relational character of apperceiving is the basis of the subjective character of thought; at an abstract level at least, this fits well with his appeal to apperception to resolve the question of unconscious representations. Apperception is criterial for conscious representations and, as noted, this would explain how those representations are a suitable basis for the application of concepts that are nothing outside the mind. Concepts are products of the mind's creative powers, and they can be applied to perceptions or conscious representations, because the latter are also products of the mind's active powers. As we have just seen, however, Tetens cannot provide this theory with the sort of observational evidence on which he had hoped to ground his entire account.

3 Essay Three: On Apperception and Consciousness, Sections 4–6

3.1 Apperceiving Apperceiving

Having presented an analogical description of apperceiving and explained its role in the creation of relational thought (thereby contrasting it with the faculty of feeling), Tetens tries to provide a more precise characterization of the elements of apperceiving. Apperceiving presupposes the presence in the mind of a representation or feeling to be apperceived (1777/1979, 1.281). This point does not require independent observation, but follows from the role of apperception in thinking. In the absence of a representation or feeling, there would be nothing for the faculty to "see." Tetens reverts to the method of observation in characterizing the elements of apperceiving and how it arises. As a preliminary, he tries to explain how we observe this activity.

> The act of apperceiving can be observed only when a thing has already been apperceived. For in the moment when one apperceives one cannot also apperceive what thereby proceeds. (1777/1979, 1.281)

The argument for this claim was given in Essay 1, in the discussion of "inner sense." Cognizers cannot apperceive their apperceiving while they are doing it, because that would require them to divide their consciousness (1777/1979, 1.46–47). For this reason, cognizers can observe their apperceiving and their thinking only "from behind" (1777/1979, 1.49).

Tetens appeals to the impossibility of the thinking faculty dividing itself in order to perform two simultaneous activities as part of his defense of Locke's introduction of inner sense. He implies that Wolff errs in having very little to say about representations of mental activities (1777/1979, 1.45). Since humans cannot apperceive and apperceive that they do, how do they know about their thinking? Locke was right to explain humans' understanding of their own mental activities in terms of an inner "sense." Inner sense is a sense, because it has the same *differentia* as outer sense. Wolff maintained that the representations of outer sense represent objects, because sensations arise in the mind as effects of those objects; this theory can be extended to mental activities.

We have already considered the basic assumption that stands behind Tetens' account of internally sensing apperceiving (thinking): a change is caused in the representations.

> No change can arise in representations that is not connected to a certain modification in the brain which belongs to it [those who identify brain and soul can substitute "soul"]. [...] Thus if a change is caused in the representations from an outwardly directed effort of the thinking power, that change is herewith connected to a change in the organ [brain or soul], which [change] can again be sensed by the soul. In this way it is comprehensible how a sensation of action on ideas in the soul could arise in the manner in which a sensation is produced from an impression that an external object creates on the [sensory] organ. (1777/1979, 1.49)

Inner sense works in the same way that outer sense does. As objects cause impressions in sensory organs that give rise to sensations that represent the objects, (mental) acts cause impressions on the mind/brain organ that give rise to sensations – which then represent the actions. These impressions remain and can be reawakened and apperceived; whence the possibility of apperceiving apperceiving and determining its properties.

Immediately after arguing that thinking can be observed only "from behind" in Essay 1, Tetens weighs the implications of this doctrine for a current controversy. He takes it to lie behind Johann Bernard Merian's critique of the *cogito*. If thinking can be observed only "from behind," then Descartes should not have said "I think" but "I have thought." Tetens thinks that this is right in a sense, although in another sense, it is sophistry.[7] Merian is correct if the *cogito* is understood as asserting that I know that I think or that I think that I think. It is, however, possible to say "I think" concurrently with the thinking, because that merely expresses the act of thinking (1777/1979, 1.48). I take Tetens' point to be that sensing thinking and then apperceiving the impression are necessary only for observing thinking and constructing theories of it. He complains that the representations of inner sense are very obscure (1777/1979, 1.45). He does not explain why this is unfortunate, but it may be because it makes the work of psychologists and philosophers difficult and controversial. Conversely, thinking itself can operate perfectly well without being observed and theorized. That is why Merian's criticism of the *cogito* might be sophistical. A cognizer who apperceives P can think P without either sensing or apperceiving his apperceiving. Since Descartes took mental activities to be transparent in that subjects who engaged in any of the various forms of thinking must be conscious that they are doing so, he would very probably reject Tetens' attempt to save him from his critics.

---

7 In my 2011, I only presented Tetens' endorsement of what he took to be Merian's critique of the *Cogito*.

3.2 The Elements (and Mechanics) of Apperceiving

Returning to Essay 3, Tetens presents the results of apperceiving apperceiving through the impressions that it leaves behind. One distinguishing feature of apperceiving is that it makes the representation preeminently lively and separated from others. (In Essay 4, this act is further divided into one of isolating or segregating and one of relating to other non-apperceived representations (1777/1979, 1.350–351)) A second distinguishing feature of apperceiving is that it involves a turning back to the representation. The powers of the soul, whether they are sensing faculties or representing ones are active, restless, inclined to move from one representation on to another. In apperceiving, the power moves on from the representation and then turns back to it. It is as though the power is bound to the representation (1777/1979, 1.281–284). This is the basis of his claim that apperceiving belongs to the species of relation of sameness and difference. The latter relation arises by going back and forth between different representations and he claims to observe a similar movement in apperceiving – not moving between representations, since this is the process of becoming conscious of representation – but moving away from the representation and back to it. Nevertheless, the back-and-forth movement in apperceiving is both the seed for and an analogue of the activity of comparing representations (1777/1979, 1.285).

Tetens claims that this sort of physical turning back to the representation is clear in many examples, but he does not give any (1777/1979, 1. 284). And, despite his efforts to show that apperceiving can be observed and so analyzed into its elements, his views about how it works seem grounded in non-self-evident theory (cf. 1777/1979, 1.vi). The doctrine that the powers of the soul are active was, as he knows, denied by "observers" such as Condillac, Bonnet, and Search. They take the thinking faculties to be like sense in being passive (1777/1979, 1.7, 1.264, 1.285). Further, it is hard to see how observation could support his claim that distancing oneself from a representation and then returning to it is an "essential factor" in producing a differentiation (1777/1979 , 1.284).

Section 5 takes up the question of the passive or active character of apperceiving, with Tetens coming down firmly on the side of action. He also repeats the surprising claim that since apperceiving is a matter of working up and making an impression or a representation

> it is without doubt an action of the *feeling* or representing faculty. (1777/1979, 1.289, my italics)

At this point, we can begin to see the basis of his disagreement with Bonnet and others. It is not so much that he thinks they err in finding commonalities between apperceiving and feeling; they err in taking the feeling faculty to be passive.

Tetens tries to explain how theorists have come to the mistaken view that apperceiving is passive. Comparing, combining and abstracting seem to be activities, but they are ascribed to the faculty of willing, because that is taken to be the faculty that determines the self-activity of the mind to some sort of efficacy. With this division, the understanding is relegated to the position of a purely passive faculty of receptivity. This, however, is an artificial division of the faculties of the soul. Why is it not better to distinguish a faculty that is self-active, but directed toward knowledge, from a self-active faculty that is directed outward to actions, that causes changes in humans and in the world that do not consist in representing and thinking? (1777/1979, 1.286) Tetens' question seems a good one. If the mind is efficacious, capable of producing representations that lead to action, why can it not also produce representations that are part of cognition? Empiricists might reply with a question of his own: If representational elements are tied to the mind's activities rather than to what the senses receive, then how are representations with those elements supposed to be applied to objects of the senses?

Besides this erring systematic division, there is also the fact that the German language distinguishes apperceiving from coming to apperceive. Coming to apperceive can happen both intentionally and in the absence of intention (1777/1979, 1.286). Sometimes we compare ideas with a view to discovering the relations in them; at other times we apperceive a relation without having tried to do so. Tetens asks: Is it not the same act of differentiating that occurs in both cases? But he does not think the issue is easy to resolve. Further, in the case of hearing the sound of a drum, apperceiving may be not just unintentional, but contrary to the subject's intention. The forced character of apperceiving may suggest that it is passive. All that really proves, however, is that the subject cannot withhold the action – and not that apperceiving is not an action. He thinks that the balance of evidence suggests that it is more reasonable to regard apperceiving as an additional action of the soul and so the faculty of apperception as active (1777/1979, 1.287–290).

3.3 Apperception and Self-Consciousness

Apperception is standardly understood as involving "self-consciousness" and this is also an element of Tetens' analysis. Earlier he had suggested that apperceiving involves distinguishing between the object and the self or the thought that a representation is in me (1777/1979, 1.273, see above pp. 18, 32). In section 5, he explains that

> in apperceiving something, we so to say in respect of this object come upon [it] as from a sleep. We grasp, apprehend it, we apprehend [*fassen*] ourselves in respect to it, think or remember [*besinnen*] ourselves and begin a new series of ideas. (1777/1979, 1.290)

In both these contexts he seems to be drawing attention to the fact that where there is an action, where there is a representation/object discerned there must also be an agent, a subject who acts, who is in some sense the correlate of the object discerned.

When Tetens explicitly takes up the question of the representation of the "I" and the identity of the "I," in Essay 5, however, he presents a very different account. He frames his theory in relation to Hume's infamous denial of a self. It is unclear whether he thinks that Hume was following the method of observation when turned his gaze inward and stumbled on only particular perceptions (Hume 1739/1978, 252). If he was, however, he did it badly, because he missed something essential. When Tetens engages in this exercise he reports that

> I feel a representation; still another, also an activity of thinking, an expression of will and so forth, and these impressions are distinguished, and actually, however, I sense still more.
>
> As often as I sense, apperceive, am directly conscious of, a representation, so am I as well conscious that this feeling of my modification is only a conspicuous feature in a much larger, more extensive, stronger (although obscure or less clear in its other elements) feeling. (1777/1979, 1.393)

Despite its unclear elements, he maintains that he is directly conscious of this large feeling. He claims further that the obscure ground of the large feeling is the same across different modifications. The concept of the identity of the I arises from the comparison of the present larger feeling with similar past feelings (1777/1979, 1.393–394).

Tetens had touched on this issue earlier in Essay 3, when he raised the question of the sense in which unconscious representations are unconscious. As noted, he claimed that undifferentiated elements of representations could be recalled by the imagination. He claims further that it is evident that all the elements of a representation, the obscure as well as the clear, leave traces behind. For that reason he asserts that

> [t]he foundation and basis of the soul consists, as Leibniz said, in unperceived representations. (1777/1979, 1.265)

With the "conscious of self" aspect of apperception, Tetens has moved away from the path of observation and embraced theory. The view that all aspects of all representations of the mind are retained by it in the form of traces could not be based on observation, but he had signaled in the Preface that the neural trace theory widely held and very probable, if not certain (1777/1979, 1.vi–vii). On the other hand, his claim Hume overlooked the large background feeling that is just as present and apperceptible as the individual feelings that he acknowledged seems to cast doubt on the method of observation itself (1777/1979, 1.393–394).

Further, insofar as Tetens' goal is to replace Hume's no-self theory with something more adequate, something that does not present the self as a product of the combination of representations into a whole by the imagination, his theory seems to fall short. In so far as the concept or idea of the identity of the self arises through acts of comparison, then it is a product of the thinking faculty and subjective for that reason. He is not presenting evidence of a perduring self, but describing how cognizers claim "same subject" through (subjective) acts of comparison. Tetens seems aware of the problem. He asserts that one consequence of his view is that the representation of my "I" is not the representation of a collection, as soldiers in a regiment. Rather the unity lies in the impression itself, in nature and not in a "made" combination (1777/1979, 1.394). The problem is that although this may be true of each apperceived representation of something, it does not seem to be true for the representation of a (continuing) "I," just because that representation is produced through comparison. Although not all relations involve comparison, comparison is a form of relating and thus a "concoction" of the thinking power (1777/1979, 1.276).

The last section of Essay 3 returns to the issue of the relation between apperceiving and feeling. It turns out that there is a close connection between apperceiving (relations) and feelings. Feelings are absolute, but there is nonetheless a feeling of relation (1777/1979, 1.291–293). He still cannot agree with Bonnet that judgments of relation are nothing more than feelings of relation, however, since it is incomprehensible to him how a feeling of relation, however clear or strong, can lead to a yes or no judgment (1777/1979, 1.291–292). Judging; for example, that the moon is not the same as the sun must be something active. Yet he has doubts about the firmness of observations in this area. Perhaps the feeling of relation is the cause that stimulates the thinking faculty into activity (1777/1979, 1.294).

4 Apperception as an Essential Element of Thinking

The topic of Essay 4 is thinking and the power of thinking. Apperceiving is not so much the *analysandum* as part of the *analysans*. Apperceiving is the first and most basic action of the thinking faculty, the faculty through which humans recognize the relations and connections among objects (1777/1979, 1.293). It is also an element in the other most important simple (i.e., non-derivative) actions of the thinking faculty (1777/1979, 1.346–347), including judging, inferring and deducing.[8] Insofar as apperceiving is necessary for forming ideas (through comparing) and ideas are necessary for judgments (that relate ideas) and judgments are necessary for inferences and deductions that relate them, this role was foreordained by the nature of apperceiving. Tetens maintains, however, that it plays a further crucial role in deductions (inferences with more than one premise).

To bring out that role, he contrasts merely placing propositions together and apperceiving the relations among them with making an inference or a deduction. The former could happen by combining simple sentences in a new judgment: A and B and C. By contrast, if someone derives C from A, then the premise and the conclusion are not so much related to each other by the thinking faculty as the conclusion is produced by the action of the thinking faculty upon its modification by the premises. The action of deriving produces a relation of ideas that had not been there before (see also 1777/1979, 1.322). (On the other hand, he maintains that deriving is an expression of the faculty of relating ideas, but one with a higher or stronger effect (1777/1979, 1.369–370)).

The producing of one proposition from others is only half of the act of inferring; if it were all, then there would be nothing but an obscure or unconscious inference. The second essential part of inferring and deducing is apperceiving the relation between the conclusion that is produced and the premise(s) from which it follows.

> This relationship consists in dependency and belongs to the relations which arise from a causal connection ... Inference is deriving one [proposition] from another, and apperceiving the dependency of the last upon the first. (1777/1979, 1.371)

Tetens' view about the requirements of deductions, or what we would call inferences seems correct. It is not enough to produce a conclusion from premises; inferring requires that the subject grasp the rational dependency of the conclusion on the premises. But how on his theory can the dependency be apperceived?

According to Tetens the act of producing the conclusion must leave a trace on the mind/brain, a trace that can be reawakened and apperceived. This "from behind" mechanism cannot, however, provide an account of the subject's appreciation of the relation of dependency between premise(s) and conclusion as she makes the inference. Since the original activity was unconscious, reawakening

---

[8] As do other scholars of this period (e.g. Kant), Tetens distinguishes deductions [*Schlusse*] which require more than one premise, from immediate inferences [*Folgerungen*] that do not.

the trace would enliven the unconscious act of producing. Apperceiving the reawakened trace – separating the impression of unconsciously producing a representation out of others from other representations – would not help. It would inform the subject of a causal dependency between her representations, but not of their rational relations. It is not possible for the subject to apperceive a trace of an act of deriving, because deriving or inferring requires apperceiving and, by hypothesis, there is no apperceiving and hence no deriving in the original act.

Tetens sees that an appreciation of rational dependence is essential for inferring or deducing, but he confuses himself and his readers by trying to segregate this appreciation from the production of the conclusion. His wording suggests that the deriving and the appreciating of the dependence relation are separate elements of a total process. The appreciation of the rational relations and the production of the conclusion can, however, be distinguished only analytically; the appreciation of the rational relations is an inseparable aspect of the act of deriving. If reasoning requires being conscious of or apperceiving relations of rational dependence between premises and conclusion and that cannot be done after the fact – by being conscious of a past unconscious action – then the apperceiving must be coeval with the act of producing the conclusion.

Inferring need not violate Tetens' principle that a mind can perform only one act at a time. Inferring would be a matter of drawing one claim from another while being conscious of or apperceiving the rational causal dependence of the conclusion on the premises. The problem with his analysis does not lie in the one mental activity at a time principle, but in his Lockean theory of mental act consciousness. Given his account of apperceiving mental acts, through reviving traces left by non-apperceived acts, it is not possible to apperceive deriving or inferring – unless they already were already conscious activities.

Descartes, Locke, and Leibniz, among many others, held that thinking was conscious or transparent. They had trouble explaining how that was possible. Leibniz backed off the perceptual model that he initially accepted, and Locke did not develop his account of inner sense. Tetens undertakes this Lockean project but does not spell out how retaining traces of mental activities that can later be objects of discernment, consciousness, provides the sort of consciousness of mental activities that is essential to their rational character. When the details are filled in, his theory does not explain how an inner sense whose contents are later apperceived accounts for mental operations, such as inferring and deducing, but how and why it is inadequate for the task. More broadly, although apperceiving the representation of a linden tree – separating out the linden tree from a background – may offer a plausible account of some aspects of conscious representation, Tetens' explanation of apperceiving apperceiving, cognizing the act of apperceiving, *via* a trace is not plausible. How can a trace left by an unconscious act explain the subject's consciousness of the linden representation as that representation is brought to consciousness?

As noted, Kant is widely believed to have made a serious study of Tetens' *Essays*. From the early 60s to the mid-70s, Kant took inner sense to be the key faculty required for the kind of cognition distinctive of humans. He is especially clear on this point in an early essay, *The False Subtlety of the Four Syllogistic Figures* (1762):

> the faculty of inner sense, that is to say, the faculty of making [*zu machen*] one's own representations the objects of one's thought. This faculty cannot be derived from any other faculty. It is, in the strict sense of the term, a fundamental faculty, which in my opinion, can only belong to rational beings. But it is upon this faculty that the entire higher faculty of cognition is based. (AA 02: 60)[9]

Although the evidence is less straightforward, he seems to have retained this view through the mid-70s.[10] As every reader of the *Critique* knows, his mature theory is very different. It is apperception and not inner sense that makes cognition possible. Inner sense plays several important roles in his epistemological theory, but one is to present a contrast case to the active faculty of apperception that is crucial to higher cognition (e.g., *CPR*, B152–153, see also AA 07: 135). It seems a reasonable interpretive hypothesis that his extensive reading of Tetens may have helped him to appreciate the problems with his original view that inner sense is the key faculty in judging and reasoning.

Some years ago, T. H. Weldon suggested that Kant was largely in agreement with Tetens' theory of inner sense. In Weldon's view, although Kant thought that apperception and not inner sense provided immediate awareness of thinking, he agreed that inner sense could still be an awareness of an awareness or awareness of a past act of perceiving (1958, 262). Kant's most explicit statement on this issue occurs in the section of the B Deduction where he contrasts inner sense and apperception:

> [S]ynthesis is nothing but the unity of the understanding's act: the act of which the understanding is conscious as an act even apart from sensibility. (*CPR*, B153)

---

[9] Reference to Kant's works other than the *Critique of Pure Reason* are given in the text by the volume and page number of Kant (1900). References to the *Critique of Pure Reason* are given by the standard A and B notation. This translation is from Walford and Meerbote 1992. Translations of the *Critique of Pure Reason* are from Pluhar 1996, except that I translate *Vorstellung* as "representation," not "presentation."

[10] According to student lecture notes (e.g., AA 28: 276), a not completely reliable source, he continued to stress the importance of inner sense through the 70s. In an important set of *Reflections*, the so-called "Duisburg Nachlaß" (1776–1778), he again mentions inner sense in connection with the use of the higher powers. See my 2011, 21, for further discussion.

This text is reflected in Weldon's interpretive claim that, for Kant, consciousness of thinking is achieved through apperception. In suggesting that cognizers can be conscious of their thinking apart from sensibility, however, Kant moves decisively away from Tetens' Lockean view of inner sense. Further, as we have just seen, Tetens' theory of how mental activity is apperceived *via* a key contribution from inner sense reveals that inner sense cannot play a role in explaining Kant's target, *viz.* the possibility of higher cognition of empirical objects. For these reasons I think it is doubtful that Kant agreed with Tetens that inner sense provides any awareness of thinking.[11] Further in introducing "inner sense" in the Transcendental Aesthetic, he presents it as the faculty by means of which the mind is aware of its states. Through inner sense the mind

> Intuits itself, or [that is] its inner state, although it gives no intuition of the soul itself as an object (*CPR*, A22/B37).

There is no hint that the faculty also registers impressions or intuitions of actions, as is expressly the case for Tetensian inner sense.

5 The One Faculty Thesis Defended

In Essay 9 (On the Fundamental Principle of Sensing, Representing and Thinking) Tetens tries to show that, despite his objections and those of others, there is one fundamental faculty of which others are mere expressions. The key to resolving the puzzle lies in recognizing that feeling or sensing cannot be a pure receptivity.

> Is this act [of apperceiving] something other than an expression of the same power to which the feeling of relations is ascribed? Is it not the effect of this faculty, in so far as it is an active

---

[11] Weldon takes Kant to agree with Tetens that inner sense provides an awareness of awareness as well as an awareness of thinking. The question of whether Kant thinks that inner sense provides an awareness of perceiving – as opposed to an awareness of perceptions – is less clear cut. See 07, 134a. Here Kant invites us to imagine that we are applying a concept or perceiving and then to consider the two different sorts of self-consciousness that is involved. Since we are invited to imagine an act of receiving an impression, perhaps this is a case of being aware of an awareness through inner sense. But the whole thing is odd, since Kant is describing the reception of sensory information as an act. Weldon may have been influenced in this discussion by Ryle's famous "one-step behind" analysis of thinking. Like Tetens, Ryle believed that an intellectual act (performance in Ryle's terminology) could only be the concern of a higher order performance and not of itself (1963, 188, originally published in 1949). For reasons we have seen, however, neither Tetens nor Ryle can adequately explain the self-awareness that permits higher level thinking itself – let alone a later commentary on it.

power, namely, in so far as it does not merely record and feel modifications, and retroact or react [*zurückwirket*] to them, but also in so far a new activity is combined with this reaction? An active faculty of sensing is thus the faculty that produces the thought of relation [...]. (1777/1979, 1.607, see also 1.609)

An obvious question to ask about this theory is whether it is faithful to Tetens' standard of finding real resolutions that display the underlying commonalities across seemingly diverse activities. It seems reasonable to object that he has found a common faculty simply by grafting an active discerning faculty onto a passive sensing one. It's not obvious how to settle such a question, however, and there are more straightforward objections to the theory.

The idea that sensory systems are not merely passive recipients of impressions but actively engaged in seeking sensory *data* has often been bruited; for example, by the psychologist J.J. Gibson (1966). That, however, cannot be Tetens' position. The relations produced by the power of apperceiving are "nothing outside the mind." Under those circumstances, the senses cannot actively look for relations that are not out there. Rather, what would be produced by Tetensian active sensing would be representations with elements that do not derive from objects. Although Tetens may still largely follow Locke's observational method, with this theory, he is denying Empiricist *credo* that nothing is in the mind that was not first in the senses. Earlier he had countered the objection that relations that are "creatures of the mind," are not in the senses, by maintaining that inner sense records the activities that relate different objects or images. Here he comes at the problem from a somewhat different angle. It is not that the (inner) sense records the activities that produce relations, but that the senses directly produce relational thoughts themselves. Either way, Tetens is giving up the cardinal virtue of Empiricism that the mind's representations are faithful to characteristics of objects outside the mind.

In the B Deduction discussion where Kant contrasts inner sense and apperception, he starts with the paradox that subjects know themselves only as they appear. This seems paradoxical because the human mind would thus be active and passive in the same transaction (*CPR*, B152–153).[12] It's not clear why this should be a problem within his theory, since he carefully distinguishes the mind's passive and active faculties. On the other hand, anyone who accepts a one fundamental faculty thesis (e.g., Tetens) will have that faculty, or its differing expressions, being active and passive in the same transaction. Kant explains that psychologists get out of the

---

12 Kant's diagnosis seems far-fetched. Presumably his readers were perplexed not about active and passive powers, but about his *prima facie* bizarre claim that humans know themselves only as appearances.

conundrum by incorrectly identifying inner sense (a faculty that registers states) and apperception (a faculty that produces states with additional representational content). In Tetens' case, the active faculty of apperception is "reduced" to a faculty of feeling that engages in active sensing. Kant objects that, in humans, the active power of the understanding/apperception is not a power of intuitions (*CPR*, B153). On the other hand, if Tetens is correct that relational ideas are "nothing outside the mind," then since the mental states that are accessed through inner sense stand in temporal relations, inner sense does not present the mind as it is – independently of the mind's way of representing its own states – but only as it appears. The contents that are accessed through inner sense would have been given special relational contents by the active powers of the mind, as Kant maintains.

Although Tetens finally comes down on the side of the one-faculty thesis, he is modest about what can be known about the fundamental faculty. The difficulty is that we could know the nature of this faculty only if we could have some idea of its first effect as a natural power. Feeling is the first expression of the power – but we have no traces of the activities that produce that first expression (1777/1979, 1.737, 1.687). Hence at the end, we are where we were at the beginning, with no idea about the original acts of the power; we cannot determine whether its activities are those of a simple immaterial thing or a bodily brain (1777/1979, 1.739).

6 Relating Tetens' Theory of Apperception to Kant's

Several scholars have drawn connections between Tetens' theories and Kant's. As just noted, Weldon maintains that Kant more or less took over Tetens' theory of inner sense. In his extensive study of the Transcendental Deduction, H. J. DeVleeschauwer argues that Tetens' *Essays* provided a psychological background that enabled Kant finally to complete his analysis of the conditions required for objective cognition in 1781. DeVleeschauwer maintains, in particular, that Kant owes his theory of the productive imagination to Tetens. He also sees important parallels between Tetens' theories and the three syntheses of the A Deduction, though he thinks there are important differences in the case of the third synthesis, that of recognition (*CPR*, A103) or of apperception (*CPR*, A94n., A115) (1939/1962, 82 ff.).

We are now in a position to take a fresh look at one question about influence. What are the relations between Tetens' views and those of his most celebrated reader on a topic that is central to both of their theories, apperception? The question is fraught, because after nearly two and a half centuries of scholarly effort, there is still no consensus on Kant's theory of apperception. I start with some fairly non-controversial points and move on to others that may be disputed.

Tetens and Kant agree on the existence of unconscious representations. Tetens holds that representations become conscious through being apperceived. Kant seems to hold a similar view. In the A Deduction, he claims that unless representations could become conscious they would be nothing for the subject as a cognitive being (*CPR*, A120, A116, A116a, cf. B131–132); and he seems to equate becoming conscious with being empirically apperceived (*CPR*, A107, A115). Like Tetens', Kant's apperceptive faculty is active. In the A Deduction, Kant calls apperception a "root faculty" (*CPR*, A114). It is possible to read this claim as akin to Tetens' view that apperception is a simple, fundamental, non-derivative faculty. Tetens tries to provide analyzes of various cognitive capacities that reveal apperceiving's role as a basic activity of the mind. Kant's argument for the root character of the faculty of apperception in the Deduction chapter seems, however, to have a different source. He introduces this "root faculty" in trying to explain a consequence of his theory, the

> strange and quite preposterous [claim] that nature should conform to our subjective basis, apperception – indeed that nature should in regard to its law-governedness depend on this basis [...] *we see nature in its unity merely in the root power for all our cognition, viz., in transcendental apperception* [...]. (*CPR*, A114, my italics)

The explanation for the preposterous claim is not that various thinking activities can be seen to be variants of apperceiving. Rather, transcendental apperception is a root power, because any representation must belong to the unity of apperception. The highest principle of cognition is the principle of the unity of apperception (*CPR*, A117n., B136), the principle that

> representations represent something in me only inasmuch as together with all others they belong to one consciousness; and hence they must at least be capable of being connected in it.) This principle holds a priori, and may be called the transcendental principle of the unity of whatever is manifold in our representations. (*CPR*, A116)

Transcendental apperception is a "root faculty" for all cognition, not because it is a simple power that is presupposed in the operations of other powers, but because the unity of apperception that it produces is a requirement for all cognitions.

In the Dialectic, Kant takes up the "one-faculty project" with which Tetens is so engaged. He considers the ideal of reducing all the powers of the soul to a single power (*CPR*, A682/B 710), but his point is largely a critical one. Some who pursue this project err in mistaking a regulative idea of reason – reason prods us to look for ever more basic faculties – for a proof that there is a single power of the simple soul. Tetens was also skeptical about merely assuming a basic power on the grounds of the simplicity of the soul. He thought the assumption could lead to superficial and incorrect analyzes of the faculties involved in cognition. On this point Tetens and Kant agree that the division of the mind into faculties must proceed on the basis of analysis and not through a pre-commitment to the result (see also Kant, AA 20: 206). Tetens thinks the analysis is mainly based on observation of the faculties' effects, whereas Kant expresses serious reservations about the trustworthiness of observation of the soul's states and activities in *Anthropology from a Pragmatic Point of View* (AA 07: 133).

Kant refers both to a faculty of apperception and to a "transcendental unity of apperception." The point of his remarks about empirical consciousness or apperception is that it presupposes the transcendental unity of apperception. Insofar as "transcendental" is understood as making reference to necessary conditions for cognition (*CPR*, A94/B126, A783/B811), there is a sense in which Tetens' Essay 4 is a "transcendental" inquiry. Its thesis is that apperceiving is one of the basic faculties required for thinking or cognition (1777/1979, 1.295). Thiel maintains that Tetens also argues that the self and its unity are necessary conditions for cognitive experience. In Essay 4, Tetens claims that a representation of the self is presupposed in judgments about objects as real, external and present (1777/1979, 1.344). In Essay 13, he argues that bringing the multiplicity of elements together in a single feeling presupposes a single substantial agent; otherwise, the elements would never form a whole (1777/1979, 2.197). As Thiel observes, Tetens' invocation of a simple substantial self to account for cognition is a metaphysical claim that Kant would not countenance (Thiel 2018, 72–74).

For Tetens, the representation of the self is necessary for judging objects. Kant understands the relation between object cognition and the unity of the self to be even closer. Most commentators agree that he claims that object cognition and the unity of apperception to mutually imply each other.[13] He expresses the view in both editions:

> The unity that the object makes necessary can be nothing other than the formal unity of consciousness in the synthesis of the manifold of the representations. (*CPR*, A105)

> The reference of representations to an object consists solely in this unity of consciousness […]. (*CPR*, B137)

In the B Paralogisms chapter he is particularly clear about the necessity of object cognition to a subject's recognition of her own unity:

---

13 See e.g, Strawson 1966, 89 ff., 98 ff., Allison 1983, 144, Cassam 1997, 36, 91.

> We are acquainted with the unity of consciousness itself only by its being for us an indispensable requirement for the possibility of experience [empirical cognition]. (*CPR*, B420, see also A107, B133)

Finally, most commentators agree that the unity of apperception requires some sort of synthesis. This point is reasonably obvious in the text:

> I am ... conscious of the self as identical, as regards the manifold of the representations given to me in an intuition, because I call them one and all **my** representations that make up **one** representation. That is tantamount to saying that I am conscious of a necessary synthesis of them. This synthesis is called the original synthetic unity of apperception. (*CPR*, B135–136)

In Kant's view the idea of an identical self does not arise through comparing feelings, large or otherwise, but through synthesizing or combining representations.

As noted, there is scholarly disagreement about exactly what the unity of apperception involves. I take a passage in the B Deduction, where Kant claims that a subject can refer to or represent her own unity only by being conscious of the synthesizing that produces it, to provide important keys to his position about what the unity involves and about how humans represent it:

> This same thoroughgoing identity of the apperception of a manifold given in intuition contains a synthesis of representations, and is possible only through the consciousness of this synthesis. For the empirical consciousness that accompanies different representations is intrinsically scattered [*zerstreut*] and without any reference to the subject's identity. Hence this reference comes about not through my merely accompanying each representation with consciousness, but through my **adding** one representation to another and being conscious of their synthesis. Hence only because I can combine a manifold of given representations *in one consciousness*, is it possible for me to represent the *identity itself of the consciousness in these representations*. (*CPR*, B133, amended translation, my italics)

When a subject (consciously) combines some representations in others, she is conscious of the dependence of the latter representations on the representations from which it was produced (my 2011, 129). Tetens gives an example of this phenomenon in discussing deductions: In a deduction, the subject produces the conclusion upon modification by the premises, the conclusion thus depends on the premises and the subject must apperceive this relation of dependency (above p. 34). I take it that Kant believes that these conditions must be met by any act of higher cognition, judging as well as inferring or deducing (see my 2011, 267–268). Insofar as a cognizer apperceives (is conscious of) some of her mental states as depending on others, however, she understands them to stand in relations of necessary connection: The judgment or conclusion could not exist without the mental states that produce it; the latter states could not be part of cognition unless they produced judgments (see my 2011, 130–131).

Hume thought that there were two ways to avoid the no-self conclusion that he could not himself escape (Hume 1739/1978, pp. 633–636). Find a constant impression of a self to which different mental states can be attached or establish that the states have a "real bond" or necessary connection across them (Hume 1739/1978, 250, 252, 259). What Kant realized was that "higher cognition" – judging and inferring – required just the sort of real bond across mental states that made them states of a single "I." Hence he realized that his analysis of empirical cognition was simultaneously an account of the synthetic unity of apperception. Mental states belong to the same "I-think" insofar as they are or can be connected to each other through acts of higher cognition.[14]

Tetens tried to explain how cognizers are able to use the concept of a self by appealing to an observable self-feeling that they could compare across different lively modifications that included the same obscure background. Kant's solution to the problem arose from a totally different method, one that used neither observation, nor "evident" metaphysical hypotheses. His "transcendental" method was concerned not just with finding the necessary conditions for the possibility of cognition, but with *a priori* representations:

> Hence the transcendental deduction of all *a priori* concepts has a principle to which the entire investigation must be directed: viz., the principle that these concepts must be recognized as *a priori* conditions for the possibility of experience (whether the possibility of the intuition found in experience, or the possibility of the thought). (*CPR*, A 94/ B126)

That is, transcendental philosophy is concerned not with just any necessary conditions for cognition, but only with conditions that involve *a priori* representations.

---

14 Since Kant accepts unconscious representations, an obvious question arises about how these states could belong to the same self as states involved in conscious judging and inferring. Kant seems to supply an answer in the A Deduction: "All intuitions are nothing for us ...if they cannot be taken up into consciousness, whether they impinge on it directly or indirectly... We are conscious of *a priori* of the thoroughgoing identity of ourselves in regard to all representations that can ever belong to our cognition. ...Such representations represent something to me only inasmuch as together with all others they belong to one consciousness; and hence they must at least be capable of being connected in it. (A116)." I take Kant's claim to be the unconscious representations participate indirectly in cognition by being combined with others in conscious representations that are consciously combined in rational cognition. Subjects would not cognize their necessary connection to other states, but would infer it and model it through the combinations they are conscious in producing.

Kant divided representations into the *a posteriori* and *a priori* and accepted Hume's view that inner sense provided no basis for an I-representation. Hence, for him, the I-think had to be *a priori*. The introduction to the *First Critique* opens by explaining how humans come to have *a priori* representations:

> In part these objects by themselves, bring about representations. In part they set in motion our understanding's activity [...]
> But even though all our cognition starts *with* experience, that does not mean that all of it arises *from* experience. *For it might well be that even our experiential cognition is composite, consisting of what we receive through impressions and what our own cognitive power supplies from itself (sensory impressions merely prompting it to do so)*. (CPR, B1–2, my italics)

That is, *a posteriori* elements of cognition come from the senses, but *a priori* elements come from the activity of the (active) faculties. The activity of the power of understanding or apperception is combining representations in inferences and judgments and recognizing the relations of dependence thereby produced. Where Tetens and Kant essentially differ is that Tetens believes that subjects can be aware of their own activities only through the traces left by the activities on inner sense, whereas, as noted, Kant maintains that

> [S]ynthesis is nothing but the unity of the understanding's act: the act of which the understanding is conscious as an act even apart from sensibility. (CPR, B153)

Kant is not claiming that the understanding non-sensibly senses or intuits the act, but that the subject is cognizant of conscious mental acts that she performs, as she is cognizant of intentional actions that she performs – not by watching herself through some sense, but just by performing the action. Through being so cognizant she represents her representations as bound together by relations of rational dependence and so as not separate and isolated, but as necessarily connected and so belonging to a single self. The relations of necessary connection are the *a priori* elements that make the I-think an *a priori* representation.

One way to see the crucial difference between Tetens' and Kant's views about the necessary unity of the cognitive self[15] is in terms of their differing ways of trying to improve on Locke's doctrine of inner sense. Tetens tries to fill in the account by positing traces of mental activities that can then be sensed, whereas Kant limits inner sense to awareness of mental states, not activities. As argued above (p. 34), Tetens' trace theory makes him unable to account for something that he recognizes as necessary to rational cognition, *viz.*, understanding that the conclusion of an in-

---

[15] Thiel (2018, 68) notes that Tetens distinguishes two senses of "soul" or "self," the psychological and the metaphysical. I am using "cognitive" to refer to Tetens' psychological sense of self.

ference does not simply come after the premises or is not simply caused by them, but is rationally dependent on them. Kant's doctrine that the only objects of inner sense are mental states and not activities leads to a different set of problems. There seem to be too many sources of information about mental states. Do cognizers know that they believe that there will not be a third world war[16] by turning their inner sense towards their belief store or by thinking about the causes of war and inferring that a third world war is unlikely (no inner sensing required)? Tetens complained about the obscurity of the representations of inner sense (1777/1979, 1.45), but perhaps both he and Kant took the theory of inner sense to be more self-evident and certain than it is. Given the many close relations between inner sense and apperception, Locke's theory created difficulties for Tetens in analyzing the role of apperception in rational thought and it led Kant to offer what is widely regarded as an undeveloped account of cognizers' knowledge of particular mental states through empirical apperception.

---

16 To borrow Evans' (1982) classic example.

Udo Thiel
Between Empirical Psychology and Transcendental Philosophy: Ernst Platner on the Feeling of Self

Abstract: This essay examines Platner's conceptual distinctions and arguments on the topic of relating to one's own self. Considering both his pre- and post-Kantian contributions the paper explains and critically evaluates Platner's position in relation to Kant and Reinhold. Platner's attempt to distinguish between different forms of relating to one's own self is to be recommended, but there are several major problems with his account. For the most part these problems are due to the fact that Platner mixes up psychological considerations with transcendental ideas.

1 Introduction

It is unfortunate that histories of the notion of self-consciousness rarely mention Ernst Platner. This neglect may be due to a mischaracterization of his approach as simply "Wolffian" and thus rather unoriginal (see, for example, Frank 2002, 39). But although his account has many problems, Platner employs conceptual distinctions and arguments that are worth considering in their own right, and they appear in various forms in present-day discussions of the topic. In this essay we shall analyze and critically evaluate Platner's contribution mainly in its relation to Kant and Reinhold. Therefore, we shall focus on the third edition of his *Philosophische Aphorismen* (1793) which contains Platner's comments on Kant and Reinhold as well as the final version of his thoughts on self-consciousness.[1] We shall also compare these post-Kantian ideas with Platner's analysis of self-consciousness in his pre-Kantian writings, especially in his *Anthropologie* of 1772.

It is plain that both the 1770s and 1790s versions of Platner's account of self-consciousness belong to the wider context of the pre-Kantian discussions of the topic, including of course those of Christian Wolff, his followers and critics. This larger context, the rather complex history of the topic from Locke to Wolff and beyond, cannot be rehearsed here,[2] however it is worth noting that even in his writ-

---

[1] Platner notes that, when he composed the 1784 edition of *Aphorismen*, he had not studied Kant's philosophy in any depth, which is why he does not comment extensively on Kant in that edition (Platner 1793, iii).
[2] Some of the relevant context is discussed in Thiel 2014.

ings from the 1770s Platner emphasized one aspect of self-consciousness that many of his contemporaries neglected – the embodied nature of consciousness. In the 1790s Platner develops new ideas on this theme, taking into account Kantian and Reinholdian perspectives, but without abandoning the earlier idea of embodiment, even if this idea is now somewhat marginalized. As we shall see, however, the problems of Platner's post-Kantian account are connected with its relation to his earlier understanding of self-consciousness.

In the 1793 edition of his *Philosophische Aphorismen* Platner describes his own general position in philosophy as a "properly understood scepticism" (Platner 1793, xv: *wohlverstandener Skeptizismus*). Rejecting a radical, Humean scepticism,[3] he characterizes his own approach as a middle way between Kant and his followers on the one hand, and Kant's critics on the other (Platner 1793, v). He calls his approach a "sceptical critique" in contrast with Kant's critical philosophy which he dubs "dogmatic" (Platner 1793, 447–450, §§ 772–774). Platner argues against Kant that we are not able to explain the nature of our own cognitive capacities.[4] He holds that we are not able to identify a priori conditions of knowledge with absolute certainty. At best we can formulate "reasonable hypotheses" (Platner 1793, x).

Platner's remarks on consciousness and self-consciousness are scattered across the logic- and metaphysic-sections of his 1793 *Philosophische Aphorismen*. There is no systematic discussion of the topic in Platner, but on the basis of an analysis of the various aphorisms in which he comments on consciousness, we can ascribe to him a distinction between four kinds of consciousness all of which involve a relating to one's own self.

1. Consciousness of representations (the "I think") (Platner 1793, 79, §126).
2. Consciousness of existence; that is, the existence of one's own soul (the "I am") (Platner 1793, 88, §145).
3. Consciousness of personality (Platner 1793, 76, § 122).
4. Consciousness as the feeling of self (*Selbstgefühl* or the *Gefühl Ich*) (Platner 1793, 88, §146).

---

[3] Arthur Wreschner (1893, 12, 109–111 et al.) claims that the sceptical aspects in the late Platner are due to the influence of G. E. Schulze's *Aenesidemus* and its critique of Reinhold and Kant. While it is true that there are similarities between some of Schulze's and Platner's criticisms of Kant, there are also significant differences. Schulze seems to advocate a return to an essentially Humean scepticism. Platner, by contrast, admires Hume (Platner 1793, 358, § 705), but rejects Humean scepticism and especially the "bundle" view of the self which he ascribes to Hume (Platner 1793, 90, § 150). See the discussion below.
[4] "Das menschliche Erkenntnißvermögen hat nicht das Ansehen sich selbst erklären zu können" (Platner 1793, 364, § 709).

As we shall see, these four types of consciousness are connected to one another in various ways, even if Platner himself does not always identify and explain these connections. We shall see also that, according to Platner, the feeling of self, *Selbstgefühl* or the *Gefühl Ich*, turns out to be the most fundamental type of consciousness and functions as a necessary condition of the other forms of consciousness.

2 Consciousness of Representations: Wolff – Reinhold – Platner

Although Platner argues for the existence of unconscious representations (Platner 1793, 32–36, §§ 28–33, and 69–71, § 113), he holds that, strictly speaking, only conscious representations should count as representations, or are "complete representations" [*völlige Vorstellungen*] (Platner 1793, 32, § 28). Obviously, then, when Platner deals with consciousness, only complete representations are at issue. Concerning these, he argues that the consciousness of representations necessarily involves the capacity to differentiate (Platner 1772, 13, § 45). Like many of his contemporaries, then, Platner follows Wolff on consciousness. Wolff argues in his *German Metaphysics* of 1720 that it is part of our consciousness of objects that we distinguish objects from one another (Wolff 1751, § 729).[5] Further, Wolff argues that in distinguishing objects from one another, we become conscious of our own act of distinguishing and, thereby, of ourselves, as distinct from the objects of which we are conscious (Wolff 1751, § 731). For Wolff, then, the act of differentiating brings along a consciousness of this act and thereby a consciousness of the subject performing that act. In this sense, consciousness involves a relating to both the subject and the object of consciousness.

These ideas are present in modified ways in both Platner's pre- and post-Kantian writings. Clearly inspired by Wolff, Platner comments in his *Anthropologie* of 1772 on the capacity to differentiate and its role for consciousness as follows:

> I am conscious of the objects of which I think as being outside me, and I distinguish them from my own person, from my own self – I compare each time the relation in which I

---

5 Wolff says here that "we are conscious of things when we distinguish them from one another" [wir ... [sind] uns alsdenn der Dinge bewust [...], wenn wir sie voneinander unterscheiden]. For a detailed account of Wolff on consciousness, see Thiel 2014, 304–314, and Thiel 2019, 201–210. The idea that consciousness is linked to the capacity to differentiate goes back to Aristotle. See, for example, Schmitt 2002, 122–130. For a general account of Platner's relation to Wolff, see Nowitzki 2007.

stand to them – hence I am always conscious of my own self, by never confusing my self with other objects. Therefore, I am conscious of my own existence. (Platner 1772, 13, § 45)[6]

In his later writings Platner explains his concept of self-consciousness by introducing the notions of clear and distinct representations. A consciousness of a representation is distinct, he argues, when the soul perceives not only the difference between itself and the object but also represents to itself the act of differentiating between subject and object. Without representing of the act of differentiating, the consciousness of the representation is not distinct but merely "clear" (Platner 1793, 79–80, § 127).[7] For Platner, all consciousness involves differentiating. However, this activity often happens so fast, he argues, that it seems to many that it does not occur at all. This should not mislead us, he insists. It remains true that there is no consciousness without differentiating, but there is of course consciousness that is not distinct; that is, that does not involve the consciousness of the act of differentiating (Platner 1793, 80, § 128).

Some of Platner's 1793 formulations are reminiscent of Reinhold's account of consciousness, and Platner explicitly appeals to Reinhold in this context (Platner, 1793, 78, § 124; 81, § 130). The concept of representation of course plays a central role in Reinhold's *Elementarphilosophie*. Possibly, like Platner, in emphasizing the centrality of concept of representation and the notion of differentiating, Reinhold was inspired by Wolffian thoughts about this matter.[8] However, unlike Wolff, Reinhold develops a theory, according to which the relations between the subject, the object, and the representation are to be expressed in a principle which is meant to function as the foundation of thought in general, and thereby, also of philosophy. Reinhold's "principle of consciousness" states that "in consciousness the representation is distinguished by the subject from both the subject and the object and related to both" (Reinhold 1791, 78).[9] Thus, representing always involves both a subject and an object, as well as the acts of differentiating and relating the repre-

---

[6] "Ich bin mir der Gegenstände die ich denke, als außer mir bewußt, und unterscheide sie von meiner Person von mir selbst – ich vergleiche jedesmal das Verhältnis in denen ich mit ihnen stehe – Also bin ich mir meiner selbst bewußt, indem ich mich niemals mit andern Gegenständen vermische. Folglich bin ich mir meines Daseyns bewußt."

[7] "Wenn die Seele den Unterschied des Gegenstandes und ihrer selbst [...] so wahrnimmt, daß sie sich wiederum die Unterscheidung vorstellt: so ist das Bewußtseyn deutlich; außerdem nur klar."

[8] Alessandro Lazzari argues that Reinhold's account of consciousness and the capacity to differentiate can be linked to Platner's early doctrine of the soul and his distinction between self and body. See Lazzari 2004, 25. It seems, however, that Platner and Reinhold draw on the same, Wolffian sources here. See Thiel 2007.

[9] "[...] dass die Vorstellung im Bewußtseyn durch das Subjekt vom Objekt und Subjekt unterschieden und auf beyde bezogen werde."

sentation with regard to both subject and object. Reinhold's principle assumes that relating to the object and relating to the subject are equiprimordial. According to Reinhold, this twofold relating to both subject and object makes representing possible in the first place. It is important to note that the relating to the subject that the principle invokes is not itself representational but rather a necessary condition of representing.

In 1793 Platner argues, seemingly following Reinhold, that a sensory representation is related by the soul "on the one hand to the external object, and to the soul as the representing subject on the other. And in this way emerges *consciousness*, which involves on the one hand *the consciousness of the object* and *self-consciousness* on the other" (Platner 1793, 77, § 123).[10] In short, Platner maintains that complete representations involve a relating both to an object and to the subject of thought or the soul (Platner 1793, 35, § 32). Platner points out that the term "soul" does not refer to a metaphysical substance here, but to a mere subject of thought (Platner 1793, 31–32, § 27). Note, however, that, unlike Reinhold, Platner calls the original relating of the representation to the subject "self-consciousness." We shall return to this issue below.

As far as the relating to an object is concerned, Platner argues that it requires a certain "connection of thought" (Platner 1793, 79, § 125: *Verbindung des Denkens*), a point with which both Kant and Reinhold could agree. If "the soul did not relate the representations to itself," Platner states, "then it could not relate them to an object either; for the latter presupposes necessarily that the representation is connected in one consciousness" (Platner 1793, 79, § 125).[11] The very act of representing, then, necessarily involves a relating to the subject. Self-consciousness, Platner says, accompanies all complete representations. It can be expressed by the *I think* (Platner 1793, 79, § 126).[12]

Further, Platner argues, that the diachronic *identity* of the thinking or representing subject, too, is a requirement for having a representation:

> Regarding self-consciousness [...]: If the soul did not look back from the last parts of the representation to the first parts and did not feel that it was it [the same soul] that had the first

---

10 "So wie das Anerkennen erfolgt und in diesem die sinnliche Vorstellung vollendet ist [...], wird die letztere bezogen einerseits auf einen äußerlichen Gegenstand, andererseits auf die Seele als auf das vorstellende Subjekt. Und so entsteht das *Bewußtseyn*, in welchem einerseits *Bewußtseyn des Gegenstandes* ist, und andererseits *Selbstbewußtseyn*."
11 "Bezieht aber die Seele die Vorstellungen nicht auf sich, so kann sie sie auch nicht beziehen auf einen Gegenstand: denn dieses setzt nothwendig voraus, daß die Vorstellung in ein Bewußtseyn verknüpft sey."
12 "Das Selbstbewußtseyn, (welches jeder völligen Vorstellung beygehet) kann ausgedrückt werden ohngefähr mit diesen Worten: *Ich denke.*"

parts, then the soul could not have the whole representation at all, and thus it could not relate it, as a whole, to itself. (Platner 1793, 79, § 125)[13]

Thus, Platner holds that without a consciousness of identity, there could be no consciousness of representations. It seems that for Platner, the consciousness of the identity of the representing subject is, like the acts of differentiating and relating, a necessary condition of the capacity to have representations. Platner does not, however, elaborate on this important point.

While Platner's comments on the consciousness of representations are reminiscent of Reinhold's account, there are important differences. Indeed, it turns out that the differences are more significant than the similarities.

First, it is plain that Platner understands the acts of relating and differentiating in empirical terms. In principle, we must be able to "perceive" [*wahrnehmen*] these acts of our soul. For Reinhold, by contrast, the relating and differentiating invoked in the principle of consciousness are to be thought of as a priori conditions. In short, Platner reads Reinhold's ideas as a piece of psychology.[14] Unlike Reinhold, Platner's comments on consciousness and representation are not meant to formulate a foundational principle.

Second, for Platner, but not for Reinhold, the notions of both the object and the subject of the representation, too, relate to empirically existing entities (Platner 1793, 77, § 123). Platner seems to undermine the empiricist and psychological nature of his account, when he notes that the relating to a subject is a necessary condition of representing. He does not elaborate, however, on the kind of necessity he has in mind.

Third, Platner is explicitly critical of aspects of Reinhold's theory. Thus, he rejects Reinhold's claim that the consciousness of representations is part of consciousness in general [*Bewußtseyn überhaupt*]. His critique assumes, however, that Reinhold's claim is of an empirical nature. Platner thinks Reinhold is saying

---

13 "Denn anlangend das Selbstbewußtseyn [...]: wenn die Seele nicht zurücksähe von den letzten Theilen der Vorstellung auf die ersten und nicht bey den letzten fühlte, daß sie es war, welche die ersten hatte: so könnte die Seele nicht die ganze Vorstellung überhaupt haben, also sie nicht als ein Ganzes beziehen auf sich."
14 "Lehrstück der Psychologie" (Platner 1793, 78, § 124). This "psychologism" is, in turn, exactly what Reinhold complains about in Platner. Reinhold writes about Platner's distinction between the consciousness of existence and the consciousness of personality as present in the 1784 edition of *Aphorismen:* "Alles was dieser Philosoph in den ersten Abschnitten seiner *Aphorismen* über das Bewußtseyn der *Existenz* und der Personalität sagt ... [ist] zwar reichhaltig an psychologischen Aufschlüssen über diese Beyden Arten des Bewußtseyns." Reinhold adds that Platner does not, however, answer the question of what consciousness is in general and simply assumes that this question has already been answered (Reinhold 1789, 322–323).

that the consciousness of a representation literally occurs in every actual consciousness we may have of an object. This is empirically false, Platner maintains. When we are conscious of a representation, this consciousness is for the most part not distinct. Most people, Platner believes, would say that they are conscious of an *object* or of a thing, but not of a representation that represents an object.[15] Most people, Platner believes, would distinguish only between themselves and the objects and know nothing of representations.

3 Consciousness of Existence

Platner's expression "consciousness of existence" stands for the soul's consciousness of *its own* existence.[16] He argues that the general concept of existence is derived from the consciousness the soul has of its own acts. He holds that "the first object to which we apply the concept of existence is our own activity and that therefore the feeling of this activity is the first empirical development of this concept" (Platner 1793, 384, § 732).[17] Platner maintains that by being conscious of its own acts the soul becomes conscious also of the power that produces those acts. In the process of thinking we are aware of this act, and we "feel" the power that produces it. The acts of the soul are (part of) the content of the consciousness or feeling of existence (Platner 1793, 381, § 728).[18] For Platner, that is why the consciousness of existence can be expressed in the formula *I am* (Platner 1793, 88, §§ 144–145).

In his pre-Kantian writings Platner argues that self-consciousness provides certainty not only of the existence but also of the nature or essence of the soul as an incorporeal substance (Platner 1772, 25–30, §§ 89–106). "That which is conscious to itself, this self, is called my soul […] Self and Soul are the same thing. Thus, the soul is a substance, a substance that is different from the whole of the

---

15 "Daher kommt es auch, daß das Wort Vorstellung nur wissenschaftlich, und nicht populär ist" (Platner 1793, 81, § 130).
16 "Bewußtseyn der Existenz […] ist das, was das Wort sagt: Gefühl der Seele von ihrem selbsteigenen Daseyn; und muß hier vorläufig unterschieden werden von dem Bewußtseyn der Persönlichkeit" (Platner 1790, 208, § 525).
17 "Ich glaube also noch immer, daß der erste Gegenstand, auf den wir den Begriff der Existenz anwenden, unser selbsteigenes Wirken ist, und also das Gefühl davon die erste empirische Entwickelung dieses Begriffes darbietet."
18 "Ich denke; und indem ich denke, bin ich mir bewußt meiner Seelenwirkungen, als meiner Thätigkeiten, und fühle mich, als die Kraft, welche diese Thätigkeiten hervorbringt. Ich fühle mich also wirkend, und dieses Gefühl meines Wirkens ist der Inhalt des Gefühls, welches ich habe von meinem Daseyn, oder von meiner Wirklichkeit und Existenz."

body, and always the same soul" (Platner 1772, 16, § 59).[19] The thesis that self-consciousness or some inner "feeling" provides evidence of the immaterial nature of the soul is, obviously, highly problematic, but the view was widespread among eighteenth-century philosophers, even among those who are typically labelled "empiricist."[20] As we shall see below, Platner does not abandon his thesis about the incorporeal nature of the soul in his *Aphorismen* of 1793 but attempts to make the thesis compatible with the moderate scepticism he adopts there.

Like the consciousness of representations, the consciousness of existence involves diachronic identity. According to Platner, I am conscious "that I am the same subject which had the present as well as the past representations of my life. Thus, all representations of my life are united into a general consciousness [of existence]" (Platner 1793, 87–88, § 143).[21] In short, both the *I think* and the *I am* are to be thought of as identical through time. It is important to note, however, that neither the *I think* nor the *I am* necessarily includes a consciousness of the self as an embodied entity. When Platner speaks of identity in relation to the consciousness of existence, he has in mind only the identity of the subject in so far as it is a representing subject. It is Platner's account of the consciousness of personality, rather, that raises the issue of embodiment.

4 Consciousness of Personality: The Embodied Nature of the Self

As indicated above, in his writings of the 1770s Platner considers as crucial the consciousness of one's own body and its spatio-temporal location. In the 1793 edition of *Aphorismen* the issue comes up in the context of Platner's distinction between the consciousness of personality on the one hand, and the consciousness of exis-

---

[19] "Das was sich bewußt ist, dies Ich heist meine Seele [...] Ich und Seele ist einerley. Also ist die Seele eine Substanz, eine von dem ganzen Körper verschiedene Substanz, und immer die nämliche Seele". See also: "Ich kann mir alle Theile meines Körpers als außer mir vorstellen. Folglich sind alle Theile meines Körpers außer mir – außer meiner Person. Ich bin kein Theil meines Körpers, und mein Körper ist außer meinem Ich" (Platner 1772, 14, § 48).
[20] See, for example, the references in Thiel 2021.
[21] "Und so wie ich die Theile jeder einzelnen Vorstellung auf mich beziehe, indem ich fühle, daß ich dasselbige Subjekt bin, welches die letztern und welches die erstern in sich hatte [...]: so bin ich mir bewußt, daß ich dasselbige Subjekt bin, welches die gegenwärtigen, und die vergangenen Vorstellungen meines Lebens hatte. Und so sind alle Vorstellungen meines Lebens vereinigt in ein allgemeines Bewußtsein, so wie bey jeder Vorstellung vereinigt sind derselben Theile in ein besonderes."

tence and the consciousness of representations on the other (Platner 1793, 90, § 150).[22] While Platner 'brackets' embodiment and the spatio-temporal aspects of the embodied self in his analysis of the consciousness of representations and the consciousness of existence, he considers them essential to the consciousness of personality.

Although Platner does not state this explicitly, it seems that he holds that the consciousness of personality presupposes both the consciousness of representations and the consciousness of existence. In his *Anthropologie* of 1772, however, he instead views the relating to one's own body as a necessary condition of self-consciousness. Here, he states:

> We are conscious of ourselves; that is, of our existence when we know the relations of the place, time, and other relations of our state. If we do not know where we are and when we are, then we are not conscious of ourselves (Platner 1772, 54–55, § 193).[23]

The soul, Platner argues here, is "never conscious of its existence, unless it thinks of itself as standing in certain relations, at least of those of place and time" (Platner 1772, 56, § 199). For Platner, the idea that self-consciousness relates to the spatio-temporal position of the subject implies that the subject must be viewed as an embodied entity. As he notes elsewhere: "If one does not feel anything of the position and situation of one's own body, then one is not conscious at all" (Platner 1772, 55, § 194). Elsewhere, he states: "the soul cannot think of itself alone, without perceiving at the same time at least one object, even if this were nothing but a single sensation of its body" (Platner 1772, 56, § 200). Accordingly, on his early account, there can be no self-consciousness without the consciousness of one's embodiment. The latter seems to be a necessary requirement for the former.

Platner was not alone in arguing that self-consciousness requires a relation to the spatio-temporal position of one's own body. Several other empiricist thinkers of the 1770s argued similarly.[24] The Göttingen philosophers Michael Hißmann and Christoph Meiners, for example, distinguish, not unlike Platner, between the consciousness of one's own existence and a self-consciousness that involves the body. Implausibly, however, they assume that it is possible to have only a consciousness

---

22 See also Platner 1790, 208, § 525.
23 "Wir sind uns unser, d. h. Unsers Daseyns bewußt, wenn wir die Verhältnisse des Orts, der Zeit und andere Verhältnisse unsers Zustands kennen. Wenn wir nicht wissen, wo wir sind und wann wir sind, so sind wir unser nicht bewußt."
24 This idea was not entirely new of course. John Locke whose account of personhood informs the eighteenth-century debate notes that consciousness relates not just to mental states but also to actions of the embodied subject. See, for example, Locke (1690/1975), 2.27, § 11 and 17. For details, see Thiel 2014, 121–139.

of one's mere existence, quite independently of a self-consciousness that includes the body.[25] Platner's 1770s account raises the related question of how his thesis: that the consciousness of the soul's existence brings along the consciousness of its incorporeal nature, sits with his other thesis: that one cannot be conscious of oneself at all, unless one is conscious of one's own body and its spatio-temporal location. He claims here both that the relating to one's own body is essential to self-consciousness, and that the consciousness of existence is a consciousness of the incorporeal soul. Platner himself did not seem to regard this as problematic.

In the *Aphorismen* of 1793 Platner does not elaborate in any detail on the consciousness of personality, but refers to his *Neue Anthropologie* and earlier editions of *Aphorismen* as well as to other writers for detailed accounts of the topic.[26] In the 1793 edition of *Aphorismen*, he gives a summary of the nature and significance of the consciousness of personality. "The consciousness of personality," Platner says here, "is a special kind of self-consciousness," pointing out that it consists of three aspects, (a) the complex feeling of the state of one's own body; (b) the equally complex feeling of our mental states, and (c) the representation of the place and time of our own self and a general view of our circumstances (Platner 1793, 76–77, § 122).[27] However, his reflections on the *I think* and the *I am* are the main focus in 1793 and linked more closely to recent ideas in Kant and Reinhold than his thoughts on the consciousness of personality. Here, the latter is not considered central but just one of several types of consciousness. Platner makes no attempt to connect his idea of a consciousness of personality with his post-Kantian ideas about self-consciousness. There is no reason to believe, however, that the idea is not consistent with his notions of the consciousness of existence, the consciousness of representations, and his account of a feeling of self or *Selbstgefühl*.

---

25 On this, see Thiel 1997, 72–74.
26 Platner mentions Sulzer, Irwing, Meiners, and M. Iganz Schmidt (Platner 1793, 76–77, § 122). See also Platner 1772, 54–57, §§ 193–201. Compare Thiel 1997, 77. For a discussion of Platner's distinction between the consciousness of existence and the consciousness of personality in the 1784 edition of *Philosophische Aphorismen*, see Wunderlich 2007, 171–176. See also Wunderlich 2018, 158–159.
27 "Das *Bewußtseyn der Persönlichkeit* ... [ist] eine besondere Art des Selbstbewußtseyns, in welchem enthalten ist 1) das unendlich viel befassende Gefühl von dem Zustande des Körpers, 2) das eben so zusammengesetzte Gefühl von dem geistigen Zustande (unsern Vorstellungen, Empfindnissen, Fähigkeiten, Neigungen u.s.w.), 3) die Vorstellung des Orts und der Zeit und die Uebersicht unserer Lebensumstände." See also Platner 1790, 315, § 754.

5 *Selbstgefühl*: The Feeling of Self

"Selbstgefühl" is a term that was used frequently in the psychological debates of the 1770s. There seems to have been no agreement, however, as to what exactly the term denotes. All that can be said about it in general terms is that it stands for some sort of immediate relating to one's own self. It seems that Johann Bernhard Basedow introduced the term into the philosophical discussions in his *Philalethie* of 1764. Johann Georg Heinrich Feder adopted the expression in his very influential *Logik und Metaphysik* (1769), and it was probably through Feder that the term became standard currency in the 1770s and 1780s.[28] The notion of a feeling of self, *Selbstgefühl*, or *Gefühl Ich*, an expression he uses in the 1793 edition of *Aphorismen*, is central in Platner's account of self-consciousness. In his *Anthropologie* of 1772 Platner does not distinguish between *Selbstgefühl* and other forms of self-consciousness and he defines *Selbstgefühl* as "one's own experience of the acts and modifications of our soul," arguing that through *Selbstgefühl* we obtain ideas of "consciousness, feeling, thinking, willing" (Platner 1772, 17–18, § 65). Further, Platner holds here that the ideas we obtain through *Selbstgefühl* lead to the notion of a soul (Platner 1772, 18, § 67), and that *Selbstgefühl* assures us of our own diachronic identity and of the immaterial nature of the soul.[29] Thus, Platner assigns *Selbstgefühl* a number of tasks, without explaining that notion in any detail and distinguishing it from other, related concepts.[30] In his writings from the 1790s, however, he has more to say about the concept of *Selbstgefühl* or *Gefühl Ich*, distinguishing this notion from those of the consciousness of existence, the consciousness of representations and the consciousness of personality. The very use of the terminology of "feeling" in this context indicates that Platner is emphasizing the empirical and, as indicated above, the immediate nature of this relating to the self, a relating to the self that is not mediated through concepts or other representations. What are his other claims, however, about *Selbstgefühl*?

Platner argues that both the consciousness of representations (the *I think*) and the consciousness of existence (the *I am*) presuppose the "simple" feeling of self, *Selbstgefühl* or *Gefühl Ich*. First, the *Gefühl Ich* is required for the *I think* of the consciousness of representations, because all parts of a representation have to be combined in the feeling of self so that they can constitute a unitary representation (Platner 1793, 87, § 143). In this sense, the *Gefühl Ich* is a "necessary condition

---

28 For the complex history of this notion, see Thiel 1997; Thiel 2021; Thiel 2018, and Frank 2002.
29 For *Selbstgefühl* and diachronic identity, see Platner 1772, 15–16, §§ 56–57, and 27, § 97.
30 This applies also, for example, to Johann Karl Wezel's account of *Selbstgefühl* in Wezel 1784–1785. On Wezel, see Gideon Stiening's analysis in Stiening 2003/4.

of all representations" (Platner 1793, 79, § 126).³¹ This argument implies that the relating to the subject that is involved in the consciousness of representations we discussed above is not the same as *Selbstgefühl*. The latter is a necessary condition of the former. Also, *Selbstgefühl* is a necessary condition also of combining a multiplicity of representations into the notion of a diachronically identical (representing) subject. Second, *Selbstgefühl* is a necessary condition of the consciousness of existence, as it makes possible "the general representation of all acts of the soul of my whole life" (Platner 1793, 87, § 143).³² Regarding the *I am*, too, without *Selbstgefühl* we would not be able to combine a multiplicity of representations into the concept of diachronically identical subject. Thus, *Selbstgefühl* is a necessary condition of the consciousness of identity.

> The feeling: *I am* [...] can be regarded as an abstraction from the repeated feeling: *I think*. [...] But in so far as the simple *Gefühl* **Ich**, which grounds both, is a necessary condition of all possible consciousness: it is also in itself the necessary condition of the consciousness of identity. (Platner 1793, 88, § 146)³³

Platner does not relate *Selbstgefühl* explicitly to the consciousness of personality, but his statement in the quoted passage that *Selbstgefühl* is "a necessary condition of all possible consciousness" implies that it is also a necessary condition of the consciousness of personality.

So far, we have looked at what Platner says about the role of *Selbstgefühl* as a necessary condition of other forms of consciousness, but what does he say about its nature? We noted that the notion of feeling employed here suggests an immediate relating to one's own self. When taking a closer look at what Platner has to say about this, however, it becomes clear that his notion of the *Gefühl* **Ich** is problematic in several respects.

---

31 "Das Selbstbewußtseyn, (welches jeder völligen Vorstellung beygehet) kann ausgedrückt werden ohngefähr mit diesen Worten: *Ich denke*. Dieses *Ich denke* aber setzt voraus das Gefühl *Ich*, als das vorstellende Subjekt: demnach ist das Gefühl *Ich* das nothwendige Bedingniß aller Vorstellungen."
32 "Gleichwie jeder einzelnen Vorstellung in mir zum Grunde liegt das Selbstgefühl *Ich* [...], in welches die gesammten Theile derselben zusammengefaßt werden [...]: so liegt es auch zum Grunde der allgemeinen Vorstellung aller Seelenwirkungen meines ganzen Lebens." As Platner himself makes clear (see note 33), "zum Grunde liegen" is to be understood in terms of a necessary condition.
33 "Das Gefühl: *Ich bin* [...] kann zwar angesehen werden, als abgezogen von dem mehrmalen wiederholten Gefühl: *Ich denke* [...]. Aber so fern das einfache Gefühl *Ich*, welches beyden zum Grunde liegt ein durchaus nothwendiges Bedingniß alles möglichen Bewußtseyns an sich selbst ist: so fern ist es auch an sich selbst das nothwendige Bedingniß des Bewußtseyns der *Identität*."

First, Platner assumes that *Selbstgefühl* exists as a mental phenomenon that can in principle be identified empirically. He provides no argument, no evidence for this assumption. Of course, Platner was neither the first nor the only eighteenth-century thinker who assumed the existence of such a feeling. Philosophers as diverse as Jean Bernard Mérian, Johann Christian Lossius and Henry Home, Lord Kames, to name only a few, all believed in the existence of an immediate consciousness or feeling of one's own self that has a special, primordial status among our mental phenomena.[34] Kames, for example holds, well before Platner, that such a feeling is a necessary condition of connecting concepts with one's own self, and so, to him, it is simply an undoubted truth that human beings have an original feeling or consciousness of their own selves that, for the most part, accompanies their ideas and representations and the actions of their soul or their body.[35] For Kames, too, however, this "original consciousness" is to be understood in empirical terms. As in Platner, Kames asserts the existence of a feeling of self but provides no argument in support of this claim. Platner, Kames and the other proponents of an immediate feeling of self may appeal to inner experience as evidence for the existence of such a feeling. This appeal, however, raises the question (as Hume would have argued) of whether such a feeling of self is in fact introspectively identifiable as a phenomenon distinct from all our other feelings or perceptions.

Second, Platner maintains both that *Selbstgefühl* is a necessary condition of all forms of (empirical) consciousness and that *Selbstgefühl* is itself an empirical phenomenon. It would seem, however, that Platner needs to explain how that, which functions as a condition of all experience, can itself be part of that experience.

Third, there is a problem concerning *Selbstgefühl*'s relation to the consciousness of representations. Strictly speaking, Platner's expression *das einfache Gefühl Ich* should be translated, not as "the simple feeling *of* self," as this conveys the idea of a duality between the self as object and a feeling that relates to this object, but as "the simple feeling *self*." Platner's expression suggests the idea of a relating that is not in any way mediated conceptually or, indeed, by any representation. Rather, as Platner insists, the *Gefühl Ich* "is presupposed by every representation" (Platner 1793, 90, § 150).[36] Platner undermines this notion of an imme-

---

[34] For Mérian and Kames, see Thiel 2014, 372–376, and 423–428. For Lossius, see Thiel 2021, 106–108.
[35] Kames 1751/2005, 231–236 (pagination of the 1751 edition). A German translation of Kames' *Essays* by Christian Günther Rauschenberg was published as *Versuche über die ersten Gründe der Sittlichkeit und der natürlichen Religion*, Braunschweig 1768.
[36] "Das Selbstgefühl *Ich* [...] ist nicht ein Haufen oder eine Reihe von Vorstellungen; denn es wird bey jeder Vorstellung vorausgesetzt." Platner uses his idea of *Selbstgefühl* to argue against the bundle theory of the self, a view that he, like many present-day commentators, ascribes to David Hume.

diate, non-representational relating to the self through the *Gefühl Ich*, however, when he elaborates on this notion, saying that "in this *Selbstgefühl*, the self is *represented* as something that is distinct from all activities of the soul" (Platner 1793, 88, § 147).[37] Platner seems to maintain that the *Gefühl Ich* is both the condition of *all* representations and itself a representation or mediated by a representation. Thus, the status of the *Gefühl Ich* and the nature of its "immediacy" remain unclear, as there is no consistent account of the latter in Platner.

This issue can help to clarify further the difference between Platner and Reinhold. For Reinhold, self-*consciousness* is a kind of representation or representing,[38] but it differs from Platner's *Selbstgefühl* and is not meant to fulfil the fundamental role that Platner ascribes to *Selbstgefühl*. For Reinhold, it is not self-consciousness but the immediate, non-representational relating to the subject that is expressed in the principle of consciousness that is fundamental and "precedes every representation."[39] Reinhold's self-*consciousness*, by contrast, is a kind of self-knowledge that presupposes the relating to the subject that is formulated in the principle of consciousness. Unlike Platner, Reinhold distinguishes clearly between this fundamental relating to the subject and a relating to the subject that is mediated through representations.

Fourth, it is difficult to reconcile Platner's account of *Selbstgefühl* as a "necessary condition of all representations" with some fundamental aspects of his general position in philosophy; that is, with his "sceptical critique." As noted above, the latter includes the statement that our cognitive faculties are not able to explain their own nature (Platner 1793, 364, § 709). If we accept this point, however, then it seems that Platner has overstepped the sceptical limits he himself has set, for

---

Applying his own conceptual distinctions, Platner argues that Hume confuses the consciousness of personality with the consciousness of existence. He holds the main reason why Hume rejects the view that the soul has an idea of itself is that he thought this would require a simple impression of the soul (Platner 1793, 90, § 150). Obviously, however, if the soul is a multiplicity of impressions, we cannot have a simple impression of it. For a detailed account of Platner's critique of Hume, see Wunderlich 2007. Wreschner 1893, 123–124, and 133, sees a similarity between Platner's *Gefühl Ich* and Tetens' idea of an "obscure" [*dunkel*] feeling of self.

37 "In diesem Selbstgefühl [...] wird das Ich vorgestellt, als etwas von allen Seelenwirkungen Unterschiedenes." Italics in the English translation are mine, U.T.

38 "Das Bewusstsein des Vorstellenden als eines solchen, das Selbstbewusstsein, hat das Vorstellende selbst zum Gegenstande." That is to say: "Beim Selbstbewusstsein wird das Objekt des Bewusstseins als identisch mit dem Subjekte vorgestellt" (Reinhold 1789, 326, 335).

39 Reinhold emphasizes that the act of distinguishing between the representation on the one hand and both the subject and the object of the representation on the other is not itself an object of a representation. Rather, he argues that the act of differentiating "precedes" every representation ["jeder ihrer Vorstellungen vorhergehen"] (Reinhold 1789, 339).

in arguing that the *Gefühl Ich* is a necessary condition of representations, and thereby of thought and knowledge in general, he clearly provides elements of an account of the nature of our cognitive faculties.

6 Logical Subject and Real Subject: Platner and Kant

So far, we have looked at Platner's understanding of *Selbstgefühl* in relation to Reinhold's account of consciousness and self-consciousness. In places, however, Platner seems to identify the *Gefühl Ich* with what he calls the "logical subject of thought" (Platner 1793, 90, § 151), thus connecting the idea to Kant's notion of the "I of apperception" (*CPR*, B 407), or the "logical self" (*RP*, AA 20: 270), rather than to Reinhold. In contrast to Kant, however, he maintains that the *Gefühl Ich* relates at the same time to "a real subject" and that it includes the consciousness of its own unity and identity. "In other words," Platner sums up, "the soul feels itself as substance," a claim that is in line with his early, pre-Kantian account.⁴⁰

Given this latter thesis it is not surprising that Platner rejects Kant's view, according to which *Selbstgefühl* (or apperception) is completely empty, as "dogmatic." Platner argues as follows. (1) It has not yet been proved that it is impossible to have a feeling of the real principle of causality of our mental faculties; (2) although the *Gefühl Ich* is the logical subject of thought, it does not follow that it "cannot at the same time also have real content"; (3) it has not yet been shown that we can only perceive what is given to our external senses (Platner 1793, 91–92, § 153). In other words, it has not been shown decisively by Kant or anyone that in *Selbstgefühl* there absolutely *cannot* be an intuition of the self as a real subject. To rule this out is simply "dogmatic."

Platner's positive account of *Selbstgefühl* as relating to a real, rather than just a logical subject is linked to his understanding of *Selbstgefühl* in representational terms, hinted at above. Platner appeals to Reinhold in this context. As noted above, for Reinhold self-consciousness represents the subject in so far as it is engaged in the activity of representing. Similarly, Platner says that through *Selbst-*

---

40 "Das Selbstgefühl *Ich* [...] weiset hin auf das logische Subjekt des Denkens, und zugleich auf ein wirkliches Subjekt; und schließt in sich Bewußtseyn der Einheit und Identität. Mit andern Worten: die Seele fühlt sich als Substanz" (Platner 1793, 90–91, § 151). Platner treats "self" and "soul" as synonyms: "Ich [...] und Seele [...] sind gleichdeutige Ausdrücke: also ist das Selbstgefühl *Ich* das Gefühl meiner Seele" (Platner 1793, 89, § 149). For differences between the 1784 and 1793 editions of *Philosophische Aphorismen* about what *Selbstgefühl* reveals, see Wunderlich 2018, 169–170.

gefühl the soul is represented in so far as it is a representing subject, and as distinct from its representations. In this sense, the soul is the representational object of *Selbstgefühl*. He argues that, as the soul "perceives" itself as an object through *Selbstgefühl*, the feeling of self cannot be "empty." Given that it is impossible to have a representation that does not relate to an object, the "representation of the representing subject," too, is not possible without the latter as a real entity to which this representation relates as an object (Platner 1793, 92, § 154).[41]

It is important to note, however, that while Reinhold's account of self-*consciousness* is indeed in representational terms, the fundamental relating to the self that is invoked in his "principle of consciousness" is *not* representational. Unlike Reinhold, Platner does not seem to distinguish between a fundamental relating to the self or subject (his *Selbstgefühl*) and representational self-consciousness. Platner also appeals to Kant's notion of inner intuition in this context (Platner 1793, 93, § 154). There is an important (and obvious) difference, however, between Kantian inner intuition (which is indeed a kind of representation) and apperception. According to Kant, pure apperception, not inner intuition, is empty.

What are we to make, however, of Platner's claim that *Selbstgefühl* is not only not empty, but has the soul, as *substance*, as its object? When dealing with Kant's critique of the paralogisms, Platner argues that the feeling of self or *Selbstgefühl* is the representation of the subject only insofar as it has representations or is engaged in the activity of representing and that on its own it provides no evidence for existence of the self as a substance. He adds that other attributes that may belong to the soul, such as immateriality, identity etc., cannot directly be derived from *Selbstgefühl* either.[42] In short, Platner seems to accept Kant's point that in *Selbstgefühl* or, in Kantian terms, apperception, there is a unity of consciousness, but

---

[41] "Wenn zugegeben werden muß, daß in dem deutlichen Bewußtseyn der Vorstellung die Seele sich bewußt ist ihrer selbst, als des Vorstellenden, und als von den Vorstellungen unterschieden; und daß also hier die Seele eine Vorstellung hat, in welcher sie selbst das Objekt ist: so wird auch zugegeben, daß die Seele sich selbst, als einen Gegenstand wahrnimmt, und daß in so fern das Selbstgefühl *Ich* nicht leer ist von allem Inhalt, sondern einen wirklichen Gegenstand hat. Denn wenn keine Vorstellung möglich ist ohne Beziehung auf einen Gegenstand; so ist ohne diese auch nicht möglich die Vorstellung eines vorstellenden Subjekts, d. h. Die Vorstellung der Seele von sich selbst." See also Platner 1790, 52–53, § 158 where Platner argues against the alleged emptiness of *Selbstgefühl*.

[42] "Wer in dem Selbstgefühl mehr sucht, als die Vorstellung des Vorstellenden, und daraus zu entwickeln hofft die Prädicate, die der Seele, außer dem Vermögen des Vorstellens, zukommen könnten; z. B. Unkörperlichkeit, Beharrlichkeit, Identität u. d. gl. der kennt nicht die Quellen dieser Prädikate" (Platner 1793, 93, § 155). See also Platner 1790, 53, § 159.

no intuition of the soul as substance.⁴³ Here, Platner's argument differs from his position in his *Anthropologie* of 1772, according to which *Selbstgefühl* provides evidence for the substantiality and even immateriality of the soul. The Kantian arguments in his *Aphorismen* of 1793 do not seem to be compatible, however, with his claim in the same edition, that *Selbstgefühl* has the soul, as substance, as its object.

Platner's account of the self or soul must be seen in the context of his "sceptical critique" of the concept of substance in general. Again, he seems to work with a Kantian position, but attempts to combine it with his earlier, pre-Kantian ideas. According to Platner, Kant attempts to show, (1) that it is not possible for us to have an objectively valid concept of substance, considered as a thing in itself, because there is nothing that corresponds to such a concept in experience (Platner 1793, 447–448, § 773), (2) that, nevertheless, we can and indeed must [*unserer Denkart nach*] pursue the idea of substance in an attempt to develop a system of reason (Platner 1793, 449, § 773). Platner argues that, unlike Kant, we must not accept (1) as an absolute truth (Platner 1793, 449–450, § 774: [*zuverlässige Wahrheit*]). This view is in line with the programme of his "sceptical critique": we cannot prove that our cognitive faculties know themselves so well as to be absolutely certain about such claims. In short, Platner leaves open the possibility that the concept of substance has objective reality for things in themselves. Platner accepts (2), however, without reservations. Yet, unlike Kant, he argues on this basis that we are justified in applying the category of substance also to "supersensible objects" (Platner 1793, 450, § 774). It is impossible for reason, Platner claims, to assume with certainty that there is nothing substantial underlying the appearances. Therefore, Platner thinks we can assume the existence of "substances as things in themselves, without however ascribing to this idea a reality that is independent of human thought, but also without ascribing to it less reality than the sensuous concept of substance" (Platner 1793, 450, § 774).⁴⁴

Applying these ideas to the question of the substantiality of the soul, Platner again attempts to marry his metaphysical, pre-Kantian ideas with the principles of a Kantian critique of reason. He states in the logic-part of *Aphorismen* that it is "a

---

43 According to Platner, Kant maintains, "daß das in dem Selbstbewußtseyn der Identität vorgegebene und, zum Behuf eines objektifen Erkenntnisses von Dingen an sich, angeführte anschauliche Gefühl von der Kraft und Selbstständigkeit unsers eigenen denkenden Wesens, nichts sey als das bey allen Vorstellungen vorausgesetzte *Ich*; und daß man in diesem Selbstbewußtseyn nur Einheit des Bewußtseyns habe, keineswegs aber sich selbst oder die Seele als Substanz anschaue" (Platner 1793, 448, § 773).

44 "[...] erkennt ... Substanzen als Dinge an sich; ohne im übrigen dieser Idee eine von menschlicher Denkart unabhängige Realität zusichern zu wollen; aber auch ohne ihr weniger Realitat, als dem sinnlichen Begriffe Substanz zuzutrauen."

universally accepted necessity of our understanding to think of the soul as a substance," adding that the question of whether this concept of the understanding proves anything about the *real* substantiality of the soul [*Selbständigkeit*] is to be dealt with in metaphysics (Platner 1793, 95, § 156).⁴⁵ In the metaphysics-part of *Aphorismen*, Platner concedes to Reinhold and Kant that we have no knowledge of our inner nature but argues that the feeling of the soul's power that is the content of *Selbstgefühl* provides an experiential base for the idea of the soul or self which our understanding cannot help but conceive of as a substance (Platner 1793, 400, § 753).⁴⁶ He points out that Kant himself says that reason necessarily applies the notion of substance to that of self-consciousness (Platner 1793, 93–94, § 155). And since Platner agrees with Kant that reason demands of us to think of the self as substance, he holds that we are entitled to do so. The idea of the soul as substance is a necessity of thought, it is a "complete, subjective belief" or conviction, and it is impossible for us to abandon this belief. We cannot but think and live by that belief (Platner 1793, 365, § 709).

For Platner, then, Kant's critique does not prove that the thinking subject cannot be a substance.⁴⁷ Indeed, Kant could happily accept this point. It is plain, however, that Platner's positive thesis, cited at the beginning of this section, that *Selbstgefühl* is a feeling of the soul as substance, cannot be derived from this negative thesis. Platner wants to say both that we cannot derive anything about the nature of the soul from *Selbstgefühl*, and that *Selbstgefühl* provides an experiential base for ascribing substantiality to the soul. While the negative thesis is compatible with the critical Kant, the positive thesis is not.

Platner thinks he can provide further details about the nature of the soul on the basis of *Selbstgefühl*. As the passage from the metaphysics-part of *Aphorismen* quoted above indicates, Platner interprets the notion of the soul, as substance, in

---

45 "So ist es doch eine allgemein anerkannte Nothwendigkeit unseres Verstandes die Seele als Substanz zu denken. Ob aber dieser Verstandesbegriff etwas beweise für die wirkliche Selbstständigkeit der Seele: das ist eine spätere Frage der Metaphysik."
46 "Ich fühle mich wie ein von meinen Seelenwirkungen unterschiedenes, unter dem Wechsel aller seiner leidendlichen und thätigen Veränderungen, beharrendes Wesen; und ich meine in dem Gefühl der Kraft, welches den Inhalt meines Selbstgefühls *Ich* ausmacht, etwas Anschauliches für die Idee *Ich* oder *Seele* zu haben, die ich nach Einrichtung meines Verstandes als Substanz denke" (Platner 1793, 400, § 753).
47 Platner rejects the claim, which he ascribes to Kant and his followers, that all philosophers prior to Kant had attempted to deduce metaphysical attributes of the soul directly from *Selbstgefühl*. He states that in order to argue for the immateriality of the soul, Leibniz and Reimarus, for example, added the point that mental acts do not appear to us as material (e. g., not as extended or shaped), and that this leads to the idea that the subject of these acts, too, is not material (Platner 1793, 93–94, § 155). On Platner and Leibniz, see Wreschner 1893, 117.

terms of a mental power or faculty. The feeling of our own mental acts gives rise to the concept of the soul as a power to perform these acts. Platner speaks of *Selbstgefühl* as the feeling of one's power in which the acts of which we are conscious originate.

> I think, and while I think I am conscious to myself of the acts of my soul as my acts, and I feel myself as that power that produces these acts. Thus, I feel myself as active, and this feeling of my activity is the content of the feeling that I have of my existence, or of my reality and existence (Platner 1793, 381, § 728).[48]

Further, Platner maintains not only that *Selbstgefühl* represents the self or soul as a substance, but also that *Selbstgefühl* is the "empirical basis for the idea that the soul is a real entity, distinct from its acts and from the body which is felt and enlivened by the soul" (Platner 1793, 89, § 149).[49] While this statement is, strictly speaking, consistent with the view that the soul itself is a material substance, it suggests that the idea of the soul's non-corporeal nature can be derived from *Selbstgefühl*.[50] The soul, Platner claims here, feels itself as the "owner" of its body (Platner 1793, 89, § 148).[51] Thus, although Platner holds that metaphysical attributes of the soul such as its immateriality cannot be deduced directly from *Selbstgefühl*, he clearly thinks that the latter provides the basis for the idea of the soul as a non-corporeal substance.

7 Immortality and Imputation

As with immateriality, Platner argues that immortality cannot be directly derived from *Selbstgefühl*. Moreover, he holds that there is no speculative proof of immortality at all. Rather, he emphasizes that immortality rests solely on God's wisdom (Platner 1793, 624, § 1025). All that can be shown philosophically is the *possibility* of an afterlife. This possibility, Platner claims, is evidenced by *Selbstgefühl*, rather than by the immateriality of the soul, as substance (Platner 1793, 627, § 1025).

---

48 "Ich denke; und indem ich denke, bin ich mir bewußt meiner Seelenwirkungen, als meiner Thätigkeiten, und fühle mich, als die Kraft, welche diese Thätigkeiten hervorbringt. Ich fühle mich also wirkend, und dieses Gefühl meines Wirkens ist der Inhalt des Gefühls, welches ich habe von meinem Daseyn, oder von meiner Wirklichkeit und Existenz."
49 "Und dieses nun ist ein empirischer Grund zu der Idee, daß die Seele etwas Wirkliches sey, und etwas theils von allen ihren Wirkungen, theils von dem durch sie empfundenen und durch sie belebten Körper Unterschiedenes."
50 See also Platner 1790, 52, § 157.
51 "Das Ich fühlt sich als der Eigenthümer des Körpers, der Körper als das Eigenthum."

Platner notes that the question of immortality relates to that of diachronic identity (Platner 1793, 626, § 1025). How does Platner account for identity? In one passage, he states that the question of identity can be answered by reference to what he has said about self-consciousness and the concept of substance, without, however, elaborating on this claim (Platner 1793, 625, § 1025).[52] Still, he engages critically with some of Kant's arguments in the Paralogism-chapter of the *Critique of Pure Reason*. According to Platner, Kant holds that it is possible that the consciousness of identity be transferred from the faculty of representation of one soul to the faculty of representation of a different soul and thus would continue to exist through a change of numerical identity. Platner asks (1), whether this is indeed possible, and (2), if this were possible, whether it would have any significant consequences. Platner answers both questions in the negative (Platner 1793, 625, § 1025; see also 93, § 155). He argues that the question of whether a "continued consciousness" [*fortdauerndes Bewußtseyn*] remains in the same substratum is irrelevant to immortality. Even if consciousness were to be transferred to a different substratum, the possibility of a "personal continued existence" on the basis of *Selbstgefühl* would remain. Moreover, this possibility cannot be proved anyway, as the question of what turns out to be real always depends on the will of God (Platner 1793, 627, § 1025).[53] Platner's distinction between the soul, as substance, and personal existence is of course reminiscent of Locke's distinction between the identity of the thinking substance and personal identity, but he does not appeal to Locke here.

Platner claims that, apart from the question of immortality, the issue of diachronic identity is important to that of imputation or the attribution of actions to a subject (Platner 1793, 626, § 1025).[54] He states that it is obvious that merit and demerit or guilt relate to our mental attitude or a "particular way of thinking and willing," and not to the continued existence of the same substance. In line with the above argument against Kant, he holds that, if a "particular way of thinking and willing" were to be transferred from substance A to B, then B is changed into A, but the object of imputation remains the same. Indeed, Planter argues, if

---

[52] "Wiefern die beharrende Persönlichkeit oder Identität der menschlichen Seele von mir als erweislich angesehen werde: das ergiebt sich aus dem, was ich einestheils über das Selbstbewußtseyn, anderntheils über die Realität des Begriffes Substanz gesagt habe."

[53] "Übrigens ist es gleichgültig, ob das fortdauernde Bewußtseyn stets in demselben Substratum verbleibet, oder aus einem in das andere übergehet. In beyden Fällen ist die Möglichkeit der persönlichen Fortdauer da; und mehr als die Möglichkeit kann hier nicht bewiesen werden, weil die Wirklichkeit allzeit, und in allen metaphysischen Hypothesen über die Natur der Seele, von dem Willen des höchsten Wesens abhängig bleibt."

[54] "Die Frage von der Identität kann doch nur in zweyerley Beziehungen wichtig seyn: in Beziehung auf die Unsterblichkeit der Seele, und in Beziehung auf die Zurechnung."

we were to abstract a "certain way of thinking and willing and being conscious" from our soul, it would be difficult to determine what remains of the latter. According to Platner, the notion of a substratum of the soul as separate from thinking, willing, and consciousness is barely intelligible (Platner 1793, 627, § 1025).[55] In any case, the identity of the soul, as substance, is not relevant, according to Platner, to questions about imputation and responsibility.

Platner does not say much about the notion of "a particular way of thinking and willing." He says that it denotes (1) the self as the "sum-total of mental powers and qualities, through which ways and degrees of thinking and sensing are possible," and (2) the self as a subject "in which certain capacities, directions, in one word, consequences, of previous states remain" (Platner 1793, 625–626, § 1025).[56] While these comments are fairly vague, at least they indicate that, like Platner's account of immortality, his analysis of imputation invokes his notion of the consciousness of personality, rather than that of a substantial soul.[57] As we saw above, the consciousness of personality includes not only "the state of our own body" but also "representations, sensations, capacities, inclinations" and a "general view of our circumstances" (Platner 1793, 77, § 122).[58]

Again, Platner's analysis of imputation may superficially sound rather Lockean, as he seems to be a saying that psychological continuity, rather than the diachronic identity of the thinking substance or soul, is relevant to imputation and to moral and legal responsibility. Unlike Locke, however, Platner does not link responsibility to the consciousness and memory of particular thoughts and actions, but rather vaguely to the mental attitude of a person. It remains unclear how our "way of thinking and willing" can function as a basis for the attribution of particular actions to a subject.

---

55 "Und was die Zurechnung betrifft: so ist es klar, daß Verdienst und Schuld sich auf eine gewissse Art zu denken und zu wollen, beziehet. Gehe nun auch diese Art zu denken und zu wollen aus A in B über: nun so wird B in A verwandelt, aber der Gegenstand der Zurechnung bleibt immer derselbige. Und am Ende, wenn ich von meiner Seele eine gewisse Art des Denkens, Wollens und Bewußtseyns abziehe: so begreife ich nicht, was das Substratum der Seele noch außer diesem allen seyn möge. Folglich kann ich mir bey einer solchen Umwandlung meines Verstandes, Willens und Selbstbewußtseyns aus einem substanziellen Substratum in das andere, gar nichts denken."
56 "Inbegriff geistiger Kräfte und Eigenschaften, in welchen Arten und Grade des Denkens und Empfindens möglich sind, [...] ein Subjekt, in welchem auch von vorherigen Zuständen gewisse Richtungen, Fertigkeiten, und mit einem Worte Folgen zurück bleiben."
57 Arthur Wreschner holds that this idea is difficult to reconcile with what Platner says elsewhere about the substantiality and immateriality of the soul (Wreschner 1893, 134).
58 "Zustand des Körpers"; "Vorstellungen, Empfindnissen, Fähigkeiten, Neigungen"; "die Uebersicht unserer Lebensumstände." See also Platner 1793, 89–90, § 149.

8 Concluding Remarks

In this essay, we have covered only some aspects of Platner's account of *Selbstgefühl* and other forms of consciousness. Clearly, more needs to be said, for example, about the reception of Platner's views and arguments in Reinhold and Fichte.[59] Here, the focus was on an explanatory and evaluative analysis of Platner's own position and its relation to Kant and Reinhold. On the positive side, we saw that Platner develops an original view of self-consciousness, taking into account earlier positions, and introducing his own conceptual distinctions between various ways in which we can be conscious of ourselves. These conceptual distinctions can be seen as a contribution to the project of a "mental geography," a project that Hume, for example, considered immensely important.[60] However, on the negative side, we saw that Platner's post-Kantian account of self-consciousness is highly problematic, as he simply combines elements of his earlier psychological approach from the 1770s with ideas derived from Kant and Reinhold. Thus, instead of developing an independent and consistent theory, in which pre- and post-Kantian ideas are critically evaluated and related to one another, Platner ends up with a mere aggregate of psychological ideas and transcendental considerations.

---

[59] Reinhold comments on Platner several times in his *Versuch einer neuen Theorie des menschlichen Vorstellungsvermögens* (Reinhold 1789), and he reviews the 1793 edition of Platner's *Aphorismen* in *Allgemeine Literatur-Zeitung* 10/4 (December 1794), columns 473–487. See Kosenina 1989, 20; Lazzari 2004, 26. Fichte comments extensively on the 1793 edition of Platner's *Aphorismen* in his lectures on logic and metaphysics (held from 1794/5 to 1799). See Fichte 1976–1977.

[60] Hume 1748/1999, 92–93: "It becomes, therefore, no inconsiderable part of science barely to know the different operations of the mind, to separate them from each other, to class them under their proper heads, and to correct all that seeming disorder, in which they lie involved, when made the object of reflection and enquiry. This task of ordering and distinguishing [...] rises in its value, when directed towards the operations of the mind, in proportion to the difficulty and labour, which we meet with in performing it. And if we can go no farther than this *mental geography*, or delineation of the distinct parts and powers of the mind, it is at least a satisfaction to go so far; and the more obvious this science may appear (and it is by no means obvious) the more contemptible still must the ignorance of it be esteemed, in all pretenders to learning and philosophy" (my italics, U.T.).

Andree Hahmann

The Debate on the Fundamental Powers of the Soul: Crusius, Platner, Kant, and Schmid

Abstract: Can a simple substance have more than one kind of power? This question leads to the core of a philosophical discussion among Kant's immediate predecessors and successors. The real focus of the debate, however, is Christian August Crusius, whose understanding of fundamental powers has strongly influenced the debate on cognitive faculties and the structure of the human mind. Crusius' main objection is directed against Wolff's assumption that simple substances can only have one power. Although Crusius assumes simple substances, he does not want to exclude the possibility that they can have several basic powers despite their simplicity. I will discuss the philosophical debate around fundamental powers and argue that this also helps to clarify Kant's methodological limitations in determining the ultimate basis of the cognitive powers of the mind.

Can a simple substance have more than one kind of power or force?[1] This question takes us to the heart of a discussion that began in the first half of the eighteenth-century and continued into post-Kantian philosophy. In this paper, I will sketch some stages of this dispute, to contribute in this way also to the elucidation of the historical context out of which Kant's *Vermögenslehre* emerged, which in turn is crucial for many aspects of Kant's philosophy. I will also point out the special role Crusius played in the development of eighteenth-century German philosophy.

It is well known that Crusius' critical assessment of Wolff's understanding of the principle of sufficient reason was very influential among eighteenth-century philosophers.[2] Less well known, however, is the fact that his understanding of fundamental powers (or basic forces: *Grundkräfte*) has strongly influenced the debate on cognitive faculties and the structure of the human mind.[3] Crusius argues against Wolff's assumption that simple substances can have only one power or force. Although Crusius subscribes to the widespread idea that there are simple

---

[1] The German is "Kraft" which can be both translated as *power* or *force*. Since we are dealing with the soul as simple substance, I will use *power* as translation. However, the same applies to simple substances that constitute matter.
[2] See the contribution of Stiening in this volume.
[3] Important exceptions include Henrich 1955; Heßbrüggen-Walter 2004; and Tester 2016.

substances, for him this does not exclude the possibility of several fundamental powers. In the following, I will discuss this view and show that Crusius made a remarkable contribution to the philosophical debate in Germany in the second half of the eighteenth-century.

My paper is divided into two parts. The first part presents Crusius' conception of power or force and explains why simple substances can have several powers despite their simplicity. In the second part, I will examine more closely the influence that Crusius' ideas on the nature of human cognition had on Kant and post-Kantian philosophy.

1 Crusius on Simple Substances and their Powers

In his *Psychologia rationalis*, Wolff asserts that the soul can ultimately have only one power:

> *Vis animae nonnisi unica est.* Anima enim simplex est (§ 48), adeoque partibus caret (§ 673 *Ontol.*) [...]. ("The power of the soul is only one. For the soul is simple (§ 48), which is why it has no parts" (§ 673 *Ontol.*)) (Wolff 1740a, § 57)[4]

Wolff justifies his assumption by referring to the simplicity of the soul as a substance. The simplicity of the soul consequently prevents a multiplicity of powers in the soul. Wolff also explains that the soul itself is this power. All activities usually associated with the soul are therefore only modifications of one and the same power (Wolff 1740a, § 60; Wolff 1751, § 53; 755). Finally, Wolff identifies this single power with the power of representation (*vis repraesentativa* or *Vorstellungskraft*).[5]

---

4 See also Wolff 1751, § 745: "Meanwhile, since it [the soul; A. H.] is a simple thing (§ 742), but in a simple thing there cannot be any parts (§ 75); so neither can there be in the soul many powers distinguished from one another [...]." ("Unterdessen, da sie [*die Seele*; A. H.] ein einfaches Ding ist (§ 742), in einem einfachen Dinge aber keine Theile seyn können (§ 75); so können auch nicht in der Seele viele voneinander unterschiedene Kräfte anzutreffen seyn [...].") For the partly problematic assumptions and argumentative background of Wolff's position, see Heßbrüggen-Walter 2004, 78–84, and Tester 2016, 428–432. For a more comprehensive discussion of Wolff's account of the soul, see Blackwell 1961.

5 Wolff, § 755: "Because, therefore, this power is the ground of all that is changeable in the soul (§ 754); so therein consists the essence of the soul [...]." ("Weil demnach diese Kraft der Grund ist von allem demjenigen, was veränderliches in der Seele vorgehet (§ 754); so bestehet in ihr das Wesen der Seele [...].") See also § 756: "Since that which makes a thing active or able to act is called its nature (§ 628); but the soul is an active being by virtue of its power, by which it represents the world (§ 753); thus this power is at the same time the nature of the soul." ("Da dasjenige, was ein Ding thätig oder vermögend etwas zu würcken machet, seine Natur genennet wird

Wolff's statements suggest three different but closely related theses: first, a simple substance can have only one power because of its simplicity. Secondly, this is the power of representation, and thirdly, the soul as a substance is this power itself. Crusius firmly rejects all three claims. In his view, it is not impossible that even simple substances have more than one power; the power of representation does not occupy a special position, and this power must not be identified with the substance itself. Crusius' critique culminates in the claim that this would make the power of representation a "general power" [*General-Kraft*] (Crusius 1745, § 70), which means that for Crusius it is not even a real power, but merely a word under which various effects are subsumed. Crucial for Crusius' critique of Wolff are therefore, on the one hand, his conception of power and, on the other, his conception of substance.[6] In what follows, I will first address his discussion of the nature of power and then of substance.

1.1 Power

In his *Entwurf der nothwendigen Vernunft-Wahrheiten* Crusius defines power as follows:

> The possibility of a thing B, which is connected to another thing A, is called a power in the thing A in the widest sense. Thus, a thing has some, and at least one, power. Therefore, if one considers any positive quality in another sense, it is a power. In fact, it is called a quality, in the sense in which the thing can be distinguished from any other thing. But it is called a power, in so far as something else is made possible, or made real, wholly or in part, by it. (Crusius 1745, § 29)[7]

(§ 628): die Seele aber vermöge ihrer Kraft, wodurch sie sich die Welt vorstellet (§ 753), ein würckendes Wesen ist (§ 754); so ist diese Kraft zugleich die Natur der Seele.") Henrich 1955, 34 points out that Wolff adopted this view from Leibniz although Wolff presents a shortened version of the Leibnizian argument.

6 In the preface to the *Entwurf der nothwendigen Vernunft-Wahrheiten* Crusius points out that his understanding of power is based on the teachings of his teacher Adolph Friedrich Hoffmann (Crusius 1745, p. XI). Unsurprisingly therefore, Crusius' criticism of the connection between the simplicity of substance and the assumption of a single power goes back to his first Latin writings. See Crusius 1740, esp. §§ I–IX. Hoffmann himself, due to an early death, never wrote a metaphysics textbook. He did, however, present the material in his lectures. Crusius refers to these lectures. The reference to Hoffmann is significant because Hoffmann closely followed his teacher Andreas Rüdiger, who also critically examined Wolff's psychology. See, for example, Rüdiger 1727. Cf. Henrich 1955, 35.

7 "Die Möglichkeit eines Dinges B, welche an ein anderes Ding A verknüpft ist, heißt in dem Dinge A in dem weitesten Verstande eine Kraft. Folglich hat ein iedwedes Ding einige, und wenigstens

It is striking that Crusius does not distinguish between possibility and reality at this point. Power includes both the possible and the actual relation to another thing.[8] Moreover, Crusius infers from a real connection of things to a power founded in one of them. Consequently, one must assume a power for each quality. So different powers can be abstracted depending on which qualities are focused on. For example, if you assume that man can write letters and books, he has a power to write. Intestines, for example, have the power to digest, and the magnet has the power to attract iron, and so on (Crusius 1745, § 70). In short, every quality, even accidental ones, derive from a power that must have produced it.[9] Crusius later limits this first definition to power in the broad sense, which he distinguishes from power in the narrow sense. We shall see, however, that this first understanding of power became influential among later philosophers.

As for Crusius' criticism of Wolff, an important point already emerges from this first understanding of power: if a substance has several qualities, it must also have several powers. But is this also true for simple substances? To answer

---

eine Kraft. Daher ist eine iedwede positive Eigenschaft, wenn man sie in anderer Absicht betrachtet, eine Kraft. Nehmlich sie heißt eine Eigenschaft, wieferne sich das Ding dadurch von irgend einem anderen unterscheiden lässt. Eine Kraft aber heißt sie, wieferne dadurch etwas anderes ganz oder zum Theil möglich, oder wirklich gemacht wird."

8 See, however, Wolff 1751, § 117: "But the power must not be mixed up with a mere capacity: for the capacity is only a possibility to do something: but since the power is a source of change (§ 115), there must be in it an effort to do something [...]. By the capacity a change is only possible; by the power it becomes actual." ("Es muß aber die Kraft nicht mit einem blossen Vermögen vermenget werden: denn das *Vermögen* ist nur eine Möglichkeit etwas zu thun: hingegen da die Kraft eine Quelle der Veränderungen ist (§ 115), muß bey ihr eine Bemühung etwas zu thun anzutreffen seyn [...]. Durch das Vermögen ist eine Veränderung bloß möglich; durch die Kraft wird sie würklich.") On Wolff's distinction between power and capacity, see Heßbrüggen-Walter 2004, 76–77, see 91 also for a discussion of the decisive differences in this matter between Wolff and Crusius.

9 Crusius 1745, § 63: "Therefore, "Therefore, one can also say that the power is the possibility of a certain thing B, linked to a substance A, by which something subsists in A, whereby B has or obtains its reality [...]. So it belongs to the concept of power [...] the concept of causality and subsistence. In fact the causality, by which A contributes something to B, is a quality subsisting in the subject A, which is also connected to the subjectum as such, if nothing is produced. Now this quality is called a power in the subject A." ("Daher kan man auch sagen, die Kraft sey die an eine Substanz A verknüpfte Möglichkeit eines gewissen Dinges B, vermöge welcher in A etwas subsistiret, wodurch B seine Wircklichkeit hat oder bekommt [...]. Es gehöret also zu dem Begriffe der Kraft [...] der Begriff der *Causalität* und der Subsistenz. Nehmlich diejenige Causalität, vermöge welcher A zu B etwas beyträgt, ist eine in dem Subjecte A subsistirende Eigenschaft, welche an das Subjectum auch alsdenn verknüpft ist, wenn nichts hervor gebracht wird. Diese Eigenschaft nun heißt in dem Subjecte A eine Kraft.") The origin of this idea also goes back to the *Dissertatio philosophica de corruptelis intellectus* (see note 6). See Crusius 1740, § IV.

this question, we need to look at Crusius' underlying metaphysics. His distinctions concerning essences and their relation to powers are particularly important here.

According to Crusius, the metaphysical essence [*metaphysische Wesen*] of a thing is responsible for its discernability.[10] Qualities contained in this essence can, according to the above explanation, also be conceived as powers. Crusius makes a further distinction between the metaphysical essence of a thing and its fundamental essence [*Grundwesen*]. The fundamental essence contains such qualities that are not themselves founded in other qualities of the same thing. For Crusius, the fundamental essence is the essence of a thing in the strictest sense and the powers that derive from the qualities of the fundamental essence are accordingly its fundamental powers.[11] He explains that the fundamental essence has at

---

10 Crusius 1745, § 17: "With each thing, one may take the word in the broad, or in the narrow sense, one must think something, by which one can distinguish it from other things. That which one thinks of one thing, and by which one distinguishes it from another, I will call the metaphysical essence of a thing." ("Bey einem iedweden Dinge, man mag das Wort im weiten, oder im engen Verstande nehmen, muß man etwas denken, dadurch man es von andern Dingen unterscheiden kann. Dasjenige, was man bey einem Dinge denket, und wodurch man es von andern unterscheidet, will ich das *metaphysische Wesen* eines Dinges nennen.")

11 Crusius 1745, § 29: "So that which is mutable in a thing has its origin in the end either from that which is enduring in it; or it is even founded in something external to it [...]. But this series cannot go on indefinitely, but one must at last reach one or several essential qualities which are not in turn founded in other qualities of the same thing. And these are called the fundamental essence, or the essence of a thing in the strictest sense [...]. The fundamental essence of a thing, then, is that which is first in it, which is not again founded in other qualities of the same thing, and in which, on the other hand, everything else has its ground, which belongs to the thing, or can belong to it, in as far as it has its ground in it, and not in external causes. [...] It should be noted here that, with good reason, I have not required a single quality for the fundamental essence of a thing, or, if it is to be a substance, only a single power. For I would accept it without any proof. It is possible that the fundamental essence of some substances is the combination of several fundamental powers." ("Das also, was in einem Dinge veränderlich ist, hat seinen Ursprung zuletzt entweder von demjenigen, was in demselben beständig ist; Oder es ist gar in etwas ausser demselben Dinge gegründet [...]. Diese Reihe aber kan nicht unendlich fortgehen, sondern man muß zulezt auf eine oder etliche wesentliche Eigenschaften kommen, welche nicht wiederum in andern Eigenschaften eben desselben Dinges gegründet sind. Und dieselben heissen das *Grundwesen*, oder das *Wesen eines Dinges in dem engesten Verstande* [...]. Das *Grundwesen* eines Dings ist also dasjenige, was in demselben das erste ist, welches nicht wiederum in andern Eigenschaften desselben Dinges gegründet ist, und darinnen hingegen alles andere seinen Grund hat, was der Sache zukommt, oder zukommen kann, in so ferne nehmlich, wieferne es in derselben und nicht etwan in äusserlichen Ursachen seinen Grund hat. [...] Man merke hierbey, daß ich mit gutem Bedacht nicht eben zum Grundwesen eines Dinges nur eine einzige Eigenschaft, oder daferne es eine Substanz seyn soll, nur eine einzige Kraft erfordert habe. Denn ich nähme solches ohne allen Beweis an. Es ist ja möglich, daß das Grundwesen einiger Substanzen in der Verbindung etlicher Grundkräfte bestehe.") See also § 70.

least one quality because otherwise the thing could not be distinguished from other things and consequently could not exist independently. However, it is not necessary for one and the same thing to have only one quality or power. This is because, as Crusius explicitly points out: "It is possible that the fundamental essence of some substances consists of the combination of several fundamental powers" (Crusius 1745, § 39).[12] He takes up this point again a little later:

> Even in the combination of several fundamental powers in a single subject, and even in a simple subject, one will not find anything inconsistent if one does not conceive of the powers as something corporeal, but realizes that innumerable many can be connected to a single subject, which do not subsist in different spaces, but in a single point of the subject, and, if it is simple, penetrate the same completely. (Crusius 1745, § 73)[13]

For Crusius, then, it is clear that a "subject" need not necessarily have only one power.

However, if one assumes that a subject must have only one power, a particular problem arises: recall that, for Crusius, a power supposedly explains the actual qualities of a thing. If the human soul, as a subject of powers, has only one power, then all human qualities and activities should be intelligible as effects of that single power. As Crusius points out, this is how Wolff has to conceive of the fundamental role of representation. The reason for this is that representation is the only thing that emerges when one abstracts from all the various mental activities, since they depend equally on representations. For Crusius, this makes the power of representation a "general-power" [*General-Kraft*] (Crusius 1745, § 70), under which one subsumes all kinds of activities of the soul. However, as Crusius points out, this "general-power" is not really a cause, because without taking into account further qualities – that is, powers – it contributes nothing to the explanation of the effects:

> […] If one believes to have found such a power of the human soul in the representative power [*vorstellende Kraft*] of the world, then that which is found therein can be understood from it.

---

12 "Es ist ja möglich, daß das Grundwesen einiger Substanzen in der Verbindung etlicher Grundkräfte bestehe."
13 "Man wird auch in der Verbindung mehrerer Grundkräfte in einem einzigen, ja in einem einfachen Subjecte nichts ungereimtes antreffen, wenn man sich nur nicht die Kräfte als etwas körperliches vorstellt, sondern mercket, daß deren unzehlig viele an ein einziges Subjectum verbunden werden können, welche nicht in unterschiedenen Räumen, sondern in ganz einerley Punkte des Subjects subsistiren, und dasselbe, wenn es einfach ist, ganz durchdringen."

Only it may be that the effect, which one abstracts, and from which one names the assumed power, is only an effect, which comes from many grounds taken together. (Crusius 1745, § 70)[14]

In short, Crusius objects that Wolff's notion of a fundamental power of representation alone is not sufficient to clearly explain the observable effects of the human soul. In his view, however, this would be necessary to call it a power in the strict sense, or a fundamental power.[15] In most mental phenomena, however, it cannot be ruled out that additional powers are involved. Thus, assuming that the power of representation serves as the common basis of all mental activities, this is not yet sufficient to make it a true "fundamental power;" that is, a power that is grounded in the essence of a thing.[16] For it cannot be excluded that the effect was only partly produced by it.

Crusius then explains how he conceives of a true fundamental power:

---

14 "[...] Wenn man sich einbildet, in der vorstellenden Kraft der Welt eine solche Kraft der menschlichen Seele gefunden zu haben, daraus sich dasjenige, was darinnen angetroffen wird, verstehen lasse. Allein es kan ja seyn, daß der Effect, den man abstrahiret, und davon man die angenommene Kraft benennet, nur eine Wirckung ist, welche von vielen Ursachen zusammen genommen herkommt."

15 Crusius 1745, § 70: "Thus we are hereby led to the concept of a power in the narrow sense, which is opposed to the mere capacity and the arbitrarily abstracted general powers. A power in the narrow sense is a possibility of other things connected to a subject, which in the same subject is a special quality, and also beyond our thoughts distinguished from others in such a way, that it is a certain something and distinguished from others, without it becoming it only by our way of looking at it, and which is also in the subject something constant. One can also call it a fundamental power. Now it cannot be denied that it is not possible to penetrate everywhere to the knowledge of these true powers belonging to the fundamental essence, but that one must often be pleased when one only knows at all what kind of effects a thing might produce, and in which substance one must look for the ground for certain effects." ("Wir werden also hiermit auf den Begriff einer Kraft *im engern Verstande* geführet, welche dem bloßen Vermögen und denen willkührlich abstrahirten General-Kräften entgegen gesetzt ist. Nehmlich eine *Kraft im engern Verstande* ist eine solche an ein Subject verknüpfte Möglichkeit anderer Dinge, welche in demselben Subjecte eine besondere, und auch ausserhalb unserer Gedanke dergestalt von andern unterschiedene, Eigenschaft ist, daß sie etwas einiges und von andern unterschiedenes ausmacht, ohne daß sie es erst durch unsere Betrachtungs-Art werden darf, und welche auch in dem Subjecte etwas beständiges ist. Man kan dieselbe auch eine *Grundkraft* nennen. Nun ist zwar nicht zu leugnen, dass sich nicht überall bis zu der Erkenntnis dieser wahren und zu dem Grund-Wesen gehörigen Kräfte hindurch dringen lasse, sondern daß man sich öfters daran begnügen lassen muß, wenn man nur überhaupt weiß, zu was für Wirckungen ein Ding aufgeleget sey, und in welcher Substanz man den Grund zu gewissen Wirckungen suchen muß.")

16 Heimsoeth 1926, 19 recognizes in Crusius' conception of fundamental powers a profound dependence on Leibniz and refers at this point to the distinction between primitive and derivative powers. It is also possible, however, that both Leibniz and Crusius emphasize different aspects of the same Aristotelian tradition. See also notes 23 and 29.

> *A true fundamental power must accord to the thing constantly,* otherwise it is a mere capacity which comes from the present mutable application of the true fundamental powers and the accidental connection of the thing with others. (Crusius 1745, § 71)[17]

According to Crusius, we are not dealing with a genuine fundamental power as long as what is attributed to the power itself cannot be clearly understood as an effect, because the causal character of the relationship remains unclear. It is therefore first necessary to determine the relevant changes in things as a constant correlation. Note that Crusius allows for differences in observable effects only in terms of intensity or direction.[18] The changes in the soul that Wolff attributes to the power of representation, however, do not satisfy this requirement.[19] If one assumes that the human soul has only one fundamental power, namely the power of representation, then all its effects or activities should be sufficiently explained by the power of representation. This means that the soul can only feel, think, reason, desire, hate, feel pain, etc. by means of this power. For Crusius, however, this makes no sense, because the differences between these activities cannot be attributed only to differences in direction or intensity, as would be the case if we were

---

[17] *"Eine wahre Grundkraft muß der Sache mit einer Beständigkeit zukommen*, sonst ist sie ein blosses Vermögen, welches von der gegenwärtigen veränderlichen Application der wahren Grundkräfte und der zufälligen Verbindung des Dinges mit andern herkommt."

[18] Crusius 1745, § 73: "What is to be a fundamental power, if the power is finite, must have no more than a continuous next effect, and its next effects must not be distinguished from one another more than in direction and degree; but the more distant effects must be comprehensible from the next one and from the different degrees and directions of it: and such must be truly shown, inasmuch as the concept of the fundamental power is to be completely clear." ("Was eine Grundkraft seyn soll, dasselbe muß, wenn die Kraft endlich ist, nicht mehr als einerley nächste Folge beständig haben und die nächsten Wirckungen derselben dürfen unter einander nicht weiter als der Direction und dem Grade nach unterschieden seyn; die fernern Wirckungen aber müssen sich aus der nächsten, und aus den unterschiedenen Graden und Richtungen derselben begreiffen lassen: und dieses muß man wircklich zeigen können, dafern der Begriff der Grundkraft völlig deutlich seyn soll.") See also Crusius 1740, § III. Tester 2016, 433 identifies eight characteristics of fundamental powers in Crusius.

[19] Crusius 1745, § 444: "[...] because the actions and changes of the understanding are more distinct than according to direction and degree: So the given power would only be a mere general power, but not yet a true physical fundamental power [...]. But there must be more than one [fundamental power; A. H.], because we can think of things of quite different determined nature." ("[...] weil aber die Actionen und Veränderungen des Verstandes mehr als der Direction und dem Grade nach unterschieden sind: So wäre die angegebene Kraft nur eine blosse *General-Kraft*, noch nicht aber eine wahre physikalische Grundkraft [...]. Mehr als eine [*Grundkraft*; A. H.] aber muß da seyn, weil wir Dinge von ganz unterschiedener determinierten Beschaffenheit dencken können.") See also the early version of this argument in Crusius 1740, § VII.

dealing with a genuine fundamental power.²⁰ Instead, one would have here only a "general-power;" that is, an abstract power to which a mere collection of effects is subsumed. But the mere subsuming of various effects under one concept does not actually explain anything for Crusius. More than that, this assumption even prevents one from "ever attaining real knowledge of the thing" (Crusius 1745, § 73).²¹ Crusius, on the other hand, emphasizes "that the very first fundamental powers of our understanding are impossible to identify by number" (Crusius 1745, § 444).²²

This makes it clear why, for Crusius, the power of representation cannot be the fundamental power of the human soul, and why Wolff mistakenly transformed a mere abstract "general-power" into a fundamental power, which is supposed to be founded in the fundamental essence of a thing and from which its essential qualities follow. Since the activities of the soul cannot be explained by a single fundamental power, one must assume a multiplicity of such powers. As we shall see below, it is Crusius' conception of substance that, in contrast to Wolff's conception, enables him to explain why it is not impossible to assume that the soul, as a simple substance, can have multiple powers.

1.2 Substance and Accident

Crusius also presents his conception of substance in the context of the discussion of the essence of things. His approach in this respect is somewhat reminiscent of

---

20 Crusius 1745, § 446: "For, assuming that thinking and willing would come from the same single fundamental power, or at least willing would depend entirely on such fundamental powers that constitute understanding taken together [...]; then either willing would have to be only a kind of thinking which would be distinguished from other kinds of thinking by content, direction or degree; or willing would have to be an adequate effect of thinking, namely from certain kinds of thinking. But both are contradictory." ("Denn gesetzt, Dencken und Wollen käme von einer einzigen Grund-Kraft her, oder wenigstens dependirte das Wollen gänzlich mit von denenjenigen Grund-Kräften, welche den Verstand zusammen genommen ausmachen [...]; so müßte entweder das Wollen nur eine Art von Dencken seyn, welche etwan von andern Arten des Denckens dem Innhalte der Direction oder dem Grade nach unterschieden wäre; oder das Wollen müßte ein adäquater Effect vom Dencken, nemlich etwan von gewissen Arten des Denckens, seyn. Es ist aber beydes widersprechend.") See also Crusius 1740, § VII–X.
21 "[...] iemals zur Erkenntnis derselben zu gelangen [...]."
22 "[...] daß sich die allerersten Grund-Kräfte unsers Verstandes der Zahl nach unmöglich ausmachen lassen [...]." In his *Weg zur Gewißheit und Zuverläßigkeit der menschlichen Erkenntniß* Crusius claims that it is impossible to "discover completely all fundamental powers of the human understanding" (Crusius 1747, § 63).

the traditional Aristotelian approaches.[23] This impression is reinforced, as we shall see, by his subsequent elaboration. In his discussion, Crusius assumes that one has to distinguish between two aspects in a complete thing: first, that which is represented as subsisting in another, and second, that in which other things subsist but which itself does not subsist in anything else. Crusius calls the first a metaphysical quality or *"accidens praedicamentale"* and the second a "metaphysical subject" (Crusius 1745, § 20). Both subject and quality are regarded by Crusius as incomplete things. Neither can exist without the other. When Crusius speaks of "substance" here, he means the complete thing composed of subject and qualities. He clarifies this thought as follows: Things can be distinguished according to their form and matter.[24] In the case of a book, for example, one can distinguish between the underlying matter and the particular form. Accordingly, one can also say that the form as a quality is inherent in the matter as a subject. But the specific matter of the book, that is, the paper, can also be distinguished into form and matter. Paper, too, is matter shaped in a certain way; that is, it consists of underlying material elements. This distinction between matter and form can be continued a little further, but according to Crusius one eventually arrives at an ultimate metaphysical subject to which the formal qualities then attach. In view of this ultimate or fundamental subject, all preceding subjects can only be regarded as relatively persistent subjects and thus as mere qualities, while only the ultimate subject is "absolute" (Crusius 1745, § 21). According to Crusius, this absolute subject exists perfectly in itself, precisely when it is not itself contained again in another subject. The relative subject, on the other hand, exists in an imperfect way insofar as it remains dependent on another subject (Crusius 1745, § 22).

Two points are of particular importance for us in the following discussion of Crusius: first, it seems to follow from this assumption that the subject as such has no special quality. Crusius therefore distinguishes in a substance between an unqualified material substrate and the intrinsic qualities of this substrate. This leads Dieter Henrich to suspect that Kant's assumption of the intrinsically unqualified *substantiale* could have drawn on Crusius' conception of substance (Henrich 1955, 40; see also Heimsoeth 1926, 25). It should be noted, however, that while Crusius allows for an ultimate metaphysical subject, which in a sense underlies all

---

[23] Heßbrüggen-Walter 2004, 88 points to Suarez.
[24] Crusius 1745, § 30, 48: "The former is called matter in the ontological understanding, or the material, while the other is called form or the formal. Both, therefore, are incomplete things, and if one abstracts them, it depends only on a particular way of looking at them." ("Das erstere nennet man die *Materie* im ontologischen Verstande, oder das materiale, das andere hingegen die *Form* oder das formale. Beydes demnach sind unvollständige Dinge, und es kömmt, wenn man sie abstrahiret, nur auf eine besondere Betrachtungsart an.")

predication, the substance itself is for him the complete thing. Even in his discussion of simple substances, he does not abandon the idea that substance consists of subject (or substrate) and quality.[25] We already know that for Crusius the qualities are based directly on powers, which in turn suggests that the substance consists of a qualityless substrate and certain powers.[26] This ambiguous understanding of substance, of course, also has a famous predecessor in Aristotle, for Aristotle already referred to the combination of form and matter, as well as form and matter in themselves (in a certain sense), as substance. The fact that such a substance, as Kant states, cannot be an object of cognition, accordingly, also applies to Aristotle's ultimate substrate: unqualified matter (see Hahmann 2009, 174–195). But if we assume that the substance as a complete thing is always at the same time a composition of an underlying substrate and its qualities, the question arises whether there can be such a thing as simple substances at all. This brings us to the second point, namely Crusius' conception of simple substance.

Contrary to what one might suppose given his conception of substance and power, Crusius actually believes that there are simple substances. He thus agrees with the Leibniz-Wolffian philosophy. Nevertheless, as we shall see in a moment, there are also crucial differences between Crusius' account and the Leibniz-Wolffian position. Consider first, however, that Crusius, analogous to his predecessors, develops the concept of simplicity from that of composition. According to this view, one can distinguish a multiplicity of parts in a real thing, even if it is a unity (i. e., one). Such a unity is therefore a whole made up of parts (Crusius 1745, § 103). And a little later in his discussion, Crusius even explicitly takes up the classical proof for

---

25 Crusius 1745, § 111: "And this is precisely what makes a substance possible when subject and power are together." ("Und eben dadurch wird eine Substanz möglich, wenn Subject und Kraft beysammen ist."); and p. 182: "This also illuminates a more elevated definition of a simple substance. A simple substance is a next subject in which a power directly subsists." ("Hiermit erhellet zugleich eine erhöhete Definition einer einfachen Substanz. Nehmlich eine *einfache Substanz* ist ein nächstes Subject, in welchem eine Kraft unmittelbar subsistiret.")

26 Crusius 1745, § 30: "As far as form subsists as a property in matter as the subject, so the last one is called materia in qua, but insofar as it is something that arises from the composition of several substances and their connection, it is called materia ex qua. One understands at the same time that the form can be an active power or something else according to what the thing is." ("Wie fern die Form als eine Eigenschaft in der Materie als dem Subjecte subsistiret, so heißt die leztere materia in qua, wiefern sie aber etwas ist, was aus der Zusammensetzung mehrerer Substanzen und deren Verbindung entstehet, so heißt dieselbe materia ex qua. Man verstehet zugleich, daß die Form eine thätige Kraft oder etwas anderes seyn könne, nachdem die Sache ist.") Identifying the form with the power or force comes quite close again to the position of Leibniz. For Leibniz, too, form or entelechy is primarily a certain activity. From this perspective, the difference between Leibniz' and Crusius' conception lies in the fact that for Crusius the form is not substantial, but accidental, and is inherent in a substrate with which it constitutes the substance.

the existence of simple substances: "Here, however, we only have to make clear that if there are composite things, there must also be simple ones" (Crusius 1745, § 111).[27]

Crucial to Crusius' further discussion is the distinction between ideal and real simplicity. The former denotes a simplicity from which no further parts can be distinguished even in thought; the latter, on the other hand, has no real or actual parts that could really be separated from it. "*True simplicity* of a thing is that constitution of it, by which it has no real part; that is, it does not consist of separable things, insofar as it does not consist of them" (Crusius 1745, § 105).[28] The strange addition, "insofar as it does not consist of them," means that Crusius does not want to exclude the possibility that further parts can be separated in thought. Accordingly, there are still parts in the substance, but these are only what Crusius calls "parts of thought" [*Gedanckentheile*] (Crusius 1745, § 104). Separation in thought and the real separation are indeed closely connected, for that which can really be separated from a thing must also be separable from it in thought. But this should not be understood to mean that everything that can be separated in thought can also be separated in fact (Crusius 1745, § 106).[29]

---

[27] "Allhier aber haben wir nur klar zu machen, daß, wenn es zusammengesetzte Dinge giebt, auch einfache seyn müssen." Cf. Wolff 1751, § 76; Wolff 1736, § 68; Baumgarten 1757, §§ 224–226.

[28] "Die *wahre Einfachheit* eines Dinges ist diejenige Beschaffenheit desselben, vermöge deren es keine wircklichen Theile hat, das ist, nicht aus trennbaren Dingen bestehet, wiefern es nicht daraus bestehet."

[29] Crusius' solution to one of the most fiercely debated problems of the eighteenth-century, namely the problem of the compatibility of the infinite divisibility of space with the assumption of simple substances as the last constituents of composite bodies, also results from this. Thus, Crusius distinguishes strictly between the realm of philosophy and that of mathematics. Consequently, the same words are understood differently in mathematics than in philosophy (Crusius 1745, § 113). Mathematics for Crusius is only concerned with the magnitudes of extended things. However, it does not address the real nature of things. "Since now in mathematics the concept of all extended quantities, which are quantitates continuae, had to be built on the concept of the mathematical point: So one cannot deny that they cannot all be together in this condition, but that the true lines, surfaces and bodies in nature are composed of the smallest substances in the same order as one imagines them in mathematics as consisting of points." (Crusius 1745, § 115: "Da nun in der Mathematik der Begriff aller ausgedehnten Grössen, welche quantitates continuae sind, auf den Begriff des mathematischen Punctes hat gebauet werden müssen: So kan man nicht leugnen, daß sie in dieser Verfassung alle zusammen nicht seyn können, sondern daß die wahren Linien, Flächen und Cörper in der Natur in eben der Ordnung aus kleinesten Substanzen zusammen gesetzt werden, wie man sich dieselben in der Mathematik als aus Punkten bestehend gedencket.") Decisive for Crusius is the respect in which something is called *simple*. Thus, he distinguishes between a metaphysical and a physical simple. The former would be simple in every respect, a definition which is fulfilled for Crusius by God (Crusius 1745, § 107), the latter is such

It is against this background that Crusius introduces his concept of simple substance: simple, by definition, is that which has no truly (i.e., physically) separable parts. A metaphysical being would thus be simple if no further qualities could be separated from it. The substance, which as such is a complete thing and thus a metaphysical subject with qualities, would be simple under this presupposition if no further substances could really be separated from it.[30] For Crusius, extended things are compound substances (Crusius 1745, § 108), which does not necessarily mean that simple substances have no extension. Even in a simple substance, parts can be distinguished in thought. It is precisely in this sense that the soul is simple: "For those who attribute only one fundamental power to the soul, as those who attribute several to it, claim the simplicity of the soul" (Crusius 1745, § 109).[31] The soul would therefore be simple even if more than one quality and, assuming Crusius' conception of power, more than one power were to be found in it. This would also prove to Crusius that the conclusion drawn by Wolff from the simplicity of the soul as a substance to the necessity of a single fundamental power is not valid:

> Thus, out of the multiplicity of mental powers and their actions, no composition of substance results, but only a multiplicity of activity, and a perfection of the subject and its essence far exceeding that of matter. (Crusius 1745, § 444)[32]

Now only Wolff's third thesis remains, according to which the power of representation is the soul itself and thus a simple substance. Crusius also rejects this thesis with the following argumentation: "First of all no power can be thought without a subject [...], therefore it cannot be the same" (Crusius 1745, § 118).[33] This conclusion, as we can now see, follows from Crusius' conception of substance, which is com-

---

"which consists of no more physical parts" (Crusius 1745, § 109: "[...] was nicht mehr als aus physicalischen Theilen besteht [...].").

30 Crusius 1745, § 107: "[...] *a substance is simple* if it is not composed of separable substances. Accordingly, a simple substance is only a single metaphysical subject which exists in perfect form for itself [...]." ("[...] *eine Substanz ist einfach*, wenn sie nicht aus trennbaren Substanzen zusammengesetzt ist. Demnach ist eine einfache Substanz nur ein einziges metaphysisches Subjekt, welches auf vollkommene Art vor sich selbst bestehet [...].")

31 "Denn es behaupten so wohl diejenigen die Einfachheit der Seele, welche ihr nur eine einzige Grundkraft zuschreiben, als diejenigen, welche ihr mehrere beylegen."

32 "So erfolget aus der Mannigfaltigkeit der geistigen Kräfte und ihrer Actionen keine Zusammensetzung der Substanz, sondern nur eine mannigfaltige Thätigkeit, und eine die Materie weit übersteigende Vollkommenheit des Subjectes und seines Wesens."

33 "Erstlich läßt sich keine Kraft ohne ein Subject [...] dencken, mithin kann sie auch dasselbe nicht seyn."

posed of a "subject" and its formal determination or power. Accordingly, power must be inherent in a "subject" and cannot subsist without this basis.

2 The Idea of a General Power in the Eighteenth Century

Crusius' criticism of Wolff's conception of the soul had a profound influence on the later development of German philosophy in the eighteenth-century. In this section we will deal with Kant and Schmid, to whom Dieter Henrich already refers.[34] However, we will also include Platner in our discussion. The treatment of Platner's position is particularly instructive for our purposes, for he initially remains unimpressed by Crusius' critique of the fundamental role he ascribes to the power of representation, but then distances himself from this view on the basis of his more thorough engagement with Kant. This indeed shows that Kant was read by his contemporaries in the light of Crusius' discussion of fundamental powers.[35]

2.1 Kant

As is well known, Heidegger refers to the introduction of the *Kritik der reinen Vernunft* to support his thesis that imagination as a special form of the power of representation is the common root of sensibility and understanding.[36] Kant seems to suggest here that the individual cognitive faculties may "perhaps spring from a common but unknown root" (*CPR*, A 15/ B 29).[37] Admittedly, Kant himself rows back in the following and instead refers to the difficulties of finding such a root. Henrich, however, has already pointed out that his reservations can be understood in two different ways (Henrich 1955, 31). Thus Reinhold, Fichte, Hegel, Cohen,

---

[34] Henrich 1955, 38 also mentions Tetens, who was also skeptical about the assumption of a single fundamental power. However, as Henrich convincingly argues, it is unlikely that Tetens had any influence on Kant in this matter.

[35] That Kant was well aware of Crusius' critique of Wolff and his conception of a fundamental power is also emphasized by Tester 2016 who focuses in particular on the Paralogism section of the *Critique of Pure Reason*.

[36] Heidegger 1991, 37. The second passage Heidegger refers to is *CPR*, A 835 / B 863. Unless otherwise noted all translations of Kant follow the Cambridge Edition of the Works of Immanuel Kant (Guyer/Wood 1992).

[37] In the *Anthropology* Kant emphasizes that it is impossible for us to cognize this common root (*Anth*, AA 07: 177).

and also Heidegger are said to have understood this to mean that the systematics of Kant's critical project does require the search for an underlying principle, although Kant did not succeed in determining this principle. Henrich now counters that it is quite conceivable that Kant resisted this project for other and deeper reasons. Indeed, Kant not only saw insurmountable difficulties in deriving the various cognitive faculties from a single principle, but even considered this undertaking impossible. This is also indicated, for example, by a passage from the first introduction to the *Kritik der Urteilskraft:*

> We can trace all faculties of the human mind without exception back to these three: the *faculty of cognition*, the *feeling of pleasure and displeasure*, and the *faculty of desire*. To be sure, philosophers who otherwise deserve nothing but praise for the thoroughness of their way of thinking have sought to explain this distinction as merely illusory and to reduce all faculties to the mere faculty of cognition [*Erkenntnisvermögen*]. But it can easily be demonstrated, and has already been understood for some time, that this attempt to bring unity into the multiplicity of faculties, although undertaken in a genuinely philosophical spirit, is futile. (*EEKU*, AA 20: 205–206)[38]

It should be noted that when Kant speaks here of faculty of cognition, he may well mean the power of representation. In fact, Kant does not use the term "power of representation" [*Vorstellungskraft*] as a technical term in his critical philosophy. However, in the *Kritik der reinen Vernunft* (*CPR*, B 130) he also calls understanding, as such, a power of representation. It should be noted that for Kant, representation is a general concept that encompasses both intuition and thought, a fact to which Heidegger draws particular attention. However, it is also clear that there is an important difference between the power of representation and the power of imagination. Although the two faculties are closely related, they are not the same thing. In some ways, the power of representation can be considered more fundamental than the power of imagination, since the power of imagination also works with representations. But despite the crucial differences between these two faculties, the general idea of a common root of intuition and understanding put forward by Heidegger shows central aspects of Crusius' so-called fundamental power, as

---

38 Kant: *EEKU*, AA 20: 205–206: "Wir können alle Vermögen des menschlichen Gemüths ohne Ausnahme auf die drei zurückführen: das *Erkenntniſvermögen* das *Gefühl der Lust und Unlust* und das *Begehrungsvermögen*. Zwar haben Philosophen, die wegen der Gründlichkeit ihrer Denkungsart übrigens alles Lob verdienen, diese Verschiedenheit nur für scheinbar zu erklären und alle Vermögen aufs bloße Erkenntnißvermögen zu bringen gesucht. Allein es läßt sich sehr leicht darthun, und seit einiger Zeit hat man es auch schon eingesehen, daß dieser, sonst im ächten philosophischen Geiste unternommene Versuch, Einheit in diese Mannigfaltigkeit der Vermögen hineinzubringen, vergeblich sey." Guyer in the English translation also refers to Wolff and the debate concerning the fundamental powers of the soul. See Guyer 2002, 358.

Henrich has already shown. But apart from that, Heidegger's interpretation is also highly problematic for several other reasons,[39] he simply overlooks the fact that Kant himself elsewhere emphasizes the unfoundedness of the assumption that the power of imagination could be the last and most original faculty of the soul, and even compares it in this respect with the power of representation. Consider the following quotation from *Über den Gebrauch teleologischer Prinzipien in der Philosophie* (cf. Henrich 1955, 32–33).

> E.g., the *imagination* in the human being is an effect that we cognize to be not the same with other effects of the mind. Therefore, the power related to this effect can only be called power of the imagination (as fundamental power). [...] Several have thought that they had to assume a single fundamental power for the sake of the unity of the substance and even have thought to gain cognition of it simply by coining the *common title* of various fundamental powers, e.g., that the fundamental power of the soul is the power of representing [*Vorstellungskraft*] the world. This would be the same as if I were to say: the sole fundamental power of matter is moving force, since repulsion and attraction both stand under the common concept of movement. Yet one desires to know whether the former could also be *derived* from the latter, which is impossible. For with respect to their specific difference, the *lower* concepts can never be derived from the *higher* ones. And as far as the unity of the substance is concerned, which appears to include the unity of the fundamental power already in its concept, this illusion rests on an incorrect definition of *power*. For the latter is not that *which* contains the ground of the actuality of the accidents (i.e., the substance) but only the *relation* of the substance to the accidents *insofar* as the former contains the ground of the actuality of the latter. But different relations may well be attributed to the substance (its unity notwithstanding). (*ETP*, AA 08: 180–181)[40]

---

[39] So, for instance, Heidegger simply ignores Kant's cautious formulation, which expressly emphasizes that this could "perhaps" be the case, i.e., under certain circumstances and not necessarily. For a still very good critical assessment of Heidegger's crucial thesis, see the early reviews in Cassirer 1931, and Levy 1932.

[40] "Z.B. die *Einbildung* im Menschen ist eine Wirkung, die wir mit andern Wirkungen des Gemüths nicht als einerlei erkennen. Die Kraft, die sich darauf bezieht, kann daher nicht anders als Einbildungskraft (als Grundkraft) genannt werden. [...] Zu der Einheit der Substanz haben Verschiedene geglaubt eine einige Grundkraft annehmen zu müssen und haben sogar gemeint sie zu erkennen, indem sie blos den *gemeinschaftlichen Titel* verschiedener Grundkräfte nannten, z.B. die einzige Grundkraft der Seele sei Vorstellungskraft der Welt; gleich als ob ich sagte: die einzige Grundkraft der Materie ist bewegende Kraft, weil Zurückstoßung und Anziehung beide unter dem gemeinschaftlichen Begriffe der Bewegung stehen. Man verlangt aber zu wissen, ob sie auch von dieser *abgeleitet* werden können, welches unmöglich ist. Denn die *niedrigern* Begriffe können nach dem, was sie Verschiedenes haben, von dem *höheren* niemals abgeleitet werden; und was die Einheit der Substanz betrifft, von der es scheint, daß sie die Einheit der Grundkraft schon in ihrem Begriffe bei sich führe, so beruht diese Täuschung auf einer unrichtigen Definition der *Kraft*. Denn diese ist nicht das, *was* den Grund der Wirklichkeit der Accidenzen enthält (das ist die Substanz), sondern ist blos das *Verhältniß* der Substanz zu den Accidenzen, *so fern* sie den Grund ihrer Wir-

Although Kant does not explicitly refer to Crusius, the above discussion clearly shows the Crusian origin of his thought: first of all, the terminology Kant uses is striking. Like Crusius, Kant also speaks of "fundamental powers." Moreover, by referring to the various faculties of the human mind, he rejects the assumption that the "power of representing the world" could be the only fundamental power. When Kant speaks here of the unity of substance, he alludes to Wolff's argument that a simple substance can have only one power because of its simplicity.[41] The closeness to Crusius, however, is most evident in Kant's argument for the rejection of a single fundamental power. According to Kant, this rejection results from a false definition of power (or force).[42] For Kant, power refers to the relationship between substance and accident. With Crusius, one could also say that the individually ascertainable qualities of a thing are powers, which is why a simple substance has as many powers as qualities; or in other words, one can attribute as many powers to it as one can ascertain relations between the substance and its accidents.

I would also like to point to a passage from the "Elementarlehre" of the *Kritik der reinen Vernunft*:

> At first glance the various appearances of one and the same substance show such diversity that one must assume almost as many powers as there are effects, as in the human mind there are sensation, consciousness, imagination, memory, wit, the power to distinguish, pleasure, desire, etc. Initially a logical maxim bids us to reduce this apparent variety as far as possible by discovering hidden identity through comparison [...]. The idea of a *fundamental power* – though logic does not at all ascertain whether there is such a thing – is at least the problem set by a systematic representation of the manifoldness of powers. The logical principle of reason demands this unity as far as it is possible to bring it about, and the more appearances of this power and that power are found to be identical, the more probable

---

klichkeit enthält. Es können aber der Substanz (unbeschadet ihrer Einheit) verschiedene Verhältnisse gar wohl beigelegt werden."

41 See once more Wolff 1740a, § 57; Wolff, 1751, § 745: "However, it is not the case that a thing that is simple can have different efforts at the same time, in that it is just as much as if a body, which in its movement is to be regarded as an indivisible thing (§ 667), should move to different regions at the same time." ("Es gehet aber nicht an, daß ein Ding, was einfach ist, verschiedene Bemühungen zugleich haben kan, indem es eben so viel, als wenn ein Cörper, der in seiner Bewegung als ein untheilbares Ding anzusehen ist (§. 667.), sich nach verschiedenen Gegenden zugleich bewegen solte.")

42 See also AA 28: 145: "The Wolfians have falsely asserted that the soul qua *simplex* is merely a power of *repraesentatio:* this arises from the false definition of power: since it is merely a *respectus*, the soul can have many *respectus*, as many are the accidents that cannot be brought back to others. Representations and desires are basic powers." ("Die Wolfianer haben falsch behauptet, daß die Seele qua simplex bloß eine Kraft der repraesentatio sei: Dies entsteht durch die falsche Definition der Kraft: da sie bloß ein respectus ist, so kann die Seele viele respectus haben, so vielerlei die accidentien sind, die nicht auf andere können gebracht werden. Vorstellungen und Begehren sind Grundkräfte.")

it becomes that they are nothing but various expressions of one and the same power, which can be called (comparatively) their *fundamental power*. [...] These comparatively fundamental powers must once again be compared with one another, so as to discover their unanimity and thereby bring them close to a single radical; that is, absolutely fundamental, power. But this unity of reason is merely hypothetical. (*CPR*, A 648–649 / B 676–677)[43]

Thus, as Henrich notes, we get the explanation for Kant's remark from the Introduction to the *Kritik der reinen Vernunft*. For in referring to the common root of the stems of knowledge, Kant by no means intends to abolish his critical separation of these stems. Rather, he is concerned, on the one hand, to maintain the explanatory openness already demanded by Crusius in the treatment of these powers and, on the other hand, to provide methodological guidance which, for its part, aims at a systematic unity in the apparent multiplicity. The necessary unity is established – following the overarching systematics of the *Kritik der reinen Vernunft* – by the "idea," which is why Kant also speaks of the "idea of a fundamental power" in this context. But although Kant's considerations are thus placed in the systematic framework of critical philosophy, the proximity to Crusius is clear. For as we have seen, Crusius also warns philosophers against rashly concluding that a single fundamental power is at work, where in reality several powers can be effective. In order to reveal the true fundamental powers; that is, powers in the narrow sense, it is necessary to carefully compare the supposed fundamental powers with one another and "thereby bring them close to a single radical, that is, absolutely fundamental power," as Kant says, even if the latter may remain undiscovered forever. As we shall see below, this methodological assumption in particular had a demonstrable influence on the development of philosophy after Kant.

---

43 "Die verschiedenen Erscheinungen eben derselben Substanz zeigen beim ersten Anblicke soviel Ungleichartigkeit, daß man daher anfänglich beinahe so vielerlei Kräfte derselben annehmen muß, als Wirkungen sich hervortun, wie in dem menschlichen Gemüte die Empfindungen, Bewußtsein [...]. Anfänglich gebietet eine logische Maxime, diese anscheinende Verschiedenheit soviel als möglich dadurch zu verringern, daß man durch Vergleichung die versteckte Identität entdecke [...]. Die Idee einer *Grundkraft*, von welcher aber die Logik gar nicht ausmittelt, ob es dergleichen gebe, ist wenigstens das Problem einer systematischen Vorstellung der Mannigfaltigkeit von Kräften. Das logische Vernunftprinzip erfordert diese Einheit soweit als möglich zustande zu bringen, und je mehr die Erscheinungen der einen und anderen Kraft unter sich identisch gefunden werden, desto wahrscheinlicher wird es, daß sie nichts, als verschiedene Äußerungen einer und derselben Kraft seien, welche (komparativ) ihre *Grundkraft* heißen kann. [...] Die komparativen Grundkräfte müssen wiederum untereinander verglichen werden, um sie dadurch, daß man ihre Einhelligkeit entdeckt, einer einzigen radikalen, d. i. absoluten Grundkraft nahe zu bringen. Diese Vernunfteinheit aber ist bloß hypothetisch."

2.2 Platner Before and After Kant

Little impressed by Crusius' criticism of Wolff and not yet touched by Kant's *Kritik der reinen Vernunft*,[44] Platner insists in the new edition of his *Philosophische Aphorismen* from 1784 that "the substance [...] is the power itself, (in the strictest sense), and the sum of the determinations or qualities; and a substantial subject, in which the qualities and the power are to exist, is a fictitious idea of imagination" (Platner 1784, § 930, 324–325). In this statement, Platner explicitly opposes Crusius' assumption of substantial subjects.[45] He argues here that such a subject must either itself be a composition of qualities and consequently an active power, or something different from the power. If, on the other hand, one assumes the latter, one must ask what it could be. Platner, along with Locke and Baumgarten, holds that only that which has an effect exists.[46] On the other hand, Platner also explicitly admits to Crusius that it would not contradict the simplicity of the substance if it had more than one power (Platner 1784, § 931, 325).[47] However, he stresses that there must be a fundamental power "on which the activity, direction and strength of the others depend" (Platner 1784, § 932, 325). The plurality of powers would thus be founded in a single – systematically ordered – fundamental power, which for Platner represents the "substantial in the narrow sense" (Platner 1784, § 932, 326: *das Substanzielle im engeren Verstande*). This is an explicit objection to Crusius, who, as already mentioned, does not want to exclude a plurality of fundamental powers on methodological grounds.

---

[44] In the new preface to the completely revised edition of his *Philosophische Aphorismen* of 1793, Platner admits that he had previously "not yet sufficiently thought through Kant's *Critique of Pure Reason*." (Platner 1793, p. III).

[45] Platner (1784, § 930, 325) refers to Crusius (1745, §§ 20 and 62), where it says (112–113): *"The power in the widest understanding is the possibility of another thing connected to one thing (§ 29). Finally, it must always be connected to a substance. Therefore, one can also say that the power is the possibility of a certain thing B which is connected to a substance A, by which in A something subsists, whereby B has its reality or obtains it (§ 59). Thus, it belongs to the concept of power, if it is to be clearly thought of, the concept of causality and subsistence."* ("*Die Kraft in dem weitesten Verstande* ist die an ein Ding verknüpfte Möglichkeit eines andern Dinges (§ 29). Zuletzt muß dieselbe allezeit an eine Substanz verknüpft seyn. Daher kann man auch sagen, die *Kraft* sey die an eine Substanz A verknüpfte Möglichkeit eines gewissen Dinges B, vermöge welcher in A etwas subsistiret, wodurch B seine Wirklichkeit hat oder bekommt (§ 59). Es gehöret also zu dem Begriffe der Kraft, wenn der deutlich gedacht werden soll, der Begriff der *Causalität* und der *Subsistenz*.")

[46] At this point Platner points to Baumgarten 1757, §§ 132 and Locke 1690, II. 23. See Platner 1784, § 930, 325.

[47] "The combination of several powers does not contradict the simplicity of substances." ("Es widerspricht der Einfachheit der Substanzen nicht, das Zusammenseyn mehrerer Kräfte.")

This position, of course, raises the problem that Platner must subsume all the faculties of the soul under a single fundamental power, which leads him, for example, to claim that both the will and human desires follow from this single fundamental power. In his view, they are effects that the ideas of good and evil have on this one fundamental power (Platner 1782, § 361, 149).[48] However, one should not infer from this that there are separate powers. On the contrary, for Platner both the understanding and the will do not exist separately from each other, but are equally based on only one fundamental power. In this context, Platner explains that for Leibniz and Wolff, the will depends essentially on the power of representation (Platner 1782, § 362, 151). In accordance with his metaphysical view of the necessary grounding of the various powers in a substantial fundamental power, he then asserts that the various powers of the soul are also ultimately grounded in a common fundamental power (Platner 1782, § 362, 149–150).[49] For Platner this fundamental power can only be the power of representation (Platner 1784, § 364, 154).[50] Consequently, he concludes that the power of representation is the sufficient basis for the knowledge of all phenomena of the will. By the power of representation he means a "spiritual being, which partly looks at ideas presented to it, that is, perceives them as something external to itself, partly compares them [...], and the latter either with ideas as characteristics, or with ideas as sensations of its own state" (Platner 1784, § 365, 154–155).[51] The idea of the good also follows

---

48 "The volitional activities, desire and abhorrence, are effects of ideas of good or evil [...]. Accordingly, activities of the will are distinguishable from the representations from which they arise. And to this extent the essence of the faculty of will does not consist in representations, but in the effects that occur upon them." ("Die Willensthätigkeiten, Begehren und Verabscheuen, sind Wirkungen von Ideen eines Guten, oder Übels [...]. Demnach sind die Willensthätigkeiten unterscheidbar von den Vorstellungen aus denen sie entspringen. Und in so fern besteht das Wesen des Willensvermögens nicht in Vorstellungen, sondern in den Wirkungen die darauf erfolgen.")
49 "Still, this distinction among representations of the will and activities of the will [...] proves nothing for a segregated independence of the power of cognition and the power of the will. For in a single being it is impossible to assume more than a single fundamental power [...] and one erroneously concludes from divisions of abstraction to a separation in the thing [...]." ("Jedennoch beweiset diese Unterscheidung unter Willensvorstellungen und Willensthätigkeiten [...] nichts für eine abgesonderte Selbstständigkeit des Erkenntniß- und Willensvermögens. Denn in einem einigen Wesen ist nicht möglich mehr denn eine einzige Grundkraft [...] und man schließt irrig von Theilungen der Abstraktion auf Trennung in der Sache [...].") See also Platner 1784, § 363, 154.
50 "The basic concept of the power of representation is a sufficient basis of knowledge of all phenomena of the power of the will [...]."
51 "[...] geistiges Wesen, welches Ideen die sich ihm darstellen theils schauet, d. i. als etwas außer sich empfindet, theils vergleicht [...], und das leztere entweder mit Ideen als Merkmahlen, oder mit Ideen als Empfindungen von ihrem eigenen Zustande [...]."

from the comparison, and so the emotions of the will also depend on it. Moreover, the power of representation also includes the striving to expand one's own power (Platner 1784, § 366, 155). But the power is extended by all ideas that promote mental and physical activity, coincide with the urge of life, or bring about the perfection of one's state. The power of the will is therefore ultimately nothing other than the endeavor of the soul to expand the power of representation (Platner 1782, § 368, 156).[52] Platner also explains all other mental activities in this way, arguing that they all depend on a supreme cognitive faculty, namely the power of representation (Platner 1782, § 373, 157).

Platner thus essentially follows the Leibniz-Wolffian conception in 1782/84, although he is familiar with Crusius' criticism, as evidenced by his explicit rejection of Crusius' view. This changes, however, in the revised and elaborated version of his *Philosophische Aphorismen* of 1793. The reason for this change, however, is not a new reflection on Crusius' critique, but his careful reading of Kant's critical work in the meantime. Platner explicitly deals with the relevant passages from Kant's work and revises his own view on the questions relevant to the problem of the fundamental powers accordingly. However, he still holds that substance is the power itself and refers to Baumgarten and Leibniz (Platner 1793, § 768, 445). In addition, however, he also considers Kant's explanation of the relationship between substance and power set out in the short text *Ueber eine Entdeckung nach der alle neue Critik der reinen Vernunft durch eine ältere entbehrlich gemacht werden soll* from 1790.[53] In this text, Kant adopts Crusius' rejection of the claim that substance is a power and further justifies it against the background of his own transcendental philosophical approach. For Platner, substance itself remains a system of subordinate powers that depend on a single fundamental power (Platner 1793, § 770, 446).[54] But in contrast to the earlier editions, in which he emphasized against Crusius that this fundamental power is the power of representation, he asserts: "But which exactly is the fundamental power: this is difficult to determine" (Platner 1793, § 771, 447).[55] Platner now explicitly refers to Kant's *Kritik der reinen*

---

52 "Accordingly, the capacity of will which always manifests itself in the production or destruction of a foreseen idea [...] is nothing other than a striving of the soul to expand its power of representation [...]."
53 Platner refers to the annotation on page 73 of the 1790 edition: Immanuel Kant: Ueber eine Entdeckung nach der alle neue Critik der reinen Vernunft durch eine ältere entbehrlich gemacht werden soll. Königsberg 1790. See accordingly *OD*, AA 08: 224.
54 "If there are several powers in the substances together [...]: however, one of them, the supreme one, must be the fundamental power on which the activity, direction, and strength of the others depend. And so a substance would be a system of inseparably connected powers subordinate to a fundamental power, and the fundamental power would be the substantial in the narrow sense."
55 "Welches aber die Grundkraft sey: das ist schwer zu bestimmen."

Vernunft and the passage already quoted above (*CPR*, B 677–678), in which Kant, as we have seen, emphasizes that it is impossible to prove that there is only one fundamental power in a substance.

This concession by Platner is noteworthy for two reasons. First, it shows that Platner, who explicitly took issue with Crusius on this question, came closer to Crusius' position after reading Kant's *Kritik der reinen Vernunft* and gave it more weight than before. Secondly, this also makes it clear that Kant's position was understood in the context of this problem. It is therefore not surprising when Platner suggests a little later, this time in agreement with Kant, that it is still permissible, even necessary, to accept this fundamental power and that this is due to the striving for systematic unity, which is founded in reason itself (Platner 1793, § 771, 447). If Platner is allowed to do this, he believes "there should be no further dispute with Mr. Schmid about this point [...]" (Platner 1793, § 771, 447).[56] With this remark, Platner refers to Schmid's *Empirische Psychologie* (1791), which not only goes back to Crusius, but also refers to the post-Kantian discussion on this topic.

2.3 Schmid

In the first part of his *Empirische Psychologie*, which deals with the "human soul, its various faculties and powers" (Schmid 1791, 153), Schmid explicitly picks up on Crusius' remarks on the problem of fundamental powers. In the introductory part of the work, he presents the basic determinations and classifications of mental faculties. If we focus on the concepts of power and substance, which are important for our question, some remarkable innovations as well as points of connection to the discussion among Schmid's predecessors become clear. Recall: crucial to Crusius' rejection of Wolff's position is his definition of power. For Crusius, power in the widest sense denotes "The possibility of a thing B, which is connected to another thing A" which is why "any positive quality" considered from a different perspective is also a power (Crusius 1745, § 29, 45–46). Crusius, in contrast to Wolff, does not distinguish between the faculties and powers of things. Schmid deviates from this right at the beginning of his explanations by explicitly emphasizing the difference between the faculties of the soul and its powers:

> We think of a subject in which these representations are inherent as its determinations, and of something that makes these determinations possible, and of something in which their real existence is founded. We call the former the faculty of the soul, the latter the power of the

---

[56] "[...] mit Herrn Schmid über diesen Punkt [...] weiter keinen Streit [*geben*; A,H.]."

soul. Both designate the relationship in which the subject of the soul is thought to certain perceived phenomena. (Schmid 1791, § I, 153–154)[57]

The quotation not only clarifies the difference Schmid sees between faculties and powers, but also introduces us to Schmid's conception of the soul as a substance. At first glance, Schmid sides with Crusius, who does not identify the substance with the power, but allows it to be composed of subject and accidents. However, if one adds the last part of the elaboration, according to which it should only be a matter of perceptible qualities; that is, appearances, it becomes clear that it is not Crusius but Kant who serves as a model here. Be that as it may, what is certain in any case is that Schmid rejects the Leibniz-Wolffian identification of substance and power in this question. This point will become important in what follows.

The soul is thus the "subject of representations" (Schmid 1791, § II, 155). If one concentrates only on the perceptible relations in the connection of representations, one is dealing with the "mind" [*Gemüth*]. The differentiation is necessary for Schmid because it allows him to distinguish between the logical and the real essence of the soul. The former comprises only the perceptible accidents or states of the soul, which are regularly arranged in this essence. The real essence, on the other hand, extends to the ultimate grounds not only of perceptible phenomena. It follows that empirical psychology concentrates exclusively on the mind [*Gemüth*] as the perceptible connection of the states of the soul.

Now one comes to the faculties of the soul when one takes a look at the conditions of the possibility of the perceived appearances (Schmid 1791, § IV, 156).[58] For Schmid, these are the "faculties of the mind [*Gemüth*] in the broadest sense" (Schmid 1791, § IV, 156). These are again distinguished into original ones on the one hand and derived ones on the other: the former include only internal conditions, while the latter; that is, the derived faculties, may also include external conditions. Both types of faculties correspond in turn to powers as reasons for their realization or "conditions of their reality" (Schmid 1791, § IV, 157).

---

57 "Wir denken uns irgend ein Subiect, dem diese Vorstellungen als seine Bestimmungen inhaeriren und in demselben ein Etwas, was diese Bestimmungen möglich macht, und Etwas, worinn ihr wirkliches Daseyn gegründet ist. Jenes nennen wir Seelenvermögen; dieses Seelenkraft. Beyde bezeichnen das Verhältnis, worinn das Subiect der Seele zu gewissen wahrgenommenen Erscheinungen gedacht wird."

58 "Die inneren Erscheinungen überhaupt, die äussern Phänomene, sofern sie zu jenen in einem gesetzmässigen Verhältnisse stehen, und die Gesetze, wornach ihr Gang und ihre Verbindung bestimmt sind, führen uns 1. Auf gewisse Bedingungen ihrer Möglichkeit – *Vermögen des Gemüthes im weitsten Sinne.*"

The derived faculties, on the other hand, as said, include external conditions. Important for our topic is the consequence that follows from this determination: namely, that a "multiplicity of appearances of the mind" necessarily leads to a multiplicity of faculties, analogous to Crusius' conclusion from the multiplicity of qualities to the underlying powers (Schmid 1791, § VII, 158). As a reminder, we are dealing with an appearing multiplicity of qualities in Schmid. It is open, however, what underlies the appearing multiplicity in reality or in itself.

What follows is Schmid's methodological innovation in comparison to Crusius' approach:

> But we, determined by the laws of our reason, relate this multiplicity to one, by linking it without distinction to the simple representation I as the subject of it, that is, by combining it in one self-consciousness. (Schmid 1791, § VII, 158)[59]

Once again, the manifold appearances suggest a multiplicity of faculties and powers, which in turn are related to only one unity. The relation between multiplicity and unity is effected by reason, which unites the various powers in a simple self-consciousness; that is, the I, which thus becomes the subject of the manifold appearances.

The Kantian origin of the thought as well as the relation to the transcendental unity of apperception are obvious. However, the reference back to Wolff and Crusius will become equally clear in the next section. For Schmid explicitly refuses to connect this unity in the determination of the state of mind [*Gemüth*] with the simplicity of substance. For "this unity [...], if it is to be recognizable, is not the unity or simplicity of the substance of the soul" (Schmid 1791, § VIII, 158).[60] With reference to the *Kritik der reinen Vernunft*, Schmid justifies this by saying that this simplicity is nothing to us as cognizant beings, since it cannot be connected with any intuition.

In the following longer note, Schmid conciliatorily refers to the previous debate between Crusius and Wolff and concedes a certain plausibility to both sides. Just as one side has proceeded correctly in accepting so many basic powers as internally distinct actions. Likewise, the other side, having pointed to the simplicity of substance, can claim the interest of reason aiming at "unity" (Schmid 1791, § VIII, 159). Schmid therefore asks: "Does one party have much reason to un-

---

[59] "Wir beziehen aber, durch die Gesetze unsrer Vernunft bestimmt, dieses Mannigfaltige auf Eines, indem wir es ohne Unterschied an die einfache Vorstellung *Ich* als das Subjekt desselben anknüpfen, d. h. in Einem Selbstbewusstein verknüpfen."

[60] "Diese Einheit [...] ist, sofern sie erkennbar seyn soll, nicht die Einheit oder Einfachheit der *Substanz* der Seele."

philosophically chide the other party's way of thinking in contrast to its own?" (Schmid 1791, § VIII, 160)[61]

This is now also the point at which Schmid makes the distinction between fundamental power and general power. Thus, Schmid understands a fundamental power to be an

> inner principle of the possibility or reality of certain phenomena which are basically identical and only prove to be different through accidental secondary determinations founded in something outside the substance, and for this very reason are attributed to different faculties and powers [...]. (Schmid 1791, § IX, 160)[62]

One can now speak of these fundamental powers in a purely comparative sense, namely whenever seemingly different expressions can be traced back to an underlying faculty. Schmid, however, does not exclude a "radical or absolute fundamental power" from which, in turn, the comparative fundamental powers emerge as a common root. In contrast to later interpreters of the *Kritik der reinen Vernunft* (see Heidegger), however, who were obviously less familiar with the previous debate on fundamental powers, Schmid now emphasizes, in agreement with Kant, to whom he also explicitly refers here, that nature hides this unity from the human being, although the human being is called upon by the maxim of reason to "seek unity" in order to bring the series of comparative fundamental powers into order (Schmid 1791, § X).[63] Schmid openly admits that these thoughts are connected with Crusius, and he explicitly refers the reader to his *Entwurf der notwendhwendigen Vernunftwahrheiten*, "where there are very readable remarks on the concept and the characteristics of the true fundamental powers" (Schmid 1791, § X, 161).

Schmid now also finds Crusius' conception of "general-power" useful, which Crusius, as we have seen above, used only negatively, that is, to reject Wolff's approach. Schmid, on the other hand, is able to gain a positive sense from the conception: The subsuming of activities under a general power contributes to the methodologically demanded unity of reason, by integrating the diversity of mental faculties and powers into a general generic conception (Schmid 1791, § XII, 163). Like Crusius, Schmid distinguishes sharply between the "general-power" and the

---

61 "Hat wohl eine Parthey viel Ursache, die Denkart der andern im Gegensatz der ihren unphilosophisch zu schelten?"
62 "[...] inneres Princip der Möglichkeit oder Würklichkeit gewisser Erscheinungen, die im Grunde identisch sind und nur durch zufällige, in etwas ausser der Substanz gegründete Nebenbestimmungen sich als verschieden zeigen und eben darum *verschiedenen Vermögen* und *Kräften* zugeschrieben werden [...]."
63 See on this, once more, Kant: *CPR*, A 648–649 / B 676–677.

fundamental power and then rejects with Crusius the Wolffian attempt to prove the *vis repraesentativa* or power of representation as the only fundamental power of the soul from which all mental motions could be derived.[64] The unification of the comparatively ascertainable fundamental powers, on the other hand, is to take place in a system of powers.

Schmid now draws attention to a fundamental confusion: a systematic unity can be justified on the one hand by a simple starting point (or "principium") and on the other by a common end:

> In such a system of mental powers [...] one can imagine, as it were, a double center: the one from which all effects proceed, the other towards which all effects aim. The one designates the first faculty and the first power in the physical or historical sense, the expression of which constitutes the physical precondition for the possibility or reality of all others. The other denotes the first faculty or the first power in the series of purposes [...] towards which everything runs and from which, again backwards, the efficacy of all other faculties and powers is modified and controlled. (Schmid 1791, § XIV, 166)[65]

Schmid already hints at his own solution here: "To the former (as will be shown in the future) sensibility will apply, to the latter reason." ["Für die erste möchte (wie künftig gezeigt wird) die Sinnlichkeit, für die letztere die Vernunft gelten."] Sensibility stands here for the power of representation, which is why Schmid continues in the second part of his *Empirische Psychologie* with an "investigation of the faculty of representation and the power of representation of the soul." But even if the power of representation is thus made a comparative fundamental power of the soul, this does not yet mean that this is at the same time the only and common root of the human powers of cognition. This assumption overlooks the second essential principle, which is based on reason as a unique power to posit ends.

Schmid also criticizes Platner at this point although he admits that all appearing effects are to be methodically traced back to this underlying root. However, this is clearly not the power of representation; this renders Platner's critique of Crusius untenable, as Schmid states, because this common root is merely assumed methodically but does not correspond to the actual nature of the thing.

---

64 See the long quotation from Crusius given by Schmid in Schmid 1791, § XII, 163–164.
65 "In einem solchen System von Gemüthskräften [...] kann man sich gleichsam einen doppelten Mittelpunkt gedenken; den Einen, von wo alle Würkungen ausgehen; den Andern, worauf alle Würkungen abzielen. Iener bezeichnet das *erste Vermögen* und die *erste Kraft in physischem* oder *historischem Sinne*, deren Aeusserung die physische Voraussetzung von der Möglichkeit oder Würklichkeit aller übrigen ausmacht. Die andere macht das erste Vermögen oder die *erste Kraft in der Reihe der Zwecke* [...] wo alles hinläuft und von da wieder rückwärts die Würksamkeit aller übrigen Vermögen und Kräfte modificirt und beherrscht wird."

3 Outlook

I want to conclude by briefly pointing out the forward-looking relevance of Schmid's discussion of fundamental powers. Shortly after its publication, his book was very favorably reviewed by Maimon in the *Magazin zur Erfahrungsseelenkunde*, edited by Maimon and Karl Philipp Moritz. In his review, Maimon particularly emphasizes the distinction between a fundamental power and a "general-power." In his view, a fundamental power means an inner principle of the possibility or reality of appearances. They are determined by the analysis of appearances in the mind [*Gemüth*]. A "general-power," on the other hand, is merely a generic term encompassing all species belonging to the same genus (Maimon 1792, 6–7). Maimon's understanding corresponds to Schmid's in this respect. What is remarkable, however, is the conclusion Maimon draws from it: In his opinion, Schmid's criticism does not only refer to Platner and Wolff, but is aimed at Schmid's colleague in Jena, Carl Leonhard Reinhold, who also calls "all kinds of effects of the soul [...] representations [*Vorstellungen*]" (Maimon 1792, 7).[66] Accordingly, the power of representation that Reinhold considers fundamental, would not be a truly fundamental power of the soul, but merely a "general-power" and thus not the absolute first principle he seeks.[67]

---

[66] "[...] alle Wirkungsarten der Seele [...] Vorstellungen nennt [...]."
[67] For Schmid's significance for the development of Reinhold's elementary philosophy, see Berger 1998; for the role of the objection related to the general-power in particular, see 166–174.

Stefan Klingner
C. C. E. Schmid on Kant's Distinction Between Sensibility and Understanding

Abstract: The essay points out some striking aspects of Schmid's interpretation of Kant and contrasts it with the reception of Kant by Fichte and Schelling in the 1790s. The focus is on Kant's distinction between sensibility and understanding, since it is central not only to Kant himself but also to the differences between Schmid's Kantianism and that of the young idealists. In a first step, the authenticity and distinctiveness of Schmid's Kantianism will be assessed; in a second step, this assessment will be clarified by looking at his engagement with the alternative interpretations of Kant by Fichte and Schelling. As will be shown, Schmid is a proponent of what could be called a "realist" Kantianism, which hardly goes beyond Kant's text and therefore does not precisely confront those systematic problems that preoccupied the young idealists.

There is little need for an extensive justification of why Kant's epistemological distinction between "sensibility" and "understanding," or between "intuition" and "concept" should be highlighted in a philosophical paper. In terms of the history of philosophy, the distinction marks the end – at least for a while – of the coexistence of epistemological empiricism and rationalism, which decisively shaped the philosophy of the early modern period and the Enlightenment. In terms of its substance, the distinction expresses the idea of the irreducibility and interdependence of the two aspects of the given and thought, which are essential for any form of cognition, in a way that is taken note of and discussed all the way up to current philosophy and probably characterizes most theoretical approaches that see themselves as "Kantian" in principle.[1]

But why should Carl Christian Erhard Schmid's reception of Kant's distinction between sensibility and understanding be the central topic of a philosophical paper, or at least a paper in the history of philosophy? Two motives for this are apparent:

---

[1] See, for example, the statements in Flach 1994, 187–188, and 192 ("Few insights have received as much circulation in philosophy, and also as much confirmation, as Kant's insight of the necessary distinction between thought and intuition," my translation), and in McDowell 1996, 3 ("One of my main aims is to suggest that Kant should still have a central place in our discussion of the way thought bears on reality"), each formulated from very different philosophical traditions.

First, Schmid is one of the first of Kant's contemporaries who not only pedantically received Kant's critical writings, but also effectively exposited them. As an interpreter of Kant who was primarily interested in authenticity and intelligibility, and as perhaps the "most important Kantian" at the University of Jena at the end of the eighteenth century, his reception of critical philosophy can be considered exemplary of early Kantianism (see Schröpfer 1995). Given the fundamental relevance of Kant's distinction between sensibility and understanding for the entire critical philosophy, his reception of this distinction should thus be instructive for a pertinent evaluation of the overall reception of Kant's philosophy among his contemporaries.

Second, it is precisely Schmid's "Kantianism" that places him in stark contrast to some other early and still well-known recipients of critical philosophy – namely the young idealists, above all Johann Gottlieb Fichte and Friedrich Wilhelm Joseph Schelling, who for their part claimed to grasp and advance not only the "letter" but the "spirit" of Kant's philosophy with their philosophical reflections.[2] While Schmid belonged to the mere "commentators of Kant" for Fichte and Schelling (Fichte 1845–1846, vol. 1, 480–490),[3] he accused the latter of "the boldest and most immodest dogmatism," "the likes of which the history of philosophy has not yet seen" (Schmid 1798, 47). Above all, he denounced their insistence on intellectual intuition as "an absolute cognitive faculty a priori," which contradicted Kant's insight into the dualistic basic structure of human cognition (Schmid 1798, 33). In view of this disagreement between the followers of the "new" philosophy, it may seem promising to ask about the relevance of Schmid's reception of Kant's distinction between sensibility and understanding for the early idealist conception of intellectual intuition.

The question of whether these two motives also provide good reason for looking at Schmid's reception of Kant's distinction between sensibility and understanding will be addressed in the following considerations. It is not possible to answer this question conclusively within the framework of an initial review of relevant passages from Schmid's writings. However, the foundation for a satisfactory answer can at least be prepared by pointing out some striking aspects of Schmid's interpretation of Kant and contrasting it with the reception of Kant by Fichte

---

[2] See, for example, Fichte's *First Introduction* (Fichte 1845–1846, vol. 1., 417–449, here 429–430), his *Second Introduction* (Fichte 1845, vol. 1, 451–518, here 479), and Schelling's *Ideen* (Schelling 1856–1861, vol. I.2, 1–343, here 221–222).

[3] Schmid is not mentioned by name in the *Second Introduction*, but for Fichte he certainly belongs to the so-called "commentators" [*Auslegern*], as his criticism of Schmid's interpretation of Kant shows, which he gives in his discussion of Schmid's "system" (see Fichte's *Vergleichung* in Fichte 1845–1846, vol. 2, 421–458, here 434–439).

and Schelling in the 1790s. The first step here will be to assess the authenticity and distinctiveness of Schmid's Kantianism, while the next step will be to clarify this assessment by looking at his engagement with the alternative interpretations of Kant by Fichte and Schelling. As will be shown, Schmid is a proponent of what could be called a "realist" Kantianism, which hardly goes beyond Kant's text and therefore does not precisely confront those systematic problems that worried the young idealists.

The structure of the following considerations is clear as well from these preliminary remarks: First, Kant's distinction between sensibility and understanding will be outlined very briefly, focusing only on some essential statements in the *Critique of Pure Reason*,[4] and then highlighting three difficulties of interpretation that arise from them (sec. 1). Following this, Schmid's presentation of this distinction in his compendium *Critik der reinen Vernunft im Grundrisse* as well as in his *Wörterbuch zum leichtern Gebrauch der kantischen Schriften* will be discussed,[5] allowing for an initial, provisional evaluation of his reception of Kant, which is also supported by consulting Schmid's later *Grundriß der Metaphysik*, published in 1799 (sec. 2). Afterwards, his criticism of the idealist theories of Fichte and Schelling will be sketched out, using his polemic in the first part of the *Physiologie*, published in 1798, as a basis (Schmid 1798, 19–49). This will be followed by a final assessment, which also takes into account the criticism of idealism, and at least a tentative answer to the question of the extent to which further engagement with Schmid's reception of Kant's epistemological criticism and its characteristic dualism might pay off (sec. 3).

1 Kant's Distinction Between Sensibility and Understanding – and its Problems

That the distinction between sensibility and understanding is of fundamental relevance for Kant's entire critical conception of cognition is already evident from the fact that he begins his *Critique of Pure Reason* with it. He states, for example, immediately in the first paragraph of the "Transcendental Aesthetics" of the first *Critique*:

---

4 See for further evidence and an overview Gava/Keller 2015, and Klingner 2015. For more recent systematic discussions, see for example Haag 2007, and Hanna 2001, 45–54, but also the older interpretation based on the concept of form in Graubner 1972.

5 The second edition of the *Grundriß* (Schmid 1788) and the third edition of the *Wörterbuch* (Schmid 1795) are used here.

> The capacity (receptivity) to acquire representations through the way in which we are affected by objects is called sensibility. Objects are therefore given to us by means of sensibility, and it alone affords us intuitions; but they are *thought* through the understanding, and from it arise concepts. (*CPR*, A 19/B 33, trans. Guyer/Wood 1998, 155)

And quite similarly he states at the beginning of the second part of the "Transcendental Doctrine of Elements," the "Transcendental Logic":

> Our cognition arises from two fundamental sources in the mind, the first of which is the reception of representations (the receptivity of impressions), the second the faculty for cognizing an object by means of these representations (spontaneity of concepts); through the former an object is *given* to us, through the latter it is *thought* in relation to that representation (as a mere determination of the mind). (*CPR*, A 50/B 74, trans. Guyer/Wood 1998, 193)

These two short quotations, to which numerous others can easily be added,[6] already provide an initially clear idea of what Kant's doctrine of sensibility and understanding involves:

1. Sensibility and understanding are *capacities* [*Vermögen*] of a cognizing subject.
2. Sensibility and understanding are *co-original* capacities [*Grundquellen*]; one cannot be reduced to the other either completely or partially.
3. Sensibility and understanding are capacities to be *distinguished* sharply: representations [*Vorstellungen*] are received ("receptivity") through sensibility; representations are produced ("spontaneity") through the understanding (see also *CPR*, A 51/B 75).
4. Representations received by sensibility are called *intuitions*, while the representations produced by the understanding are called *concepts*. The "manifold" [*Mannigfaltiges*] is given with the first, while "unity" [*Einheit*] is produced with the second (see also *CPR*, A 104–105, and B 139–140).

In addition to stressing the *co-originality* and *distinctness* of sensibility and understanding, Kant emphasizes – in the passages mentioned above, but also in several other passages – their *interrelatedness* as a necessary condition for cognition. His concise, almost formulaic statement, which is also found at the beginning of the "Transcendental Logic," is particularly well-known here:

> Without sensibility no object would be given to us, and without understanding none would be thought. Thoughts without content are empty, intuitions without concepts are blind. It is thus

---

6 See, e.g., *CPR*, A 67–68/B 92, A 119, A 126–127, B 145, A 258/B 314, A 298f./B 355. See for further references, also regarding other writings of Kant, Gava/Keller 2015, and Klingner 2015.

just as necessary to make the mind's concepts sensible (i.e., to add an object to them in intuition) as it is to make its intuitions understandable (i.e., to bring them under concepts). Further, these two faculties or capacities cannot exchange their functions. The understanding is not capable of intuiting anything, and the senses are not capable of thinking anything. Only from their unification can cognition arise. (*CPR*, A 51/B 75–76, trans. Guyer/Wood 1998, 193–194)

The three features mentioned – equal originality, distinctness, and interrelatedness – can be taken as a sufficient characterization of Kant's capacity dualism. And perhaps not all, but many of Kant's theses and conclusions can be made intelligible on this basis: for instance, his comprehensive critique of the possibility of speculative metaphysics, which made vast parts of what was understood as valid knowledge in early modern philosophy obsolete (see, e.g., Anderson 2015, 271–277); or his rejection of epistemological empiricism, which unmasks it as being naive and therefore also challenges the replacement of metaphysics by anthropology among his contemporaries;[7] and his rationalism in matters of practical philosophy, which insisted on the objective validity of moral laws and was directed against theological as well as eudemonistic and teleological conceptions of morality.[8]

Nevertheless, neither years of studying Kant's text and notes in the critical period nor extensive immersion in the profundity of a supposed "original insight" are needed to see difficulties that arise from the distinction between sensibility and understanding sketched here. Three sets of problems can be mentioned at this point, which were already recognized in the reception of Kant in late eighteenth-century German philosophy and discussed with some intensity:

(1) *Justification:* First, it is striking that Kant himself gives little information on how the fundamental distinction between sensibility and understanding itself is to be justified.[9] It is true that the genesis of Kant's distinction can be regarded as well

---

[7] See on the role of the a priori in Kant's concept of science, also with respect to an "anthropology," Sturm 2009, 146–150.

[8] See, e.g., Schneewind 1998, 517: "The natural disarray of the passions and desires is as much given in Kant's ethics as the lack of order in sensation is in the theoretical philosophy."

[9] See Heidemann 2002, 66–67, who also refers to a number of comments from older and more recent Kant scholarship, according to which the dualism remains unjustified in Kant himself. Moreover, he refers to Georg Wilhelm Friedrich Hegel's judgment in the *Vorlesungen über die Geschichte der Philosophie* that Kant's distinction is merely "empirical" and not "developed from the concept" (see Heidemann 2002, 66). The reproach of the lack of justification, which can also already be found in Johann Gottfried Herder following Johann Georg Hamann's Kant critique (on this, see Heinz 1997), may be seen as inappropriate insofar as the distinction between sensibility and understanding was generally considered trivial and at least not particularly revolutionary until eighteenth-century philosophy. This also applies to Kant critics such as Johann August Eberhard. Thus, in

researched, in that it represents a consequence of Kant's reflections on the phenomenon of incongruent counterparts, to which, as is well known, he had already referred in a small essay in 1768.[10] However this is not a philosophical justification but only a historical explanation of his development (see Heidemann 2002, 74).[11] For a justification that does not go too far beyond Kant's text, his hints at a special "isolating procedure" (see *CPR*, A 22/B 36, A 62/B 87) of the respective faculty as well as a "common root" (see *CPR*, A 15/B 29, A 124, A 835/B 863) provide some starting points based in his texts. How these hints should be interpreted and, above all, what justification they could provide, has been disputed since the publication of the first *Critique* and can be left open here. In any case, both the casualness with which Kant himself considers the problem and the self-evident way in which he introduces his distinction between sensibility and understanding in the first *Critique* and returns to it again and again seem to speak for the fact that Kant's text *alone* does not provide an answer to the question of justification.

(2) *Relation to things in themselves:* The second set of problems concerns an aspect more immanent to his theory. As is well known, Kant calls the object of knowledge resulting from the unification of sensibility and understanding "appearance" and strictly distinguishes it from an unknowable "thing-in-itself" (see *CPR*, e. g., B XXV–XXVIII, or A 41–42/B 59). At the same time, there are several remarks in the first *Critique* concerning the relation of the two capacities to a "thing-in-itself" that already caused some puzzlement in the reception of Kant among his contemporaries in late eighteenth-century German philosophy.[12] With regard to sensibility, for example, Kant is quite careful not to attribute to it a direct reference to "things in themselves." However, his repeated reference to the fact *that* "we are affected by objects" and to sensibility as the capacity for *how* "[o]bjects are [...]

---

the course of his criticism of Kant's definition of the concept of understanding, the latter writes: "As long as one has used the word understanding, one has always opposed understanding and senses, νους and αισθησις, intellectus and sensus." (Eberhard 1788–1792, vol. 3, 266, my translation; see also Eberhard's attempt to prove that the Leibniz-Wolffian philosophy is already aware of a "transcendental difference" between sensibility and understanding in Eberhard 1788–1792, vol. 3, 296–298).

10 See *DDS* 2: 380–382 (Walford/Meerbote 1992, 369–371). See also Heidemann 2018.

11 Moreover, the phenomenon of incongruent counterparts refers to empirical objects and is not brought into a direct relationship with the distinction between sensibility and understanding in Kant's *Critique of Pure Reason*. On the empirical character of incongruent counterparts (and on the supposed refutation of Kant's considerations by modern mathematics), see also Friebe 2006, 43–44.

12 On the continuity of that puzzlement in the reception of Kant's critical philosophy by the relevant passages, see also the references in Hahmann 2009, 200–202.

given to us" (*CPR*, A 19–20/B 33–34)[13] provokes questions about the relationship between "things in themselves" and that which "appears" through intuition.[14] If this relation is then understood as identity or at least similarity, then serious follow-up problems immediately arise, such as the interpretation of "affection" as a causal relation, which obviously contradicts Kant's view that causal judgments can be characterized as objectively valid only if they refer to relations between "appearances."[15] If, on the other hand, any relation of sensibility to "things in themselves" is denied, Kant's theory seems to hang strangely in the air with respect to objectivity and be nothing but an idiosyncratic variety of idealist speculation.[16] Kant is equally cautious with regard to understanding and its relation to a "thing-in-itself." On the one hand, the "pure concepts of the understanding" are "mere forms of thought without objective reality" and only their application to intuition "alone can provide them with sense and significance" (*CPR*, B 148–149; cf. *CPR*, B 305). On the other hand, from the definition of the object of cognition as "appearance" follows also the concept of objects "merely thought by the understanding," which has no objective reality, but which we cannot get rid of because of the distinction he makes (see *CPR*, B 306–B 309, and A 286/B 342–A 289/B 345). With this, however, questions about the relation between "appearance" and the "thing-in-itself" and about the status and value of mere "beings of the understanding" or a "thing-in-itself" that is a necessity of thought seem only to be self-incurred. They are problems that occur within the framework of Kant's epistemological criticism and necessarily characterize it for reasons immanent to the theory, and which remain unsolved at least when only referring to the "letter" of the first *Critique*.

(3) *Philosophical cognition:* A third difficulty arises when we ask about the possibility of the cognition claimed by Kant in his transcendental philosophical reflections. According to him, philosophical cognition is *"rational cognition* from *concepts"* (*CPR*, A 713/B 741)[17] and, within the framework of pure philosophy, does not make use of any kind of intuition.[18] Accordingly, he writes the following in

---

13 Cf. *CPR*, A 26/B 42, A 35/B 51, A 358–359, and A 494/B 522.
14 See also from the "Preface" to the second edition of the first *Critique*: "Yet the reservation must also be well noted, that even if we cannot *cognize* these same objects as things in themselves, we at least must be able to *think* them as things in themselves. For otherwise there would follow the absurd proposition that there is an appearance without anything that appears" (*CPR*, B XXVI–XXVII). See also *Pro*, § 32 (Allison/Heath 2002, 107–108).
15 See, for example, Schulze's critique of Kant's epistemology in Schulze 1792, 377–378.
16 See, for example, the notorious accusation of idealism in the Feder-Garve review of the *Critique of Pure Reason* in Garve/Feder 1782, 40.
17 On Kant's concept of philosophy, see also Klingner 2012b, 26–41, esp. 27–34.
18 It is true that for philosophical cognition the forms of intuition are of decisive relevance, namely for the schematization of the categories, the generation of some predicables and thus for the

the "Doctrine of Method" in the first *Critique* about the specific nature of transcendental philosophical cognition:

> [I]f I am given the transcendental concept of a reality, substance, force, etc., it designates neither an empirical nor a pure intuition, but only the synthesis of empirical intuitions (which thus cannot be given a priori), and since the synthesis cannot proceed a priori to the intuition that corresponds to it, no determining synthetic proposition but only a principle of the synthesis of possible empirical intuitions can arise from it. (*CPR*, A 722/B 750)

Only the a priori form of intuitions can be used in the case of philosophical cognition for the generation of synthetic judgments a priori, so that then, for example, by the application of the category of causality to the form of intuition "time," the "principle of the sequence of time according to the law of causality" can be gained and identified as objective valid (*CPR*, B 232).[19] Besides the fact that transcendental philosophical cognition characterized in this way does not really shine due to its expansiveness,[20] at least two questions are obvious at this point: If the relation to intuition is constitutive for cognition, but intuitions do not play any role for the transcendental principles, in what way are they cases of cognition? In addition, there is the question of the source of the contents of such principles: If the forms of intuition and the categories – or combinations between them – are the essential components of the content of transcendental principles,[21] then it should also be

---

formulation of the "principles of pure understanding." However, the forms of intuition are not themselves intuitions. Kant also explicitly and repeatedly points out this distinction – for instance in his characterization of the "principles of pure understanding," where he states that mathematical "principles" do not belong to transcendental philosophy, "since they are not derived from pure concepts but rather from pure intuitions (although by means of the understanding); the understanding, however, is the faculty of concepts." (*CPR*, A 159–160/B 198–199). For a detailed distinction between "form of intuition", "formal intuition" and "pure intuition", see Graubner 1972, 93–104 and 138–168.

19 See also Kant's own note on the above quotation: "By means of the concept of cause I actually go beyond the empirical concept of an occurrence (that something happens), but not to the intuition that exhibits the concept of cause in concreto, rather to the time-conditions in general that may be found to be in accord with the concept of cause in experience." (*CPR*, A 722/B 750)

20 Compared to the extent of contemporary metaphysical accounts or the idealistic systematic conceptions, the extent of the substantive output of critical philosophy – at least regarding theoretical cognition – turns out to be rather modest. For if one puts aside the critical and polemical discussion of contemporary philosophical topics, all that remains as positive doctrine are the exposition or deduction of the a priori constituents of sensibility and understanding as well as some explanations of their interaction, which results in the "principles," and finally a few brief reflections on the regulative use of reason.

21 In particular, with regard to the principle of causality, see the detailed discussion in Cramer 1985.

possible to specify how the transcendental philosopher knows about these fundamental principles. Here, too, Kant owes an answer, but makes no secret of it:

> But for the peculiarity of our understanding, that it is able to bring about the unity of apperception a priori only by means of the categories and only through precisely this kind and number of them, a further ground may be offered just as little as one can be offered for why we have precisely these and no other functions for judgment or for why space and time are the sole forms of our possible intuition. (*CPR*, B 145–146)

This raises the suspicion of a fundamental deficit of justification and accusations of a lack of reflexivity in Kant's conception (see Aschenberg 1982, 263–264). These concerns in turn also significantly motivated the post-Kantian idealist approaches to a new justification of the "beginning" and systematicity of philosophy.[22]

Whether the three complexes of problems mentioned here actually reveal difficulties that could prove Kant's conception to be fundamentally unsound from a substantive point of view does not need to be discussed here, nor do the interpretive claims that they are merely based on misunderstandings or that they can somehow be solved by Kant's own resources. The points mentioned here merely outline the horizon of problems against which Schmid's reception of Kant's distinction between sensibility and understanding will be discussed in the following.

2 Schmid on Kant's Distinction Between Sensibility and Understanding

Schmid's reception of Kant's critical writings began early. In the winter term of 1785, he had already taught on "disciplinam philosophicam, quae Critica purae rationis vocatur" at the University of Jena.[23] And at the same time, he wrote a textbook and a lexicon, which were published together in one volume in 1786 and in separate volumes from the second edition in 1788. The *Grundriß* gives above all a clearly structured overview of Kant's criticism in the manner of scholastic philosophy. Schmid successively expanded it in a second and third edition, in accordance with the publications of the second and the third *Critique*. The *Wörterbuch* again provides explanations of numerous terms arranged alphabetically, attempting to cover all relevant passages in Kant's texts. With the fourth edition in 1798, the orig-

---

22 See pointedly and with special regard to the conception of the early Fichte Hiltscher 2016, 56–73.
23 Quoted according to Hinske 1995, 2. See for the complete announcement of the lecture (including a German translation) Hinske 1995, 8–9.

inally only 127-page dictionary had reached a length of 616 pages (see Schröpfer 1995, 47–48), which illustrates Schmid's meticulousness and perseverance.

First, Schmid's comments on "sensibility" and "understanding" in the *Grundriß* and, in a second step, the corresponding entries in the *Wörterbuch*, will be compiled and considered in detail here:

(1) The *Grundriß:* If one ignores the successively added sections on the *Critique of Practical Reason* and the *Critique of Judgment*, Schmid divides the *Grundriß*, after a short "Introduction," which explicates concepts such as *cognition, philosophy*, and *critique*, like Kant himself does in his *Critique of Pure Reason*, into a "Doctrine of Elements" and a "Doctrine of Method," the first of which is divided into "Pure Aesthetics" and "Transcendental Logic," and the latter in turn into "Transcendental Analytics" and "Transcendental Dialectics."[24] Schmid thus takes Kant's division as a foundation here and prepares the content of the first *Critique* in a manner suitable to scholastic exposition by presenting it in continuous paragraphs with the customary references to preceding paragraphs. In terms of its presentation, the *Grundriß* does not differ from the legion of contemporary philosophical textbooks in this regard.

According to the "Introduction," the "critique" has the task of providing the "principle of the possibility of synthetic judgments a priori" and thus of explaining the possibility of metaphysical sciences as "pure material philosophy."[25] In doing so, the "pure doctrine of elements" will systematically demonstrate the "material conditions" of the possibility of metaphysics (see Schmid 1788, 6, § 13). According to Schmid, these material conditions are nothing less than "all representations a priori" (Schmid 1788, 6, § 13). They are to be determined "completely" in the doctrine of elements, "classified according to their sources," and their legitimate "use from principles" stated and at the same time limited (see Schmid 1788, 6–7, § 14).[26]

Schmid begins his presentation of the doctrine of elements with a thetic statement of the two sources of representations: "Human representations arise from

---

[24] By far the largest part of the second edition is the Transcendental Logic with about 140 pages (see Schmid 1788, 20–159, whereby the Analytics and Dialectics each are about 65–70 pages). The Introduction is about 6 pages (see Schmid 1788, 1–7), the aesthetics about 12 pages (cf. Schmid 1788, 7–20), and the Doctrine of Method about 7 pages (cf. Schmid 1788, 159–166). Thus, Schmid's presentation roughly corresponds to the size of the various parts of the *Critique of Pure Reason*, although the Introduction and the Aesthetics are given somewhat more space, while the Doctrine of Method is given considerably less. The second edition of the *Grundriss* also contains an account of the *Critique of Practical Reason* of 36 pages (see Schmid 1788, 167–202).
[25] Schmid 1788, 1–3 und 6 (§ 2, 4, 9 and 12). All translations are mine.
[26] The "pure doctrine of method", on the other hand, is supposed to represent the "formal" conditions of the possibility of metaphysics, that is, not the representations a priori but "the nature of their connection to the system" (Schmid 1788, 6, § 13).

sensibility and understanding" (Schmid 1788, 7, § 14). Accordingly, the doctrine of elements is to be divided into a "transc[endental] doctrine of the senses (aesthetics) and a doctrine of understanding (logic)" (Schmid 1788, 7, § 14). Directly following this, that is, in the first paragraph of the aesthetics, the terms "intuition" and "concept" are introduced. Their definition is given in three steps:
1. Representations are "in themselves modifications of the mind."
2. If they refer to an object, i.e., they have a "relation [*Beziehung*] to an object," representations are called cognitions.
3. Since the reference to the object can be either "direct" or "indirect by means of characteristics [*Merkmahle*]," all (object-referring) representations can be distinguished into those of "a single object," i.e., intuitions, and "general" ones, i.e., concepts (see Schmid 1788, 7–8, § 15).

Schmid immediately draws a consequence from this nominal definition in the next paragraph:

> Only through the faculty of intuition (§15) is it possible that representations in general, and therefore also concepts, can refer to objects, i.e., objects exist for us. Without intuition, concepts would have no reference [*Beziehung*] to objects, i.e., significance [*Bedeutung*]. Conversely, without a concept, the intuited objects [*angeschauten Gegenstände*] would have no reference to our cognition. (Schmid 1788, 8, § 16)

In this conclusion, which Schmid draws directly after introducing the difference between intuition and concept and which may prima facie seem unexciting to the Kant reader, three points are striking:

First, the consequence expressed by the first sentence ("Only through the faculty of intuition is it possible that . . .") merely explicates something that has been defined in the preceding paragraph, namely the "direct" [*unmittelbare*] reference to objects of certain representations (intuitions). Thus, obviously, neither a justification of the relevance of the difference between "direct" and "indirect" reference to the object nor an explanation of what "directness" is actually supposed to mean here is given.

Second, the notion of "reference to objects," which in the case of the "faculty of intuition" is understood as "objects being given to us," suggests a realist reading of Kant's conception of cognition. However, since Kant himself also uses – at least occasionally – similar phrases,[27] this does not reveal anything special about Schmid's reception at this point. We will have to return to this point later.

---

[27] See for instance *CPR*, A 19/B 33: "[…] the way in which we are affected by objects […]," and: "Objects are therefore given to us […]," or also *CPR*, A 50/B 74: "[…] an object is *given* to us […]."

Third, the last sentence is problematic. It is not at all evident from the preceding why "without a concept, the intuited objects would have no reference to our cognition." Since the subsequent paragraphs in the Aesthetics do not provide any information about this either, one has to be patient here and wait for the corresponding definitions and distinctions in the Logic.

In fact, Schmid gives a more detailed explanation of his understanding of Kant's distinction between sensibility and understanding in the first paragraph of the Logic. He writes:

> Sensibility [...] is a merely passive faculty of the soul [*ein sich bloß leidend verhaltendes Seelenvermögen*], which receives impressions, representations, and thereby gives objects, although only such as they must appear to us, according to the form of our intuition, in space and time. These manifold intuitions are in and of themselves not yet cognition, if they are not compared and connected to form a whole. This connection is nothing passive (affection) but an action (function) [*kein Leiden (Affection), sondern eine Handlung (Function)*], which is called thinking or judging and presupposes a non-sensible higher faculty of cognition [*ein nichtsinnliches höheres Erkenntnißvermögen*], which is called understanding in a broad sense. (Schmid 1788, 20, § 41; see *CPR*, A 77–78/B 103)

According to this passage, intuitions through which "objects" are given still have to be "connected," which then constitutes a thought or a judgment and first allows this to be called "cognition." Both Schmid and Kant also call the connective function of the mind "synthesis" (see Schmid 1788, 21, § 42). A few paragraphs later Schmid explains this as an "order of different representations under a common one and unification of them in one consciousness" (Schmid 1788, 26, § 53). Accordingly, a concept is "a representation of a representation of the object" (Schmid 1788, 26, § 53).

Schmid does not provide any further justification for Kant's distinction between sensibility and understanding in the Logic either, but at least it becomes somewhat clear here why, according to him, "without a concept, the intuited objects would have no reference to our cognition" (Schmid 1788, 8, § 16): A mere representation is not yet a cognition, since it must first be "connected" with other representations. At the same time, this reinforces the impression that, according to Schmid, the constitution of objectivity is solely due to sensibility and that the role of the understanding is merely to bring representations – which may or may not have a "direct" reference to objects – into a systematic connection with each other.[28] However, it is at least questionable whether the role of the understanding is also fulfilled in Kant's conception. Moreover, in Schmid's reception of

---

[28] Fichte then also criticizes this explicitly in his criticism of Schmid (see Fichte 1845–1846, vol. 2, 437, 455).

Kant's epistemology, no special attention is paid to those passages of the *Critique of Pure Reason* that explicitly emphasize the contribution of the understanding to the *constitution* of the object. The clearest of these passages are found primarily in the revised "transcendental deduction of the pure concepts of understanding" of the second edition of the first *Critique*, where, for example, § 17 states:

> Understanding is, generally speaking, the faculty of cognitions. These consist in the determinate relation of given representations to an object. *An object, however, is that in the concept of which the manifold of a given intuition is united.* Now, however, all unification of representations requires unity of consciousness in the synthesis of them. Consequently, the unity of consciousness is that which alone constitutes the relation of representations to an object, thus their objective validity, and consequently is that which makes them into cognitions [...]. (*CPR*, B 137, my emphasis)

Here Kant makes it quite clear that a concept refers to an object only because a representation of an object is made possible through the synthesis of a given manifold by the understanding.[29] Accordingly, the "unity of consciousness" characterized by the synthesizing function is *the* constitutively decisive ground of objectivity – and not mere sensibility.[30] By either ignoring these statements by Kant, which after all stand at a crucial point in the overall argumentation of the first *Critique*, or by taking them only in the sense of an ordering function of the understanding,[31] Schmid shows that the idea is alien to him that the epistemologically relevant interaction of sensibility and understanding could not only have a psychological, but also – and in the context of a transcendental philosophy probably above all – an epistemological meaning.

---

[29] See Graubner 1972, 204–205. See also already *CPR*, B 134–135, where the object-constituting function of the understanding is clearly emphasized: "Combination does not lie in the objects, however, and cannot as it were be borrowed from them through perception and by that means first taken up into the understanding, but is rather only an operation of the understanding, which is itself nothing further than the faculty of combining a priori and bringing the manifold of given representations under unity of apperception [...]."

[30] This thought is also found with a certain clarity in the first version of the deduction: "This relation, however, is nothing other than the necessary unity of consciousness, thus also of the synthesis of the manifold through a common function of the mind for combining it in one representation. Now since this unity must be regarded as necessary a priori (since the cognition would otherwise be without an object), the relation to a transcendental object, i.e., the objective reality of our empirical cognition, rests on the transcendental law that all appearances, *insofar as objects are to be given to us through them*, must stand under a priori rules of their synthetic unity." (*CPR*, A 109–110, my emphasis)

[31] Schmid pays little attention to the transcendental deduction in the *Grundriß* and restricts himself in his outline of its contents for the most part to the difference between "subjective" and "objective" judgments (see Schmid 1788, 35–40, §§ 70–79).

Having outlined Schmid's understanding of these terms in the *Grundriß* we can now turn to the *Wörterbuch*.

(2) The *Wörterbuch:* A look at the two relevant entries in the *Wörterbuch* confirms the previous observations. Here, too, Schmid characterizes sensibility as "the faculty of the soul to be modified by things, to be affected [*afficirt*], and thereby to receive impressions, representations of things."[32] The understanding is again in a general sense "the non-sensible, self-acting faculty of cognition, (spontaneity), or the faculty of producing and generating representations by itself"[33] – and in distinction to the power of judgment and reason more specifically "the faculty of thinking intuited objects, of forming representations and judgments of them."[34] Regarding the relationship between sensibility and understanding, Schmid makes another remark in his entry on understanding that is worth mentioning. Since the understanding is dependent on intuitions with respect to the material available to it for its connecting function, it is "in respect of the content subordinated to sensibility" (Schmid 1795, 500). But in so far as it has its own set of "laws" at its disposal, it is "independent of sensibility with respect to the form of concepts" (Schmid 1795, 500). Thus, sensibility here has priority over understanding – and this again raises the question of how the "direct" object reference of sensibility is to be understood more precisely. In order to achieve more clarity on this point, it is worth consulting Schmid's later *Metaphysik*, which is also strongly oriented towards Kant's conception, but which emancipates itself terminologically somewhat more from it.

---

32 Schmid 1795, 424: "[Sensibility is] the capacity of the soul to be modified by things, to be affected, and thereby to receive impressions, representations of things. It is therefore neither a mere modification of the understanding, as in Leibnitz, nor mere activity or stimulus [*Reitz*] of the bodily organs, whose own existence, if it is to be cognized, presupposes a receptivity in the soul itself, and which are themselves, considered as appearance, objects of sensibility, but an own essential source of representations."

33 Schmid 1795, 497: "[Understanding is] 1) in general: the non-sensible, self-acting faculty of cognition, (spontaneity), or the faculty of producing and generating representations by itself, of bringing unity into the given material of representations, of thinking objects, of judging; the faculty of concepts (they may be confused or clear), of rules, of discursive cognition; the faculty to combine a priori and to bring the manifold of given representations under the unity of self-consciousness – as distinguished from sensibility, receptivity, the passive faculty of intuitions [*dem leidenden Vermögen der Anschauungen*]. In this sense, the understanding simultaneously includes in itself the power of judgment and reason [...]."

34 Schmid 1795, 498: "[Understanding is] 2) in particular: the faculty of thinking of intuited objects, of forming concepts and judgments of them; the faculty of the unity of intuitions (appearances), which is therefore called unity of understanding; of experiential knowledge, of rules in contrast to laws. According to this concept, understanding is distinguished from reason in the narrower sense."

(3) The *Metaphysik:* The *Grundriß der Metaphysik*, published in 1799, is also written as a textbook and provides an outline of all disciplines of metaphysics, preceded by a "Critique of Reason in General" (Schmid 1799, 11) as a propaedeutic.[35] Here, only those paragraphs are relevant in which Schmid introduces the difference between sensibility and understanding – which are called "faculty of intuition" [*Anschauungsvermögen*] and "faculty of thought" [*Denkvermögen*] here (see Schmid 1799, 24, § 37) – and addresses their reference to objectivity. With regard to the first point, there is nothing new here. As in the *Grundriß* (and in the *Wörterbuch*), Schmid does not provide an explicit justification of the distinction between sensibility and understanding. Nevertheless, it is worth quoting the corresponding passage here since it shows how much Schmid remains beholden to his early reception of Kant:

> Our faculty of representation [*Vorstellungsvermögen*], as the basis of the faculty of cognition [*Erkenntnisvermögen*], includes two essentially different but equally essentially connected faculties: 1) the faculty of directly representing individual objects to us, 2) the faculty of representing the manifold of existing representations in combination. The first is called the faculty of intuition, the second the faculty of thought. (Schmid 1799, 24, § 37)

He then explicates the concept of the "faculty of intuition" in the subsequent paragraph by pointing out that the human faculty of intuition is "sensual" [*sinnlich*] and thus "bound to the condition that the object affects us" (Schmid 1799, 24, § 38). Here, too, Schmid uses rather realist vocabulary to describe the relationship of sensibility to the "object."[36] It accordingly makes sense to understand Schmid as saying the following:
1. There are objects independent of a relation (however constituted) to a cognizing subject ("things in themselves").[37]
2. These objects "affect" the faculty of intuition of a subject, whereby the subject "represents" these objects within the framework of their subjective possibilities ("forms of intuition").

---

35 See Schmid 1799, 6 (§ 11), where *Vernunftkritik* or *reine Elementarphilosophie* is called "an investigation of the first principles, by which pure material cognition becomes possible."
36 The whole paragraph is: "Our faculty of intuition is sensual, i.e., our direct representation of a single real object is bound to the condition that the object affects us." (Schmid 1799, 24, § 38)
37 See also Schmid's definition of "objects in and of themselves" [*Gegenstände an und für sich*] at the beginning of his exposition of the "metaphysical doctrine of the world" [*metaphysische Weltlehre*] in the *Metaphysik:* They are "things, which are represented simply as objects [*schlechthin als Objekte*], without any relation to a certain subject, and without those predicates, which arise only through the relation of the object to a certain representing subject, and belong to it only in this relation" (Schmid 1799, 168, § 257).

3. In order to cognize these subjectively represented objects – that is, to attribute certain predicates to them or to make judgments about certain relations between them – these representations must then be "connected" with each other (or with other, already generalized representations) according to certain laws ("categories") by the faculty of thought.

Should this roughly sketched model apply to Schmid's position, then he would understand Kant's conception of cognition in a way that could rightly be regarded as "realist." It is true that the objects spoken of in (1) are declared unknowable insofar as they do not yet stand in a relation to a subject endowed with certain capacities. And certain "material conditions" of an a priori kind must be fulfilled – the object must be given according to the a priori forms of sensibility (2) and its representation must be related to other representations according to the a priori laws of understanding (3) – so that there is a case of "cognition." However, despite the limitation of the respective cognition caused by the special capacities of cognizing subjects, their corresponding representations refer to simply existing, objects "in themselves."[38] The fact that Kant's criticism of cognition is thus understood as another variety of "metaphysical commitment" and not as a departure from metaphysical discourse is obvious and has been a common interpretative perspective even until today.[39] And as noted in the first section, this understanding can also be supported by some textual evidence. As the long history of the reception of Kant shows, however, it is only one possible interpretation and only one possible way of dealing with Kant's texts among others. In any case, Kant's epistemological criticism holds enough systematic potential to fundamentally challenge or at least rethink metaphysical discourses without having to deny philosophy its own mode of reflection and its own domain (see, for example, Rickert 1927/29; Wagner 1980; and Flach 1997).

Based on the foregoing review of relevant passages from Schmid's writings, it is now possible to provide an initial evaluation of his reception of Kant's distinction between sensibility and understanding – namely, on the basis of the first two problems this distinction entails, which were highlighted above:

Regarding the first problem, that is, the lack of a philosophical justification of the capacity dualism, it can be said that Schmid does not present any justification for it either. He does not even point to the problem, neither as a factual problem nor does he address the few hints that Kant himself gives – the procedure of "isolation" is not mentioned, nor the idea of a "common root." This thus shows in an

---

[38] Such a "realist" Kantianism is reminiscent of Alois Riehl's "Criticism" (see e.g., Riehl 1879, 18 ff.).
[39] See for example Allais 2015, 5 ff.

exemplary way how Schmid deals with Kant's text: He generally orients himself to it, systematizes the doctrines contained in it and leaves open questions aside.

Regarding the second problem, that is, the unresolved relation of the two faculties to a "thing-in-itself," Schmid's reception seems to be clearer than Kant's original. For if one takes seriously the idea that Schmid represents a realist reading of Kant's theory of cognition, then there are simply "things in themselves" that affect the faculty of cognition. Thus, they "cause" as the material every (empirical) intuition and hence objectively valid cognition.[40] Schmid does not express himself unambiguously in this sense in the considerations consulted above – like Kant himself. And of course, following Kant, he considers a cognition of "noumena" to be impossible.[41] However, all his remarks on those objects which ground our cognition can be read throughout in the sense of Kant's concept of noumena "in the negative sense."[42] That Schmid, on the other hand, cannot deal with "beings of the understanding" [*Verstandeswesen*] in the sense of "objects" of non-sensible intuition[43] is obvious in light of his realism with respect to sensibility and his empiricist understanding of the function of understanding as merely ordering. Accordingly, he believes that in rationalist conceptions, like Kant, there is above all an incorrect conception of the faculty of understanding itself at work, according to which "the sense-free understanding [. . .] thinks by intuition" (Schmid 1799, 215, § 304). This reproach, which is hardly surprising in view of Leibniz and large parts of rationalist scholastic philosophy,[44] is highly relevant for Schmid himself. For, according to him, it also applies to some of his contemporaries who believe their work to be in the "spirit" of Kant's philosophy, but who, in the "robe of critical philosophical phrases," merely "introduce a new, somewhat idealistic, dogmatism" (Schmid 1799, vi, preface).

---

40 See also Schmid 1788, 16 (§ 34), where Schmid even explicitly uses a phrase like: "intelligible causes of phenomena."
41 See Schmid 1788, 14–15 (§ 31) and 35 (§ 68); Schmid 1799, 167–168, as well as Schmid 1799, 168 (§ 259), furthermore 31 (§ 52) and 46 (§ 77).
42 See *CPR*, B 306–308, esp. 307: "Now the doctrine of sensibility is at the same time the doctrine of the noumenon in the negative sense, i.e., of things that the understanding must think without this relation to our kind of intuition, thus not merely as appearances but as things in themselves [...]."
43 See *CPR*, B 308–309: "If, therefore, we wanted to apply the categories to objects that are not considered as appearances, then we would have to ground them on an intuition other than the sensible one, and then the object would be a noumenon in a positive sense [...]; and although beings of understanding certainly correspond to the beings of sense, and there may even be beings of understanding to which our sensible faculty of intuition has no relation at all, our concepts of understanding, as mere forms of thought for our sensible intuition, do not reach these in the least [...]."
44 On the Kantian criticism of rationalism, see, for example, Klingner 2016.

3 Schmid's Kantianism and His Criticism of the "New Idealistic Dogmatism"

In this final section, the view developed so far will be made more precise by looking at Schmid's criticism of Fichte's and Schelling's idealist views. In doing so, the third of the outlined problem complexes connected with Kant's distinction between sensibility and understanding will come into focus. After all, it is precisely the struggle for a justification of philosophical reflection itself that characterizes the philosophy of German idealism (see Hiltscher 1998). This concern is characterized by an affirmative and at the same time critical relation to Kant's epistemological critique: As is well known, the "premises" are to be found to its "result[s]" recognized as correct.[45] That this not only involved going beyond Kant's text, but also reconsidering and formulating the specific nature of the "new" philosophy and its position in relation to other sciences, is shown not least by the sometimes polemical discussions between the various followers of critical philosophy in the 1790s.

Schmid deals with the early conceptions of Fichte and Schelling in several texts, but for the purpose of the following, the textual basis will be an insertion that can be found in the fifth section of the "Introduction" to his *Physiologie*, published in 1798 (see Schmid 1798, 19–49).[46] It is somewhat hidden – after all, the heading of the section is "Form of Zoonomy" (Schmid 1798, 19) – but distinguished by clear argumentative pointedness and very lucid language. The context is the question of the possibility of "zoonomy" as "cognition of animal phenomena, according to the laws of the faculty of thought, of understanding, and of reason" (Schmid 1798, 21–22).[47] Schmid insists that its form can be called "philosophical," which he takes as an occasion to respond to Fichte's criticism of his concept of philosophy presented in the *Philosophisches Journal* in 1796.[48] In doing so, Schmid dedicates nearly thirty pages to a fundamental criticism of Fichte's early reflections on "Wissenschaftslehre" and Schelling's first publications on "Naturphilosophie," which he subsequently refers to as "side considerations" [*Nebenbetrachtungen*], in order to continue with a dry exposition of the concept of a "doctrine of

---

[45] Schelling 1795/1973: "Philosophy is not yet at the end. Kant has given the results: the premises are still missing. And who can understand results without premises?" (my translation)
[46] For details on the controversy between Schmid and Fichte, see van Zantwijk/Ziche 2000, and also Frank 1997, 532–568.
[47] On the scientific context in general, see John 2001, on the term "zoonomy" 89–90.
[48] See Fichte's *Vergleichung* in Fichte 1845–1846, vol. 2, 421–458. On Fichte's criticism of Schmid in the *Vergleichung*, see also Fabianelli (forthcoming).

nature" [*Naturlehre*] (Schmid 1798, 49). He formulates the core of his criticism with the help of the Kantian terminology discussed so far:

> One [Fichte and Schelling] presupposes a mind that produces all its objects for itself, through which everything exists that is there for it; its world. In everything that it intuits, it intuits itself; its own action, which is one and the same with its object. Therefore, one does not admit any things in themselves; just as little an affection of the mind by something that it is not itself. (Schmid 1798, 30–31)

The extent to which this polemic is accurate need not be of interest here, especially since the early idealist conception of intellectual intuition is not only a factually complex idea, but above all was itself subject to historical development.[49] What is important here is what can be learned from it about Schmid's understanding of philosophy and the part it plays in his interpretation of Kant's distinction between sensibility and understanding.

According to the quote, the young idealists assume in principle a faculty of productive intuition and reject Kant's theorems of a "thing-in-itself" as well as an "affection" of sensibility. That this fundamental assumption and the rejection of two central theorems of Kant's conception do not correspond to its "letter" without further ado is obvious. But Schmid sees the decisive problem in the fact that the assumption of a productive intuition is not "proved to be true" by its advocates (Schmid 1798, 31). In so far as he himself – as has been seen – does not justify or "prove" the fundamental difference between sensibility and understanding that he advocates, this reproach seems somewhat unfair. Schmid, however, does not leave it at that: with pages and pages of quotes from Kant, he tries to demonstrate that the concept of a productive intuition is not only unproven, but "unintelligible" and that the productive intuition itself is "a thing that has no reality" (Schmid 1798, 34–35). Two arguments can be reconstructed from this criticism of the conception of intellectual intuition:

First, Schmid seems to understand the concept of productive intuition as *inconsistent*. For instance, he writes that the "enterprise" of "wanting to derive manifoldness, as such, from unity, as grounded in it," "contradicts itself already in the idea" (Schmid 1798, 45).[50] This reproach of contradictoriness, however, already presupposes a specific concept of "understanding" (or "reason"), namely that of a finite qua discursive understanding. If this is set as the only "possible" one – in the sense of being conceivable without contradiction – the concept of productive intu-

---

49 For more details see Tilliette 1995.
50 Cf. Schmid 1798, 34: "Unintelligible here means that which resists the laws of reason, where one thus runs out of understanding, that which at most can only be conceived in words or images, but not in thoughts, for example, a curved line composed of straight lines, etc."

ition would also be logically inconsistent. However, such a "logical" impossibility[51] of a non-discursive understanding would have to be shown first. Schmid, in any case, does not do this and has in Kant only a moderately suitable guarantor on this point. For according to Kant, the concepts of productive intuition and non-discursive understanding are not logically impossible.[52] They are only not correct attributions with regard to the mode of cognition familiar to us as human beings.[53] In Kant's conception, alone something like a "productive sensibility" would be impossible or unintelligible in the sense of a logical contradictoriness of the concept to be thought, since sensibility is by definition bound to the characteristic of givenness ("receptivity"). The special and philosophically relevant intuition claimed by Fichte and Schelling, however, is precisely not a sensible one, but an intellectual one – and in this point they can also consider themselves to be completely in agreement with Kant's conception.[54]

Second, Schmid refers to the *lack of empirical evidence* regarding the assumption of an intellectual intuition as "an absolute faculty of cognition" (Schmid 1798, 33; cf. 34–37). Thus, such a faculty simply does not exist "in our consciousness," and he – that is, Schmid himself – "lacks the free sense and the mental organ to intuit with this consciousness [qua intellectual intuition]" (Schmid 1798, 35, 36). However, this objection is problematic in two respects. For first of all, for Kant as well every "cognition" as a state of consciousness is already characterized by an interplay of intuition and concept, which is why transcendental philosophy must also first of all "isolate" these two "elements" in a special procedure of abstraction.[55] It is precisely this point, that sensibility, thinking and intellectual intuition are "always" "linked" with each other in the case of cognition-relevant representations, that Fichte, for example, then explicitly stresses (Fichte 1845–1846, vol. 1, 463–464; my

---

51 On the distinction between "logical" and "real possibility" see *CPR*, A 597/B 625.
52 See esp. *CPR*, B 138 and A 230/B 283. Taking up Kant's fourfold distinction of "nothing," this can also be formulated in this way: The concept of productive intuition denotes an "ens rationis" but not a "nihil negativum" (see *CPR*, A 291f./B 346–349). Even in the late *Preisschrift*, Kant still explicitly holds to this (see *RP*, AA 20: 267).
53 See a proposal for a systematization of the different uses of the concept of an "intellectual intuition" or a "intuiting understanding" in Kant Förster 2002, 176–179, as well as – partly critical of this – Klingner 2006, and the somewhat different proposal in Klingner 2016.
54 See, for example, Fichte 1845–1846, vol. 1, 471–472, and Schelling's *Abhandlungen* (Schelling 1856–1861, vol. I.1, 343–452, here 401–402).
55 See in detail and with the corresponding evidence from the *Critique of Pure Reason* Heidemann 2002.

translation).⁵⁶ Moreover, Fichte admits that the existence of intellectual intuition "cannot be demonstrated by concepts, nor, what it is, developed from concepts" (Fichte 1845–1846, vol. 1, 463; my translation). However, it is possible – and for the transcendental philosopher at the lectern even required – to lead to the "thinking of the I," that is, to intellectual intuition, by asking their respective counterpart to pay attention to the functioning of the principles of thinking in their own empirical consciousness ("action of the I").⁵⁷ With this, the cognitive access to the genuine object of transcendental philosophy is given and the question about the possibility of philosophical cognition, left open by Kant's critique of cognition, can be answered sufficiently.⁵⁸

Even if Schmid's arguments against the possibility or "reality" of an intellectual intuition may not be convincing in detail, the goal they serve must be considered above all. For the decisive point he makes here on the occasion of his question about the scientific character of a "zoonomy" against Fichte and Schelling concerns an adequate understanding of *philosophy*. Even if the differences in principle between Fichte's and Schelling's (early) conceptions of philosophy are put aside (which Schmid himself does),⁵⁹ it remains to be said that, according to him, philosophizing is precisely "not a producing, but a reflecting, a unifying, an ordering of the given" (Schmid 1798, 44). This clearly expresses what philosophical knowledge consists of for Schmid: in the systematization of empirically given things. With regard to the third problem of Kant's distinction between sensibility and understanding, the suspicion of a fundamental deficit of reasoning and the reproach of irreflexivity in Schmid's philosophical system not only present themselves but are rather justified.

Concerning the problems outlined with regard to Kant's distinction between sensibility and understanding, it can be said in summary that Schmid's reception of this distinction is (and remains) blind to at least two of the three problems associated with it:
1. The dualism of sensibility and understanding is neither justified nor problematized.

---

56 For Schelling, too, it is clear that "intellectual intuition [...] cannot occur in consciousness any more than absolute freedom can" (see *Vom Ich* in Schelling 1856–1861, vol. I.1, 149–244, here 181, my translation).
57 See Fichte's *Versuch* (Fichte 1845–1846, vol. 1, 519–534, here 522–523). See also Fichte 1845–1846, vol. 1, 458–468.
58 On the systematic function of intellectual intuition in Fichte, see Hiltscher 1998, 220–231 and in Schelling, Klingner 2012a, 191–195.
59 On Schelling's criticism of Fichte, see Klingner 2012a, 196–202.

2. Schmid completely avoids the difficulty of a coherent characterization of the nature of (transcendental) philosophical cognition. Objectively valid cognition is on the one hand "development of the necessary conditions under which an object can be sensibly intuited (given) and thought [...]" (Schmid 1798, 49–50). And on the other hand simply empirical cognition, which is then only to be ordered by understanding or reason and to be brought into connection with other empirical cognitions.
3. It is only with regard to the question of the relation between "appearance" and "thing-in-itself" that Schmid's realist Kantianism does not particularly go beyond the wording of Kant's texts, but he takes his own systematic position, which can be characterized as "realist" and remains common in the history of Kant's reception (at least in its basic features) until today.

Finally, the question remains to be answered whether the two themes mentioned at the beginning also provide good reasons for looking in detail at Schmid's reception of Kant's distinction between sensibility and understanding. The answer is: Yes. For on the one hand, it is a good illustration of how already in early Kantianism a diligent reading of Kant's writings can lead to a transcendental philosophical realism that is not particularly interested in the problem of the justification of philosophical knowledge; and on the other hand, it is able to shed further light on a discussion that was already complex in the late eighteenth century regarding the question of the systematic potential of transcendental idealism, a question that has not yet been answered with any consensus even today.

Achim Vesper

Between Hume and Kant: The Foundation of Morality in Feder's *Inquiries on the Human Will*

Abstract: This paper presents Feder's position on the foundation of morality in his four-volume *Untersuchungen über den menschlichen Willen*. First, it is shown that, in the first part of the *Untersuchungen*, Feder agrees with Hume's examination of morality both methodically and substantially. However, Feder does not follow Hume throughout the book. In the third part, he introduces a prudential consideration that differs from Hume's and explains that moral action is necessary for achieving happiness. Furthermore, Feder makes some revisions in the fourth part that were likely done in response to Kant's moral philosophy. In result, three different approaches to the justification of morality can be found in the *Untersuchungen*: Feder claims that virtue is based on (i) pleasure in the utility for oneself or others, (ii) striving for contentment in this world, or (iii) striving for inner peace after death. Although it speaks in favor of Feder's intellectual honesty that he does not overlook the shortcomings of his proposals and seeks to make improvements, he also involuntarily becomes a key witness testifying to the difficulties of an empiricist grounding of morality.

Feder made many contributions to theoretical philosophy, but his main work is a contribution to practical philosophy.[1] His *Untersuchungen über den menschlichen Willen* (*Inquiries on the Human Will*), which was published in four parts from 1779 to 1793, covers practical philosophy with an almost exhaustive breadth. He provides some insight into his motives for producing the *Untersuchungen* in the introduction to this work: It is an attempt to resolve some of the persisting disagreements in ethics. The disagreements he has in mind are those regarding the aims of human life, the grounds for the obligatoriness of moral and legal laws, and the moral quality of human nature. Although these disagreements have persisted since antiquity, Feder believes they can be resolved through an investigation of the will starting from the standpoint of observation. In his view, "self-knowledge

---

[1] Other important works by Feder in practical philosophy include a *Lehrbuch der praktischen Philosophie* (*Textbook on Practical Philosophy*) (1771) and the treatise *Über das moralische Gefühl* (*On Moral Sentiment*) (1776).

is an exceedingly necessary science" for human beings, because empirical anthropology can help to answer these traditional questions posed in practical philosophy (Feder 1785, 1).[2] This paper presents Feder's position on the foundations of morality in light of the debates at the time, in which he holds that the question of the foundation of morality can be answered through improved empirical self-knowledge.

Given his assumption that the causes of the will can only be determined by self-observation, Feder believes it is especially important to incorporate the opinions of others as any generalizations made about the will must be based on agreement with the self-observations of others.[3] According to Feder, one's own self-observation, together with the self-observation of others, plays a fundamental role for practical philosophy. But this comes with the caveat that only reports by philosophers about the causes of their will are worth consideration since ordinary people "are wary of honestly sharing the story of their heart in all regards" and are prejudiced (Feder 1785, 13). Feder also only includes philosophers here who rely on a number of examples from experience. He discounts Wolff in this regard insofar as "his principles [...] are not always deduced from sufficiently complete inductions," while he believes Shaftesbury, Hutcheson, Smith, Helvetius, and Hume offer empirically rich explanations of the will (Feder 1785, 21).

Two philosophical sources in particular stand out in Feder's considerations. Locke, as Feder admits, is an important source for his ideas: "The first idea for this enterprise arose [...] from my respect for *Locke's* work on the human mind. A similar work about the human will seemed to me to be lacking." (Feder 1825, 94) Looked at more closely, Feder takes up Locke's rejection of the view that humans have innate ideas. Like the contents of the mind according to Locke, the contents of the will according to Feder are not innate but derived from experience. In moral philosophy, this amounts to a rejection of the view that moral judgments are formed a priori through rational insight. Whereas according to Locke only the faculties by which the mind obtains contents are innate *(sensation* and *reflection),* Feder considers the drives [*Triebe*] by which the will obtains contents to be innate.

Another important source for Feder is the "science of man" that Hume calls for in the introduction to the *Treatise of Human Nature.* Hume argues here for

---

[2] All citations from the first part of the *Untersuchungen* follow the second edition.

[3] "Through all observations about himself, a man can only explore his own nature, not discover what is going on in other people, not what belongs to human nature everywhere. But if others likewise make observations about themselves, and honestly communicate them; then reasons gradually arise for drawing general conclusions. For what is found to be consistent in a great many cases can be assumed with regard to cases of which one does not have experience, until experience proves the opposite." (Feder 1785, 13).

the application of the "experimental method of reasoning" to "moral subjects"; that is, for transferring the experiential method from the natural sciences to the study of human beings.[4] According to the *Enquiry Concerning the Principles of Morals*, the search for the "foundation of ethics" and the "universal principles, from which all censure or approbation is ultimately derived" should also be guided by the experimental method and not proceed deductively (*EPM* 1.10):

> Men are now cured of their passion for hypotheses and systems in natural philosophy, and will hearken to no arguments but those which are derived from experience. It is full time they should attempt a like reformation in all moral disquisitions; and reject every system of ethics, however subtle or ingenious, which is not founded on fact and observation. (*EPM* 1.10)

Feder's project aims to reform practical philosophy in a similar way. Beyond the methodological similarities with Hume, there is also far-reaching substantial agreement with Hume. This is already evident from Feder's praise for Hume in the introduction to the *Untersuchungen*, where Feder expresses a special appreciation for Hume's *Enquiry* and defends him from the charge of moral skepticism:

> Hume, in the essay regarding his literary efforts that he left to posterity, himself declared his *Enquiry Concerning the Principles of Morals* to be the greatest of his philosophical works. It is a declaration arising from the duty of gratitude if I confess here that, in the initial development and arrangement of my concepts, this book has been of more benefit to me than any other. Far from applying here the skepticism to which he has too frequently abandoned himself in other investigations, he seems at times to have restrained his acumen for fear of making the value of virtue dubious (Feder 1785, 23).[5]

As Feder makes clear, he also considers himself indebted to Hume for the content of some of his views. In fact, the moral theory of the first part of Feder's *Untersuchungen* in particular is consistent with views expressed by Hume in the 1751 *Enquiry Concerning the Principles of Morals*.[6] In view of this, it seems strange that

---

[4] The subtitle of the *Treatise* is: "Being an Attempt to Introduce the Experimental Method of Reasoning into Moral Subjects." (Citations from *Treatise* and second *Enquiry* follow the Clarendon Edition and are given by book, part, section, and paragraph for the *Treatise* [*T*] and by book and paragraph for the *Enquiry* [*EPM*]).

[5] Feder refers to Hume's statement in *My own Life* about the second *Enquiry*: "which, in my own opinion (who ought not to judge on that subject), is of all my writings, historical, philosophical, or literary, incomparably the best." (Hume 1987, XXXVI.) On possible reasons for this assessment of Hume, see Baier 2008.

[6] The fact that Feder's *Untersuchungen* are part of the reception history of the second *Enquiry* is something that has not been discovered yet. Gawlick/Kreimendahl 1987, 115, only touch on Feder's appreciation of Hume's practical philosophy in *Über das moralische Gefühl* (*On Moral Sentiment*).

Hume, despite the laudatory address in Feder's introduction, remains a hidden hero in the *Untersuchungen* and hardly appears by name – unlike the almost ubiquitous Cicero, Hutcheson, and Smith.

Feder does not, however, simply follow in Hume's footsteps throughout the *Untersuchungen*. In the third part, he introduces a prudential consideration that differs from Hume's and explains that moral action is necessary for achieving happiness. And in the fourth part, Feder makes some revisions that were likely done in response to Kant's moral philosophy. Three different and sometimes conflicting approaches to the justification of morality can actually be seen in the *Untersuchungen*. In an overview, Feder claims that virtue is based on (i) pleasure in the utility for oneself or others, (ii) striving for contentment in this world, or (iii) striving for inner peace after death. Although it speaks in favor of Feder's intellectual honesty that he does not overlook the shortcomings of his proposals and seeks to make improvements – he also involuntarily becomes a key witness testifying to the difficulties of providing a grounding of morality based on empiricism. In what follows, I first discuss Feder's basic anthropological assumptions (1) and then turn to his grounding of morality, which is first based on Hume (2), and ultimately related to the concept of happiness (3).

1 Self-Love and Sympathy as Basic Drives

In the first book of the first part, Feder pursues the goal of identifying the basic drives governing the human will. Before that, in paragraph § 1, he discusses the relationship between the will and the understanding, which, according to him, consists in a mutual dependence. On the one hand, the will is dependent on the understanding because there are no expressions of the will without revulsion or desire aroused by ideas of the mind. On the other hand, the understanding is dependent on the will because the understanding can be directed and, for example, attention can be intentionally focused on certain objects. However, according to Feder, the dependence of the will on the understanding is stronger than the dependence of the understanding on the will, because the will cannot be exercised without the understanding, whereas the understanding can be exercised without the will.

Feder dealt with Hume several times in publications and contributed to his popularization in Germany through reviews (see literature listed in Gawlick/Kreimendahl 1987, 208, as well as Kuehn 1987).

Since, according to Feder, the understanding and the will are expressions of a unified power of the soul, the types of will can be subdivided according to the types of cognition. The two kinds of representation involved in the understanding consist of sensible representations, which "contain only those qualities that reveal themselves directly to the senses during sensation," and concepts of the understanding, which "reveal those qualities and relations that [...] are discovered by comparing several things or several consequences." (Feder 1785, 32) The division into an upper cognitive faculty with general concepts formed by observation and reflection and a lower cognitive faculty with individual concepts directly formed by influence on the sensory organs corresponds to the distinction between a sensory and a rational faculty of desire. Corresponding to the two cognitive faculties, the upper faculty of desire is characterized by continued observation and reflection, and the lower by direct sensory reference. The will, formed by deliberation, assumes the function of providing a general orientation for action in view of the multitude of existing inclinations. According to Feder, the will always has an empirical component – there is no purely rational will.

Feder's brief discussion of the problem of freedom also shows his understanding of the rational will as an empirical will that has been subjected to reflection. Like Locke and Hume, he rejects the idea that freedom requires the absence of constraints on the will and the free choice of motives for action. Instead, he holds that freedom can be attributed to a human being if they are able to act according to inclinations insofar as these inclinations are ordered by deliberation. Freedom is accordingly grounded in the ability to weigh existing motives for action through deliberation and implement the result of this deliberation in action:

> If, then, one does not want to be content with asserting freedom for *man* in general, which consists in the fact that he can bring about ideas, evaluations, resolutions, and actions with *inner power* according to his own pleasure, if the *will* is to be called free, then its freedom can be posited in the fact that it is not bound to a few impulses, but can be determined by innumerable others. This is also expressed by the terms 'arbitrariness' [*Willkühr*] and 'the faculty to choose' [*Vermögen zu wählen*]. This faculty to choose, although always according to reasons, undeniably belongs to the will. (Feder 1785, 48)

In other words, according to Feder, a human being has freedom even if they cannot produce motives for their action on their own accord. Freedom instead consists in the human ability to choose among existing impulses and act in accordance with them.[7]

---

7 Later, Feder defines freedom as "the faculty to choose" in the sense of "the ability to prefer one among several appealing, driving ideas, and to abandon oneself to it" (Feder 1786b, 154).

Moreover, Feder's theory of the will assumes that there are no ultimate objective ends of the will or "ultimate objective reasons of the will" (Feder 1785, 49). Even independently of the question of ultimate ends, Feder relativizes the importance of objective conditions for willing. Although the properties of things contribute to our willing them, according to Feder, innate human drives are the determining factor. Feder in this sense subdivides the subjective elements of human willing on the basis of a triad of (1) fixed drives as dispositions to desires, (2) desires varying between individuals as dispositions to inclinations, and (3) the actual inclinations themselves. The explanations of the drives common to all human beings on the basis of their innateness have an overriding significance for his theory of the will and moral philosophy. As Feder points out in the third chapter of the first book, the most important basic innate drive is the "drive for self-love" as a "striving for one's own welfare," which in turn can be subdivided into a "drive for pleasure" directed toward the attainment of episodic positive hedonic states and a "drive for felicity" directed toward the attainment of a permanent positive hedonic state (Feder 1785, 84–85). In this context, Feder notes that whereas drives are innate, the content of the will is not. He asserts that it is not the ideas of the human self, its welfare, its felicity, or its pleasures that bring the will to activity, but the fact

> that the *closest objects* of human willing are such inner states, which individually receive the name "well-being," and in a certain quantity the name "felicity"; that the will of man is of such a nature that by virtue of its essential directions and aspirations, the drive to pleasure, to felicity, and self-love, must be attributed to it at least as main dispositions. (Feder 1785, 85)

Feder makes a distinction between self-love here, and vanity and selfishness. Vanity represents a perverted form of self-love, because a person acting out of vanity cannot contribute to the welfare of others. He explains that an agent acting out of vanity is "driven a *mean, harmful way* by the *idea of the benefits to him.*" (Feder 1785, 86) Unlike vanity, Feder understands self-love to be compatible with acting for the benefit of others.

In the rest of the first book, Feder tries to work out the idea that self-love is not the only innate drive. Alongside the drive to self-love, sympathy, in the sense of commiseration with the states of other sentient and, above all, human beings, is a further innate human drive:

> Nature's creator has ensured that it is not as easy for us as selfishness would wish to remain insensitive and inactive regarding all the conditions and affairs of our fellow creatures, and especially man. Strange sensations are communicated to us when they vividly present themselves to our senses or even to our imagination. This is *sympathy* or *commiseration* [...]. (Feder 1785, 88)

Participation in the feelings of others comes in the forms of compassion for the unpleasant feelings of others and positive commiseration with the pleasant feelings of others. Sympathy towards present persons is mediated by the senses, whereas sympathy towards absent or imagined persons is mediated by the imagination. Feder considers it important that feelings of sympathy are a "partially involuntary participation in the condition of others" and, like pain, are beyond our control, even if they can be cultivated to a certain extent (Feder 1785, 107):

> That the sympathetic feelings do not depend entirely on our willing, that they do not arise merely from the fact that, out of intention or habit, which intention has produced, we arbitrarily put ourselves in the place of the other and seek by imagination to excite the very feelings in which the other finds themselves; this is something observation soon puts beyond doubt. The feeling that seizes us at the pain of another is often as involuntary as the pain that a falling stone or a blow causes us. (Feder 1785, 96)

Feder is likely insisting here that sympathy is not completely under our control, that it also occurs involuntarily, because the drive to sympathy can be considered a basis for an anthropological grounding of morality only if its influence cannot be weakened or even switched off through training (see, however, Feder 1785, 104–105). Feder also discusses two causal hypotheses for sympathy: While he does not completely reject the view that participation in the states of others is based on material influence on the model of the transmission of sound signals or of a contagion,[8] according to the causal explanation he favors, however, the "physical ground of sympathy" (Feder 1785, 99) lies "in the imagination and the reawakening of formerly held sensations and ideas, according to the known laws of association of ideas." (Feder 1785, 100) In summary, Feder offers the view that the will is primarily influenced by the two drives of self-love and sympathy, which are universal because of their innateness;[9] in doing so, his descriptive theory of the human will from the first part of the first book is also intended to provide the basis for the explanation of morality.

---

[8] "If it seems that the sensations and emotions of others communicate themselves to us only through sight or hearing, should the contagion, the arousing of similar emotions, come about through other ways, through exhalations that pass into us? This is a conjecture that [...] can seem nothing less than utterly reprehensible." (Feder 1985, 103.)

[9] Feder mentions further innate fundamental drives without comparable relevance for his system, such as the drive for activity, the drive for the future, and the drive for the infinite (see Feder 1985, 108–118).

2 Moral Sentimentalism

After setting out the basic drives of the human will in the first book of the first part, Feder turns to more specific drives in the second book. Before moral sentiments and drives, he discusses drives related to individual pleasure and drives related to social relations, such as those for honor, dominion, and esteem. Under the collective term "drives of very mixed relations" he finally also addresses moral drives, whereby the opening chapter *"Von den moralischen Empfindungen und Trieben überhaupt betrachtet"* ["Consideration of Moral Sentiments and Drives in General"] forms the core of the moral philosophy in the first part.

2.1 Criticism of Moral Sense Theories

§ 98 and § 99, where Feder turns to the question of the basis of moral distinctions, are relevant to the explanation of morality. Feder pursues a negative as well as a positive goal in these two paragraphs. § 98 is devoted to the critical aim of refuting views that hold there is a specifically moral sense by which simple moral sentiments are evoked.[10] The criticism is addressed at philosophers such as Shaftesbury and Hutcheson, whom Feder also praises at other points in the *Untersuchungen*. While Feder agrees with moral sense theorists that moral beliefs "do not consist in empty conceits" (Feder 1785, 386),[11] he is critical of the view that there are simple moral sentiments analogous with simple sensory sensations and that humans have a sense organ for moral sentiments analogous to bodily sense organs:

> But now it is to be examined whether these moral insights, concepts, judgments, or sensations, sentiments, as one wants to call them, taken as a whole, can ever be regarded as simple sensations and in general as effects of a sense of their own, or whether they are rather always consequences of the confluence of several sensations and ideas that arise from such grounds, none of which can be called a moral sense, a confluence that is brought about by instruction, or also by one's own observations and reflections. (Feder 1785, 387)

According to Feder, moral sentiments are not simple and do not come about through a specific sense. He points out that there are two arguments typically made for the existence of a moral sense. According to the first argument, moral

---

[10] Feder also discusses this question in *Über das moralische Gefühl* (*On Moral Sentiment*).
[11] Feder is probably thinking of Mandeville, who aims to show the concept of virtue has no content. Hutcheson develops his moral sense theory as a rebuttal to Mandeville. On Mandeville as well as Hutcheson's critique of Mandeville, see Norton/Kuehn 2006, 951–958.

judgments must be based on sentiments, because moral judgments are made "suddenly and before all reasoning" and also "cannot be derived from reasoned conclusions in the investigation and all subsequent reflection" (Feder 1785, 388). According to the second argument, moral judgments must be based on sentiments because there are also people who, like children, have moral knowledge and "for whom neither the teaching of others nor their own reasoning could provide it" (Feder 1785, 388). Feder does not consider the first argument to be conclusive because moral judgments can also be based on unconscious reasoning; and he rejects the second argument because people can also mistakenly be denied reason, and moral judgments can also be true by chance. In contrast, according to Feder, it follows from the properties of moral discourse that the use of reason contributes to the formation of moral judgments. According to Feder, we do not deal with moral disputes by saying that "we cannot say or describe" why something is wrong, but only "feel it" (Feder 1785, 393). The fact that disagreement about moral judgments triggers argumentative disputes speaks against the assumption that we become aware of moral distinctions through simple sentiments:

> From this, too, it follows that men, although they speak many languages of feeling in regard to right and wrong, yet, when they disagree with each other about this, never reject reason and leave the decision to mere feeling: as often happens, and must happen, in regard to things for which we indisputably have senses of our own. Instead, they refer to the laws, or have recourse to forms proven by experience and reason. (Feder 1785, 394)

As Feder points out in this passage, those engaged in moral disputes base their judgments on reasoning and past experience rather than on simple sentiments. With these arguments, Feder achieves his critical goal and rejects theories according to which moral ideas stem from a moral sense. On his view, moral sentiment is mistakenly thought to be simple because people are not aware of the complex conditions under which it comes about.[12]

---

[12] "Because that kind of cognition in which one is not aware of any origin from other ideas, especially when it is connected with emotions, with movements of the mind, is called sentiment, feeling, according common usage in language, which, if not always based on the most exact evaluation, is nevertheless always based on analogy, it can be accepted that, in just such a meaning of the words, a moral sentiment, a moral sense, is attributed to man." (Feder 1785, 386–387). See Norton/Kuehn 2006, 976: "[...] Feder argued that we do not have to postulate a special sense in order to account for our moral approval and disapproval. Although we are not usually aware of the multiple causes of our moral convictions, we can become aware of them."

2.2 Virtue as a Complex Entity

While § 98 is focused on rejecting moral sense theories, § 99 contains Feder's own position. According to him, moral concepts and judgments are based neither on reason nor on inclination alone; moreover, the inclination involved cannot be traced to just one of the two drives for self-love or sympathy. Feder develops his own view based on the question: "What is the cause of pleasure in virtue and of displeasure in vice?" (Feder 1785, 395) He starts here from the dialectic that on the one hand it cannot be explained "where the charms of virtue come from" when moral judgments result from reason, and on the other hand it cannot be explained why moral judgments are disputed, when moral judgments are used to express sentiments (Feder 1785, 395). In other words, Feder turns to the question of how the cognitive claim of moral judgments can be related to the aspect of pleasure that is necessary for their efficacy in action.

According to his solution, a course of action is considered virtuous if it is judged by the understanding to have utility: "Virtue is generally presented to everyone as *useful*, as the ground of one's own happiness and common welfare, through instruction and experience." (Feder 1785, 397) Moreover, a representation of the understanding is always connected with an inclination of the will if the content of the representation consists in utility. First and foremost, according to Feder, virtue aims at utility for oneself, "at the promotion of the purest and most lasting pleasure" (Feder 1785, 397). However, the concept of self-love as the foundation of morality quickly reaches a limit, even though "representations of the benefits of virtue are very often explicitly used as motives" (Feder 1785, 397). Feder points out that, on the one hand, virtue often requires sacrifice and, on the other, actions are viewed with favor even without expected or even hypothetical utility for oneself. Thus he states that "virtuous actions and characters still please us even when they have no consequences for us at all, when they are presented to us in the history of the most distant times, or in fictions that we also consider to be such," and asks, "why do we also love or admire and hold in high esteem the righteousness of an enemy who is harmful to us?" (Feder 1785, 398) According to Feder, these facts suggest "that these representations [derived from self love] of the utility of virtue, should be accepted as merely one, not the only, ground of inclination" (Feder 1785, 398). Instead, he argues for a view according to which virtue is complex, and moral inclinations "arise from several drives, self-interested and disinterested taken together, that do not originally and necessarily aim at it [virtue] [...]." (Feder 1785, 396). On his view, in addition to self-love, as a reason for taking pleasure in virtue, there is sympathy, due to which even actions with positive consequences for others please us. Thanks to sympathy, "the lover of virtue takes pleasure in the virtue of other people [...] even if it does not bring him any benefit." (Feder 1785, 399). Sympathy contributes to the approval or disapproval of actions and even extends to the enjoyment of morally meritorious actions in the past and in narrative literature, or even to character traits that are harmful to us but beneficial to their owner or to third parties.[13]

Feder in short argues for a utilitarian principle of moral evaluation, with reason having a role in the assessment of utility. According to him, the objects of moral evaluation consist of character traits or intentions to act, whereby he understands character traits that are useful for one's own or others' well-being as virtues, character traits that are harmful for this purpose as vices, actions that are useful for this purpose as morally commanded, and actions that are harmful for this purpose as morally forbidden. However, Feder's utilitarian principle for moral evaluation cannot be detached from its sentimentalist framework. According to him, the idea of a benefit triggers an inclination only because we like the utility for us due to self-love as well as the utility for others due to sympathy. Moral sentiment is based on the perception that an action or character trait promotes one's own good or the good of others, in which all human beings have an interest by virtue of their natural constitution. Feder conceives of moral judgments as complex entities based on a combination of inclinations and reason, with inclinations arising from both self-love and sympathy.

2.3 Feder as a Humean Partisan

Upon closer examination, it becomes clear that Feder takes both the basic outlines and details of his argument from Hume. Hume opens his second *Enquiry* with the controversy regarding whether moral judgments are based on reason or emotion.[14] On the one hand, according to Hume, the fact that we argue about moral judgments suggests that moral judgments have a basis in reason;[15] on the other hand, the fact that virtue pleases and vice displeases suggests that moral judg-

---

13 However, useful actions accompanied by bad intentions can displease, and useless actions accompanied by good intentions can please. Feder explains this by the fact that a bad intention indicates a bad character, and a good intention indicates a good character (see Feder 1785, 401).
14 "There has been a controversy started of late, much better worth examination, concerning the general foundation of MORALS; whether they be derived from REASON, or from SENTIMENT." (*EPM* 1.3)
15 "Moral distinctions, it may be said, are discernible by pure *reason:* Else, whence the many disputes that reign in common life, as well as in philosophy, with regard to this subject: The long chain of proofs often produced on both sides; the examples cited, the authorities appealed to, the analogies employed, the fallacies detected, the inferences drawn, and the several conclusions adjusted to their proper principles." (*EPM* 1.5)

ments have a basis in sentiments, because reasoning is incapable of causing pleasure or displeasure.[16] Hume provides his answer to the controversy raised in the introduction later in the first appendix, "Concerning Moral Sentiment," where he considers the conflict between reason and inclination to be superficial:

> One principal foundation of moral praise being supposed to lie in the usefulness of any quality or action; it is evident, that *reason* must enter for a considerable share in all decisions of this kind; since nothing but that faculty can instruct us in the tendency of qualities and actions, and point out their beneficial consequences to society and to their possessor. (*EPM* App. 1.2)

Also, according to Hume, moral judgment consists in the determination of utility by reason. Although reason is necessary for the perception of utility, it cannot produce the pleasure in utility. According to Hume, it is only in conjunction with a sentiment that the perception of a utility can trigger a liking or disliking of a character trait or action and lead to moral approval or disapproval:

> But though reason, when fully assisted and improved, be sufficient to instruct us in the pernicious or useful tendency of qualities and actions; it is not alone sufficient to produce any moral blame or approbation. Utility is only a tendency to a certain end; and were the end totally indifferent to us, we should feel the same indifference towards the means. It is requisite a *sentiment* should here display itself, in order to give a preference to the useful above the pernicious tendencies. (*EPM* App. 1.3)

Although a utility is identified by the understanding for a particular purpose, the appreciation of the utility is transferred from the appreciation of the purpose given by a feeling. Here, the purpose of utility associated with a positive feeling is not only for one's own good, but also for the good of others. Since character traits and actions that serve the interests of others are also praised, the feeling responsible for the appreciation of virtue cannot be attributed to self-love alone:

> Usefulness is agreeable, and engages our approbation. This is a matter of fact, confirmed by daily observation. But, *useful?* For what? For somebody's interest, surely. Whose interest then? Not our own only: For our approbation frequently extends farther. It must, therefore, be the interest of those, who are served by the character or action approved of; and these we may conclude, however remote, are not totally indifferent to us. By opening up this principle, we shall discover one great source of moral distinctions. (*EPM* 5.16)

---

[16] "On the other hand, those who would resolve all moral determinations into *sentiment*, may endeavor to show, that it is impossible for reason ever to draw conclusions of this nature. To virtue, say they, it belongs to be *amiable*, and vice *odious*. This forms their very nature or essence. But can reason or argumentation distribute these different epithets to any subjects, and pronounce beforehand, that this must produce love, and that hatred?" (*EPM* 1.6)

Because utility for others is also approved without utility for oneself, according to Hume there must be a principle of benevolence or sympathy as a source of moral distinctions in addition to the principle of self-love. In this regard, Hume treats sympathy in the *Treatise* as a mechanism by which the mental states of others are communicated and which leads to the adoption of the attitudes of others.[17] In the *Enquiry*, on the other hand, he generalizes the principle of sympathy to a principle of appreciation of the utility for a society or humanity as a whole.[18] Hume bases his argument for the principle of sympathy on the observations that even a utility for past persons and an imagined utility for literary characters is pleasing, although there can be no hidden utility for oneself; as he notes, it even happens that utility for others is pleasing, although it is associated with disadvantages to oneself.

Feder adopts this line of argumentation without qualification. He argues alongside Hume for a grounding of morality in human nature that is uniformly endowed with self-love and sympathy.[19] These two principles are responsible for the fact that moral evaluation refers to utility and that both utility for oneself and utility for others are valued.[20] In doing so, Feder also occasionally shifts between an understanding of sympathy as a causal mechanism for the transmission of mental states and as commiseration with the welfare of all people.[21] Moreover, it

---

17 "The minds of all men are similar in their feelings and operations; nor can anyone be actuated by any affection, of which all others are not, in some degree, susceptible. As in strings equally wound up, the motion of one communicates itself to the rest; so all the affections readily pass from one person to another, and beget correspondent movements in every human creature." (*T* 3.3.1.7)

18 See *EPM* 5.17: "That everything, which contributes to the happiness of society, recommends itself directly to our approbation and good-will." As well as *EPM* App. 1.3: "This sentiment can be no other than a feeling for the happiness of mankind, and a resentment of their misery; since these are different ends, which virtue and vice have a tendency to promote. Here, therefore, *reason* instructs us in the several tendencies of actions, and *humanity* makes a distinction in favour of those, which are useful and beneficial."

19 Cf. Norton/Kuehn 2016, which – however with a view primarily to the artificial virtue of justice – refers to a *two foundations-theory* in Hume with the two sources of self-love and sympathy.

20 It is debatable to what extent it can be claimed that Hume was a utilitarian. Although moral evaluation according to Hume is based on the evaluation of utility, unlike Bentham and Mill he does not develop a utilitarian calculus, nor does Feder. See among others Pauer-Studer 2007, 300–305; Rosen 2003, 29–57.

21 The understanding of sympathy as universal commiseration in human welfare is expressed in this passage: "No man can be indifferent to another; each is the object of natural sympathy and benevolence, and of general notions of justice and equity. Restricted to a part of mankind, however important it is to us as the object of special duties, they would always be in danger of becoming mixed up with injustice." (Feder 1793, 244)

is consistent with Feder's appeal to the second *Enquiry* that Hume assigns greater importance to reason in it than in the *Treatise*. Thus, according to the *Enquiry*, judgments of moral facts are comparable to judgments of artistic beauty, for which, in contrast to judgments of natural beauty, a contribution of reason is constitutive (see *EPM* 1.9). Feder, however, shares with Hume not only his grounding of morality but also the criticism of the alternative theories of ethical egoism on the one hand and moral sense theories on the other.[22] It is pretty clear that overall Feder is attempting to breathe new life into Hume's moral philosophy in the first part of the *Untersuchungen*.[23] Nevertheless, Feder's claim that Hume was only "the inspiration for the initial development" of his view on moral philosophy is not entirely misleading (Feder 1785, 23). This can be seen from the fact that the third and fourth parts of Feder's *Untersuchungen* contain variants on the grounding of morality in which he departs from Hume.

3 Morality as a Means to Happiness

By the appearance of the third part of the *Untersuchungen* in 1786, it becomes clear that Feder's moral philosophy has some internal tensions. Although he repeats his intention to "seek out with the greatest possible precision the grounds of justice and morality as they lie in *human nature*" (Feder 1786b, VIII) and reaffirms his view that man "by virtue of the unalterable fundamental law of his nature" strives for happiness and also feels the urge "to restrict himself according to other people's needs and to promote other people's good" (Feder 1786b, 1). At the same time, however, Feder tries to prove that the pursuit of our own well-being alone already gives us a ground to act morally. Unexpectedly, Feder makes the concept of happiness more specific by means of a doctrine of goods, according to which a good necessary for one's own happiness is lost through morally reprehensible action. On the basis of a prudential consideration (although he does not refer to it as such), Feder apparently wants to dispel the doubt that sympathy constitutes

---

[22] On Hume's rejection of egoistic explanations, see e.g., *EPM* 5.16 and on the critique of moral sense theories, see T 3.3.6.3. Hume and Feder share a common path with Hutcheson in arguing against ethical egoism. On Hume's critique of ethical egoism, see, among others, Baillie 2000, 147–152.

[23] Brandt, 1989, 254, on the other hand, sees Feder as being in common opposition alongside Kant to empiricist moral philosophy: "In contrast to Hutcheson, Hume, and Smith, both hold in judgment to the possibility of rational value judgments." However, it is wrong to infer from Feder's critique of *moral sense theories* that he rejects moral sentimentalism as a whole. Like Hume, Feder criticizes *moral sense* views based on alternative sentimentalist assumptions.

too weak a resource for obeying moral duties because it is based primarily on relations of proximity between persons and, moreover, is susceptible to distortions.[24] According to Feder, the power of sympathy extends so far that it cannot be successfully ignored even by agents primarily concerned with self-interest.

3.1 Contentment in This World

The discussion of happiness, contained in the fourth book of the third part, starts from a distinction between pseudo-goods and true goods, whereby a pseudo-good "deprives happiness as a whole of more than it brings it" and is therefore "better dispensed with" (Feder 1786b, 110). According to Feder, the false belief that something is a good has particularly harmful consequences for the conduct of life: "Nothing is more deceptive than the appearance of happiness and misery, on which the judgments of most people are based!" (Feder 1786b, 8) Feder denies a simple equivalence between the concepts of the good and the pleasant here: "There are certainly kinds of pleasures or pleasant feelings, with the conception of which reason in well-ordered minds has so adverse and deterrent ideas, and so firmly connected; that it cannot well be demanded that they should think of them under the idea of something good at all." (Feder 1786b, 87) As Feder points out, not all kinds of pleasure can be regarded as good, such as, for example, episodic pleasures that cause displeasure later. Rather, only that "which in itself, that is, in its natural, own effect, with appropriate behavior, causes man more pleasant than unpleasant sensations" falls under the concept of "good" (Feder 1786b, 109). According to Feder, something is a true good precisely when it has a positive long-term effect on happiness. Health, love, respect from others, or external objects necessary for the satisfaction of natural needs are examples of goods that usually cause more pleasant than unpleasant sensations (Feder 1785, 109). Even if these goods do not guarantee permanently pleasant states, they at least make the occurrence of such states probable.

---

24 Elsewhere, Feder concedes that sympathy has limits. According to him, it follows from the causal explanation he advocates based on the association of ideas "that persons of different age, sex, and station do not sympathize with each other quite as well as those who are less dissimilar and unequal." (Feder 1785, 101) Moreover, he considers access to the mental states of others through sympathy to be particularly prone to error because it is based on imagination: "If, however, according to the reason first indicated, sympathy arises from the imagination, it is understandable how easy it is for one to miss the sensations of the other by a long way."
(Feder 1785, 103–104)

Feder moreover claims that among all goods, internal ones are more valuable than external ones: "The most important goods and evils, on which man's happiness depends most, are those which he keeps in himself and has most in his power." (Feder 1786b, 14) According to him, the higher value of internal goods is supported by the fact that people in the same environment differ in their happiness and that we can change the influence of the environment on our happiness through imagination (Feder 1786b, 15–16). External goods in contrast are susceptible to abuse and are "very subject to change and transience" (Feder 1786b, 17). Unlike external goods, internal goods – such as a developed mind – are characterized, according to Feder, by the fact that they contribute to happiness under all circumstances and are therefore valuable for all people. Feder concludes from this that only internal goods have intrinsic value: "*Internal goods*, then, are what determine the true value of everything that is outside the soul for every human being. [...] Those goods alone have a decided value *in themselves*." (Feder 1786b, 111) Among all internal goods, the virtuous will again has a superior value for one's own happiness. For the will must here be mentioned "all the more [...], the more man can *always be satisfied* with this his will, as far as he recognizes it, and does not afterwards, when he has acted, have to look back on it with remorse and displeasure" (Feder 1786b, 111). According to Feder, the virtuous will enjoys an advantage over other goods because it provides contentment without remorse. And in this regard, he turns to a new aspect of moral phenomenology, claiming that immoral action leads to later remorse. Moral action is required for all human beings striving for happiness because the superior good of contentment is lost through remorse.

Feder expands his moral philosophy by introducing a prudential consideration into the grounding of morality. All human beings according to him have a reason for moral action, which consists in the avoidance of remorse as an inner sanction. He believes that moral action is in one's own interest and that we should comply with the demands of morality simply because of our pursuit of happiness. Feder probably supplements his explanation of morality from anthropologically universal predispositions with a prudential explanation in order to prove there is a reason for virtue even to someone like Hume's *sensible knave*, who follows virtue only when it recognizably serves his self-interest (*EPM* 9.22).[25] Hume says about the sensible knave that he actually has no reason to act virtuously if he is deaf to moral feelings involving sympathy with others: "If his heart rebel not against such pernicious maxims, if he feel no reluctance to the thoughts of villainy or baseness, he has indeed lost a considerable motive to virtue; and we may expect, that his

---

25 On the *sensible knave*, see Darwall 1995, 309–317.

practice will be answerable to his speculation." (*EPM* 9.23) Unlike Hume, Feder believes that even an exclusively egoistically motivated person has a ground to act according to virtue. Perhaps Feder discovers in Hume the potential for a rebuttal to the egoist, considering the outlook following the passage about the *sensible knave* at the end of the *Treatise*:

> who can think any advantages of fortune a sufficient compensation for the least breach of the *social* virtues, when he considers, that not only his character with regard to others, but also his peace and inward satisfaction entirely depend upon his strict observance to them; and that a mind will never be able to bear its own survey, that has been wanting in its part to mankind and society? (*T* 3.3.6.6)

Without elaborating further, Hume assumes a close relationship between virtue and happiness here. He emphasizes that virtue contributes to glory and promotes inner peace and contentment. Feder follows Hume's gesture here by regarding remorse as a negative internal sanction for unvirtuous action and the achievement of contentment as the positive reward for virtuous action. However, according to Feder, even the sensible knave has a motive to act virtuously, which consists in avoiding later remorse. According to his conception, the power of sympathy is so great that it cannot be willingly overcome and breaks through at the latest in remorse for one's own moral lapses.

One can, however, also look at Feder's reasoning with some skepticism: Regarding the good of contentment, he says that it trumps all other goods and therefore must not be risked. But on critical examination it would not be implausible to include a lack of remorse in the weighing of goods. One can imagine for example that the powerful tyrant is able to compensate for inner remorse with new pleasures. It is rational for him to accept remorse as an internal sanction if, by virtue of his power, he can acquire a greater sum of pleasurable enjoyment without the limitations placed by virtue. It is not clear why remorse should not be rationally acceptable as the price that has to be paid for other pleasures.

3.2 Inner Peace after Death

In the third section of the fourth part, entitled *"Von der Tugend als dem höchsten Zweck bey der Bildung des Willens"* ("On Virtue as the Highest Purpose in the Formation of the Will"), published in 1793, Feder refers to a consensus among philosophers, insofar as they are not moral skeptics, according to which "of all goods [...] virtue has the highest value" (Feder 1793, 231). This position is also open to philosophers who attribute the value of virtue to self-interest according to Feder:

> For this is also readily admitted by those who, in their investigations of human nature, believe to have found that the *most general basic drive of the will* lies in the desire for *well-being* and the abhorrence of *evil*, in that they recognize virtue as the most essential *condition* and the most important *ground* for lasting well-being or happiness [...]. (Feder 1793, 231–232)

Feder should not have overlooked the fact that, according to this line of reasoning, virtue does not have the highest value, but rather its value is subordinate to that of happiness. Notwithstanding this, he is particularly concerned in part four with the question of whether his own position does justice to the absolute value of morality and therefore makes a number of revisions to his own approach. Although Feder does not refer to Kant, it is likely that he feels pressured to make changes because of arguments in the *Critique of Practical Reason*.[26]

Two arguments are pertinent to Kant's critique of conceptions of morality based on sympathy: The arguments against sympathy as a source of morality are that (i) what is morally right and wrong is unreliably determined by sympathy, and (ii) actions performed solely out of sympathy have no moral value. Both claims can be found in a passage of the *Critique of Practical Reason* in which Kant denies that the inclination toward what conforms with duty has a role in both moral judgment and moral motivation.

> Even an inclination to what conforms with duty (e.g., to beneficence) can indeed greatly facilitate the effectiveness of moral maxims but cannot produce any. For in these everything must be directed to the representation of the law as determining ground if the action is to contain not merely legality but also morality. Inclination is blind and servile, whether it is kindly or not; and when morality is in question, reason must not play the part of mere guardian to inclination but, disregarding it altogether, must attend solely to its own interest as pure practical reason. Even this feeling of compassion and tender sympathy, if it precedes consideration of what is duty and becomes the determining ground, is itself burdensome to right-thinking persons, brings their considered maxims into confusion, and produces the wish to be freed from them and subject to lawgiving reason alone. (*CPrR*, 5: 118, trans. Gregor 2015)

As Kant makes clear here, morality attaches to an action only if it is performed out of respect for the law; moreover, unlike rational deliberation, sympathy is an unreliable means of determining what is morally right.

Surprisingly, Feder seems to accept both arguments directed against the positive understanding of the inclination toward duty. First, he subscribes to the view that inclinations form a source of error in moral judgments. This is expressed

---

[26] Feder is familiar with Kant's practical philosophy, as can be seen, among other things, from his review of the *Critique of Practical Reason* and his essay *Über die kantische Moraltheologie* (*On Kantian Moral Theory*), both published in *Philosophische Bibliothek*. See Brandt 1989, and as a historical source Werdermann 1794.

in his remarks on the "Influence of the inclinations and passions on the judgments of the intellect": "Thus it can happen that people, with a pronounced dutiful zeal for the good, do not cast a sharp judging eye on their overly strong inclination, reassure themselves with sham reasons in their justification, and thus gradually put their moral feeling to sleep and numb their reason here." (Feder 1793, 260) Correspondingly, with his definition of virtue as "the prevailing inclination, according to the best possible knowledge, to do what is right," he now foregrounds the cognitive side of moral judgments in the knowledge of benefit and harm (Feder 1793, 238).[27]

Feder also agrees with Kant that an action acquires moral value only when it is performed out of a consciousness of duty. Among other things, he says that moral value concerns the "inner reason of actions"[28] and is to be determined "according to the purity and sublimity of motives" (Feder 1793, 253) with only the consciousness of duty being an appropriate reason for action. Feder subscribes to Kant's conception of moral value and endorses the view that motives for action arising from a charitable inclination as well as from prudence have no authentic moral value:

> The absolute essence of virtue requires that the thought of *duty* and *right* be the governing motive, the highest motive that is decisive over all others. In this way it rises above lawful behavior out of servile fear of punishment or selfish mercenary service, as well as lawful behavior, which is based on blind natural instinct, on automatism or unenlightened and therefore uncertain feelings. (Feder 1793, 253)

According to Feder, the absolute value of virtue is lost if it is attributed to fear of sanctions or even to feelings that arise for human beings due to their natural constitution. Unlike in the previous parts of the work, Feder now assumes that grounding morality on natural drives or the avoidance of sanctions compromises the value of morality.

Nevertheless, there are clear differences of opinion that remain between Feder and Kant. First, contrary to Kant, Feder asserts that the motivating drive for moral action is not reason but a moral drive. According to Feder's new explanation, agents acting out of a sense of duty follow a "drive to do everything that is

---

[27] The difference between Feder and Kant in their views on the content of the principle of moral evaluation also persists. Brandt 1989, 254–255, also points this out: "The difference between Feder and Kant lies in the determination of reason: Feder is utilitarian in orientation and believes he has a concept of the respective utility which can be universalized, to which reason can refer with its moral imperatives."

[28] "In general, however, the concept of virtue must not be considered merely in terms of the outward behavior of people, whether it is lawful, useful, and decent; but rather in terms of the inner reason for the actions. Because *moral* value is based mainly on this." (Feder 1793, 238)

right" (Feder 1793, 247). Feder introduces a moral drive of his own, but one that is artificial in contrast to the natural drives of self-love and sympathy, in order to do justice to the autonomy of morality. Second, according to Feder, agents acting out of a sense of duty constitute only the telos of moral development. Even if, on his view, the motive for moral action ideally consists in a sense of duty, moral agents realistically require some motivational help:

> But can a man's virtue, with this its essential ground, *entirely dispense* with the help of other natural impulses, with the thought of external, temporal advantage or disadvantage, human approval or disapproval, with encouraging examples and exhortations, also with the hope of compensation in a future life, for that which he sacrifices, tolerates, is deprived of here for duty? Or are such outlooks and perspectives necessary for its support and encouragement from time to time, even often? (Feder 1793, 253–254)

Assuming a realistic picture of moral agents, it is clear, according to Feder, that a ground for moral action external to morality is required in the pursuit of happiness in this world or even after death. Feder states in general that "the most general indomitable basic drive of the human will […] is always that of well-being" and that virtuous action benefits personal well-being (Feder 1793, 342–343). He thus considers it certain that "virtue is the surest and best way even to the possession of external goods" (Feder 1793, 343), even though "the ways of virtue are not the only ones that lead to the attainment and quiet possession of the goods of happiness" (Feder 1793, 343). While virtue is only the best means for acquiring external goods, there are internal goods that cannot be obtained without virtue. According to Feder, even the perfectly virtuous person acts in accordance with virtue because they know the value of virtue for the internal goods of satisfaction and inner peace: "For he has felt it and realized that satisfaction, that inner peace departs from him when he acts contrary to these immutable laws of his inner judge, reason." (Feder 1793, 281)

Compared to the third part, however, Feder weakens the view that the desire for contentment provides reasons to act morally for all agents. Presumably, Feder has come to the conclusion that an agent who is indifferent to the suffering of others will regard the threat of losing his contentment through remorse as empty.[29]

---

[29] This hearkens back to Kant's criticism of the view attributed to Epicurus that felicity constitutes the highest good and is acquired through virtue: "the virtuous Epicurus – like many morally well-disposed men of this day who nevertheless do not reflect deeply enough on their principles – fell into the error of presupposing the virtuous disposition in the persons for whom he wanted first of all to provide the incentive to virtue." According to Kant, virtue cannot be justified to the skeptic by the fact that it helps to reassure the soul. Kant considers this argument unsuccessful because an agent without moral feeling will also deny that immoral action harms contentment through neg-

According to Feder's new argument, however, there is a good that is superior to contentment and that consists in inner peace: "But what is the possession of all happiness and what is all fame among men against the inner peace which virtue alone provides?" (Feder 1793, 344) In contrast to the concept of contentment, the concept of inner peace refers to the survival of the soul after death. While the pursuit of contentment in this world is not a strong enough reason for acquiring virtue, the desire for inner peace after death trumps all other goods because of its supra-temporal nature. Moreover, even an agent without feelings of sympathy must be concerned about their inner peace after death, since it depends on the intervention of God and not the agent's own feelings. Feder recognizes in inner peace a sufficiently strong reason for virtuous action, because immoral agents must fear not being accepted into communion with God. Feder resorts to God as an external sanctioning authority because it provides agents a prudential reason that is decisive over other reasons.[30]

Feder brings his argument together in an answer to the question of whether the reference to a state after death brings into play "lower drives of fear or reward-seeking unworthy of virtue" (Feder 1793, 384). In doing so, he again criticizes the idealized notion of subjects that are motivated to moral action by a sense of duty alone:

> It is always unfounded to expect and demand everywhere that which is conceivable according to separate concepts and can at most be real in the case of individual subjects under special internal and external conditions. That pure, sublime virtue, which is ready and willing for every duty, solely because these duties are based on truth and directed to the best in the whole, is not a mere ideal, but has real possibility and reality in single individuals in mankind. But how does the real condition of the vast majority of people, in all successive stages of life, and under manifold external conditions, relate to this ideal? Is it not better to protect

---

ative moral feelings: "But the question is, how is such a disposition and cast of mind in estimating the worth of one's existence possible in the first place, since prior to this no feeling at all for moral worth as such would be found in the subject? If a human being is virtuous he will certainly not enjoy life unless he is conscious of his uprightness in every action, however fortune may favor him in the physical state of life; but in order to make him virtuous in the first place, and so before he esteems the moral worth of his existence so highly, can one commend to him the peace of mind that would arise from consciousness of an uprightness for which he as yet has no sense?" (*CPrR*, 5: 116, trans. Gregor 2015)

30 However, Feder would like to dispel the impression that this is a prudential reason for morality because, according to him, prudence refers "merely to the external affairs of this life" and the skill to "make one's happiness in the world" (Feder 1793, 402). While prudence aims at external good, wisdom aims at internal good and is "not merely restricted to this life" (Feder 1793, 402). It is clear here that Feder is merely distinguishing prudence in the choice of means to acquire external goods from prudence in the choice of means to acquire internal goods.

weak reason, by explaining to it the inner reasons of duty, as far as this can be done, and making these venerable, until reason becomes strong enough to let this alone determine itself against the passions by the frightfully great ideas of religion [...]? (Feder 1793, 385)

According to Feder, it is important for their moral development that immoral agents must fear for their admission to communion with God after death.[31] The utility of the religious motivation consists in the fact that, fearing the loss of inner peace after death, agents fulfilling their moral duty progressively internalize the value of the moral duty and develop a moral drive.

However, one may ask why God should enforce moral duties that are not established by God himself. It is obvious to think that God helps moral laws be enforced because these laws owe their content to his will. Feder in fact indicates that he is open to explanations that attribute the content of morality to divine will rather than to human dispositions, and in doing so revises the core of his project. He changes his conception and drops the thesis, which was originally central to his view, that natural human dispositions form the basis for the explanation of morality both in terms of its content and its obligatory character.

4 Conclusion

It is clear that Feder's view changes during the course of the *Untersuchungen*. The extent of this change can be gauged by comparing it with Hume's view again. In large part, the *Untersuchungen* follow Hume in explaining virtue on the basis of principles of human nature. According to Hume, one advantage of a naturalistic explanation over a theological explanation is that it is compatible with scientific progress, and growth in knowledge does not threaten the stability of morality.[32] Hume's goal is to establish a secular ethics that also does not privilege monastic virtues related to future salvation. Clearly, Feder sees himself as participating in this project, at least at the beginning of the *Untersuchungen*; later, however, he abandons the project of a secular ethics pursued by Hume and uses religious beliefs to justify morality. Feder begins as a partisan fighting alongside Hume and, as the work progresses, moves to prudential theories related first to happiness in this

---

[31] Apparently, Feder is inspired by Kant's moral theology in the postulates. Unlike Kant, however, the correspondence between happiness and morality is not the content of a postulate in Feder, but of a conviction held with a claim to knowledge.

[32] Schneewind 1998, 375, describes this fact, which is central to Hume, as follows: "They [the moral sciences] enable us to understand why a descriptive natural science of causal connections, and a morality of useful and agreeable motives have nothing to fear from the advance of knowledge. Religion and the harmful morality associated with it, by contrast, are likely to lose their hold on us."

world and then in the afterlife.[33] Although Feder's transformation from a naturalist to moral theologian within a single work is a curiosity, his change of position can teach us something about the weaknesses of grounding morality on empiricist tenets. The fact that Feder's views did not become more widely accepted in philosophy in his time in Germany need not be due to the impediments of external circumstances – it could also be due to the lack of coherence of his views.[34]

---

[33] Responding to the German version of this paper, Stefano Bacin has recently criticized my thesis that Feder's conception of morality is strongly linked to Hume. Contrarily, he claims: "Feder's *Untersuchungen* provide not so much an investigation of the dynamics of moral approbation in the wake of the Scottish sentimentalists, but rather an examination of the various elements of appetition and desire, closer to Wolff than to Hume." (Bacin 2018, 238) I agree that elements from various traditions play a role in Feder's theory. Nevertheless, I think that the adoption of some of Hume's views is crucial for Feder's project and that my paper gives sufficient support for this claim.
[34] See in contrast Röttgers 1984.

Part II: **Influences**

Tinca Prunea-Bretonnet
Crusius and Kant on Distinctness, Certainty, and Method in Philosophy

Abstract: In this chapter, I analyze Crusius' methodological commitments in his treatises on logic and metaphysics, and their reception in Kant's *Preisschrift* of 1764. I begin with an examination of Crusius' definition of philosophy and the resulting distinction between mathematics and philosophy in the narrow sense, on which he bases his considerations of the methods relevant to philosophical enquiry. I argue that the importance of analysis is emphasized by Crusius' novel and influential divisions of distinctness and certainty, which, alongside his treatment of probability, were to play an important role in controversies over method up to the 1760s. I then examine Kant's *Inquiry Concerning the Distinctness of the Principles of Natural Theology and Morality* in light of Kant's explicit endorsement of the Crusian views. I argue that, despite undeniable borrowings, Kant revises Crusius' position by more firmly advocating the role of analysis as an appropriate philosophical method and rejecting the latter's 'supreme rule' of truth. The *Inquiry* thus testifies to Kant's crucial debt to Crusius' philosophy and to his endeavor to take a novel standpoint on the certainty and on the specific method of metaphysics, a standpoint that, in the early 1760s, is not yet free of tensions and ambiguities.

In 1761 the Berlin Academy published one of its most famous prize questions, which focused on the problem of method in philosophy and asked for a detailed account of certainty and distinctness [*evidence*] with respect to "metaphysical truths in general."[1] It had a huge impact on the philosophical community, not only in Prussia but in Europe in general, comparable with the impact of the two prize essays published in 1764, namely Moses Mendelsohn's *Treatise on the Evidence in Metaphysical Sciences* [*Abhandlung über die Evidenz in metaphysischen*

---

[1] "On demande, si les vérités métaphysiques en général et en particulier les premiers principes de la Théologie naturelle et de la Morale sont susceptibles de la même évidence que les vérités mathématiques, et au cas qu'elles n'en soient pas susceptibles, quelle est la nature de leur certitude, à quel degré elle peut parvenir, et si ce degré suffit pour la conviction?" ("One wishes to know whether the metaphysical truths in general and the first principles of *Theologiae naturalis* and morality in particular, admit of distinct proofs to the same degree as geometrical truths; and if they are not capable of such proofs, one wishes to know what the genuine nature of their certainty is, to what degree the said certainty can be brought, and whether this degree is sufficient for complete conviction?")

Wissenschaften],[2] which won the first prize by endorsing a Wolffian perspective, and especially Kant's *Inquiry Concerning the Distinctness of the Principles of Natural Theology and Morality* [*Untersuchung über die Deutlichkeit der Grundsätze der natürlichen Theologie und der Moral*], which was awarded the *accessit* for advancing an anti-Wolffian standpoint.

Favorable to English, Scottish, and French enlightened ideas, Pierre-Louis Moreau de Maupertuis, the influential president of the Berlin Academy after its reorganization by Frederick the Great in 1744–1746, had promoted these movements in Prussia while attempting to discredit the "Leibnizian-Wolffian" philosophy. Several significant members of the Academy supported Maupertuis in this endeavor, albeit without reaching a consensus within the Academy, where Wolffian disciples, such as Jean Henri Samuel Formey or Johann Georg Sulzer, were also active (on this debate, see Prunea-Bretonnet 2015). Thus, the institution regularly rewarded anti-Wolffian responses and favored competing views. By 1761, however, after both Wolff's and Maupertuis' demise (in 1754 and 1759, respectively), the standpoints defended within the speculative philosophy class had reached a certain balance and common ground (see also Prunea-Bretonnet 2022). As regards the philosophical method, scholars no longer supported the exclusive relevance or even pre-eminence of the synthetic method, unless it had at least been preceded by an analytic section. Indeed, analysis emerged as the method of choice for philosophy and theology in most of the essays submitted for the 1763 academic prize (see Tonelli 1959); furthermore, with respect to the exclusive use of the synthetic (demonstrative or "mathematical") method in philosophy, an explicit anti-Wolffian attitude prevailed on the philosophical scene. This is why, despite the fact that Sulzer managed to award the academic prize to Mendelssohn's essay that was clearly inspired by Wolff, it is Kant's anti-Wolffian *Inquiry* that embodied the novel take on method and effectively closed the era of the demonstrative method promoted by Wolff and his disciples. Interestingly enough, Kant claimed to defend a Crusian viewpoint in his essay.

In this chapter, I will examine the role played by Christian August Crusius' conception in the controversy about method in philosophy around the mid-century, and its reception in Kant's prize essay of 1764. I argue that Crusius' treatment of distinctness [*Deutlichkeit*] and certainty [*Gewißheit*], and his views on the distinction between mathematics and philosophy had a decisive influence on Kant's account in the *Inquiry*. In order to shed light on this relationship, I will first examine

---

[2] *Dissertation qui a remporté le prix proposé par l'Académie royale des sciences et belles-lettres de Prusse sur la nature, les espèces, et les degrés de l'évidence avec les pièces qui ont concouru* (Berlin, 1764); reprint in Mendelssohn 1972. For a summary in English, see Walford/Meerbote 1992, 276–286.

Crusius' account of the task, specificity, and appropriate method of philosophy (§§ 1 and 2), and his treatment of distinctness and probability (§ 3), as elaborated in his treatises on logic and metaphysics. I will then analyse the reception of these methodological theses in Kant's prize essay by discussing Kant's aims in the *Inquiry* (§ 4), views on the distinction between mathematics and philosophy (§ 5), and the role granted to principles (§ 6). I will conclude with a general assessment of Kant's relationship to Crusian philosophy.

1 The Definition and the Division of Philosophy According to Crusius

From 1743, Crusius became one of the main challengers of the Wolffian system. Representative of the Thomasian school, he was the heir of the more intellectualist movement supported by Andreas Rüdiger (1673–1731) and a disciple of August Friedrich Müller (1684–1761) and Adolph Friedrich Hoffmann (1703–1741), as he explicitly declares in the prefaces to his main treatises on logic and metaphysics. Crusius gave a consistent and in many respects original expression to Hoffmann's anti-Wolffian methodological stance. Like his teacher, he was familiar with Wolff's works, and the controversy against Wolff shaped the way in which he articulated his own writings. Scholarship agrees in considering Crusius' critique as decisive for the decline of Wolffianism (Tonelli 1969, xx). For many years, even after 1752 when he devoted himself almost exclusively to theology, Crusius' philosophy represented a competing doctrine to Wolffianism and enjoyed an undeniable longevity in university education as well.[3] As his philosophical system was founded on his opposition to Wolff and structured by the – sometimes implicit but always present and precise – criticism of his theses, one can surely speak of an indisputable "contamination" at the doctrinal level (see Carboncini-Gavanelli 2001).

The activity of the Academy did not seem to have attracted Crusius' attention, not even in its combat against Wolffian philosophy. Nevertheless, he was indirectly present in the Academy at least twice: first in 1755, when his disciple Adolf Friedrich Reinhard won the prize for an essay on optimism, and in 1763, when Kant's essay on distinctness was awarded the *accessit*.[4]

Crusius' opposition to Wolff is manifest from the first paragraphs of his treatise on logic, titled *Path to the Certainty and Reliability of Human Cognition* [*Weg*

---

[3] For details on the University Albertina in Königsberg, see Oberhausen/Pozzo 1999.
[4] Three other memoirs for 1763 (nos. 2, 13 and 25) implicitly or explicitly mention Crusian doctrines. I thank Paola Basso for this information.

zur Gewissheit und Zuverlässigkeit der menschlichen Erkenntniss]. He mentions the Wolffian distinction between historical and philosophical knowledge (see Wolff 1996), while arguing against Wolff that philosophy cannot be defined as merely "the science of the reasons [*Gründe*] of things" (Crusius 1747, §§ 1–4). He also rejects the Wolffian claim that we cognize something with certainty only if we are able to unveil its cause, hereby preparing the path for a redefinition of both certainty and the philosophical investigation of existence.[5]

On Crusius' account, philosophy in the broad sense should be understood as the science investigating "in as much as possible" [*so viel möglich*] the reasons of things "with evidence and certainty" *and* the existence of some things or state of affairs; as such, philosophy also relies on perception and experiences [*Erfahrungen*] (Crusius 1747, § 10). As some of its objects escape our capacity of investigation into their causes [*Realgründe*], Crusius argues, they should be considered according to their existence. Therefore, philosophy, while being concerned with the unchanging truths of reason [*unveränderlichen Vernunftwahrheiten*], also addresses the truths that can be obtained through the consideration of the natural things [*natürliche Dinge*] in the world. Among these unchanged or necessary truths, Crusius mentions the necessarily given (or existing [*vorhanden[e]*]) beings, or that which should happen in every world. In this endeavor, philosophy should aim to be true and thorough [*gründlich*], go beyond the mere existence of things, be useful, insightful and rise above common sense (Crusius 1747, § 3). Philosophy in the broad sense is said to comprise two sciences: one that deals with magnitudes of extension [*Grössen der Ausdehnung*] and is called mathematics, and the other, called philosophy in a narrow sense. He divides the latter into, on the one hand, metaphysics, which is concerned with the necessary theoretical truths of reason, and, on the other hand, *Disciplinalphilosophie*, which deals with the truths that are either contingent or practical.[6] We should note that metaphysics is said to also comprise "the highest reasons of all practical truths" (Crusius 1747, § 11).

In his treatise *Outline of the Necessary Truths of Reason* [*Entwurf der nothwendigen Vernunft-Wahrheiten*], Crusius advances a negative definition of metaphysics as "the science of those necessary truths that are something else than determinations of extended magnitudes" (Crusius 1745, § 4). He confers to metaphysics the eminence of the fundamental science containing the first reasons of all the other sciences (Crusius 1745, § 6). Crusius takes up the common division of metaphysics in ontology (or general metaphysics) and the three disciplines of special

---

[5] On Crusius' (and Rüdiger's) reception of Wolff, see Ciafardone 1983.
[6] On his account, the *Disciplinalphilosophie* deals with three objects: bodies, the nature and the use of the understanding [*Verstand*], and the truths which concern our will (Crusius 1747, § 13).

metaphysics: natural theology, cosmology and pneumatology. However, he does not endorse the order advanced in this respect by Wolff (cosmology, psychology, theology; cf. Wolff 1996, §§ 55 sq.); rather, aiming to highlight the distinction between the theoretical and practical branches of philosophy understood in a narrow sense, he speaks of "theoretical" natural theology and "metaphysical" cosmology and pneumatology.

As a science based on the necessary and the actual – and no longer on the possible, as Wolff defines it (Wolff 1996, § 29) – philosophy is determined by the limited nature of human understanding. It must, therefore, start from given existences or *individuata* (Crusius 1747, §§ 3–4) and be satisfied with probability. This is also why, according to Crusius, thought cannot account for the unity of the whole reality by applying a single principle, but it imperatively needs several principles (to the principle of contradiction, he adds the principle of inseparables and that of incompatibles). And this is also why, constrained to start from existence and to verify its conclusions in experience, philosophy must deal with many unanalyzable and indemonstrable concepts.

After having included mathematics within philosophy understood in a broad sense, Crusius seeks to highlight the distinction between mathematics and philosophy "in the narrow sense" and devotes several decisive paragraphs of his *Logic* to the crucial differences in the objects and methods of these two sciences. Notably, the differences listed in § 10 of the *Path* would find a large echo in the 1760s owing to Kant's reception in the *Inquiry*. On Crusius' account, mathematics is concerned with quantities or magnitudes and its objects are simple; their qualities are essential (not accidental). Thus, the addition or removal of a quality produces a new being. In mathematics, it is therefore possible to abstract a definition from a single example, which is impossible in philosophy where we deal with qualities. Mathematics, through definitions, generates its object. Moreover, it disregards the moral consideration of final ends [*moralische Betrachtung der Endzwecke*] (Crusius 1747, § 10) and the efficient causes [*wirkende Ursachen*], which is unthinkable in philosophy, where the essence [*Wesen*] of things most often depends on them. Mathematics seldom appeals to the division into species, as its objects are usually too simple for that, and proceeds by demonstration, drawing necessary conclusions from necessary principles – whereas in philosophy "one would be gravely mistaken" if one thought that it is necessary to proceed likewise or that it is profitable for the perfection of philosophy to always [*allezeit*] choose demonstration (Crusius 1747, § 10). Mathematics is based on a single principle, that of contradiction, while philosophy requires several principles; mathematics only uses syllogisms, something that is neither possible nor advantageous in philosophy.

This comparison allows Crusius to conclude that anyone who reflects on these crucial differences will understand that the use of the mathematical method has been only partially beneficial to philosophy, having sometimes caused considerable damage despite the wish of "famous men" to help this science:

> Moreover, whoever properly reflects on these differences, will understand why philosophy, beyond the benefit that it has drawn in some [of its] parts, has also suffered prejudice in others, due to the fact that certain famous men thought to remedy the verbiage which has occasionally spread in philosophy, by making use of the mathematical method [in this discipline], but have not always paid sufficient attention to the distinct nature of the two sciences. (Crusius 1747, § 10)[7]

2 Philosophy and Its Methods

Any attempt to assess the proper method in philosophy ought to necessarily take into account this distinction, Crusius argues, and his elaborate reflection on methodology is indeed based on this initial comparison. He devotes a long chapter of his *Logic* [*Von dem Nachdencken und Lehrart*] (Crusius 1747, §§ 566–584) to a precise and subtle account of the analytic and synthetic methods. He claims that the aim of thinking [*Nachdencken*] is to widen [*erweitern*] our knowledge of truth; thinking is based on one or several fundamental thoughts [*Grundgedancken*] that constitute its beginning and object. Crusius defines thinking as the effort to reach a more distinct, more complete, more certain or more extensive knowledge of the truth (Crusius 1747, § 566). The way we proceed is crucial, he argues, and therefore a "logical" theory of method is very helpful even if the common or "natural" intellect [*natürliche Verstand*] is also apt to reflect on this issue. According to this logical approach, there are two main but inherently distinct kinds of thinking [*Hauptarten des Nachdenckens*]. The first is the analytic (or "decomposing," "resolving" – [*auflösend, zergliedernd*]) method, which starts with fundamental thoughts and attempts to reach a more complete knowledge of these thoughts by "going back" to their simplest elements and increasing their distinctness, completeness, and certainty (Crusius 1747, §§ 571–572). The second kind is the synthetic or unifying [*zusammensetzend[e]*] method, which seeks to produce new knowledge by moving forth [*fortgehen*] from known truths towards truths that are not contained in the *Grundgedancken*. Crusius further distinguishes between a "resolving" analytic

---

[7] "Wer übrigens diese Unterschiede wohl überleget, der wird begreiffen, warum die Philosophie ausser dem Nutzen, den sie in einigen Stücken gezogen hat, in andern auch wiederum Schaden dadurch gelitten habe, nachdem einige berühmte Männer dem hin und wieder eingerissenen Gewäsche in der Philosophie dadurch abzuhelfen gedacht haben, dass sie sich in derselben der mathematischen Lehrart haben bedienen wollen, dabey sie aber auf die unterschiedene Natur beyder Wissenschaften nicht allezeit aufmerksam genug gewesen sind."

method and a "proving" one; the latter collects proofs while the former has two components: the "merely resolving or pure" [*bloß zergliedernde oder reine*] method, which seeks to make the fundamental thoughts or concepts more distinct [*deutlicher*]; and the "determining" [*determinierend[e]*] method, which also aims to determine them further (Crusius 1747, § 574). This last type of the analytic resolving method is in fact, Crusius argues, a mixed [*gemischt[e]*] procedure, because the synthetic way of thinking is involved in adding further determinations. He regards it as more important than other methods, especially for philosophical topics, and devotes two further paragraphs to the investigation of its features. On Crusius' account, distinctness is related to the analytic procedure – a point to which I shall come back.

The synthetic method is said to include three subdivisions: the geometrical or mathematical method, which deals with possible beings or with their relations (Crusius 1747, § 578), the physical [*physikalische*] method and the "moral" one. The last two deal with existent beings, that is, with experiences or existences (the physical method), and with the final aims of things (the moral method) (Crusius 1747, § 581). Crusius proposes to call these two latter subdivisions the "philosophical synthesis" (Crusius 1747, § 578). In the physical method we always start with experiences and examine their causes and further consequences; on his account, this is the proper approach in disciplines such as natural philosophy, medicine and revealed theology (Crusius 1747, § 580). He emphasizes here the limits of the geometrical method, which can be used only when we deal with possible beings or relations among possible beings (or essences), and not with really existing beings.

Two crucial aspects should be underlined here: the relationship between the analytic and synthetic methods and the specific use of each subdivision. Crusius insists on the fact that each discipline and topic should be assigned a particular kind of method according to its "nature" [*Natur*]. The correctness and fruitfulness of any scientific endeavor depend on the appropriate identification and application of these methods.[8] For instance, in § 584 of the *Path* he explains that with respect to existences [*Existenzen*] we should employ either the analytic determining method or the synthetic physical or moral one, or a combination thereof. Essences, however, should be examined with the help of the mathematical method (which is synthetic) or of the analytic resolving or determining method.

Moreover, when combining the two main methods, one should always keep in mind that the analytic procedure grounds the synthetic one and must always be

---

[8] "Eine iedwede Sache muß nach derjenigen Methode überdacht und abgehandelt werden, welche ihre Natur leidet" (Crusius 1747, § 584).

applied first: it is impossible to acquire new knowledge if the "fundamental thoughts" are not distinct and properly known. In the "orderly way" of thinking, the two methods go together, but the analytic one has epistemic primacy and can stand by itself. While the synthetic method definitely enriches the analytic procedure, Crusius argues, it cannot exist without it.[9] On his account, in philosophy the two methods are most of the time combined.[10] It is imperative to correctly discern, Crusius argues, what principles and axioms are involved in these procedures. For instance, the principle of identity and that of the indiscernibles are specific to analysis, while the principle of causality belongs to the synthetic method (Crusius 1747, § 583).

3 Distinctness and Probability

In his *Logic*, Crusius devotes an important part of the chapter "On the completeness of concepts" (Crusius 1747, §§ 166–199) to the question of distinctness [*Deutlichkeit*], advancing a nuanced classification that allows him to expand on the differences between mathematics and philosophy, further clarify his understanding of the role of analysis, and denounce the most common errors committed by philosophers in this domain. The same topic is dealt with more succinctly in his *Metaphysics* (Crusius 1745, §§ 7–8), where his main target is unsurprisingly the Wolffian school.

Let us look closer at this classification, as it will prove particularly influential in the debates on method up to the 1760s.[11] According to Crusius, human understanding has access to only three kinds [*Arten*] of distinctness (Crusius 1747, §§ 171–173; Crusius 1745, § 8). At the lower limit of our cognitive faculty he situates the "common distinctness" [*gemeine Deutlichkeit*], which is specific to unanalyzed concepts issued from experience and representing the matter of our reflections. A

---

9 "Es ist vor bekannt anzunehmen, daß man nicht eher zu neuen Gedancken fortgehen soll, bis die Grundgedancken genugsam deutlich sind, und ihre Wahrheit untersuchet worden"; and "Das synthetische Nachdenken kan nicht eher, wenigstens nicht gründlich, angewandt werden, als bis die Grundgedancken deutlich sind, und ihrer Realität oder Möglichkeit nach, welche man ihnen zuschreibet, vor bekannt angenommen werden können. [...] *Das analytische Nachdencken wird fruchtbarer, wenn das synthetische hinzu kommt. Das synthetische aber kan ohne irgend ein vorher gegangenes analytisches gar nicht seyn* " (Crusius 1747, § 573 and § 583, my emphasis).
10 On the methodological theories within the Thomasian school and in the first half of the eighteenth century, see Tonelli 1976.
11 Cassirer regards this classification as the starting point of the "fight" [*Streit*] against Wolff's methodology; see Cassirer 1974, vol. 2, 532.

concept that is distinct in this way can be differentiated [*unterschieden*] from any other concept. Crusius gives here the example of colors (Crusius 1745, § 8). This kind of distinctness is sufficient for every-day life, he argues, and, if our conscience is not ignored or contradicted, it can also be attained in the moral domain.

At the higher end [*oben*] (Crusius 1745, § 8), Crusius places the "logical" or "abstractive" distinctness [*logikalische oder die Deutlichkeit des Abstractionsweges*], which is obtained through the analysis or resolution [*Zergliederung*] of compound concepts acquired through the senses. Our senses, he claims, are "touched" or moved [*rühret*] by composite things [*zusammengesetzte Dinge*]; thus, our first representation is of a *concretum* (Crusius 1747, § 172). All the determinations that do not belong to the concept in question are left out until we remain only with "what belongs to" the it (Crusius 1745, § 8; Crusius 1747, § 172). Thus, through analysis, we attain the simplest concepts. Crusius insists that this kind of distinctness is specific to ontology (defined as the science that must attain the "most simple concepts" [*allereinfachsten Begriffe*]), as well as to metaphysics in general, and denies that the lack of definitions or the absence of an ascribable cause bring along obscurity in metaphysics (Crusius 1745, §§ 7–8). Whether after having obtained the simplest concepts we should proceed according to the synthetic method remains to be established, he argues, in a statement that announces Kant's own apparent hesitation on this subject. Further clarifications in this respect will be brought by his theory of principles. Between these two limits [*extrema*] (Crusius 1745, §§ 7–8), he situates the third type of distinctness; that is, the distinctness "of essential content" [*die Deutlichkeit des wesentlichen Inhaltes*]. This latter kind makes it possible to become aware of what differentiates a concept from other concepts, that is, of its parts and determinations. It is obtained by decomposing the representation of the content of a concept and also – in other sciences than ontology – through the definition of a concept.

Crusius laments the errors and confusions that stem from the conflation of these types of distinctness and from the desire to attain one or the other type in domains that are not suited for that precise kind of distinctness. Ontology in particular, if it does not aim at logical distinctness but pursues other goals, becomes obscure, difficult [*schwer*] and futile: instead of grounding knowledge on simple and distinct concepts, it acquires "mere relative and negative" ones, which lead to "pure circles and empty words" (Crusius 1745, § 8).

For a correct understanding of metaphysics, Crusius argues, we should moreover admit that we cannot rely exclusively on proofs and demonstrations: on the one hand, because of the limited character of our intellect, and on the other hand, because we are also dealing with concepts that stem from experience and do not rely on the principle of contradiction alone. As soon as we leave the realm of possibility and make use of the principle of sufficient reason or of another fundamental principle, probability must be considered as satisfying and sufficient. Nevertheless, he holds, metaphysics should be regarded as capable of attaining certainty because "[c]ertainty is simply something in the intellect" [*Gewissheit ist bloss etwas im Verstande*] (Crusius 1745, § 10). Thus, Crusius disjoins certainty from necessity: not only does necessity belong to the thing [*Sache*] and certainty to our mind, he contends, but we are apt to reach certainty even if we do not have a distinct insight into the necessity of a thing or state of affairs.[12] Therefore, not strictly dependent on necessity and demonstration, as Wolff and his school advanced, certainty is perfectly compatible, on Crusius' account, with probability. This is a crucial statement for the decades to come, and especially for the 1763 prize essays.

While a detailed account of his rich and subtle analysis of probability developed in chapter 9 of the *Outline*, is beyond the scope of this essay, Crusius' notion of "moral certainty" (Crusius 1745, §§ 360–361) must be mentioned here, because it will directly influence Kant's *Inquiry*. Experience provides only probable knowledge, according to Crusius, but we can sometimes be certain of it even if its opposite can be conceived of and is not contradictory. Probable knowledge (or the knowledge acquired through probability, [*Erkenntnisweg der Wahrscheinlichkeit*]) stemming from experience can be divided into three types: (1) the *verisimile*, which is probable in a narrow sense, that is, more plausible than its opposite; (2) the credible ([*probabile*] or [*glaubwürdige*]), which deserves to be considered true; and (3) the "morally certain," which we cannot consider otherwise than true and certain. Thus, experience can provide a precise kind of knowledge that we take to be certain even if its necessity cannot be demonstrated. Crusius gives the example of the existence of the city of Athens (Crusius 1745, §§ 360–361) and claims that this precise type of certainty founded on experience should be added to the types of certainty grounded on demonstration and analyzed in § 359 of the *Outline*.[13]

---

[12] "Eine deutliche Erkenntniß der Notwendigkeit einer Sache giebt zwar eine Gewißheit; aber es folgt nicht umgekehrt, daß man nicht eher Gewißheit habe, bis man die Nothwendigkeit deutlich einsiehet" (Crusius 1745, § 10).

[13] Crusius establishes a distinction between geometrical demonstration and what he calls the "disciplinale" demonstration, which he explains as follows: "Dahingegen [haben] die Neuern die Erfahrungen, den Satz von der zureichenden Ursache, und andere Sätze, welche unter den andern und den dritten Grundsatz der Vernunft gehören, in der Demonstration zugelassen [. . .]. Sie haben nemlich wahrgenommen, daß sonsten der Begriff der Demonstration in den Wissenschaften, welche reale Objecte, und nicht bloß mögliche Begriffe, z. E. Grössen, betrachten, nicht nützlich werde; und daß doch, wenn man ihn nützlich machet, der Gewißheit nicht nothwendig etwas abgehe, sondern nur dasjenige beobachtet werde, was die Natur solcher Objecte nicht anders leidet" (Crusius 1747, § 521).

A decisive element of Crusius' doctrine becomes manifest in this account, namely the fact that truth is founded on a *datum* of "inner sensation" [*innerliche Empfindung*] (Crusius 1745, §§ 8, 16; Crusius 1747, § 172), also called the "highest mark of truth" [*obersten Kennzeichen der Wahrheit*] (Crusius 1745, § 15). It is this inner conviction that tells us that "that which cannot be thought otherwise than true is true," while "that which cannot be thought otherwise than false is false (Crusius 1747, §§ 256, 261; cf. Crusius 1745, § 15). Interestingly, he explicitly associates logical or abstractive distinctness with a finer and more accurate inner sensation.

In a similar way, Crusius grounds the other ontological principles in the essence of the intellect [*Wesen des Verstandes*],[14] and justifies this foundation by positing a "natural drive to perfection" inherent to our soul, of which the "drive to truth" [*Wahrheitstrieb*] is a consequence (Crusius 1747, § 256). The principle of sufficient or determining reason applies to existing things, but the three "highest" principles apply to both possible and actual or existing things: the principle of contradiction, the principle of inseparables ([*Grundsatz der nicht zu trennenden*]: that which cannot be thought without each other, can neither exist without each other), and the principle of incompatibles ([*Grundsatz der nicht zu verbindenden*]: that which cannot be thought with each other or next to each other, can neither be with or next to each other). Even if Crusius hereby maintains the homogeneity between the ontological and epistemological realms by positing that the same principles apply to both domains, he emphasizes the foundational role of the intellect with respect to principles. To these fundamental principles, he adds not only the principle of sufficient or determining reason, but also numerous "material" principles involved in the cognition of existing beings and indemonstrable by our intellect (Crusius 1747, § 259). He highlights in his treatises the importance of experience, of the actual [*wirklich*] and the given, as well as the limitations of our cognitive powers – a rather common theme at the time. Nevertheless, his appeal to experience is not grounded on induction, but mostly on an abstractive and analytic procedure, as we have seen, and his emphasis on "inner sensation" does not testify to an empiricist commitment as such, his standpoint remaining within a ra-

---

14 "[W]as sich nicht ohne einander denken läßt, das ist auch in der That mit einander verbunden: Man kan diesen den Grundsatz des nicht zu trennenden nennen. Und was sich nicht mit und neben einander denken läßt, das kan auch in der That nicht mit einander verbunden werden; Dieses kan der Grundsatz der nicht zu verbindenden heissen." (Crusius 1745, § 14). See also Crusius 1745, § 15: "Das allerhöchste Kennzeichen aber, der möglichen und wirklichen Dinge, ist das Wesen des Verstandes, daß nehmlich dasjenige nicht möglich oder wirklich sey, was sich nicht also denken läßt; und daß hingegen dasjenige möglich sey, was sich denken läßt; dasjenige aber gar nicht wirklich sey, bey dessen Leugnung man mittelbar oder unmittelbar etwas zugeben müßte, was sich nicht als wahr denken läßt [...]."

tionalist framework. Despite this fact, his methodological views will have a large echo up to the 1760s, and this especially in a context where the new physics and empiricist theses were favored. The significance granted to inner experience as a criterion of truth, however, will turn out to have a mixed reception and even be contested, notably in Kant's pre-critical philosophy.

4 Kant's Preisschrift on Distinctness

Kant's prize essay titled *Inquiry Concerning the Distinctness of the Principles of Natural Theology and Morality* [*Untersuchung über die Deutlichkeit der Grundsätze der natürlichen Theologie und der Moral*], written in all likelihood during the last weeks of 1762, expresses his clearly anti-Wolffian convictions. Despite a hasty drafting, it summarizes a methodological perspective that had been long in the making and articulates the defining arguments of Kant's philosophy circa 1762–1764, thus belonging to a group of closely related writings whose chronological ordering remains controversial. Kant once again sides here with doctrines opposed to the Wolffian school, namely to the use of the mathematical method in philosophy (see Hinske 1998, 108–111). He shows a deep concern for the question of method, in which he had placed for more than a decade the only hope of "saving" metaphysics from the serious crisis it was going through.[15] While other influences are undoubtedly relevant for Kant's methodological position – such as the perspective promoted by the Berlin Academy (cf. Campo 1953, 312 sq.) – it is the role played at the time by Crusius' conception that seems particularly significant and will be addressed in the following sections.

Kant had been reading Crusius' works for at least a decade, without however abandoning all critical distance. Even if his admiration for the latter would not pass the test of Kant's mature philosophical thought, it is indisputable that Crusian philosophy was still decisive for Kant in 1762, and some of Crusius' intuitions would prove consequential in the elaboration of central critical theses. Kant came fairly early into contact with his writings: by 1755, he had closely read a Crusian text published in Leipzig in 1743, *Dissertation on the Use and Limits of the Principle of Determining Reason, Commonly Called Sufficient Reason* [*Dissertatio philosophica de*

---

[15] See Kant's letter to Lambert from December 31, 1765 (AA 10: 55–61). Lambert, who wrote a draft in response to the prize question but did not send the essay, told Kant "The method that your writings exhibit, sir, is undeniably the only method that one can use with security and progress" (Letter to Kant, February 3, 1766, AA 10: 63). Lambert's essay was published by K. Bopp in 1918 under the title *Über die Methode die Metaphysik, Theologie und Moral richtiger zu beweisen*. I use the English translation provided in Walford/Meerbote 1992.

usu and limitibus principii rationis determinantis, vulgo sufficientis]. The *New Elucidation of the First Principles of Metaphysical Cognition* [*Principiorum primorum cognitionis metaphysicae nova dilucidatio*] (1755) discusses in detail the theses developed by Crusius in this essay and takes up the criticism of the supremacy of the principle of contradiction in Wolffian philosophy. At the beginning of the 1760s, Kant also became aware of Crusius' main treatises, that is of his *Ethics* [*Anweisung vernünftig zu leben*] (Leipzig, 1744), *Metaphysics*, and *Logic*.

In a 1760 letter to L. E. Borowski,[16] Kant wrote that he wanted to keep for some time the copy of Crusius' *Metaphysics* that Borowski had lent him, in order to read it more thoroughly before purchasing his own copy. It is thus legitimate to situate in the early 1760s the more attentive reading of Crusius' treatises and closely link the development of Kant's reflection of the time to certain central theses encountered there. Crusius' thought was familiar to Kant thanks to the previous reading of the *Dissertation on the Use and Limits of the Principle of Determining Reason*, but the overall picture and the finer details of his conception became accessible to him only from 1760 onward. His admiration for Crusius was still intact in 1762, and Kant, who in the *New Elucidation* and in later works used to call him "the celebrated Crusius" (see, for instance, AA 1: 393, 396, 397; AA 2: 168), "the most distinguished and penetrating Crusius" (AA 1: 398, 405), "this great man," one of the "most penetrating philosophers of our time" (AA 1: 128), pays him homage in the *Inquiry*:

> I have deemed it necessary here to mention the method of this new philosophy. It quickly became so famous and it has been so widely admitted to have been instrumental in clarifying many of the things we know that it would have been a major omission not to have mentioned it in a work which is concerned with metaphysics in general. (*IC*, AA 2: 293)

The very core of Kant's argumentation about philosophical method and the certainty attainable in metaphysics is related to the Crusian approach. Kant establishes a real kinship with his predecessor:

> I shall briefly indicate the true character of the first fundamental truths of metaphysics; at the same time, I shall offer a brief account of the true content of Crusius' method, which is not as different from that of the philosophy contained in this treatise as may, perhaps, be thought. (*IC*, AA 2: 294)

Indeed, he invokes Crusius in the last paragraph of the third reflection devoted to metaphysical certainty and chooses to present his own conclusions in a double movement of endorsement and revision of Crusius' theses. In the introduction

---

[16] Letter to Ludwig Ernst Borowski, June 6, 1760 (AA 10: 33).

to his *Inquiry*, Kant sets himself the goal of showing "the true degree of certainty to which [metaphysics] may aspire, as well as the path by which the certainty may be attained" (*IC*, AA 2: 275). The method he wishes to establish is meant to achieve the highest possible degree of certainty in metaphysics and is regarded as an essential condition to fully grasp "the nature of this kind of conviction [*Überzeugung*]" (*IC*, AA 2: 275). As we can see, from the very first lines we come up against an ambiguity that will remain constant throughout the text: is metaphysical certainty (or philosophical certainty – Kant will unify the two) different in *kind* from other types of certainty, or only in *degree*?

To articulate this new method, which he considers apt to "unite reflective minds in a single effort" (*IC*, AA 2: 275), Kant implicitly appeals to two fundamental theses of Crusius' thought, namely the requirement to rely on the given, that is, on experience, and the conviction of the fundamental limitation of human understanding, incapable of grasping reality in its ultimate determinations. Kant presents his methodological reflection as grounded only on principles which he regards as "assured, based on experience and on the consequences which immediately follow." The first step he takes is to carefully distinguish between the method proper to mathematics and the method suitable for philosophy, since, Kant argues, "nothing has been more detrimental to philosophy than mathematics, and in particular, the imitation of its method in contexts where it cannot possibly be employed" (*IC*, AA 2: 283). In order to illustrate this radical heterogeneity, Kant makes a detailed comparison between the two disciplines and their specific procedures, a comparison that presents an obvious kinship with the paragraphs devoted to this question in Crusius' *Metaphysics* (Crusius 1745, § 115) and *Logic* (Crusius 1747, § 10).

5 Philosophy and Mathematics

The differences between philosophy and mathematics are deemed "substantial and essential" (*IC*, AA 2: 280, 283) and they concern the acquisition of knowledge, the specific object and task of each science, as well as the features of the certainty that they can attain. On Kant's account, mathematics constructs its concepts through arbitrary combination and starts with the definition, which gives the concept of the object. Philosophy, on the contrary, where the concept of a thing is given at the outset but "confusedly or in an insufficiently determinate fashion", proceeds by abstraction "from knowledge that analysis has made distinct" (*IC*, AA 2: 276). Thus, the proper task of philosophy is to render given concepts determined and complete through analysis; the task of mathematics, whose approach is synthetic, is to combine and compare constructed concepts of magnitude in order to establish what can be further inferred. Mathematics uses signs instead of things and considers universal rules *in concreto*, while philosophy uses words and represents the universal *in abstracto*; it focuses on the "thing itself." In mathematics, there are very few, if any, unanalyzable concepts, because the mathematician "defines by arbitrary combination, and the thought of that object first becomes possible in virtue of that arbitrary combination" (*IC*, AA 2: 280). The approach is entirely different in philosophy and necessarily presupposes analysis. In the analysis of a confusedly-given concept, philosophy inevitably arrives at a considerable number of concepts that are unanalyzable or partially unanalyzable, and the indemonstrable propositions which constitute its foundation as a science are also infinite. In mathematics, on the contrary, there are only a few indemonstrable propositions, Kant argues. Philosophy deals with *data* that the intellect perceives immediately and that serve to form a primitive, indemonstrable judgment. The studied object is likewise distinct: in mathematics, it is magnitude (*IC*, AA 2: 282), in philosophy, quality. "There are infinitely many qualities which constitute the real object of philosophy, and distinguishing them from each other is an extremely strenuous business" (*IC*, AA 2: 282).

On Kant's account, the method that allows philosophy to achieve the highest possible degree of certainty is based on two rules: (1) one should never start with definitions, but first seek in the given concept what one is immediately certain of, draw conclusions from it and acquire true and certain judgments; and (2) what is known as certain must be distinguished from other cognitions: immediate judgments about the object must be "distinguished" by relating them to what was first encountered as certain in it, and these judgments should become the foundation of further inferences (*IC*, AA 2, 285).

Kant advances here an analytic process inspired explicitly not only by Crusius, but also by the Newtonian method, an exemplary methodological paradigm in the eighteenth century: "The true method of metaphysics is basically the same as that introduced by Newton into natural science" (*IC*, AA 2: 286). "Likewise," metaphysics, defined as "a philosophy which deals with the first foundations of our knowledge," must ground its approach, according to Kant, on experiential data. It must seek, by a "certain" or "immediate and self-evident inner consciousness" (*IC*, AA 2: 286), the marks of the given concept. Even if the nature or complete essence of a thing may not be grasped by our finite understanding, these marks are sufficient to allow reliable further inferences about the thing itself.

Mathematics and metaphysics are undoubtedly two distinct sciences, each with its specific object and method. Kant consequently denies the universal character of the demonstrative method and supports the possibility of scientificity independently of demonstration. Nevertheless, the relationship between philosophy and mathematics remains ambivalent in the *Inquiry:* even if Kant argues for the heterogeneity of these two sciences and philosophy is associated with physics on account of the role conferred to experience and data, mathematics continues to embody the ideal and the model of scientificity.[17]

6 The Ambivalent Role of Crusius' Methodology: the Theory of Principles

The question of the general or rational principles on which metaphysical certainty is based is treated by Kant in close connection to Crusius' position. In line with Crusius, Kant disputes the pre-eminence of the principle of contradiction and holds that there are two formal principles which "together constitute the supreme universal principles, in the formal sense of the term, of human reason in its entirety" (*IC*, AA 2: 294): the principle of identity for affirmative propositions, and the principle of contradiction for negative propositions. To these, Kant adds what he calls, following Crusius, *material* principles – and it is here that Crusius' valuable contribution is most evident. Material principles are defined as indemonstrable propositions, they are said to be very numerous and immediately subsumed under the first formal principles. Moreover, they constitute "the foundation of human reason and the guarantor of its stability." They provide, on Kant's account, "the stuff of definitions and, even when one is not in possession of a definition, the *data* from which conclusions can be reliably drawn" (*IC*, AA 2: 295).

In the third consideration dealing with the nature of metaphysical certainty, Kant defends three theses: metaphysical certainty (1) is of a different nature than mathematical (geometrical) certainty, but (2) can attain the same degree as the certainty of the fundamental truths of rational knowledge in general, and (3) is sufficient to produce conviction. Without endorsing the rather elaborate classification of certainty in Crusius' *Logic*, Kant adopts its central statements. He agrees with Crusius (Crusius 1745, § 234) that, despite a clear difference in kind, philosophical certainty is just as "assured" and "complete" as geometric certainty. Even the negative Kantian definition of certainty is inspired by the negative form proposed by Crusius: "One is certain if one knows that it is impossible that a cognition should be false" (*IC*, AA 2: 290).

For all these reasons, Kant insists, including the means by which we attain it, mathematical certainty is different in kind from metaphysical certainty (see, for example, *IC*, AA 2: 290–291). Less intuitive, using general and abstract concepts, and built on confused given concepts, metaphysical certainty is more difficult to

---

[17] On mathematics as *Wissenschaftsideal*, see Engfer 1982, 55–51.

achieve and more prone to error. Kant presumably attempts here, even if still hesitantly, to shield certainty from a conviction understood only in a subjective, psychological way. It is through "rational," "general" principles that metaphysics can be certain, and experience is said to provide many examples.[18] However, because of the limitation of our intellect, caution is needed: one must never venture to judge and give definitions hastily, but must seek certain and distinct knowledge.

After having established the radical distinction of the methods, tasks and objects in mathematics and philosophy, and argued for the specificity of the proper philosophical method, Kant thus concludes in a somewhat puzzling way that certainty in each of these sciences can attain the same degree. He holds that the formal and material *grounds* of certainty are not "different in kind" in metaphysics and geometry: the formal element is governed in both sciences by the principle of contradiction, and both sciences ground their inferences on indemonstrable foundations which are equally certain: mathematics on definitions, metaphysics on indemonstrable propositions which "provide the primary data." This is why, on his account, the certainty in both sciences "may be just as great" (*IC*, AA 2: 296) and suffices to produce conviction:

> Metaphysics therefore has no formal or material grounds which are different in kind from those of geometry [...]. Metaphysics is as much capable of the certainty which is necessary to produce conviction as mathematics. The only difference is that mathematics is easier and more intuitive in character." (*IC*, AA 2: 296)

It seems, nevertheless, that in the last statement, Kant weakens the difference between metaphysical certainty and mathematical certainty, a difference that he had attempted to argue for throughout the *Inquiry*. Still captive of his admiration for Newton and for the mathematical model, Kant remained convinced that mathematical certainty is the scientific ideal to be pursued in all domains. At the point in which he postulates the radical distinction between the logic realm and reality, between the possible and the actual, and regards the proper philosophical method as the only way to save metaphysics, Kant seemingly still hesitates. I believe, however, that Kant endorses here Crusius' understanding of certainty: independent of necessity or demonstration, certainty is said to be attainable in other sciences than mathematics because it ultimately belongs to the intellect. The means to achieve it might be different, but its degree can be the same, as is its result, namely conviction. Nevertheless, the absence of Crusius' nuanced division of certainty which takes into account the distinction between metaphysics and math-

---

[18] On the question of experience in the *Inquiry*, see De Boer 2021.

ematics, prevents Kant's conclusion in this respect from being fully consistent and coherent with his claims about the specificity of the philosophical method.

Similarly, in the end, Kant's methodological position seems to lack clarity and to fail to advance an uncompromising solution. In the conclusion to the second reflection, he apparently maintains an undecided use of the synthetic method in metaphysics, even if he clearly advances the epistemic primacy of analysis. In a controversial statement that echoes Crusius' views on the collaboration between the two main methods, he writes:

> Metaphysics has a long way to go yet before it can proceed synthetically. It will only be when analysis has helped us towards concepts which are understood distinctly and in detail that it will be possible for synthesis to subsume compound cognitions under the simplest cognition, as it happens in mathematics (*IC*, AA 2: 290).

Many commentators consider this passage to prove that Kant fails to set himself free from the rationalist frame of the Wolffian school,[19] despite his ambition to articulate a novel, Newtonian, account of the philosophical method. I rather hold his conclusion on the proper method in philosophy to ironically dismiss the synthetic procedure associated with Wolff's position and to signal the beginning of a new period – and this despite the undeniable influence of Crusius' suggestion to combine both methods. Kant's feelings on the matter are arguably more poignant in the original German: "*Es ist noch lange die Zeit nicht, in der Metaphysik synthetisch zu verfahren.*" Thus, his intention in the *Inquiry* is, in my view, not to complete the analytic method by a synthetic procedure in the future, but, on the contrary, to depart from Crusius' more consensual methodological views by radicalizing their spirit and clearly arguing for analysis – and analysis alone – as the proper philosophical method.

Let us underline, by way of conclusion, a final aspect of the relationship between Kant and Crusius, as it appears in the *Inquiry*. Despite the admiration and praise abundantly displayed and the numerous borrowings, Kant does not consider Crusius' conception a consistent metaphysical theory after all. His verdict is clear: "Metaphysics is arguably the most difficult of all human knowledge, but one has never yet been written" (*IC*, AA 2: 283). What Kant contests in the first place is the relevance of the highest principle that grounds certainty and in fact the whole theory of truth in Crusius's philosophy: "What cannot be thought as other than true is true" (*IC*, AA 2: 294, 295). For Kant, to postulate such a principle amounts to making subjective conviction the criterion of truth, to mistaking a "feeling of conviction" which Kant defines as the "avowal" of the truth of these in-

---

[19] See, for instance, De Vleeschauwer 1962; see also Friedman 1992, 21 (n33).

demonstrable principles for the ground of truth, for "an argument" that establishes the truth of cognitions. Kant agrees with Crusius that the "correctness" of the supreme material principles can be "established by appealing to the nature of our understanding" and also holds that their indemonstrable character means not only that they are immediately thought under the formal principles, but also that "they cannot be thought in any other way" (*IC*, AA 2: 294) and that their status (of supreme material principles) is "obvious to every human understanding" (*IC*, AA 2: 295). Nevertheless, he explicitly rejects Crusius' "highest mark of truth" (Crusius 1745, § 15):

> It is my conviction, however, that a number of the principles adduced by Crusius are open to doubt, and, indeed, to serious doubt. This celebrated man proposes setting up a supreme rule to govern all cognition and therefore metaphysical cognition as well. The supreme rule is this: *what cannot be thought as other than true is true, etc.* However, it can easily be seen that this proposition can never be a ground of the truth of any cognition (*IC*, AA 2: 298).

Regrettably, Kant does not give further details on this point. He merely brings up this issue, but does not insist here on this weakness of Crusius' doctrine – although it is so central that it calls into question the whole edifice – nor does he propose a convincing alternative to Crusius' criterion of truth.[20]

In the following years, Crusius' principle of truth proved to be the main stumbling block which caused Kant to distance himself from his predecessor and adopt an increasingly critical attitude. He would call this rule, almost every time he mentions its author, an "occult quality" invalidating all Crusian logic and justifying the rejection of his position. It was indeed impossible for Kant to endorse, especially in the critical period, a logical conception so decisively based on psychological criteria. Critical remarks against Crusius were to become more and more sarcastic and follow a reverse trend to those about Wolff. Moreover, Kant never chose a Crusian textbook in his teaching, despite the fact that many of the professors at the Albertina based their lessons on Crusius' works. His admiration for Crusius did not survive beyond 1770.

---

20 Contrast with Friedman 1992, esp. 22–24.

Marion Heinz
Johann Georg Sulzer and the Beginnings of Kant's Doctrine of Three Faculties

Abstract: This work takes up the question discussed in older research as to whether Sulzer can be regarded as the inventor of the doctrine of the three faculties and whether he gave the decisive impulse for Kant's doctrine. The publication of Herder's notes on Kant's lectures on metaphysics provides a decidedly improved textual basis for addressing this problem. They enable us to see the significance of Kant's early critique of Baumgarten's doctrine of perfection for the development of his three-part distinction of faculties.

The "excellent and thoughtful" Sulzer (*CPR*, A 741 / B 769); Sulzer, who "among those who have written in prose, [is] almost the only one who has combined intellect with beauty" (Pinder 1998, 313, 345); one "should read Sulzer, and especially his theory of the fine arts" (AA 14: 843) – comments like these from Kant's earliest to his latest writings and lectures show in how much esteem he held Sulzer. There is no doubt, then, that Kant held the philosopher from Berlin in high regard, as shown not least by his sending him his dissertation *De mundi sensibilis atque intelligibilis forma et principiis* (1770). Sulzer's response from December 8, 1770, certainly proves this high regard was reciprocal: The older, more established, man praises the inaugural dissertation saying: "that you [Kant] would give philosophy a new impetus with these concepts" only to add admonishingly: "If you would take the trouble to develop each completely and to show its application in some detail" (AA 10: 111–112).[1] To Sulzer, it obviously seemed as if both were constructing from different sides the same, still wavering a theory of morality. Sulzer continues:

> I would like to know from you whether we can hope to see your work on the metaphysics of morals soon. This work is highly important in the still wavering theory of morality. I have also attempted something of this kind in which I undertook to resolve this question: What is the physical or psychological difference between the soul that is called virtuous and that which is vicious? I have sought to discover the actual predispositions to virtue and vice in the first

---

1 According to a letter to Mendelssohn of April 8, 1766, the *Träume eines Geistersehers* had already have been given to Sulzer: "Ich habe durch die fahrende Post einige Träumerey an Sie überschickt und bitte ergebenst nachdem Sie beliebet haben ein Exemplar vor sich zu behalten die übrige an die Herren: Hofpred: Sack. Oberconsist: R: Spalding. Probst Süsmilch: Prof: Lambert: Prof. Sultzer u. Prof. Formey gütigst abgeben zu lassen." (AA 10: 68)

https://doi.org/10.1515/9783110793857-008

manifestations of ideas and sensations, and I believe that I have undertaken the investigation all the less in vain, since it has led me to rather simple and easily grasped concepts, which can be applied to teaching and education without effort or difficulty. (AA 10: 111–112)[2]

But beyond these expressions of interest and esteem, are there any substantive similarities between Sulzer and Kant? How does Kant relate to Sulzer's philosophy, what was important to him in it, what did he accept and what did he reject?

Early research contended Sulzer influenced Kant primarily in two respects. First, Sulzer's doctrine of the three faculties is said to have provided the decisive impetus for Kant's doctrine of the three faculties of the mind (Palme 1905; Springorum 1929, 20).[3] Secondly, Sulzer's aesthetics is seen as a model for certain elements of Kant's philosophy of the beautiful (Tumarkin 1933; Vesper 2006). Another general point of agreement[4] lies in the two figures establishing a common front against the intellectualism of Leibniz-Wolff's philosophy on the one hand and Hume's skepticism on the other (see Tumarkin 1933, 98–107). For both philosophers, empirical psychology and the anthropological turn that originated around the middle of the eighteenth century were of eminent importance.

1 Baumgarten and the Doctrine of Three Faculties

This paper is devoted to the beginnings of Kant's three-faculties doctrine and will take up considerations from previous studies, which could not be concluded satisfactorily due to the deficient status of the textual corpus. At that time, the resolution of the question of Kant's models for this doctrine was seen as dependent on "the publication of the lectures in the Akademie edition, [where] the material will be made generally accessible in a sufficient manner" (Tumarkin 1933, 59). The pub-

---

2 "Ich wünschte wol von Ihnen zu erfahren, ob wir Hoffnung haben können ihr Werk über die Metaphysik der Moral bald zu sehen. Dieses Werk ist bey der noch so wankenden Theorie der Moral höchst wichtig. Ich habe auch etwas in dieser Art versucht in dem ich unternommen diese Frage aufzulösen: Worin besteht eigentlich der physische oder psychologische Unterschied der Seele die man tugendhaft nennt, von der, die Lasterhaft ist. Ich habe gesucht die eigentlichen Anlagen zur Tugend und zum Laster in den ersten Äußerungen der Vorstellungen und der Empfindungen zu entdecken, und glaube die Untersuchung umsoweniger ganz vergeblich unternommen zu haben, da sie mich auf ziemlich einfache und leicht zu faßende Begriffe geführt hat, die man ohne Mühe und Umwege auf den Unterricht und die Erziehung anwenden kann."
3 Alfred Baeumler disputes Sulzer's influence on Kant on this point. See Baeumler 1923, 134.
4 For a general assessment of Sulzer's importance in the history of philosophy, see Riedel 1994; Proß; Stiening 2004; Zelle 2010; Décultot 2006.

lication of all of Kant's lecture notes that have been discovered [*alle auffindbaren*] – with the exception of a part of the notes on physical geography – puts us in a privileged position. We can see how scanty the material available for those first investigations was, the darkness in which Kant's development lay, from Palme's statement that, despite some hints in the *Critique of Pure Reason*, only Kant's letter to Reinhold from December 28, 1787, should be taken as the "first definite statement by Kant on the threefold division of the faculties" (Palme 1905, 57). That letter clearly states: "For the faculties of the mind [*Gemüt*] are three: the faculty of cognition, the faculty of pleasure and displeasure, and the faculty of desire" (AA 10: 514).[5] With the publication of Herder's lecture transcripts from the years 1762 to 1764,[6] the now available texts promise to shed light on the genesis of this doctrine as these earliest surviving lecture transcripts already document Kant's considerations on an independent capacity for pleasure and displeasure. Given that Sulzer is frequently mentioned in this context, we might also expect to see whether and how Sulzer's doctrine was a model for Kant. However, the editors of Kant's lectures on anthropology, Reinhardt Brandt and Werner Stark, conclude that it was not Sulzer, but Baumgarten who was Kant's source. Kant could not find this "triadic division of cognition, feeling and desire [...] in complete clarity in the empirical psychology of Baumgarten [...], but he could find it in his *Ethica*" (AA 25: XXV; see also Baum 2006). That this structure can already be found in Herder's postscript to Kant's practical philosophy (see AA 27: 1–89) suggests Kant learnt of it through the textbook on which he based his lectures, namely Baumgarten's *Ethics*. This leads them to their conclusion that this doctrine was already "secured as familiar" around this time (AA 25: XXV).[7] This seemingly proved the assumption that Sulzer played a role in the development of this doctrine wrong.

---

5 "Denn der Vermögen des Gemüts sind drey: Erkenntnisvermögen Gefühl der Lust und Unlust und Begehrungsvermögen."
6 First published Irmscher 1964. Now also published as part of the Academy Edition: *Vorlesungsnachschriften Herders: Über Logik* (AA 24: 3–6), *Über Moralphilosophie* (AA 27.1: 3–89), *Über Metaphysik* (AA 28.1: 5–166, 843–849, 850–931), *Über Mathematik und Über Physik* (AA 29.1,1: 49–66, 69–71). One problem – this should be said in advance – is that the Herder postscripts written between August 1762 and November 1764 can hardly be differentiated and dated precisely. For this, see the introduction by Irmscher (1964, 7–14), in particular 12: "Alle Nachschriften, einschließlich des Geographie-Heftes, sind zwischen dem 21. August 1762 und dem 22. November 1764 entstanden, als Herder Königsberg verließ."
7 On Kant's theory of the soul's faculties, see Heßbrüggen-Walter 2004.

The practical philosophy lecture notes that Brandt and Stark drew upon are most likely those from the winter semester of 1763/64, where Kant taught practical philosophy using Baumgarten's *Ethica Philosophica*.[8] We read there:

> 3 main concepts in the soul: (1) Cognition: to hold phenomena before true or false: thus, theoretical philosophy. (2) Feeling presupposes cognition of phenomena of pleasure and displeasure: is mostly new, distinct from cognition: it expresses the relation of an object to all our powers [...]. (3) Desire presupposes both: (a) imagination, (b) reference to desire and displeasure: the particular: (1) the prevision of a possibility through my power. (AA 27: 12)[9]

In fact, this is early evidence for the introduction of a third faculty alongside the two common faculties of cognition [*facultas cognoscitiva*] and desire [*facultas appetitiva*] – although, surprisingly, it is presented without any claim to originality. Kant implicitly applies the distinctions between three different subject-object relations: The object determines the representation and thereby makes it true or false. Accordingly, the ability to know is attributed to the soul. If the object is considered in relation to the "entire powers" of the subject, it appears as pleasurable or unpleasurable. We thus find a separate faculty, distinct from cognition, which merely presents the effect of the object in relation to the "entire powers" of the subject. It is not how the object is that is determined in feeling but rather how it affects the subject. And finally, the subject is conceived as the ground of the object by means of the representation and the feeling of pleasure. However, a functional distinction between the faculties of the soul does not rule out the dependence of one on another. Hence the faculty of feeling is represented as conditioned by the faculty of cognition, and the faculty of desire as conditioned by both the faculty of cognition and the faculty of feeling. The object itself must be cognized in order to be represented in relation to the "entire powers" of the subject and in order to be able to be desired the representation of the object in feeling must be related to the subject and its powers. When Kant states: "What relates to feeling is in general practical: for the sum of the greatest possible pleasure is the ground of all desires" (AA 27: 12),[10] this is *cum grano salis* still compatible with Wolff, but not with the prior def-

---

[8] See Irmscher 1964, 13, 99. For critical comments, see Gerhard Lehmann's *Kommentar* in AA 27: 1046–1049.

[9] "3 Hauptbegriffe in der Seele: (1) Erkenntnis: Phaenomena vor wahr oder falsch halten: so die theoretische Philosophie. (2) Gefühl sezt Erkenntnis voraus Phaenomena lust und Unlust: ist meistens neu, von Erkenntnis unterschieden: es drukt die beziehung eines Gegenstandes auf unsere Gesamte Kräfte aus [...]. (3) Begierde sezt beides voraus: (a) Vorstellung, (b) beziehung auf lust und Unlust: das besondere: (1) die Praesvision einer Möglichkeit durch meine Kraft."

[10] "Was beziehung aufs Gefühl hat ist allgemein praktisch: denn die Summe der gröstmöglichen Lust ist der Grund aller Begierden [...]."

inition of feeling as a faculty that renders the presentations of the object accessible only with respect to their effect on the subject.

Nevertheless, we can ask whether Kant could have adopted this doctrine in empirical psychology from Baumgarten. At first sight, it seems unlikely that this idea originated from Baumgarten because it can be found neither in the *Metaphysics* nor in the *Ethics* [*Ethica philosophica*]. It can be maintained in support of the thesis of Kant's dependence on Baumgarten that this threefold structure is less clear in empirical psychology, which is a part of Baumgarten's metaphysics, than in his *Ethica philosophica*. This means it is also present in empirical psychology, just it is not so easily recognizable there (see AA 25: XXV). It should be noted, however, that the chapter on pleasure and displeasure in Baumgarten's *Metaphysics* is entitled *facultas appetitive* (see Baumgarten 1779, synopsis).[11] As in Wolff, it is thus integrated into the investigations of the faculty of desire, which already speaks against the plausibility of assuming that Kant simply adopted the doctrine from Baumgarten. However, Baumgarten's *Ethica philosophica* supposedly provides the main testimony to this: It "discusses in the field of duties towards oneself first the *'cura intellectus'* (§§ 221–225), then the *'cura voluptatis et taedii'* (§§ 226–234) and afterwards the *'cura facultatis appetitivae'* (§§ 235–241) [...]; the arrangement in the 'Synopsis' proceeds differently, giving the usual dichotomy of *'facultas cognoscitiva'* and *'appetitiva'* and assigning to the latter – as usual – *'voluptas'* and *'taedium'*" (AA 25: XXVI, note 2).[12] The threefold structure of duties towards oneself thus bears the entire burden of proof for the thesis of the existence of a threefold doctrine in Baumgarten. However, the stated discrepancy between text and synopsis is not of any substantive relevance. This is merely due to the trivial fact that certain levels of the subheadings in the synopsis are not included in the text. Apart from these questions of arrangement and structure, it should be noted that Baumgarten nowhere speaks of a *facultas voluptatis et taedii* analogous to the faculties of cognition and desire. Baumgarten also does not speak of a *sensus*

---

[11] If one can speak of a special position of the chapter on pleasure and displeasure, then this is only insofar as it is placed before the discussion of the individual *facultates* of the faculty of desire – *inferiores* or *superiores* – and thus belongs to the empirical psychology of the faculty of desire "*in genere*" and not "*in specie.*" In Wolff's empirical psychology, the chapter on desire and displeasure is the first subchapter of *De Facultatis appetendi parte inferiori*, see Wolff 1738a, 387–440.

[12] It "erörtert im Bereich der Pflichten gegen sich selbst zuerst die 'cura intellectus' (§§ 221–225), sodann die 'cura voluptatis et taedii' (§§ 226–234) und danach die 'cura facultatis appetitivae' (§§ 235–241) [...]; anders verfährt die Gliederung in der 'Synopsis,' die die übliche Zweiteilung von 'facultas cognoscitiva' und 'appetitiva' vorsieht und der letzteren – wie üblich – 'voluptas' und 'taedim' zuordnet [...]."

voluptatis et taedii.¹³ Pleasure and displeasure are ontologically determined exclusively as a condition, or status, of the soul (see Baumgarten 1779, § 655).¹⁴ According to Baumgarten, these specific states of the soul arise *ex intuitu perfectionis or imperfectionis* (Baumgarten 1779, § 655). And like other states of the soul, these can also be sensed (Baumgarten 1779, § 655).¹⁵ But this obvious does not require Baumgarten to claim there is a special faculty that is related to these states alone. Hence, we cannot say that Kant simply discovered this doctrine in Baumgarten. And differences between Baumgarten and Kant clearly emerge when we look more closely at the passage from the empirical psychology that Kant discusses. For Baumgarten, pleasure and displeasure are determined as states of the soul that arise from intuition,¹⁶ that is, they arise from vague notions of perfection or imperfection and are thus conditioned and determined by properties of the object. However, Kant, as indicated in Herder's postscript to practical philosophy, thought that pleasure is a way in which the subject is determined that is completely independent of the objective determinations of the object (see AA 27: 12).¹⁷ This claim has no equivalent in Baumgarten's philosophy.

2 Sulzer's Theory of Delight [*Vergnügen*]

Sulzer's great achievement is considered to be the subjectification of pleasure and displeasure and the liberation of these phenomena from the intellectualism of Wolffian philosophy. And according to older scholarship, this "making the emotional function independent" (Palme 1905, 41) suggests Sulzer is the decisive model for Kant's doctrine of the three faculties. For instance, after a detailed discussion of other possible sources, Palme claims that Kant was neither driven to the tripartite division by Tetens' conception of the faculty of feeling nor by Mendelssohn's doctrine of the faculty of approval, "but by adopting Sulzer's opposition be-

---

13 But Leibniz does say *"voluptas est sensus perfectionis,"* see Letter to Wolff from 21 February 1705 in Gerhardt 1860, 18; see also Schwaiger 1995.

14 For the concept "status," see Baumgarten 1779, § 205. Meiers' translation of § 655 is unclear: "Der Zustand der Seele, welcher aus dem Gefallen entsteht, ist das Vergnügen [*voluptas*], welcher aus dem Missfallen entsteht, das Missvergnügen (*taedium*)." See Meier 1783, 152, § 482. Pleasure and displeasure are not defined, so the way pleasure and enjoyment are supposed to be different remains an open question. This is especially irritating because Baumgarten uses these expressions synonymously for the state of the soul arising from the contemplation of perfection, see Baumgarten 1779, § 655.

15 Baumgarten translates *sentire* with *empfinden*, see Baumgarten 1779, § 534.

16 For the notion *cognitio intuitive*, see Baumgarten 1779, § 620.

17 It is there stated: "bei einer Art des Erkenntnisses verschiedene Gefühle."

tween cognition and 'feeling'" (Palme 1905, 59).[18] Can this view be maintained in light of the publication of Herder's lecture transcripts? First, let me briefly sketch Sulzer's position.[19] Dissatisfied with Wolff's theory of pleasure (Sulzer 1773, vol. 1, 5; see also Sulzer 1762), Sulzer, in the first part of his *Investigation concerning the Origin of Pleasant and Unpleasant Sensations* [*Untersuchung über den Ursprung der angenehmen und unangenehmen Empfindungen*], outlines a new "general theory of pleasure" (Sulzer 1773, vol. 1, 4) that retains Wolffian principles. This is supposed to indicate the true source of all pleasure for the first time and to be able to derive all the different kinds of pleasure from it as their uniform ground [*Grund*] (Sulzer 1773, vol. 1, 4). On this account, Wolff's empirical psychology, which succeeded in an exemplary way in deriving all the intellectual faculties of the soul from the active fundamental drive, is supplemented – while preserving its systematic unity – by a theory of pleasure (Sulzer 1773, vol. 1, 11). The fruitfulness of Wolff's monistic approach is proven all the more in that Sulzer wants to found pleasure, which is genuinely different from the intellectual faculties, in the soul itself, in its basic power alone. Like Wolff, Sulzer too considers the power of representation [*Vorstellungskraft*] to be the soul's only basic power. This consists in thinking, which means "to bring forth ideas, or, if one wishes, to take up ideas and compare them with each other; that is to think" (Sulzer 1773, vol. 1, 5).[20]

Wolff defines pleasure as "intuiting [*Anschauen*] perfection" (Wolff 1751, § 404),[21] thus delimiting the generic term *representation* [*Vorstellung*] by the two characteristics of perfection as both an object of representation [*Gegenstand der*

---

[18] "[...] sondern durch die Adoption der sulzerschen Entgegensetzung von Erkennen und 'Empfinden' naturgemäß zu der Dreiteilung gedrängt wurde." See also Springorum 1929, 14–19.

[19] Sulzer's progress, which Palme considered so important, between the first *Untersuchung über den Unterschied der angenehmen und unangenehmen Empfindung*. (1751/52; in Sulzer 1773, vol. 1, 1–98) and the later treatise *Anmerkungen über den verschiedenen Zustand, worinnen sich die Seele bei Ausübung ihrer Hauptvermögen, nämlich des Vermögens, sich etwas vorzustellen, und des Vermögens zu empfinden, befindet* (1763; in Sulzer 1773, vol. 1, 225–244) are not considered in the following. Although the later treatise progresses in clarity and precision in many points, it cannot be considered as a central source for the upcoming investigation of the beginnings of Kant's theory of three faculties. While it is certain that Kant knew the first treatise – it is also listed in Warda's book list – no such evidence can be provided for the second treatise. Moreover, it cannot be determined exactly how its date of publication relates to the date of the lectures transcribed by Herder. See Gerhard Lehmann's *Anmerkung* zu AA 20: 137, here 494–495; Rischmüller 1991, 102. See also Reich 2001b, 297. Whether Kant also knew the second treatise is unclear. Extremely illuminating are also the chapters *Empfindung* (vol. 1, 31–36) and *sinnlich* (vol. 2, 1083–1088) in Sulzer 1792–1799.

[20] "Ideen hervorzubringen, oder wenn man will, Ideen aufzunehmen und mit einander zu vergleichen; das heißt zu denken."

[21] For Wolff's account of pleasure, see Schwaiger 1995; see also Vesper 2008.

Vorstellung] on the one hand and intuitiveness [*Anschaulichkeit*] as degree of logical perfection of representation on the other. In short, what defines the conception of pleasure is the specific object qua perfection, understood as "the unity of the manifold" (Wolff 1751, § 152).

Sulzer objects to this: "Unity, diversity, concordance of the parts, make an object pleasant to us only insofar as they have a beneficial relationship to the effective power of the soul" (Sulzer 1773, vol. 1, 39).[22] The determinations of the object, which are accessible to cognition and which qualify it as perfect, are not completely irrelevant, but they become significant only under a certain condition with regard to the excitation of pleasure or displeasure: namely their relation to the "effective power of the soul" (Sulzer 1773, vol. 1, 39) itself. By asserting that the decisive condition for the emergence of pleasure and displeasure is the reference of the object to the activity of the soul, Sulzer postulates a new dimension to the causal relationship as compared with Wolff. Not only does the soul as the power of representation cause all the changes in it (that is, it is the cause of representations), but the representations as the effects of the power of representation in turn have an effect on the activity or action of the soul itself. The promotion or inhibition of the activity of the soul, that is, the change in the degrees of its vividness [*Lebhaftigkeit*], are the second level inner-soul effects that are caused by the representation of objects (see also Sulzer 1773, vol. 1, 1–13, 18–20).[23] Thus Sulzer ascribes a power to the representations themselves. A corresponding capacity to suffer attests to the existence of a power of representation [*Vorstellungskraft*] that is to be fundamentally distinguished from the modifiability of its representations.[24] Sulzer speaks of the soul being irritated,[25] touched,[26] or moved[27] and uses these terms

---

[22] "Einheit, Mannichfaltigkeit, Uebereinstimmung der Theile, machen uns einen Gegenstand nur insoferne angenehm, als sie auf die wirksame Kraft der Seele eine vortheilhafte Beziehung haben." Here the beautiful is being discussed; but as the remarks on p. 22 indicate, this applies generally.
[23] Without considering this new dimension of intrapsychic causality, the difference to Wolff on this point remains unclear. See Stöckmann 2009, 215. Stöckmann points out that Sulzer's program of returning pleasure to the power of representation might well appear to be a kind of radicalization of Wolff's rationalist project.
[24] The power of representation must be considered passive if it is not the sufficient reason for its representations. But this must be distinguished from the aforementioned being affected insofar as it is still a modification of its representation whereas the aforementioned affection reflects a modified degree of its activity.
[25] For "Reiz," see Sulzer 1773, vol. 1, 18; see note 2, 5.
[26] For the notion "rühren" see Sulzer 1773, vol. 1, 22, 97. Sulzer's dynamization of the inner-soul, his modeling of the soul as a space of moving and moving forces, is hardly conceivable without Wolff's new determination of the relationship between psychology and physics (see Sulzer 1773, vol. 1, 4). Sulzer's model of psychology projects an inner-soul dynamic analogous to the interactive

to describe the affections of the soul that while produced by representations [*Vorstellungen*] are nonetheless different from the representations [*Vorstellungen*] themselves.²⁸ In view of this special type of changes in the soul, Sulzer obtains his new definition of pleasure and displeasure as the ways in which the soul is accessible to itself in its effectiveness and through which objects first become experienceable as pleasant or unpleasant.

Terminologically, the difference between pleasure and displeasure on the one hand and representations of objects on the other hand is marked – not always sharply – by the use of the term "sensation"²⁹ for pleasure and displeasure, and the term "representation" for representations of objects (see Sulzer 1773, vol. 1, 12–13, 53). It is already to some extent clear that the specific difference between sensation and representation consists in the difference between the origin of their contents and the reference of the corresponding predicates. The contents of representations are conceived as originating from the object itself and as belonging to it. Sensations, on the other hand, contain something that is grounded in the nature of the subject. What is sensed is how the soul acts. This does not mean, however, that this is a cognition; that is, an objective representation of a special object qua soul. It is clear especially from the later remarks in his *General Theory*

---

relations between bodies: Just as the movement of bodies can be increased or decreased by other bodies, so the activity of the soul is influenced by ideas or representations. The vividness of its activity is an analogue to the speed of moving bodies. See Sulzer 1773, vol. 1, 19. On the relation of psychology and physics in Wolff and also on Sulzer's reference to Wolff's remarks on the concept of velocity in psychology and physics, see Torra-Mattenklott 2002, 71–74, and 118–124. On the paradigm of Wolffian psychology in comparison with Leibniz, see also Engfer 1988.

27 See, e.g., Sulzer 1773, vol. 1, 9–10, 22.

28 In these metaphors, originally taken from rhetoric but transposed by Sulzer into the field of biology, we can detect his perhaps most important role model for his innovations vis-à-vis Wolff, Abbé Dubos (see Dubos 1719). In Sulzer and Dubos, the soul is presented as a living being in need of nourishment: the soul's drive is primarily directed towards activity as such, such that boredom must appear as the greatest evil. See Stöckmann 2009, 220–221. Sulzer's dependence on Dubos and De Pouilly deserves a separate investigation. On De Pouilly and Sulzer, cf. Altmann 1969, 92 ff. See also Bamberger 1929/1971.

29 See Sulzer 1773, vol. 1, 11–14, 22. Unfortunately, Sulzer's first treatise on this subject fails to use terminology precisely and consistently. Hence sensory impression is also called sensation, but the term is mostly used with the qualification "sinnlich" (see Sulzer 1773, vol. 1, 53). "Moralische Empfindung" is used as a translation for "moral sentiment." However, we also find "Empfindniß," a term that goes back to Thomas Abbt (see Sulzer 1773, vol. 1, 89, 92–3). The term representation, which is synonymous with "Handlung der Seele" (Sulzer 1773, vol. 1, 229), is divided in the later notes as a generic term into representation in a narrow sense or cognition and sensation. Sensations are representations which are pleasant or unpleasant or cause desire and disgust.

of the Fine Arts [*Allgemeinen Theorie der schönen Künste*][30] that Sulzer altogether denies that sensations have an intentional object.[31] In other words, they are not representations of the states of the soul in the inner sense. Sensations are modes of experiencing the soul in the light of its disturbed or undisturbed activity.[32] For their part, they may modify the activity of the soul as a promoting or inhibiting impulse.[33] "Sensation is therefore an action of the soul that has nothing in common with the object that produces or causes it. [...] One does not sense the object, but oneself" (Sulzer 1773, vol. 1, 229).

The genus "sensation" is further determined by Sulzer in two respects, namely with regard to the kind and the degree of the soul's activity. The activity of the soul is categorized generically as inhibited or free. This is the reason underlying the division of the generation of kinds of sensation into "pleasant" or "unpleasant" (see Sulzer 1773, vol. 1, 11–12). All differentiations within the species can be acquired through gradual differences. "The very same sensation, depending on whether it is stronger or weaker, is called pleasantness, pleasure, joy, delight" (Sulzer 1773, vol. 1, 11).[34] "Delight [*Vergnügen*] is distinguished from mere contentment" by its greater degree of vividness [*Lebhaftigkeit*] (Sulzer 1773, vol. 1, 11).[35]

But it is questionable whether we are justified in regarding Sulzer as the originator of the doctrine of three faculties. In my opinion, Sulzer presents a two- and not a three-faculties theory. Sulzer's attempt to distinguish the faculty of sensation

---

[30] See the chapter *Empfindung* in Sulzer 1792–1799, vol. 1, 312–316. . See also the chapter *sinnlich* in Sulzer 1792–1799, vol. 2, 1083–1088.

[31] See also Barth 2010, 193, where Sulzer's contribution to the development of the doctrine of three faculties is also mentioned.

[32] The way the soul relates to its sensations is sometimes referred to by Sulzer as sensing (Sulzer 1773, vol. 1, 18, 59). Sensations are not *eo ipso* conscious, but they can be made conscious, brought to the center of attention or remembered. It is also possible for one sensation to give rise to another.

[33] In the chapter *sinnlich* in the *Allgemeinen Theorie der schönen Künste*, the reference to the subject defining the sensation is understood more concretely as "approaching" in a double sense: the sensations are directed towards the changed state of our own power brought about by agitation, either in such a way that we enjoy it, i.e., would like to remain in it, or in such a way that we dislike it, and would like to leave it. The consciousness of this effect also approaches this effect in the sense that it expresses itself effectively – as persistence or change of the state. "Hier ist uns nichts von uns verschiedenes, nichts als außer uns sich veränderndes gegenwärtig: wir fühlen allein uns selbst; unsere uns gefallende oder missfallende Existenz." Sulzer 1792–1799, vol. 2, 1084.

[34] "Eben dieselbe Empfindung wird, nachdem sie stärker oder schwächer ist, Annehmlichkeit, Vergnügen, Freude, Entzücken genannt."

[35] The relation between comfort [*aisance*] and pleasure from the class of pleasant sensations deserves special attention: If pleasure, in contrast to comfort, is presented as a kind of spiritual desire, it cannot, contrary to how it seems, be qualitatively different from "contemplative" comfort. Pleasure differs from contentment by its degree of vividness. See Sulzer 1773, vol. 1, 13.

from the faculty of imagination is clear. For to assume that the action of the basic force, which is thought to be modifiable through representations, is the origin of sensations of pleasant and unpleasant, means nothing other than to claim an ability to be affected by representations such that through them the subject itself becomes perceptible as modified by its own effects.[36] This remains the case with Wolff's assumption that the power of representation is the basic power of the soul. This latter, however, is claimed to be the origin of sensations and the origin (cf. Sulzer 1773, vol. 1, 18) of representations in a fundamentally different way. Already the title of the later treatise – *Notes on the different state in which the soul finds itself when exercising its main faculties, namely the faculty of imagining something and the faculty of feeling* [Anmerkungen über den verschiedenen Zustand, worinn sich die Seele bey Ausübung ihrer Hauptvermögen, nämlich des Vermögens sich etwas vorzustellen, und des Vermögens zu empfinden] – shows the consistent development of this new approach in terms of a psychology of faculties. As clear as the separation of the faculty of sensation from the faculty of representation is, the later treatise especially also shows that Sulzer advocates a doctrine of two and not of three faculties. The aim of tracing *all* changes of the soul back to these two faculties is stated programmatically, without, however, being elaborated in detail:

> As varied as the effects of the soul seem to be, they all result from the use of two faculties, which are the sources of all its other determinations and changes. One is the faculty of representation, or of knowing the properties of things; the other, the faculty of feeling, or of being moved in a pleasant or unpleasant way. (Sulzer 1773, vol. 1, 225)[37]

He intends to ground the faculty of desire in the faculty of sensation (see Sulzer 1773, vol. 1, 92–93). The *conditio sine qua non* of all practical activities of the soul is the capacity for self-feeling. Whereas the theoretical ideas are "as if outside of us" and "are not accompanied by any consideration of ourselves"; the practical

---

36 It may be doubted whether Sulzer understood the ontological implications of his doctrine, according to which modi of the soul (representations) can cause modi of a completely different kind (degrees of activity of force), which in turn must be able to be represented in some way, without, however, being able to be regarded as caused by the power of representation in the same way as representations. For an analysis of Wolff's and also Kant's theory of faculties, see Heßbrüggen-Walter 2004, for Wolff, see 55–84.

37 "So mannichfaltig auch die Wirkungen der Seele zu seyn scheinen, so laufen sie doch alle auf die Anwendung zweyer Vermögen, welche die Quellen aller ihrer übrigen Bestimmungen und Veränderungen sind, hinaus. Das eine ist das Vermögen, sich etwas vorzustellen, oder die Beschaffenheiten der Dinge zu erkennen; das andere, das Vermögen zu empfinden, oder auf eine angenehme oder unangenehme Art gerührt zu werden."

ideas "are such in us that we do not become aware of them other than with the sensation of ourselves which accompanies their representation" (Sulzer 1773, vol. 1, 234; see also 239).

3 Sulzer and Kant's Theory of Three Faculties

In Herder's transcript of Kant's logic lectures, themselves given following Meier's excerpt from the *Vernunftlehre* (1752) – in WS 1762/63 at the earliest (see Irmscher 1964, 43) – we read the following of Meier under the heading "*Von der Weitläufigkeit der gelehrten Erkenntnis*" in § 41:

> It is a basic impulse of the human soul to expand the field of ideas (Sulzer seeks to make it the first basic impulse) This is different from the other kinds of knowledge. It is not formal, but material. The formal of cognition is very much based on the material. With the less one can do nothing, and thus he lacks major grounds of distinction; one must therefore, *ceteris paribus*, also strive for expansiveness. (AA 24: 6)[38]

With this statement, Kant is obviously referring to (while also cautiously distancing himself from) Sulzer's 1751 academic writing *Investigation concerning the Origin of Pleasant and Unpleasant Sensations* [*Untersuchung über den Ur-sprung der angenehmen und unangenehmen Empfindungen*], in which the soul is defined as an incessant endeavor "that, as it were, sets everything in motion for the production of ideas" (Sulzer 1773, vol. 1, 9).[39] However, around this time Kant already opposed the view that the soul is a power. We accordingly read on a loose page [*lose Blatt*] from the Herder manuscripts the following concerning the *Psychologia rationalis*:

> The Wolfians have falsely asserted that the soul qua *simplex* is merely a power of *repraesentatio*: this arises from the false definition of power: since it is merely a *respectus*, the soul can have many *respectus*, as many are the accidents that cannot be brought back to others [*die*

---

[38] "Es ist ein Grundtrieb der menschlichen Seele, das Feld der Ideen zu erweitern (Sulzer sucht es zum ersten Grundtrieb zu machen) Dies ist von den übrigen Arten der Erkenntnis unterschieden. Es ist kein formale, sondern materiale. Das formale der Erkenntnis beruht sehr auf dem materialen. – Mit desto weniger kan einer nichts machen und also fehlen ihm große Unterscheidungsgründe; – man muß also ceteris paribus auch nach der Weitläufigkeit zu streben."

[39] See also Sulzer 1773, vol. 1, 5: "[U]nd mithin ihre [sc. der Seele] wesentliche Thätigkeit nur in Hervorbringung von Ideen bestehen kann."

nicht auf andere können gebracht werden.]. Presentations and desires are basic powers. (AA 28: 145)[40]

The error in the definition of power implies yet another one, namely making a certain, special effect of the soul into its general essence. And this is obviously also the case with Sulzer. It is thus clear that Sulzer's attempt to establish a general theory of pleasure on the basis of Wolffian monism in psychology is not compatible with Kant's views (see AA 27: 4). Around this time, Kant already had an independent doctrine of feeling, understood as the faculty of pleasure and displeasure, which is not coincidentally presented in the most detail in his critical discussion of Baumgarten's doctrine of the *iudicium* in sectio IX of the empirical psychology. For Kant's restructuring [*Umbildung*] of the faculties of the mind [*Gemütsvermögen*] takes place within the context of a critique of Wolff's and Baumgarten's metaphysics of perfection.[41] Kant tries to correct the deficiencies in Baumgarten's concept of *iudicium* and in the concept of perfection, which is indispensable to its definition, by taking recourse to the faculty of feeling, which is defined as the faculty of pleasure and displeasure. Insofar as it is on the basis of feeling that a form of judgment genuinely different from logical judgment becomes possible, Kant can also directly say: "Feeling is not to cognize things, but with pleasure etc., not *facultas judicandi* (logical) but *dijudicandi*. [...] It is not to explain" (AA 28: 74)[42] – and that means that this faculty is a basic faculty that cannot be traced back to anything else.[43]

---

40 "Die Wolfianer haben falsch behauptet, daß die Seele qua simplex bloß eine Kraft der repraesentatio sei: Dies entsteht durch die falsche Definition der Kraft: da sie bloß ein respectus ist, so kann die Seele viele respectus haben, so vielerlei die accidentien sind, die nicht auf andere können gebracht werden. Vorstellungen und Begehren sind Grundkräfte."
41 Unfortunately, I could not take into account Dieter Henrich's paper (1963) which only came into my hands after the completion of this contribution. Henrich shows that Kant's "früheste Ethik" can only be understood against the background of his criticism of Leibniz's conception of theodicy in the *Einzig möglichen Beweisgrund zu einer Demonstration des Daseyns Gottes* and his resulting revisions of Wolff's and Baumgarten's metaphysics of perfection. Henrich's reconstruction of the beginnings of Kant's independent ethics predates the publication of Herder's lecture transcripts; however, they are fully confirmed by the evaluation of these texts begun here, which does not concern the genesis of Kant's ethics. Henrich's contribution deals more thoroughly than was possible here with the theological and ontological foundations for Kant's critique of Wolff-Baumgarten's conception of perfection; one should also refer to the lucid remarks on the moral-philosophical section of the Preisschrift *Untersuchungen über die Deutlichkeit der Grundsätze der natürlichen Theologie und der Moral*. This article is indispensable for reviewing the context in which the early Kant's doctrine of three faculties emerged.
42 "Gefühl ist nicht Dinge zu erkennen, sondern mit Lust etc. nicht facultas judicandi [logisch] sondern dijudicandi. [...] Es ist nicht zu erklären."

In his very first commentary on sectio IX of Baumgarten's empirical psychology, Kant criticizes the one-sidedly intellectualistic treatment of the faculty of judgment: "so far merely theoretical cognition: now to a matter which actually presupposes not only cognition, but also feeling" (AA 28: 73).[44] Accordingly, *dijudicatio* cannot be discussed, as in Baumgarten, as a kind of cognition under the heading *facultas cognoscitiva inferior* (see Baumgarten 1779, § 606; Meier: 1783, § 451). This error has its deeper source in Baumgarten's inadequate understanding of perfection. According to Baumgarten, the defining factor for the act of judgment is the knowledge of things with respect to their perfection or imperfection.[45] And the criterion of perfection is the agreement of the manifold: "when the manifold of a thing is recognized as either coherent or incongruous, its perfection or imperfection is recognized" (Baumgarten 1779, § 452, 139).[46] Kant now criticizes this as a merely formal determination that does not provide "*das materiale, die Vorstellung von dem Einen, wozu zusammengestimmt wird*" (AA 28: 73), and he himself sets out to consider precisely this. Kant then explains, with reference to the use of language, that "we also express perfect by good: it pleases. To examine it more closely: all predicates can be attributed to a thing only the predicate of good and evil merely in relation to conceiving beings" (AA 28: 73).[47]

Perfection is thus made dependent on that which is represented as good by rational beings – be it by God or by other rational beings – that is, it is itself a purpose or good for a purpose. Being good is not a determination of things in themselves, but a determination that is relative to a rational subject and it can only be

---

43 The extent to which Kant prefigures Mendelssohn's doctrine of the faculty of approval in this needs to be investigated separately. See Mendelssohn 1785/1973, 61–240.; see also Mendelssohn 1757/1971, 168, where Mendelssohn already speaks of a basic ability to love and to loathe that is genuinely different from the power of representation. If my view is correct, however, loving and loathing are brought into connection through the operation of comparing, which is similar to judgment, only in the *Morgenstunden* (Mendelssohn 1785/1973, 63). See also Vogt 2005.
44 "[...] bisher blos theoretische Erkenntnis: jetzt zu einer Materie, die eigentlich nicht nur das Erkennen voraussetzt, sondern auch das Gefühl."
45 Baumgarten 1779, § 651, 241: "Per facultatem diiudicandi alicuius vel perfectionem vel imperfectionem percipio [...]." See also Meier 1783, § 451, 139: "Ich stelle mir die Vollkommenheiten und Unvollkommenheiten der Dinge vor, das ist, ich beurteile (diiudicio), folglich habe ich ein Vermögen zu beurtheilen [....]."
46 "[...] wenn das Mannigfaltige einer Sache entweder als zusammenstimmend oder als nicht zusammenstimmend erkannt wird, so wird ihre Vollkommenheit oder Unvollkommenheit erkannt."
47 "vollkommen drücken wir auch aus durch gut: es gefällt: Näher untersucht: alle Prädicate können einem Dinge zukommen nur das Praedicat des Guten und Bösen blos in Beziehung auf vorstellende Wesen." Good and evil are not to be understood here in the restricted moral sense, but in the broad sense of bonum and malum as transcendentals, cf. Baumgarten 1779, § 100.

attributed to things by means of this relation.[48] The determinations that belong to things in themselves can be recognized; but what is good is determined by feeling, which latter is to be distinguished from the cognitive faculty because it is a faculty of pleasure and displeasure. What is good is what arouses pleasure or enjoyment. The concept of the good disappears without representing, sensible beings: "but if he [the human] had no feeling at all, it would not even be possible that something good or bad should be in regard to him" (AA 28: 74).[49]

The dependence of perfection on the concept of the good and the dependence of this on feeling impacts Wolff's and Baumgarten's concept of perfection in that perfection is no longer to be understood as an objective determination of an object accessible to cognition. The perfection of an object rather becomes determinable through the relationship of the object to a subject, to its faculty of desire and to its faculty of feeling. In this way, the relationship stated by Wolff and Baumgarten between perfection and good, as well as that between perfection and pleasure, is turned upside down. The perfection posited with it or through it [*die mit ihr bzw. durch sie gesetzte Vollkommenheit*] defines the goodness of a thing in Baumgarten's ontology: "*Bonum est, quo posito ponitur perfectio. Ergo omne ens est bonum*" (Baumgarten 1779, § 100, 28).[50] The entity is either already a *perfectum* as such in the transcendental or metaphysical sense and, insofar as it contains the reason for this, it is a *bonum* or, insofar as it contributes to the perfection of a being, it is relatively a *bonum* (see AA 27: 5, 16). Kant questions this ontological connection between perfection and goodness, which was established by Leibniz's doctrine of divine choice as the ground of the real world as the most perfect and best. Goodness cannot be defined by an objective determination qua perfection, and it is consequently not an object of knowledge.[51] Inversely, the good, which is to be inferred from sources other than cognition – namely, feeling – makes it possible to determine something as perfect. The purposes of rational beings represent the material unity with which the manifold agrees and that Kant thinks is lacking in Baumgarten.[52] Like the moral sense philosophers, Kant defines the good by re-

---

48 It becomes obvious with the example of the knife as an artifact that its being good can only be determined by its purpose; the purpose is therefore the material unity of perfection that Baumgarten misses – and not the concept, cf. AA 28: 73.
49 "[h]ätte er [der Mensch] aber gar kein Gefühl, so wäre es gar nicht möglich, daß in Ansehung seiner was guts oder böses sein sollte."
50 See also Meier 1783, § 79, 26: "Dasjenige, was so beschaffen ist, daß wenn es gesetzt wird, zugleich eine Vollkommenheit gesetzt wird, ist gut (bonum); folglich sind alle Dinge wesentlich gut."
51 It also follows that volition is not to be determined by the knowledge of the good.
52 Mendelson, against Sulzer, also teaches the necessity of referring to the final purpose of things in order to grasp their perfection, cf. Mendelssohn 1755/1871, 59–60 (5. Brief).

course to pleasure. And this at the same time reverses the relationship between pleasure and perfection as defined by Wolff and Baumgarten. It is not perfection that grounds pleasure, but pleasure is the ground for determining something – actions and characters – as perfect.

By grounding the predication of "perfect" on the basis of the concepts of good and pleasure which are themselves relative to a subject, Kant can also improve upon Baumgarten's doctrine of *iudicium* and can provide the veritable ground of the distinction between judgment and logical judgment. At this time, Kant understood judging as comparing:

> To compare something as a characteristic mark with a thing is *to judge*. The thing itself is the subject; the characteristic mark is the predicate. The comparison is expressed by means of the copula *is* or *are*. When used absolutely, the copula designates the predicate as a characteristic mark of the subject. If, however, it is combined with the sign for negation, the copula then signifies that the predicate is a characteristic mark which is incompatible with the subject. (*FS*, AA 2: 47; Walford/Meerbote 1992, 89)[53]

If the predicates good and pleasurable are not determinations that belong to the thing itself, but can only be attributed to it through its representation related to the subject, the reason for the connection between the subject and predicate concepts cannot lie in the understanding.[54] In so far as the criterion for whether something is a bonum or not ultimately consists in whether it is immediately pleasing, it is feeling that is to be used as the faculty of judging things. "When I consider things in this relation to my pleasure and displeasure: so I do not judge logically, as if I were comparing things with each other, but I predicate things with feeling" (AA 28: 74).[55]

These few hints from Herder's lecture notes on metaphysics correspond to what Kant wrote in the 1764 "*Preisschrift*" on the distinctness of the principles

---

[53] "Etwas als ein Merkmal mit einem Dinge vergleichen heißt urtheilen. Das Ding selber ist das Subject, das Merkmal das Prädicat. Die Vergleichung wird durch das Verbindungszeichen ist oder sind ausgedrückt, welches, wenn es schlechthin gebraucht wird, das Prädicat als ein Merkmal des Subjects bezeichnet, ist es aber mit dem Zeichen der Verneinung behaftet, das Prädicat als ein dem Subject entgegen gesetztes Merkmal zu erkennen giebt."

[54] On the non-logical distinction justified by feeling cf. *FS*, 2: 60; AA 28: 79.

[55] "Wenn ich die Dinge in dieser Beziehung auf meine Lust und Unlust betrachte: so dijudiziere ich nicht logisch, alsdenn vergleiche ich die Sachen untereinander, sondern praedicire die Sachen mit dem Gefühl." See also: "Hätte er aber gar kein Gefühl [...], was guts oder böses sein sollte. – Freuden des Himmels, wenn sie jemand nicht rühren, sind sie auch nicht gut [...]. Kurz dies Gefühl ist nicht Dinge zu erkennen [...], nicht facultas judicandi [logisch], sondern dijudicandi. Es ist nicht [...] Vorstellung selbst, sondern eine Folge etc. [...] kurz man kann sich von der Beschaffenheit der Sache keinen Schluss machen, obs gut sei – es kommt auf die Reizbarkeit der Teile an." (AA 28: 74)

of natural theology and morality [*Über die Deutlichkeit der Grundsätze der natürlichen Theologie und der Moral*],⁵⁶ which was published in the context of his discussion of the first grounds [*Gründe*] of morality. A twofold "ought" is to be distinguished there: "[E]ither I ought to do something (as a *means*) if I want something else (as an *end*), or I *ought immediately* to do something else (as an *end*) and make it actual. The former may be called the necessity of the means [*necessitas problematica*], and the latter the necessity of the ends [*necessitas legalis*]" (*IC*, AA 2: 298; Walford/Meerbote 1992, 272).⁵⁷ While the first necessity refers to rules of skill that are not suitable principles of morality, the second necessity refers to the binding force that is necessary for ethics. In the case of the *necessitas problematica*, the intended is to be obtained through cognition; but where no end is presupposed, the intended is therefore not a means for the attainment of this end. In this case "it is impossible, by contemplating a thing or a concept of any kind whatever, to recognize or infer what one ought to do" (*IC*, AA 2: 299; Walford/Meerbote 1992, 273).⁵⁸ The question of the sources from which the formal rules of the ultimate good ("perform the most perfect action in your power"; see *IC*, 2: 299; Walford/Meerbote 1992, 273)⁵⁹ and the corresponding rule of omission are to be acquired may be left undecided here.⁶⁰ Through an allusion to moral-sense philosophy, Kant makes unmistakably clear that moral philosophy has to appeal to feeling [*das Gefühl*] as the capacity to sense [*empfinden*] the good in order to be able to find the unprovable material principles of practical knowledge: "It is only recently, namely, that people have come to realize that the faculty for representing the *true* is *cognition*, while the faculty for sensing [*empfinden*] the *good* is *feeling*, and that the two faculties are on no account to be confused with each other" (*IC*, AA 2: 299; Walford/Meerbote 1992, 273).⁶¹ As in the lecture notes on met-

---

56 See *IC*, 2: 273–301, in particular § 2. Cf. on this, as well as on Kant's criticism of Wolff's critique of perfection Schmucker 1961, in particular chapter II, 52 ff.
57 "Ich *soll* nämlich entweder etwas thun (als ein Mittel), *wenn* ich etwas anderes (als einen Zweck) will, oder ich *soll unmittelbar* etwas anders (als einen Zweck) *thun* und wirklich machen. Das erstere könnte man die Nothwendigkeit der Mittel (necessitatem problematicam), das zweite die Nothwendgkeit der Zwecke (necessitatem legalem) nennen."
58 "aus keiner Betrachtung eines Dinges oder Begriffes, welche es auch sei, möglich zu erkennen und zu schließen, was man thun solle."
59 "Thue das Vollkommenste, was durch Dich möglich ist."
60 See Schmucker 1961, 73 ff., and his justified dissociating of Kant from Hutcheson concerning this point.
61 "Man hat es nämlich in unseren Tagen allererst einzusehen angefangen: daß das Vermögen, das Wahre vorzustellen, die Erkenntniß, dasjenige aber, das Gute zu empfinden das Gefühl sei, und daß beide ja nicht miteinander müssen verwechselt werden." Hutcheson is explicitly mentioned shortly afterwards (*IC*, AA 2: 300).

aphysics, the good is understood here as a subject-relative predicate. Kant explains the simple concepts of the good and the unprovable judgments formed from them as an "immediate effect of the consciousness of the feeling of pleasure combined with the representation of the object" (*IC*, AA 2: 299; Walford/Meerbote 1992, 273).[62] Hence it is ultimately the pleasure in the representation of the object that decides what is good and it is by means of this that we attain the unprovable material principles of practical philosophy.

In the *Preisschrift* as in the postscripts to the lectures on Metaphysics, "perfect" is a derivative predicate: If an action is immediately represented as good by moral feeling, it is not thought of as a means from which a good different from it can be recognized as its end. This action is not called "perfect," but good in itself. "Perfect" is an action only when it can be derived as a means from an end which is itself analytically contained in it (cf. *IC*, AA 2: 299; Walford/Meerbote 1992, 273). With this restriction of the term "perfect," Kant draws the terminological consequence from his insight [*sachlichen Einsicht*] that Wolff and Baumgarten can only think perfection in the sense of the indirectly good. Hence we read in Herder's postscript to practical philosophy: "[Baumgarten] omits to define [moral perfection], according to the taste of the philosophy of Wolf, which continually based perfection on the relation between cause and effect, and thus treated it as a means to ends grounded in desire and aversion" (AA 27: 16; Heath/Schneewind 1992, 10).[63] As documented in Herder's postscripts, Kant can, however, also speak of moral perfection (see AA 27: 16) as good in itself. But this concept too is to be defined only in relation to the subject.

That the faculty of sensing [*empfinden*] the moral good is not to confused with the faculty of cognition as the faculty of true representations is – as already said – emphasized as being Francis Hutcheson's eminently important discovery, made "only recently," that is, after Wolff. Furthermore, the feeling [*Gefühl*] of the good is indissoluble, that is, it does not allow any reduction to other representations. Moreover, the feeling of pleasure is connected with the representation of an object which, as a moral object, triggers "many simple sensations [*Empfindungen*] of the good" (*IC*, AA 2: 299; Walford/Meerbote 1992, 273)[64] and evil in us. But this is not a faculty of representation akin to the faculty of cognition. Nevertheless, an open question here is whether the first principles of obligation belong to the cognitive

---

[62] "unmittelbare Wirkung von dem Bewusstsein des Gefühls der Lust [verbunden] mit der Vorstellung des Gegenstandes."
[63] "Baumgarten unterlässt es, die sittliche Vollkommenheit zu bestimmen; nach dem Geschmack der Philosophie des Wolf, die stets die Vollkommenheit auf den Respekt zwischen Ursache und Folge bauete und also bloß als Mittel zu Zwecken in Lust und Unlust ansah."
[64] "[...] viele einfache Empfindungen des Guten."

faculty or to feeling [*Gefühl*] as a faculty, which constitutes the first intrinsic ground for the faculty of desire, and thus is also a different faculty from it (cf. *IC*, AA 2: 300). With this two-sided demarcation of the faculty of feeling from the faculty of cognition and the faculty of desire, the published text confirms what could also been seen in Herder's postscripts: In the early 1760s, Kant already has a doctrine of three faculties for which no immediate predecessors can be discerned.

Nevertheless, Kant's lectures on metaphysics confirm a certain proximity to Sulzer with respect to the doctrine of feeling: Their common opposition to the doctrine of pleasure as knowledge of perfection that was advocated by Wolff and his school is obvious. Like Sulzer, Kant separates feeling as a faculty of pleasure and displeasure from the faculty of cognition. "Feeling is the property [i.e., not quality, but *proprium*, attribute] of a being capable of pleasure and displeasure" (AA 28: 78).[65] More precisely, it is a *receptivitas* (see AA 28: 75) of the subject, the faculty of being so moved or irritated by objects as to give rise to a distinct class of predicates that characterize not the things themselves but our "relation to the things" (see AA 28: 99; Mendelssohn 1761/1971, 131–132). For Kant, pleasant and unpleasant, beautiful and ugly, good and evil are predicates that do not belong to the thing in itself, but are attributed to it by means of the reference of the representations to the subject and its capacity to be moved to pleasure or displeasure through them (see AA 28: 66–67, 89). Free actions as the objects of moral philosophy also move the subject to pleasure or disgust. In contrast to the physical feeling, however, moral feeling is general and uniform.[66]

Kant's comments on Sulzer in the Herder post-scripts reveal both sympathy for him personally and agreement with certain aspects of the doctrine of pleasure;[67] but there is nothing to indicate that Sulzer's theory of sensations was the decisive model for Kant's conception of feeling. One of the consequences of Kant's aforementioned skepticism concerning monistic approaches in metaphysics and moral philosophy is that, due to the Crusian premises of his psychology, Kant can-

---

65 "Gefühl ist die Eigenschaft [d.h. hier nicht Qualität, sondern Proprium, Attribut] eines Wesens, das der Lust und Unlust fähig ist."
66 See AA 27: 4; Heath/Schneewind 1992, 4: "Pleasure in free actions directly is called moral feeling. We have a moral feeling, which is (1) universal (2) unequivocal." ["[D]ie Lust an freien Handlungen unmittelbar heißt Moralisches Gefühl. wir haben ein Moralisches Gefühl: dies ist (1) allgemein (2) einstimig."]
67 In particular, Sulzer's achievements in the field of aesthetics as a science of taste are to be appreciated; this discipline analyzes taste understood as "the sensual feeling [...] where the impression touches immediately without judgment of reason" ("das sinnliche Gefühl [...] wo der Eindruck unmittelbar rührt ohne Urteil der Vernunft" AA 28: 75).

not gain anything from Sulzer's innovation that is invoked against Wolff or from Sulzer's explanation of pleasure by way of reference to the being-active of the power of representation. Sulzer's derivation of pleasure from the activity of the power of representation does not meet with Kant's approval: "Sulzer says that what facilitates and promotes the natural efficacy of the soul touches me with pleasure. This says only that it promotes the natural striving after pleasure" (*ROBS*, AA 20: 137; Frierson/Guyer 2011, 158).[68] When an object "moves me with pleasure," it is not the action of the soul understood as the power of representation as a whole that is promoted but rather merely the natural striving for pleasure itself. This means, however, that a special faculty of pleasure has to be always presupposed., to which the striving for an appropriately pleasure-increasing object accords.

As Mendelssohn clearly saw, Sulzer's doctrine of pleasure means an anthropologization and subjectivization of Wolff's metaphysics of perfection, and against this Mendelssohn sought to reassert the objective concept of perfection (see Moses Mendelssohn 1755/1971; Altmann 1971, 102–103). Kant takes a completely different path when he abandons the ontological justification for the good and the pleasurable in an ontology of perfection. This questioning of the Wolffian metaphysics separates being and ought. It accordingly paves the way towards a new moral philosophy that, unlike Wolff's, does not aim at considering the means for promoting the objectively given end of perfection as a doctrine of prudence (see again AA 27: 16).

---

[68] "Sultzer sagt das rührt mich mit Vergnügen was die natürliche Wirksamkeit der seele erleichtert u. befördert. Dieses sagt nur daß es die natürliche Bestrebung nach Vergnügen befordere." See also AA 27: 4; Heath/Schneewind 1992, 3: "(2) It is said that the pleasure we have in [the welfare of others] is merely our own end, and a more refined self-interest. Responsio: the pleasure itself presupposes (1) a power of having it; (2) I cannot explain pleasure by means of pleasure. I will pleasure means, merely: I have pleasure in pleasure, and thus already presupposes a certain feeling. So there are merely lower grades of it." ["(2) sagt man: – Das Vergnügen, waz wir daran haben, ist blos unser Zweck und ein feinrer Eigennutz Responsio das Vergnugen selbst sezt (1) eine Kraft, es zu haben, voraus (2) das Vergnügen kan ich nicht durch Vergnügen erklären. Ich will das Vergnügen: heißt bloß: ich habe Vergnügen am Vergnügen: sezt also ein gewißes Gefühl schon voraus. Dies sind also blos niedrige Ränke."]

Paolo Pecere
Lambert, Kant and Solidity: A Matter of Method

Abstract: Kant's "metaphysics of corporeal nature" in the *Metaphysical Foundations of Natural Science* (1786) introduced new and important methodological insights to Kant's philosophical system. In this paper, I consider Kant's original connection of metaphysical, mathematical and empirical elements of natural science against the background of his earlier connection to Lambert in the 1760s. By focusing on one significant example – the account of "solidity" – I will argue that Lambert's works and his correspondence contain the first position of the problem of a new method of metaphysics of corporeal nature which Kant himself was starting to face at the same time. In this perspective, Kant's solution of the problem in the *Metaphysical Foundations* appears as a late critique and rethinking of Lambert's approach.

1 Introduction: A Matter of Method

Ernst Cassirer pointed out that Lambert had introduced a "peculiar and new point of view in the problem of knowledge," that is, the idea that we can take empirical concepts and then, without questioning their "psychological origin," discover in them "certain universal relations" and thus set the basis for a priori knowledge concerning these concepts (Cassirer 1999, 453). As Lambert puts it, experience "provides at best an occasion [*Veranlassung*], in order to see whether and how far one can prove a priori" (Lambert 1770, § 6).[1] Gereon Wolters has focused on this topic in his seminal study on Lambert's theory of scientific knowledge, maintaining that "as far as I can see, Lambert is the first in the history of exact sciences and their methodology to establish the *program of a protophysical basis*" (Wolters 1980, 85). This program concerns the formulation of definitions and/or postulates concerning the unities of measure in the exact sciences (e.g., extension, duration, mass), leading from the basic sensations corresponding to these magnitudes to the first scientific propositions. For example, Lambert asks "whether the first propositions of mechanics can be proved [*erweisen*] necessarily and a priori, as Euclid has done with regards to the geometrical propositions" (Lambert 1770, § 1). This investigation

---
[1] On the a priori and a posteriori investigation concerning propositions and properties see Lambert 1764, Dianoiologie, § 634–665.

takes place in a section of mechanics that Lambert calls "dynamics," starting from the concepts of "solidity" and "force," and it provides an opportunity to test the limits of Locke's empiricist methodology. "Solidity," listed by Lambert among the *Grundbegriffe* of science, had been already considered by Locke as a simple idea derived from experience. While recognizing the importance of Locke's analysis, Lambert objected that the latter "had looked for the simple concepts, but he missed the application of the method of establishing doctrinal systems [*Lehrgebäude*]" (Lambert 1771, § 14). Locke "proceeds entirely a posteriori" with his "anatomy of concepts" (Lambert 1764, Alethiologie, § 29), and thus misses the a priori moment in the foundations of empirical science, which can be conceived following the model of geometry.

> It seems that he lacked the method, or at least the idea, to try *what the geometers had done with respect to space, in regard to the other simple concepts as well.* (Lambert 1771, § 10; italics mine)

Now, it is well known that Lambert's foundational attempt provided a substantial inspiration for Kant's analogous investigation on the possibility of a metaphysics of nature at the time of their correspondence, between 1765 and 1771, and beyond. Kant himself would recognize the authority of Lambert for the "claims subsequently presented in the *Kritik der reinen Vernunft* in their whole context" (AA 10: 278).[2] Alison Laywine has convincingly argued that Lambert's conception of postulates and their use in the foundations of natural science may have been a model for Kant's transcendental analytics (Laywine 2010). But if we take the cue from the concepts of solidity and force it makes all the more sense to consider Kant's own account of "pure physics" in the *Metaphysical Foundations in the Natural Science* (*MNS*), published in 1786, as a late assessment of the issues formulated by Lambert. Starting from a puzzling reference to Lambert, I will compare both the latter and Kant's accounts of solidity as alternative methodological solutions to the same foundational problem concerning concepts and principles of natural science.

---

2 Indeed, Kant was planning to dedicate the *Critique* to Lambert. See *R* 5024, AA 18: 64: "(for the dedication.) You have honored me with your letters. The effort to provide a concept of the method of pure philosophy at your request has led to a series of considerations, developing the concept that was still obscure to me, and as the prospects expanded with the progress, the answers were postponed indefinitely. This writing can serve as an answer, as far as the speculative part is concerned. As it is due to your requests and suggestions, I wished that it might fully belong to you by endeavoring to incorporate it into your work."

2 Kant on Lambert and Solidity

Kant's critical reference to Lambert's account of solidity appears in the *Remark* to *Theorem* 1 of the "Dynamics" chapter of the *Metaphysical Foundations in the Natural Science*.

> Lambert and others called the property of matter by which it fills a space *solidity* (a rather ambiguous expression), and claim that one must assume this in every thing *that exists* (substance), at least in the outer sensible world. According to their ideas the presence of something *real* in space must already, through its concept, and thus in accordance with the principle of noncontradiction, imply its resistance, and bring about that nothing else can be simultaneously in the space where such a thing is present. But the principle of noncontradiction does not repel a matter from advancing to penetrate into a space where another is found. Only when I ascribe to that which occupies a space a force to repel every external movable that approaches, do I understand how it contains a contradiction for yet another thing of the same kind to penetrate into the space occupied by such a thing. (*MNS*, AA 4: 497–498, the translation of *Metaphysical Foundations of Natural Science* is taken from Friedmann 2004)

The concluding sentence refers to Kant's own alternative view, exposed in the theorem. Rather than to "solidity" (an expression that he considers suitable for "rigid" bodies; *MNS*, AA 4: 527), Kant refers to the empirical property of "impenetrability" [*Undurchdringlichkeit*], manifested by a resistance to penetration [*Eindringen*]. According to the theorem, "matter fills space not by its mere *existence*, but through a *particular moving force*." It is useful to quote Kant's "proof" [*Beweis*] of this theorem, as an example of how he moves from the empirical property of impenetrability to dynamics by means of a priori inferences.

> Penetration into space (in the initial moment this is called a striving to penetrate) is a motion. Resistance to motion is the cause of its diminution, or even of the change of this motion into rest. Now nothing can be combined with a motion, which diminishes it or destroys it, except another motion of precisely the same movable in the opposite direction (Phoron. Prop.) [...] But the cause of motion is called a moving force. Thus matter fills its space through a moving force, and not through its mere existence. (*MNS*, AA 4: 497)

Given the sensory experience of resistance to penetration (empirical element), Kant applies the phoronomical theorem of the composition of motions (mathematical element),[3] thus inferring the need to introduce a cause of this resistance,

---

3 For its proof see *MNS*, AA 4: 490.

which turns out to be, by definition, a moving force.[4] Kant will successively qualify this force as a fundamental repulsive force.

This argumentative context can help us understand why Kant decides to single out Lambert among those who argue for the fundamental solidity of matter. Besides Locke, who was Lambert's source, these "others" include a large number of mechanistic natural philosophers.[5] From the physical point of view, indeed, this conception corresponds to the attribution to matter of an "absolute impenetrability," which is "nothing more nor less than an occult quality. For one asks what the cause is for the inability of matters to penetrate one another in motion, and one receives the answer: because they are impenetrable" (*MNS*, AA 4: 502). Absolute impenetrability, together with "absolute homogeneity," forms the basis of the "mechanical philosophy of nature," which "under the name of *atomism*, or the *corpuscular philosophy*, always retained its authority and influence on the principles of natural science, from Democritus of old, to Descartes and even to our time" (*MNS*, AA 4: 533). This philosophy has the advantage of representing empty spaces and vacuum in bodies with mathematical evidence but pays this advantage with several shortcomings for mathematical physics besides its empty explanation of impenetrability (e.g., it gives too much power to the imagination in positing these empty spaces for the explanation of different densities). Kant's "dynamical mode of explanation," on the contrary, is "much more appropriate and conducive to natural philosophy, in that it leads directly to the discovery of matter's inherent forces and laws" (*MNS*, AA 4: 533), whereby resistance can be traced back to a cause and "estimated in regard to its degrees" (*MNS*, AA 4: 503).

The mechanical philosophy with absolutely hard particles, empty spaces, and no inherent forces could be attributed to major physicists of the time. In the first *Critique*, indeed, Kant writes that this is the way "most mathematical and mechanical investigators of nature" explain different densities (*CPR*, A 173/B 215). These scientists include Newton and Euler, who are often discussed in the *Remarks* of the *MNS*. After all, one of the objectives of Kant's *MNS* was to provide the sketch of a new "metaphysical part" to be included in treatises of mathematical physics (*MNS*, AA 4: 478). It is puzzling, in this regard, that Kant names Lambert in his *Remark* about solidity. As I will argue, this suggests that Kant is raising a *methodological* rather than a *physical* issue, concerning his new conception of a metaphysics of corporeal nature. In order to introduce this argument, let us first consider Lambert's view.

---

[4] For a detailed account of Kant's general methodology in the *MNS* see Pecere 2009, 321–391; Friedman 2013, 1–33, 564–580.
[5] For a list of alternatives see Pollok 2001b, 229–231.

3 Lambert's Principles of Solidity

Lambert's accounts of solidity in the *Neues Organon* and the *Architektonik* present an intertwining of empirical and rational elements, which will form the starting point of Kant's successive rethinking. In the *Neues Organon* Lambert introduces the empirical concept of matter as follows:

> The concept of *matter*, which we have directly through *feeling*, makes us ascribe to matter a *solidity* and *firmness* or *impenetrability*. (Lambert 1764, *Alethiologie*, § 19)

He argues that, given simple concepts, which can be thought for themselves, we can immediately deduce a corresponding set of principles [*Grundsätze*]. In this particular case, we get principles of "solidity" and "force," including the principle stating that "every solid excludes any other solid from the place where it is" (Lambert 1764, *Alethiologie*, § 94). This suggests that the latter principle can be derived by a pure logical inference and thus be grounded on the principle of contradiction.

A similar and more detailed account can be found in the *Architektonik*. Here Lambert lists different *Grundsätze* which can be applied to "material solids" with no contradiction [*ohne Widerrede*]:

The concept of solidity also gives us some principles that are applied to material solids without objection
1. The solid fills a space as far as it can.
2. The solid excludes other solids from the place where it is.
3. The solid has three dimensions of space.
4. Space cannot be more than filled with solid.
5. The solid has an absolute density, and therefore it is a unit that is unchangeable. (Lambert 1771, § 88)

In Lambert's text we find a principle of impenetrability (n. 2 above) and more striking correspondences with Kant's later account:
1. These propositions can be derived by "the collection and immediate comparison [*Vergleichung*] of simple concepts," and thus merely depend on the principle of contradiction. (Lambert 1771, § 76)
2. The term "solidity" has a number of different meanings, including metaphysical ones ("The word *solidity* is already made metaphorical and transcendent in various ways").It can mean "volume" in geometry, "rigidity" in physics and it can also have a metaphorical meaning regarding "scientific" or "grounded" knowledge (Lambert 1771, §§ 92–93). We can even conceive of a "solidity" of spiritual substances, although we don't have any simple concept of the latter

(remember Kant's observation that his principle is valid "at least in the outer sensory world" (Lambert 1771, § 90).
3. The solid has "absolute density" (principle n. 5 above), a claim that will be thoroughly criticized by Kant (see below § 4).

From these close correspondences we can conclude that Kant was taking Lambert's texts in close consideration when he was writing his *Remark*. Hence, we can wonder why Kant examines Lambert's *methodological* works in the *MNS* and why, while focusing on method, he spells out his disagreement with Lambert concerning the physical concept of *solidity* in particular.

4 Solidity from the Physical Point of View

Lambert's systematic treatment of the fundamental concepts of mechanics is better understood against the background of Newton's. In the *Principia mathematica* Newton considers density as an essential property of matter (hence invariable) and derives mass by multiplying density and volume. Force, on the other hand, is a variable quantity and thus no essential property (Newton 1726/1972, 39–40 (Definitiones, I)). Newton then introduces a cinematic measure of force, which is applied to the study of gravity, leaving open the issue of the cause of force (Newton 1726/1972, 298 (Lib. I, Sect. XI, Prop. LXIX, Scholium)). Regarding the resistance to motion (inertial mass) he defines a *vis inertiae* of matter (Newton 1726/1972, 40 (Definitiones, III), cf. Newton 1730/1956, 397 (Query 28)). The ontological relevance of solidity is highlighted in *Query 31* of the *Opticks* (starting from the Latin edition of 1704), where Newton argues that God has created "solid, massy, hard, impenetrable Particles" (Newton 1730/1956, 400). The connections among density, mass, force and solidity require the discussion of a number of different conjectures about ether and microscopic forces, without leading to a conclusive theory: this problematic legacy would be shared by Newtonian scientists of the eighteenth century.

In this context, Lambert submits an empirical foundation of mechanical concepts, arguing that both density (see above) and force depend on solidity, which is in turn given with the sensation of touch. Hence he adds a number of principles of "Dynamics" to the principles of solidity:

> We get this concept [of force], as well as the concept of *solidity*, from feeling, because we feel that we must use more or less *force* to set a body or the solid in motion or to change or completely stop its motion. From this flow the following principles, which [have been] adopted in Dynamics.

1. The solid is in itself at rest, or without motion.
2. The solid is set in motion by another solid.
3. Every change in the movement of the solid is caused by another solid which directly touches the moving solid.
4. In free space, the solid, once set in motion, maintains its direction and speed.
5. The motion is proportional to the force with which the solid is set in motion, and follows the direction in which the force is applied (Lambert 1771, § 94).

To sum up: the sense of touch, by the feeling of impenetrability, is the source of both the concepts of density (and hence mass) and of inertia (the resistance to the impressed motion whose coefficient is mass – our inertial mass). These concepts are sufficient to establish the mathematical analysis of motion, while the first cause of motion is left out of the physical picture. A similar, radically mechanistic system of concepts had been recently defended by Euler: impenetrability is the source of mechanical action in impact or pressure; action is transmitted by impact or pressure according to a coefficient (inertial mass) which can be empirically measured. Force is given by multiplying mass by the impressed acceleration, while the Newtonian expression *vis inertiae* (for inertial mass) has to be avoided (see, e.g., Euler 1736, vol. 1, §§ 56–74). This approach to mechanics, in fact, would be much more successful than the dynamical one entertained by Kant and others. In this perspective, Lambert appears as just one among many mechanistic scientists following Newton and Euler.

But Lambert's account, albeit it does not envisage any repulsive force, shares an element with the Kantian account: Lambert grants that density may have an originally different degree, allowing for the explanation of specific gravity of bodies with no hypothetical dissemination of void in bodies:

> A completely different question that arises here is this: whether a completely filled space could not be even more densely filled, or whether the solid that fills it could be brought into an even smaller space, or whether all solids are equally dense and thus an absolute and unchangeable unit in this regard? These questions relate to the second, fourth, and fifth principles, which are based on the well-known and accepted concept of the impenetrability of matter in mechanics [...]. We obtain the concept of solidity through sensation, and this does not provide us with the internal differences of solidity. In the concept we have of it, there seems to be no impossibility that solids could have different degrees of internal density. (Lambert 1771, § 91)

This alternative theory of density would involve a modification of Lambert's own principle n. 2, which establishes absolute density. In this perspective Lambert appears closer to Kant than the other mechanistic physicists. Indeed, this open-mindedness regarding the explanation of density casts a shadow on Lambert's claim that his axiomatization of solidity is a "grounding principle of metaphysical truth" and possesses "geometrical necessity" (Lambert 1771, § 298, 313). Michael Friedman has argued that this open-mindedness is a reason why Kant singles out Lambert in his defence of the dynamical conception and points out that "this very open-mindedness exposes deep problems and tensions in Lambert's overall view" on the a priori principles, concerning in particular "how such explicitly non-analytical or non-definitional a priori judgments are possible" (Friedman 2013, 128).

I agree with Friedman's suggestion that here Kant's procedure of bringing the concepts of logic "into relation with both pure and empirical intuition" determines the divergence between Kant's and Lambert's views (Friedman 2013, 129). Hence, I conclude that the reason for Kant's choice of Lambert as the first example of a supporter of solidity *cannot* lie in Lambert's physical opinions about density. Kant was rather interested in Lambert's methodological reflection on the intertwining of empirical, metaphysical, and mathematical elements of physics. In order to highlight the points of agreement and disagreement regarding method we need to consider Lambert's and Kant's approach in more detail.

5 Lambert's Method: the Possibility of Concepts and the Role of Examples

Lambert, in his first letter to Kant (1765), notes the "similarity" between the latter's views in the *Beweisgrund* (1763) and his own views in the *Neues Organon* (Lambert 1782, 335). Then he addresses the issue of the method of metaphysics, arguing that Wolff was mistaken in granting a fundamental role to definitions without investigating the possibility of the corresponding objects. A better model is the method followed by Euclid in geometry, where definitions are just a kind of "nomenclature," while the possibility of the corresponding objects (geometrical figures) is merely hypothetical and has to be proved "synthetically:"

> In Euclid, definitions are, as it were, only nomenclature, and the expression *per definitionem* is no more valid for him than the expression *per hypothesin*. *Wolf* also seems not to have noticed enough how careful *Euclid* is, and how he himself arranges the presentation in order to prove the *possibility* of the figures and determine their *limits*. One should not begin with metaphysical concepts if one does not want to get lost and confused in an endless analysis, but rather follow Euclid's method of synthesis. (Lambert 1782, 338)[6]

---

[6] That Lambert considers Euclid, rather than Wolff, as the "true auctoritas" for realizing his foundational project has been highlighted by Basso 1999, in part. 1–2. For the proximity of Lambert's project to the Leibnizian idea of the *ars characteristica* see Pasini 2005.

Kant replies that there was indeed "a lucky agreement in our methods" (Lambert 1782, 341), mentioning the similar role played by constructions in mathematics according to the *Deutlichkeit*. The agreement concerning metaphysics is not clearly spelled out, but Kant mentions his project to write a book on the "proper *Method of Metaphysics*:" this ambitious project is temporarily shelved because he lacks "examples, of how the correct method should work," and he has decided to "give precedence to smaller works." Then he mentions two "ready" writings, the "Metaphysische Anfangsgründe der natürlichen Weltweisheit" and the "metaph. Anf Der praktischen Weltweisheit," which will present examples of the new method. By this separate exposition "the main work will not be burdened with too many and inadequate examples" (Lambert 1782, 342).

Lambert (December 3, 1766) replies that Kant's procedure of introducing the new method by the exposition of positive and negative examples is a good one, and that he has followed the same method in the *Dianoiologie*; for example, in the illustration of the relation between form and matter of knowledge. While these concepts do not raise issues in their logical meaning, when applied in metaphysics they have led to "controversies and hypotheses." In this regard, Lambert submits a number of propositions concerning the transition from simple to complex concepts:

1. Form provides principles, while matter provides axioms and postulates.
2. Form requires starting with simple concepts because they, being simple, cannot have an internal contradiction or be inconceivable in themselves.
3. Axioms and postulates actually only occur with simple concepts, as compound concepts are not a priori conceivable in themselves. The *possibility of composition* must first follow from principles and postulates. (Lambert 1782, 348; italics are mine)

In the following passage, Lambert explains in more detail this transition and the role played by axioms and postulates:

> After these sentences, I have no hesitation in saying that Locke was on the right track in seeking the simple in our knowledge. One must only leave out what is mixed in with the use of language [...] The concept of *duration*, and likewise the concepts of *existence, motion, unity, solidity*, etc., have something simple that is peculiar to them, and which can very well be thought of as separate from the many concepts of relationship that occur with them. They also give *axioms* and *postulates* for themselves, which lay the foundation for scientific knowledge and are absolutely of the same kind as the Euclidean. (Lambert 1782, 349)

According to Lambert, metaphysics begins with simple concepts derived from experience. These simple concepts can be listed in any order ("in the order, in which it occurs to me"), but it is crucial to separate their different meanings and to exclude those who can find no empirical support and are merely suggested by the corresponding word – as we have seen above with "solidity" (Lambert 1782, 349). Here Lambert follows Locke's teaching on language and definitions. Given the refined list of simple concepts the corresponding axioms and postulates can be logically derived. Axioms and postulates guide the formulation of propositions from simple concepts and hence they are the "ground" of scientific knowledge, just as it happens in geometry: on this point Lambert departs from Locke and introduces a domain of a priori inference in philosophy.

An important difference between philosophy and geometry lies in the potentially misleading form of language with regards to reference: contrary to geometry, in philosophy we face the risk of formulating judgements with a predicate which is not uniformly applied to the subject, for example, "the watch is made of gold" when only the watch-case is made of gold. In this regard Lambert hopes that Kant's contributions will help and will be published soon. He is optimistic concerning the development of this new method of philosophy, underscoring that examples will play a crucial role in this enterprise. He then focuses on the analogy between geometrical figures and philosophical examples, arguing that:

> a genuine method can best and most surely be shown by the presentation of *real examples* with all individualities, since, on the other hand, expressed logically, it would easily remain too abstract. [...] *Examples do the same service that figures do in geometry, because these too are actually examples or special cases.* (Lambert 1782, 351; italics are mine)

The correspondence will reprise after the publication of Kant's *Dissertation* in 1770. The new exchange will focus on the reality of time, and, while Lambert will briefly point out that metaphysics can be exposed in merely abstract terms and then applied to phenomena, the role of examples will not be discussed anymore.

Yet it is interesting, in this regard, to examine Lambert's letter to Holland of November 21, 1765. In this letter Lambert comments again on Euclid's method. Euclid sets forth nominal definitions (as a "nomenclature") and then, first, he "requires the unconditioned possibility of straight lines and circles of any magnitude and position," and second, *ex concessis postulatis*, he shows the "universal and unconditioned possibility of the equilateral triangle." Lambert concludes by examining the analogous procedure in the case of metaphysics, where terms are abstract and their meaning cannot be "put in front of the eyes."

> In his proofs, Euclid does not need the expression *per definitionem* any differently than the expression *per hypothesin*. Because until the possibility of the concept is proven, the definition remains only a hypothesis. If it is clear in itself, or even by a single example, that there are at least some such figures which the definition indicates, then the definition may be foreshadowed [...] But the conditions of its possibility must follow from principles and postulates.

This is the case of the triangle [...] In my opinion, this is the way Euclid deals with definitions and concepts. It should also be applied in metaphysics. However, in this field, one cannot visualize the abstract *thing* itself, but must be content for the most part with *words* and *concepts*. (Lambert 1782, 30)

The impact of these conceptions on Kant's parallel investigation in the 1760s is not easily assessed. In the *Deutlichkeit* (written in 1762) Kant already maintained that mathematics can show the possibility of its concepts *"in concreto"* by means of constructions, while philosophy deals with signs and cannot follow this method, thus facing the risk of using empty concepts (*IC*, AA 2: 278–279). He will hold this view of definitions in philosophy until the *Architectonic* chapter of the first *Critique*. However, one wonders what did Kant make of Lambert's ideas about the synthetic method and the role of examples in metaphysics. These ideas have probably influenced Kant's development of the unpublished material on the "metaphysical principles," and he could have given a fresh look at Lambert's published correspondence before writing the *MNS*. As matter of fact, Lambert's ideas are closely connected to the issues addressed in the *MNS*.

Hence, we can put forward the following hypotheses:
1. The *MNS* can be considered as the definitive version of the material announced by Kant in the 1760s as a "metaphysics of natural philosophy." The book would reformulate physical doctrines which had been already anticipated in previous writings (e. g., the conceptions of fundamental forces and inertia), but first of all it would address the problem of the method of metaphysics and its epistemological importance for natural science, which is the main topic of the *Preface*. In this regard, the model first provided by Lambert would provide an important background for Kant's theory.
2. The concept of solidity was the main topic of confrontation with Lambert's methodological ideas. Indeed, according to Kant, impenetrability offers the first empirical property of any physical object (*MNS*, AA 4: 510, quoted below, § 6), and Lambert similarly associates solidity with "Ding" or "etwas Reales" (Lambert 1771, § 57). Moreover, the explanation of impenetrability corresponds to the dynamical theory of matter, which is, since the *Monadologia physica*, Kant's favorite example of "metaphysics combined with geometry" (*MP*, AA 1: 473).

In this regard, it is important to mention a major shift in Kant's thought occurred around the time of his correspondence with Lambert. In the 1750s and early 1760s Kant grounds natural philosophy on a theory of physical monads as point-like centers of repulsive and attractive forces, and explains the originally variable density of bodies through the interplay of these forces (hence, in Kant's system of concepts, density is not a primitive magnitude anymore). In the *Prize Essay* (written in 1762) Kant quotes the *analysis* of the concept of impenetrability as an example of metaphysical method, that leads with intuitive certainty to the action of force. Later Kant would replace physical monadology with a different dynamical theory, grounded on the representation of matter as a continuum. I cannot address here the details of this turn[7] (note that Lambert brackets the role of monads in the systems of scientific concepts. This may have provided an important example for Kant; Lambert 1771, § 90). What matters for our purposes is that Kant, in the *MNS*, maintains that force (thus also density and mass) cannot be derived by analysis of concepts: the representation of motion in pure intuition involves a *synthetic* passage in both cases. As a result of Kant's abandonment of monadology in the 1760s, the dynamical theory – with its methodological background – would need a complete rethinking. Let us now elaborate on these hypotheses, starting from Kant's methodical framework of the *MNS*.

6 Metaphysics of Nature: from Lambert to Kant

Let me review the main steps of Lambert's scientific method. First, there is an empirical moment, consisting in the collection of simple concepts, derived from sensation (e. g., solidity and force from the sensation of touch). Second, by following Euclid's model, principles and postulates are derived from simple concepts. These establish the "possibility of composition," or the "conditions of possibility" of concepts. Third, these principles and postulates are grounds of scientific propositions. For example, from solidity we get principles of dynamics, such as the law of inertia. This inference is grounded on "logical truths," which in turn presuppose – in a Wolffian fashion – the "metaphysical truth" of the existence of God, lest that logical truth becomes an "empty dream." This is also the ultimate ground of the solidity of bodies:

> Therefore, the proposition that there are necessary, eternal, unchanging truths implies that there must be a necessary, eternal, unchanging *intelligent suppositum*, and that the object of these truths, namely the solid and the forces, have a necessary possibility to exist. (Lambert 1771, § 299)

Of course, Kant breaks with this metaphysical approach in his critical philosophy (for this transition compare Cassirer 1999, 457). Still, he retains much of Lambert's original insights when introducing his new "metaphysics of nature," in the *MNS*.

---

[7] For my account see Pecere 2016. For a broader contextualization also see Pecere 2009, 34–143.

Kant separates a transcendental part of this doctrine from a second more specific part.

> [It] concerns itself with a particular nature of this or that kind of thing, for which an empirical concept is given, but still in such a manner that, outside of what lies in this concept, no other empirical principle is used for its cognition (for example, it takes the empirical concept of matter or of a thinking being as its basis, and it seeks that sphere of cognition of which reason is capable a priori concerning these objects). (*MNS*, AA 4: 470)

So far, there is a close analogy with Lambert's method: Kant starts with empirical concepts – for example, impenetrability of matter – and then derives knowledge a priori. But here we find an entirely different way of conceiving the role of mathematics, which provides not merely a methodological model, but also a necessary element of the new metaphysics. This change depends on the role of pure intuition for scientific knowledge in general and the thesis that pure rational principles are necessary but insufficient for "proper natural science," as "there can be only as much *proper* science as there is mathematics therein" (*MNS*, AA 4: 470). This intuitive component of knowledge is necessary for establishing the *possibility* of concepts:

> Hence, in order to cognize the possibility of determinate natural things, and thus to cognize them a priori, it is still required that the *intuition* corresponding to the concept be given a priori, that is, that the concept can be constructed (*MNS*, AA 4: 470).

Hence Kant disagrees with Lambert's way of proving the possibility of concepts through simple empirical concepts and logical inferences. In the light of Kant's procedure, indeed, some of the principles listed by Lambert turn out to lack apodictic validity. This novel conception requires the *construction* of these properties in space, but since pure intuition of natural objects is impossible, Kant's metaphysics of bodily nature establishes the possibility of the mathematical *construction* of the properties belonging to the concept of matter.

> But in order to make possible the application of mathematics to the doctrine of body, which only through this can become natural science, principles for the *construction* of the concepts that belong to the possibility of matter must be intoduced first. Therefore, **[1]** a complete analysis of the concept of matter in general will have to be taken as the basis, and this is a task for pure philosophy – which, for this purpose, makes use of no particular experiences, but only that which it finds in the isolated (although intrinsically empirical) concepts itself, **[2]** in relation to the pure intuitions of space and time, **[3]** and in accordance with laws that already essentially attach to the concept of nature in general, and is therefore a genuine *metaphysics of corporeal nature*. (*MNS*, AA 4: 472; my numeration in bold characters)

Here Kant summarizes the three elements of his new "metaphysics of bodily nature," as it is exposed and applied in the *MNS*:
1. The analysis of the properties belonging to the *empirical* concept of matter, as the basis to seek "that sphere of cognition of which reason is capable a priori concerning these objects" (*MNS*, AA 4: 470).
2. The schematization of these properties through motion as the "basic determination" of any material object (*MNS*, AA 4: 476), which can be represented a priori in intuition, as a pure synthesis of space and time, thus rendering a *mathematical* science of nature possible in general.
3. The elaboration of the principles of this construction in a "pure part" of physics corresponding to these properties. This includes the *transcendental* principles of the intellect, and further *metaphysical* principles, elaborated by the intellect starting from the empirical concept of matter, "that make the concept of their proper object, namely, matter, a priori suitable for application to outer experience, such as the concept of motion, the filling of space, inertia, and so on" (*MNS*, AA 4: 472). These metaphysical principles include the explanation of the filling of space through the action of a fundamental force.

Let me examine in more detail the connection of these three elements with special regard to the example examined above in § 2 (*Dynamics, theorem* 1). Kant points out that the concept of impenetrability is given "by means of the sense of feeling," which "provides us with the quantity and figure of something extended, and thus with the concept of a determinate object in space, which forms the basis of everything else one can say about this thing" (*MNS*, AA 4: 510). The transition from the *sensation* of impenetrability to the *concept* of the filling of space requires the application of the category of quality, and the corresponding principle of intensive magnitudes (degree): thus, we get the representation of the filling of space as a magnitude that can have a determinate degree. The possibility of constructing this concept, in turn, can be examined a priori in pure intuition by schematizing resistance as a motion opposing penetration. The result is one of Kant's non-pure, a priori synthetic principles of metaphysics: "matter fills space, not through its mere *existence*, but through a particular *moving force*."

This is the proposition to which Kant's remark about Lambert is appended. We can now draw some conclusions about Kant's remark.

First, Kant's insistence on the ambiguity of the word "solidity," while evoking Lambert's views on terminological clarity – originally meant to avoid transcendent meanings –, also implies a number of corrections to the latter's analysis of the concept. Sense experience of impenetrability, which is a first meaning of "solidity," is not sufficient to establish a primitive concept of science. Only by the understanding of solidity as the filling of space, as a special case of intensive magnitude, does resistance to penetration become accessible to mathematical analysis. Kant's account contributes to the issue whether density is originally variable or not – a question that Lambert rightly considered unsolvable on the ground of sensation, but then left open – by developing a model of matter with originally variable density. Thus, Kant's remark can be considered as both a critique and an original development of Lambert's idea that experience can provide the "occasion" for the "a priori reasoning," based on the fundamental concept of solidity (see above § 1).

But solidity is just an example – albeit a fundamental one, due to the empirical precedence of the corresponding experience. The formation of the concepts of inertia and mass, which Lambert derived as well from the experience of resistance to motion, requires the application of principles of relations in the pure part of mechanics. In the *Mechanics* chapter Kant first introduces the conditions to represent a material substance as a quantity of matter (mass) which is constant in time and manifests itself in impact and resistance to force. Here the application of the transcendental principle of causality leads to the metaphysical principle that the cause of motion must be external to the moved substance, the *lex inertiae*. Thus, material substance and inertia (as lack of activity), through the combination of metaphysics and mathematics, appear as new concepts derived from the original experience of touch.

On the whole, Kant's new "principles for the construction of the concepts that belong to the possibility of matter" (*MNS*, AA 4: 472) – meant to connect a priori sense experience and mathematical physics – can be considered as a rethinking of Lambert's idea of "principles and postulates" dealing with the "possibility of composition." The difference is that Lambert thinks to an elaboration of empirical concepts by means of logical inference which is *analogous* to mathematical construction, but does not require the use of spatial intuition, while Kant, after having defended the idea of an entirely analytical metaphysics in the *Deutlichkeit*, now introduces synthesis in pure space-time as the procedure that has to connect empirical concepts and metaphysical principles, thus establishing the possibility of mathematical constructions in physics.

Kant's view of the systematical meaning for general metaphysics of these examples concerning bodies also echoes Lambert's ideas. Remember that Lambert had repeatedly argued that his new principles would provide metaphysics with "examples," which would play the same role of figures in Euclidean geometry, that is, to establish the possibility of defined objects. In the *MNS* Kant assigns a strikingly similar role to examples in metaphysics:

> It is indeed very remarkable [...] that general metaphysics, in all instances where it requires examples (intuitions) in order to provide meaning for its pure concepts of the understanding, must always take them from the general doctrine of body, and thus from the form and prin-

ciples of outer intuition; and, if these are not exhibited properly, it gropes uncertainly und unsteadily among mere meaningless concepts. This is the source of the well-known disputes, or at least obscurity, in the questions concerning the possibility of a conflict of realities, of intensive magnitude, and so on, in which the understanding is taught only by examples from corporeal objective reality, that is, meaning and truth. And so a separated metaphysics of corporeal nature does excellent and indispensable service for *general* metaphysics, in that the former furnishes examples (instances *in concreto*) in which to realize the concepts and propositions of the latter (properly speaking, of transcendental philosophy), that is, to give a mere form of thought sense and meaning. (*MNS*, AA 4: 478)

This exhibition [*exhibitio, Darstellung*] of concepts plays a crucial role in critical philosophy in general, as Kant also points out in the new *General remark to the Analytic of principles* in the second edition of the *Critique* (*CPR*, B 288–294).[8] Again, mere sensation is a necessary but not sufficient condition of the objective reality of concepts. Therefore, critique of transcendent metaphysics and foundation of natural science coincide in the new metaphysics of bodily nature. Concerning the foundational side of the project, Kant points out the epistemological failure of allegedly empiricist accounts of science by mathematical physicists:

> Hence all natural philosophers who have wished to proceed mathematically in their occupation have always, and must have always, made use of metaphysical principles (albeit unconsciously), even if they themselves solemnly guarded against all claims of metaphysics upon their science. Undoubtedly they have understood by the latter the folly of contriving possibilities at will and playing with concepts, which can perhaps not be presented in intuition at all [...]. All true metaphysics is drawn from the faculty of thinking itself, and is in no way fictitiously invented on account of not being borrowed from experience. Rather, it contains the pure actions of thought, and thus a priori concepts and principles, which first bring the manifold of *empirical representations* into the law-governed connection through which it can become *empirical cognition*, that is, experience. Thus these mathematical physicists could in no way avoid metaphysical principles, and, among them, also not those that make the concept of their proper object, namely, matter, a priori suitable for application to outer experience, such as the concept of motion, the filling of space, inertia, and so on. But they rightly held that to let merely empirical principles govern these concepts would in no way be appropriate to the apodictic certainty they wished their law of nature to possess, so they preferred to postulate such [principles], without investigating them with regard to their a priori sources. (*MNS*, AA 4: 472)

This charge of inconsequence is directed – among other possible targets – to Newton's epistemology in the *Principia*, and Kant will indeed argue that Newton was "at variance with himself" when he denied that gravity is an essential property of matter (as Kant argues in *MNS*, 4: 515). In this perspective, Lambert's approach

---

[8] I provide more details on *exhibitio* in Pecere 2009, 185–202, 208–277, and Pecere 2015.

appears once more controversial. He submitted an important insight by recognizing the importance of connecting the empirical basis of science with a priori reasoning, but his derivation of principles, lacking any reference to intuition as the source of synthetic judgments, is inadequate (in the quoted passage, indeed, Kant may have been hinting at Lambert's use of the concept of "postulate," which corresponds to the content of Kant's new metaphysical principle).

I think that Kant directly refers to this limit of Lambert's approach in the final passage of the *Remark* on solidity that we have been examining, where he addresses the "mathematician:"

> Here the mathematician has assumed something, as a first datum for constructing the concept of matter, which is itself incapable of further construction. Now he can indeed begin his construction of a concept from any chosen datum, without engaging in the explication of this datum in turn. But he is not therefore permitted to declare this to be something entirely incapable of any mathematical construction, so as thereby to obstruct us from going back to first principles in natural science. (*MNS*, AA 4: 498)

Here is the point of the methodological disagreement with Lambert: the latter considered absolute solidity as a primitive concept, thereby excluding the possibility of its construction (hence absolute impenetrability is an "empty concept"). But this impossibility, in turn, "obstructs" the natural scientist "from going back to first principles," that is, to infer the activity of force by mathematical construction and thus to establish the objective reality of impenetrability as a consequence of natural laws. From a physical point of view, as we have seen, this produces a number of additional problems, while the dynamic philosophy envisaged by Kant reduces phenomena to laws. From the more fundamental metaphysical point of view, Lambert fails to provide an adequate account of the intertwining of logical, empirical, and mathematical elements in natural science, thus also failing to justify the *necessity* of natural science, and this failure affects his treatment of the most basic empirical concept of natural science, that is, impenetrability of matter.

7 Conclusions

My examination of the disagreement between Kant and Lambert on solidity does not end up in a merely negative result. We have seen that Lambert's methodological writings not only influenced and inspired Kant in the 1760s, but – what has not been sufficiently highlighted – also provided a significant legacy for Kant's methodical elaboration of a metaphysics of nature in criticism, long after the correspondence and Lambert's death. This slow elaboration is not uncommon in Kant's writings, especially in his long and uninterrupted work on natural sciences.

We can thus confidently conclude that Lambert's seminal insights about "protophysics" and methodology set the background for Kant's mature conception of the metaphysics of bodily nature. Among the many points of agreement we have found: the preliminary analysis of the empirical concept of matter, the role of examples against the confusions and illusory references of transcendent metaphysics, the model of Euclid's mathematical postulates for the establishment of a metaphysics of natural science. In this context, moreover, Lambert also suggests the analogy between geometrical figures and metaphysical examples, which will be developed by Kant in his theory of "principles for the construction" of matter.

Although Lambert provides the bricks and the project for the new metaphysical building, as it were, his work appears unaccomplished from Kant's point of view, because it does not spell out how empirical and a priori elements can form a properly scientific; that is, mathematical doctrine. Lambert's conception of solidity in particular, is an example of the failure to provide a transition from the empirical basis to mathematical physics and hence to justify the latter's exemplary function for metaphysics.

Arguably Kant may have been wrong regarding the alleged heuristic value of dynamism, as the successive history of physics shows that dynamical conceptions of matter have not provided a full reduction of the impenetrability of matter to elementary forces (or fields). Anyway, whatever we may think of Kant's solution to the problem of solidity and of its greater influence in the history of philosophy of science, it is Lambert who has to be credited for having posited this foundational problem in the framework of post-Newtonian natural sciences, thus introducing the idea of a new methodological connection between empirical, mathematical and metaphysical elements of natural science.

Heiner F. Klemme
Johann Georg Sulzer's "Mixed Doctrine of Morals": A Contribution to the History of the Development of Kant's Ethics Between 1770 and 1785

Abstract: Johann Georg Sulzer is not an important moral philosopher. However, in a letter from 1770, he asks Immanuel Kant a question that Kant seems to have thought about ever since: Why do the doctrines of virtue have so little influence on human action? It was not until preparing his *Groundwork for the Metaphysics of Morals* (1785) that Kant found a convincing answer to it: because previous moral doctrines (including Sulzer's "mixed doctrine of morals") did not strictly distinguish between pure and empirical concepts, they failed to realize that pure reason itself is practical. In the first two sections of the paper, I present the basic principles of Sulzer's moral philosophy. In the third section, I outline Kant's response to Sulzer. I argue that Kant's new account of motivation in the *Groundwork* is accompanied by a redefinition of his doctrine of the highest good, as presented in the *Critique of Pure Reason* (1781).

1 Introduction

The Swiss philosopher and long-time member of the Prussian Academy of Sciences Johann Georg Sulzer is widely known and esteemed as the author of the *Allgemeine Theorie der schönen Künste* (*General Theory of the Fine Arts*, 1771–1774). However, he is by no means an original moral philosopher.[1] Although Sulzer's eth-

---

[1] Sulzer did not write a monograph on ethics. Relevant to the presentation and criticism of his ethical views are, above all, the following works, collected in 1773 in his *Vermischte philosophische Schriften* in German translations from French: (1) the fourth section of his "Untersuchung über den Ursprung der angenehmen und unangenehmen Empfindungen" (first published in 1751), which bears the title "Von den moralischen Vergnügungen" (77–98); (2) "Erklärung eines psychologisch paradoxen Satzes: Daß der Mensch zuweilen nicht nur ohne Antrieb und ohne sichtbare Gründe sondern selbst gegen dringende Antriebe und überzeugende Gründe handelt und urtheilet" (first published in 1759; 99–121); (3) "Psychologische Betrachtungen über den sittlichen Mensch" (first published in 1769, 282–306); (4) "Versuch über die Glückseligkeit verständiger Wesen" (first published in 1754, 323–247); (5) "Versuch, einen festen Grundsatz zu finden, um die Pflichten der Sit-

ics are neither original nor ingenious, his moral psychology is not entirely irrelevant to the development of modern ethics. First of all, his ethics stand for a particular type of philosophy in Germany, known as popular philosophy [*Popularphilosophie*]. Like skepticism, popular philosophy distrusts metaphysics. Yet, unlike radical skepticism, it does not abandon the claim to opinion justified by reason; rather it attempts to bridge the gulf between metaphysical problems and empirical research by means of common sense. It takes the problems of metaphysics seriously, but does not rely on abstract concepts and the deductive method. Secondly, although not groundbreaking in itself, popular philosophy is philosophically important insofar as it puts its finger in the wound of metaphysics; for example, concerning the question of why metaphysics is still not a science? Likewise, Sulzer's ethics, though insignificant in itself, puts its finger in the wound of moral theory: Why is it that no doctrine of virtue can motivate people to do what they acknowledge as their duty? It is this question, I will argue, that had a significant impact on the development of Kant's moral philosophy.

Sulzer draws Kant's attention to positions of "popular moral philosophy" (*GM*, AA 4: 392),[2] which Kant contends must be overcome within the framework of a "pure practical philosophy, or (if one may use a name so decried) [...] metaphysics of morals" (*GM*, AA 4: 410), in order to understand and improve our "common" moral practice. That Sulzer may have exerted this influence on Kant is hinted at in a note in the *Groundwork to the Metaphysics of Morals* (written in 1784 and published in 1785). In order to understand the impact and meaning of this note, it might be helpful to discuss Kant's overall objective in the *Groundwork*. In this work, Kant aims to contribute to the improvement of morals through an analysis of the supreme moral principle, the Categorical Imperative. Accordingly, he emphasizes the merits of his "metaphysics of morals,"[3] in distinction to a theory of morality in which reason and feeling, anthropology and psychology, physics and theology are mixed together. Accordingly, if we want to understand the nature of our moral obligations and improve our moral practice, we could not be worse advised than to propound a "mixed doctrine of morals" [*vermischte Sitten-*

---

tenlehre und des Naturrechts zu unterscheiden" (first 1755, 389–398). On Sulzer's life and work, see Guyer 2016.

2 English translations of Kant's work stem from the *Cambridge Edition of the Works of Immanuel Kant* (general editors Paul Guyer and Allen W. Wood).

3 "A metaphysics of morals is therefore indispensably necessary, not merely because of a motive to speculation – for investigating the source of the practical basis principles that lie a priori in our reason – but also because morals themselves remain subject to all sorts of corruption as long as we are without that clue and supreme norm by which to appraise them correctly." (*GM*, AA 4: 389–390)

lehre] (*GM*, AA 4: 411).⁴ Thus, in Kant's view, Sulzer's "science of happiness" (Sulzer 1773, 3) fails in its attempt to promote our practice of virtues. It is incapable of discerning that the ground of our moral obligations and the sole moving principle of our moral agency lies in pure reason. Not only does pure reason motivate us to act out of respect for the moral law, but the purity of our disposition, that is, our respect for the moral law, is also the measure of the morality of our actions.[5]

Considered from the perspective of the *Groundwork*, however, Sulzer's "mixed doctrine of morals" would be of interest as a mere foil only if Sulzer's views were not also relevant to the history of the development of Kant's ethics between 1770 and 1785. I clarify this relevance in section 4. Before doing so, I sketch Sulzer's main ethical principles (wisdom, justice, and magnanimity) in section 2 and discuss their philosophical significance in section 3.

2 Sulzer's Ethical Views

As a typical representative of a variety of eudaemonism in Germany mainly shaped by Gottfried Wilhelm Leibniz[6] and Christian Wolff,[7] Sulzer assumes as a matter of course that ethics describes virtues that enable us to achieve the "highest happiness" and the "highest perfection" (Sulzer 1773, 347). It is self-evident to Sulzer that God created the world as a system whose "end" (Sulzer 1773, 3) is the happiness of human beings. However, a human being can achieve this end only on the basis of proper empirical observations about the state and use of the soul's faculties. Because this "physics of the soul" (Sulzer 1773, 100) is a "science of happiness" (Sulzer 1773, 3), it must devote itself primarily to the analysis of our pleasures. We must recognize the "true value" (Sulzer 1773, 3) of pleasures "in order to be happy, and to be able to decide on the means by which we should procure them" (Sulzer 1773, 4). Sulzer assumes that the soul is happy precisely when its activity accords with its vocation, which consists in thinking.[8] Pleasure depends on thinking prop-

---

[4] In the first section of his essay "On the commons saying" (1793), Kant argues as against the popular philosopher Christian Garve that the denial of the motivational force of pure concepts "is the death of all morality." (*OCS*, AA 8: 285)
[5] "For, in the case of what is to be morally good it is not enough that it *conform* with the moral law but it must also be done *for the sake of the law*" (*GM*, AA 4: 390).
[6] Actually, Leibniz formulated a utilitarian calculus of happiness even before Jeremy Bentham and John Stuart Mill. See Hruschka 1991.
[7] On Wolff, see Schwaiger 1995, and Klemme 2009.
[8] Thinking is "our essential activity, the basic impulse of all our undertakings, of all our free actions" (8–9; cf. 91).

erly. Among the three possible kinds of pleasures – sensual, intellectual, and moral – the latter have priority: "If someone enjoyed all sensual and intellectual pleasures but lacked the moral ones, he would be deprived of the best part of happiness and would not know precisely the most exquisite thing in the existence of a thinking being" (Sulzer 1773, 98).

Sulzer holds a realist position on moral reasons: the "reality of the reasons of morality" is based on the "nature of our sensations" (Sulzer 1773, 285). But what distinguishes moral sentiments from other sentiments? In Sulzer's view, moral pleasures are "the consequence and the reward of good actions and virtuous dispositions" (Sulzer 1773, 77). If there were no pleasure in virtue, no one would act virtuously. The prospect of pleasure, then, is the motive of our virtuous actions. That virtue causes a moral pleasure cannot be denied earnestly, according to Sulzer. But what objects cause moral pleasure? In answering this question, Sulzer makes use of the concept of "moral goods" (Sulzer 1773, 84), which are characterized by the fact that they "make the natural activity of our soul more perfect" (Sulzer 1773, 85) or facilitate it. As an example, he points to the moral good of friendship. Friendship evokes in us a moral pleasure because it stimulates us to think and enlivens our minds. The enlivening of our minds pleases us because the mind finds its natural vocation in the free production of ideas. However, not only do we take pleasure in goods which directly promote the activity of our own minds, the happiness of other persons also gives us moral pleasure. If we perceive that a person derives moral pleasure from his friendship with other persons, this indirectly enlivens our minds.[9]

For Sulzer, the "beneficent hand" of God explains the active interest we take in the good of others. God wants us to pursue the happiness of our fellows as earnestly as our own happiness:

> On the basis of our theory, it is clear that the precious germs of virtue have been planted in our souls by the very beneficent hand to which we owe the inclinations that aim at our preservation; and that we act no less according to our nature when we follow the inclination to virtue than when we follow the impulse to other pleasures. Man is determined by his very nature to strive after the happiness of other beings capable of happiness as much as after his own. (Sulzer 1773, 91)

---

9 "I observe, then, that every rational being is determined by his nature to take part in all good and evil that concerns others, without any previous deliberation. The distinct idea of a good must necessarily awaken a pleasant sensation, even if this good itself does not belong to us; for ideas have the same effect, only weaker, than things themselves." (Sulzer 1773, 85) We simply have "a natural inclination [...] to take part in the good and evil of others." (Sulzer 1773, 86)

Accordingly, a virtuous person promotes the "double happiness" (Sulzer 1773, 92) of his fellows and himself by following the "voice of nature" (Sulzer 1773, 93). In connection with this, Sulzer points out that a pleasant moral sensation arises in us only when we view other people's happiness from a certain perspective. Although Sulzer does not frame the issue in these terms, we can describe this perspective as the perspective of impartiality (cf. Sulzer 1773, 88). We adopt this perspective when we identify with another person, when we regard him as a part of ourselves. If we judge impartially, we take the perspective of humanity as a whole.[10]

Sulzer could have argued that while happiness in the form of moral sentiments is the reward of virtue, a life without pain is not possible even for the most virtuous human being, since it is metaphysically impossible for God to create anything perfect. As God's creatures, we could attain supreme happiness, but we could never attain perfect happiness. However, Sulzer chooses to argue otherwise. In accordance with the principle that we can be obligated only to such acts as we are able to perform, he holds that we are capable of perfect virtue and thus of perfect happiness in this world. It is a realistic option for us humans to live a "perfectly happy life" (Sulzer 1773, 324) with only pleasant sensations. Our pain felt today is a necessary condition for perhaps reaching perfection tomorrow. Our pain is based either on internal or external causes. If our moral character contradicts "the eternal laws of order" and is "repugnant to moral beauty" (Sulzer 1773, 326), pain arises just as in the case of desires that we cannot realize because of the external circumstances of our actions. Yet, according to Sulzer, the absence of pain does not mean that we are happy. In particular, our moral pleasures presuppose a certain activity.[11] If we want to overcome pain, then we must improve our cognition of the moral order of the world. If we recognize this order, then we act according to it and to our vocation.

If perfect happiness is possible in this world, why did God not create human beings as happy from the beginning? Sulzer argues that God created the best "moral constitution" (Sulzer 1773, 323) in the world. Yet, he was not at liberty to "give finite beings [...] the highest degree of happiness" (Sulzer 1773, 355), because he cannot create beings that are both finite *and* perfect. However, our finitude does not entail that we cannot attain perfect virtue and happiness. It is up to us to acquire knowledge that leads to happiness "in a certain time" (Sulzer 1773,

---

10 "As soon as one has become accustomed to regard the rest of mankind as a part of oneself, one is a friend of the whole human race, and feels pleasure at its welfare." (Sulzer 1773, 97)

11 "They demand a constant, attentive care to know the condition of other rational beings, and an ability to be effective in them. This presupposes a perfect moral goodness in rational beings themselves, and the most exact connection between them. For without this connection, moral goodness could not express itself at all." (Sulzer 1773, 330; cf. 328)

337).¹² If we have acquired perfect knowledge, then we will be perfectly happy: a knowing person does not feel any pain.¹³ Sulzer claims, then, that we are finite creatures that can gradually acquire perfect knowledge and, thus, perfect happiness.

While the "honest man [...] finds the path of virtue" (Sulzer 1773, 283), the evil man misses it. The evil man performs actions that are "contrary to his natural and immutable inclinations" and thus violates the "proposition of wisdom" (Sulzer 1773, 287). Because everyone strives for happiness, but the bad action makes one unhappy, the evil person does not will evil at all. Evil has no independent reality, but represents a deficient form of good. In a note to the 1755 German translation of Hume's *Enquiry concerning Human Understanding*, Sulzer states, "[...] thus evil will disappear entirely from creation, and one will have to say that evil is only a lesser degree of good, that the most evil being is distinguished from the good only by a lesser degree of good" (Hume 1748/1755, 237).

If the pursuit of evil is based on ignorance, the problem of its imputability looms. To avoid this, Sulzer resorts to Hume's conception of the compatibility of freedom and necessity. The evil person acts voluntarily because no one forces him to act in a way that is evil: "What more do you want in order to be free than to do only what you yourself *do gladly*. Now, even though our volition is a necessary consequence of preceding ideas, it is not, for this reason, any less our own work and our own impulse" (Hume 1748/1755, 234).¹⁴

Besides the "proposition" or the "*principium* of wisdom," Sulzer mentions the "principle of justice" (Sulzer 1773, 287) and the principle of magnanimity. With the principle of justice, Sulzer indicates our mutual obligations, invoking the "natural equality of men" (Sulzer 1773, 287), an equality that, for Sulzer, has the status of an axiom. He argues that, according to the necessities to which human beings are subject by virtue of their own nature, every human being owes certain things, to which he consequently has claims. Entitlements denote rights. By virtue of the equality of human beings, I must concede my rights to others. These rights oblige me to uphold justice: "Since the reasons are the same on both sides, it would be inconsistent and contradictory to draw opposite conclusions from them. And

---

12 "The nature of a finite being does not permit it to attain that degree of perfection which is necessary to the highest happiness, without first having passed through a certain number of lower degrees, where it sometimes felt pleasure, sometimes pain." (Sulzer 1773, 335)
13 "[...] the more perfect the faculties of a finite being are, the more secure it is from pain, and the more capable it is of enjoying every kind of pleasure. From this, then, it follows (all other circumstances being equal) that the more time it has utilized to make its knowledge more perfect, the more it approaches the highest bliss" (Sulzer 1773, 339).
14 On Sulzers reception of Hume, see Klemme 2018b.

this is what is just as established and certain as the principle of wisdom." (Sulzer 1773, 287) However, the knowledge of our duties towards other persons develops a motive force only if it is also felt: "The truth, to be felt, must touch the soul, as it were, and assimilate itself to it, if I may so express myself." (Sulzer 1773, 295) We feel an obligation when our knowledge is accompanied by an emotional state of discomfort that we wish to overcome. For example, if I recognize the misery of my neighbor, this evokes in me unpleasant sensations which I wish to overcome by some righteous action.

While justice aims at the prevention of evil and the bad, the third moral principle of magnanimity aims at the promotion of good: "Justice seeks to make human beings equal to one another, magnanimity to make all into a single individual, for it is really nothing else than the propensity and inclination to see and feel one's advantage and one's best merely in the advantage and best of the whole human race" (Sulzer 1773, 305).

3 The Philosophical Significance of Sulzer's Ethics

Reading and studying Sulzer's ethical writings is not an end in itself. In moral philosophy, we seek conceptual clarifications, original descriptions, and surprising perspectives. However, this is not to be found in Sulzer's writings. Those who wish to learn about the presuppositions and cornerstones of pre-Kantian eudaemonism would be well advised to read Leibniz, and will find in Wolff an author who devotes himself more extensively and with greater energy to the connection between happiness and perfection than Sulzer.[15] Those who wish to understand what options are available to a theory of morality that seeks to combine happiness, sentiment, and teleology should study Francis Hutcheson or, if they are willing to let happiness take a back seat and dispense with teleology altogether, David Hume. Problems and alternatives that have been discussed at length in the context of British moral philosophy from Hobbes to Adam Smith are neither solved nor not taken up by Sulzer. In his observation of his own mental processes and operations, Sulzer takes himself to find for his arguments a firm ground which needs no external instruction and cannot be shaken by any dissenting opinion. Is there really a "supreme happiness" in *this* world, in which supreme perfection and supreme pleasure harmonize? Did Leibniz not already raise justifiable doubts about this view in his *Nouveaux Essais*, via Theophilus:

---

15 See, among others, Mori 1993 for further details.

> I doubt that a greatest pleasure is possible; I am inclined to believe that it can increase *ad infinitum*, for we do not know how far our knowledge and our organs can be developed in the course of the eternity which lies before us. So, I would think that *happiness* is a lasting pleasure, which cannot occur without a continual progress to new pleasures. (Leibniz 1765/1985, II, § 41, 305; trans. Remnant/Bennett 1996)

And does Thomas Hobbes not hold in his *Leviathan* that there can be no permanent state of happiness at all, because man is moving matter? If Hobbes were right in his view that new desires arise after we have satisfied our previous ones, everything Leibniz and Sulzer say about happiness would be wrong. But Sulzer does not even begin to inform his readers of this important alternative to his conception of happiness, and accordingly shows no interest in rejecting it. Nor does he discuss Hume's conception of justice as an artificial virtue as an alternative to his own claims. Hume denies that human beings possess universal benevolence, much less a magnanimity that levels the difference between ourselves and others in practical terms. Sulzer's silence on the principle of sympathy, which, according to Hume, is more characteristic of our moral nature than any other, is surprising, as is the absence of any reference to Smith's notion of an impartial spectator. Sulzer would thus hardly be worth remembering as an author of ethical writings if his "science of happiness" had not been deemed worthy of explicit criticism by Kant. With a view to Kant's ethics, based on the categorical imperative, Sulzer's remarks gain an unexpected relevance for the problem-oriented historiography of modern ethics.

4 Sulzer's Question and Kant's Answer

In the second section of the *Groundwork* ("Transition from popular moral philosophy to metaphysics of morals"), Kant emphasizes the necessity of a "completely isolated *metaphysics of morals*, mixed with no anthropology, theology, physics, or hyperphysics and still less with occult qualities (which one might call hypophysical)" (*GM*, AA 4: 410). This metaphysics is not only of central importance for knowledge of our duties, but also precisely as "a desideratum of the utmost importance for the actual fulfillment of their precepts." (*GM*, AA 4: 410) As evidence of the relevance of metaphysics to our actions, Kant adds the following observation:

> For the pure thought of duty and in general of the moral law, mixed with no foreign addition of empirical inducements, has by the way of reason alone (which with this first becomes aware that it can of itself be practical) an influence on the human heart so much more powerful than all other incentives, which may be summoned from the empirical field, that reason,

in the consciousness of its dignity, despises the latter and can gradually become their master […]. (*GM*, AA 4: 410–411)

Whoever, on the other hand, advocates "a mixed doctrine of morals" and mixes incentives of feeling, inclination and rational concepts, makes the mind "waver between motives that cannot be brought under any principle, that can lead only contingently to what is good and can very often also lead to what is evil." (*GM*, AA 4: 411)

In a note to this text, Kant refers to the author who asked the right question, but unfortunately gave the wrong answer:

I have a letter from the late excellent Sulzer in which he asks me what the cause might be that the teaching of virtue, however much they contain that is convincing to reason, accomplish so little. By trying to prepare a complete answer I delayed too long. However, my answer is simply that the teachers themselves have not brought their concepts to purity, but, since they want to do too well by hunting everywhere for motives and to moral goodness, in trying to make their medicine really strong they spoil it. For the most ordinary observation shows that if we represent, on the other hand, an action of integrity done with steadfast soul, apart from every view to advantage of any kind in this world or another and even under the greatest temptations of need or allurement, it leaves far behind and eclipses any similar act that was affected in the least by an extraneous incentive; it elevates the soul and awakens a wish to be able to act in like manner oneself. Even children of moderate age feel this impression, and one should never represent duties to them in any other way. (*GM*, AA 4: 411)

Unfortunately, it is not clear from this passage when Sulzer, who died in 1779,[16] wrote Kant this letter. What has survived, however, is a letter dated December 8, 1770, in which Sulzer addresses a problem that fits very well with Kant's note in the *Groundwork*.[17] In this letter, Sulzer expresses a request to Kant and reports on the latest outcome of his work:

I really wished to hear from you whether we may hope to see your work on the Metaphysics of Morals soon. This work is of the highest importance, given the present unsteady state of moral philosophy. I have tried to do something of this sort myself in attempting to resolve the question, 'What actually is the physical or psychological difference between a soul that we call virtuous and one that is vicious?' I have sought to discover the true dispositions to virtue and vice in the first manifestations of this investigation as less futile, since it has led me to concepts that are simple and easy to grasp, and which one can effortlessly apply

---

[16] In the annotated edition of the *Grundlegung*, edited by Chr. Horn, C. Mieth, and N. Scarano, Sulzer's death is erroneously dated 1799 (see Horn/Mieth/Scarano 2007, 201).
[17] Otto Schöndörffer (1986, 822), in contrast to the Akademie edition and Werner Stark (Kant 2004, 32), doubts that Kant refers to this letter of Sulzer.

to the teaching and raising of children. But this work too is impossible for me to complete at present. (AA 10: 112; Zweig 1999, 121)[18]

Sulzer addressed the question he mentions in his letter to Kant in his "Psychological Reflections on the Moral Man," first published in 1769, claiming that "mere reflection [...] is sufficient" to "guide us to wisdom; but it is not sufficient to beget the virtue of justice." (Sulzer 1773, 301) If "one wants to be just according to principles," it is true that one must have made a "very simple conclusion of reason [...]: all men are equal to one another; consequently they all have the same natural claims." (Sulzer 1773, 301) But "reasoning alone is not sufficient to beget justice in the heart of man." (Sulzer 1773, 302) For "truth to be efficacious," something must be added:

> [one] cannot be just [...] until one has attained to that degree of reason which transforms the conception or cognition of the true into sensation. That truth, which constitutes the ground of justice, must be incorporated into the soul in such a way that it can be felt as one of its modifications; so that in the case of everything that seems to be contrary to this truth, not only does the intellect notice the contradiction, but also the soul feels the compulsion and the violence that is done to it by it, just as it feels them when it is compelled by a sensual feeling to admit something that is contrary to its nature. (Sulzer 1773, 302–303)

The reason "why it is so rare to find truly just persons, and why there are a hundred compassionate and benevolent persons compared with one just person" is because we feel the "strength of evidence" and of "truth" (especially when it concerns the needs of other persons) only "through long habit and practice" (Sulzer 1773, 303).

Why does Kant refer in his *Groundwork*, written in 1784 and published in 1785, to a letter request of Sulzer's dating back to 1770, in which he refers to an article of his published in 1769? One answer to this question can undoubtedly be seen in Kant's taking Sulzer's request as an opportunity to point out the peculiarities of his "metaphysics of morals" as opposed to the "mixed doctrine of morals," which was the preferred variety of moral philosophy in Germany after the death of Christian Wolff in 1754. Philosophers realized that Wolff's strategy of providing ethics with a scientific foundation by means of the mathematical method is not convincing. It is not enough to think rational. Rational concepts must somehow

---

[18] In his influential study "Kant and the Ethics of the Greek" on Kant's "Platonic" turn in moral philosophy between 1767 and 1770, Klaus Reich (2001a) does not address Sulzer and the problem of moral motivation.

reach our hearts, too.¹⁹ In this way, Sulzer was quite right, according to Kant, to see that there must be a connection between concepts and feeling [*Gefühl*] if it is to be possible for us to act morally on the basis of principles. But, Kant argues, Sulzer failed to clarify this connection. The motive of our virtuous striving does not rest on the prospect of our happiness and well-being, nor is the feeling of respect a feeling, "inclination," or a "desire" (Sulzer 1773, 305). Whoever wants to understand how a "truth" can motivate us must present the moral law in its "purity and rigor" (*GM*, AA 4: 405), independent of all empirical elements. Only then does pure practical reason, in the form of a feeling of respect wrought in us by it, develop its highest motivational force. Accordingly, Sulzer takes the wrong path with his psychologization of morality. Anyone who wants to understand the moral law in its normative and motivational dimension needs a metaphysics of morals, not an empirical science of the soul. Those who cast doubt on the "purity and rigor" of the moral law undermine morality. The more anthropology, theology, and physics we mix into the theory with the intention of making it more palatable, the less we achieve our practical goal of improving morality.²⁰

If we turn to Kant's answer to Sulzer from a developmental perspective, the question arises why Kant did not already answer Sulzer's question in the *Critique of Pure Reason* (1781).²¹ My thesis is that Kant does not answer this question then because at this point he had not yet found a completely convincing answer at that point. It is true that, for Kant in 1781, it is certain that the moral law is based on pure reason.²² But at this point in his philosophical development, Kant had not yet

---

19 Earlier in his career, Kant himself was very near to a "mixed doctrine of morals" at one point. On Kant's struggle for a new moral philosophy in the 1760s and its context, see Klemme 2018a.
20 Kant never tires of emphasizing the practical relevance of pure reason. Thus, at another point in the *Groundwork*, Kant argues as follows: "From what has been said it is clear that all moral concepts have their seat and origin completely a priori in reason, and indeed in the most common reason just as in reason that is speculative in the highest degree; that they cannot be abstracted from any empirical and therefore merely contingent cognitions; that just in this purity of their origin lies their dignity, so that they can serve us as supreme practical principles; that in adding anything empirical to them one subtracts just that much from their genuine influence and from the unlimited worth of actions; [...]." (*GM*, AA 4: 411).
21 On some central aspects of Kant's theory of moral motivation between 1775 and 1785, see Klemme 2006 (with further references).
22 This observation is already made by Kant in his inaugural dissertation *De mundi sensibilis atque intelligibilis forma et principiis of* 1770: "Moral philosophy, therefore, in so far as it furnishes the first *principles of judgement*, is only cognized by the pure understanding and itself belongs to pure philosophy. Epicurus, who reduced its criteria to the sense of pleasure or pain, is very rightly blamed, together with certain moderns, who have followed him to a certain extent from afar, such as Shaftesbury and his supporters." (*ID*, AA 2: 396, § 9) and in the mid-70s in his lectures on moral philosophy [*Nachschrift Kaehler*] (cf. Stark 2004, 32) and on anthropology. Thus, in *Anthropologie–*

seen how pure reason can motivate us without making a direct reference to happiness.[23] Quite along these lines, Kant admits in his note on Sulzer that his answer to his question was "delayed" because he tried "to prepare a complete answer" (*GM*, AA 4: 411 note). In other words, Kant's own perception is that he did not seem to be able to answer Sulzer's question publicly until 1785.

The key concept for understanding Kant's overcoming the remnants of popular philosophical eudaemonism in favor of a theory of respect and autonomy is the concept of worthiness. Whereas in the *Critique of Practical Reason* (published at the end of 1787) and in the *Critique of Judgment* Kant relates the concept of worthiness solely to the question of the object of our moral *hope*, in 1781 he relates the concept of "*worthiness to be happy*" (*CPR*, A 806/B 834) instead to the question "*What shall I do?*" (*CPR*, A 805/B 833). This question is answered by the following imperative: "*Do that by which you become worthy to be happy.*" (*CPR*, A 808–809/B 836–837) This concept of happiness then leads to the question of the object of my moral hope: the "system of morality" is "inseparably combined with the system of happiness, though only in the idea of pure reason" because "everyone has cause to hope for happiness in the same measure as he has made himself worthy of it in his conduct" (*CPR*, A 809/B 837). In other words, if I could not hope to become happy through my virtuous actions, I could not prove worthiness of happiness either. One can prove worthiness only of that which one can attain. The categorical command of pure reason to prove myself worthy of happiness would otherwise be empty. I would have no motive to act morally.

The answer to the question of the relation between the worthiness of happiness and the hope of happiness will continue to accompany Kant's thinking. But the answer he gives in the *Groundwork* differs significantly from the one he gives in the *Critique of Pure Reason*. In his writings published from 1785 onwards, Kant is emphatic that neither the validity nor the objective motivational power of

---

Friedländer Kant states: "The faculty of acting in accordance with principles and maxims is based on this, that the human being can act in accordance with concepts, but the concepts must become an incentive for him. True, the concepts are not in themselves incentives, for what is an object of understanding, can indeed not be an object of feeling, yet they can still serve to rouse feeling to act in accordance with these concepts; then one acts in accordance with principles and maxims." (AA 25: 649)

23 It is noteworthy that in the *Kaehler Nachschrift*, Kant seems at first to notice the motivating power of pure reason, but in the following sentence establishes a relation to the good pleasure of God: "And a pure moral ground has a greater incentive than when it is mixed with pathological and pragmatic *motivis*, for such *motiva* have more motive force for sensibility, but the understanding pays heed to the universally valid motive force. Morality, to be sure, is unappealing, it is not so pleasing and enjoyable, but it is a relation to the universally valid satisfaction, it must in fact please the highest being, and that is the strongest motive." (Stark, 2004, 32–33)

pure reason can be undermined by doubts about the object of our *hope*.[24] These later responses, then, emphasize a difference between the question of moral ought and moral hope in a way that is not found in the *Critique of Pure Reason*. In this work, Kant argues that, through reason, we must distance ourselves from our immediate sensible stimuli and allow ourselves to be guided by "considerations about that which in regard to our whole condition is desirable; i.e., good and useful" (*CPR*, A 802/B 830). But such a formulation is alien to his later work, in which he refers to autonomy and the feeling of respect. With these concepts, the immediate connection between ought and worthiness of happiness is cut in 1785.

Against the background of these central developmental aspects of Kant's thought, Sulzer certainly makes a contribution, if not to the genesis, then at least to the problem of modern ethics. For Sulzer drew Kant's attention as early as 1770 to a problem whose solution Kant would not succeed in solving until after the publication of the *Critique of Pure Reason*. Formulated in the terminology of Kant's moral-philosophical lectures from the 1770s: pure reason is not only the *principium dijudicationis*, it is also the *principium executionis* of morality (see Stark 2004, 55 ff.). The motive force of pure reason, however, becomes clear to us only when we seek out the principle of morality in a metaphysics of morals and also reject the "mixed doctrine of morals" of popular philosophers with respect to moral motivation. We then recognize that the feeling which makes us take heed of the voice of pure reason in us, even subjectively, has been brought about by this reason itself. It was only with the theory of respect presented in 1785 that Kant, according to his own self-understanding, succeeded in cutting the Gordian knot in the relationship between reason and feeling in the area of the doctrine of motivation as well. Only in the *Groundwork* did Kant find the key to the transition "from a popular philosophy, which goes no further than it can by groping with the help of examples, to metaphysics (which no longer lets itself be held back by anything empirical and, since it must measure out the whole sum of rational cognition of this kind, goes if need be all the way to ideas, where examples themselves fails us)" (*GM*, AA 4: 412). And because the popular philosopher Johann Georg Sulz-

---

24 See, for example, Kant's discussion of "a righteous man (like Spinoza) who takes himself to be firmly convinced that there is no God" (*CPJ*, AA 5: 452) in § 87 of the *Critique of Judgment*, as well as his remarks in the essay "On the common saying": "The incentive which the human being can have before a goal (end) is set for him can obviously be nothing other than the law itself through the respect that it inspires (without its being determined what end one may have and may attain by complying with it). For the law with respect to what is formal in choice is indeed all that remains when I have left out of consideration the matter of choice (the goal, as Mr. Garve calls it)." (*OCS*, AA 8: 282 note)

er asked the right question at the right time in Kant's philosophical development, Kant thanks him in the form of a note. It is not enough to build your system of virtues and duties on pure concepts of reason. You must also show how pure reason can motivate you to act according to its concepts. Kant's answer in the Groundwork is that pure reason is practical because it causes the feeling of respect in us. This feeling bridges the gap between pure reason and the human condition (desires and inclinations). However, the feeling of respect does not entail that people will always act out of respect for the moral law. The feeling of respect binds us to the voice of pure reason. It is the means of pure reason to obligate us through necessitation. However, at the end of the day, we act out of respect for the moral law. We have the choice to do good or evil. Why we choose the vicious action although we know better is inexplicable to Kant (Klemme 2013).

Gabriel Rivero
Dependence and Obedience: Crusius' Concept of Obligation and its Influence on Kant's Moral Philosophy

Abstract: Although it is undisputed that Crusius had a decisive influence on the development of Kant's practical philosophy, if one considers the specific question of obligation [*Verbindlichkeit*], his influence becomes less obvious. In this paper, I argue that the relevance of Crusius' notion of obligation is nuanced and, accordingly, highlight that Kant's reception of Crusius contains both positive as well as negative aspects. This becomes especially clear in two essential components of Kant's notion of obligation: moral necessitation and the self-legislating character of the will. In this regard, I argue that Kant develops a new concept of moral necessitation [*moralische Nötigung*] on the basis of his positive reception of Crusius' critique of Wolff. The negative dimension, viz. Kant's critical reception, refers to Crusius' application of the concept of dependence. In contrast to Crusius, Kant reinterprets the dependence of the will, which does not consist in the dependence upon an external lawgiver. In this way, Kant's reinterpretation of the concept of dependence represents an important step towards his conception of the autonomy of the will.

Although it is undisputed in secondary literature that Crusius had a decisive influence on the development of Kant's practical philosophy, the exact nature of his influence and its extent and duration are the subject of controversial discussion. In this sense, interpreters have attributed Crusius' influence either to the introduction of the distinction between formal and material elements of practical philosophy (see Menzer 1899, 305), to the importance of drives [*Triebe*] for action (see Henrich 1963), or to the priority of will over understanding (see Schmucker 1961, 81). It cannot be denied that these questions were crucial to Kant's practical philosophy, and accordingly it can be assumed that Crusius must have been an important inspiration for Kant.

If one considers the specific question of obligation [*Verbindlichkeit*] rather than the field of practical philosophy in general, the influence of Crusius becomes

---

Funding note: Funded by the Deutsche Forschungsgemeinschaft (DFG, German Research Foundation) – Project number 388570675. I am indebted to Sonja Schierbaum and John Walsh for their suggestions.

https://doi.org/10.1515/9783110793857-011

less obvious. There are basically two divergent interpretations: One position proceeds from the thesis that Crusius' influence can be excluded in every respect, since he advocated a theologically-shaped concept of obligation about which Kant was always skeptical (Schwaiger 2011, 146). According to this approach, Kant's idea of autonomy serves as decisive evidence that a theologically-shaped concept of obligation cannot in principle be considered valid. Rather, this approach holds that Alexander Baumgarten and/or Christian Wolff should be viewed as the most influential authors for the Kantian term "obligation" because they introduced an autonomous conception of morality based on the concept of perfection. The opposing interpretive approach emphasizes that despite Crusius' moral-theological notion of obligation, its relevance for Kant cannot be denied. According to this interpretation, Crusius is significant because he defines an attribute of the principles of morality on the basis of the idea of God's absolute authority, which produces an intrinsic obligation and is not based either on the idea of happiness or perfection. So, if neither perfection nor happiness are the central concepts for the moral judgment of an action, then it suggests that Crusius' idea of an absolute authority valid in itself, despite the implied theological elements, has similarities with Kant's idea of the absolute validity of the categorical imperative (see Fricke 2018; also Schmucker 1961, 85).

If we consider these interpretations from a critical perspective, it becomes clear that they both look at the influence of Crusius one-sidedly and therefore come to wrong results in each case, either by completely negating his influence or by completely affirming it. In what follows I will show that the one-sided negative assessment of Kant's reception of Crusius results in the failure to appropriately treat important elements of Crusius' practical philosophy that are undoubtedly significant for Kant's conception of obligation.[1] The one-sidedly positive appraisal – because it postulates that Kant adopts Crusius' theory almost without any criticism – leads to an oversimplification of the development of Kant's practical philosophy as well as a levelling of the differences between the two authors.[2] In

---

[1] This tendency is most noticeable in Schwaiger's interpretation, which attempts to relativize Crusius' influence in favor of Baumgarten's. In this regard Schwaiger disregards the importance of the concept of dependence for Kant's practical thought since he merely considers it from the implicit theological aspects. Cf. Schwaiger 1999, 48–49.

[2] As Fricke 2018, 61, for example, writes: "Aus der Lehre von der moralischen Gesetzgebung durch Gott übernimmt Kant Lehren, die für seine eigene Theorie von zentraler Bedeutung sind, allen voran die Lehre von der Notwendigkeit und Objektivität der moralischen Verpflichtung, d.h. die Konzeption der moralischen Pflicht als universaler Rechtspflicht und die daraus folgende Unterscheidung zwischen einer genuin moralischen Handlungsmotivation und einer Motivation, die aus der Selbstliebe und dem Glücksstreben erwächst."

contrast to the aforementioned interpretations, I argue that the relevance of Crusius' notion of obligation is nuanced and, accordingly, highlight that Kant's reception of Crusius contains both positive as well as negative aspects. This becomes especially clear in two essential components of Kant's notion of obligation: moral necessitation and the self-legislating character of the will.

The positive dimension proposed here is linked to Crusius' critique of incorporating psychological elements into the determination of obligation, which was characteristic for the practical philosophy of the Wolffians. In this regard, I argue that Kant develops a new concept of moral necessitation [*moralische Nötigung*] on the basis of his positive reception of Crusius' critique of Wolff. The negative dimension, viz. Kant's critical reception, refers to Crusius' application of the concept of dependence. Two points regarding this critique prove to be relevant. On the one hand, Kant still considers this concept to be important with respect to obligation insofar as in 1785 he defines the latter in connection with the dependence of the will which is not absolutely good.[3] On the other hand, however, Kant strongly criticizes Crusius' conception of the relation of the human will with respect to God's laws such that Kant ultimately reinterprets this relation. In contrast to Crusius this relation does not consist in the dependence upon an external lawgiver. Thus, a second important element of Kant's conception of obligation arises, namely the self-legislating character of the will.

In summary, one can say that Kant, due to his positive reception of Crusius, emphasizes the non-psychological determination of the constraining character of the law (critique of psychology). The autonomous character of the will emerges from his negative reception of Crusius insofar as the dependence of the will follows from a self-legislated law (critique of theology). This double-character of Kant's reception of Crusius manifests how he positions his new concept of obligation in his practical philosophy as an original alternative to Wolffian naturalism as well as to the voluntarism of the Pietistic tradition.[4]

In this paper I will address this proposed impact of Crusius on Kant's practical thought on the basis of the *Preisschrift* of 1762/64, the *Träume eines Geistersehers* (1766) and the *Vorlesung Kaehler* from the mid-1770s. This text is structured in two parts. The first part presents the elements of the positive reception, which will be clarified on the basis of Crusius' voluntarist notion of obligation and his

---

[3] The fact that the concept of dependence is an essential component of obligation is demonstrated by its definition in *GM*, AA 4: 439: "The dependence upon the principle of autonomy of a will that is not absolutely good (moral necessitation) is *obligation*." On Kant's concept of obligation in his pre-critical period see Rivero 2017. For Kant's conceptions of obligation and dependence during the critical period see Rivero 2018.
[4] On Wolff's concept of obligation, see Hüning 2002; see also Hüning 2018.

critique of the psychologizing components of the necessitating character of law in Wolff. The second part examines the negative reception, on the basis of which Kant's re-interpretation of the concept of dependence can be clarified.

1 The Positive Reception: The Critique of a Psychologically-Based Concept of Obligation

1.1 Crusius' Critique of the Conflation of Psychological and Normative Components of Obligation

One of the essential definitions of the concept of obligation in the Wolffian tradition consists in establishing the correlation between cognition of a (objective) law of nature and the (subjective) motive of an action which arises from that cognition. The idea of an active obligation stems from this correlation between motive and law (cf. Wolff 1754, § 35. See also Baumgarten 1760, § 10 and 11, and Eberhard 1786, § 35 and 36). A few presumptions however underlie this correlation, which lies at the heart of the Thomasians' and Pietists' criticism of Wolff. First, the normative and rational character of the law of nature is presumed to be valid in itself, by virtue of which the moral value of an action can be objectively determined. This means that at the normative level, the moral value of an action does not derive from commanding determinations, which externally ascribe moral character to the action. Instead, this value is based on conformity to the law of nature, that is, to the principle of perfection, whereby good or evil actions in themselves are defined as duties that ought to be done or omitted.[5] The second presumption refers to the level of motivation in which mere cognition of the natural law is a sufficient motive for action.[6] Thus, the obligating character of an action results from this close connection of normative and motivational levels insofar as the underlying motives for action have a causal power.[7] These two fundamental characteristics of Wolff's moral philosophy – the autonomy of moral law on one hand and intellectualism on the other – would be disapproved by the Pietistic, Thomasian tradition.[8] According to Pietistic theology, Wolff's conception of the autonomy of the law

---

[5] Cf. Wolff 1733, § 5: "[...] so sind sie vor und an sich selbst gut oder böse, und werden nicht erst durch GOTTES Willen dazu gemacht." See Wolff 1754, §§ 13–14.
[6] Wolff 1733, § 6: "Die Erkäntniß des guten ist eine Bewegungs-Grund des Willens."
[7] In this way, the moral principle is: "Thue was dich und deinen oder anderer Zustand vollkommener machet; unterlaß, was ihn unvollkommener machet." Wolff 1733, § 12.
[8] On the general debate between the Thomasians and Wolff, cf. Arndt 1989.

identifies law and lawgiver, which ultimately leads to the charge that Wolff's philosophy is atheistic. Intellectualism in turn is construed as leading to the abolition of human freedom since it establishes a mechanical connection between law and motive. This critical interpretation of Wolff's moral philosophy is most clearly found in the work of Joachim Lange (cf. Lange 1734). Two basic strategies can be discerned in his critique: one refers to the logical mistakes that seem to be found in Wolff's arguments. In this respect, Lange objects multiple times that Wolff argues either circularly or simply tautologically. Lange's other strategy consists in fabricating proximity between the Wolffian system and that of Spinoza so that the common objections against Spinozism would also apply to Wolff. Even this brief mention of Lange's criticism of Wolff already indicates what will guide Crusius' remarks in connection with this subject. Like Lange, Crusius argues for the separation of law and lawgiver and takes up the same critical standpoint towards intellectualism, which in his view abolishes human freedom. However, a closer examination proves that Crusius pursues a different strategy than Lange in his critique of Wolff. For Crusius, the recourse to identifying Wolff with Spinoza is not relevant at all; likewise, he does not focus on logical objections (cf. Carboncini 1989). The characteristic feature of his critical approach consists much more in the fact that it is conceptualized in terms of a theory of faculties.

This becomes clear when Crusius claims that a separate theoretical science, whose object would be exclusively the knowledge of nature and the attributes of the will, should necessarily precede practical philosophy (Crusius 1744, § 1). Starting from this claim, we can distinguish several of his general points of criticism aimed at Wolffianism. One of the first consists in Crusius introducing a theory of human faculties, which asserts a transcendental separation between cognitive and appetitive faculties. As a second point of criticism, Crusius emphasizes the priority of the will in this division. Based on the idea that the will is not a faculty that may be reduced to understanding, one realizes that mere knowledge of perfection does not allow for the justification of the necessity of an action. This is the third point of criticism. At this point, the question arises how relevant these points of criticism could be for the conception of obligation. A closer inspection proves that two notable aspects for the determination of obligation follow from these points of criticism. The first aspect refers to "de-psychologizing" the relation between will and law, which was characteristic for the Wolffians. The second aspect entails a new understanding of law, which by its nature should be considered in conjunction with the aforementioned "de-psychologization" of the relation between will and law. In the following, I will elaborate on both these latter aspects, namely: (a) de-psychologization and (b) understanding of the law.

(a) *"De-psychologization" and moral necessitation.* Crusius' critique of Wolff reveals, first and foremost, that drives become significantly more important for the determination of action because the will, as opposed to the understanding, is conceived as an independent faculty. Of the three drives mentioned by Crusius – the drives of perfection, moral love and conscience – the drive of conscience [*Gewissenstrieb*] is undoubtedly most germane to the question of obligation. Since conscience is defined as a drive, Crusius draws the conclusion that it does not concern theoretical judgments of the understanding, and consequently should also not be mistaken for consciousness in general nor with the epistemic consciousness of perfection or imperfection.[9] Hence, Crusius points out that conscience is not related to the Latin term *conscientia* but to the term *religio* (Crusius 1744, § 132). The question regarding indebtedness [*Schuldigkeit*] with respect to divine law should be explained with neither consequentialist nor naturalist reasons and hence should also not be conceived as a consciousness that yields a determining motive. Accordingly, indebtedness is neither linked to weighing utility or damages, nor is it equivalent to a motive or to be confounded with coercion, fear or hope (Crusius 1744, § 133). The reason such indebtedness arises and becomes discernible consists solely in obedience.[10]

Aside from the theologically implied elements in Crusius' conceptions of indebtedness and obedience, it follows from the drive of conscience that the will immediately submits itself to a law. This is accordingly predicated on the direct regard for the legal character of the command itself. If the submission of the will ensues merely on the basis of the legal character of the command without considering other conditions, then an obligation arises, which cannot be traced back to any other ground than the absolute authority of the law and the engendered indebtedness towards this law. Crusius calls this "legal obligation," viz. "obligation of virtue," which differs from "obligation of prudence" in that the former is not directed towards arbitrary ends grounded in human nature but is based on reasons that refer back to the law.[11]

If this is so, then a *necessitating, imperative* character must be attributed to the obligation of virtue, on the basis of which the will is immediately subjected to the

---

9 "Daß das Gewissen kein bloß theoretisches Urtheil des Verstandes sey, sondern seinen Grund in einem Triebe des Willens haben müsse, kann man auch schon daraus urtheilen, weil es erfreuet und ängstet [.]" (Crusius 1744, § 132).
10 "Der Gewissentrieb ist also bloß ein Trieb, gewisse Schuldigkeiten, das ist, solche allgemeine Verbindlichkeiten zu erkennen, die man aus Gehorsam zu beobachten hat[.]" (Crusius 1744, § 133)
11 Crusius 1744, § 162: "Nemlich dasjenige, worauf sich die moralische Nothwendigkeit eines Thuns und Lassens gründet [...] wird entweder nur in gewissen schon vorher von uns begehrten Endzwecken gesucht [...]; so will ich die Pflicht, welche, und wiefern, sie sich darauf gründet, eine Pflicht der Klugheit § 161 nennen[.] Oder der Grund der moralischen Nothwendigkeit liegt in einem Gesetze und in unserer Schuldigkeit, dasselbige zu erfüllen; so will ich dergleichen Pflicht eine Pflicht der Tugend nennen."

law. This is what I originally identified as the "de-psychologization" of the relation between action and law; the particular relevance of which – from a Kantian perspective – lies in the disclosure of an important aspect of obligation: purely moral necessitation grounded in the law. Two important aspects can be taken here in regard to the necessitating character of the law: on the one hand the reason for the observance of the law results from the authority of the law itself;[12] on the other, it follows from the former that the moral necessity of the law – in the sense of active obligation – is not established by an epistemological, causal connection between the psychologically conditioned notion of good and obligatory action. This ultimately means that psychology may not function as the link between the law and the will.[13]

Crusius comments extensively on this aspect in the footnote to paragraph 164 of his *Anweisung*. He first criticizes the fallacious conflation of psychological and normative elements of obligation. He claims that the question of the validity of obligation on the one side and the question of the way in which an action is initiated via effective causes on the other must be separated.[14] Crusius calls into question the Wolffian claim that nature obligates us by saying that such an expression in principle merely constitutes a theoretical proposition, which can only elucidate what and how we want something, but not why we should want it. Psychology can only give an explanation as to how the causal and empirical connection between law and motive occurs in action, that is, an account for the *genesi physica* of action, as Crusius calls it. Hence, he claims that no justification of the ought

---

12 This is the reason why, for example, Fugate emphasizes the proximity between Kant's and Crusius' conceptions of moral obligation: "Crusius is brought to this notion of freedom in order [...] to make sense of our actual inner experience of moral struggle and choice, and our actual experience of the sort of absolute duty or moral obligation we know the moral law to be invested with. His conception of freedom [...] makes it possible to understand the moral law as what Kant calls a categorical imperative, precisely because it invests us with the capacity to act from the thought of the law alone[.]" See Fugate 2010, 281.
13 At this point, Fugate critically points out that Crusius' notion of freedom leads to an absolute subjectivism in which the connection between law and will, or freedom and law no longer exist. "There are simply no resources within Crusius' concept of freedom to explain how freedom *qua* freedom could possibly be motivated to adopt any particular law, let alone the moral law." Fugate 2010, 281–282. Notably, Fugate does not consider the aspect of obligation, which precisely establishes such a connection through the idea of absolute authority.
14 Crusius 1744, § 164: "Man verwirret die Entstehungsart einer Handlung aus ihren wirckenden Ursachen mit der Verbindlichkeit. Z.E. Wenn man sagt, die Natur verbinde uns durch die Vorstellung des Guten; denn diese Vorstellung, worinnen wir etwas vor ein Gut halten, treibe uns an, danach zu streben [...]. Dieser Satz gehört zur genesi physica der Actionen des Willens."

is given,[15] and it is therefore necessary to discuss the normative question totally independent of psychology.[16]

Hence, an alternative to Wolffian practical philosophy emerges, since a non-psychological notion of the necessitating character of the law leads to the fact that the imperative authority to execute or omit a certain action originates neither in the mere cognition of perfection, nor in the implicit cognition of the consequences of an action. It is thus, to use Lange's expression, the orientation toward the pure law and not toward the action and its consequences that reveals obligation.[17]

(b) *The law*. At this point, the conception of law should be more closely examined. At first glance, Crusius' remarks regarding the law appear to be a long way from being able to provide positive elements for the Kantian conceptions of obligation and law. A few aspects are nevertheless quite relevant.[18] The first noteworthy feature of a law is the correlation with the *will*, which is established in Crusius' work (cf. Crusius 1744, § 165). As opposed to Wolff, who defines law as a rule toward which free actions should be directed (cf. Wolff 1733, § 16), Crusius' considers the idea of the will of a lawgiver to be a determining authority. The second noteworthy feature concerns the *universality* of the will. This universal will, in turn, postulates – as the third feature – the *autonomy* of the lawgiver such that this lawgiver can be designated the sovereign (cf. Crusius 1744, § 165).

Although Kant's conception of obligation is distant from the ideas of the will, obedience, and indebtedness, explicated above, Crusius' observations prepare the way for an important advancement apropos the non-psychological notion of moral necessitation, which Kant later defines as the will's dependence upon the moral law. This already appears in Kant's pre-critical phase, particularly from 1762–1764, when he understands obligation in connection with the necessity of ends.

---

[15] Crusius 1744, § 164: "Bei der Verbindlichkeit [] will man nicht wissen, wodurch eine Handlung geschiehet, denn die bösen und guten Actionen haben ihre zureichenden wirckenden Ursachen; sondern man verlangt zu wissen, ob und warum etwas geschehen soll, oder darf."

[16] Upon closer examination, an identical distinction and an equally valid critique can be seen in the preface to Kant's *Groundwork* in which Kant, like Crusius, reproaches Wolff for having investigated the empirically and psychologically determined will, but not the pure will. Cf. *GM*, AA 4: 390. In this regard, we could speak of a long-term effect of Crusius on Kant. Cf. Baum 2018, 179–180.

[17] Lange 1734, 23: "Ob nicht ein Gesetz eher seyn müße, als eine Handlung, damit es dieselbe als eine allgemeine Regel und Richtschnur dirigiren könnte?"

[18] In section 2 I go into further detail on the aspect criticized by Kant.

1.2 Kant's Positive Reception Exemplified by the *Preisschrift* of 1762/1764: Obligation as the Necessity of Ends

In general, the *Preisschrift* – as far as practical philosophy is concerned – holds an ambivalent stance towards Crusius (cf. Henrich 1957, 64).[19] On the one hand, Kant relies on some of Crusius' arguments to reinforce his critical position against Wolffianism. A clear example of this is Kant's reference to a necessary distinction between the faculty of cognizing what is true from sensing the good (cf. Crusius 1744, § 165). On the other hand, it becomes apparent that Kant criticizes Crusius in two regards: first, Kant still does not maintain a theologically-grounded notion of obligation and, second, he limits the "double character" of obligation, which he adopts from Crusius, to an aspect of virtue that he interprets in the *Preisschrift* as the necessity of ends – as opposed to the non-obligating necessity of means.[20]

On closer inspection of this last point, however, it becomes apparent that despite Kant's critical standpoint, a positive element emerges, which in principle speaks for a Crusian influence in the *Preisschrift*. This is demonstrated by the fact that Kant – insofar as he conceived the notion of obligation as something that is exclusively derived from the necessity of ends – de-psychologizes the concept of obligation and hence implicitly that of necessitation as well.[21] In this way, in accordance with Crusius and against all tendencies to incorporate psychological elements into the grounding of obligation, Kant emphasizes that the obligating character of practical principles is characterized by one essential feature: the *immediacy* of their validity.

The fact that an action is immediately represented as good indicates that the moral necessity of an action does not depend upon empirical or arbitrary ends. Moreover, this shows that a mediation based on mere reason (which is typical for Wolffianism) between objective natural law and subjective knowledge, whereby the good is discerned, is of no importance. The reason for this is that Kant limits the guiding principle of perfection – even if he considers it to be valid – to a merely formal significance so that no motivating effect can be attributed to the insight into perfection. In this sense, Kant calls into question the correlation between motive and action, which determines active obligation and unites the objective natu-

---

[19] Klemme argues against this position by relativizing Crusius' relevance in the *Preisschrift* and by attempting to emphasize the proximity to Wolff's position. See Klemme 2018a, 301–302.
[20] *IC*, AA 2: 298: "The first kind of necessity does not indicate any obligation at all."
[21] Schwaiger rightly points out, against the common interpretation of the *Preisschrift*, that Kant's distinction between the necessity of means and ends is not influenced by Crusius. Cf. Schwaiger 1999, 52–54. However, to claim that Kant's distinction is based on Baumgarten's *Initia* is misleading. This would deny Kant's anti-psychological point of view that he assumedly adopted from Crusius.

ral law and the subjective motives brought about by reason. In short, according to the Kant's standpoint of 1762/1764, the obligating character of the principles of action cannot exclusively be traced back to a clear cognition acquired through reason, which actively motivates obligating action.[22] Instead of cognition as the motive for action, Kant claims that it is rather consciousness of the feeling of pleasure or displeasure that brings about the immediacy of the practical principles and can supplement the formal character of the principle of perfection (*IC*, AA 2: 299). Kant tries to draw a parallel between practical and theoretical principles; in this way, he makes the claim, just as in the case of theoretical cognition, that the mere definition of terms should not be the methodological starting point. Rather, empirical and "certain propositions" [*sichere Erfahrungssätze*] can guarantee the validity of principles. The immediacy of the principles of practical philosophy mentioned by Kant also leads to the presumption that "the supreme rule of all obligation" is indemonstrable (*IC*, AA 2: 299).

How the formal and the material relate to one another is not, however, clearly enough explained in the *Preisschrift* and Kant concludes his considerations with an open question, namely, whether the faculty of cognition or feeling is that which determines the principles of practical cognition. Assuming that Kant would have chosen the first option, it would be certain that he would not make a case for a purely intellectualist notion of obligation since immediacy and indemonstrability are considered to be essential features of practical principles. A conception focused merely on feeling would be equally implausible because this would result in a purely psychological definition of obligation in an empirical sense. The moral feeling postulated by Kant instead provides a direct experience of the good, which complements the formal principle of perfection. Only then can a moral necessity of ends be expressed. In this sense, it can be assumed that neither the psychological components of Wolffian intellectualism nor the psychological-empirical components of moral sense theory are decisive for Kant's understanding of practical philosophy around 1762/1764. Instead, he appears at this time to have attempted to develop a theory of material and formal principles which have a certain proximity to Crusius' remarks regarding the drive of conscience. For in both cases, immediacy is postulated as the instance of recognizing the obligating character of an action and, likewise, in both cases such recognition is not regarded as a merely conceptual recognition brought about by understanding or reason.

---

[22] *IC*, AA 2: 299: "For it is impossible, by contemplating a thing or a concept of any kind whatever, to recognize or infer what one ought to do[.]"

2 The Negative Reception: The Critique of a Theologically-Based Conception of Obligation

2.1 Crusius' Notion of Dependency as Obedience and Indebtedness

As already mentioned at the outset, Wolff's justification of obligation does not trace back to an authority of the will of a lawgiver, but rather to an objective, autonomous natural law. Crusius' use of the concept of dependence is in this sense a clear indication of how he develops his theory as distinct to Wolffianism and hence closely orients himself towards a voluntarist notion of moral law. It becomes clear that Crusius follows the critique of Wolf made by the Thomasians and continues some of their arguments that had already been put forward by, for instance, Joachim Lange. But in contrast to Lange, Crusius developed – in addition to his critique and own conception of obligation – an extensive theory of the will and drives.[23]

If we turn to Crusius' idea mentioned in the previous section, namely to understand conscience as *religio* instead of *conscientia*, and consider it in relation to the concept of dependence that he uses to define obligation, then it turns out that a triad of elements – the foundation of which ultimately amounts to a theologically-based conception of obligation – determines action. First, the divine law; second, obedience; and third, indebtedness. Contrary to Wolffianism, which identifies the *law* with the *law of nature*, Crusius rather presumes an equation of *law* and *universal will*, by virtue of which the law itself and the act of its generation by its lawgiver can be distinguished.[24] From this follows, first, that the demanding character of the law takes on the character of a command and, second, that this character generates a relationship of indebtedness underlying this command, whereby it ultimately gains unconditional and imperatival validity (Crusius 1744, § 133).

What has been said suggests that the obligation of the law presupposes a lawgiver, whose basic characteristic is its independence [*Selbständigkeit*]. From its independence, it follows both that it can qualify as a (self-)lawgiver and also that the laws she enacts are unconditionally valid for the human will (Crusius 1744, § 165). Moreover, the obligation towards the law presupposes that obligation essentially

---

23 See section 1.1.
24 Crusius 1744, § 165: "Ein Gesetz ist ein allgemeiner Wille eines mächtigern, welcher nicht wiederum einen andern mächtigern über sich hat[.]"

has a "determining-determined" relationship in which one acts as a sovereign (by virtue of its independence) and the other as a subordinate (by virtue of its dependence). This also gives rise to a submission based on a relationship of debt and hence defines an unconditional duty. If we look again at the Kantian definition of obligation from 1785,[25] it becomes obvious how Crusius – despite his theological background – supplies the precursors for central concepts of Kant's practical philosophy insofar as elements such as law/will, submission [*Unterwerfung*], and duty assume a decisive function for him. It is now necessary in the following section to pursue the question as to how Kant reinterprets the concept of dependence in the course of his intellectual development such that the terms just mentioned can acquire a truly Kantian significance.

2.2 The Negative Reception Exemplified by Kant's Reinterpretation of the Concept of Dependence in *Dreams* (1766) and in the *Kaehler Lecture* (1774/5)

2.2.1 The Dreams of a Spirit-Seer

An initial phase of the re-interpretation of the concept of dependence is depicted in the *Dreams of a Spirit-Seer* from 1766. The first subtle modification of the concept of dependence – the impact of which on the terms of law, submission, and duty is relevant – refers to its characterization as a "felt" or "sensed" [*empfundene*] dependence (cf. *DSS*, AA 2: 334). That Kant speaks in the context of the *Dreams* of a "felt" dependence is explained by his intention to subject metaphysics in general, and the concept of spirit [*Geist*] in particular, to a critique. In this sense, Kant attempts to show that the concept of spirit – like all other concepts of metaphysics – has no validity if it is not based on experience. In accordance with the *Preisschrift* of 1762/64, he raises the claim that metaphysical concepts should be based on empirical and certain propositions [*sichere Erfahrungssätze*]; in contrast to the *Preisschrift*, Kant however uses a method in *Dreams* that employs skeptical elements and is supposed to reveal the limits of human reason.[26] The application of this method produces important results which concern, among others, practical cognition. In this respect, Kant's reference to the impossibility of using a pure concept implies that sensible and intellectual representations are considered dissimilar [*unglei-*

---

25 See note 3.
26 Accordingly, Kant's definition of metaphysics in the *Dreams* is: "a science of the *limits of human reason.*" *DSS*, AA 2: 368. See also Moses Mendelssohn's letter from 1766 (see AA 10: 70).

chartig] (cf. Rumore 2007, 187–233). Since the dissimilarity of these representations leads to the fact that no gradual distinction between them is possible, it is necessary to differentiate between two regularities that can be described as laws of nature and laws of freedom.[27]

This distinction points to a specific characteristic of Kant's standpoint in 1766 because – according to his observations – sensible and intellectual representations, viz. laws, are cognizable neither a priori nor a posteriori considered in isolation.[28] Kant's way out of this problematic position now appears to be to speak about the impact of intellectual or pure representations on the sensible world without, however, needing to address the ontological constitution of the intelligible world. Human cognition shows its limits in this sense through the characteristic features of human reason, which indeed postulate an order of things but cannot prove it.[29] This is the case with the assumption of the existence of the soul and its participation in a spirit-world (see *DSS*, AA 2: 329–341). Although the soul can be postulated as a pure, indivisible entity that, as such, participates in the spirit-world, it does not follow from this that the human being can have a direct – and to this extent pure, metaphysical – cognition of the soul and its participation in that world. As a sensible dependent being, however, the human being is capable of visualizing such a participation through a sensation (see *DSS*, AA 2: 324) so that – without overstepping the limits of human reason – the human being can be conscious of her participation in two worlds.

In the context of this reflection on the spirit-world, Kant develops his conception of a sensed dependence, which he identifies as a relation between one's own intentions, viz. self-interest, and the common good (see *DSS*, AA 2: 334). Kant writes as follows:

> We recognize that, in our most secret motives, we are dependent upon the *rule of the general will*. It is the rule which confers upon the world of all thinking beings its *moral unity* and invests it with a systematic constitution, drawn up in accordance with purely spiritual laws. We sense within ourselves a constraining of our will to harmonize with the general will. To call this sensed constraining *moral feeling*, is to speak of it merely as a manifestation of that which takes place within us, without establishing its causes. (*DSS*, AA 2: 335)

---

27 "This *immaterial world* may therefore be regarded as a whole existing in its own right; the parts of that immaterial world stand in a relation of reciprocal connection and community with each other, even without the mediation of corporeal things; it follows that this latter relation is contingent and only belongs to some of the parts." *DSS*, AA 2: 330. See Gutiérrez-Xivillé 2018b.
28 In this sense, Lothar Kreimendahl speaks of an "empirically founded" metaphysics in Kant around 1766. Cf. Kreimendahl 1990, 125–126.
29 On the distinction between human knowledge and human reason, see Rivero 2014, 86–110.

This quotation discloses multiple aspects of the reinterpretation of the concept of dependence, which affects the concepts of law, submission, and duty.

Law. In accord with Crusius, Kant's explanations represent the universal, viz. the law, as a rule of the will by means of which a unity of thinking natures is established by subjugating the private will. This general rule has a necessitating character that manifests itself as a determining relation of dependence. In contrast to Crusius, however, the cause of the law is not questioned – due to the limit of human reason – so that the specific relevance that Crusius assigns to the authority of the independent lawgiver in order to determine the obligating character of an action does not play a role here at all. This is because according to the Kantian standpoint, the cause of the accord between the universal and the private will, which is created by a law, is not "discernable."

What follows from this is that in contrast to Crusius, the independence of the lawgiver for Kant is not a decisive element in order to be able to guarantee the imperative character of submission. It can be presumed that as a result of the reinterpretation of the concept of dependence, the independence of the law becomes the center of Kant's consideration. That it is possible to assume such an autonomy of the law is in principle due to the fact that the moral unity, which guarantees the "sensed" participation in the spirit-world, leads to the insight that the laws of morality are considered to be their own class independent from nature, which Kant calls "merely spiritual laws." If that is the case, one can conclude that Kant succeeds in taking an important step towards the idea of the autonomy of the law insofar as the obligating necessity of the law is not derived from the authority of the lawgiver; instead, mere universality, on the one hand, and the validity of the moral law isolated from the senses, on the other, seem to be the characteristics which give rise to moral necessitation with regard to the private will and the resulting conformity with the universal will.[30]

Submission. If Kant deduces the submission of the private will to the universal will from the mere universality of the law "without establishing its causes", then submission is, phenomenologically considered, grounded on moral feeling. At the basis of this conception – according to which the unifying effect of the law appears as a phenomenon and manifests itself as a "moral feeling" (*DSS*, AA 2: 335)   Kant avoids using voluntarist concepts; for example, command, even though he continues to make use of the concept of dependence.

Duty. Crusius' concept of conscience as *religio* instead of *conscientia* leads – as demonstrated in the previous section – to a conception of duty as indebtedness;

---

[30] In the *Bemerkungen*, Kant presents the same view. Cf. *ROBS*, AA 20: 145. See also Edwards 2018, 188–189.

that is, to a relation determined by the idea of obedience and hence to a commitment understood according to the model of perfect legal duty (see Fricke 2018, 59). Although Kant's remarks in *Dreams* do not allow us to pursue this idea further, he in principle provides the preconditions to avoid such a Crusian conception of duty despite his use of dependence. Finally, Kant does not use the terms lawgiver, obedience, nor command, but instead speaks of motives which he furnishes with the attribute "secret."

2.2.2 The Kaehler Lecture

As progressive as these conceptions of the concept of dependence may appear in *Dreams*, they still receive a revision shortly thereafter in Kant's inaugural dissertation of 1770. The reason for this lies in the fact that Kant's method around 1770 specifies and radicalizes the distinction between pure and sensible ideas already sketched in *Dreams* in such a way that a transcendental distinction is drawn between sensibility and understanding. The radicality of this methodical approach bans the language of a felt dependence in the context of practical philosophy, as was the case in *Dreams*. Instead, Kant makes use of a terminology in keeping with the introduction of a "pure part" of practical philosophy and in which the *ideal* becomes the leading concept of practical philosophy (see *ID*, AA 2: § 9; cf. also AA 10: 97).

The notion of practical philosophy as a pure part of the system represented in his *Dissertatio* is later more precisely determined in the *Kaehler Lecture* from the mid-1770s. In this lecture, new elements in the determination of dependence appear, the consequences of which are of great importance for the concepts of law, submission, and duty.

Law. Just as in *Dreams*, the independence of the law from that of the lawgiver is presupposed in the *Kaehler Lecture*.[31] But in contrast to *Dreams*, in which the impact of the law as the appearance of a feeling was central for the determination and establishment of the dependence of the private will, in the *Kaehler Lecture* – under the influence of the method of the *Dissertatio* – the insight into the validity of a general rule derived from pure reason ultimately proves to be decisive.[32] In this regard, Kant develops a conception of law that is exclusively grounded on

---

[31] Stark 2004, 79: "Vom moralischen Gesetz ist also kein Wesen auch das göttliche nicht ein Urheber, denn sie sind nicht aus der Willkür entsprungen, sondern sind practisch nothwendig[.]"
[32] Stark 2004, 267: "Diejenige principia [...], die allgemein, beständig und nothwendig gelten sollen, können nicht aus der Erfahrung, sondern aus reiner Vernunft abgeleitet werden." Cf. also Gutiérrez-Xivillé 2018a, 139–216.

the universality of the rule (Stark 2004, 68). This universal character of the rule is at the same time the reason for its morally imperatival feature. In this sense, Kant can clearly distinguish between pragmatic and categorical imperatives (Stark 2004, 53 and 58), and between the principle of appraising obligation and the principle of its performance (Stark 2004, 55–56).

Submission. Such a sharp distinction between the principle of appraisal, on the one hand, and the principle of performance on the other, however, makes the question of the submission of the will particularly incisive. Kant states in the lecture, "The submission of our will to the rule of universally valid ends is the inner goodness [*Bonitaet*] and absolute perfection of free choice" (Stark 2004, 30). It follows from Kant's observations that the subjection of the will to a law must be interpreted in such a way that it is based only on an internal determination which only requires the subjective principle of action to be in accordance with universal ends. Thus, Kant presumes contra Crusius that the goodness [*Bonitaet*] of the action and its necessitating character are not a result of the dependence of the will on another;[33] rather, it consists in the formal character of conformity with "universal ends." The will should subject itself to a law that is only valid by virtue of the principle of appraisal of the understanding.[34] This means that the exercised necessitation is to be judged as moral because the, in principle, merely subjective necessity of one's own end qualifies as a universal end.[35] The necessity of an action is to be understood as a *necessitatio* instead of a *necessitas* so that the will subjects itself to a rule; that is, makes itself dependent upon a rule that the will imposed on itself.

Duty. Turning towards the concept of duty, it follows from the previous elements (the formal universality of the law, the goodness of the action as agreement of ends and, the necessity of action as "making necessary") that Kant had to arrive at a new conception of duty. Duty can express – contra Wolffianism – neither a mere necessity of the law because duty implies a necessitation ("making necessary") nor – contra Crusius – the result of a mere indebtedness insofar as the necessity of an action follows from the law itself: from obligation. In this sense, it must be emphasized that the relation implied by the concept of duty cannot be interpreted in the sense of a legal relationship; rather, it concerns a relation that establishes itself by a specific relationship to itself: as self-determination and self-legislation.

---

[33] Stark 2004, 37–38: "Crusius meynt, alle Verbindlichkeit beziehe sich auf die Willkür eines andern. [A]llein ich werde necessitirt durch ein arbitrium internum aber nicht durch ein arbitrium externum; also durch die nothwendige Bedingung der allgemeinen Willkür[.]"

[34] Stark 2004, 68: "Da nun der Verstand das Vermögen der Regel und der Urtheile ist, so besteht die Moralitaet in der Unterordnung der Handlung überhaupt unter dem principio des Verstandes."

[35] Kant calls this process the "necessitation" [*Notwendigmachung*] of the random, subjective principles of action. Cf. Stark 2004, 29.

In other words, the legal model interprets the relation on which duty is based as a commitment to something that allows the obligating power of law to emerge from the relation to a third term, to its choice, command, and authority. On the contrary, Kant's model of duty does not merely address such an obligation to the law; rather, its characteristic feature consists in being a *self-obligation, self-determination* and a *self-legislation*. In this sense, the law does not arise from the relation to a third term, but from the relation to itself. What constitutes duty is agreement with oneself and one's own humanity – the dignity of one's own self.

As has become clear from what has been said above, Kant's reinterpretation of the concept of dependence inherited from Crusius reveals a change in the concepts of law/will, submission, and duty, which, from a developmental perspective, represents an important step towards Kant's own conception of the autonomy of the will. In the case of the positive reception of Crusius' conception of obligation, Crusius' conception leads Kant to the non-psychologically understood notion of the moral necessitation of the will. In the negative reception, another noteworthy concept is illuminated from the perspective of its historical development: the autonomy of the will. Such a result can only be achieved if, in contrast to the current interpretations, the influence of Crusius' conception of obligation on Kant is not merely generalized in one direction or the other, but seen to consist in various, properly differentiated, aspects. This was precisely the aim of this essay.

Part III: **Controversies**

Stefanie Buchenau
Human Dignity: The Garve-Kant Controversy

Abstract: The aim of this article is to shed a new light on the Kantian notion of *Menschenwürde*, or human dignity, as a universal entitlement to respect and institutional protection. By reconstructing Kant's controversy with Christian Garve in the *Groundwork*, it shows that this notion possesses multiple dimensions beyond the strictly ethical and political, that it lies at the very core of Kant's philosophy and that Kant himself participated in a wider Enlightenment debate and collective reinterpretation of it, based on modern social, economic and aesthetic premises. The first part offers an attempt to locate Garve's position in his 1783 translation and detailed philosophical commentary on Cicero. Garve's attempt to translate Cicero's *De Officiis* from the Roman Age into German civil society conduces him to put special emphasis on the importance of self-esteem as grounded not on the affiliation to a particular social class but on a universal human honor and a novel idea of human vocation and self-perfectioning. This perspective, in turn, sheds new light on the systematic relation between the notions of dignity, freedom and God, which Garve had already sketched in his 1772 Ferguson commentary and which he developed in 1783, while adding important ideas on what he calls "interest", "participation" and human education through art and aesthetics.
The second part describes Kant's response to Garve and traces the two thinkers' lifelong dialogue. As shows his *Groundwork*, originally set up as an "Anti-Garve", Kant elaborates on a number of fundamental ideas first outlined by Garve.

The Enlightenment marks a central stage in the *Begriffsgeschichte* of human dignity, illustrated by the emergence of a new composite noun: *Menschenwürde*. Of course, this *Menschenwürde* concept slowly emerging as a new translation of the Latin expression *dignitas hominis* and the German expression *Würde des Menschen* did not at that time enjoy its current constitutional status. Notwithstanding its innovative claims, the French *Déclaration des droits de l'homme et du citoyen* [Declaration of the rights of man and of the Citizen] of 1792 employed the term *dignité* in a rather traditional and established sense, asserting that "humans and citizens are admitted to all public dignities, offices, and positions [*toutes dignités, places et emplois publics*]."[1] But despite the differences in usage, a novel idea was

---

[1] *Déclaration des droits de l'homme et du citoyen*, 1792, § 6: "All the citizens, being equal in its eyes,

beginning to take shape: that humans never lose their dignity or their right to respect, however humane or inhumane their actions and behavior;[2] and that political institutions and universal human rights should guarantee them protection of this dignity.

The German philosopher Christian Garve (1712–1798) appears to have played a major role in this history. As a modern interpreter of Cicero, he was himself an important thinker on human dignity, taking an active part in what Johan von der Zande called the "eighteenth Century Cicero Renaissance" (see van der Zande 1995 and 1998) In 1783, he translated and commented on over 800 pages of Cicero's classic treatise on dignity, *De officiis* [*On Duties*]. In this commentary, entitled *Philosophische Anmerkungen und Abhandlungen zu Ciceros Büchern von den Pflichten* [*Philosophical Annotations and Treatises on Cicero's Books of Duties*], Garve gave a new direction to the Enlightenment debate on human dignity and vocation [*Bestimmung*]. In his commentary, he made a first and very tangible attempt to transfer the ancient notions of *honestas*, *dignitas*, and *officium* from the Roman Republic to the modern, political, and economic present and its civil society. Garve lays out the "Stoic" fundamentals for this commentary as early as 1772 in the postface of his translation of Adam Ferguson's *Principles of Moral Theory*. He subsequently expounded on the humanities, the educational program for a man and citizen of the world, and his own aesthetic program of *Teilnehmung* and participation in a number of later writings.

But Garve's work has even wider significance. Not only is he a thinker on dignity in his own right, he is also preparing the way for Kant's thought on dignity and practical philosophy. The two philosophers maintained a lifelong dialogue, and in addition, Kant on several occasions expressed his high esteem for his Breslau colleague, calling him a "worthy scholar" and a "philosopher in the genuine sense of that word" (*MM*, AA 6: 206, and *OCS*, AA 8: 278). As a matter of fact, Garve seems to have exerted an early and deep influence through his 1772 Ferguson commentary and to have been instrumental in shaping Kant's systematic and critical approach in the first *Critique*, which Garve reviewed with Feder in 1782.[3] While Kant was clearly disappointed by Garve's unwillingness to engage with Kant's moral philosophical theses in this review and by his sharp criticism of a

---

are equally admissible to all public dignities, places, and employments, according to their capacity and without distinction other than that of their virtues and of their talents."

2 From the overwhelming secondary literature on the topic, see in particular Rosen 2012; Waldron 2012. On Kant, see Sensen 2011. Sensen already points out Cicero's influence on Kant.

3 An abridged version of the review was published 1782 in the supplement to the *Göttinger Gelehrten Anzeigen* (Garve/Feder 1782), the unabridged version followed a year later in: *Allgemeine Deutsche Bibliothek*, supplement to volume 37 to 52, 2nd section, Fall 1783, 838–862.

set of Kantian premises, this disappointment did not end the philosophical dialogue between the two thinkers.[4] On the contrary, Garve continued to provide Kant with philosophical impulses, in his Cicero commentary of 1783. These are directly reflected in several of Kant's writings. While there was no further epistolary correspondence until 1798, the philosophical exchange between the two philosophers continued intensively. Only a short time later, according to a report by Hamann, Kant drafted his *Groundwork for a Metaphysics of Morals*, as a response to Garve; an "Anti-Garve." On February 18, 1784, this anti-critique against Garve was mentioned for the first time in a letter from Hamann to Scheffner.

> According to rumours, our dear Professor Kant, who has bought the painter Becker's house, is working on an anti-critique – although the title has not yet been determined – against Garve's Cicero as an indirect answer to the same review in the monthly *Allgemeine Deutsche Bibliothek*. His intention was also to deliver something about beauty in the *Berl. Monatsschrift*.[5]

Finally, on May 2, in a letter to Herder, Hamann claims that this Anti-Critique has been transformed into "a prodromum on morality"; that is, preparation or groundwork. And indeed it is in the *Groundwork* that Kant argues most directly with Garve. But even in the later essay *Über den Gemeinspruch. Das mag in der Theorie richtig sein taugt aber nicht für die Praxis* [*On the Common Saying: This may be correct in Theory but is of no Use in Practice*], Kant goes into their earlier discussion about freedom. Traces of the same discussion can also be found in several other important writings, for example in the *Idee zu einer allgemeinen Geschichte in weltbürgerlicher Absicht* [*Idea for a Universal History from a Cosmopolitan Point of View*], and in the second and third *Critiques*. Garve, for his part, views himself as a "whetstone" allowing Kant to sharpen his own arguments. He believes that in this role, he "has not been entirely useless […] to others," even though he "has done little as a cutting instrument" (Garve 1798, XIII).[6]

---

[4] When Garve emerged from *incognito* status in 1783 and revealed in his letter that he was the (co-)author of the Göttingen review, Kant made no secret of his annoyance and displeasure in his reply dated August 7, 1783. But he also clearly expressed his admiration for Garve: he had long revered in the person of Garve "an enlightened philosophical mind and a taste purified by erudition and knowledge of the world." And when Garve explained to him that the review had been radically shortened and mutilated by his colleague [Feder] without his consent and apologized for errors, Kant accepted the apology.

[5] See Hamann to Herder, February 18, 1784 and May 2nd, 1784. In: Johann Georg Hamann, *Briefwechsel*, ed. by Arthur Henkel, 7 vol., Francfort 1955–1979, vol. 5, p. 127 ff. and 143 ff.

[6] Garve writes: "When I reflect on the history of my life, I believe that I may indeed claim the merit which Horace, out of excessive modesty, considered to be his only one: I believe that I have not been entirely useless as a whetstone for others, even if I have done little as a cutting in-

So far, Garve's importance to Kant has been very inadequately grasped. Although his strategic role as an addressee for the polemic in the *Groundwork* has been formally acknowledged in almost all commentaries, it has been constantly downplayed.⁷ As Jens Timmermann, here representing a more general attitude in Kant research, writes: "the *Groundwork* is too complex […] to be inspired by two second-rate philosophers (i.e., Cicero and Garve)" (Timmermann 2007, xxviii). An overly narrow systematic approach to Kant seems to have prevented the reconstruction of their dialogue. Kant's readers tend to overlook the fact that Kant sought and pursued the discussion with Garve precisely to highlight the particular features of his own reading of Cicero and to give a more tangible form to his own thoughts on dignity. Examining Garve's commentary can therefore help to articulate the major affinities and differences, while providing a key to Kant's sometimes cryptic theses. It emerges clearly that Kant is participating in a wider debate and in a collective reinterpretation of concepts of dignity [*dignitas*], honor [*honestas*], and propriety [*proprietas*] based on new social, economic, and aesthetic premises.

1 Garve's Commentary

Like earlier scholasticism and certain traditions of Jewish philosophy carried on in the eighteenth century by eminent figures such as Moses Mendelssohn and Salomon Maimon, Garve practices philosophy as translation *and* commentary. Basically, he asserts, he has spent his life commenting on other people's works. While allowing him to connect with earlier traditions of thought and to apply old ideas to new debates, this favorite genre of his, the philosophical commentary, did not exclude originality. As Garve explains, foreign texts offered him the opportunity and the stimulation he needed to develop his own thought:

> It is true that I need occasions [*Veranlassungen*] for all my ideas, and that the thoughts of others, which I examine, most often offer me this kind of occasion. As far back as I remember, my most distinguished thought has consisted in interpreting, disputing, confirming the teaching I received from others. (Garve 1785a, preface, 4)⁸

---

strument. Although I have not enriched the sciences with great and new discoveries in my writings, I have made some readers think" (Garve 1798, XIII).
7 On the relationship between Garve and Kant, see also Stern 1884; Stolleis 1972; Melches Gilbert 1994.
8 See also Wölfel 1987.

In Garve's eyes, it is precisely the foreignness, difference, and need for comparison and translation that allows a clarification of his own concepts. "Everything that prompts us to compare favors reflection," he writes. Whereas the Cicero translation is a commissioned work, fulfilling a spoken wish of Frederick the Great and earning Garve 3000 *Reichsthaler*, the attached commentary is not. It is an independent philosophical work that aroused great interest among his contemporaries before posterity contemptuously turned its back on Garve's "annotation philosophy" and *Unphilosophie* (see Schleiermacher 1800, 136). Apparently, only Garve's contemporaries were still willing and able to appreciate his implicit arguments and his subtle and indirect participation in the Enlightenment debates via his commentary.[9] For Garve is not interested in Cicero's "Roman dress" but rather in the larger ideas, arguments, and concepts, especially those drawn from the Stoic tradition. As Garve puts it in the introductory chapter of his commentary:

> Insofar as it deals with duties, Cicero's present writing contains precisely those ideas which, in the whole field of human knowledge, are least the exclusive property of any man or age and least may wear the dress of this age. (Garve 1783, unpag.)[10]

Just as Cicero translated Greek philosophy and its concepts into the context of the Roman Republic in 44 B.C., Garve intends to translate them into the 1783 German civil society. Such a translation however requires not only a return to and reflection on the Stoic core, but also a deeper engagement with Ferguson and the development of thought from the treatise itself and Garve's 1772 commentary. For in Garve's view, Ferguson is essentially Stoic,[11] which explains why Garve's commentary on Ferguson introduces Cicero and his *De finibus* via the opposition between Epicureanism and Stoa. In Garve's view, the ideas need to be stripped of their Roman dress, to be presented in such a way as to "produce on the German reader the same effect as those expressed in the Latin original produced on the Roman" (Garve 1783, preface, unpag.). Garve's annotations are "only in a few places necessary to understand Cicero. Most often they explain those details that only cause difficulties for those who understand Cicero best." (Garve 1783, preface).

---

9 Presumably, Mendelssohn encouraged Garve to translate Cicero. See Mendelssohn's letter to Garve in Mendelssohn 1977.
10 In the following sections, I will refer to this first edition (which Kant read) rather than to the new edition of 1787/88.
11 Garve 1798, 158: "Ferguson's system is basically the genuine Stoic, purified of sophistry, exaggerations, and paradoxes, and brought back to its essential content, which is: that man can find his happiness only in the ever-increasing perfection of his whole nature – and that he can increase this perfection only by an uninterrupted series of beneficent and patriotic acts, performed with prudence and courage, throughout life."

1.1 Self-Esteem as the Foundation of Freedom

Garve's Cicero commentary shows that human dignity is also a philosophical concern for him. Engaging in an anthropological reflection and transferring the social and hierarchical model of dignity to a higher level, he defines dignity as a human prerogative and honor [*Ehre*].

In modern civil society, honor "cannot simply be reserved for the nobility," as Garve states in a later chapter of his treatise on the "way of life" [*genus vitae*]. To consider honor as an attribute of nobility would express a "prejudice of pride, persisting in this class itself together with the associated rituals, the bloody feuds and duels of honor" (Garve 1783, vol. 1, 249). This has restricted the meaning of these concepts, "which are in themselves general, to a certain social class and status, and for this very reason they have become more deeply rooted, they have been held more sacred, because they have at the same time become distinctive signs of this class" (Garve 1783, vol. 1, 250–251). This prejudice can and must be fought and eradicated by a general "convention" of all states or by a continuing Enlightenment. For

> as long as the word honor still expresses something that is the property of a class, not the prerogative of man, as long as there is an honor of which one cannot say on what part of the being, on what quality, on what human act it is based, which is based merely on a name and public opinion (and the honor of the nobleman, defended with the sword, is precisely of this kind), then it will necessarily be destroyed by every attack, and it cannot be saved in any other way than by the downfall of the attacker. (Garve 1783, vol. 1, 250–251)

In a nutshell: honor is not to be reserved for a certain class. It is first and foremost a right and privilege of all humans. More precisely, the honor or dignity of a particular class depends on its foundation in a universal human honor or dignity. Human dignity must be, as in some respects Cicero already thought, the condition for civic dignity.

Just like his Enlightenment contemporaries (Spalding, Mendelssohn, Herder), Garve conceived of such dignity or of "this sublimity of the soul, by virtue of which man regards every other man as his equal, and happiness, status, wealth as insignificant advantages" as an object of feeling rather than of theoretical and distinct reasoning. His originality here consists first of all in a more radical return to Cicero's Stoic model of dignity and world citizenship.

Already for Cicero, humans play two roles and possess two dignities: on the one hand, a dignity as citizens, and on the other hand, a dignity as human beings, distinguishing them from brute animals. Cicero develops this idea in the opening chapter of *De officiis*.

> We must realize also that we are invested by Nature with two characters [*personis*], as it were: one of these is universal, arising from the fact of our being all alike endowed with reason and with that superiority which lifts us above the brute [*quarum una communis est ex eo, quod omnes participes sumus rationis praestantiaeque eius, qua antecellimus bestiis*]. From this all morality and propriety are derived [*a qua honestum decorumque trahitur*], and upon it depends the rational method of ascertaining our duty [*officii*]. The other character is the one that is assigned to individuals in particular. (Cicero: *De officiis*, I, 107; trans. Walter Miller)

Humans possess human dignity as citizens of the world. In this pattern, man/humanity is considered as a being destined to develop his own merit, distinction, difference, and dignity through and in the fulfillment of his office [*officium*] itself:

> [T]he entire command of the commodities produced on land is vested in mankind. We enjoy the fruits of the plains and of the mountains, the rivers and the lakes are ours, we sow corn, we plant trees, we fertilize the soil by irrigation, we confine the rivers and straighten or divert their courses. In fine, by means of our hands we essay to create it were a second world within the world of nature [*quasi alteram naturam efficere*]. (Cicero: *De natura deorum*, II, 152; trans. H. Rackham)

In both roles, humans are agents. The "praiseworthy role of virtue lies in activity", states Cicero in *De officiis* (I, 7, 21). In *De finibus*, he elaborates on the human constitutive drive for activity. Humans are born to intervene in nature, to cultivate nature, to tame it, to subdue it, and thus to establish a balance of forces (Cicero: *De finibus*, V). The same drive for activity leads them into society, where they find an appropriate territory for human activity, self-perfection, and differentiation. Humans develop and perfect themselves by perceiving their role as citizens, dealing with their peers, adapting their behavior to each other, and interacting with each other.

From these general premises follow a set of new philosophical consequences in a world which has abandoned ancient finalism in favor of modern openness. Garve includes among these consequences humanity's characterization not by a purpose but by a "destination" or "vocation" [*Bestimmung*] and an infinite tendency toward greater perfection, or, to use Rousseau's term, "perfectibility." Note that Garve explicitly introduces the term "perfection" in his account: "The ultimate end, say [the Stoics], toward which all men strive, even without knowing it, is to make themselves more perfect" (Garve 1783, 12).

Moreover, according to Garve, it is enough that one's virtue be grounded in a *subjective self-esteem, sense* or *feeling* of one's worth, because this self-esteem is the *practical* condition of the expression of power. "[E]very being that feels itself, that is conscious of itself, must care most of all what it is itself"; man "must think himself to be something [*muss sich selbst für Etwas halten*]" (Garve 1783, vol. 1, 56).

> Without a consciousness of his dignity [*Bewusstsein seiner Würde*], neither rising above external things nor a very lively expression of power is possible for him. Perhaps this is necessary to make him capable of effort; self-esteem is then a motive for summoning his forces to prove himself according to his dignity. Perhaps *pride* and *courage* are only consequences of one and the same cause; both may arise from a feeling of strength [*Kraft*], which, insofar as man compares himself with his peers, makes him eager to rise above them and disinclined to submit to them, and insofar as he is involved with external things, makes him bolder in the face of danger and more indifferent to external advantages. (Garve 1783, vol. 1, 57–58)

This perspective, in turn, sheds new light on the systematic relation between the notions of dignity, freedom, and God, anticipating Kantian perspectives. The first sketch of this novel articulation can be found in the opening passages of the commentary on Ferguson of 1772, and it is taken up and developed in the Cicero commentary of 1783/84. Already in 1772, Garve turns his attention to the philosophical concept of freedom. Its possibility, he argues, cannot be philosophically established. "The inscrutability [*Unergründlichkeit*] of this matter is proven; it constitutes one of the limits of our understanding" (Ferguson 1772, 289–290). Nevertheless, the notion can claim practical validity to the extent that humans have a sense of merit and guilt.

> There is a sense [*Empfindung*] of merit and demerit in human actions, in addition to the sense of usefulness and harmfulness: the latter sense can be found in many creatures other than humans; the former is found in none: what, then, does the human being have that neither the machine nor the animal has, for which he alone can be praised and blamed? The difference between the machine and the living being is to be expressed in the schools by the word spontaneity, and the difference between the animal and the human being by the word freedom. (Ferguson 1772, 289–290)

Garve takes this thought further by drafting a program which Kant was to develop in greater detail later. Instead of continuing to vainly demonstrate the possibility of freedom, it aims at showing more clearly in what way freedom sets a "limit" [*Gräntze*] to any knowledge. For this purpose, it is necessary to "present as honestly and impartially as possible the two systems of freedom that are possible and prevailing"; instead of seeking to overcome the difficulties, what is needed is to "show that difficulties really exist in both, that these difficulties cannot be removed; and that so far all attempts to do so either merely conceal these difficulties or postpone them." But it must also be shown that, notwithstanding the impossibility of proving freedom theoretically,

> human senses [*Empfindungen*] of right and wrong are immutable and certain, and not dependent on any system; and that, whether we can explain human freedom or not, we

must always distinguish happiness from merit, and the sense of pleasure we take in an object from the sense of approval we give to an action. (Ferguson 1772, 290–291)

In Garve's view, between the system of fatalism and the "freedom of indifference" there is an "invaluable point of union. We all believe in the existence of virtue. This belief is earlier than all systems; it gave rise to them in the first place; to justify it we invented the systems." In his Cicero Commentary, eleven years later, Garve asserts that "one must be able to imagine that nature enables humans to judge for themselves the goodness of their action; that humans, in spite of all the inexplicability of freedom, have at their disposal "common concepts" according to which their freedom is "completely certain [*ausgemacht*] and comprehensible" (Garve 1783, vol. 1, 68). For humans as rational beings must be able to produce by their own power or out of themselves [*sponte*] that which is desirable for its own sake [*propter se*] or in itself.

1.2 The Natural History of the Stoa

Garve emphasizes that Cicero and "the Ancients" were already using a method borrowing elements from natural history based on this practical questioning of the conditions of one's own activity and virtue (see in particular Cicero: *De officiis*, I, 11–15, and *De finibus*, V). Like eighteenth-century *naturalistes*, they based their method on observation and comparison, starting from external, anatomical, and other characteristics:

> The method chosen by the Ancients is the most natural and best. They begin with the natural history of man, take him, as it were, at his birth, observe the structure of his body, the movements of his limbs, the first aspirations [*Triebe*] of the soul, which are expressed by these; they lead him through the various stages of old age and observe the growth, the changes of form, the expressions of those first instincts, at the same time as his body and the faculties of his mind. In this way they distinguish what art and what nature have produced in man, what he is according to his first disposition, and what he is in his fullest maturity. They supplement this method with comparison. They believe that they are observing the peculiarity of human nature best when they notice differences from those natures that are most similar to man but still below him. (Garve 1783, 11)

This perspective and method, which according to Garve is already peculiar to the Stoics, in its turn provides new grounds for refuting Epicureanism. It consists in directing the view first to the primary impulses of nature ([*prima invitamenta naturae*] Cicero: *De finibus*, V, 17). From this practical perspective, the Epicurean thesis that man's purpose in nature is to achieve pleasure and avoid pain proves untenable. It seems far more plausible to posit a natural purpose and drive, common to all human beings, toward self-love, self-preservation, and self-perfection. For observation reveals that every living being is dear to itself by nature, and no one is an enemy to himself. This self-love or self-esteem shows itself in the general fear of death and in the general drive for self-preservation: a desire for things that are useful to him and a desire for recognition. As mentioned above, such a drive characterizes not only humans but all natural beings:

> [there] is a common stock [*gemeinsamer Bestand*] in all, and not only in living beings, but also in all the things which nature nourishes, multiplies, and sustains. In this, as we see, that which arises from the earth brings forth from itself, as it were, by its own power, much that is important for life and growth, so that it reaches the highest end in its kind. (Cicero: *De finibus*, V, 26)

But in contrast with other living beings, humans are unique in going beyond this natural purpose and reaching perfection *by their own power*. This natural history thus leads to self-knowledge, a knowledge of one's own virtue and capacity for *self-determination*, which is peculiar to humans because it "belongs" to them and does not concern external things.

1.3 God as Sovereign [*Oberherr*]?

According to Garve, Christianity can help to conceive this universal and equal human dignity by stipulating a divine creator and judge. This, however, requires some revision to the extent that the old Augustinian two-world doctrine proves to be incompatible with the new idea of self-perfection. For Garve (just as for his contemporaries Mendelssohn or Herder), human self-perfection as a continuous process must begin in this world and carry on in the afterlife. Furthermore, it must be possible to reconcile Christian humility and dignity. The Christian religion, as Garve finds, does not allow for such compatibility. While acknowledging the possibility of equality and freedom in faith, it forgets dignity. "Beyond the virtue of humility, which religion preaches [...]," people have forgotten, "to recommend the noble feeling of human worth [*das edle Gefühl seines Werths*], which can co-exist with humility, and without which few virtues can exist." According to Garve, virtue comprises four cardinal virtues, namely prudence, justice, courage, and temperance, to which is added wisdom as the power to "direct" oneself. Among these virtues, courage has been neglected in recent times. Assuming that nature has intended humans to express their power and take action, such courage presupposes first of all notions of the self and of self-esteem, or, as Garve elsewhere puts it, "of that sublime elevation [*Erhabenheit*] of the soul, by virtue of which humans regard themselves as equal, and happiness, status, wealth as insignificant advantages."

From Garve's perspective, the Stoa and Cicero can offer new insights here. They allow certain attributes and functions of the ancient gods to be transferred to the Christian God. It is in this sense that Garve reinterprets God in the sociology of religion sections of the second volume of his commentary. The latter is, among other things, a lawgiver and judge who directs his gaze to the whole of the human character.

> Since they [the Ancients] regarded virtue as the natural state of an uncorrupted and sufficiently developed human spirit, they could not possibly find the reason why virtue is good and the actions flowing from it are obligatory in mere obedience to a Sovereign. They could not view positive rewards as necessary motives for what they regarded as happiness itself, nor punishments as deterrents from that which constitutes human misery. Virtue, according to them, was indeed in accordance with the will of God, and thus became more venerable, more certain of its immanent reward. But that which made it virtue, i.e., good, lay in our nature, not in our relation to anything but ourselves, not even to the supreme being. (Garve 1783, vol. 2, 18)

Nature or God or the lawgiver in the realm of all rational beings [*Gesetzgeber im Reiche aller Vernunftwesen*] must be able to will that I can esteem myself and that I am able to take credit for my actions. Under these circumstances, it must be possible to think that nature encourages man to form a character and moral character expressing itself in resistance to nature. In certain respects, Cicero and the Stoa had already reached the same conclusion. Garve employs this ancient idea, adapting it to a Christian model and distinguishing the perspectives of the divine lawgiver from those of the human judge, in terms of modes of observation and underlying principles. Whereas the human judge judges the individual act with a view to consequences, the divine gaze is on the whole of character or disposition, virtue in its first seat, the state of a perfect soul, and true moral duty. "He sees what I am, and how I became what I am, and He makes my destination depend on this foundation with the greatest justice which is at the same time the greatest benevolence" (Garve 1783, vol. 1, 38). His judgment of human morality, character, disposition, or "will" presupposes reference to the "whole human being" [*den ganzen Menschen*] "as he has gradually formed himself" (Garve 1783, vol. 1, 34), to his behavior and propriety [*Aufführung und Schicklichkeit*]. The opposition between a divine and a human viewpoint replaces the former opposition between perfect and imperfect duties, which Garve abandons as being a mere "school-subtlety" (Garve 1783, vol. 1, 39). "Belief in a God does not create the idea of virtue, but it sets it in place [*fixiert*], because it assures us of the existence of an absolute goodness" (Garve 1783, vol. 2, 28).

In principle, such a virtue amounts to a "love of honor" [*Ehrliebe, honestas*]; it is linked to the claim to respect and public recognition, even if it first presupposes self-respect: "Strength [*Kraft*], where it exists, brings forth the feeling of dignity, just as, conversely, strength is awakened by this feeling: – it therefore also produces the desire to be recognized by others in this dignity, that is, to be honored by them, or to be raised [*erhoben*] above them" (Garve 1783, vol. 2, 59). Such an urge for activity and to express one's strength tends to lead humans into society. As Garve writes (with Cicero and against Rousseau), man "is formed only by society and he only finds in society the objects of his virtues" (Ferguson 1772, 301). But Garve modernizes Cicero's political philosophy by transforming Cicero's static notion of rank[12] into a more dynamic one and by introducing into German philosophy new socio-critical, sociological, and state-economic perspectives whose influence extends to and beyond Hegel (see Waszek 1988). He draws above all on the insights of the English and Scottish philosophers, who, in his opinion, "have more access in their country to certain objects which concern governmental affairs" and "matters of politics and state economy."[13]

1.4 Dignity, Value, and Price

Cicero was correct in his observation that man in society strives for honor and recognition, for rank, distinction, and differentiation. In the eyes of eighteenth-century philosophers, this love of honor [*Ehrliebe*] is even the condition for human self-perfection. For as Garve points out, with Ferguson and other Scottish state economists, it is the love of honor and the need for recognition in society that produces certain human needs and drives in the first place.

> As soon as man enters into contact with his equals, not only to seek protection in association with them, but also to enjoy the pleasures of life in social gatherings, as soon as and only then does his circle of needs become larger. He now wants food, not only for himself, but for those who live in company with him and better food to tempt them to enjoy being with him. […] [He wants] clothes that not only cover him but adorn him, give him a look and reputation. [*Ansehen*] […] always more for the sake of others than for himself. […]. (Garve 1783, vol. 1, 47)

---

[12] Viktor Pöschl already emphasizes a certain dynamic dimension of Cicero's own concept of dignity, insofar as public offices in the Roman Republic were in principle accessible to every man. But there are nonetheless some major differences from the civil society of the eighteenth century. See Pöschl 1989.

[13] Garve 1785a, preface, quoted in the introduction, IX, XI. Garve contributed to the dissemination of these writings in German-speaking countries by translating several English-language philosophers such as Adam Ferguson and Edmund Burke.

Creating new needs in society, human ambition or *Ehrliebe* leads to an increase in diligence and wealth. By producing new *means*, it allows man to set new *ends* for himself. The value that his labor possesses is thus not absolute, but relative, to be determined in terms of needs and demand. It is precisely the increase in needs that contributes to the technical perfection of humankind and the forming of new capabilities.

But ambition or *Ehrliebe* also has its own dangers. The fact that "public esteem acquires a value" even represents in some respects, as Rousseau thought, the first step toward inequality and also the first step toward vice: "from these first preferences arose vanity and contempt on the one hand, shame on envy on the other" (Rousseau 1750/1997, 166). Garve indirectly concedes to Rousseau that human socialization can imply alienation and can increase and cement the distance between humans. Garve already emphasizes this danger in his early essays *Betrachtung einiger Verschiedenheiten in den Werken der ältesten und neueren Schriftsteller, besonders der Dichter* [*Consideration of Some Diversities in the Works of the Most Ancient and Recent Writers, Especially the Poets*] (Garve 1779) and *Über den Charakter der Bauern und ihr Verhältnis gegen die Gutsherren und gegen die Regierung* [*On the Character of the Peasants and Their Relationship Against the Lords of the Manor and Against the Government*] (Garve 1796). He observes, that the classes have "separated themselves from each other." "Each distances himself from those who are below him, and those who are above him cannot be approached" (Garve 1796, 5).[14] Of course, humans sometimes happen to transgress these distances between classes. The motives for such social mobility are either ambition ("self-interest") in the lower class, curiosity ("the desire to be amused") in the higher class, or true openness and a "nobler less restricted way of thinking on both sides." But in all these cases "the interaction remains cold, without that frankness and confidentiality which alone can grant us knowledge of foreign hearts and afford us in our intercourse with them a source of observation." The separation of the classes can be traced back to economic factors: "Wealth creates a far greater difference among people than rank," Garve aptly observes, and he adds: "and it

---

14 "Far more striking (than the differences in the provinces) are those differences, subject to far fewer exceptions, which in every nation separate the different classes from each other, since the inequality of these classes has been fixed by a series of generations, has given to each its own occupation, has bound each more together within itself, and has separated it from the rest. Between the manners of high society in all the European capitals, there is a resemblance such that, if one were suddenly transferred from the societies of one to those of others, it would only feel like passing from the crowd of a given place to the crowds of others. Between the customs of the nobleman, the bourgeois, and the peasant, in France as well as in Silesia, there is a dissimilarity that strikes everyone's eyes as soon as he passes from one class to the other."

is only because both are generally united among us that the separation of the classes has risen to the highest level" (Garve 1796, 5). For the difference in rank, in contrast to the difference in property, is temporary:[15]

> The commanding person can only show his relation to the obeying person under certain circumstances, and as long as the kind of action occurs that he knows how to command. On the other hand, the difference that wealth makes is constant and extends to everything. Dwelling, household utensils, clothing, the expense of the table, the costliness of the pleasures, everything that the rich man has and does is different from what the poor man has and does. (Garve 1796, 5)

Differences in possessions, however, deepen and cement differences in rank, because they are constantly in view: "The rich man, therefore, can never lose sight of his elevation, and the poor man of his lowliness. From these two differences in rank and property, and from the "long separation," there finally arises a difference in "decency and manners, in the manner of behaving and expressing oneself." These manners, in turn, are "the first thing by which we measure a man's excellence and merit," so "arbitrarily, too, these terms are linked sometimes to one way, sometimes to the opposite way of doing and saying something. From the incomprehensibility of the concepts of one class for the other, it follows that all bonds of communication are broken, and that all possibility of bonding is suspended" (Garve 1796, 99–100). "If, then, the communication of ideas can be the only bond of society once self-interest is silenced and needs are satisfied, there is no longer any such bond among members of a nation who speak a language foreign to each other and can neither be loved nor esteemed by each other" (Garve 1796, 99–100). Cicero does not yet see this danger. His language also attests to this blind spot, which in Garve's eyes, does not allow adequate comprehension and analysis of these social mechanisms.

While the eighteenth century is seeing the classes "separate" from each other such that the distances have become unbridgeable and the "general bond of communication has been torn away," in the Roman republic, despite the fixed order of rank and subordination in the execution of public affairs, a kind of equality, mutual intercourse, and general activity prevailed. Garve points out that in ancient times almost all members of a state, a republic, were known to each other. They "all had a certain common interest, affairs that often brought them together, public meetings where they became thoroughly acquainted with each other; festivities in which they all took part." The hierarchy prevailing at the time did not diminish this proximity based on shared interests. For respective rank did not determine

---

15 About the evolution of differences in wealth: Garve 1785b.

the actual being, but only the task, order, and subordination in the "execution of public affairs." "Commanding and obeying were very strict on those occasions where it was actually important to fulfill the duties of one's rank. But as soon as these occasions had passed, a kind of equality was restored" (Garve 1796, 99–101).

Probably because the problem of class hierarchies and division did not present itself with such brisance, Cicero did not feel the need to distinguish between the drives for perfection and for sociability. He still thought that a man's humanity, his human honor in social interaction, was always plainly visible, allowing empathic bonds to be formed. That is why he was primarily concerned with the dignity and duties and offices [*officii*] of the nobility. He wrote mainly "for the higher classes" and neglected the remaining active classes of society.

> The remaining active classes of society, which produce or provide society's requirements, this so vast, so indispensable, and so estimable part of mankind does indeed seize the general rules of virtue, which are common to all classes because of the equal nature of mankind, but it misses, for the most part, the application of these rules to its circumstances and conditions. (Garve 1783, vol. 1, 8)

More generally, he gave "too much importance to the particular duties of man" and neglected to "properly elaborate the universal ones."

> Duties, those by which man improves his own internal or external condition, are only briefly indicated. Domestic life is not considered other than insofar as it is the transition to civil life and the reason for it. The duties of religion are completely omitted. (Garve 1783, vol. 1, 9)

In our modern society, however, Cicero's outmoded concepts require revision.

1.5 Participation, Interest, and Communication

As suggested by Garve Cicero himself already formulated a rudimentary idea of human honor or dignity as *honestas, dignitas,* and *humanitas*. In *De oratore*, Cicero combines the educational program of humanity and reason with the education of the citizen, statesman, and orator. This man and citizen does not prepare himself directly for a specific office, but he must master all subjects to a certain degree, so that he can relate to his fellow citizens and have an effect on them through his speech and deeds: however, in his historical context, Cicero does not yet see the need for an educational program that deals specifically with training for "participation" [*Teilnehmung*].

Garve sees a gap in the curriculum here. The individual must be educated to become a human being on the one hand and a citizen on the other. According to Garve, however, he becomes a human being only *by learning to put himself in the place of his fellow citizens*, given the separation of the social classes and worlds and their distance from one another. In this sense, he must develop a sense or feeling of general participation for the sake of the community and to properly express his honor.

Garve, who deplores the lack of a German equivalent for "interest" in his Ferguson translation[16] and struggles with the difficulties of translating the term, is apparently one of the first to translate the term from English into German. By "interest" he understands "the partaking of everything, insofar as it has a direct influence on our person, and on this alone." Interest is in his eyes, according to the Latin root, an *inter-esse:* the ability to take the place in the world that allows us to judge the usefulness of things for the perfection of mankind:

> Everything that is to move us must be related to us, but not to everyone directly; many only by means of human society, on which it has an influence and that, in turn, has an influence on us. Everything that we should desire must be useful to us; but not everything is useful insofar as it acts upon us and makes our condition more agreeable; many things are useful insofar as they act upon society, thereby making our nature more perfect.(Ferguson 1772, 333)[17]

Garve believes that art, what the eighteenth century called the fine arts, can fill this gap in Cicero's educational program. In his eyes, art serves above all to train for "participation" [*Teilnehmung, Teilnahme*] and to educate man aesthetically. Plays and novels "transport us back into human society", "from which we are to a certain extent excluded; because they show us people of all ranks, acting and speaking in far more important performances of their lives than we ourselves have the opportunity to see [...]."[18] They provide us in fiction with *"the pleasure of being among human beings and among human beings of all kinds, which we have lost in reality"*; and they therefore at the same time supplement that part of our knowledge which we can no longer gather through experience."[19] This aesthetic education for participation in turn ensures that we understand the language and concepts of our fellow citizens in general; that they have true "popularity." It

---

16 Ferguson 1772, 332: "We have no word for 'interest'. It is not 'advantage,' for this merely indicates the object which stirs interest; not 'self-interest,' for this is the tendency of the soul always to be governed by its interest."
17 See also the later essay *Über das Interessierende* and Doris Bachmann-Medick's analysis of Garve's concept of interest in Bachmach-Medick 1989, 164–243, in particular 189.
18 Garve 1779, 104–105.
19 Garve 1779, 130.

contributes to forming a collective interest that goes beyond individual interests. This leads to a broadening of one's own point of view to include other human points of view, without the need for ascension to a divine perspective.

This program of participation links directly with the Enlightenment aesthetic and moral sense tradition.[20] Garve engages with these traditions, with Burke, Lessing, and Herder, even in his early reviews. At the same time, it differs from their model of *humaniora* in one crucial aspect. It is concerned with the formation of an aesthetic sympathy and "participation" for the sake of human duty and dignity, like Cicero's own program.

2 Kant's "Anti-Garve"

Anyone familiar with Kant's argumentation will recognize central parallels between the two philosophical projects. Garve's profound influence on Kant is demonstrated not only by words and concepts such as "good will" [*guter Wille*], "disposition," [*Gesinnung*], "interest," and "participation" [*Teilnehmung*] drawn from Garve, but by fundamental practical, philosophical, and aesthetic perspectives on virtue, honor, and dignity. Kant, too, is a modern Ciceronian, although for his part he emphasizes this proximity less explicitly, cultivating a very different philosophical style and introducing a new technical terminology.[21] Already the early writings and the lectures on *Physical Geography* and on *Anthropology* bear traces of Kant's engagement with Cicero and the Stoa and of his attempts to redefine humans as world-citizens, actors, and players in the game of nature. Initially, Kant seems to have developed this thinking in relative independence from Garve. But by ascribing to the practical justification of dignity as self-esteem the same signifi-

---

20 See in particular the bipartite Essay *Einige Gedanken über das Interessierende* (Garve 1771/72).
21 Garve had confessed that he had at times become "unwilling to read, because I believed it must be possible to make truths intended to bring about important reforms in philosophy more easily comprehensible to those who are not altogether unaccustomed to reflection." The new language "makes the deviation from the thoughts of others [...] appear greater than it really is." He holds to the view "that the whole of your system, if it is really to become useful, must be expressed in a more popular way, and if it contains truth, it can also be expressed in a popular way" (AA 10: 331–332). Kant confesses in the reply that this issue, which he had carefully thought through for more than 12 years, was not tangible [*fasslich*] enough. Lack of popularity was "a just reproach that one (could) make to his writing, for indeed (every) philosophical writing (must) be capable of the same, otherwise it conceals, above a haze of apparent acumen, presumably nonsense," AA 10: 339 ff. (I am henceforth referring to the translations of the Cambridge edition, unless indicated otherwise). Kant tries to refute this reproach in the *Prolegomena*, but also in the *Groundwork* and in a number of other writings.

cance for the justification of philosophical ideas, Kant in 1781 does directly address Garve's philosophical challenge. With his third antinomy and the philosophical refoundation of the apodictic certainty of law and practical validity of freedom, he develops the philosophical program outlined by Garve in 1772.[22] He explains that while we do not grasp the practical necessity of the moral imperative, we do grasp its "incomprehensibility" [*Unbegreiflichkeit*], which is "all that is to be demanded of philosophy" (*GM*, AA 4: 463). In his own *Anthropology*, moreover, Kant also adopts a "Stoic" and pragmatically oriented view of natural history. From the outset, such natural history enquires into humans' causality and spontaneity, into dispositions, drives, or, as Kant puts it, into the characteristic marks of the faculty of desire. Setting out from nature, this inquiry then turns to character as a mode of feeling and thought and as "the distinctive mark of man as a rational being endowed with freedom." In this context, furthermore, Kant conceives of dignity as a virtue and, at the same time, as a certain form of "inner respectability" [*honestas interna*] and a just self-esteem [*iustum sui aestimium*]. Such self-esteem is intrinsically linked to one's own self-love, developing out of it and in interaction with one's fellow human beings. This idea is found first in the *Observations*, and later, in a revised form, in the *Anthropology* and the *Metaphysics of Morals*.

Similarly to Garve, Kant furthermore views this conception of honor and self-respect as incompatible with a certain Christian virtue or perspective on dignity as humility and with the Christian ideas of a divine ruler and judge who rewards good actions and punishes bad ones: in Kant's eyes, man is a spontaneous and active being. God or nature requires him to develop his virtue all by himself, entirely from his own power and spontaneity. The Christian perspective on a divinely legitimized human dignity thus loses relevance. In a reversal of the previous perspective, a certain reasonable belief in a completely independent being follows from the binding force of the moral law.

Kant develops this thought in the *Idee zu einer allgemeinen Geschichte*, which once again attests to Garve's deep influence. Garve's argumentation pattern is also recognizable in Kant's perspective on nature as a stepmother and the best of all mothers, determining man to determine himself. As Kant explains in his *Idee zu einer allgemeinen Geschichte*, Nature's intention was to make humans develop

---

[22] In the later writing *Über den Gemeinspruch* (*OCS*, AA 8: 285), Kant adds that Garve fails to grasp freedom and nature as two opposing antinomic concepts: "Hr P. Garve makes (in his notes on Cicero's Book of Duties, 69, edition of 1783) the strange confession worthy of his acumen: 'Freedom, according to his most intimate conviction, will always remain indissoluble [...] Since a proof of it cannot be given on merely theoretical grounds [...] consequently only on morally practical ones,' one must wonder why Mr. G. did not take recourse to the concept of freedom in order to save at least the possibility of such imperatives."

their dispositions out of themselves, so that they can claim "the merit for it and owe it to themselves" (*IUH*, AA 8: 21). In this redefinition of the exemplary role of God as a lawgiver and as a creative principle (Nature) that determines man to determine himself, Kant and Garve are unanimous.

Finally, Kant also adopts the idea of human dignity as an office or virtue that must precede dignity of status. This office commands that one must direct one's actions toward a higher social and moral norm of perfection and morality, and create the political, legal, and material conditions necessary for the attainment of this ideal *in this world*. This infinite task of self-perfection is a collective one, involving and encompassing the whole of humanity.

Such human dignity, however, presupposes a certain degree of participation [*Teilnehmung*]. Reflecting on one's own *decorum* and the propriety of conduct and speech requires first being able to put oneself in the place of everyone else. Kant formulates this insight in his early writing *Beobachtungen über das Gefühl des Schönen und Erhabenen* of 1764, before turning to the same question in the elaboration of his aesthetic program in the *Critique of Judgment*. Here again, he seems to take inspiration from Garve's thoughts on "interest" and from his aesthetic program of participation.

This aspect of Kant's aesthetics has rarely been recognized. While the importance of the so-called humanity formula has been pointed out, Kant's aesthetic humanity has so far been widely disregarded. Kant subscribes to Garve's idea that the perfection of humanity cannot be achieved by improving political and social institutions alone; it also requires aesthetic education. In his *Logik*, he outlines a program of *humaniora*, or education of humanity.

> A part of philology is *humaniora*, by which is understood knowledge of the ancients, which promotes the union of science with taste, polishes away the roughness, and promotes the communicability and urbanity which humanity entails. (*JL*, AA 9: 45)

Kant also transfers the formation of a general "sense of participation" to art. His definition of art extends to other objects beyond the representation of anthropological concerns, but he also thinks that the contemplation of the beautiful invites us to put ourselves in the place of everyone else and to cultivate an "aesthetic pluralism" (*Anth*, AA 7: 127).

> The propaedeutics to all beautiful art, insofar as it is designed for the highest degree of perfection, does not seem to lie in prescriptions, but in cultivating the faculties of the mind through those precognitions which are called *humaniora*; presumably because humanity means, on the one hand, the general sense of participation [*Teilnehmungsgefühl*], and on the other hand, the capacity to communicate intimately and universally; which qualities, com-

bined, constitute the sociability peculiar to humanity and which distinguishes it from animal limitation. (*CPJ*, AA 5: 355)

Because such an aesthetics is designed for the education of man, it is far from being elitist. On the contrary, it should be seen as a guarantee of the popularity and validity of philosophy in general. The same aesthetic humanity [*humanitas aesthetica*] also appears in two passages of Kant's *Metaphysik der Sitten*. There he states that sympathetic feeling is a duty [*theilnehmende Empfindung ist überhaupt Pflicht*]. A *humanitas aesthetica* or "receptivity to the common feeling of pleasure and pain" must underlie the *humanitas practica*, or the ability and will to communicate one's feelings to one another (*MM*, AA 6: 456). A little later, Kant interprets *humanitas aesthetica* in more detail, namely as mutual love and esteem – benevolence, respectability, and decorum. Cultivating them is a "duty of virtue" and involves the need "to have intercourse with one's moral perfections" [*officium commercii, sociabilitas*], "not to isolate oneself"; and to regard one's own aesthetic "circle" or "horizon" (*JL*, AA 9: 41) also "as one that constitutes the part of an all-embracing cosmopolitan attitude" (*MM*, AA 6: 473). Being practically aesthetic, such a perception is at the same time sufficient to reflect on decorum, propriety, honor, and human dignity. There is no need for a higher, "divine" point of view.

2.1 Divergences

But why then does a polemical tone prevail in the *Grundlegung*, despite these deep affinities? Probably not for personal reasons: not because Kant was still angry over Garve's review of the first *Critique*. On the contrary, the *Grundlegung* seems to testify to Kant's high regard for Garve and his desire for reconciliation. The polemic seems to be philosophical in nature. For Kant here provides the second part of his answer to the philosophical challenge posed by Garve in 1772. And therefore, in a certain sense, he argues with and against Garve; with him, insofar as Garve in his own philosophy of human dignity is already undertaking a central reinterpretation of Christian human dignity; against him, insofar as Garve (according to Kant) does not consider all the logical consequences. Kant seems to reproach Garve for continuing to argue too anthropologically and in contradiction to his own Stoic and popular philosophical principles.

Kant takes particular offense at the assumption of a "guardian nature" (*GM*, AA 4: 425) that endows man with fixed capacities or an "implanted sense." Morality should not be anchored in any arbitrarily determinable "human nature" and a "special natural disposition of mankind," in a feeling, a tendency, a direction. For "what is derived from the special natural disposition of humanity – what is derived from certain feelings and propensities, even, where possible, from a special tendency that would be peculiar to human reason and would not have to hold necessarily for the will of every rational being – that can indeed provide a maxim for us, but not a law" (*GM*, AA 4: 425). Kant also criticizes the grounding of morality and one's own self-esteem in a mere feeling. In "philanthropy and sympathetic benevolence to do good, or to be just from love of order," one does not find "the genuine moral maxim of our conduct, the maxim befitting our position among rational beings, as human beings" (*CPrR*, AA 5: 82). Garve furthermore does not distinguish clearly enough between morality and happiness. Finally, he does not take into account the principle that self-love and love of honor must be antagonistic, and that one's self-determination with respect to higher collective ends must be based on self-constraint. "Respect is properly the representation of a worth that infringes upon my self-love. Hence there is something that is to be regarded as an object neither of inclination nor of fear, though it has something analogous to both" (*MM*, AA 6: 401).

Abandoning these old assumptions is what, in Kant's eyes, allows him to wipe the slate clean and to meet Garve's challenge philosophically. Kant holds that popularity can only be achieved indirectly, via the subtleties of metaphysics. For only through metaphysics and the sources of virtue and *honestas* in pure practical reason is it possible to refer to the divine principle of the morality of pure reason, "which corrects the whole "principle of action and brings it in conformity with universal ends." To find such a principle, Kant in the *Groundwork* starts from the "common" concept of duty and good will, which is already inherent to common sense and does not need to be taught but merely "clarified" (*GM*, AA 4: 393, 397). This new perspective allows him to found self-activity, self-legislation, and self-determination as the "ground of the dignity of human and every rational nature" in *reason* as a *faculty of universal legislation* instead of in a mere feeling and in a mere inclination (*GM*, AA 4: 436).

Dignity cannot be conceived thereby, neither from an individual viewpoint, as a quality of an ideal individual such as the wise man (Stoa), nor from a view of the divine as lawgiver and judge (Garve). Rather, it requires the new, collective, and fictitious ideal of a realm of ends. Kant defines this realm as "a systematic connection of rational beings by common objective laws, i.e., a realm which, because these laws have as their intention the very relation of these beings to each other, as ends and means." This realm of ends is composed of human beings and higher beings. These "are all under the law that each of them should never treat itself and all others merely as means, but always at the same time as ends in themselves" (*GM*, AA 4: 433 ff.). The sovereign of this realm of ends differs from his subjects in that he is not subject to the will of any other. He stands on an equal footing with them, insofar as he is also subject to the law, while being a lawgiver.

With this understanding of dignity as worthiness, Kant is invoking an aspect of the old dignity, *dignitas*, including honorableness, *honestas*. The dignity and reason of man consists in a general respectability, "worthiness," and "suitability" [*Tauglichkeit*], which all rational beings ascribe to him. Now it is this respectability that establishes his dignity as an unconditional value. Thus, Kant writes in a famous passage of the *Groundwork*:

> In the realm of ends everything has either a *price*, or a *dignity*. What has a price can be replaced by something else as its *equivalent*; what, on the other hand, is raised above all price, and therefore admits of no equivalent, has a dignity.
>
> What is related to general human inclinations and needs has a *market price*; that which, even without presupposing a need, is in accordance with a certain taste, i.e., with a delight in the mere purposeless play of our mental powers, has a fancy price; but that which constitutes the condition under which alone something can be an end in itself has not just a relative worth, i.e., a price, but an inner worth, i.e., dignity.
>
> Now morality is the condition under which alone a rational being can be an end in itself, since only through this is it possible to be a law-giving member in the realm of ends. Hence morality and humanity, insofar as it is capable of morality, is that which alone has dignity. (*GM*, AA 4: 434 ff.)

2.2 Conclusion: Garve's Reservations

This Kantian thought has its own potential, but also its own difficulties. Garve highlights both aspects in retrospect when he resumes the argument with Kant in 1798. He now sends him his new translation of Aristotle, which contains an Excursus entitled *Übersicht der vornehmsten Principien der Sittenlehre*. As the enclosed letter shows, "in this last, saddest period," he turns to Kant as a human being and a friend. "This hidden and tacit connection, which has existed among us for a long time, is meant to be strengthened even more toward the end of our lives" (Garve to Kant, mid-September 1798, AA 12: 255). In the spirit of the program of participation outlined above, he lets the aging and suffering Kant feel his sympathy, which Kant clearly appreciates.[23] At the same time, Garve also resumes the philosophical argument.

In the joined treatise, Garve speaks very highly of Kant's idea of dignity: "This idea of the dignity of man, often itself presented with force and dignity of expression in the midst of metaphysical speculation, by the greatness and prominence it contains, carries the reader away with it, and has won me to it as well" (Garve

---

[23] Kant to Garve, Königsberg, September 21, 1798: "I hasten to report, dearest friend, the [...] reception of your loving and soul-strengthening book and letter [...]."

1798b, 243). Garve is especially enthusiastic about the formula of ends used by Kant to express this claim:

> No principle peculiar to Kant's morals has so completely won my approval from the first moment I became acquainted with it: none has seemed to me, on longer and closer consideration, so useful for application in daily life, or to arouse awareness of my duties toward other people in moments of temptation, than the sentence: treat every human being as an end in himself, none as a mere means for you and for the attainment of your ends. (Garve 1798b, 250)

It offers "moral teachings for active and social life," condemns "slavery, tyranny, and violence," guards "against pride and arrogance toward lower persons and against servility toward higher persons" (Garve 1798b, 252–253).

But Garve also formulates several reservations. For example, he takes offense at Kant's distinction between happiness and being worthy of happiness.

> For my part, I confess that I understand this division of ideas very well in my head, but that I do not find this division between desires and aspirations in my heart, that it is even incomprehensible to me how any human being can become aware of having purely separated his desire for happiness itself, and thus of having performed the duty quite disinterestedly.[24]

And Garve raises an even more fundamental objection. He again criticizes Kant for his artificial language's disrespect for popular use, which, in his view, masks possible inconsistencies and contradictions by giving certain old words an entirely new, counterintuitive meaning. These include terms such as "form" and "substance," but also "dignity": Garve adds that this term corresponds to a certain philosophical meaning, but not to the popular use of the word: he could not "conceal from himself on examination that it is similar to the Stoics' description of their sage who is blissful even in Phalari's furnace, which is also attractive and heartrending in the writings of Antonin and Epictetus." However, this notion is "too little supported by reasons, experience and facts [...] to grant conviction."

In this assessment, it is evident that Garve is aware of the radical nature of Kant's interpretation. Since Kant founds dignity on the mere universality or form of a law, it follows that it is revealed precisely in the renunciation of one's own nature, inclinations, and pursuit of happiness. This foundation is, at the same time, a demolition of the old concept, insofar as it strips it of its original *personal* dimension. According to Garve, this interpretation requires too great an "effort of the mind" for it to be "completely grasped, to be recalled [...], and to have a great influence on our actions" (Garve 1798b, 244).

---

24 Kant tries to counter this objection in the first section of *Über den Gemeinspruch*.

Dieter Hüning

"These Objections are Therefore Nothing but Misunderstandings": Kant's Critique of Garve in His Essay *On the Common Saying*

Abstract: The relationship between Kant and Garve is a history of persistent misunderstandings on Garve's part, and thus a history of failed communication. The paper will focus on Kant's criticism of Garve in the essay *On the Common Saying*, in which Kant responds in particular to the moral-philosophical considerations that Garve had put forward in his commentary on his translation of Cicero's *De officiis*. The focus of Kant's criticism is Garve's mixing of moral reasoning and empirical psychology. Because Garve believes that abstraction from happiness would deprive the will of any possible motivation, he denies the possibility of pure reason becoming practical in itself. It is true that Kant also considers the pursuit of happiness to be a psychological triviality, but no moral value is attached to this pursuit. Only that will which can be determined solely by the representation of the moral law deserves to be called moral.

1 Kant and Garve: A Story of Persistent Misunderstandings

If one wanted to write a history of the development of Kant's critical philosophy, one could do so in view of his criticism of popular philosophy and his relationship to Christian Garve. At the same time, it would be a history of continuous misunderstandings on the part of popular philosophy and, in this respect, the history of a failed communication. The dispute with the Breslau philosopher follows Kant from the publication of the *Critique of Pure Reason* to the death of Garve in December 1798. As is well known, the dispute begins with Garve's review of the *Critique of Pure Reason* in the *Göttingische Anzeigen von gelehrten Sachen* of January 19, 1782, which resulted in a strong reaction from Kant in the *Prolegomena*. There, Kant accuses the anonymous reviewer of being incapable of "thinking beyond his school metaphysics" (*Pro*, AA 4: 373, Allison/Heath 2002, 161) and therefore of having completely misunderstood the critical idealism of the *Critique of Pure Reason*. After Garve had at least partially acknowledged the review, although he had inaccurately placed the main blame for the misunderstandings on Feder, the review's editor,[1] Kant wrote him a friendly letter in which he paid Garve a few superficial compliments, calling him an "enlightened philosophical spirit" [*einen aufgeklärten philosophischen Geist*] and attesting to his "refined taste, the product of wide reading and worldly experience" [*einen durch Belesenheit und Weltkenntnis geläuterten Geschmak*] (AA 10: 336; Zweig 1999, 195). The letter also makes clear why Kant is evidently lenient on Garve, asking him to use his "position and influence" to "encourage" the "enemies" of his theory to examine the *Critique of Pure Reason* as closely as possible (AA 10: 340; Zweig 1999, 198).

If we may believe Hamann's report, Garve's translation and commentary of Cicero's *De officiis* provided the immediate occasion for Kant to compose the *Groundwork of the Metaphysics of Morals*. Since the mid-1760s, Kant had frequently announced the publication of a "Metaphysics of Morals" [*Metaphysik der Sitten*]. On January 11, 1782, Hamann reported in a letter to his publisher Hartknoch: "Kant is working on the Metaphysics of Morals." However, on January 19, 1782, Garve's review of the *Critique of Pure Reason* appeared in the *Göttingische Anzeigen von gelehrten Sachen*. The review also mentions the "way in which the author finally wants to give reasons for the common way of thinking [*gemeinen Denkart*] on moral concepts, after he has withdrawn the speculative ones from it" (Garve/Feder 1782, 46). However, the reviewer does not want to go into this in more detail, because he "could find himself in it least of all" (Garve/Feder 1782, 46). Moreover, the reviewer does not recognize in the author's expression and presentation the usual method of moral reasoning, "namely to link the concepts of truth and the most general laws of thought to the most general concepts and principles of legal behavior, which has its basis in our nature" (Garve/Feder 1782, 46). Kant refers to this suggestion concerning his moral reasoning in preparatory notes to his *Prolegomena*. He notes there that the reviewer seems to have neither pursued nor encountered the principle of morality any more than the principles of the possibility of metaphysics (AA 23: 56). A little later, the same preparatory work states:

---

[1] Whereby the main misunderstanding of taking Kant's transcendental philosophy for an idealism à la Berkeley rests on Garve's side, see the letter from Jakob Sigismund Beck to Kant, Nov. 10, 1792, in which Beck reports from his talk with Eberhard: "Professor Garve was here a while ago, and Professor Eberhard told me something of his conversations with him about the Critical Philosophy. He says that even though Garve strongly defends the Critique he was still forced to admit that Critical Idealism and Berkeleyan Idealism are entirely the same" (Zweig 1999, 438; AA 11: 384: "Der Professor Garve war vor einiger Zeit hier, und Herr Pr. Eberhard hat mir einiges von seinen Gesprächen mit ihm, in Beziehung auf die critische Philosophie mitgetheilt. Er sagt, daß so sehr auch Garve die Critick vertheidigt, so habe er doch gestehen müssen, daß der critische Idealism und der Berkleysche gänzlich einerley seyn"). In contrast, Bernd Ludwig believes "that its harsh criticisms [of the Göttingen review] and the attempt to associate Kant with Berkeley had their origin in Feder" (Ludwig 2007, 184).

> Moralists have long ago recognized that the principle of happiness never gives a pure morality, but only a doctrine of prudence that is interested in its benefits. [...] Now the question is, how is a categorical imperative possible? Whoever solves this problem has found the true principle of morality. The reviewer will probably dare as little to do this as to the important problem of transcendental philosophy, which has a striking similarity with that of morality. I will present the resolution in a short while. (AA 23: 60)[2]

After Garve had revealed himself as the author, or co-author, of the Göttingen review on July 13, 1783, and after Kant had taken note of Garve's *Cicero* edition in the fall of 1783, he apparently believed that he could no longer hesitate with the publication of his moral philosophy. In a letter to Herder of February 8, 1784, Hamann connects this intention with Garve's edition of *Cicero*:

> Kant shall work on an anti-criticism, whose title he himself does not know yet, about Garve's Cicero. I visited him 8 days ago today. He studied Garve but did not think of a refutation. (Hamann 1965, vol. 5, 123)[3]

On March 25, 1784, another letter from Hamann to Herder says:

> The anti-criticism will not be directed against Garve's review directly, but actually against his Cicero, and by means of it will become a satisfaction for the latter. (Hamann 1965, vol. 5, 134)[4]

On May 2, 1784, Hamann notes in a further letter to Herder:

> The anti-criticism about Garve's Cicero has turned into a prodomus of morality [i.e., the Groundwork of the Metaphysics of Morals, D.H.]. (Hamann 1965, vol. 5, 147)[5]

The critical discussion of Garve continued in the following years: both in the essay *On the Common Saying: That May be Correct in Theory, but it is of no Use in Practice*, as well as in the appendix of *Toward Perpetual Peace: A Philosophical Project*.

---

[2] "Es haben schon längst Moralisten Eingesehen[,] daß das Princip der Glückseeligkeit niemals eine reine Moral[,] sondern nur eine Klugheitslehre die sich auf ihren Vortheil versteht[,] gebe. [. . .] Nun ist die Frage[,] wie ist ein categorischer Imperativ möglich[,] wer diese Aufgabe auflöset[,] der hat das echte princip der Moral gefunden. Der Rec: wird sich vermutlich eben so wenig daran wagen[,] wie an das wichtige Problem der Transcendental philos.[,] welches mit jenem der Moral eine auffallende Aehnlichkeit hat. Ich werde die Auflösung in Kurzem darlegen."
[3] "Kant soll an einer Antikritik – doch er weiß den Titel selbst noch nicht – über Garves Cicero arbeiten. Ich besuchte ihn heut vor 8 Tagen. Er studirte im Garve, dachte aber nicht an eine Gegenschrift."
[4] "Die Antikritik wird nicht unmittelbar gegen die Garvesche Rezension, sondern eigentlich gegen seinen Cicero gerichtet seyn, und vermittelst dessen eine Genugthuung für jene werden."
[5] "Die Antikritik über Garvens Cicero hat sich in einen Prodomus der Moral verwandelt."

The correspondence between the two philosophers ends with Garve's transmission of the book *Outline of the Most Noble Principles of the Doctrine of Morals* [*Uebersicht der vornehmsten Principien der Sitten-Lehre*], dedicated to Kant, in September 1798 and Kant's immediate reply on September 21, 1798, in which Kant takes a great interest in Garve's serious illness, but not without referencing the "pain like that of Tantalus" that the still unresolved problem of the "Transition from the metaphysical foundations of natural science to physics" causes him (AA 12: 257; Zweig 1999, 551). However, even in this letter Kant feels compelled to clarify what the systematic starting point of the *Critique of Pure Reason* had been. Unlike Garve suspected (see Garve 1798b, 339), it was:

> not the investigation of the existence of God, immortality, and so on, but rather the antinomy of pure reason – "The world has a beginning; it has no beginning, and so on, right up to the 4th: There is freedom in man, vs. There is no freedom, only the necessity of nature" – that is what first aroused me from my dogmatic slumber and drove me to the critique of reason itself, in order to resolve the scandal of ostensible contradiction of reason with itself. (AA 12: 257; Zweig 1999, 552)[6]

In light of Garve's continued misunderstandings of Kant's philosophical intentions, it is all the more surprising to hear that Kant felt so close to the Breslau philosopher, the self-declared "preacher of the general sense of man," this "enemy[...] of all genuine philosophy," who never wanted to be more than "a popular philosopher" (Garve 1798a, 1) and a "whetstone for others" (Garve 1798a, unpaginated dedication). Kant met him on a personal level with appreciation or indulgence, while other critics, such as Feder, Eberhard, Rehberg or Gentz felt the full force of his polemics. In his letter to Garve from August 7, 1783, one of the reasons for the considerable gentleness with which Kant treats Garve becomes clear:

> Garve, Mendelssohn, and Tetens are the only men I know through whose cooperation this subject [e. g., the solution of "the general problem, how synthetic a priori knowledge is possible," D.H.] could have been brought to a successful conclusion before too long, even though centuries before this one had not seen it done. (AA 10: 341; Zweig 1999, 199)[7]

---

[6] "Nicht die Untersuchung vom Daseyn Gottes, der Untersterblichkeit etc., ist der Punct gewesen[,] von dem ich ausgegangen bin, sondern die Antinomie der r. V.: Die Welt hat einen Anfang –; sie hat keinen Anfang etc bis zur vierten: Es ist Freyheit im Menschen, – gegen den: es ist keine Freyheit, sondern alles in ihm ist Naturnothwendigkeit; diese war es welche mich aus dem dogmatischen Schlummer zuerst aufweckte und zur Critik der Vernunft selbst trieb, um das Scandal des scheinbaren Widerspruchs der Vernunft mit ihr selbst zu heben."

[7] "Garve, Mendelsohn u. Tetens wären wohl die einzige[n] Männer die ich kenne, durch deren Mitwirkung diese Sache in eben nicht langer Zeit zu einem Ziele könnte gebracht werden, dahin es Jahrhunderte nicht haben bringen können."

To return to the role that Garve had played in the creation of the *Groundwork of the Metaphysics of Morals*, although his name no longer appears in the *Groundwork*, the moral philosophical positions he put forward in his notes to the Cicero translation provide, to a certain extent, the background to Kant's own attempt at an "identification and corroboration *of the supreme principle of morality*" (*GM*, AA 4: 392; Timmermann 2011, 13). According to Kant's formulation, this is the quite limited justificationary task of the *Groundwork*. Already in the preface to the *Groundwork*, Kant – in order to avoid the suspicion that his moral philosophy depended on Wolff's *philosophia practica universalis* and thus did not "have to open up an entirely new field" – drew attention to the specifics of his starting point: his ethics was only about a will "that is completely determined from a priori principles, without any empirical motivating grounds, and could be called a pure will" (*GM*, AA 4: 390; Timmermann 2011, 9). In this abstraction from all empirical motives, Kant sees the decisive difference of his ethics from Wolff (and the popular philosophy that followed him), because Wolff "took into consideration [...] willing generally, with all actions and conditions that belong to it in this general sense" (*GM*, AA 4: 390; Timmermann 2011, 9). It is precisely for this reason that Wolff and his successors would have failed to "distinguish grounds of motivation that, as such, are represented completely a priori by reason alone and are actually moral, from empirical ones, which the understanding elevates to general concepts merely by comparing experiences." (*GM*, AA 4: 391; Timmermann 2011, 11) This lack of distinction had the consequence that "their concept of obligation [...] is anything but moral," but instead had been merely psychologically determined, that is, related to happiness as the final purpose of all actions (*GM*, AA 4: 391; Timmermann 2011, 11).[8] According

---

8 See Garve 1798b, 376–377: "If a principle, i.e., a generally true proposition, which states a supreme rule for human actions, is to move the will of men to really follow this rule, then the presentation which lies in the principle, and which merely brings into his mind an object different from it and indifferent to it, must necessarily be brought into connection with another presentation of man, of a state of his own which is [...] pleasing to him, in such a way that he sees that he can hope to attain a similar state by following the rule. [...] And since happiness is nothing else than the sum of many good things: so happiness is necessarily the last end, and the hope for it the first mainspring of human actions." ("Wenn ein Princip, d.h. ein allgemein wahrer Satz, der eine höchste Regel für menschliche Handlungen aussagt, den Willen der Menschen bewegen soll, dieser Regel wirklich zu folgen: so muß nothwendig die Vorstellung, die im Principe liegt, und die ihm bloß ein von ihm verschiedenes, und ihm gleichgültiges Objekt ins Gemüth bringt, mit einer andern Vorstellung des Menschen, von eiem ehmahls [...] wohlgefälligen Zustande seiner selbst, dergestalt in Verbindung gebracht werden, daß er einsieht, daß er von der Befolgung der Regel einen ähnlichen Zustand zu hoffen habe. [...] Und da die Glückseligkeit nichts anders ist, als die Summe von vielem Guten: so ist Glückseligkeit nothwendig der letzte Endzweck, – und die Hoffnung auf sie die erste Triebfeder der menschlichen Handlungen.").

to Kant, however, moral philosophy is not about the factual actions of human beings and the corresponding empirical motives; it has nothing to do with the questions of empirical psychology or empirical motivation. Rather, its object is a pure idea of reason: the idea of a will "that is completely determined from a priori principles" (*GM*, AA 4: 390; Timmermann 2011, 19).

2 Christian Wolff's Account of Obligation

Kant's critical note that Wolff's concept of obligation is anything but moral requires further explanation. It does not only concern Wolff, but also the action-theoretical considerations of Garve. It is true that Garve is not a Wolffian in the strict sense, because his temporal distance from Wolff was too great, along with the influence on him of the Stoic doctrine mediated by Cicero and the social philosophy of the Scots. But the already mentioned circumstance of linking the (normative) question of obligation on the one hand with the psychological question of motivation for action on the other is characteristic of the Wolffian legacy in Garve's writings. In this respect, it seems appropriate to sketch this Wolffian background. According to Wolff, the reason for the possibility of being bound to an action as a duty is based on the natural orientation of the will towards the good: "appetitus in genere est inclinatio animæ ad objectum pro ratione boni in eadem percepti" (Wolff 1738a, § 579).[9] Here, Wolff makes use of the traditional concept of *appetitus rationalis*, by which he, like the scholastics, meant the will "in the narrower sense" (Wolff 1740a, § 155, and Wolff 1751, § 492). That the will is directed in this way towards the good is due to the fact that the conception of the good produces in us a feeling of pleasure, just as the conception of evil produces one of disgust. The will's relation to actions in accordance with duty, which promote the good, is therefore not external to the will, but immanent. Accordingly, Wolff defines the *obligatio naturalis* as that obligation "quæ in ipsa hominis rerumque essentia atque natura rationem sufficientem habet" (Wolff 1738a, I.2, § 129). Since, therefore, all morality is directly anchored in the nature of man, a rational man does good

---

[9] Cf. *Thomas* 2004, 173–174: "According to Wolff, the will, by virtue of its own essence and nature, is given a supreme and ultimate purpose by which all of its particular purposes and actions are determined. It is the natural striving for perfection that guides the will and, according to Wolff's conception, commits an acting subject to certain obligatory actions." ("Nach Wolff ist dem Willen aufgrund seines eigenen Wesens und seiner Natur ein höchster und letzter Zweck vorgegeben, durch den alle seine besonderen Zwecksetzungen und Handlungen bestimmt werden. Es ist das den Willen leitende natürliche Streben nach Vollkommenheit, das zufolge der Wolffschen Konzeption ein handelndes Subjekt an bestimmte Pflichthandlungen bindet.").

and refrains from evil not "in view of the reward and out of fear of punishment," but because he gives himself the law of action on the basis of the presentation [*Vorstellung*] of the good, without needing any further motive apart from the insight into the moral quality of an action (Wolff 1733, § 38). The will of human beings is such that the knowledge of good associated with an action is a "motive of the will [...] that we will it," just as, conversely, the knowledge of evil is "a motive of not wanting, or of loathing something" (Wolff 1733, §§ 6–7).[10] In this respect, obligation is identical with the motivation of the will by the presentation of the good or evil associated with an action. Therefore, for Wolff, morality does not consist in the external motivation, by threats and rewards, of an external law-giving will, but in the internal determination of the will by the acting subject itself, that is, in the autonomous orientation of one's own will to the demands of the natural law:

> Because we recognize by reason what the law of nature wills to have; so, a rational man needs no further law [than the natural], but by means of his reason he is himself a law to himself. (Wolff 1733, § 24)[11]

In view of the motivation-theoretical interpretation of the concept of obligation, however, one can say with good reason that Wolff's ethics – at least as far as the concept of obligation is concerned – represents a *continuation of empirical psychology*. For in Wolff's intellectualistic theory of the will, the will appears as the "inclination of the mind (*Gemüth*) towards a thing for the sake of the good that we think we perceive in it" (Wolff 1751, §§ 492–493). In contrast, non-willing is the "withdrawal of the mind (*Gemüth*) from a thing for the sake of the evil that we think we perceive in it" (Wolff 1751, §§ 492–493). The presentation of the good or the perfect produces in us a pleasure, which Wolff defines as "a beholding of perfection" (Wolff 1751, § 404). The pleasure of the presentation of the perfect,

---

[10] In his *Anmerkungen zur Deutschen Metaphysik* (Wolff 1740b, § 155) and (Wolff 1751, § 492), Wolff points out that he understands by the will "in the narrower sense" like the scholastics the "rational desire" [*appetitus rationalis*]. Cf. Wolff 1738a, § 586: "Repræsentatio boni est ratio sufficiens appetitus; repræsentatio mali ratio sufficiens aversationis." On the systematic problems associated with this intellectualist view of free will, cf. Wolff 1949, 109ff.

[11] "Weil wir durch die Vernunft erkennen, was das Gesetz der Natur haben will; so braucht ein vernünftiger Mensch kein weiteres Gesetz, sondern vermittels der Vernunft ist er ihm selbst ein Gesetz.") Cf. Wolff 1738b, vol. 1, § 268: "Homo ratione valens & utens sibimetipsi lex est." Cf. *Schröer* 1988, 213: "The key to the core of the Wolffian moral foundation thus lies in the thesis that the rational human being, by virtue of his reason, is himself the law and does not need any further laws beyond that." ("Der Schlüssel zum Kern der Wolffischen Moralbegründung liegt somit in der These, der vernünftige Mensch sei kraft seiner Vernunft sich selbst das Gesetz und brauche darüber hinaus keine weiteren Gesetze."). See also *Clara Joesten: Wolffs Grundlegung der praktischen Philosophie*. Leipzig 1931, pp. 27ff.

for its part, becomes the driving force of the performance of moral acts. This *psychologization of the concept of obligation*, which can be observed in Wolff's ethics and which pursues the goal of "combating the purely positivistic conception of obligation," is indeed – as Clemens Schwaiger has pointed out – a profound innovation in the modern theory of obligation.[12] In view of this psychologization of the concept of obligation, however, the question arises of whether the *specifically normative aspect* of obligation, namely that it is an imperative or moral necessity, is not dissolved into psychology or into corresponding motivation-theoretical considerations. For Wolff claims precisely that the will is determined by the presentation of the good, so we are dealing here only with the motivational causality of actions, their psychological necessity conditioned by the presentation, but not with any kind of moral necessity. Therefore, the question arises of how, if the will is determined by the presentation of the good, this psychological causality of actions actually differs from a moral coercion of some kind.[13]

Garve, in his *Uebersicht der vornehmsten Principien der SittenLehre*, criticizes Wolff's moral philosophy for having formulated the "concept of perfection in such a general and abstract way" that it could no longer function as a moral principle (Garve 1798b, 176–182), but in terms of theory of action, Garve sticks to this school philosophical understanding of motivation throughout his life, which was additionally reinforced by his reception of Scottish moral philosophy (Ludwig 2007, 188). He even interprets Cicero's *De officiis* in light of the *philosophia practica universalis*.[14] In contrast, the assumption of Bernd Ludwig, who in his instructive essay on *Kant, Garve, and the Motives of Moral Action* has tried to place Kant's theory of moral motivation into a larger philosophical-historical context of the establishment of a new conception of causality in Newton's *Principia Mathematica* and the moral-philosophical reflections of Samuel Clarke that follow from it, does not seem plausible to me (Ludwig 2007, 190 ff.).

---

12 *Schwaiger* 2000, 251–252: "Obligation is equal to motivation – this is, in a nutshell, Wolff's solution to the problem of obligation." ("Obligation ist gleich Motivation – so lautet, auf eine Kurzformel gebracht, Wolffs Lösung des Verbindlichkeitsproblems.")

13 I have addressed this problem in more detail elsewhere, cf. *Hüning* 2004, 158 ff.

14 Garve 1787, 10: "Cicero first divides all moral science into two main parts: into the doctrine of the highest good [...] and into that of the duties [...]. This division is common to all sects of the ancient philosophers since Socrates; it is also not foreign to the moderns [...]. That first part, in fact, examines the general grounds of all obligation, and the essence of virtue: that is our general practical philosophy." ("Cicero theilt zuerst alle moralische Wissenschaft in zwey Haupttheile: in die Lehre von dem höchsten Gute [...] und in die von den Pflichten [...]. Diese Eintheilung ist allen Secten der alten Philosophen seit dem Socrates eigen; – sie ist auch den Neuern nicht fremde [...]. Jener erste Theil untersucht nämlich, die allgemeinen Gründe aller Verbindlichkeit, und das Wesen der Tugend: das ist unsre allgemeine praktische Philosophie.").

3 The Role of Dogmatic Metaphysics in Kant's *Groundwork*

As we have seen, Kant's claim that the school philosophical conception of obligation is anything but moral was all too well founded. In this respect, an insurmountable boundary line is drawn here between the moral philosophy of popular philosophy and Kant's critical ethics. Thus, it is all the more surprising that Kant, despite this resounding criticism, complies with the school philosophical understanding of moral philosophy in the second section of the *Groundwork* to an astonishing degree, at least further than would actually be possible according to the *Critique of Pure Reason*. In the following, I draw on a groundbreaking essay by Manfred Baum entitled *Metaphysics in Kant's Moral Philosophy* (Baum 2020, 313–332), which in turn is based upon Klaus Reich's paper *Kant and the Ethics of the Greeks* (Reich 2001a, 138–139).

Accordingly, we find in the second section of the *Groundwork* a kind of thought experiment, in which Kant introduces the question of "how to derive the supreme moral law as a categorical imperative for man, given a dogmatic metaphysical assumption" (Baum 2020, 319).[15] This claim is remarkable insofar as Kant had already pointed out in the first section that the unconditioned worth of actions is not derived from intentions and ends that a human being can have, but only from the formal "principle of the will," in fact "regardless of the ends that can be effected by such action" (*GM*, AA 4: 400; Timmermann 2011, 29). This formal principle, which demands "universal conformity of actions with law," is of course nothing other than the categorical imperative: "I ought never to proceed except in such a way *that I could also will that my maxim should become a universal law*" (*GM*, AA 4: 402; Timmermann 2011, 3). One must wonder why Kant, despite the proof that the categorical imperative is the sought-after principle of the intrinsically good will, now additionally discusses the possibility of deriving the categorical imperative from presuppositions of dogmatic metaphysics by linking the same with the idea of humanity as an end in itself. The moral law can then be formulated as follows:

> So act, that you use humanity, in your own person as well as in the person of any other, always at the same time as an end, never merely as a means. (*GM*, AA 4: 429; Timmermann 2011, 87)

---

15 "[…] wie man das oberste Sittengesetz als kategorischen Imperativ für den Menschen ableiten kann, wenn man eine dogmatisch-metaphysische Annahme zu Grunde legt."

The dogmatic metaphysical premises upon which this end-in-itself formula is based are stated by Kant as follows:[16]

1. But suppose there were something *the existence of which in itself* has an absolute worth, that, as an *end in itself,* could be a ground of determinate laws, then the ground of a possible categorical imperative, i.e., of a practical law, would lie in it, and only in it alone.
2. Now I say: a human being and generally every rational being *exists* as an end in itself, *not merely as a means* for the discretionary use for this or that will. (*GM*, AA 4: 428; Timmermann 2011, 85)

From this, Kant draws the conclusion:

3. If, then, there is to be a supreme practical principle and, with regard to the human will, a categorical imperative, it must be such that, from the representation of what is necessarily an end for everyone, because it is an *end in itself,* it constitutes an *objective* principle of the will, and hence can serve as a universal practical law. The ground of this principle is: *a rational nature exists as an end in itself.* (*GM*, AA 4: 428–429; Timmermann 2011, 85/87)

Distinguishing himself from a vast number of interpreters, Manfred Baum has emphasized that, according to Kant, the "ground of this principle is a proposition of dogmatic metaphysics which does not stand up to a critique of pure reason in its metaphysical assertions" (Baum 2020, 320).[17] In support of his claim, Baum refers to Kant's lecture on natural law (the so-called *Naturrecht Feyerabend*), which Kant delivered at the same time that he was working on the *Groundwork*. There, Kant made the dogmatic-metaphysical basis of why man can be regarded as an end in itself knowable by claiming that man is the "end of creation" (*Zweck der Schöpfung*; AA 27: 1319). In his essay, Baum criticizes the vast

> flood of publications [...] in which one finds quotations from the rest of the 2nd section of the *Groundwork*, from which it is assumed that, in search of the basic assumptions of Kant's moral philosophy, one finds in them that which explains and makes intelligible the general categorical imperative with its accursed formalism. (Baum 2020, 319)[18]

---

[16] In this, I also follow the reconstruction by Manfred Baum (see Baum 2020, 319–320).
[17] "[...] [dass der] 'Grund dieses Princips' ein Satz der dogmatischen Metaphysik ist, der einer Kritik der reinen Vernunft in ihren metaphysischen Behauptungen nicht standhält."
[18] "[...] Flut der Veröffentlichungen [...], in denen man Zitate aus dem Rest des 2. Abschnitts der *Grundlegung* findet, von denen angenommen wird, dass man, auf der Suche nach den Grundannahmen der Kantischen Moralphilosophie, in ihnen dasjenige finde, was den allgemeinen kategorischen Imperativ mit seinem verwünschten Formalismus erklärt und verständlich macht."

The fact that Kant in the second section of the *Groundwork* in fact only conducts a thought experiment to make his moral principle more understandable to readers with a popular philosophical background and does not present his own philosophical position can be seen, as Manfred Baum also points out, from the lecture on natural law from 1784/85. There, Kant specifies the metaphysical background of the corresponding considerations, according to which only man "can be regarded as an end in himself" (*als Zweck an sich selbst angesehen werden kann*), and that is because man is the "end of creation:" "in the world of ends, there has to be an ultimate end, and that is the rational being" (AA 27: 1319).[19] The reason why Kant argues at all within the framework of metaphysical premises, to the rejection of which the *Critique of Pure Reason* was dedicated, Manfred Baum sees in Kant's popular pedagogical intention to bring "the frightening abstractness of his doctrine of the supreme moral law" closer to the readers in this way (Baum 2020, 320–321).[20] I would put the emphasis differently here: it seems to me that Kant's intention is rather to show that even if one starts, as Garve does, from premises of dogmatic metaphysics or from the idea of a purposeful arrangement of the world, one can make plausible the necessity of an unconditionally valid moral law that abstracts from the pursuit of happiness.

4 Garve's Note from 1792

If Kant had hoped to have dissuaded Garve and other representatives of school philosophy from eudaemonism by his extensive concession in the second section of the *Groundwork*, Garve disabused him of this hope a few years later.

Before I discuss Kant's criticism in detail, I would like to emphasize that Kant refers critically to Garve in two respects in his essay *On the Common Saying*:
1. In the first section, Kant takes a long note by Garve on the "happiness of sentient creatures" as the final purpose of the world, which Garve had added to his treatise *On Patience* (*Ueber die Geduld*) of 1792 (Garve 1792, 111–116), as the occasion for a renewed criticism. This note serves as a fundamental clarification of the relationship between moral philosophy and eudaemonism, or duty and happiness. Already on July 30, 1792, Kant announces to Johann Erich Biester, the editor of the *Berlinische Monatsschrift*, a moral treatise "on Herr

---
19 "[…] in der Welt der Zwecke muss doch zuletzt ein Zweck seyn, und das ist das vernünftige Wesen."
20 "[…] die erschreckende Abstraktheit seiner Lehre vom obersten Sittengesetz."

Garve's recently expressed opinion about my moral principle" (AA 11: 350; Zweig 1999, 423).[21]

2. But this is only one aspect of the reference to Garve found in the essay *On the Common Saying*. The general problem of the essay, namely the relation between theory and practice, also very likely has Garve's remarks on this topic as its starting point. Now, Kant does not deny that "between theory and practice there is required, besides, a middle term connecting them and providing a transition from one to the other," insofar as the said connection must be accomplished by "an act of judgment" (*OCS*, AA 8: 275; Gregor 1996, 279).

However, Kant considers it a "scandal of philosophy" when this difficulty of connection is transformed by a "would-be expert" [*Klügling*] into the assertion of an opposition of theory and practice, by admitting that theory retains "its value in the schools (perhaps only to exercise the mind)," while asserting that, in relation to practice, "when one goes into the world one becomes aware that one has been pursuing empty ideals and philosophic dreams" (*OCS*, AA 8: 276–277; Gregor 1996, 279–280). This *Klügling*, of whom Kant speaks here, is no one else than Garve. Garve, in fact, in his treatise *Some Scattered Considerations about Morality in Politics* [*Einige zerstreute Betrachtungen über die Moral der Politik*], which he had appended to his notes on the Cicero translation (see Garve 1788, 165 ff.),[22] claims that "in the political arena, self-interest plays a far more praiseworthy and lauded role," that is, politicians should pursue their interests in power or the purpose of the state without major moral concerns, whereas "all the moralist can say about this [...] are pious wishes, which generally seem ridiculous to those who are at the helm and have to do with business" (Garve 1788, 197). Further, Garve explains:

> This much, however, is obvious: that in no kind of business are the general principles, which reason recognizes as right, [...] and which can therefore be regarded as truths, if anything is true, so much in contradiction with general practice; in contradiction even with what the necessity of the circumstances, and the situation, in which old errors and abuses have placed the states, seems to require as a duty in individual cases; as in political business. (Garve 1788, 198)[23]

---

21 "[...] über Hrn Garve [...] neuerdings geäußerte Meynung von meinem Moralprincip."
22 Kant knew these notes or treatise, for he quotes from it in his *Toward Perpetual Peace* (cf. *TPP*, AA 8: 385; Gregor 1996, 350).
23 "So viel leuchtet indessen ein: daß bey keiner Art von Geschäften, die allgemeinen Grundsätze, welche die Vernunft für richtig erkennt, [...] und die man also für Wahrheiten ansehen kan, wenn irgend etwas wahr ist, so sehr im Widerspruche sind mit der allgemeinen Praxis; im Widerspruche selbst mit dem was die Nothwendigkeit der Umstände, und die Lage, worein alte Irrtümer und

Kant now instructs Garve that, with regard to the problem of the relation between theory and practice, there is a fundamental difference between an empirical "theory, which concerns objects of intuition," and a theory "in which objects are represented only by means of concepts," and this is especially the case with the speculative "objects of philosophy" (*OCS*, AA 8: 276; Gregor 1996, 280). In the case of such objects, however, it is quite possible that they can be thought without contradiction and "irreproachably (on the part of reason)," but at the same time they cannot be "*given*" in experience and thus can prove to be "empty ideas" (*OCS*, AA 8: 276; Gregor 1996, 280). Again, however, the case is different with moral philosophy as a "theory that is based on the *concept of duty*," because here "the concern about the empty ideality of this concept quite disappears" (*OCS*, AA 8: 276; Gregor 1996, 280). For moral philosophy is not about how people actually act, but about how they ought to act; its counterfactual concepts (such as the concept of duty) cannot therefore be refuted by reference to a contradictory experience: The laws of moral philosophy are "laws of what *ought to happen*, even if it never does, i.e., objective practical laws" (*GM*, AA 4: 427; Timmermann 2011, 83). This is the reason for the independence of moral philosophy from empirical psychology, but it is equally true that appealing to experience cannot support moral reasoning, because "it is clear that no experience can give occasion to infer even just the possibility of such apodictic laws [like the categorical imperative, D.H.]" (*GM*, AA 4: 408; Timmermann 2011, 45).

5 Kant's Critique of Garve in the First Part of His Essay *On the Common Saying*

I now proceed to the presentation of Kant's criticism in the first section of the essay *On the Common Saying*. The first part of Kant's "reply to some objections by Professor Garve" (*OCS*, AA 8: 278; Gregor 1996, 281) deals with Garve's misunderstandings concerning Kant's moral principle (*OCS*, AA 8: 278–284; Gregor 1996, 278–286). The second part deals with the actual topic, the "supposed conflicting interests of theory and of practice in philosophy" (*OCS*, AA 8: 284; Gregor 1996, 286).

Mißbräuche die Staaten gesetzt haben, in einzelnen Fällen als Pflicht zu erfordern scheint; – als bey den politischen Geschäften."

5.1 Kant's Criticism of Garve's Erroneous Presentation of His Moral Principle

As already mentioned, Kant's criticism in the first part of the section devoted to Garve in the *Gemeinspruch*-essay was prompted by a note from Garve in his *Essays on Various Topics from Morals and Literature* [*Versuche über verschiedne Gegenstände aus der Moral und Literatur*], published in 1792. Garve claimed there,
1. that, firstly, he himself considered happiness to be an indispensable element of motivation,
2. that, secondly, by considering "the observation of the moral law, completely without regard to happiness" as the "only final purpose of the Creator," Kant has created a fundamental problem of motivation, along with the problem of a deficient metaphysical anchoring of his moral philosophy (Garve 1792, 111). For even the "virtuous person, in his disinterested obedience to the moral law, could nor should […] never lose sight of that aspect [of happiness]," because "otherwise he would completely lose the transition to the invisible world, to the conviction of the existence of God and of immortality, which, according to the theory of these philosophers themselves, is absolutely necessary to give the moral system support and stability" (Garve 1792, 111);
3. and that he, thirdly, could understand Kant's "division of ideas" of happiness and virtue, according to which the "virtuous person […] incessantly strives to be worthy of happiness, but […] never strives to be happy" (Garve 1792, 111–112), in *abstracto*, i.e., in his "head," but not in his heart. Such "subtle differences of ideas," as Kant's ethics obviously presuppose, contradict the findings of empirical psychology, according to which it is completely "incomprehensible" "how any human being can become aware of having purely separated his desire to be worthy of happiness from the desire for happiness itself, and thus of having practiced duty completely unselfishly" (Garve 1792, 112).

In his answer to these objections, Kant first emphasizes the independence of his ethics from any special purpose, as he did in the *Groundwork*. Garve misunderstood this abstraction from the purposiveness of the moral principle because he did not distinguish between moral reasoning and empirical psychology. That the pursuit of happiness is a guiding motive of action for all human beings is considered trivial by Kant. In this respect, happiness is also a legitimate, for it is a "natural," purpose of action. Therefore, in his ethics he also does

> not fail to remark the human being is not thereby required to *renounce* his natural end, happiness, when it is a matter of complying with his duty; for that he cannot do, just as no finite

rational being whatever can; instead, he must *abstract* altogether from this consideration when the command of duty arises. (*OCS*, AA 8: 278; Gregor 1996, 281–282)

Garve's second misunderstanding concerns the role of the highest good in Kant's ethics. The need for the assumption of a "highest good possible in the world (universal happiness combined with and in conformity with the purest morality throughout the world)" as well as the "belief […] in a moral ruler of the world" is not, as Garve assumes, an expression of "a deficiency in moral incentives" (*OCS*, AA 8: 279; Gregor 1996, 282). Such thoughts are rather effects of the will's orientation to the moral law, but not the condition under which "the universal concept of duty first gets 'support and stability' […], that is, gets a sure basis and the requisite strength of an *incentive*" (*OCS*, AA 8: 279; Gregor 1996, 282). Therefore, in the question of the moral principle, "the doctrine of the *highest good* […] can be completely passed over and set aside" (*OCS*, AA 8: 280; Gregor 1996, 283).

In summary, Kant states: "These objections are therefore nothing but misunderstandings (for I do not care to take them as misrepresentations)" (*OCS*, AA 8: 281; Gregor 1996, 283). In Kant's view, they are human, all too human, because they explain themselves. Here, Kant basically repeats his critique from the *Prolegomena*: from "the human propensity to follow one's accustomed course of thought even in appraising the thoughts of others, and thus to carry the former over into the latter" (*OCS*, AA 8: 281; Gregor 1996, 283). It is the "old refrain" that Garve sings, namely that happiness "constitutes the basis of all objective necessity in acting and hence of all obligation" (*OCS*, AA 8: 284; Gregor 1996, 286). Hence, Garve thinks that the abstraction from happiness would deprive the will of all possible motivation.

Subsequently, Kant sums up Garve's "dogmatic assertion of the opposite" (*OCS*, AA 8: 281; Gregor 1996, 284) in the following points:

1. A person acts in relation to the presentation of the respective states to be achieved, preferring in his decision the state that appears to him as a *good state*: "a series of such good states is the most general concept expressed by the word *happiness*" (*OCS*, AA 8: 281; Gregor 1996, 284).
2. All motives in general arise from happiness; according to Garve, this also applies to the "observance of the moral law" (*OCS*, AA 8: 281; Gregor 1996, 284).

Kant sees in the notion of the good state, which a human being strives for in comparison to a worse one, only a "play upon the ambiguity of the word *the good*" (*OCS*, AA 8: 282; Gregor 1996, 284). The good condition of Garve could only be "a state that is relatively better but in itself evil" (*OCS*, AA 8: 282; Gregor 1996, 284). The goodness of such a state is only based upon a comparison with other possible states, and so it is desired merely conditionally, namely under the condition of the respective end. The state, however, which is based upon compliance with the moral law, which in turn determines the will merely in form, not in matter, "is not merely a better state, but the only one that is good in itself." Kant emphasizes at this point that the goodness of this special state is "from another sphere altogether, where ends that may present themselves to me (and so too their sum, happiness) are not taken into consideration at all" (*OCS*, AA 8: 283; Gregor 1996, 288). While all ends, or all matter of the will, originate from the sphere of sensibility, the formal determination of the will by the moral law is based exclusively on the legislation of practical reason.

Of course, Kant also holds that "the will must have *motives*" (*OCS*, AA 8: 283; Gregor 1996, 288). The crucial point here is whether the will is determined by empirical reasons – that is, by objects that are connected to it vis-à-vis the feeling of pleasure or displeasure – or by the "unconditional *law* itself" (*OCS*, AA 8: 283; Gregor 1996, 288). In this case, it is also clear that such a purely rational motive is not related to physical feelings or to happiness.

5.2 Kant's Critique of Garve's Determination of the Relationship Between Theory and Practice

In the second part of his argument with Garve, Kant now goes into more detail about the actual point of contention, the relationship between theory and practice (cf. *OCS*, AA 8: 286–290; Gregor 1996, 284–289). Garve had raised the problem in his remark "that no one can become aware with certainty of *having performed his duty* quite unselfishly" (*OCS*, AA 8: 284; Gregor 1996, 286). This is also the opinion of Kant, because such certainty would require "a perfectly clear representation of all the associated representations and considerations attached to the concept of duty by imagination, habit, and inclination," which no human being can ever achieve (*OCS*, AA 8: 284; Gregor 1996, 286). But Garve's problematization is only a pseudo-objection, since moral philosophy is not concerned with the question of how, and on the basis of what motives, an action is taken, but how an action should be taken. In this respect, there is no problem at all, for every agent has the clearest consciousness that he *"ought to perform* his duty quite unselfishly" and without regard for conflicting motives of happiness (*OCS*, AA 8: 284; Gregor 1996, 286).

As for the already mentioned division of the ideas of morality and happiness, of which Garve had claimed that he could not find "in his heart," Kant attributes this confession to Garve's inability to understand the underlying problem of reconciling "the possibility of categorical imperatives (such as those of duty are) – with the usual principles of psychological explanation (all of which have the mechanism of natural necessity as their basis)" (*OCS*, AA 8: 285; Gregor 1996, 287). To put it more clearly, Kant was convinced that Garve was incapable of grasping the fundamental moral philosophical problem of the possibility of categorical imperatives as such in the first place because of his adherence to the school philosophical way of psychological explanations, which always remain related to the empirical nature of man and thus to a world that is thoroughly determined by causal laws.

Also, the impossibility of a proof of freedom, which Garve emphasizes in his notes to the Cicero translation, turns out to be a pseudo-problem (cf. Garve 1787, 69; *OCS*, AA 8: 285; Gregor 1996, 287). In fact, no theoretical proof can be given for the "reality" of freedom, "either in an immediate or in a mediate experience," because an act of freedom would be the very abolition of the causality of nature, which is at the same time the condition for the possibility of experience at all (*OCS*, AA 8: 285; Gregor 1996, 287). On the other hand, a proof of freedom can very well be given on moral-practical grounds. Such a proof does not extend our knowledge of the real world, but formulates a necessary condition of moral action in general. That the assumption of the universal applicability of causality and natural necessity in theoretical philosophy can very well exist with the assumption of freedom for moral purposes, Kant had already shown in the discussion of the third antinomy in the *Critique of Pure Reason* and in the *Groundwork*.[24]

Kant concludes his critique of Garve with the assertion that, in the rejection of Garve's objections lies "a clear proof that everything in moral philosophy that is correct for theory must also hold for practice" (*OCS*, AA 8: 288; Gregor 1996, 289). Admittedly, the truth of morality is not confirmed by historical experience, for here it is shown that the maxims of action are predominantly drawn from self-interest. But our common, inner experience of having an awareness of the moral law, and therefore of also being aware that we can act morally "because [we] ought to," confirms the moral law (*OCS*, AA 8: 287; Gregor 1996, 289). That the "historical experience up to now has still not proved the success of the doctrine of virtue,"

a) is, on the one hand, also due to pseudo-philosophers like Garve, who start from the wrong premise, "that the incentive derived from the idea of duty in itself is much too fine for the common concept" to have a motivating effect on the will,

b) and, on the other, it is also because of the fact that one made "a principle of education and homiletics to give preference to the aspiration for happiness" without realizing that such rules for the promotion of happiness are not commands and have no obligatory force. (*OCS*, AA 8: 288; Gregor 1996, 289)

---

[24] *GM*, AA 4: 456; Timmermann 2011, 141: "that no true contradiction can be found between freedom and natural necessity of just the same human actions."

Garve remained faithful to the school philosophical positions with which he was academically socialized until the end of his life. For this reason, his misunderstanding of the theoretical intentions and significance of Kant's critical philosophy is equally enduring. Despite Kant's repeated wake-up calls, Garve persisted in his dogmatic slumber, so that he did not rise above the role he had ascribed to himself: to be a mere whetstone for others.

Gideon Stiening
The "Entire Human Being" Rather Than "Pure Reason": Feder's *Philosophische Bibliothek* and His Review of the *Kritik der praktischen Vernunft*

Abstract: J. G. H. Feder (1740–1821) was engaged in a bitter confrontation with the philosophy of Immanuel Kant since the 1780s. After the review of the *CPR* written with Christian Garve and Kant's vigorous reaction in the *Prolegomena*, Feder concentrated primarily on a critical interpretation of Kant's practical philosophy, which he published primarily in his journal *Philosophische Bibliothek* (1788–1791), which he edited with C. Meiners. The anti-Kantian studies in this journal show not that Feder did not understand Kant at all – as has long been assumed by Kant-scholars – but rather that he fundamentally rejected the secular orientation of Kant's Moral Philosophy. In his critique of Kant's practical apriorism, Feder went so far as to suspect a secret Catholicism in Kants so called 'return of practical metaphysics.'

> From this I concluded in my earliest systems, and still consider it a good conclusion: *The fruit of the Lord is the beginning of wisdom.* (Feder 1825, 252)[1]

1 Against the "Downplaying of the *Erfahrungsphilosophie* [Philosophy of Experience]"

Johann Georg Heinrich Feder did not underestimate the implications of his confrontation with Kantian philosophy. As he wrote in his autobiography, in which he evidently aimed to legitimate his critique of Kant's philosophy, both in general and in its specifics:

---

[1] Feder quotes Psalm 111:10: "Hieraus folgerte ich in meinen frühesten Systeme, und halte es noch immer für eine gute Folgerung: *Die Frucht des Herrn ist der Weisheit Anfang*."

> Because I foresaw that I would be attacked from several sides, it seemed to me that a *Philosophical Library* [*Philosophische Bibliothek*] of my own was as necessary as *a standing army* in political feuds. (Feder 1825, 123)²

At the time, in the late 1780s, Feder indeed foresaw being attacked from different fronts. This is because he was responsible for the notorious 1782 review of the *Critique of Pure Reason* (Garve/Feder 1782, 40), which had provoked Kant's angry retort in the *Prolegomena*. Kant accused the reviewer of having conducted a superficial reading of the text and of demonstrating a profound lack of understanding.³ Although Christian Garve had written the original draft of the review, which appeared anonymously in the *Göttingischen Gelehrten Anzeigen*, Feder added, as he freely admitted, the accusation of Berkeleyan subjective idealism to the considerably abridged final version.⁴ This addition was the straw that broke the camel's back: Kant had not shied away from attesting to the Göttingen reviewer's impatience and bad temper, in the end extending a challenge to him and daring him to lift the mask of anonymity.⁵

Without explicitly admitting it, Feder accepted the challenge and soon produced a monographic critique of transcendental philosophy, in which he not only repeated the accusation of subjective idealism but also sought to expose Kant's apriorism as bad metaphysics (see Feder 1787; see also Hahmann 2018). Despite some positive reviews,⁶ however, Feder quickly realized that the "spectre" of a new metaphysics could not be handled in a single monograph. Instead, he planned to launch a journal – a type of publication that promised to reach a larger audience, especially if it came from Göttingen (see Marino 1995, 40 ff.).

The journal project gave rise to the *Philosophical Library* [*Philosophische Bibliothek*] in 1788. Feder founded, organized, and authored the *Philosophical Library* with his friend and colleague, Christoph Meiners. The project was clearly and exclusively directed against the growing influence of Kant and Kantian philosophy, which emerged at the end of the 1780s and extended both to academic philosophy and to the philosophically interested public (see Schröpfer 2003; Bondeli 2014). Thirty years later, Feder would still refer to the journal as a "standing army" in political disputes with Kant. Thus, Feder put all his eggs in the basket of the *Philosophical Library*, against this "enemy of war." This was a war he would ultimately

---

2 "Weil ich voraussah, daß ich von mehreren Seiten würde angegriffen werden; so schien mir eine eigene *Philosophische Bibliothek* so nöthig, als bey den politischen Fehden *eine stehende Armee*."
3 Immanuel Kant: Prolegomena zu einer jeden künftigen Metaphysik, die als Wissenschaft wird auftreten können. In: AA 4, 372–380.
4 On the peculiar events surrounding this review, see Nowitzki/Roth/Stiening 2018a.
5 Kant: Prolegomena (see note 4), 378 seq..; see Polloka, XXIII ff.
6 See the review in: Allgemeine Deutsche Bibliothek 86 (1789), 355–380.

lose, however: following the fourth volume, the library had to be discontinued due to lack of sales. Until 1791, hardly anyone was interested in an empiricist critique of Kant's transcendental philosophy. How could it have come to this?

In his autobiography, Feder admits that by the end of the 1780s he had realized what a dangerous opponent he was facing – one who was receiving support from unexpected directions. A few lines after his comparison of the journal to a standing army, he writes:

> By the way, my, and certainly many others' thoughts have often been preoccupied with the synchronism of revolutionary aspirations in the political and in the scholarly world. It will not occur to any informed contemporary to assert that one of these revolutions has produced the other. But that the political condition of the time has had some influence on the events among the philosophers, not only with respect to what has been asserted but also with respect to the way in which it was put forward, can hardly be denied. (Feder 1825, 127)[7]

One must read these insinuations carefully.[8] Feder does not claim that Kant's philosophy promoted or even caused a political revolution. He clearly distances himself from the counter-Enlightenment conservatism exemplified by Friedrich Gentz[9] and Augustin Barruel (Barruel 1800, 23 ff.). Feder claims, however, that it was the turmoil of the revolutionary age, this supposed revaluation of all values, that made a successful reception of Kant's "confusions" possible. According to Feder's suggestion, there must have already been great cultural-political confusion in order for Kant's philosophy to have had a convincing effect. For all his anti-revolutionary and anti-Kantian verve, Feder moved methodologically within the framework of the historiography of philosophy that he had practiced in the 1770s and that was enforced by other authors toward the end of the eighteenth century – authors like Wilhelm Gottlieb Tennemann, who considered the social- and political-historical contextualization of philosophical theory both possible and necessary (see

---

[7] "Übrigens hat mein, und gewiß auch manches Anderen, Nachdenken oft beschäftigt der Synchronismus der revolutionären Strebungen in der politischen und in der gelehrten Welt. Daß die eine dieser Revolutionen die andere erzeugt habe, wird keinem unterrichteten Zeitgenossen zu behaupten einfallen. Aber daß der politische Zustand der Zeit einigen Einfluß gehabt hat auf die Ereignisse unter den Philosophen, nicht nur in Ansehung dessen *was*, sondern auch in Ansehung der Art, *wie* man es zu behaupten gesucht hat, ist kaum zu verkennen."
[8] In any case, the passage must be interpreted more precisely than Zwi Batscha (1989, 64) does. Batscha interprets Feder's statement in a way that brings it close to the conservative thesis of the outbreak of revolution through the spirit of enlightenment, but it is precisely this correlation that Feder explicitly rejects.
[9] Gentz 1793, vol. 2, 183: "Der Philosoph formt Systeme, der Pöbel schmiedet Mordgewehre daraus. Es kann kein schrecklicher Schwerdth in den Händen eine ungebildeten Menschen geben, als ein allgemeines Princip."

Tennemann 1798–1819, vol. 1, XLV–LXI). The sociology of knowledge of the 20th century, which also followed a methodological empiricism, proceeded in the very same way and thus belonged – albeit unwittingly – to the same tradition as Feder (see Knoblauch 2005, 256 ff.).

Nevertheless, this attempt to depotentiate Kant in terms of real history from the spirit of the revolutionary critique of the early nineteenth century is at the same time the view of one who, from a much later perspective, still considered himself to have lost the war. Feder wrote his autobiography around 1815 and thus, as he explicitly emphasizes, at a time when authors like Jakob Friedrich Fries were once again giving order to philosophy – in direct contrast to Kant (Feder 1825, 123, note *).

Although Feder had managed to defend himself against his first defeat in 1783 by means of his journal, his second defeat consisted in the discontinuation of the *Philosophical Library* in 1791. This latter blow was final. Consequently, Feder experienced severe psychosomatic symptoms (hypochondria), which could only be remedied (in part) by walks with his friend Christoph Meiners and a trip to the Harz mountains with Meiners, the natural philosopher and physician Johann Friedrich Gmelin and the university preacher and (extraordinary) professor of theology Johann Gottlob Marezoll.[10] It is only thanks to Meiners that Feder did not give up his professorship.

Any pity one might feel toward Feder is likely to dissipate when one considers the sentimental passages of his autobiography, however. In these passages, one can well imagine the two *Göttingeners* in 1787, planning their journal on their walks together and eagerly devising how to destroy the metaphysician from Königsberg. Yet they clearly and considerably overestimated their power (see also Albrecht 2014, 255) – as did many other authors of the time, including Georg Forster (see Stiening 2012b), Johann Gottfried Herder (who was reluctant to admit his own hubris; see Riedel 1989), and Jacob Friedrich Abel (see Pietsch 2011, 123 ff.), who failed in his critical examination of Kant. Of these, only Feder would be made to pay for his attempt by the verdict of posterity, handed the fate of being "rightly forgotten."[11]

The generally sparse literature on Feder, which is mostly focused on the early review of the *Critique of Pure Reason*, has tried to provide a psychological explanation for this scientific-political fact. Accordingly, Zwi Bascha writes that although Feder was a happy person, he did not understand Kant's philosophy until the end of his life (Batscha 1989, 63 ff.). This assessment, according to which Feder was sim-

---

10 This journey is described in Meiners 1794.
11 This had already been emphasized by Erdmann 1878, 10.

ply too weak-minded to understand Kant, traces back to an older opinion according to which Feder's criticism – which was undeniably wrong – had constituted a kind of lèse-majesté (see Erdmann 1878, 87 ff.; Vorländer 1992, 415; von Selle 1937, 176 ff.; and Wundt 1945, 291–292). A methodically reflected history of ideas and philosophy, however, must and can do without such judgments.

Luigi Marino's assessment was much more nuanced; his reference to Feder's engagement with Kant's practical philosophy is noteworthy, for it makes clear that Feder was by no means the ignorant reader of Kant he was often judged to be. Other research in recent decades points in a similar direction (Zimmerli 1983; Röttgers 1984; Brandt 1989; and Rachold 1999), and thus it is worth tracing these indications back to Feder's critique of Kant's ethics. The epistemological interest in doing so belongs to both the history of ideas and the history of philosophy: from the perspective of the history of ideas, the goal is to reconstruct the forms and content of the critique of eudaemonistic enlightenment directed at Kant; from the perspective of the history of philosophy, it is to examine whether this critique is coherent; that is, the systematic quality of the argument. In the following, I will attempt to answer this question on the basis of the detailed discussion of Kant's *Critique of Practical Reason* from the first volume of the *Philosophical Library*.

2 The *Philosophische Bibliothek* as Critical Instrument

Prior to analyzing and interpreting Feder's philosophical critique of Kant's ethics, I will first outline the four volumes of the journal in terms of their structure, authorship, and methodological contours. In this way, I will examine the scientific instruments with which Feder and Meiners attacked Kantianism. First, it should be noted that the project of founding a journal was by no means unusual in the late eighteenth century; neither Feder and Meiner's attempt to reach a broader readership for a specific scientific topic nor their journal's specifically anti-Kantian orientation would have been out of the ordinary. Philosophical journals and newspapers were being founded more frequently than ever before at the time, especially in the latter third of the eighteenth century (see Habel 2007). Like Feder and Meiners's project, they ran for an average of two to four years, producing approximately 200 to 500 copies (see Marti 2014, 31). Against this background, the *Philosophical Library* was by no means a failure, but Feder was unaccustomed to being "average:" since the early 1770s, he had considered himself as occupying a position at the pinnacle of European research, a self-assessment that was confirmed by many colleagues (see Nowitzki/Roth/Stiening 2018b).

The new Göttingen journal was not exactly original in terms of its anti-Kantian thrust, however: Johann August Eberhard also founded the *Philosophisches Magazin* in 1788, a publication devoted exclusively and explicitly to a critique of Kantian philosophy – albeit from a Leibnizian perspective.[12] Eberhard had an even longer run: after the magazine was discontinued in 1792, he founded a new journal, the *Philosophisches Archiv*, which remained in circulation until 1795.

The question of the authorship of the contributions to the *Philosophical Library* is straightforward (although in no way insignificant). As Feder, in his role as editor, writes in the preface to the first volume:

> We make ourselves known not only as editors, but as authors of this library; because we have as yet no reason to count on contributions from those with whom it would be an honour and pleasure for us to work together. (Feder/Meiners 1788–1791, vol. 1, VII)[13]

At first glance, this announcement seems surprising and slightly presumptuous. Reading Falk Wunderlich's study of Göttingen empiricism and materialism (Wunderlich 2012), one can understand why the two Göttingeners still believed they could put a stop to the strange activity of transcendentalism in the late 1780s. Many of their friends and combatants, from Herder (via Forster and Wieland) to Platner, Abel, Tittel, von Selle, Maaß and Schulze, were *on their side* against the "metaphysical spectre" from Königsberg. Feder and Meiners, however, claimed to simply be the leaders of this broader movement, which viewed itself as a species of enlightenment against a new obscurantist apriorism. Their position in the intellectual life of the 1770s certainly legitimized this assumption (cf. Riesbeck 1784/2013, 490).

The journal's format makes this interest in holding a prominent position in the anti-Kantian movement of the late 1780s – from which the Enlightenment was to be renewed – more than clear. By no means was criticism of Kant cited as having prompted the publication of the journal, and its content was not limited to critical accounts of Kant or Kantian themes. Rather, its four sections included systematic "treatises" (I) and detailed reviews of "foreign writings" (II) that seemed weighty and influential to the two Enlightenment thinkers (or were to be made so). This

---

[12] Eberhard 1788–1792. For the outline and objectives of this journal, see Gawlina 1996, 48 ff. On the philosophical substance of the controversy, see Stiening 2012a.

[13] "Wir machen uns nicht bloß als Herausgeber, sondern als Verfasser dieser Bibliothek bekannt; weil wir bis jetzt noch keine Ursache haben, auf Beyträge derjenigen zu rechnen, mit welchen in Gemeinschaft zu arbeiten uns Ehre und Vergnügen seyn würde."

includes, for example, Thomas Reid, whose common-sense theory had a lasting influence on Feder (Brandt 1989, 259 ff.), Pierre-Paul Leroy de Barincourt and his pamphlet on sovereignty,[14] and Jacques-Antoine-Hippolyte de Guibert's work on constitutional law and state prudence [*Staatsklugheit*],[15] the latter of whose political theories are also presented (as well as their relevance post-1789). Jacques Henri Bernardin de Saint Pierre's bestseller *Études de la nature* is also given detailed attention.[16] New publications in European philosophy were also presented and subjected to criticism; accordingly, Cornelis de Pauw's *Recherche philosophiques sur les Grecs* was torn apart by Meiners (Meiners had already revealed himself as a racist in his publications about the Indians).[17]

In addition, there are extensive reviews of "Teutsche Schriften" (III), as well as short announcements on European philosophy (IV). Apparently, Feder had had these two sections with reviews of foreign and German-language publications specifically in mind when he founded the journal. This is noted in the preface to the first volume:

> In the reviews in the G[elehrten] A[nzeigen], in which I have participated since 1769 according to my ability and will continue to do so, one is forced for various reasons to be so careful about abbreviations that many remarks, which arise during the reading of a book and could be useful to some for the better use of that book, must be half or completely suppressed and omitted. (Feder/Meiners 1788–1791, vol. 1, IV)[18]

Never again should Feder be accused of having insufficiently abridged his review of Kant. Moreover, Feder wanted space for his own defensive project. Above all, the section of detailed reviews of German-language texts is revealing in that, although many authors of his "own" empiricist-popular-philosophical Enlightenment circle are presented (e.g., Schulze, Garve, Abel, Tittel, and many more), no distinctly anti-Kantian faction is to be found. Rather, also here clear, even quite drastic criticism is exercised; thus, the following is said of Herder's *Ideen zur Philosophie und Geschichte der Menschheit*:

---

14 Leroy de Barincourt 1788, reviewed in Feder/Meiners 1788–1791, vol. 3, 67–83.
15 de Guiberts 1790, reviewed in Feder/Meiners 1788–1791, vol. 4, 87–104.
16 Saint-Pierre 1788, reviewed in Feder/Meiners 1788–1791, vol. 4, 104–129. On this book, which is famous throughout Europe, see König 2010.
17 de Pauw 1771; see also Zantop 1999, 66 ff.
18 "Bey den Recensionen in den hiesigen G[elehrten]. A[nzeigen]. an denen ich seit 1769 nach Vermögen Antheil genommen habe und ferner nehmen werde, ist man durch mancherley Gründe genöthigt, so auf Abkürzungen bedacht zu seyn, daß viele Bemerkungen, die beym Lesen eines Buches entstehen, und zum bessern Gebrauch desselben manchen nützlich seyn könnten, halb oder ganz unterdrückt und weggelassen werden müssen."

> We have read this third part of the investigations on the history of the human race with even greater pleasure than the first two. The language of the famous author develops and purifies itself more and more from mystical swelling, without losing the richness of new, and often surprisingly beautiful images. (Feder/Meiners 1788–1791, vol. 1, 96)[19]

Further "praise" is not offered, however; in what follows, Meiners, the author of this review, formally picks apart Herder's text with regard to the coherence of the empirical data – without touching on its historical-philosophical elements in anything more than a peripheral way. In short, Herder, who in 1788 would have had sufficient reason to join this front against Kant (see Stiening 2014), was rejected by Feder and Meiners as a potential combatant in the struggle against Kantianism. Thus, Feder's aim with this journal was by no means only to gain "satisfaction" in the face of Kant's harsh criticism in the *Prolegomena*; it was clearly above all geared toward forming an Enlightenment position that was ignited by criticism of Kant – the self-enlightenment of the Enlightenment, as it were, in the guise of a refutation of Kant. However, this scientific-political goal was not to be pursued at any price, but only on the basis of common premises. Herder, for all his pretended empiricism and open hostility to Kant, had no place in this context.

3 Empirical versus Transcendental Freedom: On the Critique of Kant's Ethics

Feder's philosophical and political interests can clearly be seen in his critical examination of Kant's *Critique of Practical Reason*. The review is noteworthy not only because of its length (37 printed pages; Feder/Meiners 1788–1791, vol. 1, 182–218) but also due to its specific methodology, which was unusual compared to the customs of the time (see Urban 2004): in a total of 36 sections, Feder presents what he considers to be the central theses, premises, and lines of evidence of the *Critique* and then comments on them in a section that is also visually; that is, typographically, highlighted. This procedure is justified as follows:

> In order to be able to make an appropriate judgment about this new product of Kant's genius – it is more than a simple revision of the Groundwork of the Metaphysics of Morals (Grund-

---

[19] "Wir haben diesen dritten Theil der Untersuchungen über die Geschichte des menschlichen Geschlechts mit noch größerm Vergnügen, als die beyden ersten gelesen. Die Sprache des berühmten Verfassers bildet und reiniget sich immer mehr von mystischem Schwulste, ohne an Reichthum neuer, und oft überraschend schöner Bilder zu verlieren."

legung der Metaphysik der Sitten) – and its relation to the doctrines of other philosophers, it is necessary to highlight the main propositions on which the author builds and by which he proceeds, and to accompany them individually with notes. (Feder/Meiners 1788–1791, vol. 1, 182)[20]

First, it must be noted that Feder's comment on the difference between the *Groundwork* (1785) and the second *Critique* (1788) is accurate (see Höffe 2002, 1 ff.). Moreover, on the basis of this statement he provides a philosophical commentary on the systematic essentials of the *Critique of Practical Reason*. Kant proceeded similarly in his review of Herder's *Ideas* (AA 8: 43–66). In his commentaries, Feder examines the logical coherence of the arguments and methodological stringency of the text. But he also elaborates on and justifies systematic differences. These various commentaries are sometimes more, sometimes less, convincing; however, one cannot find a "water-soup philosophy [*Wassersuppen-Philosophie*]" (Lichtenberg 1787/1967).

3.1 "Diese gibt es nicht" – Feder's Critique of Kant's Apriorism

Without further ado, Feder shifts from these decisive systematic differences to Kant's practical philosophy and to his philosophy in general. First, he aptly summarizes one of Kant's central claims from the preface of the *Critique of Practical Reason*, according to which we would do away with reason altogether if we did not presuppose knowledge a priori.[21] Feder comments on this claim, which is crucially distinct from his approach and on which he had already elaborated in *On Space and Causality* [*Über Raum und Caussalität*] (see Feder 1787, IXff.). Against the background of his pretended anti-apriorism, however, he cautiously notes: "It only depends on what knowledge a priori is supposed to mean." (Feder/Meiners 1788–1791, vol. 1, 183) Feder then clarifies:

> Concepts and principles before all experience, before all sensation, and independent of them? *These do not exist*; and also K[ant] basically does not assert them. For the concepts, which he

---

[20] "Um über dieses neue Product des Kantischen Genies – es ist mehr als eine bloße Umarbeitung der Grundlegung der Metaphysik der Sitten – und das Verhältniß desselben zu den Lehren anderer Philosophen, ein angemessenes Urtheil fällen zu können, ist es nöthig, die Hauptsätze, auf welche der Verf. baut, und durch die er fortführt, auszuheben, und einzeln mit Anmerkungen zu begleiten."

[21] However, Kant points out that to deny reason a priori is contradictory because this is done with the instruments of reason. See *CPrR*, AA 5: 12.

calls a priori, are, according to his own explanation, by themselves, without any connection with experience, empty forms of thought without any content. (Feder/Meiners 1788–1791, vol. 1, 183; emphasis by G.S.)[22]

It can hardly be denied that Feder herewith grasps a crucial difference between his position and Kant's: his own epistemological empiricism assumes, as it had in 1767 and would continue to do so in 1815, that *nihil est in intellectu, quod non prius fuerit in sensu* and thus that concepts and principles are always to be reconstructed from their empirical genesis; that is, from the experiences of the knower. This is why he believes that there can be no concepts and principles prior to experience. This is also why he conducted extensive *investigations* into the various empirical influences on the constitution of the *human will* [*Untersuchungen über den menschlichen Willen*].[23] However, Kant had already distinguished between the genesis and the validity of concepts in the introduction to the first edition of the *Critique of Pure Reason*, where he emphasized that although he agrees that *nihil est in intellectu, quod non prius fuerit in sensu*, to this must be added *nisi intellectus ipse*, which must and can do without the dogmatism of metaphysics (*CPR*, A 1). It was one of the aims of the first *Critique* to prove the validity of such transcendental concepts and principles. In this respect, Feder's remark that "even Kant's a priori insights cannot do without experience" is imprecise but not at all clouded by ignorance. His attempt at appropriation was not ignorant but rather calculating.

Following this commentary, Feder extends an interpretive olive branch to Kant that seems to gently level their fundamental differences:

> But if knowledge a priori means a combination of representations into judgments and conclusions, according to the subjective and objective reasons of human knowledge, in relation to certain objects and events that have not occurred to experience, nor will occur in the future, or that occurred before our experience, or that are otherwise outside of it, then knowledge a priori certainly constitutes the essence of reason. For all foresight and all reasoning is based on it. (Feder/Meiners 1788–1791, vol. 1, 184)[24]

---

[22] "Begriffe und Grundsätze vor aller Erfahrung, aller Empfindung, und unabhängig von ihnen? *Diese gibt es nicht*; und auch K[ant]. behauptet sie im Grunde nicht. Denn die Begriffe, die er a priori nennt, sind, nach seiner eigenen Erklärung, an sich selbst, ohne Verbindung mit Erfahrung, leere Denkformen ohne allen Inhalt."

[23] See Feder 1779–1793, here 1782 (vol. 2).

[24] "Heißt aber Erkenntnis a priori eine Verbindung von Vorstellungen zu Urtheilen und Schlüssen, nach Maaßgabe der subjectiven und objectiven Gründe der menschlichen Erkenntniß, in Beziehung auf gewissen Gegenstände und Ereignisse, der Erfahrung nicht vorgekommen, noch künftig, oder vor unserer Erfahrung vorgegangen, oder sonst außer derselben befindlich sind: so macht freylich das Erkennen a priori das Wesen der Vernunft aus. Denn alles Vorhersehen und alles Schließen beruht darauf."

Yet this interpretation is of course a poisoned chalice insofar as it raises specific forms of knowledge or the empirical universal to the a priori, which is precisely what Kant explicitly rejected:

> Empirical universality is therefore only an arbitrary increase in validity from that which holds in most cases to that which holds in all, as in, e.g., the proposition "All bodies are heavy," whereas strict universality belongs to a judgment essentially; this points to a special source of cognition for it, namely a faculty of a priori cognition. Necessity and strict universality are therefore secure indications of an a priori cognition, and also belong together inseparably. (*CPR*, B 4, trans. Guyer/Wood 1998)[25]

This is not difficult to understand, and Feder also clearly understood this distinction; he just thought it was wrong.[26] In fact, his "offer" is about a fundamental critique of Kant's *Critique of Pure Reason* when he states in what immediately follows:

> On the contrary, this very Critique [of Pure Reason] restricts the ability of reason to know something about objects outside experience far more than it seems to be restricted to others. (Feder/Meiners 1788–1791, vol. 1, 184)[27]

This first comment suggests an important motive for Feder's furore against Kant: on the one hand, Kant's apriorism (because it is actually prior to and independent of all experience) is supposedly a form of rationalism. Consequently, it threatens to do away with important achievements of European empiricism. Hegel will correctly deny this objection when he is opposing the contemporary reproach to call Kant a "Prussian Hume" (Hegel 1817/1986, 112–147). On the other hand, according to Feder, this field of a priori knowledge is extensionally all too limited because, among other things, he denies that the objects of natural theology can be cognized by theoretical reason but also rejects dogmatic reference to the universal validity of the *principium rationis sufficientis* and the principle of contradiction. Above all, the impossibility of a reference of speculative reason to "God and immortality" (*CPrR*, AA 5: 5) may have promoted Feder's efforts against Kantianism.

---

25 "Die empirische Allgemeinheit ist also nur eine willkürliche Steigerung der Gültigkeit, von der, welche in den meisten Fällen, zu der, die in allen Fällen gilt, wie z. B in dem Satz: alle Körper sind schwer, wo dagegen strenge Allgemeinheit zu einem Urteile wesentlich gehört, da zeigt sich diese auf einen besonderen Erkenntnisquell desselben, nämlich ein Vermögen des Erkenntnisses a priori. Notwendigkeit und strenge Allgemeinheit sind also sichere Kennzeichen einer Erkenntnis a priori und gehören auch unzertrennlich zueinander."
26 This connects him to authors such as Michel Foucault, among others; see Stiening 2009.
27 "Vielmehr schränkt eben diese Critik [der reinen Vernunft] das Vermögen der Vernunft, von Gegenständen außer der Erfahrung etwas zu erkennen, weit mehr ein, als es anderen eingeschränkt zu seyn scheint."

Feder thus puts the whole thing right at the beginning of his review: both the experiential foundation of all knowledge and the decisive condition for having a happy life, securely founded knowledge of the existence of God and the certainty of one's own immortality, are endangered by Kant. The latter is thus portrayed as a bad – because godless – metaphysician.[28]

Even if this theological judgment (especially its normative component) may be dubious, Feder identifies an actual point of difference between his position and Kant's and thus engages with a central constellation of late Enlightenment thought: the unproblematic relation between empiricist epistemology and methodology, on the one hand, and religious conviction, on the other, had already been demonstrated by Locke, who thus also became the preferred reference for a stream of late Enlightenment thought that rejected strict Wolffianism and its rational theology.[29] This constellation was central to Hamann, Jacobi, and Herder, as well as to Ernst Platner and Johann Georg Sulzer. Their often only pretended empiricism by no means prevented them from viewing theological convictions as pure beliefs. Like Feder, they were searching for a solid connection between empiricism and religion, which is precisely where Kant got in their way.

3.2 Subjective versus Objective Happiness

This is also true of Kant's rejection of happiness as a principle of morality, which was indeed bound to upset almost every "Enlightenment philosopher" of the late eighteenth century, since this critique of eudaemonism "crushed" a *fundamentum inconcussum* of pre-critical Enlightenment anthropology (see Mori 1993; Kang 2015). For Feder, as well as for Platner and Sulzer, man is determined by the fact that he *firstly* consists of body and soul and their unity and *secondly* strives for happiness and can only become good through this striving. Thus, in his early Anthropology for Physicians and Worldly Wisdom [*Anthropologie für Ärzte und Weltweise*], Platner defines man's happiness as the "whole intention of his being" (Platner 1772, 12, § 43: "ganze Absicht seines Daseyns"), and Sulzer presupposes quite naturally that "all rational beings strive for perfect happiness" (Sulzer 1773/81, vol. 1, 323: "alle vernünftigen Wesen nach einer vollkommenen Glückseligkeit trachten"). Likewise, Feder states in the third part of his *Investigations on the Human Will* [*Untersuchungen über den menschlichen Willen*]: "Every human being

---

28 This accusation of atheism – subtle in Feder's case – had already been raised against Kant for some time in the controversies of the 1780s, especially in connection with the Spinoza debate, for example by Jacobi, Hamann, and Herder, but also by Mendelssohn in 1785. See Irrlitz 2010, 35.
29 With respect to immortality beliefs, this is shown in Hüning/Klingner/Stiening 2017.

strives for happiness by virtue of the unalterable fundamental law of his nature." (Feder 1786b, 1)[30] Feder's efforts consisted precisely in taking into account the growing insights into the physical conditions and realizations of human happiness since the 1750s in a "physics of the human heart" (Feder 1775, 4) such that both the materialistic hedonism of La Mettrie and the moral egoism of Helvetius (Feder 1775, 90) could be prevented. Feder's extensive reflections on sympathy with others based on the instinct for sociability (Feder 1779, 349 ff.), which was originally laid out in the nature of man in the same way as self-love (Feder 1779, 88 ff.), were undertaken for precisely this reason. At the same time, his aim was to associate the legitimate sensuality of the "original determinations of the human heart" (Feder 1779, 58) with the supersensuality of the highest good and the prospect of eternal happiness, which are only possible in the happiness of the virtuous and in hope for the grace of God (Feder 1779, 298 ff.).

For such a conception of practical philosophy – which Feder, like the bulk of late Enlightenment philosophers, scientists, and artists (see Grunert 1998), wholeheartedly supported – the following sentences pose a significant challenge:

> All material practical principles as such are, without exception, of one and the same kind and come under the general principle of self-love or one's own happiness. [...] Thus, all material principles, which place the determining ground of choice in the pleasure or displeasure to be felt in the reality of some object, are wholly *of the same kind* insofar as they belong without exception to the principle of self-love or one's own happiness. [...] That is to say, in what each has to put his happiness comes down to the particular feeling of pleasure and displeasure in each and, even within one and the same subject, to needs that differ as this feeling changes; and a law that is *subjectively necessary* (as a law of nature) is thus *objectively* a very *contingent* practical principle, which can and must be very different in different subjects, and hence can never yield a law because, in the desire for happiness, it is not the form of lawfulness that counts but simply the matter, namely whether I am to expect satisfaction from following the law, and how much. Principles of self-love can indeed contain universal rules of skill (for finding means to one's purposes), but in that case they are only theoretical principles (such as, e.g., how someone who would like to eat bread has to construct a mill). But practical precepts based on them can never be universal because the determining ground of the faculty of desire is based on the feeling of pleasure or displeasure, which can never be assumed to be universally directed to the same objects. (*CPrR*, AA 5: 22–26; trans. Gregor 2015)[31]

---

30 "Nach Glückseligkeit strebt jeder Mensch vermöge des unabänderlichen Grundgesetzes seiner Natur." Of course, the list could easily be extended.
31 "Alle materialen praktischen Principien sind, als solche, insgesammt von einer und derselben Art, und gehören unter das allgemeine Princip der Selbstliebe oder eigenen Glückseligkeit. [...] Worin nämlich jeder seine Glückseligkeit zu setzen habe, kommt auf jedes sein besonderes Gefühl der Lust und Unlust an, und selbst in einem und demselben Subject auf die Verschiedenheit des Bedürfnisses nach den Abänderungen dieses Gefühls, und ein *subjectiv nothwendiges* Gesetz [als Naturgesetz] ist also *objectiv* ein gar sehr *zufälliges* praktisches Princip, das in verschiedenen Sub-

With the demonstration of the mere subjectivity of the principles of happiness, the foundations of eudaemonistic ethics, and thus of Feder's ethics, eroded. Only if man's natural striving for happiness could be standardized – the possibility of which Kant did not deny, but the moral necessity and thus legitimacy of which he rejected – could the educational programs of popular philosophy and the theories of legitimacy of a literature of the Enlightenment be sustained and expanded. Thus, it was not only Feder's entire work since the mid-1760s that was at stake with Kant's critique of eudaemonism. Wieland's, Lessing's, and Nicolai's life's work was also vulnerable insofar as one of the great aims of these Enlightenment thinkers was to establish an ethics that could ground duty without resorting to God as a guarantor, that established virtue for its own sake as the condition of the worldly promise of happiness – all without promoting atheism.[32] Kant, however, proved to this Enlightenment that its commitment to happiness as a goal of action was incoherent, even dangerous (see Kang 2015 97 ff.). This constellation of conflicts is likely one of the decisive reasons for the widespread opposition to Kant's philosophy which lasted well into the 1790s (see Lazzari/Bondeli 2014).

In his review, however, Feder reconstructs Kant's view (which necessarily irritated him), completely accurately at first:

> The maxim to seek one's own happiness cannot therefore be considered a law, because everyone has his own happiness as his object, which is different from that of the other and so also contradicts it – that is, there is no general law in it. (Feder/Meiners 1788–1791, vol. 1, 189–9)[33]

Subsequently, however, this challenge is countered (with the full force of the deeply irritated) with the claim that reason and truth are also ultimately subjective. Thus, Feder is prepared to use radical scepticism, which he had always rejected, in his defence against Kant's fundamental critique.[34] This willingness to raise rad-

---

jecten sehr verschieden sein kann und muß, mithin niemals ein Gesetz abgeben kann, weil es bei der Begierde nach Glückseligkeit nicht auf die Form der Gesetzmäßigkeit, sondern lediglich auf die Materie ankommt, nämlich ob und wieviel Vergnügen ich in der Befolgung des Gesetzes zu erwarten habe. Principien der Selbstliebe können zwar allgemeine Regeln der Geschicklichkeit [Mittel zu Absichten auszufinden] enthalten, alsdann sind es aber bloß theoretische Principien [z. B. wie derjenige, der gerne Brot essen möchte, sich eine Mühle auszudenken habe]. Aber praktische Vorschriften, die sich auf sie gründen, können niemals allgemein sein, denn der Bestimmungsgrund des Begehrungsvermögens ist auf das Gefühl der Lust und Unlust, das niemals als allgemein auf dieselben Gegenstände gerichtet angenommen werden kann, gegründet."

32 Glinka 2012 examines this development towards a secular ethics.
33 "Die Maxime, seine eigene Glückseligkeit zu suchen, kann darum nicht für ein Gesetz gelten, weil jeder seine eigene, von der des andern verschiedene, und ihr so widerstreitende Glückseligkeit dabey zum Gegenstand hat – also kein allgemeines Gesetz dabey ist."
34 See Feder,1769, 221 ff., here above all arguments against the "Erzzweifler Bayle."

ical doubt in situations of conflict also connects Feder with many authors of the late Enlightenment, such as Wieland and Wezel, who at base advocated a moderate scepticism but who could radicalize themselves when things became more serious (see Ilbrig 2007; Stiening 2012c). Thus, Feder could state in the immediate aftermath, with all the – now again non-sceptical[35] – authority of an Enlightenment patriarch:

> But just as, in spite of all individuality and all deviations of men in regard to their concepts and judgments, they nevertheless unite in certain common concepts and principles, so also, in spite of all egoism, self-love, their inclinations and intentions soon unite in some, and gradually in more and more, points of the common good. And this is precisely the purpose of morality, to bring people, where possible, to the point where they imagine and seek their wellbeing, their satisfaction, their highest good, in the promotion of the common good, according to the best possible knowledge, and thus in the faithful performance of their duties. (Feder/Meiners 1788–1791, vol. 1, 190)[36]

This critique, which is unconvincing because it does not refute Kant's arguments but simply opposes them with an alternative conception which is justified by its supposedly unquestionable factuality, shows once again how fundamentally and momentously Kant had struck the ethicists of the Enlightenment. For Feder, practical scepticism and egoism are overcome by man's natural inclinations; that is, by human nature, which is moral in itself. Thus, morality can be guaranteed in man's striving for happiness, which is directed toward the *bonum commune*. While Kant had already shown in 1784 that "self-love and sociability"[37] can only be conceived as two contradictory inclinations of man,[38] Feder remained convinced, with Gro-

---

35 Such passages in particular suggest to refer Kant's following point also and in particular to Feder: "*Consequent* zu sein, ist die größte Obliegenheit eines Philosophen und wird doch am seltensten angetroffen. Die alten griechischen Schulen geben uns davon mehr Beispiele, als wir in unserem *synkretistischen* Zeitalter antreffen, wo ein gewisses *Coalitions system* widersprechender Grundsätze voll Unredlichkeit und Seichtigkeit erkünstelt wird, weil es sich einem Publikum besser empfiehlt, das zufrieden ist, von allem etwas und im ganzen nichts zu wissen und dabei in allen Sätteln gerecht zu sein" (*CPrR*, AA 5: 24).
36 "Aber gleichwie bey aller Individualität und allen Abweichungen der Menschen in Ansehung ihrer Begriffe und Urtheile, sie sich doch bey gewissen gemeinen Begriffen und Grundsätzen vereinigen: so vereinigen sich auch, bey allem Egoism, der Selbstliebe, ihre Neigungen und Absichten dennoch bald bey einigen, und allmählig bey immer mehreren Punkten des *gemeinen Besten*. Und das ist eben der Zweck der Moral, die Menschen, wo möglich, dahin zu bringen, daß sie ihr Wohlseyn, ihre Zufriedenheit, ihr höchstes Gut, in Beförderung des gemeinen Besten, nach bestmöglicher Erkenntniß, und also in getreuer Ausübung ihrer Pflichten, sich vorstellen und suchen."
37 On this constellation of problems in eighteenth-century philosophy, science, and literature, see Vollhardt 2001, and Kempe 2004.
38 See Kant's demonstrations of an "ungeselligen Geselligkeit" in *IUH*, AA 8: 20–21.

tius and Pufendorf, that self-love and sympathy can exist without conflict and co-originally in (and indeed *as*) the nature of man.³⁹ This counter-position is justified in a later passage as follows:

> And now it can be seen how far the concept of the good must be derived from a preceding law, not serve as its basis. (a) All good is based on a law of nature; the reason for pleasant and unpleasant things lies in nature and the relations of things. (b) Thus also in respect and approval, to which the true, the reasonable, when it is recognized, determines us, there lies a natural law at the bottom, the law by virtue of which the contradictory cannot be imagined, thus also cannot be approved and desired; but what is unanimous, possible, real. (c) Laws of reason, then, lie especially at the bottom of ideas of the highest good and true goods. d) But at the bottom of all positive rules of reason of definite objective content, whether they concern duties toward us or toward others, lie and must lie concepts of the good. The relation to the good of the individual or of the whole is the ratio legis; according to which the fitness or reprehensibility of all rules and laws is, and must be, judged. (Feder/Meiners 1788–1791, vol. 1, 202)⁴⁰

Two things should be noted regarding this sharp juxtaposition of critical and eudaemonistic ethics: first, it becomes clear that Feder's moral theory has a specifically political component insofar as it ties the moral disposition of the individual as virtue to the social *bonum commune* and thus to the *ratio legis* – as well as to the state – without, however, explicitly articulating this. Kant's strictly subjective conception of happiness, on the other hand, cannot be exploited politically, if at all negatively, insofar as the individual should be protected from any state or communal instrumentalization of his needs. Thus, Kant's warning against orientating the state's purposes to a common good – which necessarily remains without criteria⁴¹

---

39 On the insurmountable problems associated with this conception, see Stiening 2016.

40 "Und nun wird eingesehen werden können, *in wiefern* der Begriff vom *Guten* von einem vorhergehenden *Gesetze* abgeleitet werden, nicht diesem zum Grunde dienen müsse. (a) Bey allem Guten liegt ein *Naturgesetz* zum Grunde; in der Natur und den Verhältnissen der Dinge liegt der Grund des Angenehmen und Unangenehmen. (b) Also auch bey der *Achtung* und *Billigung*, wozu das Wahre, Vernünftige, wenn es erkannt wird, uns bestimmt, liegt ein Naturgesetz zum Grunde, das Gesetz, vermöge dessen das Widersprechende nicht vorgestellt, also auch nicht gebilliget und begehrt werden kann; wohl aber das Einstimmige, Mögliche, Reelle. (c) Vernunftgesetze liegen also insbesondere zum Grunde, bey den Vorstellungen vom höchsten Gut, und wahren Gütern. (d) Aber bey allen positiven *Vorschriften* der Vernunft von bestimmtem objectiven Inhalt, mögen sie die Pflichten gegen uns oder gegen andere betreffen, liegen zum Grunde und müssen zum Grunde liegen Begriffe vom Guten. Das Verhältniß zum Wohl der Einzelnen oder des Ganzen ist die ratio legis; nach welcher die Tauglichkeit oder Verwerflichkeit aller Vorschriften und Gesetze beurtheilt wird, und werden muß."

41 See also *CF*, AA 7: 87: "Wohlfahrt aber hat kein Princip, weder für den, der sie empfängt, noch der sie austheilt [der eine setzt sie hierin, der andere darin]; weil es dabei auf das *Materiale* des Willens ankommt, welches empirisch und so der Allgemeinheit einer Regel unfähig ist."

– is vividly demonstrated by Feder's obdurate adherence to political eudaemonism:

> A government established on the principle of benevolence toward the people like that of a *father* toward his children – that is, a *paternalistic government* [imperium paternale], in which the subjects, like minor children who cannot distinguish between what is truly useful or harmful to them, are constrained to behave only passively, so as to wait only upon the judgment of the head of state as to how they *should* be happy and, as for his also willing their happiness, only upon his kindness – is the greatest *despotism* thinkable (a constitution that abrogates all the freedom of the subjects, who in that case have no rights at all).[42]

This critical analysis, however, also applies to any political ethics that is oriented towards the *bonum commune* because in it the criterion must likewise remain undetermined, and therefore the postulate of setting aside one's own for the interests of the general must remain undetermined and thus boundless.

On the other hand, this nature is unmistakably moral in man only to the extent that it is thus created, from which it becomes clear why this empiricism, in its practical dimension, needs theology – or at least theonomic arguments, to which it is oriented – for only God as the creator of humanity can guarantee the fundamental morality of natural man. In itself, nature is only that eternally "devouring, eternally ruminating monster" experienced by the lovestruck Werther (Goethe 1774/1988, 53). It is only as creation that it can contain a normative order, which is not to be produced by people but only to be realized. From the perspective of this strain of Enlightenment thought, Kant's criticism of eudaemonism is not only joyless – as argued by Schiller, who both famously and falsely thought that Kant did not grant people the right to be happy (see Schiller 1795/1973, 466)[43] – but also godless. Feder believed that Kant's critique of eudaemonism rendered him an atheist and "crusher" of human pleasure in its moral sense. Thus, he writes:

> The idea of God, by its nature, works not only through fear and hope, but also through gratitude, reverence and trust, obedience to his laws. Reason and all laws of nature and all good impulses in human nature acquire more authority and weight when theoretical reason does not leave it doubtful whether they are the work of chance, or of blind necessity, or of the high-

---

42 *OCS*, AA 8: 290–291: "Eine Regierung, die auf dem Princp des Wohlwollens gegen das Volk als eines Vaters gegen seine Kinder errichtet wäre, d. i. eine *väterliche Regierung* [imperium paternale], wo also die Unterthanen als unmündige Kinder, die nicht unterscheiden können, was ihnen wahrhaftig nützlich oder schädlich ist, sich bloß passiv zu verhalten genöthigt sind, um, wie sie glücklich sein *sollen*, bloß von dem Urtheile des Staatoberhaupts und, daß dieser es auch wolle, bloß von seiner Gültigkeit zu erwarten: ist der größte denkbare Despotismus."
43 On this misunderstanding of Schiller, see Vesper 2018, and Stiening 2020.

est wisdom and goodness. Faith in God and a different life moderates attachment to the goods of this earth, and thereby removes one of the main obstacles to virtue; without making it subject to fear of punishment or reward-seeking and self-serving. (Feder/Meiners 1788–1791, vol. 1, 215)[44]

Once again, Feder's interpretation is not completely wrong, although it is tendentious. Feder recognized that Kant's ethics would make his position impossible, a position he had held, scientifically and ideologically, for decades. It is more than understandable that he sought to resist this with all means available. That he wrongly judged Kant's philosophy is much less understandable. In any case, however, Feder's "critique" of Kant remains significant, even beyond the late eighteenth century.[45]

3.3 Feder's Criticism of Autonomy as the "Self-Rule of the Will"

The significance of this is proven again by Feder's analysis of what he calls the ninth main theorem of the *Critique of Practical Reason*, a "main point of our author's system." In fact, this section is about Kant's concept of autonomy, which Feder quite rightly interprets as being central to Kant's ethics (see O'Neill 2002). First, he faithfully reconstructs Kant's argumentation:

> A will to which the mere *legislative form* of maxims alone can serve as a law must be a *free* will, that is, one that is independent of the empirical law of causality. Such a will has *autonomy; heteronomy*, on the other hand, is when the inclinations and the material of the law connected with them determine the will. This, then, is the freedom of the will, which it is determined not only without the participation of sensual impulses, but with the rejection of all of

---

[44] "Die Idee von Gott wirkt ja, ihrer Natur nach, nicht bloß durch *Furcht* und *Hoffnung*, sondern auch durch Dankbarkeit, Ehrfurcht und Vertrauen, Gehorsam gegen seine Gesetze. Vernunft und alle Naturgesetze und alle guten Antriebe in der menschlichen Natur bekommen mehr Auctorität und Gewicht, wenn die theoretische Vernunft es nicht zweifelhaft läßt, ob sie das Werk des Zufalls, oder einer blinden Nothwendigkeit, oder der höchsten Weisheit und Güte seyn. Glaube an Gott und ein anderes Leben mäßiget die Anhänglichkeit an die Güter dieser Erde, und räumt dadurch ein Haupthinderniß der Tugend weg; ohne darum diese von Furcht vor Strafen abhängig oder lohnsüchtig und eigennützig zu machen."

[45] For this peculiar criticism of Kant, which emerges from a specific tendency in anthropological research, see for example Garber 2002, 202–204, and Riedel 2004.

them, and with a cessation of all inclinations, *insofar* as they can be contrary to that law, only by the law. (Feder/Meiners 1788–1791, vol. 1, 190–191)⁴⁶

Once again, Kant's thought is on the whole accurately represented, although at the end of the passage the reference to an alleged "cessation of all inclinations" would seem to be overstated. In his commentary on this passage, Feder also remains rather restrained at first; he wants to deal primarily with the concept of freedom, which he seeks to explain in a first analytical step through a philosophical-historical contextualization:

> It [i.e., the concept of freedom] is by no means entirely new, or opposed to the otherwise usual concepts, but can, *considered in itself* [i.e., here independently of the justification of its validity], be declared to be one and the same as what the Stoic calls freedom, and what is otherwise called *higher moral freedom*. (Feder/Meiners 1788–1791, vol. 1, 191)⁴⁷

This connection to Stoicism, especially with regard to the concept of autonomy, is not very convincing, even though it has also been advocated by more recent Kant interpreters (see Brandt 2007, 139 ff.).⁴⁸ The decisive reason for the historicizing demarcation, however, consists in Feder's own theory of freedom, which he shows to be an empirical one; that is, based on observation and experience, informed by the latest scientific research. This conception concludes that the will is always determined by a multitude of ideas, sensations, and feelings, to which it yields to varying degrees. The crucial point for Feder is that the human will never makes decisions on the basis of pure self-rule without such empirical motivations. Although it is capable of resisting certain motivations,

> this cannot in the least justify the opinion that an expression of the will can take place against all representations and without all determining sensation or representation. Many attentive

---

46 "Ein Wille, dem die bloße *gesetzgebende Form* der Maximen allein zum Gesetze dienen kann, muß ein *freyer*, das heißt von dem empirischen Gesetze der Caussalität unabhängiger seyn. Ein solcher Wille hat *Autonomie*; *Heteronomie* ist es hingegen, wenn die Neigungen und die mit ihnen in Verbindung stehende Materie des Gesetzes die Willkühr bestimmt. Darinnen besteht also die Freyheit des Willens, daß derselbe nicht bloß ohne Mitwirkung sinnlicher Antriebe, sondern mit Abweisung aller derselben, und mit Abbruch aller Neigungen, *so fern* sie jenem Gesetze zuwider seyn können, bloß durchs Gesetz bestimmt werde." In this context, see also Bacin 2018.
47 "Er [d. i. der Begriff der Freiheit] ist keineswegs ganz neu, oder den sonst gewöhnlichen Begriffen entgegen gesetzt, sondern kann, *an sich betrachtet* [und d. h. hier unabhängig von der Begründung seiner Geltung], für einerley erklärt werden mit dem, was der Stoiker Freiheit nennt, und was sonst die *höhere moralische* Freyheit genannt wird."
48 Christoph Horn 2008 on the other hand, provides an interpretation that emphasizes the differences.

observers, to whom I may add myself, affirm that they have never been able to become aware of *such* independence, *such* self-dominance of the will in themselves. And it is very easy to understand how those who want to assert the opposite, on the basis of their experience, can have been too hasty in their judgment, for they only pay attention to some of what was going on in them and not, as they should have, to everything that was active. (Feder 1779, 47)[49]

This sheds light on how Feder interpreted Kantian autonomy, namely as radically arbitrary self-rule of the will. Such "decisionism," which is not in fact a feature of Kantian autonomy, would necessarily have been met with resistance from Feder due to his unrestricted empiricism. Above all, Feder was reacting critically to a conception of freedom that must also have seemed politically problematic to him insofar as such freedom, even if only external, is unconditional and thus cannot (as Feder thought) be directed toward or limited by the common good. In general, for Feder, the "drive to freedom" does not belong to the higher natural purposes of man, because these are instead to be found in the drives to self-love and sociability. But whoever complies with the drive for freedom unconditionally, because it can only be found outside of society as absolute unconditionality, is, according to Feder, going against nature: "The human being who desires to be completely free resists nature rather than following a true natural drive" (Feder 1779, 463).[50]

Once again, Kant's conception of autonomy and Feder's critique of it reveal the fundamental differences between the two philosophical systems rather than a lack of understanding on Feder's part, for the Stoicism reproach is grounded in a primarily polemical motivation. Feder's arguments indicate the direction in which his critique is fundamentally aimed: with the concept of "higher moral freedom," it becomes apparent that Kant is to be declared a voluntaristic wolf in transcendental sheep's clothing. In the first part of the *Untersuchungen über den menschlichen Willen*, we read:

---

[49] "Aber dieß kann doch im geringsten nicht die Meynung rechtfertigen, daß eine Willensäußerung gegen alle Vorstellungen und ohne alle bestimmende Empfindung oder Vorstellung erfolgen könne. Sehr viele aufmerksame Beobachter, denen ich mich herinn zugesellen darf, versichern, daß sie einer *solchen* Unabhängigkeit, einer *solchen* Selbstherrschaft des Willens sich bey sich selbst nie haben bewußt werden können. Und es läßt sich sehr leicht begreifen, wie diejenigen, die das Gegentheil, vermöge ihrer Erfahrung, behaupten wollen, in ihrem Urtheile sich dabey übereilet haben können, indem sie nämlich nur auf einiges, was in ihnen vorging, nicht, wie sie gesollt hätten, auf alles, was rege war, Acht geben."
[50] "Der Mensch, der ganz frey zu seyn begehrt, sträubt sich gegen die Natur vielmehr, als daß er einem wahren Naturtriebe folgte."

> For this [i.e., higher moral freedom] consists in nothing else than the complete dependence of the will on the idea of duty, which can be recognized by reason, and the independence of sensual stimuli and impulses. Thus, the wise man alone is free, and the vicious fool is the slave of his body and his passions. (Feder/Meiners 1788–1791, vol. 1, 190–191)[51]

However, Feder had already rejected the freedom of the Stoic sage in 1779 as contradictory and politically problematic: the "sage as the Stoic thought of him" can remain indifferent to external freedom as an unrestricted ruler of his own happiness because he could be indifferent to "whether he should be slave or king" (Feder 1779, 466). Feder clearly identifies inner with outer freedom, which he otherwise knows to distinguish, for programmatic purposes: the distinction between law and ethics (see Dörflinger/Hüning/Kruck 2017), which had been disputed since Thomasius and was first and foremost sufficiently substantiated by Kant, must be undermined by eudaemonism in order to be able to connect the happiness of the individual with the *bonum commune*. In 1788, Christian Garve demonstrated that this could and should only succeed at the price of the unconditional identification of the former with the latter (see Garve 1788). Nevertheless, Schiller would follow him in this (see Schiller 1795/1993, 588 ff.).

3.4 Freedom in Experience: Feder's Critique of the Two Realms Doctrine

In the course of his argument, Feder remains particularly troubled by the peculiar construction of Kant's doctrine of the two realms, a criticism that will be discussed here in conclusion. Once again, it is apparent that Feder understood Kant very well but did not fundamentally agree with this model of ethics:

> In this, then, K[ant] differs from others in his concept of freedom, that he presents this freedom as not directly recognizable from experience, but only demonstrable from the existence and nature of the moral law, and at the same time as a deviation from the law of causality. But the freedom that is demonstrable from the existence and nature of a moral law contains no exception or deviation from the law of causality; and is directly recognizable from experience. (Feder/Meiners 1788–91, vol. 1, 192–193)[52]

---

51 "Denn diese [d. i. die *"höhere moralische* Freyheit"] besteht in nichts anderm, als in der völligen Abhängigkeit des Willens von der durch die Vernunft erkennbaren Vorstellung der Pflicht, und der Unabhängigkeit von sinnlichen Reizen und Antrieben. So ist der Weise allein frey, und der lasterhafte Thor ist Sklave seines Körpers und seiner Leidenschaften."
52 "Darin unterscheidet sich also K[ant] mit seinem Begriffe der Freyheit von andern, daß er diese Freyheit als aus der Erfahrung unmittelbar nicht erkennbar, sondern nur aus dem Daseyn und der Natur des moralischen Gesetzes erweislich, und zugleich als eine Abweichung vom Gese-

Again, it is the programmatic anti-empiricism of Kant's conception of freedom that provokes (and indeed must provoke) Feder's resolute opposition, since he had outlined such an empiricist theory of freedom in his *Investigations on the Human Will* [*Untersuchungen über den menschlichen Willen*], in which "observation alone" was to decide whether the human will is free (Feder 1779, 45). After rejecting the strictly voluntaristic idea of a criterion-less and thus unconditional "self-power of the will" – as quoted above – Feder develops the following alternative model in the first volume of his opus magnum:

> If, then, one is not content to assert freedom for man in general, which consists in the fact that he can, with *inner strength*, bring about ideas, judgments, resolutions, and actions according to his own pleasure; if the *will* is to be called free, then its freedom can be placed in the fact that it is not bound to a few impulses, but can be determined by innumerable others. This is also expressed by the name of the *faculty of choice* [*Willkühr*]. This capacity to choose, although always according to reasons, undeniably belongs to the will. (Feder 1779, 47)[53]

For Feder, human freedom is thus neither exposed to the determinism of a closed natural causality nor arbitrary in the sense of complete indeterminacy, which would contradict the basic law of traditional metaphysics, *nihil sine ratione*, also shared by Feder.[54] He consequently advocates a conception of the moderate compatibility of nature and freedom, both of which are subject to empirically observable causality to varying degrees.[55] Against this background, Feder must have above all been disturbed by Kant's idea that one must conceive of "the will [...] as independent of all empirical conditions" (*CPrR*, AA 5: 31) in order to coherently preserve freedom and moral responsibility. This quite "alienating" assumption – as Kant himself described it – evoked Feder's resolute objection:

---

tze der Caussalität vorstellig macht. Allein die Freyheit, die aus dem Daseyn und der Natur eines moralischen Gesetzes erweislich ist, enthält keine Ausnahme oder Abweichung vom Gesetze der Caussalität; und ist unmittelbar aus der Erfahrung erkennbar."

53 "Wenn man sich also nicht begnügen will, für den Menschen überhaupt Freyheit zu behaupten, die darinn besteht, daß er mit *innerer Kraft* Vorstellungen, Beurtheilungen, Entschließungen und Handlungen nach Wohlgefallen bewirken kann; wenn der *Wille* frey heißen soll: so kann die Freyheit desselben darinn gesetzt werden, daß er nicht an einige wenige Antriebe gefesselt ist, sondern durch unzählich viele bestimmt werden kann. Dieß drückt auch der Name der *Willkühr* oder des Vermögens zu wählen aus. Dieß Vermögen zu wählen, obgleich immer nach Gründen, kömmt dem Willen unleugbar zu."

54 See also Leibniz's argumentation in Leibniz 1710/1968, 125, § 44.

55 For a typology of theories of freedom with respect to Kant, see Brandhorst/Hahmann/Ludwig 2015, 9 ff. According to this model, Feder's conception roughly corresponds to that of Bieri 2001.

Not only has it been irrefutably demonstrated by a great many thorough philosophers, who are well enough known and need not be named, that even if everything is done on decisive grounds, the moral concepts of duty, merit, guilt, and punishability persist in the most complete way; but I also do not see how the author, according to his own most peculiar concepts and principles of morality and moral law, can arrive at a concept of freedom that is not subject to the law of causality and is not directly recognizable from experience. According to his system, morality is based on the fact that the will can be determined by the *form* of the moral law, or by the idea of *duty* as *duty*, and at least has *respect* [*Achtung*] for it, independent of the other interests of the inclinations. This admitted, what then follows from it? That the will is not under the law of causality? Is not the *representation* of duty, together with the *nature of the will*, the *cause*, and the respect [*Achtung*], where the inclination and resolution are not determined according to duty, the *effect*? And is not this causality recognizable from experience as well as any other? (Feder/Meiners 1788–1791, vol. 1, 193)[56]

Again, Feder's objection, which seems to be primarily concerned with saving the one world in which it is possible to conceive of freedom and necessity, seems to be characterized not at all by dull ignorance but by an interest in supporting a theory of freedom that takes into account the empiricist epistemological and methodological principles that he outlined. Feder understood Kant – but nothing of the latter's theory of free will and moral responsibility was met with his approval.[57]

---

56 "Nicht nur ist es von sehr vielen gründlichen Philosophen, die bekannt genug sind, und nicht brauchen genannt zu werden, unwiderleglich dargethan worden, daß wenn gleich alles aus entscheidenden Gründen erfolgt, die moralischen Begriffe von Pflicht, Verdienst, Schuld, Strafbarkeit, aufs völligste dabey bestehen: sondern ich sehe auch nicht ein, wie der Verf. nach seinen eigensten Begriffen und Grundsätzen von Sittlichkeit und sittlichem Gesetze auf eine Freyheit schließen könne, die dem Gesetze der Caussalität nicht unterworfen, und aus der Erfahrung unmittelbar nicht erkennbar seyn soll. Die Sittlichkeit beruht nach seinem System, wie sich aus dem Bisherigen schon ergeben hat, und aus dem Folgenden weiter erhellen wird, darauf, daß der Wille durch die *Form* des moralischen Gesetzes, oder durch die Vorstellung der *Pflicht* als *Pflicht*, bestimmbar ist, wenigstens *Achtung* dafür hat; unabhängig vom anderweitigen Interesse der Neigungen. Dieß zugegeben; was folgte nun daraus? Daß der Wille dabey nicht unter dem Gesetz der Caussalität stehe? Ist denn hier nicht die *Vorstellung* von Pflicht, nebst der *Natur des Willens*, *Ursache*; und die Achtung, wo nicht Neigung und Entschließung nach der Pflicht sich zu bestimmen, *Wirkung*? Und ist diese Caussalität nicht aus der Erfahrung erkennbar; so gut als irgend eine andere?"
57 Only Kant's thoughts on the sacredness of the will elicit Feder's emphatic agreement: "All this is wonderful, especially the latter!" ("Herrlich dieß alles, besonders das Letztere!" Feder/Meiners 1788–1791, vol. 1, 213).

3.5 Feder's Summary: Rationalistic, Unproven and with a Tendency towards Atheism

At the end of his review, Feder once again summarizes the decisive moments of Kant's moral philosophy by stating that "everything in which the author differs from other moralists boils down to three points." These include:

1. The *"Principle of Morality"*, in which for Feder the fundamental difference between late Enlightenment anthropology and metaphysical-rationalistic transcendentalism is once again crystallized:

> But here [in the Principle of Morality] all difference comes only from the fact that *Kant* [...] has *pure reason* before his eyes; and the others the *whole* man with all his inclinations. (Feder/Meiners 1788–1791, vol. 1, 216)[58]

There is no clearer formulation of the difference that anthropologists assumed to exist between themselves and Kant, and more precisely the misunderstanding – but by no means the lack of understanding – of Kant's philosophy that this Enlightenment would publicly cultivate: the notion that he prioritized *pure reason over the whole man*.

2. As a second important difference between Kant's ethics and "all other" philosophical theories Feder isolates the *theory of freedom of the will*, which he interprets rationalistically and thus rejects as a threat to all empiricist achievements in ethics, and thus any ethics at all:

> For this [i.e., the determination of free will by human representations] is something we all know and teach; and we know that this attribute of humanity is increased by exercises of wisdom, and weakened by following sensual impulses. But this freedom is supposed to be (a) an exception to the law of causality; and (b) to follow as such from the essence of morality. This, however, K[ant] has not yet proved. (Feder/Meiners 1788–1791, vol. 1, 217–218)[59]

Once again, Feder primarily rejects Kant's two-realms doctrine and doubts its scientific status. At the very least, he considers these theses insufficiently proven.

---

[58] "Aber hier [beim "Princip der Sittlichkeit"] kömmt aller Unterschied nur daher: daß *Kant* [...] die *reine Vernunft* vor Augen hat; und die anderen den *ganzen Menschen* mit allen seinen Neigungen."

[59] "Denn dieß [d. i. die Bestimmung des freien Willens durch die menschlichen Vorstellungen] wissen und lehren wir alle; und wissen, daß dieß Attribut der Menschheit durch Übungen der Weisheit erhöht, und durch Befolgung sinnlicher Triebe geschwächt werde. Aber diese Freyheit soll α) eine Ausnahme von dem Gesetze der Caussalität seyn; und β) als eine solche aus dem Wesen der Sittlichkeit folgen. Dieß nun aber hat K[ant]. noch nicht bewiesen."

3. Third, Feder views the following theoretical feature as having significance for Kantian philosophy and thus at the same time formulates his decisive objection. Again, it concerns God and immortality as features of any practical philosophy:

> [T]he *reasons of faith in God and another life*; which K[ant], like the rest of us, considers essential conditions for the fortification of the moral system, or pract[ical] reason. Only a) he denies that *theoretical* philosophy contains sufficient reasons for this; but finds them only in the moral nature of man, or in practical reason; b) it seems that he does not want to have *motives* (*Beweggründe*) for virtue taken from it; but only regards them as a prerequisite, without which practical reason would not be consistent or explainable. (Feder/Meiners 1788–1791, vol. 1, 218)[60]

Once again, it is the reproach from his review of the *Critique of Pure Reason*, namely the unknowability of God and human immortality, that Feder makes the focus of his critique. With their purely practical function, God and immortality would become mere presuppositions of theoretical coherence and would thus, according to Feder, be degraded. Once again, he accuses Kant of atheism and amoralism – an accusation that Jacobi also makes in letters from the same time (see Stolzenberg 2004). He does concede that Kant considers God and immortality important, but *this* practical reason does away with both and thus with any possible binding force of morality. At such points the critique becomes gloomy; it is – as throughout – by no means unintelligent and for that reason dangerous. Not only but also because of these outbursts, which show that an alleged "self-enlightenment of the Enlightenment"[61] turned out to be the "raving drivel of the counter-enlightenment" (Laermann, 1985). When it comes to a critique of Kant, to study Feder is definitely worthwhile.

---

60 "[D]ie *Gründe des Glaubens an Gott und ein anderes Leben*; die K[ant]. wie wir andern auch, für wesentliche Bedingungen zur Befestigung des Moralsystems, oder der prakt[ischen]. Vernunft hält. Nur a) leugnet er, daß die *theoretische* Philosophie hinreichende Gründe dazu enthalte; sondern findet diese lediglich in der sittlichen Natur des Menschen, oder in der praktischen Vernunft; b) scheint es, daß er nicht *Beweggründe* zur Tugend hergenommen wissen wolle; sondern nur als Voraussetzung sie betrachte, ohne welche die praktische Vernunft nicht consequent, oder nicht erklärbar seyn würde."
61 For one of the more ambitious works to feature this thesis, see van Hoorn 2004; Garber/Thoma 2004. See also Borchers 2011.

Rudolf Meer
"On this Occasion, I cannot but [...] speak a few words with Mr. Kant": On the Meiners-Kant Controversy 1786

Abstract: Starting from an analysis of Christoph Meiners's preface of *Grundriß der Seelen-Lehre* (1786), the paper illuminates facets of the early polemic against Kant's *Critique of Pure Reason*. However, it does not claim to present the development of reception in its diachronic details. At its core is the debate that took place in 1786. In this year (or shortly before or after) not merely Meiners published a polemic against Kant but also Dietrich Tiedemann, Gottlob August Tittel, Johann Georg Heinrich Feder, Hermann Andreas Pistorius, Johann Georg Adam Forster, and Johann Daniel Metzger. In this context, the high standards and revolutionary character that Kant, but especially his friends and students, attributed to the first Critique proved to be the main 'stumbling block'. This led to the polarization that is noticeable everywhere in Meiners's text, but also in the defense of Kant. The resulting confrontation made a more appropriate discussion of the *Critique of Pure Reason* impossible and led to the fact that, beginning with Reinhold's letters, Kant's philosophy remained largely misunderstood.

1 Introduction

In the preface of his *Grundriß der Seelen-Lehre* (1786),[1] Christoph Meiners formulated a polemic against the *Critique of Pure Reason*, which represents a climax of early Kant criticism.[2] He stated numerous resentments that were repeatedly voiced in the course of Kant's reception. From a greater distance to the so-called Meiners-Kant controversy and from a historical perspective, two skeptical questions can be raised: firstly, do we learn anything from Meiners' polemic against the *Critique of Pure Reason* – perhaps about what should be opposed to it? In terms of content,

---

[1] The preface of *Grundriß* is not numbered throughout. The first four double pages are labeled a2, a3, a4, a5, after which the counting stops. To make it easier to find the quoted passages, the numbering started in the book is continued, and the double pages are differentiated as a and b. Therefore, page a2 is followed by b2, a3, b3, etc. In research literature, numbering in Roman numerals is also occasionally found.
[2] Unless a translation is indicated, translations from German are mine. Except for the titles of Kant's writings, I refer to the original German-language titles of books, papers, and journals.

the answer is no. The preface is conceived as a pamphlet in which any subtleties are quickly thrown overboard. If, however, the larger context is taken into account, especially the situation in Göttingen of 1786, it can be paradigmatically reconstructed as to how a classic of the history of philosophy started its way through intellectual history. Secondly, there is also the question of whether we could better understand Meiners' philosophical position from his polemic. The more favorable answer for Meiners is no, since his drafts on anthropology and empirical psychology go much further in philosophical depth than the combative tone of the preface suggests. Meiners as well as Johann Georg Heinrich Feder, Michael Hißmann but also Gottlob August Tittel, Georg Forster, Johann Daniel Metzger were the spokesmen of the so-called "Popularphilosophie [popular philosophy]."[3] It emerged with the claim to overcome Wolffian philosophy with John Locke, David Hume, and George Berkeley, as well as the sensualist and mechanist extensions of empiricism by Charles Bonnet, Étienne Bonnot de Condillac, and Claude-Adrien Helvétius. Nevertheless, it quickly became evident that they did not have the philosophical means to overcome or reconcile the antagonisms that came to a head in the second half of the eighteenth century. This becomes particularly clear in their critique of Kant.[4]

Although the *Critique of Pure Reason* rose to become the philosophical classic par excellence in the second half of the nineteenth and in the twentieth century, its early history of impact[5] must be described as quite "bumpy." In research, this has already been presented in detail in large-scale studies. Some of the most important results can be found in the works of F. Beiser (1987) and L. H. Pietsch (2011).[6] The paper takes its starting point from those studies. However, it does not claim to present the development of reception in its diachronic details. Starting from the preface of *Grundriß*, it rather attempts to illuminate facets that appear in the polemic against Kant's *Critique of Pure Reason* in 1786 and which became "templates" of anti-Kantianism.[7] In this context, the high standards and revolutionary character that Kant, but especially his friends and students, attributed to the first Critique proved to be the main "stumbling block." Only a few years after its pub-

---

[3] On the relationship between self-attribution and attribution to others as "Popularphilosophie," see, among others Böhr 2003, 35–36; Nowitzki 2018, 384. For the historical classification and wide-ranging expression of "Popularphilosophie" in Germany, see Beiser 1987, 165–192; van der Zande 1995; Pietsch 2011, 90–100; Wunderlich 2012; Longo 2015; Zimmerli 1983; Röttgers 1984.
[4] See among others, Gideon Stiening in the present volume; Albrecht 2014, 255.
[5] For historical sources, see Landau 1991; Hausius 1793; Malter 1990.
[6] See also Hinske 1995; Hinske 2005; Kuehn 1992; Goldenbaum 2004, 105; Sassen 2000, 1–49; Petrus 1994, 289–292. Older investigations can be found in Erdmann 1878, 105; Vorländer 1992, 415.
[7] Explicitly developed is Meiners's position in Pietsch 2011, 90–100, 119–140; Kuehn 1987; Kuehn 1996; Cramer/Patzig 1994, 86–91; Marino 1995, 145–245; Thiel 1997; Wunderlich 2005, 90–101.

lication, it was inevitable for Kant's contemporaries to take a stand on this book. This led to the polarization that is noticeable everywhere in Meiners's text, but also in Kant's defense. The resulting confrontation made a more appropriate discussion of the *Critique of Pure Reason* impossible and, beginning with Reinhold's letters, led to the fact that the whole movement of those "going beyond Kant always dealt with a great unknown. This unknown was none other than Kant himself" (Ebbinghaus 1968, 3).

2 The Contexts of the Controversy

After the *Critique of Pure Reason* had initially attracted little or no attention, it increasingly came into focus from 1784 onward (Motta 2018, 105; Saner 1967, 129; Beiser 1987, 177). Like few philosophical works, the 1781 book claims to establish philosophy in a completely new way (Saner 1967, 128). Kant not only develops the claim of a "change in the ways of thinking" or rather an "alteration in our way of thinking" (*CPR*, B XVI; *KrV*, B XIX),[8] but also parallels his progress in metaphysics with the greatest possible scientific achievements. While this self-assessment of the author may only partially correspond to the actual historical references of the first Critique, it nevertheless predetermined the "fate" of the book. There were only two options in opposition to it: to ignore or refute it. In that sense, it should be noted that Kant as the author of the *Dreams of a Spirit-Seer* (1766) enjoyed great prestige in Göttingen and was readily quoted and reviewed by Feder as well as Meiners and Hißmann (Nowitzki/Roth/Stiening 2018a, 1).

After the first review of the *Critique of Pure Reason* by Christian Garve, which was revised by Hißmann and Feder and published in the *Göttingische Anzeigen von gelehrten Sachen*, the tactics of ignoring was increasingly and deliberately used in Göttingen. It was hoped that the "scholastic tone" of the first Critique would not appeal to a wider audience. In 1786, Meiners formulates this retrospectively as follows:

> When the *Critique of Pure Reason* first appeared, I told all those who feared the detrimental effects of this work that they could be reassured on that score, because, by the subtlety of his reasoning [*Spitzfindigkeit seiner Räsonnements*] and by the obscurity of his language, Mr. Kant had ensured that his writing would neither make a great impression nor cause considerable harm. I believe that our nation differs from the idle or depraved Greeks at the time of the ancient Sophists and the later dialecticians, and that our age differs from the centuries of

---

8 Kant's texts are quoted according to the Cambridge Edition.

the scholastics by so many degrees that our contemporaries could not possibly find pleasure in such musings and in such language. (Meiners 1786, a8–b8)

In public, however, the impression increasingly arose that the Göttingen philosophers were bowing to the judgment Kant pronounced in the *Prolegomena* (Pietsch 2011, 90). Moreover, the strategy of ignoring was no longer viable from the middle of the decade. With this in mind, Kant urges his reviewers in the *Prolegomena* quite decisively as follows: "[S]o my *Critique* must either be accepted or a better one put in its place, and therefore it must at least be studied; which is the only thing I ask for now" (*Pro*, AA 4: 379). Consequently, the critics were left with radical opposition only.

On the basis of this situation, Meiners notes with regret in 1786 that the "philosophical spirit of our nation" has taken an unmistakable "turn" in recent years (Meiners 1786, a8). "Kant's writings have found enthusiastic admirers [*laute Bewunderer*] in some public teachers of philosophy, and have maddened the minds of a much greater number of raw, or half-educated youths." (Meiners 1786, b8)

Even before the publication of Reinhold's *Briefe über die Kantische Philosophie*, the polemics had come to a head around 1786. In addition to Meiners's scathing review, Dietrich Tiedemann's *Ueber die Natur der Metaphysik; zur Prüfung von Hrn. Professor Kants Grundsätzen* (1785) became the starting point for this polemic. In 1786, Gottlob August Tittel published the text *Ueber Herrn Kant's Moralreform*, in which he sharply attacks the *Groundwork of the Metaphysics of Morals*. In the same year, Johann Georg Heinrich Feder polemicized against Kant in the third volume of his *Untersuchung über den menschlichen Willen* (1786, VI–X), but without explicitly mentioning Kant's name. In addition, Feder announced his book *Ueber Raum und Caussalität zur Prüfung der Kantischen Philosophie* with which he wanted to counteract the so-called "dissolute addiction to doubt [*ausschweifende Zweifelsucht*]" (1787, XI). After the counterattacks of the Kantians, Feder defended Meiners for his position in the preface of *Grundriß* (Feder 1787, XXIII). This criticism was also supported by Hermann Andreas Pistorius. He published a review of the *Prolegomena* in the *Allgemeine deutsche Bibliothek* as early as 1784. In it, he criticized the theory of space and time and deepened it with reference to Schultze's *Erläuterungen* in a paper from 1786 also published in the journal *Allgemeine deutsche Bibliothek*. In 1788, Pistorius reviewed Meiners' *Grundriß* in the same organ and confirmed the "accusation of skepticism" against Kant. In 1786, Johann Georg Adam Forster published in explicit demarcation to Kant's *Determination of the Concept of a Human Race* the paper *Noch etwas über die Menschenraßen* in the *Anzeiger des Teutschen Merkur*. In this context, it is also worth mentioning Johann Daniel Metzger's contribution *Ueber die sogenannten Menschenracen* (1786).[9]

While in 1782 it was still the idealism reproach that served as the master argument against the *Critique of Pure Reason*, in 1786 the skepticism reproach[10] formed the core of the criticism. The preface of Meiners' *Grundriß* is set in these historical contexts, culminating in its tone and sharpness of polemic.

3 Meiners's Kant Critique from 1786

The preface of *Grundriß der Seelen-Lehre* cannot be read as a composed argumentation, but rather as a catalog of possible polemics against the first *Critique*. These are directed against the form and some contents, but especially against possible consequences of the study of this book. Six main attacks can be differentiated.
1. The style of writing: Meiners's master argument is a critique concerning the form of presentation. Kant's language reveals that the *Critique of Pure Reason* is written in the spirit of the "Greek sophists and dialecticians" (Meiners 1786, b8). Furthermore, he uses the "language of the scholastics" (Meiners 1786, b8). In this sense, Kant neither provided a single new doubt "against the most sublime truths" nor did he present a single "new, only somewhat probable paradox" (Meiners 1786, b9). Only "for the sake of his new language" does he appear to have "properly examined the foundations of the whole edifice of human knowledge [*Grundlagen des ganzen Gebäudes menschlicher Kenntniße*] and would be able to shake [*erschüttern*] them" (Meiners 1786, b9).

    From Meiners's point of view, it was merely the choice of language rather than the content of Kant's philosophy that made it so dangerous. "But he liked to hide his thoughts in dark, mostly impenetrable clouds of new artistic expressions that were quite peculiar for him." (Meiners 1786, a15–b15) And furthermore we read:

    > In my experience, Mr. Kant could have raised many more apparent doubts [*scheinbare Zweyfel*] against the grounds of human knowledge, and against the noblest doctrines of morality and natural religion, and still would have done less harm than he does now, had he written in a more comprehensible language that did not consume so much noble time and energy. (Meiners 1786, b15)

---

9 For the philosophical contexts in Göttingen see Wunderlich 2012, 84.
10 For the background of the pantheism controversy, see Pietsch 2011, 77–89.

Consequently, the *Critique of Pure Reason* reformulates the sophistical musings in a new language.[11] However, Kant's followers misinterpreted the effort required to study the *Critique of Pure Reason* as a sign of quality. The "extraordinary applause" (Meiners 1786, b8), with which the *Critique of Pure Reason* was received by the public,

> shows either a sad ignorance in the history of the older and newer sophists and doubters, or a complete forgetfulness or misjudgment of the ultimate purpose of all genuine worldly wisdom [*Weltweisheit*], or perhaps unmanly fear [*unmännliche Furcht*]. (Meiners 1786, b8–a9)

2. The function of reason and philosophy: In terms of content, Meiners's criticism against Kant's book from 1781 primarily focuses on the position and role of philosophy. He writes that it is not Kant's doubts about the "many opinions" (Meiners 1786, a9) which are incontrovertible for most of mankind, nor his pleasure with "transcendental speculations" that bother him about this undertaking. "By this alone, Mr. Kant has incurred the displeasure [. . .] that he accepts pure reason, also apart from pure mathematics, as a source or a principle of true knowledge [*wahrer Erkenntniß*], without having proved its reality and validity in the least" (Meiners 1786, a9).

3. Exaggerated doubt and skepticism: From Meiners's point of view, the abstraction traceable to the role of reason results in an antagonism of opinions, and thus, in skepticism. He reminds his readership that Kant took Hume as his model, although Hume's doubt can be turned against Kant's skepticism: "I must not be reminded that Mr. Kant's writings would not find a more dangerous and severe judge than the man he has chosen as his hero or model." (Meiners 1786, a12) Accordingly, the "most important and most striking objection that can be raised against exaggerated skepticism [*übertriebenen Skeptizismus*]" (Meiners 1786, a11) as formulated by Hume: "One need only ask such a skeptic what his intention is, and what he intends to achieve by all his sophistical investigations" (Meiners 1786, a11). By these questions alone, "the doubter will at once be silenced" (Meiners 1786, a11) because s/he can claim no beneficial influence on man for his type of philosophy. This was also the reason why Hume rejected "exaggerated skepticism [...] altogether" (Meiners 1786, b11) and pleaded for a "moderate doubt" (Meiners 1786,

---

[11] This objection against the form can also be found, among others, in Pistorius' *Rezension zu Schultzes Erläuterungen* (Landau 1991, 338) and in Selle 1788. See also Zimmerli 1983, 60–61; Petrus 1994, 289–292.

a12).¹² Already the "first and simplest event or matter of life" will make the doubts of the skeptic disappear "and will leave him about every point of theory as well as of practical life just where the other wise of the world [*Weltweisen*] stand with all those who do not care at all about philosophical investigations" (Meiners 1786, b12–a13). With Hume and against Kant, Meiners thus sums up:

> It is true that one has no great cause to fear such a sad revolution as extreme skepticism [*der äußerste Skepticismus*] seems to threaten; nature will always triumph over these musings. (Meiners 1786, b12)

This is also the reason why these kind of philosophers have so far enjoyed only "a momentary reputation [...] which was a fruit of the whim or ignorance of their century; but none of them have been able to stand the fairer judgment [*gerechtern Urtheil bestehen*] of posterity" (Meiners 1786, a14–b14).

4. Disregard for common sense: The role of reason in the philosophical system leads Kant "to speak of the first truths of natural religion and of the doctrine of moral as mere hypotheses, which, to use his words, have no validity as opinions in themselves, albeit in relation to opposing transcendent presumptions" (Meiners 1786, a9–b9). According to Meiners, Kant admits that he was only concerned with abstract speculations. Therefore, he had read the function of weighing reasons and counter-reasons of natural religion in Kant's *Critique of Pure Reason* with "an awkward feeling [*peinlicher Empfindung*]" (Meiners 1786, a10):

> It is not at all a question of what is advantageous or disadvantageous for the common being [*gemeinen Wesen*], but only how far reason can go in its speculation that abstracts from all interest, and whether one should count on it at all, or rather discard it in favor of the practical. (Meiners 1786, a10)

Consequently, Kant's considerations lack any understanding of the fact that the "general best could suffer through such doubts and speculations" (Meiners 1786, a10). In this sense, Meiners interprets Kant's skepticism negatively, turning it against common sense. This is evident at both the micro and macro level, that is, among those who devote themselves to the study of the *Critique of Pure Reason* as well as the societies that are imbued with these thoughts.

---

12 Remarkably, Kant never relates his conception of skepticism to that of Hume. Rather, he refers to the ancient skeptics such as those of the Academy and Pyrrhon of Elis (Fukuda 2018, 125). See also Kant's references to Hume in the *CPrR*, AA 5: 52–53.

5. Demagogy: Following Meiners, Kant puts much emphasis on "the speculations independent of all experience, or as he puts it, cognition of pure reason" (Meiners 1786, a15). The confidence expressed in this, in contrast to Hume, has seduced the young people.

> [I]nexperienced youths, who did not yet know how artificially words had been played with in previous centuries, offered all their strength to investigate the meaning of inscrutable words [unergründliche Wörter]; but they wasted strength and time in fruitless efforts. (Meiners 1786, b15)

To prove this, Meiners reports several concrete cases in the preface: There are

> hopeful young men [...] whom Mr. Kant's critique for a time completely withdrew from the useful sciences to which they were to devote themselves, or whom it even stole the tranquility of mind [Ruhe ihres Gemüths], and probably even more than this. One of these young men was so tortured by the darkness that prevails in Mr. Kant's last writings and by the doubts, insoluble to him, against truths on which he had hitherto founded virtue and happiness that he began to doubt the reality of his feelings, finally falling literally into a madness [förmliche Verrücktheit]. (Meiners 1786, b10)

According to Meiners, this example proves the actual effects of the antinomian structure of Kant's argumentation. These are accepted by Kant, but especially by his followers.[13]

6. Incitement to revolution: What leads to confused youths and misguided scholars on a small scale brings political instability on a large one. In this sense, Meiners for the first time links Kant's "change of thinking" with political revolution (Pietsch 2011, 218), a topos that will gain weight especially during the French Revolution (Losurdo 1987). He establishes a connection between philosophical and political subversion. Meiners reproaches Kant and the Kantians for preparing the ground for the general revolution.

> I even notice that similar sentiments are gradually creeping into the minds of people from the wide world [großen Welt] who govern other people [...] and are preparing everything for the general revolution with which Europe is threatened, and by which the small remnant of the noble sentiments of the ancient Greeks and Romans can easily be destroyed. (Meiners 1786, a18)

In his parallelization of philosophical and political subversion, Meiners brings Leibniz into play as a guarantor against Kant. However, he radicalizes the con-

---

[13] Following Meiners' example, the negative consequences of studying the *Critique of Pure Reason* were repeatedly emphasized in the reception of Kant. However, Meiners's reference to these examples was also interpreted negatively (see Pietsch 2011, 223).

sequences to be drawn from this: "I subscribe again to all these statements of Leibniz, only the latter seems to me too fearful, or at least neither suited to our age nor our present fatherland." (Meiners 1786, a18) Meiners suggests the following reaction:

> One has a right to take measures against harmful doctrines that are dangerous to morals and piety, but at the same time, one must carefully guard against attributing such doctrines to other people to their detriment as long as one does not have the most obvious evidence in hand. (Meiners 1786, a17)

Strictness must therefore be exercised against that doctrine on which demonstrable crimes are based. "These must not be tolerated at all, and one must try to stifle them by force" (Meiners 1786, a17): One has a right to kill [*vernichten*] a poisonous animal [*giftiges Thier*], however innocent it may be" (Meiners 1786, b17).

To summarize these six points, it can be said that Meiners' polemic against Kant's *Critique of Pure Reason* consists of a compilation of various, in part contradictory, accusations that are merely marginally developed or substantiated on Kant's text. In this sense, the *Critique of Pure Reason* remains entirely in the wake of old sophistical speculations and scholastic arguments, while also making use of a newly invented language. It leads to exaggerated doubt and skepticism, but at the same time refutes itself and lacks any penetrating power. It is completely harmless because of its language, but simultaneously the cause of confused youth and emerging political revolutions. It presents itself as new and critical while referring to already known points of view, without, however, doing justice to them or bringing any innovations according to its content.

4 Meiners' Alternative Draft in the Preface of *Grundriß*

Although the preface of *Grundriß der Seelen-Lehre* is a text in itself, primarily as an opportunity to give enough space to the polemic against Kant, it must also be seen in connection with the rest of the book. In that sense, then, it is not merely a critique on Kant's approach, but also an attempt to critically posit Meiners's own project in distinction to it. He consequently ties his critique of Kant to the claim he pursues with the book, which is to form a counter-project to the *Critique of Pure Reason*. In doing so, the outline of *Grundriß der Seelen-Lehre* manifests a "clear move away from materialism" (Wunderlich 2012, 74, 89) which is replaced by a substance-dualistic theory (Meiners 1786, 15–66). Although this is not made explicit in the preface, the criticism on Kant provides a favorable opportunity to critically delimit the newly formulated position.

Following the Göttingen professor, philosophy is a "science of man" (Meiners 1786, b2) or, in other words, a

> collection of knowledge in which the nature of man is examined, not only in so far as he feels, thinks and speaks, desires and detests, but also in so far as he can, by his way of feeling and thinking, desiring and acting, either himself become happy or unhappy, or make others happy or unhappy, in manifold domestic and civil relations. (Meiners 1786, b2)

Therefore, mathematics and natural history (he distinguishes between "Naturkunde" and "Naturgeschichte") are separated from philosophy, because they have a different content and a different way of teaching. Philosophy itself falls into two "main sections: theoretical philosophy and practical philosophy" (Meiners 1786, a3). Theoretical philosophy examines man as a sentient, thinking, and speaking creature. "The theory of man now, considered as a feeling, thinking, and speaking creature, I give the name doctrine of soul [*Seelen-Lehre*], or psychology" (Meiners 1786, b3). Practical philosophy, on the other hand, thematizes man as a wanting, desiring, and loathing being. This results in an interplay between psychology or the theory of the soul and philosophy.

> Although psychology is generally concerned with the explanation of various kinds of beauty and ugliness, and of pleasant or unpleasant sensations which are produced in us by them, it leaves the more detailed discussion of these objects to the theory of the *schönen Wissenschaften* [*belles lettres*]. In a similar way, it shows in detail the origin, nature, and various kinds of deduced concepts [*abgezogenen Begriffe*]; on the other hand, it leaves the investigation of the origin and reality of the most important general concepts to metaphysics and natural religion. (Meiners 1786, b3–a4)

Psychology further falls into four main parts, "the order of which is determined by the nature of the human mind itself" (Meiners 1786, a4) and which are developed in the main parts of *Grundriß der Seelen-Lehre*. Accordingly, experience is the only "real source of knowledge" (Meiners 1786, a5), pure reason or pure understanding, on the other hand, do not constitute a source of knowledge.[14]

> I do not envy anyone for the treasure trove of wisdom [*Fund-Grube der Weisheit*] he discovers in pure reason, and for the treasures he thinks he has found through it; only do not blame me

---

[14] This is the common denominator of the criticism on Kant put forward in 1876, which resulted from a larger-scale reception of British philosophy and a distancing from Wolff.

and others for following our convictions and at the same time following in the footsteps of the greatest men. (Meiners 1786, a6)

In order to characterize his own point of view positively, Meiners recommends reading "graspable works [*faßliche Werke*]," which do not start from "supposed axioms [*vermeyntlichen Axiomen*], and arbitrary definitions" (Meiners 1786, a6). More precisely, it says:

> I therefore recommend, apart from the doctrine of reason by Feder and Reimarus [...] the *Essai de Psychologie*, and the *Essai analytique* by Bonnet, or [...] Condillac's *Traité des sensations*, and his writing *sur l'origine des connoissances humaines*; furthermore Beattie's *Philosophische Versuche und Moralische und kritische Abhandlungen*: Gerard's writings on genius, Basedow's *Philalethie*, also Irwing's *Erfahrungen über den Menschen*, and the first volume of Search's *Licht der Nacht*. (Meiners 1786, a6–b6)

After a thorough reading and study, Locke's *Essay Concerning Human Understanding* should follow. This work is "the main book for the researcher of the soul" (Meiners 1786, a7), but is not for the beginning, because of its "excessive nature." Moreover, Locke should be read together with Leibniz' commentary *Nouveaux Essais sur l'entendement humain*. "[I]f one has the desire and the time" (Meiners 1786, b7) the writings of Johann Georg Sulzer, Moses Mendelssohn, Johann Heinrich Lambert, Johann August Eberhard, Joachim Heinrich Campes, and Ernst Plattner are recommended. Merely if "one has filled one's memory with useful knowledge and strengthened one's powers by reading and contemplating the books mentioned so far, then one can venture to read the works of Sextus, Berkeley, Hume, and Kant without danger" (Meiners 1786, b7).

5 The (Missing) Answer from Kant

Already in *Grundriß der Seelen-Lehre*, Meiners challenged Kant to partake in a public debate when he said: "I cannot blame Mr. Kant if he regards these remarks of mine about his way of philosophizing as an attack which he must try to repel as best he can according to the right of self-defense." (Meiners 1786, a16) Furthermore, he also determined the way he envisioned the dispute when saying that Kant "may answer in the very spirit in which I have judged him, and that he may not be hasty in his conjectures about my motivations that have moved me to make public statements about his writings" (Meiners 1786, a16–b16).

Furthermore, from inner circles, Kant was also called upon to respond to Meiners' polemics. On January 3, 1786, Schütz wrote to Kant: "What has struck me more than all other writings so far against the Critique of Pure Reason is the attack by Mr. Meiners in Göttingen in the preface to his Psychology" (AA 10: 369–370). In addition, Friedrich Victor Leberecht Plessing wrote in a letter to Kant dated January 16, 1787:

> I hope that you, honorable gentleman [*Eurer Wohlgeboren*], will emphatically punish the wanton and indeed evil-hearted attack that Meiners dared to make on you the other day. This writer no longer knows how to set any limits to his rash judgments [...]. How much more has this man sunk with me by portraying your writings as dangerous to religion and morals. (AA 10: 474)

Kant registered the polemics against his *Critique of Pure Reason* and, for some time, played with the idea of writing a defense against Feder and Tittels. Among other things, this can be seen in a letter from Johann Erich Biesters dated June 11, 1786. "You write to me concerning a defense you intend to publish against attacks by Mr. Feder and Mr. Tittel. It will, like everything from your pen, be instructive and pleasing to the public." (AA 10: 457) After taking an explicit stand against his critics in the *Prolegomena* and subsequently in the second edition of the *Critique of Pure Reason* (cf. Motta 2012), he later interferes only with isolated remarks or indirectly in the controversies. In the *Critique of Practical Reason* (1788), there are some marginal notes that defend the critical project against the accusation of skepticism (*CPrR*, AA 5: 3, 50–54).[15] In *What does it mean to orient oneself in thinking?* Kant formulates in a footnote (presumably) as a point against Meiners as follows:

> Likewise, another scholar finds *skepticism* in the *Critique*, even though precisely the starting point of the *Critique* is firmly to posit something certain and determinate in respect of the range of our cognition *a priori*. Similarly [he finds] a *dialectic* in the critical investigations, whereas the aim is to resolve and forever eliminate the unavoidable dialectic in which pure reason becomes involved and entangled when it is employed dogmatically everywhere. The Neoplatonists, who called themselves "eclectics" because they knew how to find their own conceits all over the place in other authors – if they had previously put them in there – proceeded in just this way; hence nothing new happens under the sun. (*WOT*, AA 8: 143)

Kant's reticence can be explained by the fact that he had already built up a network in the 1770s that he could activate in this controversy (Nowitzki/Roth/Stiening 2018a, 2). It included in particular Christian Gottfried Schütz and Carl Christian Erhard Schmid in Jena, Johannes Bering in Marburg and Ludwig Heinrich von Jakob

---

[15] See also Kant's references to the *Critique of Practical Reason* in his letter to Schütz from June 25, 1787 (AA 10: 490); Kant's letter to Jakob from September 11, 1787 (AA 10: 494); Kant's letter to Reinhold from December 28, 1789 (AA 10: 514).

in Halle.¹⁶ This support was encouraged by two organs: the *Allgemeine Literatur-Zeitung* and the *Gothaische gelehrte Zeitung*.¹⁷

In 1787, three articles appeared that explicitly defended Kant against Meiners' attacks.

1. Published in the *Allgemeine Literatur-Zeitung* on April 5–7, 1787: Lemgo in der Meyerschen Buchhandlung: Grundriß der Geschichte der Weltweisheit von C. Meiners, Professor der Philosophie in Göttingen 1786.

The anonymous author is Christian Jacob Kraus.¹⁸ According to him, Meiners "rendered a severe judgment [*ein peinliches Gericht gehegt*]" (Landau 1991, 534) in the preface, which is based on two hypotheses: the *Critique of Pure Reason* "contains nothing but sophistical musings in scholastic language, and its connoisseurs [*Liebhaber*] read it with such pleasure merely because they like subtlety [*Spitzfindigkeit*] and verbiage [*Wörterkram*]" (Landau 1991, 534). Behind this critique, however, there is nothing but "boasting" (Landau 1991, 536), because the book contains, quite contrary to the author's self-assessment, merely "a series of scant descriptions of the lives [*kahle Lebensbeschreibungen*] of these wise of the world [*Weltweisen*] with few indications of their doctrines" (Landau 1991, 536). For this reason, it is merely "improper science" (Landau 1991, 553).

The review forms a substantial critique of central assumptions of the book. These are directed in particular against Meiners' reconstruction of the ancient history of "world wisdom" and the consequences drawn from it. The only thing that could help against these fallacies and prejudices is "the critical method of philosophizing, which consists in the most honest, acute, most unbiased application to our entire cognitive faculty" (Landau 1991, 550). This is the method, so the reviewer polemically, which "every wise man follows for himself and in silence" and which, through Kant's writings, has become "in these last years among the German nation, more than ever publicly and generally" (Landau 1991, 550).¹⁹

---

16 For Kant's circle of scholars, see Pietsch 2011, 93.
17 On the essential role of the journals in the controversy between Kant and the Göttingen philosophers, see Stiening's contribution in the present volume.
18 As late as November 1786, Schütz offered Kant to write a review of Meiners' *Grundriß* (AA 10: 569–570). However, the latter decided in favor of Christian Jacob Kraus as reviewer (Pietsch 2011, 96). Kraus reported that Kant had been "bitterly offended [*gekränkt*] by Meiners from Göttingen" and had "asked him for a defense [*Schutzschrift*]" (Malter 1990, 309). On the relationship between Kant and Kraus, see Stark 1987, 172.
19 For Meiners's reaction to this review, see Stark 1987, 172.

2. In March 1787, published anonymously, appeared a missive to Professor Meiners in Göttingen concerning his attack against Kant's system of philosophy was published anonymously in the *Neue Litteratur und Völkerkunde* 1 (1787), 221–242.

The author of this review is Ludwig Heinrich Jakob, who, however, denied the authorship.[20] With a polemical tone but a high level of expertise, he endeavored to reassure Meiners about his alleged "philanthropic fear" (Jakob 1787, 221). For this reason, he states the "known means, which have always been used by such campaigners who were more interested in receiving the applause of the public, which has no voice at all in the matter" (Jakob 1787, 222). In terms of content, the reviewer repeatedly relates Meiners's objections to Kant's response to the "reproach of idealism" in the *Prolegomena*. Moreover, he develops his counterarguments starting from the questions structuring the *Prolegomena*: "How is pure mathematics, pure natural science and metaphysics in general possible?" In doing so, he addresses two accusations in great detail: first, in the *Critique of Pure Reason* there are merely known or unproven and arbitrary assertions; second, the doubts raised "against sacred truths [*geheiligte Wahrheiten*]" have caused great harm. Thereby, the reviewer admits that the *Critique of Pure Reason* is written in a "cumbersome, and often not easily graspable new terminology," but that this terminology is "extremely assertive [*äußerst bestimmt*]" (Jakob 1787, 230). In particular, with reference to Meiners's repeatedly emphasized "most sublime truths" or "sanctified truths," the reviewer argues:

> Who has sanctified the sanctified truths? The unholy judgment of men. Not from God is the knowledge of God in the provisions of the philosophical system and the Christian faith. From teachers of the school, and teachers of the church, we have the fundamental truths of religion, in the determination, in the expressions, the proofs which constitute the faith of the great multitude [*grossen Haufen*], and which only the teacher of the school, the teacher of the church, has sanctified. (Jakob 1787, 237)

For this reason, the reviewer asks again polemically: why should the metaphysician not examine the foundations of theology?

3. An article by an unnamed scholar on Meiners' *Grundriß der Seelen-Lehre* appeared in the first volume of *Philosophische Annalen: Grundriß der Seelen-*

---

[20] See: Kurze Nachrichten in: Gothaische gelehrte Zeitungen, 24. September 1788, 632. For the identity of the reviewer, see Reinhold's letter to Kant on March 1, 1788 (AA 10: 529).

lehre von C. Meiners, Professor der Philosophie in Göttingen. Lemgo 1786 in der Meyerschen Buchhandlung.

With reference to the already published reviews of *Grundriß*, three points are made against Meiners' publication: firstly, the reviewer criticizes Meiners' determination of philosophy, especially its lack of "scientificity" (Landau 1991, 524–525), and contrasts it with Kant's determination as the "science of concepts." Since Meiners does not know the difference between "pure" and "empirical knowledge," "he must therefore necessarily mix all these things together" (Landau 1991, 525). Secondly, the reviewer criticizes Meiners's tone. "[I]t only seems as if Mr. M., through the few pages that declaim against K., only wanted to show how a sophistical lecture should be set up" (Landau 1991, 527). And it goes on to say: "No truly, even if Kant had only applied his practiced art to build up sophismata, it would have required more than a preface to destroy his edifice [*Bau*]" (Landau 1991, 528). From all the attacks, the reviewer concludes: "[O]ne can hardly believe one's eyes when opening the quoted passages, and it almost cannot be otherwise than that a malicious person has given Mr. Meiners a mutilated copy [*verstümmeltes Exemplar*] of the Critique" (Landau 1991, 530). Thirdly, the reviewer characterizes Meiners's attempts in the field of empirical psychology and anthropology as "unsuccessful;" they "are based only on subjective judgments" (Landau 1991, 533).

Summarizing all three reviews, it can be stated that the reactions to Meiners' preface of *Grundriß der Seelen-Lehre* are as sharp as the attack itself. In terms of content, no reasons are elaborated that could have prompted Meiners to polemicize so decidedly against it. As Meiners demanded, the reviewers responded "in the very spirit" (Meiners 1786, a16–b16) in which he judged Kant.

6 Summary

Apart from the improper tone that pervades the entire preface, Meiners raises two points in the preface of *Grundriß der Seelen-Lehre* that are still relevant today. With his frequently repeated statement that the *Critique of Pure Reason* is not so new, he firstly reclaims the historical context from which the book emerged. Even if Meiners' contextualizations seem to be prejudiced and wrong, it is a historical fact that the *Critique of Pure Reason* emerged from a wide variety of influences at the end of the eighteenth century and was made possible by them in the first place. Kant and his followers deliberately emphasize the uniqueness of the *Critique of Pure Reason*, thus denying its historical context. This prevented a productive reception located in philosophical-historical contexts. The lack of engagement with transcendental philosophy, especially with its empirical aspects, eventually led to German idealism. Secondly, the *Critique of Pure Reason* is in fact characterized by conceptual creations or transformations that few philosophers before Kant had accomplished. The characteristic style, which may be justified on its merits, makes it difficult for contemporaries to understand the book and creates an endless loop of interpretive approaches to this day. Nevertheless, it is worthwhile examining Kant's revolutionary claim to philosophy, especially with a critical view to his contexts. There is no need to argue further for the latter here. Rather, it should be emphasized that Meiners' work also deserves critical reception beyond the controversy with Kant.

Andreas Brandt
Meiners's Critique of Kant

Abstract: Meiners's examination of Kant's philosophy is presented on the basis of the relevant writings. Meiners criticizes Kant's a priori claims and idiosyncratic terminology, which he considers mannered and quirky. He disputes the originality of this philosophy, attributing it to earlier thinkers, particularly among the Cambridge Platonism (Cudworth). It is shown that, on the one hand, Meiners makes some astute analyses and valid objections, but, on the other hand, does not fully grasp the depth of the theory, misunderstands it on many points and remains superficial.

When informed readers consider the relationship between the philosophers from Göttingen and the philosophy of Immanuel Kant, they will probably think first of the so-called *Göttingen Review* of the first edition of the *Critique of Pure Reason* (1781), which – based on a draft by Christian Garve – was edited by Johann Georg Heinrich Feder and published in January 1782 (Garve/Feder 1782; cf. Polloka 2001, XXIII–IV; Petrus 1994). However, this is only the best-known of the efforts of philosophers from Göttingen to engage with Kant. Whether Feder and his student and friend Christoph Meiners, who had been full professors in Göttingen since 1768 and 1775 respectively and represented a tendentially empiricist popular philosophy, wanted to make Göttingen a "center of anti-Kantianism" remains to be seen, but both philosophers wrote critical works on Kant (cf. Cramer/Patzig 1994). In this context, Meiners, unlike Feder, dealt with Kant relatively late and presumably initially reluctantly, but then thoroughly, reserving the entire second volume of his *Universal Critical History of Ancient and Modern Ethics* [*Allgemeine kritische Geschichte der älteren und neueren Ethik*] from 1801 for a critique of Kant's ethics. In order to provide a more complete picture of Meiners's reception (or non-reception) of this philosophy, I will also discuss Meiners's earlier role as co-editor and reviewer of the *Philosophical Library* [*Philosophische Bibliothek*] as well as his critique of Kant in the preface to *Outline of the Doctrine of the Soul* [*Grundriß der Seelenlehre*] from 1786.

1 The Philosophical Library

The project of a separate review journal, planned and carried out jointly by Feder and Meiners and lasting for four years (from 1788 to 1791), pursued the purpose of making new works known – especially those from abroad that were not easily accessible but seemed interesting to the editors because of their basic empiricist view.[1] In addition, the journal provided the editors with the opportunity to publish longer, more detailed reviews than the usual short form afforded by other journals.[2] At the same time, Feder and Meiners took advantage of the opportunity to publish their own systematic treatises in the first section of a yearbook. This was followed by reviews, first of foreign, then of German-language literature, as well as brief literature announcements.

The division of labor between the two reviewers is made evident by their characteristic choice of topics in the four realized volumes, although only some of the articles are signed (with the initials F. and M.). In spite of Meiners's significant and extensive knowledge of literature and foreign languages, Feder was generally the more diligent reviewer and also the stronger systematic philosopher of the two. For the first two volumes, Feder wrote the major systematic articles introducing the volumes, *On Subjective and Objective Truth* [*Über subjective und objective Wahrheit*], *Conformity Between All Truths* [*Übereinstimmung aller Wahrheiten untereinander*] (Feder/Meiners 1788–1791, vol. 1, 1–42) and *On the Concept of Substance* [*Über den Begriff der Substanz*] (Feder/Meiners 1788–1791, vol. 2, 1–40). Feder probably also wrote the corresponding essays in volumes 3 and 4, and he reviewed the majority of genuinely specialized new publications in philosophy. In contrast, topics of empirical psychology, anthropology, cultural and social history predominate in Meiners's work.[3] Both reviewers deal with German and foreign literature (English, French, even Italian) with a command of old and new languages.

For the consideration of the reception of Kant in the journal, Feder's reviews of the *Critique of Practical Reason* (Feder/Meiners 1788–1791, vol. 1, 182–218) and the *Critique of the Power of Judgment* (Feder/Meiners 1788–1791, vol. 4, 180–194) are particularly important, as are the treatises introducing the 3rd volume: *Attempt to Present the Kantian System as Briefly as Possible* [*Versuch einer möglichst kurzen Darstellung des Kantischen Systems*] (Feder/Meiners 1788–1791, vol. 3, 1–13) and *On the Kantian Moral Theology* [*Über die Kantische Moraltheologie*] (Feder/Meiners 1788–1791, vol. 3, 13–66). Since these two texts are anonymous, Meiners's authorship cannot be ruled out. However, various textual criteria make this highly unlikely. First, the text says: "Three years have passed since I appeared as an opponent of

---

[1] For more about the intentions and implementation of this project, see the contribution of Gideon Stiening in this volume.
[2] Cf. the preface to Feder/Meiners 1788–1791, vol. 1, III–IV.
[3] Examples by Meiners from volume 1 are Rabaut Saint-Étienne 1787; Leclerc de Sept-Chênes 1787; Brandes 1787.

Kantian philosophy" (Feder/Meiners 1788–1791, vol. 3, 61).[4] What could be meant here? Feder had already commented on Kant on various occasions. The *Göttingen Review* appeared in 1782, eight years before this text. In a review in the 1st volume (1788) of the *Philosophical Library*—only two years earlier than the text in question—Feder dealt with Kant's *Critique of Practical Reason*.[5] Feder's book *On Space and Causality to Review the Kantian Philosophy* [*Ueber Raum und Caussalität zur Prüfung der Kantischen Philosophie*] from 1787 was a major independent publication and is the only one of his works that fits chronologically and must therefore be the one he means. Meiners's *Outline of the Doctrine of the Soul* (1786), however, which includes a Kant critique in its preface, would also fit chronologically, but it is too selective and superficial in its critique to be considered. But more importantly, the content argues against Meiners's authorship when compared with his original contributions directed against Kant (see below). The first text offers a neutral presentation, divided into 25 shorter paragraphs, of the main content of the first Critique. It intentionally contains no discussion of problems or commentary and was written only at the request of student listeners, as a note on p. 2 states. The second text deals with Kant's moral theology, largely omitting the foundations of ethics (possibly because Feder had already reviewed the *Critique of Practical Reason* in the first volume of the journal?). We can clearly detect an effort to do justice to Kant's argumentation. The presentation is easily understandable and avoids the most controversial and misleading aspects of Kant's theory. Instead, it emphasizes similarities with other classical ethics, in particular with Stoic ethics. Kant's criterion of conformity of maxims to their conceived lawful universality, for example, is interpreted as conformity to the nature of things (Feder/Meiners 1788–1791, vol. 3, 24). Finally, in this view colored by Stoic thought, we find a critique of the core moral-theological argument, in which an irresolvable dilemma is seen: Either the moral law is not adequate to human nature (a mere ideal of reason), in which case it cannot necessarily oblige man; or it is adequate to nature, in which case no further conclusions can be drawn that go beyond nature (Feder/Meiners 1788–1791, vol. 3, 42–48). The overall modest tone of the treatise is more similar to Feder's *Göttingen Review* than to the more polemical contributions undoubtedly written by Meiners. It follows, then, that Feder is the sole author of the Kant criticism within the joint project of the *Philosophical Library* and that Meiners's critique takes place elsewhere.

---

4 "Es sind nun drei Jahre her, dass ich als Gegner der kantischen Philosophie aufgetreten bin."
5 Immanuel Kant: *Critik der practischen Vernunft*. Riga 1788 (in: AA 5, 1–163). In this paper, the English translation by Mary Gregor is used (Immanuel Kant: *Critique of Practical Reason*. Trans. and ed. by Mary Gregor. Revised Edition. Cambridge 2015).

2 The Preface to the *Outline of the Doctrine of the Soul*

The *Outline of the Doctrine of the Soul* (Meiners 1786) is the only philosophical-systematic draft Meiners wrote besides his numerous and extensive historical "outlines" [*Grundrisse*]. It is typical for Meiners that it concerns psychology. In order to better understand the critique of Kant contained in the preface, let us briefly consider the character and layout of the work. In the preface, Meiners explains the position of psychology within philosophy or the system of sciences in general. The systematics of the work, however, raise some serious questions. First, the focus of the concept of philosophy on anthropology is clear. Although it is reminiscent of Hume's *Treatise*, Meiners traces it back to the Socratic tradition:

> I therefore declare philosophy, with the wisest of the Greeks,[6] to be a science of man, or a collection of knowledge, in which the nature of man is investigated, not only in so far as he feels, thinks and speaks, desires and detests, but also in so far as, in various domestic and civil relationships, by his manner of feeling and thinking, desiring and acting, he can either himself become happy or unhappy, or make others happy or unhappy. (Meiners 1786, preface, 2)[7]

Mathematics, natural science, and natural history are excluded. Natural history would also include medicine and thus assume too large a scope (Meiners 1786, preface, 3). Philosophy is divided into theoretical and practical philosophy. Since it is understood as anthropology, it treats man according to his theoretical and practical aspects; that is, theoretical philosophy treats him as a sentient, thinking, speaking being, and thus also as a desiring and detesting one. However, this belongs more closely to the topics of ethics and is therefore more appropriately placed in the general part of practical philosophy. It remains unclear how Meiners classifies metaphysics and natural theology (which actually transcend the anthropological framework, but which Meiners does not deal with).

---

6 I.e., Socrates. Cf. the paragraph after next, beginning: "Wenn man mit dem Sokrates [...]" (Meiners 1786, 2 of the preface, which is not paginated in print).

7 "Ich erkläre daher die Philosophie mit dem Weisesten unter den Griechen als eine Wissenschaft des Menschen, oder als eine Sammlung von Kenntnißen, worinn die Natur des Menschen untersucht wird, nicht nur in so ferne er empfindet, denkt und redet, begehrt und verabscheut, sondern auch in so ferne er in mannichfaltigen häuslichen und bürgerlichen Verhältnißen durch seine Art zu empfinden und zu denken, zu begehren und zu handeln entweder selbst glücklich oder unglücklich werden kann, oder andere glücklich oder unglücklich machen kann."

Meiners presents theoretical philosophy as a "doctrine of the soul" (psychology). It is divided into four main parts, each of which is described by Meiners with a number of topics and which can be summarized as follows: (1) doctrine of the inner sense (phenomenology of consciousness), (2) soul and powers of the soul, (3) philosophy of language (language and writing; logic and dialectics), (4) epistemology (abilities and limits of understanding, truth and error) (Meiners 1786, preface, 5–8). The descriptions correspond quite closely to the four parts of the *Outline*.

In epistemology Meiners shows himself to be a committed empiricist: Experience and history are taken as the only sources of knowledge, except in mathematics (Meiners 1786, preface, 8). From his didactic recommendations it becomes clear that Meiners treats his sources from contemporary German, French and English literature as equally valuable, not shying away from newer foreign languages. For beginning students he recommends (Meiners 1786, preface, 9–12) epistemological and psychological works by Feder[6] (1786), Reimarus (1756), Bonnet (1755, 1760), Condillac (1746, 1754), Beattie (1770, 1783), Gerard (1776), Basedow (1764), Irving (1777–1785), and Search (1771–1772). Locke's *Essay concerning Human Understanding* is cited as the central work and main book, alongside Tetens' *Versuche über die menschliche Natur* (1777), if they were not so broad. Locke, however, must be supplemented by Leibniz' "commentary" (i.e., the *Nouveaux Essais sur l'entendement humain*). It is not recommended that beginners study the works of Sextus, Berkely, Hume, and Kant, which should be reserved for those who already stand firmly on empiricist ground (Meiners 1786, preface, 12). This selection of literature sufficiently proves that Meiners stands in a different intellectual environment, a different scientific culture than Kant, who comes from the school philosophy of the Leibniz-Wolff tradition.

This provides the background for his critique of Kant. A brief look at the main text of the *Outline* shows that Meiners used both classical and modern literature, but did not consider Kant. He engaged with Plato, Aristotle, and Cicero, as well as with a wide range of German, French, and English contemporaries. Mendelssohn, Wolff, Tetens, Lambert, Reimarus, and Feder are among the German authors. However, there is no trace of Kant. Only in the preface does Meiners address Kant. Apparently, he feels compelled to comment on Kant's philosophy in light of his growing influence. However, this is done rather as one reacts to an annoying alien element, a nuisance.

Meiners generally criticizes Kant for the obscurity or artificiality of his language and the overly subtle nature of his reflections [*Grübeleien*]. He had hoped that the great inaccessibility of the writings would prevent their success. When he realized his mistake, however, he blamed the readership for it. He accused the readers of a "sad ignorance" of the history of the older and newer sophists and skeptics, a "complete forgetfulness or misjudgment of the ultimate purpose of all genuine worldly wisdom," or perhaps an "unmanly fear." There are four more specific objections to Kant:

1. that he accepts pure reason also apart from pure mathematics as a source or a principle of true knowledge, without having proved its reality and validity in the least:
2. that he further speaks of the first truths of natural religion and the doctrine of morals as mere hypotheses, which, to use his words, have no validity as opinions in themselves, but only in relation to opposing transcendent assumptions, since he at the same time establishes the arbitrary propositions and declarations as irrefutable axioms and without any proof:
3. that he does not even raise a single new important doubt against the most sublime truths, or against the reasons and criteria of human knowledge, not even a single new, only somewhat probable paradox, and yet, merely for the sake of his new language, gives himself the appearance as if he had first properly investigated the foundations of the entire structure of human knowledge, and could then undermine them:
4. that he finally does not even remain the same in his elevations of pure reason, but declares it in several places to be just as void and unreliable as he is otherwise accustomed to declare experience and empirical knowledge to be (see Critique of Pure Reason p. 642 and Metaphysics of Morals p. 126). (Meiners 1786, preface, 15–17, numbering added)[8]

In short: (1) to assert synthetic judgments a priori from mere concepts without proof of their possibility. For this, Meiners would have had to deal with Kant's transcendental proofs of the chapter on principles in the first *Critique* as well as

---

8 "[1] daß er die reine Vernunft auch außer der reinen Mathematik als eine Quelle oder ein Principium wahrer Erkenntniß annimmt, ohne ihre Wirklichkeit und Gültigkeit im geringsten bewiesen zu haben: [2] daß er ferner von den ersten Wahrheiten der natürlichen Religion und der Sittenlehre als von bloßen Hypothesen spricht, die, um mich seiner Worte zu bedienen, keine Gültigkeit als Meinungen an sich selbst, sondern nur in Beziehung auf entgegengesetzte transcendente Anmaaßungen haben, da er doch zugleich die willkührlichen Sätze und Erklärungen, als unumstößliche Axiomen und ohne allen Beweis festsetzt: [3] daß er auch nicht einen einzigen neuen wichtigen Zweyfel wider erhabensten Wahrheiten, oder wider die Gründe und Kriteria der menschlichen Erkenntniß, nicht einmal ein einziges neues, nur einigermaaßen wahrscheinliches Paradoxon vorbringt, und sich dennoch, bloß um seiner neuen Sprache willen, das Ansehen gibt, als wenn er zuerst die Grundlagen des ganzen Gebäudes menschlicher Kenntnis gehörig untersucht hätte, und erschüttern könnte: [4] daß er sich endlich in seinen Erhebungen der reinen Vernunft nicht einmal gleich bleibt, sondern sie an mehrern Stellen für eben so nichtig, und unzuverlässig erklärt, als wofür er sonst die Erfahrung und Erfahrungs-Kenntniße zu erklären zu erklären pflegt (Man sehe Kritik der reinen Vernunft S. 642 und Metaphysik der Sitten S. 126)."

the transcendental deduction of the categories, which claim to provide exactly this: The principles of pure understanding are justified by the proof that they constitute conditions of the possibility of experience.[9] Admittedly, this is not a progressive, deductive proof, and it is likely that Meiners would not have accepted Kant's transcendental proof upon closer examination.

(2) No objective proof of propositions of morality and natural religion is provided, only statements as "hypotheses." Meiners presumably means the status of the propositions as practical postulates (freedom of will as implication of the obligatory nature of the moral law; immortality of the soul and the existence of God as implications of the possibility of the highest good), which cannot be proved by theoretical means. Objections (1) and (2) seem to contradict one another, for (1) criticizes Kant's assumption of certain synthetic judgments a priori, while in (2) he seems to insist on them on the contrary, for what are the first truths of natural religion and the moral doctrine but certain synthetic judgments a priori?

But Meiners's point is to contrast this lack of objective provability with the fact that elsewhere Kant unquestioningly posits arbitrary definitions and unproven propositions (axiomatic positings). Examples of this are given in the note: the concepts of space and time (*CPR*, A 23–30), then in the preface to the *Groundwork of the Metaphysics of Morals* on the obligatory nature of moral laws, on page 70 on humanity as an end in itself; "most of all, however, in what he puts forward about the knowledge that man has of himself p. 106 about pure reason p. 126 and about the incomprehensibility of the first law p. 128." (Meiners 1786, preface, 16)[10] The criticism seems justified, but must be considered in more detail in any case.

In the section on space and time in the *Critique of Pure Reason*, namely within the metaphysical discussions of the concepts of space and time, Kant does indeed provide arguments for the asserted qualities of these concepts, namely as subjective presentations (forms of intuition) a priori, even if individual arguments are fraught with problems (*CPR*, A 23–36/B 33–53). What Meiners considers to be arbitrary explanations or axiomatic settings, should be explained in more detail. Most likely, the doctrine of two-sources of cognition (intuition and thinking) could be regarded as an unexplained presupposition that forms a basic decision of the whole theory. When Kant writes at the beginning of the transcendental logic: "Our cogni-

---

9 See *CPR*, A 156/B 195: "The possibility of experience is therefore that which gives all of our cognitions a priori objective reality." ("Die Möglichkeit der Erfahrung ist also das, was allen unsern Erkenntnissen a priori objective Realität giebt.") Cf. *CPR*, A 771/B 799 (trans. by Guyer/Wood 1998).
10 "[...] am meisten aber in dem, was er über die Kenntnis, die der Mensch von sich selbst hat S. 106 über reine Vernunft S. 126 und über die Unbegreiflichkeit des ersten Gesetzes S. 128 vorbringt."

tion arises from two fundamental sources in the mind [...]" (*CPR*, A 50/B 74),[11] one must wonder how we know this. Are they psychologically ascertainable facts, or propositions a priori, or propositions of a transcendental psychology, which justify other propositions a priori? What exactly are their sources in each case? Meiners, however, does not dig that deeply into the problem.

More clearly identifiable is Meiners's point of criticism with respect to passages in the *Groundwork of the Metaphysics of Morals*. In its preface, the obligatory nature of practical laws is located a priori in pure reason and "cleansed" of all empirical anthropology (*GM*, AA 4: 388; trans. by Timmermann 2011), without Kant plausibly justifying this decision. It goes without saying that Meiners, as a philosophical anthropologist and empiricist, felt particularly challenged here. The same applies to the introduction of the "principle of humanity and of every rational nature as such, *as an end in itself*," which, according to Kant's own information, is not derived from experience (*GM*, AA 4: 430), but is not proven either; furthermore with Kant's claim that man always knows himself only as appearance and not in itself (*GM*, AA 4: 451), as well as in the incomprehensibility assertion with reference to the necessity of the categorical imperative (*GM*, AA 4: 463); the claim to necessary validity of a principle a priori actually requires corresponding evidence.

Objection (3) is difficult to interpret because Meiners does not specify the points in question, but only makes a sweeping negation of the originality of Kant's critical achievements. In his view, Kant's claim to have first shaken the foundations of metaphysics is unjustified, since the critical objections to the possibility of transcendent metaphysics have long been anticipated by English and French empiricism, and Kant merely uses new language that feigns originality. This reproach also seems at least partially justified, and the appreciation of Kant's original achievement needs more intensive discussion.

Objection (4) refers to the dialectical fallacies of pure reason, whose fallacious character is acknowledged in Kant's theory and does not really conflict with the justified propositions a priori. Here Meiners does not seem to have sufficiently understood the theory; presumably he does not believe Kant's a priori claims anyway and is not inclined to distinguish within this class yet.

More fundamental is Meiners subsequent criticism of Kant's views of the ultimate purpose of philosophizing. Meiners takes it for granted that the investigations of natural theology should have a relation to the common good of mankind. He is downright embarrassed by Kant's answer to the question whether the doubts and speculations undertaken in theoretical philosophy (for example, in the cri-

---

[11] "Unsere Erkenntnis entspringt aus zwei Grundquellen des Gemüts [...],"

tique of the proofs of God or immortality) could be detrimental to the "general best" (Meiners 1786, preface, 17) Kant says:

> For the issue is not what is advantageous or disadvantageous to the common good in these matters, but only how far reason can get in its speculation in abstraction from all interest, and whether one can count on such speculation at all or must rather give it up altogether in favor of the practical. (*CPR*, A 746/B 744–745)

Meiners compares this attitude with that of Hume in his *Enquiry concerning Human Understanding*, in which experiments are rejected, "to endeavor the refutation of any hypothesis, by a pretense of its dangerous consequences to religion and morality." (Hume 1975, 8.2, 96) For Kant, as for Hume, it is clear that investigations of theoretical metaphysics are committed to truth alone and must take place without regard to practical, especially religious, purposes. What distinguishes Hume from Kant, according to Meiners, is the practical harmlessness of Hume's skepticism. In practical life, in society, it immediately falls away as soon as one stops thinking theoretically (Meiners 1786, preface, 22–27). For Kant, on the other hand, theoretical speculation was decidedly more important than experience and had therefore misled young, immature and half-educated people into fruitless discussions about the most abstract concepts, thus wasting their time and damaging their sound judgment (Meiners 1786, preface, 27–29). According to Meiners, philosophy should be comprehensible and promote human happiness.

3 The Appendix on Kant to Meiners's *History of Ethics*

In its second part, Meiners's *Universal Critical History of Ancient and Modern Ethics* (1800–1801) finally brings an extensive, thorough critique of Kant. This is the second volume of a history of ethics, in the first of which Meiners treats the important ancient and modern ethical theories up to Kant. In addition to the purely historical account, the subtitle promises to examine systematic questions: "Is there really a science of life? What should be its content, its method?"[12] The outline shows that approaches of a systematic comprehension of the historical material are used as a basis to arrive at a systematic position. The most important peculiarities of the old and new ethics – including their methods – are assessed and com-

---

12 Title page of the 1st and the 2nd part: "Gibt es dann auch wirklich eine Wissenschaft des Lebens? Wie sollte ihr Inhalt, ihre Methode beschaffen seyn?"

pared with each other. The first section discusses the question of the existence of ethics; the latter contains suggestions on how to shape the limits, content, and mode of teaching ethics, as well as remarks on the teachers and followers of ethics – altogether an extraordinarily broad, substantial program.

The conception of an entire second volume, which, in contrast, deals exclusively with Kant's ethics, is striking and obviously corresponds to a desideratum explained in the preface of the first volume. It is a matter of assessing Kant's originality (which Meiners doubts), but also of avoiding partiality resulting from ignorance of other positions. Meiners sees among Kant's followers a certain school or sectarianism and intolerance of other positions, which, in fact, is not new in the history of philosophy but, in this particular case, is partly rooted in Kant's particular way of thinking (see below). As a counterbalance, he recommends a broad, calm scholarship that expands one's view and takes into account the relative right of all significant philosophies; the work is dedicated to this purpose (Meiners 1800–1801, vol. 1, IV–XIII). In the preface to the second volume, he is even more explicit: He has made every effort to "discover the defects of Kant's ethics and the infirmities of its author, as a writer," not for the pleasure of polemics, but because he considers this ethics "as harmful, as empty, and groundless," but assures a fair, objective examination (Meiners 1800–1801, vol. 2, III–IV).

The second volume contains six sections. The first two merely make comparative observations with the intention of disputing the originality of Kant's design. The first section concerns Kant's predecessors in theoretical philosophy, the second those in practical philosophy, with a very different methodological approach in the two sections. Sections 3–6 provide Meiners's systematic discussion of Kant's ethics and are central in this respect. In what follows, a survey of all six sections is provided.

(1) The content of the historical comparisons of the first section cannot be reproduced in detail. Meiners treats the positions in question in the first half within the framework of a detailed exposition of epistemological problems, stylistically oriented on Locke's *Essay*, in which the historical positions are embedded. The general line of argument consists in showing that since antiquity certain basic questions have been answered by one philosophical party in one way, by another in a different manner, and that Kant occupies only a certain position in the already existing spectrum of answers: for instance, in the question whether man knows by his senses or by his reason, or in the question whether the senses (through which we believe in the existence of an external world) represent things as they are. Ancient skeptics, for example, had already claimed that they do not, a position taken in modern times by many authors beginning with Malebranche (Meiners 1800–1801, vol. 2, 6). That the way of teaching or proving mathematics is entirely different from that of all other disciplines has also been known for millennia, al-

though some philosophers have imitated it without hesitation (Meiners 1800–1801, vol. 2, 31), etc. It is striking to what extent the epistemological treatise becomes independent and how Kant does not appear in it at all, at least not explicitly. It seems that Meiners first wants to offer a historical introduction to the field in order to provide a background for uninformed readers of Kant.

This historical-epistemological sketch ends in the middle of the section (Meiners 1800–1801, vol. 2, 41). Only then does Meiners discuss Kant, whose position he summarizes in a few paragraphs (Meiners 1800–1801, vol. 2, 42–44). They mainly concern the opposition between the passivity of sensibility and the activity of understanding, which is the source of the unity and necessity of determinate cognitions. The extract condensed again in the final paragraph claims:

> The most general, or last results of the noblest doctrines of critical philosophy are these: our senses supply us with nothing but scattered, or torn, and confused impressions of things whose true nature is entirely unknown to us. It is our mind alone that collects the scattered sensory impressions and combines the manifold of them into a certain unity. It does this according to laws that are created and essential to it. The knowledge of the original forms of the mind constitutes the only necessary and generally valid knowledge of man, which we cannot expect from experience. (Meiners 1800–1801, vol. 2, 42)[13]

Instead of supporting his presentation with original Kant passages, Meiners makes sure to agree with secondary authors (Buhle, Aenesidemus, Garve) to ensure that these are really Kant's basic positions (cf. Meiners 1800–1801, vol. 2, 42). Meiners writes as if he does not have a copy of the *Critique of Pure Reason* at hand – in the whole section there is no indication that he knows the original passages, while in other sections he excerpts extensively.

He finds the doctrine of the passivity and scatteredness of sensory impressions and the activity of the mind establishing unity and justifying the generality and necessity of certain cognitions prefigured in Cudworth, Clarke, Wollaston, and Price. He judges Cudworth as particularly perceptive in the opposition of understanding and reason, more precisely: in the exposition of the unreliability of experience and the reality and infallibility of the knowledge of reason independent of

---

[13] "Die allgemeinsten, oder letzen Resultate der vornehmsten Lehrsätze der kritischen Philosophie sind diese: unsere Sinne liefern uns weiter nichts, als zerstreute, oder abgerissene, und verworrene Eindrücke von Dingen, deren wahre Beschaffenheit uns gänzlich unbekannt ist. Unser Geist ist es allein, der die zerstreuten sinnlichen Eindrücke sammelt, und das Mannichfaltige derselben zu einer gewissen Einheit verbindet. Er thut dieses nach Gesetzen, die demselben anerschaffen und wesentlich sind. Die Erkenntniß der ursprünglichen Formen des Geistes mache die einzige nothwendige und allgemein gültige Erkenntniß des Menschen aus, dergleichen wir von der Erfahrung nicht erwarten dürfen."

all experience (precisely the conception of the Cambridge Platonists), and he apparently sees in it the prototype of Kant's philosophy. Twenty pages of excerpts from Cudworth's *Treatise Concerning Eternal and Immutable Morality* (1731) are presented as evidence (Meiners 1800–1801, vol. 2, 48–68).[14] A second set of excerpts, almost as long, concerns Richard Price (Meiners 1800–1801, vol. 2, 69–81); it, too, revolves mainly around the relationship between the activity of the intellect and the passivity of sensibility. Further excerpts contain passages from Leibniz's *Nouveaux Essais*, which – against Locke's denial of innate ideas – propagate the existence of intellectual ideas in us, which are distinct in contrast to the confused ideas of the senses (similar to Cudworth's view).

It seems that Meiners has over-extended himself somewhat with this topic. The extraordinarily extensive evidence from Cambridge Platonism and Leibniz is apparently intended to show that earlier philosophers also taught the existence of pure intellectual knowledge, and apparently Meiners believes that Kant merely translated this fact into the new terminology of synthetic judgments a priori. But it was not Kant's goal to establish the existence of synthetic judgments a priori but to explain how they are possible. This problem does not occur at all in Meiners's text, and certainly not in Kant's solution to it.

(2) Considerably more tangible because of the clear reference to the Cudworth school are the remarks in the second section. Methodologically, it differs from the first like night and day, since from the outset it works with original Kant passages, comparing these to those of the Cambridge school. Following his usual method of excerpting extensively, Meiners presents the important passages from the *Groundwork of the Metaphysics of Morals* and the *Critique of Practical Reason* (Meiners 1800–1801, vol. 2, 85–114), to then show that their principles are just as unoriginal as those of Kant's theoretical philosophy. He restricts himself to the most important position, namely again to Cambridge Platonism: "I am satisfied if I have shown that what were considered the most peculiar principles of Kant's morality were, several ages ago, doctrines of the Cudworthian school." (Meiners 1800–1801, vol. 2, 114)[15] For the sake of brevity, other authors such as Samuel Clarke or Wollaston are omitted, while Price is used as a controlling authority. The selected passages prove the intellectualist position of this school, which recognizes only reason as the source of good and right, in contrast to moral-sense theorists such as Hutcheson, Shaftesbury, Hume, and Smith.

---

[14] Meiners translates into German from Mosheim's Latin translation, since the English original was not available to him.

[15] "Ich bin zufrieden, wenn ich dargethan habe, daß das, was man als die eigenthümlichsten Principien der Kantischen Moral betrachtete, schon vor mehreren Menschenaltern, Lehren der Cudworthischen Schule waren."

In line with the Platonist position, ethical intuitionism is assumed to refer to the simple ideas of the good and the right – an intuition of ideas or intellectual intuition that is actually absent in Kant, although this does not bother Meiners. Cudworth writes:

> The words right and wrong, or morally good and morally evil denote simple ideas, and these simple ideas must therefore be assigned to a faculty of immediate perception. (Meiners 1800–1801, vol. 2, 116)[16]

The opinion that such an ethical intuition could come from sensibility is rejected. Benevolence is also interpreted in an intellectualist way, with Cudworth recognizing two kinds of benevolence, one instinctive and one rational, which are identical with the morally good. Beginning on p. 142, Meiners summarizes the points of agreement between the two positions, which he sees primarily in the existence of a moral law anchored in the immutable nature of things. He formulates the common content of this law thus:

> The law, namely, to act in such a way that both the acting nature and all other rational natures are satisfied with the action, or can approve of it. (Meiners 1800–1801, vol. 2, 143)[17]

To what extent this is an appropriate interpretation of the categorical imperative and what criteria for concrete actions could be derived from it are questions that cannot be investigated here.

Kant's and Cudworth's views on moral value and moral motivation have much in common. Actions have value insofar as they conform to the moral law. The pleasure of practicing virtue can never be a motivator of action. Meiners sees the main difference in the fact that, according to Kant, there is an unbridgeable gap between aspiration and reality, and that Kant, under the title of a pure practical reason, demands a blind faith in propositions that, from a theoretical standpoint, are mere ideas and incomprehensible (Meiners 1800–1801, vol. 2, 145; cf. below).

Despite these similarities, it cannot be said that Kant only repeats positions of the Cambridge school. Meiners fails to recognize that Kant's ethics, despite its intellectualism and apriorism, cannot be called Platonist. Kant's position is a critical rationalism that recognizes no higher source of knowledge beyond what can be ra-

---

[16] "Die Wörter Recht, und Unrecht, oder moralisch Gutes, und moralisch Böses bezeichnen einfache Ideen, und diese einfachen Ideen müssen daher einem unmittelbaren Wahrnehmungs-Vermögen zugeeignet werden."
[17] "Das Gesetz nämlich, so zu handeln, dass so wohl die handelnde, als alle übrige vernünftige Naturen mit der Handlung zufrieden seyn, ober sie billigen können."

tionally discussed. This is true at least up until the position of the *Groundwork*, which demands a deduction of the highest moral principle. How, on the other hand, the doctrine of the fact of reason in the *Critique of Practical Reason* is to be judged remains open. What is certain is that Kant rejects intellectual intuition as a source of knowledge and that the "fact of reason" does not have the character of a clear intuition but of a dark feeling, which, however, remains theoretically unexplained. Therefore, the appropriateness of Meiners's Kant-Cudworth comparison is certainly still open to debate.

(3) The third section, however, hits the mark systematically. In it, Meiners examines Kant's reasons for assuming pure moral knowledge, and he finds both Kant's conceptualization vacillating and indeterminate and the theses associated with it unfounded or contradictory. He criticizes Kant for explaining neither how he conceives of the status of moral concepts and propositions a priori, nor which and how many concepts there are, nor on what grounds Kant declares them to be a priori. How can Kant call the moral principle a necessary proposition a priori and at the same time assert its unknowability? "Of which axiom or theorem of pure mathematics has anyone ever dared to assert that it is universally valid, and necessary, and yet that the possibility of it is incomprehensible?" (Meiners 1800–1801, vol. 2, 162–163).[18] If the apriority and necessity of the principle are asserted, corresponding evidence should be visible, but Kant asserts the opposite. Meiners's questions are justified, but in part also easy to answer (and Meiners could have done this himself). With respect to the first objections, Kant can be credited with the fact that the *Groundwork* (in the first two parts) is not, in methodological terms, a systematic theory that is proven in logical steps, but an analytic exposition that, starting from common moral consciousness, gradually develops its determinations in order to provide a proof or deduction of its principles only afterwards (in the third part). As far as apriority is concerned, Kant conceives of the concept of duty as strictly normative, i.e., non-empirical, and he attempts to develop the formulas of the categorical imperative purely formally from the generality of the concept of law or from the structure of an unconditional purpose, without assumptions of empirical relevance, although it remains questionable whether and how he succeeds in doing so. The unknowability thesis, however, remains a serious problem.

Ambiguity is also found in the formulas of the categorical imperative. Meiners gives three possible interpretations of the law formula. In the first, one is required

---

[18] "Von welchem Axiom oder Theorem der reinen Mathematik hat man es je zu behaupten gewagt, daß es allgemein gültig, und nothwendig, und doch die Möglichkeit desselben unbegreiflich sey?"

to act as one believes all rational beings would or must act in the same situation in which one finds oneself. This would be wrong according to Meiners, "because what is lawful and obligatory in every case varies according to the diversity of natures, status, sex, age, occupations, situations, and relations to other men as much as what the laws of propriety and prosperity require of every man." (Meiners 1800–1801, vol. 2, 164)[19] The objection is plausible under the given interpretation, but the legal formula does not require acting as all *would* or *must* actually act in a certain situation, but that all *could* act in this way in this situation without a contradiction arising. Therefore, the first interpretation proposed by Meiners is flawed. The second states: "Act as you believe all rational beings would and must act if they were not merely in your situation, but entirely you, entirely what you are" (Meiners 1800–1801, vol. 2, 164).[20] In such an interpretation, the principle is a mere plaything, for: "What good does it do if I identify all other rational beings with myself in thought, or to put them completely in my place, if I do not know how to act in my place?" (Meiners 1800–1801, vol. 2, 165)[21] However, how Meiners comes to this mistaken interpretation remains a mystery because the law formula universalizes over all rational beings not under the counterfactual condition that they would have my qualities, but that they would have their own qualities. Only the third interpretation seems reasonable, namely as an impartiality principle:

> Detach yourself from yourself, put yourself in the place of reasonable, informed, and impartial spectators, and then act every time in such a way that such reasonable, informed, and impartial spectators can be satisfied with your way of acting, or can sympathize with it. (Meiners 1800–1801, vol. 2, 165)[22]

Then, however, it would coincide with Adam Smith's rule or the *Golden Rule*. Smith's rule of the "impartial spectator" (Smith 1751/1979, 3.1, 148–150), which Mei-

---

19 "[...] weil das, was in jedem Fall recht- und pflichtmäßig ist, sich nach der Verschiedenheit der Naturen, des Standes, des Geschlechts, des Alters, der Beschäftigungen, Lagen und Verhältnisse zu andern Menschen eben so sehr abändert, als das, was die Gesetze der Schicklichkeit und des Wohlstandes von jedem Menschen fordern."
20 "Handle so, wie du glaubst, daß alle vernünftige Wesen, wenn sie nicht bloß in deiner Lage, sondern ganz du, ganz das wären, was du bist, handeln würden und müssten."
21 "Was hilft es mir, alle übrige vernünftige Wesen in Gedanken mit mir zu identificiren, oder ganz in meinen Platz zu versetzen, wenn ich nicht weiß, wie ich auf meinem Platze handeln soll?."
22 "Reisse dich von dir selbst los, versetze dich in die Stelle vernünftiger, unterrichteter, und unparteyischer Zuschauer, und handle dann jedesmahl so, daß solche vernünftige, unterrichtete, und unparteyische Zuschauer mit deiner Art zu handeln zufrieden seyn, oder damit sympathisiren können."

ners apparently uses as a template, provides an abstraction from personal interests and thus results in a debatable principle of fairness, but it lacks the aspect of generalization, i.e. the generally conceived practice, which first generates the inconsistency of impermissible maxims (e.g., the institution of the promise, which disappears if no one keeps it), which, however, also leads to well-known problems of application. The fact that Kant himself distinguished the *Golden Rule* from the categorical imperative and criticized it as insufficient is not considered.[23] Meiners has seen the problems of interpretation and application of the legal formula, but his discussion only scratches the surface of the actual problems; these kinds of objections are self-made.

Meiners finds the principle (already objected to in the *Outline*) underlying the formula of the ends of the categorical imperative no less ambiguous: "*a rational nature exists as an end in itself*" (*GM*, AA 4: 429). If it is the highest end, how can it (also) be used as a means? Rather, it should never be used as a means (Meiners 1800–1801, vol. 2, 166). One may ask how Meiners does justice to the fact that in social intercourse; for example, in services, we actually use people as means although we recognize their existence as an end unto itself. Meiners also finds it unclear whether Kant is talking about the whole of rational nature; that is, the whole notion of all rational beings, or about each individual (Meiners 1800–1801, vol. 2, 166). If Kant were speaking about the purpose of the human species, one could demand that some sacrifice themselves for others, and then the formula of ends [*Zweckformel*], which demands that humanity be treated in every person as an end, would be meaningless. Meiners could very easily draw the consequence here that for this very reason the final end is not to be thought as a generic end, but as a final end in each person – again a difficulty that is self-imposed.

Concerning the formula of general legislation, Meiners only remarks that it is not understandable how such a weak and limited creature as man could presume that his will is general law for all rational beings, including even God (*GM*, AA 4: 434). What man can do, he can do only in individual conditions, which are very different from those of other men. How can such a demand be made a priori as a necessary proposition? (Meiners 1800–1801, vol. 2, 167)

Kant's concept of a pure practical reason appears new and idiosyncratic. Meiners's main reproach here is that the explanation of this novel concept is inade-

---

[23] *GM*, AA 4: 430: "Let it not be thought that the trivial quod tibi non vis fieri etc. can serve as the benchmark or principle here. For it is, though with various limitations, just derived from the latter; it can be no universal law, for it does not contain the ground of duties to oneself, not of duties to love others (for many a man would gladly agree that others should not benefit him if only he might be exempt from showing them beneficence), finally not of owed duties to one another; for the criminal would argue on this ground against the judges who punish him, and so on."

quate and – in part –inconsistent. On the one hand, Kant equates reason with the will,[24] on the other, he distinguishes them from each other.[25] On the one hand, Kant finds it incomprehensible that pure reason could be practical,[26] on the other, he believes he can demonstrate this "from the 'common use of reason.'"[27] This indeterminacy could still be excused with reference to the *Groundwork*, but not in the *Critique of Practical Reason*, which explicitly has the investigation of this capacity as its central task: "To write a whole book about a hitherto undiscovered power of the human soul, and in this book neither to determine what this power is, nor why it is!" (Meiners 1800–1801, vol. 2, 174)[28]

For a more detailed analysis, Meiners takes up the passages on the primacy of practical reason over theoretical reason. He finds several questions unanswered: What is reason, especially: what is pure practical reason, or why is it practical? How can theoretical and practical reason be one and the same reason and yet subordinate to each other under different names? How can the one know nothing of the other, and how can the other impose its propositions? Can principles of pure practical reason really exist and what do they consist in? It must be said, however, that Meiners plays a bit deaf at times; with a little analytical or interpretive effort, much could be clarified. In fact, Kant says at this very place that reason is the faculty of principles and has a speculative and a practical use. Kant formulated the highest principle in § 7 of the *Critique of Practical Reason* and there also explained – or at least asserted – reality on the basis of the fact of moral consciousness. One gets the impression that Meiners is mainly concerned with looking through passages for actual or supposed contradictions and searching for missing definitions or justifications. Since he lines up passages from writings spanning 15 years (from the first *Critique* to the *Metaphysics of Morals*), it is easy for him to find what he is looking for. After all, in doing so he reveals factual inconsistencies—true or apparent, synchronic or diachronic—that have long been the subject of Kant scholarship.

---

24 *GM*, AA 4: 448: "Reason [...] must consequently, as practical reason, or as the will of a rational being, by herself be viewed as free."
25 *GM*, AA 4: 431: "from this now follows the third practical principle of the will, as the supreme condition of its harmony with the universal practical reason."
26 *GM*, AA 4: 461: "But any human reason is entirely unable to explain *how pure reason can be practical.*"
27 Cf. *CPrR*, AA 5: 91: "But that pure reason [...] is practical of itself alone: this one had to be able to show from the *most common practical use of reason.*"
28 "Ein ganzes Buch über eine bisher unentdeckte Kraft der menschlichen Seele zu schreiben, und in diesem Buche weder zu bestimmen, was diese Kraft, noch warum sie sey!"

Why did Kant distinguish so strongly between theoretical and practical reason? Meiners finds an explanation in the fact that the doctrine of the antinomies of the *Critique of Pure Reason* presents speculative reason as antinomian, dialectical, misleading, apparent, and that practical reason should be separated from it as much as possible. Moral law must be simple and unambiguous, or, as Meiners puts it, reason must be given a "brighter and friendlier mask" than the "black and fearful theoretical" one. Accordingly, the primacy of practical reason over theoretical reason is given the form of a figurative battlefield of the two Reasons, or as a struggle between the good and the evil principle – an unnecessary dramatization and allegorization with the aim of caricaturing the debate.

Meiners particularly disapproves of the fact that Kant did not assume, in fact explicitly denied, any natural relationship of reason to human happiness: If happiness were the purpose of nature, "then she would have made very bad arrangements for this in appointing the creature's Reason as the accomplisher of this purpose" (*GM*, AA 4: 395). Meiners himself follows concepts of ancient eudaemonist ethics by assuming, in contrast to Kant, rather a harmony of the guidance of reason and happiness. He thus follows the optimistic trend of Enlightenment philosophy, which Kant opposes – not only in his discussion of the concept of happiness, but also in his doctrine of radical evil and in his overall more pessimistic, less harmonious anthropology. Meiners disagrees: Kant's views sprang from a "morose whim" [*grämliche Laune*]; (Meiners 1800–1801, vol. 2, 186). Meiners's personification of reason delivers an eight-page accusation, which states, for example:

> All rightly famous experts on mankind and historians have proved from the history of all centuries and peoples that from time immemorial man has become all the more man, i.e., the more perfect and happy, the more he has exercised his noblest powers of reason and understanding. That true enlightenment has not only promoted virtue and happiness in entire peoples, and reduced vice and misery, it has also made individuals more content with their fate, more moderate in fortune, more patient and steadfast in misfortune; that, finally, it is not education, but miseducation, or the lack of education of reason and understanding, that has spread or increased moral corruption and misery. (Meiners 1800–1801, vol. 2, 191)[29]

---

[29] "Alle mit Recht berühmte Menschenkenner, und Geschichtforscher bewiesen aus der Geschichte aller Jahrhunderte, und Völker, daß der Mensch von jeher um desto mehr Mensch d. i. um desto vollkommner, und glücklicher wurde, je mehr er seine edelsten Kräfte, die Vernunft, und den Verstand übte: daß wahre Aufklärung nicht nur in ganzen Völkern Tugend und Glück befördert, Laster und Elend vermindert, sondern auch einzelne Menschen zufriedener mit ihrem Schicksale, mäßiger im Glück, geduldiger und standhafter im Unglück gemacht: daß endlich nicht die Bildung, sondern die Mißbildung, oder der Mangel von Bildung der Vernunft und des Verstandes Sittenverderbniß und Elend verbreitet, oder vermehrt haben."

In Meiners's rhetorical enthusiasm, his arguments sometimes overshoot the mark. Kant does not consider reason fundamentally incapable of governing the will, as Meiners suggests in the course of the speech (Meiners 1800–1801, vol. 2, 188).

(4) In the fourth section, Meiners examines Kant's views on the will and freedom of man. As a textual basis, no fewer than 30 passages from *Critique of Pure Reason* A 802 f., *Groundwork* I, and *Critique of Practical Reason* (19 printed pages) are quoted before he discusses them critically. Meiners asks,

1. whether these passages, and the propositions contained therein, follow one another in their natural order,
2. whether they agree with each other,
3. whether and to what extent they are really new, or only seem to be new, true or false, or at least harmonizing with the ways of thinking of the greatest sages of old and new times, or deviating from them. (Meiners 1800–1801, vol. 2, 197; numbering added)[30]

Regarding 1: according to Meiners, Kant should have first defined the concept of the will and the concept of the good – he obviously demands a scholastic presentation according to the synthetic method, while Kant, on the contrary, assures that the procedure in parts 1 and 2 of the *Groundwork* is analytical.

Regarding 2: It remains correct that Kant's different will-theoretical explanations – about will, brute and free choice [*Willkür*], lower and upper desire, practical and transcendental freedom, freedom in positive and negative meaning – are spread over different writings and are not always free of contradictions among each other, as the extensive research on these topics shows (e. g., the so-called "canon problem" within the first *Critique*; cf. Josifović 2015; Schönecker 2005). Meiners's cited evidence shows these inconsistencies extensively. He simplifies matters, however, in that he lists Kant's descriptions of the will without context and is content to note the differences. He does not bother at all to analyze factual correspondences or differences, but stops at the wording of the formulations and prefers to draw the devastating conclusion,

> no famous worldly-wise man [*Weltweiser*] of old or new times has confused the doctrine of the will and the freedom of man to such a degree, has changed the meanings of the words will, freedom, and free choice [*Willkühr*] so often and so arbitrarily, and has contradicted

---

30 "[1.] ob diese Stellen, und die darin enthaltenen Sätze in ihrer natürlichen Ordnung auf einander folgen, [2.] ob sie mit einander übereinstimmen, [3.] ob und in wie fern sie wirklich neu, oder nur neu scheinend, wahr, oder falsch, oder wenigstens mit den Denkarten der größten Weisen alter und neuer Zeit harmonirend, oder davon abweichend sind."

himself so often and so palpably, as Mr. K. and all this without presenting the slightest new truth or only the slightest new paradox. (Meiners 1800–1801, vol. 2, 225)[31]

Regarding 3: Meiners comes to the conclusion that the most important Kantian positions can be found pre-formed in Cudworth's school. Likewise, the Kant criticism of his contemporaries (Garve etc.) is shaped by the English debate subsequent to Cudworth. Garve merely repeats the objections of Hume and Smith (again, this is supported with numerous and extensive citations). Against the view that pure reason is the exclusive source of concepts of the good, anthropological motivations such as empathy, gratitude, passion, commitment are pointed out as sources of value judgments. In this, Meiners largely follows Hume and Smith. He finds sufficient evidence here that the Kantian doctrine of reason as the sole source of moral value is at least one-dimensional and ignores important aspects of moral anthropology.

The investigation of the doctrine of free will is placed on a broad basis, drawing on ancient sources on the well-known problem of *fatum* (Epicurus, Carneades, Chrysippus, Cicero). In keeping with his empiricist approach, Meiners favors a concept of comparative freedom and rejects Kant's transcendental freedom. (This would not be elucidated without Kant's theory of transcendental idealism either and Meiners is not willing to accommodate Kant.) In modern terms, Meiners takes a compatibilist position. He regards the freedom to choose for rational reasons and to override immediate sensory impulses as an empirical fact that is as certain as sensory perceptions. He considers the problem of reconciling with this the fundamental determination by (internal or external) natural causes to be an artificial aggravation arising from wrong mechanistic models, to which Kant is also subjected. If the latter describes the merely comparative freedom of the will determined by internal natural causes as equivalent to the "freedom of a turnspit" (*CPrR*, AA 5: 97), he ignores the fact that the human will is very different from a turn-spit (a mechanical device) and should not be interpreted according to this mechanistic model. The fact that there are no causeless events in the human brain does not mean that we are in fact wind-up dolls or resemble them; rather, we are and remain living beings who have the experience of choosing between alternative actions. Meiners's critique of the use of misleading models, similes, and thought experiments is original and consistent with considerations of contemporary philosophy (see, e.g., Dennett 2015). Indeed, it is permissible to ask whether

---

31 "[…] daß kein berühmter Weltweiser der alten, oder neuen Zeit die Lehre von dem Willen, und der Freyheit des Menschen in einem solchen Grade verwirrt, die Bedeutungen der Wörter, Wille, Freyheit, und Willkühr so oft und so eigenmächtig verändert, und sich selbst so oft und so handgreiflich widersprochen hat, als Herr K. und alles dieses, ohne die geringste neue Wahrheit, oder nur das geringste neue Paradoxon vorzubringen."

Kant's theory of freedom is tied to a causal theory placed in a mechanistic worldview.

(5) In the fifth chapter, Meiners discusses the affective components of respect [*Achtung*], self-love, selfishness, and self-conceit [*Eigendünkel*]. Kant's concept of respect is examined in its contexts, and there, too, Meiners notes an ambiguous, inconsistent usage that deviates from ordinary usage. In particular, he criticizes that, according to Kant's own statement, feeling belongs to sensibility, but the feeling of respect is a presentation of a value that is detrimental to our self-love. It is an intellectual, only conceivable, not sensibly receptive relation. Kant himself conceded this. He claims that respect is a feeling produced by reason;[32] but in Meiners's opinion, Kant should have cleared up this riddle. Kant's version of the terms self-love, selfishness, and self-interest is also criticized as an arbitrary deviation in the use of language. Meiners counters Kant with his own view, which is developed on the basis of a broad recourse to ancient and more recent sources as well as investigations of the use of language. In discussing self-love, Meiners is motivated by his own systematic psychological interests, and Kant's position is not really considered for the remainder of the section. Meiners primarily examines the difference between self-love and selfishness, which Kant allegedly confused. He argues that there is an innate self-love that is as natural as benevolence and that has nothing to do with selfishness (egoism). He finds the attempts to reduce the disinterested incentives to the self-interested ones (Epicurus, Hobbes) unconvincing and theoretically confused. Instead Meiners recognizes disinterested affects such as benevolence and gratitude as original incentives, and supports his views with extensive quotations, this time from Hume's *Enquiry concerning the Principles of Morals* (Meiners 1800–1801, vol. 2, 284–293).

(6) The sixth and final chapter completes his critique of Kant with various supplementary aspects: enumeration of further paradoxes, reflections on the first principles of morality and on Kant's way of writing, but also on the effects of Kant's philosophy.

The reflections on the first principles of morality turn out to be unexpectedly substantial, since Meiners here betrays much of his own view of an adequate ethical theory. He rejects the entire modern effort to search for a supreme principle of moral theory, preferring the ancient question of man's highest good or ultimate end. In spite of the different answers provided by ancient philosophy as to what the highest good consists in, he at any rate finds the question clear and unambig-

---

[32] Cf. *CPrR*, AA 5: 73: "Consequently, respect for the moral law is a feeling that is produced by an intellectual ground, and this feeling is the only one that we can cognize completely a priori and the necessity of which we can have insight into."

uous, in contrast to the modern question as to the first principles of ethics. For this is where the difficult questions of appropriate formulation and justification and of the derivability of concrete duties arise, including the relation of the principle to the highest good. Meiners holds that – in particular – Kant's strict separation of moral principle and highest good is a fundamental error.

Meiners remarks about Kant's "style of writing" [*Schreibart*] are few, but disparaging. He cites linguistic errors and barbarisms: Kant "often uses one preposition instead of another, or with a different case than the rules of our language prescribe, declines and conjugates incorrectly, and sullies the language with a tangled mass of barbarous words to denote concepts for which equally good, or even better, expressions were available." (Meiners 1800–1801, vol. 2, 318)[33] In lieu of concrete examples of these claims, Meiners offers two particularly repulsive examples of Kant's expansive, overlong sentence periods – true syntactical monstrosities indeed.[34] He has no misgivings about "declar[ing] Mr. Kant, as the author of the aforementioned works, to be the worst writer that Germany has produced among its worldly wise men since the times of Thomasius" (Meiners 1800–1801, vol. 2, 318).[35] It is worth noting – only in passing and without going into details – the enormous contrast with which today's Kant interpreters regard the *Groundwork* as especially clear and readable (cf. Horn/Mieth/Scanaro 2007, 111) or as a text of "almost outstanding clarity and beauty" (Schönecker 2015, 7) – apparently Meiners was used to other literary standards.

More important than these shortcomings, however, are – in Meiners's opinion – the influence on the thinking style and writing style of youthful students, namely the danger of acquiring a "similar incomprehensibility and indeterminacy of terms and expressions," as well as of imitating the apodictic attitude of mind with which Kant discards other philosophies "with proud contempt" and talks about his philosophy as the only possible one (Meiners 1800–1801, vol. 2, 321).

Meiners concurs with the judgment of the Wittenberg theologian and philosopher Franz Volkmar Reinhard (1802). Reinhart cites the indisputable merits of Kant's philosophy – for example, that it reproaches the empiricists for their superficiality and the rationalists for their presumption, as well as the dogmatists for

---

[33] "[...] braucht häufig eine Präposition statt einer anderen, oder mit einem anderen Casu, als die Regeln unserer Sprache vorschreiben, Er decliniert und conjugiert unrichtig, und befleckt die Sprache mit einem Wuste barbarischer Wörter zur Bezeichnung von Begriffen, für welche ebenso gute, oder noch bessere Ausdrücke vorhanden waren."

[34] Both passages are from the *Groundwork*, see AA 4: 388.21–389.04 (20 lines of the AA) and the whole section 443.03–19 (17 lines).

[35] "Herrn Kant, als Urheber der genannten Werke, für den schlechtesten Schriftsteller zu erklären, welchen Deutschland unter seinen Weltweisen seit Thomasii Zeiten hervorgebracht hat."

the uncertainty of their principles and the skeptics for their lack of principles. Reinhart regards a gloomy anthropology torn apart by Kant's dualisms as a deficiency: Man appears here as a being whose powers of cognition are entirely limited to experience, and "a reason which absolutely does not recognize these limits"; which has a radical evil in itself and a moral law about it, which demands unconditional obedience, which rejects every consideration of one's own advantage as unworthy and which man can never fully satisfy. Such a disharmonious nature appears rather as a "composite product of chance, than as the masterpiece of a creating wisdom." About the effects of Kantian philosophy Reinhart writes (Meiners quotes verbatim):

> The spirit of critical philosophy subtracts from experience and destroys the taste for thorough scholarship, for ancient languages, for the studio of history, and for the knowledge necessary for the business of life. It makes claims, and cannot do otherwise than make claims to infallibility. It inculcates in its disciples: The free man may not recognize any other moral law than what he prescribes for himself. Indeed, through his reason, he prescribes laws to nature and to the entire realm of rational beings. Such principles must inevitably produce pride, intolerance, and revolutionary addiction in the empty heads of young people. (Meiners 1800–1801, vol. 2, 323)[36]

Meiners merely adds the psychological theses that Kant's (and to a greater extent Fichte's) philosophy educates its disciples either to romanticism [*Schwärmerei*] or to unbelief. Those who have a warm heart, who are attracted by "splendid words" about a realm of purposes, and tend to disdain experience (one thinks, for example, of Schiller) are educated to romanticism; those who possess a "twisted head organized for empty musings [*Grübeleien*]" and thus become even more twisted and emotionally cold are educated to unbelief (Meiners 1800–1801, vol. 2, 327). With these remarks Meiners returns to his aim mentioned in the prefaces of resisting recent Kantian fads.

---

36 "Der Geist der kritischen Philosophie zieht von der Erfahrung ab, und vernichtet den Geschmack an gründlicher Gelehrsamkeit, an alten Sprachen, an dem Studio der Geschichte, und an den zu den Geschäfften des Lebens nöthigen Kenntnissen. Sie macht Ansprüche, und kann auch nicht anders, als Ansprüche auf Unfehlbarkeit machen. Sie schärft ihren Jüngern ein: der freye, Mensch dürfe kein anderes sittliches Gesetz anerkennen, als was er sich selbst vorschriebe. Ja er schreibe durch seine Vernunft so gar der Natur, und dem ganzen Reiche vernünftiger Wesen Gesetze vor. Solche Grundsätze müssen in den leeren Köpfen von jungen Leuten nothwendig Stolz, Unduldsamkeit, und Revolutionssucht hervorbringen."

4 Conclusion

Meiners's Kant critique has two facets. On the one hand, much of it is justified, both from an internal and external point of view. Meiners reveals internal flaws in the elaboration of the theory and, externally, offers theoretical alternatives available to him through his extensive knowledge of the history of philosophy. On the other hand, in his internal critique of Kant's theory, he is too often lax. He is far too much at home in ancient eudaemonist ethics and in contemporary English and French moral psychology, as well as convinced of his empiricist and popular philosophical approach, to find any pleasure in an a priori "metaphysics of morals" modeled after the rationalist patterns of Wolffianism. Therefore, he makes little effort to thoroughly understand the difficult theoretical structures of transcendental idealism, but is satisfied with a statement of the (supposed) contradictoriness and unnaturalness of Kantian conceptualization and theorizing. His polemical intentions are sometimes detrimental to his own arguments; his interest in discovering theoretical deficiencies sometimes prevents understanding. Moreover, it must be said that Meiners (unlike his friend Feder) lacked philosophical and systematic faculties. His writings consist largely of excerpts that present plenty of material to the audience, but elaborate little from it. The analytical treatment turns out to be relatively paltry compared to the sprawling volume of quotations presented.

Meiners's knowledge of both ancient literature and modern English and French literature, of old and new foreign languages, and of cultural history far exceeds Kant's, who was more of a natural scientist and metaphysician. Meiners is not a master of speculative thought and systematic philosophy. Instead, he read widely, if manically, and thus he possesses a broad, cosmopolitan, experience-saturated view beyond the narrow limits of academic philosophy. He shows that there are good reasons to cultivate quite different views in moral philosophy than Kant's obligatory ethics, which is overstretched by a priori claims of necessity. Kant's ethics has only gradually conquered its dominant position in German philosophy and was quite controversial in the contemporary context. In comparison to the occasional operational blindness of Kant scholarship, which reveres Kant's *Groundwork* as one of the most important texts of modern ethics[37] and cannot get enough scholarly commentary on it (Schönecker/Wood 2002, 7), Meiners offers a distance that is still refreshing today and that for once takes the philosopher from Königsberg off his traditional pedestal and suggests the question whether inveterate Kantians perhaps enjoy an all too one-sided diet.

---

37 According to Allison Kant's *Groundwork* "is widely regarded as the most important work in modern moral philosophy" (Allison 2011, 1).

Abbreviations of Kant's Works

Except for the *Critique of Pure Reason*, Kant's works will be cited using the abbreviations along with the volumes and page number following the "Akademie-Ausgabe" (AA; Kant 1900 ff.). The *Critique of Pure Reason* is cited according to the page numbers in the first edition of 1781 ('A') and/or the second edition of 1787 ('B').

Anth	Anthropology from a Pragmatic Point of View (AA 7: 117–333)
CF	The Conflict of the Faculties (AA 7: 1–116)
CPJ	Critique of the Power of Judgment (AA 5: 165–485)
CPR	Critique of Pure Reason
CPrR	Critique of Practical Reason (AA 5: 1–163)
DDS	Concerning the Ultimate Ground of the Differentiation of Directions in Space (AA 2: 375–383)
DSS	Dreams of a Spirit-Seer Elucidated by Dreams of Metaphysics (AA 2: 317–373)
EEKU	First Introduction to the Critique of the Power of Judgment (AA 20: 193-251)
ETP	Concerning the Employment of Teleological Principles in Philosophy (AA 8: 157–184)
FS	The False Subtlety of the Four Syllogistic Figures Demonstrated by M. Immanuel Kant (AA 2: 47–61)
GM	Groundwork of the Metaphysics of Morals (AA 4: 385–463)
IC	Inquiry Concerning the Distinctness of the Principles of Natural Theology and Morality, Being an Answer to the Question Proposed for Consideration by the Berlin Royal Academy of Sciences for the Year 1763 (AA 2: 275–301)
ID	On the Form and Principles of the Sensible and the Intelligible World (Inaugural Dissertation) (AA 2: 385–419)
IUH	Idea for a Universal History with a Cosmopolitan Aim (AA 8: 15–39)
JL	Jäsche Logic (AA 9: 1–150)
MM	Metaphysics of Morals (AA 6: 205–493)
MNS	Metaphysical Foundations of Natural Science (AA 4: 467–565)
MP	The Employment in Natural Philosophy of Metaphysics combined with Geometry, of which Sample One Contains the Physical Monadology (AA 1: 473–487)
OCS	On the Common Saying: That May Be Correct in Theory, but It Is of No Use in Practice (AA 8: 273–313)
OD	On a Discovery Whereby Any New Critique of Pure Reason Is to Be Made Superfluous by An Older One (AA 8: 185–252)
R	Reflection (and number) (AA 14–19)
ROBS	Remarks in the Observations on the Feeling of the Beautiful and the Sublime (AA 20: 3–192)
Pro	Prolegomena to Any Future Metaphysics That Will Be Able to Come Forward as Science (AA 4: 253–383)
RP	What Real Progress Has Metaphysics Made in Germany Since the Time of Leibniz and Wolff? (AA 20: 253–351)
TPP	Toward Perpetual Peace. A Philosophical Project (AA 8: 343–386)
WOT	What Is Orientation in Thinking? (AA 8: 133–147)

Bibliography

1 Kant's Works

Allison, Henry, and Peter Heath, eds. 2002. *Immanuel Kant: Theoretical Philosophy after 1781.* Cambridge: Cambridge University Press.
Friedman, Michael, trans. and ed. 2004. *Immanuel Kant: Metaphysical Foundations of Natural Science.* Cambridge: Cambridge University Press.
Frierson, Patrick, and Paul Guyer, eds. 2011. *Immanuel Kant: Observations on the Feeling of the Beautiful and Sublime and Other Writings.* Cambridge: Cambridge University Press.
Gregor, Mary, trans. and ed. 1996. *Immanuel Kant: Practical Philosophy.* Cambridge: Cambridge University Press.
Gregor, Mary, trans. and ed. 2015. *Immanuel Kant: Critique of Practical Reason.* Cambridge: Cambridge University Press.
Guyer, Paul, and Allen W. Wood, trans. and eds. 1998. *Immanuel Kant: Critique of Pure Reason.* Cambridge: Cambridge University Press.
Guyer, Paul, ed. 2000. *Immanuel Kant: Critique of the Power of Judgment*, translated by Paul Guyer, and Eric Matthews. Cambridge: Cambridge University Press.
Heath, Peter, and J. B. Schneewind, trans. and eds. 1997. *Immanuel Kant: Lectures on Ethics.* Cambridge: Cambridge University Press.
Horn, Christoph, Corinna Mieth, and Nico Scarano, eds. 2007. *Immanuel Kant: Grundlegung zur Metaphysik der Sitten.* Frankfurt am Main: Suhrkamp.
Irmscher, Hans Dietrich, ed. 1964. *Immanuel Kant. Aus den Vorlesungen der Jahre 1762 bis 1764. Aufgrund der Nachschriften Johann Gottfried Herders.* Köln: Kölner Universitäts-Verlag.
Kant, Immanuel. 1900 ff. *Kants gesammelte Schriften, Akademie Ausgabe.* Berlin: De Gruyter.
Pinder, Tillmann, ed. 1998. "Logik Hechsel." In *Immanuel Kant: Logik-Vorlesung. Unveröffentlichte Nachschriften II*, 269–501. Hamburg: Meiner.
Pluhar, Werner, trans. 1996. *Immanuel Kant. Critique of Pure Reason: Unified Edition.* Indianapolis: Hackett.
Schöndörffer, Otto, ed. 1986. *Immanuel Kant: Briefwechsel*, dritte Auflage. Hamburg: Meiner.
Stark, Werner, ed. 2004. *Vorlesung zur Moralphilosophie.* Berlin, New York: De Gruyter.
Timmermann, Jens, ed. 2011. *Immanuel Kant: Groundwork of the Metaphysics of Morals*, translated by Mary Gregor, and Jens Timmermann. Cambridge: Cambridge University Press.
Walford, David, and Ralf Meerbote, trans. and eds. 1992. *Immanuel Kant. Theoretical Philosophy 1755– 1770.* Cambridge: Cambridge University Press.
Zweig, Arnulf, trans. and ed. 1999. *Immanuel Kant: Correspondence.* Cambridge: Cambridge University Press.

2 Eighteenth-Century Literature

Barruel, Augustin. 1800. *Denkwürdigkeiten zur Geschichte des Jakobinismus. Nach der in London 1797 erschienenen französischen Original-Ausgabe ins Teutsche übersetzt von einer Gesellschaft verschiedener Gelehrter*, vol. 1. Münster, Leipzig: Waldeck.

Basedow, Johann Bernhard. 1764. *Methodischer Unterricht der Jugend in der Religion und Sittenlehre der Vernunft nach dem in der Philatelie angegebenen Plan*. Altona: Iversen.

Baumgarten, Alexander Gottlieb. 1757. *Metaphysica*. Halle: Hemmerde.

Baumgarten, Alexander Gottlieb. 1760. *Initia philosophiae practicae primae*. Halle: Hemmerde.

Baumgarten, Alexander Gottlieb. 1779. *Metaphysica*, seventh edition. Halle: Hemmerde.

Beattie, James. 1770. *An Essay on the Nature and Immutability of Truth, in Opposition to Sophistry and Scepticism*. Edinburgh: W. Creech.

Beattie, James. 1783. *Dissertations. Moral and Critical*. Edinburgh: W. Strahan, T. Cadell, and W. Creech.

Bonnet, Charles. 1755. *Essai de psychologie*. ESTC Number: T153414.

Bonnet, Charles. 1760. *Essai analytique sur les facultés de l'âme*. Copenhague: Philibert.

Bonnot de Condillac, Étienne. 1746/1947. "Essay on the Origin of Human Knowledge." In *Oeuvres philosophiques de Condillac*. Paris: Georges LeRoy.

Bonnot de Condillac, Étienne. 1746. *Essai Sur L'Origine Des Connaissances Humaines*. Amsterdam: Mortier.

Bonnot de Condillac, Étienne. 1754. *Traité des sensations*. Londres, Paris: Bure l'aîné.

Brandes, Ernst. 1787. *Ueber die Weiber*. Leipzig: Weidmanns Erben und Reich.

Crusius, Christian August. 1740. *Dissertatio philosophica de corruptelis intellectus a voluntate pendentibus*. Leipzig: Langenhemius.

Crusius, Christian August. 1744. *Anweisung vernünftig zu leben, darinnen nach Erklärung der Natur des menschlichen Willens die natürlichen Pflichten und allgemeinen Klugheitslehren im richtigen Zusammenhange vorgetragen werden*. Leipzig: Gleditsch (Reprint: *Christian August Crusius, Die philosophischen Hauptwerke*, vol. 1, edited by Giorgio Tonelli. Hildesheim: Olms).

Crusius, Christian August. 1745. *Entwurf der nothwendigen Vernunft-Wahrheiten wiefern sie den zufälligen entgegen gesetzt werden*. Leipzig: Gleditsch (Reprint: *Christian August Crusius, Die philosophischen Hauptwerke*, vol. 2, edited by Giorgio Tonelli. Hildesheim: Olms).

Crusius, Christian August. 1747. *Weg zur Gewißheit und Zuverläßigkeit der menschlichen Erkenntniß*. Leipzig: Gleditsch (Reprint: *Christian August Crusius, Die philosophischen Hauptwerke*, vol. 3, edited by Giorgio Tonelli. Hildesheim: Olms).

Cudworth, Ralph. 1731. *Treatise Concerning Eternal and Immutable Morality*. London: James and John Knapton.

de Guiberts, Jacques-Antoine-Hippolyte. 1790. *De la force publique considerée dans tous ses rapports*. Paris: Gattey.

de Pauw, Cornelius. 1771. *Recherches philosophiques sur les Américains, ou Mémoires intéressants pour servir à l'Histoire de l'Espèce Humaine. Avec une Dissertation sur l'Amérique & les Américains*. London 1771.

Dubos, Jean-Baptiste. 1719. *Reflexions critiques sur la poesie et sur la peinture*, 3 vols. Paris: Mariette.

Eberhard, Johann August. 1786. *Sittenlehre der Vernunft. Zum Gebrauch seiner Vorlesung. Verbesserte Auflage*. Berlin: Nicolai.

Eberhard, Johann August. 1788–1792. *Philosophisches Magazin*, 4 vols. Halle: Gebauer.

Eberhard, Johann August. 1792–1795. *Philosophisches Archiv*, 2 vols. Berlin: Matzdorf.

Euler, Leonhard. 1736. *Mechanica sive motus scientia analytice exposita*, 2 vols. Petropoli: ex typographia Academiae Scientiarum.
Feder, Johann Georg Heinrich. 1769. *Logik und Metaphysik, nebst der philosophischen Geschichte im Grundrisse.* Göttingen, Gotha: Dieterich.
Feder, Johann Georg Heinrich. 1775. *Lehrbuch der praktischen Philosophie*, third edition. Hanau: Leipzig.
Feder, Johann Georg Heinrich. 1779. *Untersuchungen über den menschlichen Willen, dessen Naturtriebe, Veränderlichkeit, Verhältnis zur Tugend und Glückseligkeit und die Grundregeln, die menschlichen Gemüther zu erkennen und zu regieren. Erster Theil.* Göttingen, Lemgo: Meyer.
Feder, Johann Georg Heinrich. 1782. *Untersuchungen über den menschlichen Willen. Zweiter Theil.* Lemgo: Meyer.
Feder, Johann Georg Heinrich. 1785. *Untersuchungen über den menschlichen Willen, dessen Naturtriebe, Verschiedenheiten, Verhältnis zur Tugend und Glückseligkeit und die Grundregeln, die menschlichen Gemüther zu erkennen und zu regieren. Erster Theil. Zweyte verbesserte Auflage.* Göttingen, Lemgo: Meyer.
Feder, Johann Georg Heinrich. 1786a. *Logik und Metaphysik*, sixth edition. Göttingen: Meyer.
Feder, Johann Georg Heinrich. 1786b. *Untersuchungen über den menschlichen Willen. Dritter Theil.* Lemgo: Meyer.
Feder, Johann Georg Heinrich. 1787. *Ueber Raum und Caussalität zur Prüfung der Kantischen Philosophie.* Göttingen: Dieterich.
Feder, Johann Georg Heinrich. 1793. *Untersuchungen über den menschlichen Willen. Vierter Theil.* Lemgo: Meyer.
Feder, Johann Georg Heinrich, and Christoph Meiners, eds. 1788–1791. *Philosophische Bibliothek*, 4 vols. Göttingen: Dieterich.
Ferguson, Adam. 1772. *Grundsätze der Moralphilosophie, übersetzt und mit einigen Kommentaren versehen von Christian Garve.* Leipzig: Dyck.
Fichte, Johann Gottlieb. 1845–1846. *Sämmtliche Werke*, edited by Immanuel Hermann Fichte. Berlin.
Fichte, Johann Gottlieb. 1976–1977. *Gesamtausgabe*, vol. II, 4, edited by R. Lauth, and H. Gliwitzky. Stuttgart Bad Canstatt: Fromman-Holzboog.
Forster, Georg. 1786/1974. "Noch etwas über die Menschenraßen." In *Georg Forsters Werke. Sämtliche Schriften, Tagebücher, Briefe, vol. 8: Kleine Schriften zu Philosophie und Zeitgeschichte*, 130–156. Berlin: Akademie.
Garve, Christian. 1771/72. "Einige Gedanken über das Interessierende." *Neue Bibliothek der schönen Wissenschaften und der freyen Künste* 12 (1): 1–42, and 13 (1): 5–50.
Garve, Christian. 1779. "Betrachtung einiger Verschiedenheiten in den Werken der ältesten und neueren Schriftsteller, besonders der Dichter." In *Christian Garve: Sammlung einiger Abhandlungen*, 116–197. Leipzig: Dyck.
Garve, Christian. 1783. *Philosophische Anmerkungen und Abhandlungen zu Cicero's Büchern von den Pflichten.* Breslau: Korn.
Garve, Christian. 1785a. *Anhang einiger Betrachtungen über Johann Macfarlands Untersuchungen die Armuth betreffend.* Leipzig: Weidmann und Reich.
Garve, Christian. 1785b. *Johann MacFarlands Untersuchungen über die Armuth, die Ursachen derselben und die Mittel ihr abzuhelfen.* Leipzig: Weidmann und Reich.
Garve, Christian. 1787. *Philosophische Anmerkungen und Abhandlungen zu Cicero's Büchern von den Pflichten. Anmerkungen zu dem Ersten Buche. Neue verbesserte und mit einigen Anmerkungen vermehrte Ausgabe.* Breslau: Korn.

Garve, Christian. 1788. *Philosophische Anmerkungen und Abhandlungen zu Cicero's Büchern von den Pflichten. Anmerkungen zu dem Dritten Buche. Neue verbesserte und mit einigen Anmerkungen und einer Abhandlung über die Verbindung der Moral mit der Politik vermehrte Ausgabe.* Breslau: Korn.

Garve, Christian. 1788. *Abhandlung über die Verbindung der Moral mit der Politik.* Breslau: Korn.

Garve, Christian. 1792. "Ueber die Geduld." In *Christian Garve: Versuche über verschiedene Gegenstände aus der Moral, der Literatur und dem gesellschaftlichen Leben. Erster Theil*, 1–116. Breslau: Korn.

Garve, Christian. 1796. "Über den Charakter der Bauern und ihr Verhältnis gegen die Gutsherren und gegen die Regierung." In *Christian Garve: Vermischte Aufsätze, welche einzeln oder in Zeitschriften erschienen sind. Erster Theil*, 1–229. Breslau: Korn.

Garve, Christian. 1798a. *Eigene Betrachtungen über die allgemeinsten Grundsätze der Sittenlehre.* Breslau: Korn.

Garve, Christian. 1798b. *Uebersicht der vornehmsten Principien der Sittenlehre.* Breslau: Korn.

Garve, Christian, and Johann Georg Heinrich Feder. 1782. "Critik der reinen Vernunft. Von Immanuel Kant. 1781." *Zugabe zu den Göttingischen Anzeigen von gelehrten Sachen* (January 19, 1782): 40–48.

Gentz, Friedrich. 1793. *Betrachtungen über die Französische Revolution. Nach dem Englischen des Herrn Burke neu bearbeitet mit einer Einleitung, Anmerkungen, politischen Abhandlungen.* 2 vols. Berlin: Vieweg.

Gerard, Alexander. 1776. *Versuch über das Genie*, translated by Christian Garve. Leipzig: Weidmanns Erben und Reich (original *An Essay on Genius*. London: W. Strahan, T. Cadell, and W. Creech, 1774).

Gerhardt, Carl Immanuel, ed. 1860. *Briefwechsel zwischen Leibniz und Christian Wolff. Aus den Handschriften der Koeniglichen Bibliothek zu Hannover.* Halle: Schmidt.

Goethe, Johann Wolfgang. 1774/1988. "Die Leiden des jungen Werther." In *Johann Wolfgang Goethe: Werke. Hamburger Ausgabe*, edited by Erich Trunz, vol. 6. München: DTV.

Hamann, Johann Georg. 1965. *Briefwechsel*, 5 vols., edited by Arthur Henkel. Frankfurt am Main: Insel.

Hausius, Karl Gottlob, ed. 1793. *Materialien zur Geschichte der critischen Philosophie. In drey Sammlungen. Nebst einer historischen Einleitung zur Geschichte der Kantischen Philosophie.* Leipzig: Breitkopf.

Hume, David. 1739/1978. *A Treatise of Human Nature*, edited by P. H. Nidditch (revision of L. A. Selby-Bigge), second edition. Oxford: Oxford University Press.

Hume, David. 1748/1755. *Philosophische Versuche über die menschliche Erkenntnis. Als dessen vermischter Schriften Zweyter Theil. Nach der zweyten vermehrten Ausgabe aus dem Englischen übersetzt und mit Anmerkungen des Herausgebers begleitet*, edited and translated by Johann Georg Sulzer. Hamburg, Leipzig: Grund & Holle.

Hume, David. 1748/1999. *An Enquiry Concerning Human Understanding*, edited by Tom. L. Beauchamp. Oxford: Oxford University Press.

Hume, David. 1975. *Enquiries Concerning Human Understanding and Concerning the Principles of Morals*, edited by Peter Nidditch. Oxford: Oxford University Press.

Hume, David. 1987. *Essays Moral, Political, and Literary*, edited by Eugene F. Miller. Indianapolis: Liberty Classics.

Irving, Karl Franz von. 1777–1785. *Erfahrungen und Untersuchungen über den Menschen*, 4 vols. Berlin: Verlag der Realschulbuchhandlung.

[Jakob, Ludwig Heinrich]. 1787. "Sendschreiben an Herrn Professor Meiners in Göttingen, über dessen Angriff gegen Kants System der Philosophie." *Neue Litteratur und Völkerkunde* 1: 221–242. Online: http://ds.ub.uni-bielefeld.de/viewer/rest/pdf/mets/2097609_001.xml/LOG_0029/Sendschreiben_an_Herrn_Professor_Meiners_in_Gttingen_ber_dessen_Angriff_gegen_Kants_System_der_Philosophie.pdf (07.03.2023).

Kames, Henry Home, Lord. 1751/2005. *Essays on the Principles of Morality and Natural Religion*, edited by Mary Catherine Moran. Indianapolis: Liberty Fund.

Lambert, Johann Heinrich. 1764. *Neues Organon oder Gedanken über die Erforschung und Bezeichnung des Wahren und dessen Unterscheidung von Irrthum und Schein*. Leipzig: Wendler.

Lambert, Johann Heinrich. 1770. "Gedanken über die Grundlehren des Gleichgewichts und der Bewegung." In *Johann Heinrich Lambert: Beyträge zum Gebrauche der Mathematik und deren Anwendung. Zweyter Theil*, 363–628. Berlin: Verlag des Buchladens der Realschule.

Lambert, Johann Heinrich. 1771. *Anlage zu Architectonic oder Theorie des Einfachen und des Ersten in der philosophischen und mathematischen Erkenntniß*. Riga: Hartknoch.

Lambert, Johann Heinrich. 1782. *Deutscher gelehrter Briefwechsel*, edited by Johann III Bernoulli. Berlin: Bernoulli.

Landau, Albert, ed. 1991. *Rezensionen zur Kantischen Philosophie 1781–1787*. Bebra: Landau.

Lange, Joachim. 1734. *Philosophische Fragen aus der neuen mechanischen Morale*. Halle: Fritsch.

Leclerc de Sept-Chênes, Nicolas-Marie. 1787. *Essai sur la religion des anciens Grecs*. Genève: Barde, Manget, Et Comp.

Leibniz, Gottfried Wilhelm. 1710/1968. *Die Theodizee*. Translated and edited by Arthur Buchenau, second edition. Hamburg: Meiner.

Leibniz, Gottfried Wilhelm. 1765/1985. *Neue Abhandlungen über den menschlichen Verstand*, frz./dt., edited by Hans Heinz Holz. Darmstadt: Wissenschaftliche Buchgesellschaft.

Leibniz, Gottfried Wilhelm. 1765/1996. *New Essays Concerning Human Understanding*, translated and edited by P. Remnant, and J. Bennett. New York: Cambridge University Press.

Leibniz, Gottfried Wilhelm. 1969. *Philosophical Papers and Letters*, translated and edited by L. E. Loemker, second edition. Boston: D. Reidel.

Leroy de Barincourt, Pierre-Paul. 1788. *Principe fondamental du droit des Souverains*. Geneve.

Lichtenberg, Georg Christoph. 1787/1967. "Brief an Georg Forster vom 24. Dez. 1787." In *Georg Christoph Lichtenberg: Schriften und Briefe*, edited by Wolfgang Promies, vol. 4, 722. München: Hanser.

Locke, John. 1690/1975. *Essay Concerning Human Understanding*, edited by P. H. Nidditch. Oxford: Clarendon Press.

Maimon, Salomon. 1792. "Einleitung zur neuen Revision des Magazins zur Erfahrungsseelenkunde." *Gnothi Sauton oder Magazin zur Erfahrungsseelenkunde als ein Lesebuch für Gelehrte und Ungelehrte* 9 (3): 1–28.

Meier, Georg Friedrich, trans. and ed. 1783. *Alexander Gottlieb Baumgarten: Metaphysik*. Halle: Hemmerde.

Meiners, Christoph. 1786. *Grundriß der Seelen-Lehre*. Lemgo: Meyer.

Meiners, Christoph. 1794. "Einige Bemerkungen über den Harz. Geschrieben im Oktober 1791." In *Christoph Meiners: Kleine Länder- und Reisebeschreibung. Zweytes Bändchen*, 7–79. Berlin: Spener.

Meiners, Christoph. 1800–1801. *Allgemeine kritische Geschichte der ältern und neuern Ethik oder Lebens-Wissenschaft*. 2 vols. Göttingen: Dieterich.

Mendelssohn, Moses. 1755/1971. "Über die Empfindungen." In *Moses Mendelssohn: Gesammelte Schriften. Jubiläumsausgabe*, vol. 1, 41–123. Stuttgart-Bad Cannstatt: Frommann-Holzboog.

Mendelssohn, Moses. 1757/1971. "Betrachtungen über die Quellen und die Verbindungen der schönen Künste und Wissenschaften." In *Moses Mendelssohn: Gesammelte Schriften. Jubiläumsausgabe*, vol. 1. Stuttgart-Bad Cannstatt: Frommann-Holzboog.

Mendelssohn, Moses. 1761/1971: "Rhapsodie oder Zusätze zu den Briefen über die Empfindung." In *Moses Mendelssohn: Gesammelte Schriften. Jubiläumsausgabe*, vol. 1, 381–424. Stuttgart-Bad Cannstatt: Frommann-Holzboog.

Mendelssohn, Moses. 1764/1972. "Abhandlung über die Evidenz." In *Moses Mendelssohn: Gesammelte Schriften. Jubiläumsausgabe*, vol. 2, 267–328. Stuttgart-Bad Cannstatt: Frommann-Holzboog.

Mendelssohn, Moses. 1783/1977. "An Christian Garve, April 22, 1783." In *Moses Mendelssohn: Gesammelte Schriften. Jubiläumsausgabe*, vol. 13, 102–103 Stuttgart-Bad Cannstatt: Frommann-Holzboog.

Mendelssohn, Moses. 1785/1973. "Morgenstunden oder Vorlesungen über das Daseyn Gottes." In *Moses Mendelssohn: Gesammelte Schriften. Jubiläumsausgabe*, vol. 3.2. Stuttgart-Bad Cannstatt: Frommann-Holzboog.

Newton, Isaac. 1726/1972. *Philosophiae naturalis principia mathematica*, the third edition with variant readings, edited by Alexandre Koyré, and I. Bernhard Cohen. Cambridge: Cambridge University Press.

Newton, Isaac. 1730/1956. *Opticks or, a treatise of the reflexions, refractions, inflexions and colours of light*, based on the fourth edition. New York: Dover.

Pistorius, Hermann Andreas. 1784. [Review of] "Prolegomena zu einer jeden künftigen Metaphysik." *Allgemeine deutsche Bibliothek* 59 (2): 322–356.

Pistorius, Hermann Andreas. 1786. "Erläuterung von Herrn Prof. Kants Critik der reinen Vernunft." *Allgemeine deutsche Bibliothek* 66 (1): 92–103.

Pistorius, Hermann Andreas. 1788. [Review of] "Grundriss der Seelenlehre." *Allgemeine deutsche Bibliothek* 80 (2): 459–474.

Platner, Ernst. 1772. *Anthropologie für Aerzte und Weltweise*. Leipzig: Dyk (Reprint Hildesheim: Olms 2000).

Platner, Ernst. 1790. *Neue Anthropologie für Aerzte und Weltweise*. Leipzig: Crusius.

Platner, Ernst. 1782. *Philosophische Aphorismen nebst einigen Anleitungen zur philosophischen Geschichte. Anderer Theil*. Leipzig: Schwickert.

Platner, Ernst. 1784. *Philosophische Aphorismen nebst einigen Anleitungen zur philosophischen Geschichte. Erster Theil. Neue durchaus umgearbeitete Ausgabe*. Leipzig: Schwickert.

Platner, Ernst. 1793. *Philosophische Aphorismen nebst einigen Anleitungen zur philosophischen Geschichte. Erster Theil. Ganz neue Ausarbeitung*. Leipzig: Schwickert.

Rabaut Saint-Étienne, Jean-Paul. 1787. *Lettres à Monsieur Bailly sur l'histoire primitive de la Gréce*. Paris: de Bure l'aîné.

Reimarus, Hermann Samuel. 1756. *Die Vernunftlehre, als Anweisung zum richtigen Gebrauche der Vernunft in der Erkenntniß der Wahrheit, aus zwoen ganz natürlichen Regeln der Einstimmung und des Wiederspruchs hergeleitet*. Hamburg: Bohn.

Reinhold, Karl Leonhard. 1789. *Versuch einer neuen Theorie des menschlichen Vorstellungsvermögens*. Prag, Jena: C. Widtmann, and J.M. Mauke.

Reinhold, Karl Leonhard. 1791. *Ueber das Fundament des philosophischen Wissens*. Jena: Mauke.

Riesbeck, Johann Kaspar. 1784/2013. *Briefe eines reisenden Franzosen über Deutschland*, edited by Heiner Boehncke, and Hans Sarkowicz. Berlin: Die Andere Bibliothek.

Rousseau, Jean-Jacques. 1750/1997. "Discours sur l'Origine et le Fondement de l'Inégalité entre les Hommes." In *Jean-Jacques Rousseau: The Discourses and other Political Writings*, translated and edited by Victor Gourevitch, 113–239. Cambridge: Cambridge University Press.

Rüdiger, Andreas. 1727. *Herrn Christian Wolffens Meinung von dem Wesen der Seele und eines Geistes überhaupt, und D. Andreas Ruedigers Gegen-Meinung*. Leipzig: Heins.

Saint-Pierre, Jacques Henri Bernardin de. 1788. *Études de la nature*. Paris: Didot & Mequignon.

Schelling, Friedrich Wilhelm Joseph. 1795/1973. "Schelling an Hegel, Brief vom 6. Januar 1795." In *Schelling: Briefe und Dokumente*, edited by Horst Fuhrmans, vol. 2, 57. Bonn: Bouvier.

Schelling, Friedrich Wilhelm Joseph von. 1856–1861. *Sämmtliche Werke*, edited by Carl Friedrich August Schelling. Stuttgart, Augsburg: Cotta.

Schiller, Friedrich. 1793/1993. "Über Anmut und Würde." In *Friedrich Schiller: Sämtliche Werke*, edited by Gerhard Fricke, and Herbert G. Göpfert, ninth edition, vol. 5. München: Hanser.

Schiller, Friedrich. 1795/1993. "Über die ästhetische Erziehung des Menschen in einer Reihe von Briefen." In *Friedrich Schiller: Sämtliche Werke*, edited by Gerhard Fricke, and Herbert G. Göpfert, ninth edition, vol. 5, 570–669. München: Hanser.

Schleiermacher, Friedrich. 1800. "Garves letzte von ihm selbst herausgegebene Schriften." *Athenaeum*, 3 (1): 129–139.

Schmid, Carl Christian Erhard. 1788. *Critik der reinen Vernunft im Grundrisse*. Jena: Cröker.

Schmid, Carl Christian Erhard. 1791. *Empirische Psychologie*. Jena: Cröker.

Schmid, Carl Christian Erhard. 1795. *Wörterbuch zum leichtern Gebrauch der kantischen Schriften nebst einer Abhandlung*. Jena: Cröker.

Schmid, Carl Christian Erhard. 1798. *Physiologie, philosophisch bearbeitet. Erster Band*. Jena: Akademische Buchhandlung.

Schmid, Carl Christian Erhard. 1799. *Grundriß der Metaphysik*. Altenburg: Seidler.

Schulze, Gottlob Ernst. 1792. *Aenesidemus oder über die Fundamente der von dem Herrn Prof. Reinhold in Jena gelieferten Elementar-Philosophie*. Helmstedt.

Search, Eduard. 1771–1772. *Das Licht der Natur*, trans. by Johann Christian Polykarp Erxleben. Göttingen, Gotha: Dieterich.

Selle, Christian Gottlieb. 1788. *Grundsätze der reinen Philosophie*. Berlin: Himburg.

Smith, Adam. 1759/1979. *The Theory of Moral Sentiments*, edited by David Daiches Raphael, and Alexander Lyon Macfie. Oxford: Oxford University Press.

Sulzer, Johann Georg. 1762. *Theorie der angenehmen und unangenehmen Empfindungen*. Berlin: Nicolai.

Sulzer, Johann Georg. 1773. *Vermischte philosophische Schriften. Aus den Jahrbüchern der Akademie der Wissenschaften zu Berlin gesammelt*. Leipzig: Weidmanns Erben und Reich.

Sulzer, Johann Georg. 1773/81. "Versuch über die Glückseligkeit verständiger Wesen." In *Johann Georg Sulzer: Vermischte philosophische Schriften. Aus den Jahrbüchern der Akademie der Wissenschaften zu Berlin gesammelt*, 2 vols. Leipzig: Weidmanns Erben und Reich.

Sulzer, Johann Georg. 1792–1799. *Allgemeine Theorie der schönen Künste in einzelnen, nach alphabetischer Ordnung der Kunstwörter aufeinanderfolgenden, Artikeln abgehandelt. Neue vermehrte zweyte Auflage*, 4 vols. Leipzig: Weidmann.

Tennemann, Wilhelm Gottlieb. 1798–1819. *Geschichte der Philosophie*. 11 vols. Leipzig: Barth.

Tetens, Johann Nicolaus. 1777. *Philosophische Versuche über die Menschliche Natur und ihre Entwicklung*. Leipzig, New York: Weidmanns Erben und Reich (Reprint Hildesheim: Olms, 1979).

Tiedemann, Dietrich. 1785. "Ueber die Natur der Metaphysik; zur Prüfung von Hrn. Professor Kants Grundsätzen." *Hessische Beyträge zur Gelehrsamkeit und Kunst* 1: 113–130, 233–248, 464–474.

Tittel, Gottlob August. 1786. *Ueber Herrn Kant's Moralreform*. Frankfurt, Leipzig: Pfähler.
Werdermann, J.G.K. 1794. "Feder und Kant. Versuch zur Aufhellung einiger streitigen Punkte in den Gründen der Moralphilosophie." *Berlinische Monatschrift* 1: 309–338.
Wezel, Johann Karl. 1784–1785. *Versuch über die Kenntniß des Menschen*, 2 vols. Leipzig: Dyk.
Wolff, Christian. 1733. *Vernünfftige Gedancken von der Menschen Thun und Lassen*, fourth edition. Frankfurt, Leipzig 1733 (Reprint: Christian Wolff, *Gesammelte Werke*, I.4, Hildesheim: Olms).
Wolff, Christian. 1736. *Philosophia prima, sive Ontologia, methodo scientifica pertractata, qua omnis cognitionis humanae principia continentur*. Frankfurt, Leipzig: Renger (Reprint: Christian Wolff, *Gesammelte Werke*, II.3, edited by J. École, Hildesheim: Olms).
Wolff, Christian. 1738a. *Psychologia empirica, methodo scientifica pertractata*. Frankfurt, Leipzig: Renger (Reprint: Christian Wolff, *Gesammelte Werke*, II.5, edited by J. École, Hildesheim: Olms).
Wolff, Christian. 1738b. *Philosophia practica universalis methodo scientifica pertractata*. Frankfurt, Leipzig: Renger 1738 (Reprint: Christian Wolff, *Gesammelte Werke*, II.10–11, edited by W. Lenders, Hildesheim: Olms).
Wolff, Christian. 1740a. *Psychologia rationalis*. Frankfurt, Leipzig: Renger (Reprint: Christian Wolff, *Gesammelte Werke*, II.6, edited by J. École, Hildesheim: Olms).
Wolff, Christian. 1740b. *Der Vernünfftigen Gedancken von Gott, der Welt und der Seele des Menschen, auch allen Dingen überhaupt, anderer Theil, bestehend in ausführlichen Anmerckungen*. Frankfurt am Main: Andreä und Hort.
Wolff, Christian. 1751. *Vernünftige Gedancken von Gott, der Welt und der Seele des Menschen, auch allen Dingen überhaupt*, eleventh edition, Halle: Renger (Reprint: Christian Wolff, *Gesammelte Werke*, I.2, edited by Charles A. Corr, Hildesheim: Olms).
Wolff, Christian. 1754. *Grundsätze des Natur- und Völckerrechts*. Halle: Renger (Reprint: Christian Wolff, *Gesammelte Werke*, I.19, edited by Marcel Thomann, Hildesheim: Olms).
Wolff, Christian. 1996. *Discursus praeliminaris*, edited by Günter Gawlick, and Lothar Kreimendahl. Stuttgart-Bad Cannstatt: Frommann-Holzboog.

3 Secondary Literature

Albrecht, Michael. 2014. "Johann Georg Heinrich Feder." In *Die Philosophie des 18. Jahrhunderts, vol. 5.1: Heiliges Römisches Reich Deutscher Nation. Schweiz. Nord- und Osteuropa*, edited by Helmut Holzhey, and Vilem Mudroch, 249–255. Basel: Schwabe.
Allais, Lucy. 2015. *Kant's Idealism and his Realism*. Oxford: Oxford University Press.
Allison, Henry E. 1983. *Kant's Transcendental Idealism: An Interpretation and Defense*. New Haven: Yale University Press.
Allison, Henry E. 2011. *Kant's Groundwork for the Metaphysics of Morals. A Commentary*. Oxford: Oxford University Press.
Altmann, Alexander. 1971. 1969. *Mendelssohns Frühschriften zur Metaphysik*. Tübingen: Mohr Siebeck.
Altmann, Alexander. 1971. "Einleitung." In *Moses Mendelssohn: Gesammelte Schriften. Jubiläumsausgabe*, vol. 1. Stuttgart-Bad Cannstatt: Frommann-Holzboog.
Anderson, R. Lanier. 2015. *The Poverty of Conceptual Truth: Kant's Analytic/Synthetic Distinction and the Limits of Metaphysics*. Oxford: Oxford University Press.

Arndt, Hans Werner. 1989. "Erste Angriffe der Thomasianer auf Wolff." In *Christian Thomasius 1655–1728. Interpretationen zu Werk und Wirkung*, edited by Werner Schneiders, 257–286. Hamburg: Meiner.

Aschenberg, Reinhold. 1982. *Sprachanalyse und Transzendentalphilosophie*. Stuttgart: Klett-Cotta.

Bachmann-Medick, Doris. 1989. *Die ästhetische Ordnung des Handelns. Moralphilosophie und Ästhetik in der Popularphilosophie des 18. Jahrhunderts*. Stuttgart: Metzler.

Bacin, Stefano. 2018. "Kant and Feder on the Will, Happiness and the Aim of Moral Philosophy." In *Kant and his German Contemporaries. Vol. 1: Logic, Mind, Epistemology, Science and Ethics*, edited by Corey W. Dyck, and Falk Wunderlich, 232–249. Cambridge: Cambridge University Press.

Baeumler, Alfred. 1923. *Das Irrationalitätsproblem in der Ästhetik und Logik des 18. Jahrhunderts*. Halle: Niemeyer.

Baier, Annette C. 2008. "Enquiry concerning the Principles of Morals: Incomparably the Best?" In *A Companion to Hume*, edited by Elizabeth S. Radcliffe, 293–320. Malden, Oxford: Wiley.

Baillie, James. 2000. *Hume on Morality*. London, New York: Routledge.

Barth, Roderich. 2010. "Von Wolffs 'Psychologia empirica' zu Herders 'Psychologie aus Bildwörtern': Beobachtungen zur Umformung des Seelenbegriffs der Aufklärung." In *Über die Seele*, edited by Katja Crone, Robert Schnepf, and Jürgen Stolzenberg, 154–173. Frankfurt am Main: Suhrkamp.

Basso, Paola. 1999. *Filosofia e geometria. Lambert interprete di Euclide*. Firenze: La Nuova Italia.

Batscha, Zwi. 1989. "J. G. H. Feder zwischen Aristokraten und Demokraten." In *Zwi Batscha: "Despotismus von jeder Art reizt zur Widersetzlichkeit." Die Französische Revolution in der deutschen Popularphilosophie*, 57–125. Frankfurt am Main: Suhrkamp.

Baum, Manfred. 2006. "Gefühl, Begehren und Wollen in Kants praktischer Philosophie." *Jahrbuch für Recht und Ethik* 14: 125–141.

Baum, Manfred. 2018. "'Pflicht! Du erhabener, großer Name.' Betrachtungen zu Pflicht und Verbindlichkeit bei Kant." In *Aufklärung, vol. 30: Pflicht und Verbindlichkeit bei Kant. Quellengeschichtliche, systematische und wirkungsgeschichtliche Beiträge*, edited by Gabriel Rivero, 165–188. Hamburg: Meiner.

Baum, Manfred. 2020. "Metaphysik in Kants Moralphilosophie." In *Manfred Baum: Kleine Schriften vol. 2: Arbeiten zu Kants praktischer Philosophie*, edited by Dieter Hüning, 313–332. Berlin, Boston: De Gruyter.

Baumanns, Peter. 1997. *Kants Philosophie der Erkenntnis. Durchgehender Kommentar zu den Hauptkapiteln der "Kritik der reinen Vernunft."* Würzburg: Königshausen & Neumann.

Beck, Lewis White. 1969. *Early German Philosophy: Kant and His Predecessors*. Cambridge, MA: Harvard University Press.

Beiser, Frederick C. 1987. *The Fate of Reason. German Philosophy from Kant to Fichte*. Cambridge (Mass.), London: Harvard University Press.

Berger, Andreas. 1998. "Systemwandel zu einer ‚neuen Elementarphilosophie'? Zur möglichen Rolle von Carl Christian Erhard Schmid in der Entwicklung von Reinholds Elementarphilosophie nach 1791." In *Athenäum. Jahrbuch für Romantik* 8: 137–210.

Bieri, Peter. 2001. *Das Handwerk der Freiheit. Über die Entdeckung des eigenen Willens*. München: Hanser.

Blackwell, Richard J. 1961. "Christian Wolff's Doctrine of the Soul." *Journal of the History of Ideas* 22 (3): 339–354.

Böhr, Christoph. 2003. *Philosophie für die Welt. Die Popularphilosophie der deutschen Spätaufklärung im Zeitalter Kants*. Stuttgart-Bad Cannstatt: Frommann-Holzboog.

Bondeli, Martin. 2014: "Der Kantianismus." In *Die Philosophie des 18. Jahrhunderts, vol. 5.2: Heiliges Römisches Reich Deutscher Nation. Schweiz. Nord- und Osteuropa*, edited by Helmut Holzhey, and Vilem Mudroch, 1075–1082. Basel: Schwabe.

Borchers, Stefan. 2011. *Die Erzeugung des 'ganzen Menschen'. Zur Entstehung von Anthropologie und Ästhetik an der Universität Halle im 18. Jahrhundert*. Berlin, New York: De Gruyter.

Bouterwek, Friedrich. 1805. *Immanuel Kant. Ein Denkmal*. Hamburg: Hoffmann.

Brandhorst, Mario, Andree Hahmann, and Ludwig, Bernd. 2015. "Einleitung." In *Sind wir Bürger zweier Welten? Freiheit und moralische Verantwortung im transzendentalen Idealismus*, edited by Mario Brandhorst, Andree Hahmann, and Bernd Ludwig, 7–34. Hamburg: Meiner.

Brandt. Reinhard. 1989. "Feder und Kant." *Kant-Studien* 80: 249–264.

Brandt, Reinhard. 2007. *Die Bestimmung des Menschen bei Kant*. Hamburg: Meiner.

Buchenau, Stefanie. 2015. *The Founding of Aesthetics in the German Enlightenment. The Art of Invention and the Invention of Art*. Cambridge: Cambridge University Press.

Campo, Mariano. 1953. *La genesi del criticismo kantiano*. Varese: Magenta.

Carboncini, Sonia. 1989. "Die thomasianisch-pietistische Tradition und ihre Fortsetzung durch Christian August Crusius." In *Christian Thomasius 1655–1728. Interpretationen zu Werk und Wirkung*, edited by Werner Schneiders, 287–304. Hamburg: Meiner.

Carboncini-Gavanelli, Sonia. 2001. "Christian August Crusius und die Leibniz-Wolffsche Philosophie." In *Autour de la philosophie wolffienne*, edited by Jean École, 263–278. Hildesheim: Olms.

Carl, Wolfgang. 1989. *Der schweigende Kant: Die Enwürfe zu einer Deduktion der Kategorien*. Göttingen: Vandenhoeck & Ruprecht.

Cassirer, Ernst. 1931. "Kant und das Problem der Metaphysik." *Kant-Studien* 36: 1–26.

Cassirer, Ernst. 1974. *Das Erkenntnisproblem in der Philosophie und Wissenschaft der neueren Zeit*, 4 vols. Darmstadt 1974 (Reprint).

Cassirer, Ernst. 1999. *Das Erkenntnisproblem in der Philosophie und Wissenschaft der neueren Zeit, Zweiter Band*. Gesammelte Werke, vol. 3. Hamburg: Meiner.

Ciafardone, Raffaele. 1983. "Von der Kritik an Wolff zum vorkritischen Kant. Wolff-Kritik bei Rüdiger und Crusius." In *Christian Wolff 1679–1754*, edited by Werner Schneiders, 289–305. Hamburg: Meiner.

Cohen, Hermann. 1971. *Kants Theorie der Erfahrung*. Berlin: Dümmler.

Cramer, Konrad. 1985. *Nicht-reine synthetische Urteile a priori. Ein Problem der Transzendentalphilosophie Immanuel Kants*. Heidelberg: Winter.

Cramer, Konrad, and Günther Patzig. 1994. "Die Philosophie in Göttingen 1734–1987." In *Die Geschichte der Verfassung und der Fachbereiche der Georg-August-Universität zu Göttingen*, edited by Hans-Günther Schlotter, 86–91. Göttingen: Vandenhoeck & Ruprecht. URL: https://www.uni-goettingen.de/de/zur+geschichte+des+philosophischen+seminars/70420.html (06.03.2023).

Dahlstrom, Daniel O., ed. 2018. *Kant and his German Contemporaries. Vol. 2: Aesthetics, History, Politics, and Religion*. Cambridge: Cambridge University Press.

Darwall, Stephen L. 1995. *The British Moralists and the Internal 'Ought': 1640–1740*. Cambridge: Cambridge University Press.

Décultot, Élisabeth. 2006. "Metaphysic que ou physiologie de beau?" *Revue germanique internationale* 4: 93–106.

Dennett, Daniel C. 2015. "Please Don't Feed the Bugbears." In *Daniel C. Dennett: Elbow Room. The Varieties of Free Will Worth Wanting*, New Edition, 1–22. Cambridge (Mass.), London: MIT Press.

DeVleeschauwer, H. J. 1962. *The Development of Kant's Thought*. New York: Thomas Nelson and Sons.

Dörflinger, Bernd, Dieter Hüning, and Günter Kruck, eds. 2017. *Das Verhältnis von Recht und Moral in Kants praktischer Philosophie*. Hildesheim: Olms.
Dyck, Corey W. 2014. *Kant and Rational Psychology*, Oxford: Oxford University Press.
Dyck, Corey W., and Falk Wunderlich, eds. 2018. *Kant and his German Contemporaries. Vol. 1: Logic, Mind, Epistemology, Science and Ethics*, Cambridge: Cambridge University Press.
de Boer, Karin. 2020. *Kant's Reform of Metaphysics. The Critique of Pure Reason Reconsidered*. Cambidge: Cambridge University Press.
de Boer, Karin. 2021. "Kant's Inquiries into a New Touchstone for Metaphysical Truths." In *The Experiential Turn in Eighteenth-Century German Philosophy*, edited by Karin de Boer, and Tinca Prunea-Bretonnet, 274–296. London: Routledge.
de Boer, Karin, and Tinca Prunea-Bretonnet, eds. 2021. *The Experiential Turn in Eighteenth-Century German Philosophy*. London: Routledge.
Ebbinghaus, Julius. 1968. "Kantinterpretation und Kantkritik." In *Julius Ebbinghaus: Gesammelte Aufsätze, Vorträge und Reden*, 1–23. Darmstadt: Wissenschaftliche Buchgesellschaft.
Edwards, Jeffrey. 2018. *Autonomy, Moral Worth, and Right. Kant on Obligatory Ends, Respect of Law, and Original Acquisition*. Berlin, Boston: De Gruyter.
Engfer, Hans-Jürgen. 1982. *Philosophie als Analysis. Studien zur Entwicklung philosophischer Analysiskonzeptionen unter dem Einfluß mathematischer Methodenmodelle im 17. und frühen 18. Jahrhundert*. Stuttgart-Bad Cannstatt: Frommann-Holzboog.
Engfer, Hans-Jürgen. 1988. "Konzeption des Psychischen und der Psychologie zwischen Leibniz und Wolff." In *Wegbereiter der Historischen Psychologie*, edited by Gerd Jüttemann, 23–27. München, Weinheim: Beltz, Psychologie Verlags Union.
Erdmann, Benno. 1878. *Kant's Kriticismus in der ersten und in der zweiten Auflage der Kritik der reinen Vernunft*. Leipzig: Voss.
Evans, Gareth. 1982. *The Varieties of Reference*, edited by John McDowell, Oxford: Clarendon Press.
Fabianelli Faustino. Forthcoming. "Intelligibler Fatalismus und Grundlegung der Philosophie. Zur Auseinandersetzung zwischen Johann Gottlieb Fichte und Carl Christian Erhard Schmid." In *Carl Christian Erhard Schmid (1761–1812): Spätaufklärung im Spannungsfeld zwischen Leibniz und Kant*, edited by Marion Heinz, and Gideon Stiening. Berlin, Boston: De Gruyter.
Feder, Karl August Ludwig, ed. 1825. *J. G. H. Feder's Leben, Natur und Grundsätze. Zur Belehrung und Ermunterung seiner lieben Nachkommen, auch Anderer die Nutzbares daraus anzunehmen geneigt sind*. Leipzig: Schwickert.
Flach, Werner. 1994. *Grundzüge der Erkenntnislehre: Erkenntniskritik. Logik. Methodologie*. Würzburg: Königshausen & Neumann.
Flach, Werner. 1997. *Grundzüge der Ideenlehre: Die Themen der Selbstgestaltung des Menschen und seiner Welt, der Kultur*. Würzburg: Königshausen & Neumann.
Flach, Werner. 2002. *Die Idee der Transzendentalphilosophie: Immanuel Kant*. Würzburg: Königshausen & Neumann.
Förster, Eckart. 2002. "Die Bedeutung von §§ 76, 77 der Kritik der Urteilskraft für die Entwicklung der nachkantischen Philosophie [Teil 1]." *Zeitschrift für philosophische Forschung* 56: 169–190.
Förster, Eckart. 2011. *Die 25 Jahre der Philosophie: eine systematische Rekonstruktion*. Frankfurt am Main: Klostermann.
Frank, Manfred. 1997. *"Unendliche Annäherung." Die Anfänge der philosophischen Frühromantik*. Frankfurt am Main: Suhrkamp.
Frank, Manfred. 2002. *Selbstgefühl*. Frankfurt am Main: Suhrkamp.

Fricke, Christel. 2018. "Die Quadratur des Kreises. Kants Moralphilosophie und ihr crusianisches Erbe." In *Aufklärung, vol. 30: Pflicht und Verbindlichkeit bei Kant. Quellengeschichtliche, systematische und wirkungsgeschichtliche Beiträge*, edited by Gabriel Rivero, 51–72. Hamburg: Meiner.

Friebe, Cord. 2006. "Substanz/Akzidens-Ontologie inkongruenter Gegenstücke." *Kant-Studien* 97: 33–49.

Friedman, Michael. 1992. *Kant and the Exact Sciences*. Cambridge: Harvard University Press.

Friedman, Michael. 2013. *Kant's Construction of Nature*. Cambridge: Cambridge University Press.

Fugate, Courtney David. 2010. "Moral Individuality and Moral Subjectivity in Leibniz, Crusius, and Kant." In *Cultivating Personhood: Kant and Asian Philosophy*, edited by Stephen R. Palmquist, 273–284. Berlin, Boston: De Gruyter.

Fukuda, Kiichiro. 2018. "Feders Vorwurf des Skeptizismus gegen Kant." In *Johann Georg Heinrich Feder (1740–1821): Empirismus und Popularphilosophie zwischen Wolff und Kant*, edited by Hans-Peter Nowitzki, Udo Roth, and Gideon Stiening, 123–138. Berlin, Boston: De Gruyter.

Funke, Gerhard. 1979. *Von der Aktualität Kants*, Bonn: Bouvier.

Garber, Jörn. 2002. "Die Bestimmung des Menschen in der ethnologischen Kulturtheorie." In *Aufklärung, vol. 14: Aufklärung und Anthropologie*, edited by Karl Eibl, Norbert Hinske, Lothar Kreimendahl, and Monika Neugebauer-Wölk, 161–204. Hamburg: Meiner.

Garber, Jörn, and Thoma, Heinz, eds. 2004. *Zwischen Empirisierung und Konstruktionsleistung: Anthropologie im 18. Jahrhundert*. Tübingen: Niemeyer.

Gava, Gabriele, and Pierre Keller. 2015. "Sinnlichkeit." In *Kant-Lexikon*, edited by Marcus Willaschek, Jürgen Stolzenberg, Georg Mohr, and Stefano Bacin, 2113–2117. Berlin, Boston: De Gruyter.

Gawlick, Günter. 1985. "Einleitung." In *Hermann Samuel Reimarus: Die vornehmsten Wahrheiten der natürlichen Religion*, 2 vols., edited by Günter Gawlick, 9–50. Göttingen: Vandenhoeck und Ruprecht.

Gawlick, Günter, and Lothar Kreimendahl, eds. 1987. *Hume in der deutschen Aufklärung. Umrisse einer Rezeptionsgeschichte*. Stuttgart-Bad Cannstatt: Frommann-Holzboog.

Gawlina, Manfred. 1996. *Das Medusenhaupt der Kritik. Die Kontroverse zwischen Immanuel Kant und Johann August Eberhard*. Berlin, New York: De Gruyter.

Glinka, Holger. 2012. *Zur Genese autonomer Moral. Eine Problemgeschichte des Verhältnisses von Naturrecht und Religion in der frühen Neuzeit und in der Aufklärung*. Hamburg: Meiner.

Goldenbaum, Ursula. 2004. "Die öffentliche Debatte in der deutschen Aufklärung 1697–1796. Einleitung." In *Appell an das Publikum. Die öffentliche Debatte in der deutschen Aufklärung 1687–1796*, edited by Ursula Goldenbaum, Part 1, 1–118. Berlin: Akademie.

Graubner, Hans. 1972. *Form und Wesen. Ein Beitrag zur Deutung des Formbegriffs in Kants "Kritik der reinen Vernunft."* Bonn: Bouvier.

Grunert, Frank. 1998. "Die Objektivität des Glücks. Aspekte der Eudämonismusdiskussion in der deutschen Aufklärung." In *Aufklärung als praktische Philosophie*, edited by Frank Grunert, and Friedrich Vollhardt, 351–368. Tübingen: Niemeyer.

Grunert, Frank, Andree Hahmann, and Gideon Stiening. 2021. "Introduction." In *Christian August Crusius (1715–1775). Philosophy between Reason and Revelation*, edited by Frank Grunert, Andree Hahmann, and Gideon Stiening, 1–17. Berlin, Boston: De Gruyter.

Gutiérrez-Xivillé, Ana-Carolina. 2018a. *Kants ethischer Autonomiebegriff*. Berlin, Boston: De Gruyter.

Gutiérrez-Xivillé, Ana-Carolina. 2018b. "Vier Phasen in Kants moralphilosophischen Werdegang." In *Natur und Freiheit. Akten des XII. Internationalen Kant-Kongresses*, edited by Violeta Waibel, Margit Ruffing, and David Wagner, 3177–3185. Berlin, Boston: De Gruyter.

Guyer, Paul. 2016. "Sulzer, Johann Georg (1720–1779)." In *The Bloomsbury Dictionary of Eighteenth-Century German Philosophers*, edited by Heiner F. Klemme, and Manfred Kuehn, 762–766. London: Bloomsbury.

Haag, Johannes. 2007. *Erfahrung und Gegenstand. Das Verhältnis von Sinnlichkeit und Verstand.* Frankfurt am Main: Klostermann.

Habel, Thomas. 2007. *Gelehrte Journale der Aufklärung. Zur Entstehung, Entwicklung und Erschließung deutschsprachiger Rezensionszeitschriften des 18. Jahrhunderts*. Bremen: edition lumière.

Hahmann, Andree. 2009. *Kritische Metaphysik der Substanz. Kant im Widerspruch zu Leibniz*. Berlin, New York: De Gruyter.

Hahmann, Andree. 2018. "Feder über die letzten Gründe der menschlichen Erkenntnis im Raume." In *Johann Georg Heinrich Feder (1740–1821): Empirismus und Popularphilosophie zwischen Wolff und Kant*, edited by Hans-Peter Nowitzki, Udo Roth, and Gideon Stiening, 87–103. Berlin, Boston: De Gruyter.

Hanna, Robert. 2001. *Kant and the Foundations of Analytic Philosophy*. Oxford: Oxford University Press.

Hegel, Georg Wilhelm Friedrich. 1817/1986. "Enzyklopädie der philosophischen Wissenschaften." In *Georg Wilhelm Friedrich Hegel: Werke in 20 Bänden*, edited by Karl Markus Michel, and Eva Moldenhauer, vol. 8. Frankfurt am Main: Suhrkamp.

Hegel, Georg Wilhelm Friedrich. 1836. *Vorlesungen über die Geschichte der Philosophie*, edited by Karl Ludwig Michelet, vol. 3. Berlin: Duncker und Humblot.

Heidegger, Martin. 1976. *Wegmarken*, edited by Friedrich-Wilhelm von Herrmann. Frankfurt am Main: Klostermann.

Heidegger, Martin. 1991. *Kant und das Problem der Metaphysik*, Gesamtausgabe, vol. I.3. Frankfurt am Main: Klostermann 1991.

Heidemann, Dietmar H. 2002. "Anschauung und Begriff. Ein Begründungsversuch des Stämme-Dualismus in Kants Erkenntnistheorie." In *Aufklärungen. Festschrift für Klaus Düsing zum 60. Geburtstag*, edited by Kristina Engelhard, 65–90. Berlin: Duncker & Humblot.

Heidemann, Dietmar H. 2018. "Der Raum ist kein empirischer Begriff. Zu Kants erstem Raumargument." *Con-Textos Kantianos. International Journal of Philosophy* 7: 19–43.

Heimsoeth, Heinz. 1926. *Metaphysik und Kritik bei Chr. A. Crusius. Ein Beitrag zur ontologischen Vorgeschichte der Kritik der reinen Vernunft im 18. Jahrhundert*. Berlin: Deutsche Verlagsgesellschaft für Politik und Geschichte.

Heinz, Marion. 1997. "Herders Metakritik." In *Herder und die Philosophie des deutschen Idealismus*, edited by Marion Heinz, 89–106. Amsterdam, Atlanta: Rodopi.

Henrich, Dieter. 1955. "Über die Einheit der Subjektivität." *Philosophische Rundschau* 3 (1): 28–69.

Henrich, Dieter. 1957. "Kant und Hutcheson." *Kant-Studien* 49: 49–69.

Henrich, Dieter. 1963. "Über Kants früheste Ethik." *Kant-Studien* 54: 404–431.

Heßbrüggen-Walter, Stefan. 2004. *Die Seele und ihre Vermögen: Kants Metaphysik des Mentalen in der "Kritik der reinen Vernunft."* Paderborn: Mentis.

Hiltscher, Reinhard. 1998. *Wahrheit und Reflexion. Eine transzendentalphilosophische Studie zum Wahrheitsbegriff bei Kant, dem frühen Fichte und Hegel*. Bonn: Bouvier.

Hiltscher, Reinhard. 2016. *Einführung in die Philosophie des deutschen Idealismus*. Darmstadt: Wissenschaftliche Buchgesellschaft.

Hinske, Norbert. 1968. "Die historischen Vorlagen der kantischen Transzendentalphilosophie." *Archiv für Begriffsgeschichte* 12: 86–113.

Hinske, Norbert. 1995. "Das erste Auftauchen der Kantischen Philosophie im Lehrangebot der Universität Jena. Aus den Vorlesungsverzeichnissen und -ankündigungen der Jahre 1784–1789."

In *Der Aufbruch in den Kantianismus. Der Frühkantianismus an der Universität Jena von 1785–1800 und seine Vorgeschichte*, edited by Norbert Hinske, Erhard Lange, and Horst Schröpfer, 1–14. Stuttgart-Bad Cannstatt: Frommann-Holzboog.

Hinske, Norbert. 1998. *Zwischen Aufklärung und Vernunftkritik. Studien zum Kantischen Logikcorpus.* Stuttgart-Bad Cannstatt: Frommann-Holzboog.

Hinske, Norbert. 2005. "Kant im Auf und Ab der katholischen Kantrezeption. Zu den Anfängen des katholischen Frühkantianismus und seinen philosophischen Impulsen." In *Kant und der Katholizismus. Stationen einer wechselhaften Geschichte*, edited by Norbert Fischer, 189–205. Freiburg: Herder.

Höffe, Otfried. 2002. "Einführung in die Kritik der praktischen Vernunft." In *Immanuel Kant. Kritik der praktischen Vernunft*, edited by Otfried Höffe, 1–23. Berlin: Akademie.

Höffe, Otfried. 2011. *Kants Kritik der reinen Vernunft: die Grundlegung der modernen Philosophie.* München: C.H. Beck.

Horn, Christoph. 2008. "Kant und die Stoiker." In *Stoizismus in der europäischen Philosophie, Literatur, Kunst und Politik. Eine Kulturgeschichte von der Antike bis zur Moderne*, edited by Barbara Neymeyr, Jochen Schmidt, and Bernhard Zimmermann, vol. 2, 1081–1104. 2 vols. Berlin, New York: De Gruyter.

Hruschka, Joachim. 1991. "The Greatest Happiness Principle and Other Early German Anticipations of Utilitarian Theory." *Utilitas* 3: 165–177.

Hüning, Dieter. 2002. "Gesetz und Verbindlichkeit. Zur Begründung der praktischen Philosophie bei Samuel Pufendorf und Christian Wolff." In *Gedächtnisschrift für Dieter Meurer*, edited by Eva Graul, and Gerhard Wolf, 525–544. Berlin: De Gruyter.

Hüning, Dieter. 2004. "Wolffs Begriff der natürlichen Verbindlichkeit als Bindeglied zwischen empirischer Psychologie und Moralphilosophie." In: *Christian Wolffs Psychologie*, edited by Oliver-Pierre Rudolph, and Jean-François Goubet, 145–169. Tübingen: Niemeyer.

Hüning, Dieter. 2018. "Christian Wolffs Konzeption der Verbindlichkeit. Eine Antizipation der Ethik Kants?" In *Aufklärung, vol. 30: Pflicht und Verbindlichkeit bei Kant. Quellengeschichtliche, systematische und wirkungsgeschichtliche Beiträge*, edited by Gabriel Rivero, 15–34. Hamburg: Meiner.

Hüning, Dieter, Stefan Klingner, and Gideon Stiening, eds. 2017. *Aufklärung, vol. 29: Das Problem der Unsterblichkeit in der Philosophie, den Wissenschaften und den Künsten des 18. Jahrhunderts.* Hamburg: Meiner.

Husserl, Edmund. 1956. *Erste Philosophie (1923–1924). Erster Teil. Kritische Ideengeschichte*, Husserliana vol. 7, edited by Rudolf Boehm. Den Haag: Nijhoff.

Ilbrig, Cornelia. 2007. *Aufklärung im Zeichen eines "glücklichen Skeptizismus." Johann Karl Wezels Werk als Modellfall für literarisierte Skepsis in der späten Aufklärung.* Hannover: Wehrhahn.

Irrlitz, Gert. 2010. *Kant-Handbuch. Leben und Werk*, second edition. Stuttgart, Weimar: Metzler.

John, Matthias. 2001. "Carl Christian Erhard Schmid und die Naturwissenschaften." In *Naturwissenschaften um 1800. Wissenschaftskultur in Jena-Weimar*, edited by Olaf Breidbach, and Paul Ziche, 83–95. Weimar: Böhlaus Nachfolger.

Josifović, Saša. 2015: "Das 'Kanon-Problem' in Kants Kritik der reinen Vernunft." *Kant-Studien* 106: 487–506.

Kang, Ji-Young. 2015. *Die allgemeine Glückseligkeit. Zur systematischen Stellung und Funktion der Glückseligkeit bei Kant.* Berlin, Boston: De Gruyter.

Karampatsou, Marialena. 2023. *Der Streit um das Ding an sich. Systematische Analysen zur Rezeption des kantischen Idealismus 1781–1794.* Berlin, Boston: De Gruyter.

Kempe, Michael. 2004. "Geselligkeit im Widerstreit. Zur Pufendorf-Kontroverse um die socialitas als Grundprinzip des Naturrechts in der Disputationsliteratur in Deutschland um 1800." *Jahrbuch für Recht und Ethik* 12: 57–71.

Kitcher, Patricia. 2011. *Kant's Thinker.* Oxford: Oxford University Press.

Klemme, Heiner F. 2009. "Werde vollkommen! Christian Wolffs Vollkommenheitsethik in systematischer Perspektive." In *Christian Wolff und die Europäische Aufklärung*, edited by Jürgen Stolzenberg, and Oliver-Pierre Rudolph, vol. 3, 163–180. Hildesheim: Olms.

Klemme, Heiner F. 2013. "Kants Erörterung der 'libertas indifferentiae' in der *Metaphysik der Sitten* und ihre philosophische Bedeutung." In *Internationales Jahrbuch des Deutschen Idealismus/International Yearbook of German Idealism vol. 9/2011: Freiheit/Freedom*, edited by Fred Rush, and Jürgen Stolzenberg, 22–50. Berlin: De Gruyter.

Klemme, Heiner F. 2018a. "Der Grund der Verbindlichkeit. Mendelssohn und Kant über Evidenz in der Moralphilosophie (1762/64)." *Kant-Studien* 109: 286–308.

Klemme, Heiner F. 2018b. "Die Bedeutung der 'Schattenphilosophie' für die 'Philosophie der deutschen Schule.' Über Johann Georg Sulzers Auseinandersetzung mit David Hume (1755)." In *Johann Georg Sulzer – Aufklärung im Umbruch*, edited by Elisabeth Décultot, and Philipp Kampa, 92–99. Berlin, Boston: De Gruyter.

Klingner, Stefan. 2006. "Kant über den endlichen Verstand, den intuitiven Verstand und Gott." In *Die Vollendung der Transzendentalphilosophie in Kants Kritik der Urteilskraft*, edited by Reinhard Hiltscher, Stefan Klingner, and David Süß, 163–181. Berlin: Duncker 6 Humblot.

Klingner, Stefan. 2012a. "Schelling über die Torheit des Transzendentalphilosophen." In *Friedrich Wilhelm Joseph Schelling. Neue Wege der Forschung*, edited by Reinhard Hiltscher, and Stefan Klingner, 187–206. Darmstadt: Wissenschaftliche Buchgesellschaft.

Klingner, Stefan. 2012b. *Technische Vernunft. Kants Zweckbegriff und das Problem einer Philosophie der technischen Kultur.* Berlin, Boston: De Gruyter.

Klingner, Stefan. 2015. "Verstand." In *Kant-Lexikon*, edited by Marcus Willaschek, Jürgen Stolzenberg, Georg Mohr, and Stefano Bacin, 2522–2524. Berlin, Boston: De Gruyter.

Klingner, Stefan. 2016. "Kants Begriff einer intellektuellen Anschauung und die rationalistische Rechtfertigung philosophischen Wissens." *Kant-Studien* 107: 617–650.

Knoblauch, Hubert. 2005. *Wissenssoziologie.* Konstanz: UVK-Verl.-Ges.

König, Torsten. 2010. *Naturwissen, Ästhetik und Religion in Bernardin de Saint Pierres Études de la nature.* Frankfurt am Main: Lang.

Kopper, Joachim. 1984. *Die Stellung der "Kritik der reinen Vernunft" in der neueren Philosophie.* Darmstadt: Wissenschaftliche Buchgesellschaft.

Kosenina, Alexander. 1989. *Ernst Platners Anthropologie und Philosophie.* Würzburg: Königshausen & Neumann.

Kreimendahl, Lothar. 1990. *Kant. Der Durchbruch von 1769.* Köln: Dinter.

Kuehn, Manfred. 1987. "Hume in the Göttingische Anzeigen. 1739–1800." *Hume Studies* 1, 46–73.

Kuehn, Manfred. 1987. *Scottish Common Sense in Germany, 1768–1800.* Kingston, Montreal: McGill-Queen's University Press.

Kuehn, Manfred. 1992. "Kant's Critical Philosophy and Its Reception – the First Five Years (1781–1786)." In *Cambridge Companion to Kant and Modern Philosophy*, edited by Paul Guyer, 630–663. Cambridge: Cambridge University Press.

Kuehn, Manfred. 1996. "The German Aufklärung and British Philosophy." In *British Philosophy and the Age of Enlightenment*, edited by Stuart Brown, 309–331. London: Routledge.

Laermann, Klaus. 1985. "Das rasende Gefasel der Gegenaufklärung. Dietmar Kamper als Syndrom." *Merkur* 39: 211–220

Langlois, Luc. 2019. "Der Begriff der Verbindlichkeit bei Baumgarten und sein Einfluss auf Kants Moralphilosophie." In *Aufklärung, vol. 30: Pflicht und Verbindlichkeit bei Kant. Quellengeschichtliche, systematische und wirkungsgeschichtliche Beiträge*, edited by Gabriel Rivero, 35–50. Hamburg: Meiner.

Laywine, Alison. 2010. "Kant and Lambert on the geometrical postulates in the reform of metaphysics." In *Discourse on a new method. Reinvigorating the marriage of history and philosophy of science*, edited by Mary Domski, 113–133. Chicago: Open Court.

Lazzari, Alessandro. 2004. "Zur Genese von Reinholds 'Satz des Bewußtseins.'" In *Philosophie ohne Beynamen. System, Freiheit und Geschichte im Denken Karl Leonhard Reinholds*, edited by Martin Bondeli, and Alessandro Lazzari, 21–38. Basel: Schwabe.

Lazzari, Allesandro, and Bondeli, Martin. 2014. "Kants Gegner." In *Die Philosophie des 18. Jahrhunderts, vol. 5.1: Heiliges Römisches Reich Deutscher Nation. Schweiz. Nord- und Osteuropa*, edited by Helmut Holzhey, and Vilem Mudroch, 1121–1151. Basel: Schwabe.

Levy, Heinrich. 1932. "Heideggers Kantinterpretation. Zu Heideggers Buch 'Kant und das Problem der Metaphysik.'" *Logos* 21: 1–43.

Longo, Mario. 2015. "The Göttingen School and Popularphilosophie." In *Models of the History of Philosophy, vol. 3: The Second Enlightenment and the Kantian Age*, edited by Gregorio Piaia, and Giovanni Santinello, 515–695. Dordrecht: Springer.

Losurdo, Domenico. 1987. *Immanuel Kant. Freiheit, Recht und Revolution*. Köln: Pahl-Rugenstein.

Ludwig, Bernd. 2007. "Kant, Garve, and the Motives of Moral Action." *Journal of Moral Philosophy* 4 (2): 183–193.

Mackie, John Leslie. 1976. *Problems from Locke*. Oxford: Clarendon Press.

Malter, Rudolf, ed. 1990. *Immanuel Kant in Rede und Gespräch*. Hamburg: Meiner.

Marino, Luigi. 1995. *Praeceptores Germaniae. Göttingen 1770–1820*. Göttingen: Vandenhoeck & Ruprecht.

Marti, Hanspeter. 2014. "Vermittlungsinstanzen des aufklärerischen Gedankenguts und seiner Kritik." In *Die Philosophie des 18. Jahrhunderts, vol. 5.1: Heiliges Römisches Reich Deutscher Nation. Schweiz. Nord- und Osteuropa*, edited by Helmut Holzhey, and Vilem Mudroch, 26–39. Basel: Schwabe.

McDowell, John. 1996. *Mind and World*, second edition. Cambridge, Mass.: Harvard University Press.

Melches Gilbert, Carlos. 1994. *Der Einfluss von Christian Garves Übersetzung Ciceros "De officiis" auf Kants "Grundlegung der Metaphysik der Sitten."* Regensburg: Röderer.

Menzer, Paul. 1899. "Der Entwicklungsgang der Kantischen Ethik in den Jahren 1760 bis 1785." *Kant-Studien* 2: 290–322.

Messer, August. 1923. *Kommentar zu Kants Kritik der reinen Vernunft*. Stuttgart: Strecker und Schröder.

Metzger, Johann Daniel. 1786. "Ueber die sogenannten Menschenracen." *Medicinischer Briefwechsel* 2: 41–47.

Meyer, Jürgen Bona. 1870. *Kants Psychologie*. Berlin: Wilhelm Hertz.

Mori, Massimo. 1993. "Glück und Autonomie. Die deutsche Debatte über den Eudämonismus zwischen Aufklärung und Idealismus." *Studia Leibnitiana* 25 (1): 27–42.

Motta, Giuseppe. 2012. "'Das Phantom des Berkleyischen Idealisms.' Su alcuni riferimenti a J. G. H. Feder nella Critica della ragion pura." *Studi Kantiani* 25: 59–69.

Motta, Giuseppe. 2018. "Elemente des Kritizismus in Feders Logik und Metaphysik." In *Johann Georg Heinrich Feder (1740–1821): Empirismus und Popularphilosophie zwischen Wolff und Kant*, edited by Hans-Peter Nowitzki, Udo Roth, and Gideon Stiening, 105–122. Berlin, Boston: De Gruyter.

Nagl, Ludwig. 1981. "Einleitung." In *Zur Kantforschung der Gegenwart*, edited by Peter Heintel, and Ludwig Nagl, 1–22. Darmstadt: Wissenschaftliche Buchgesellschaft.

Natterer, Paul. 2003. *Systematischer Kommentar zur Kritik der reinen Vernunft. Interdisziplinäre Bilanz der Kantforschung seit 1945*. Berlin, New York: De Gruyter.

Norton, David Fate, and Manfred Kuehn. 2006. "The Foundations of Morality." In *The Cambridge History of Eighteenth-Century Philosophy*, edited by Knud Haakonssen, 2 vols., 941–986. Cambridge: Cambridge University Press.

Nowitzki, Hans-Peter. 2007. "Platner und die Wolffsche Philosophietradition." In *Aufklärung, vol. 19: Ernst Platner. Konstellationen der Aufklärung zwischen Philosophie, Medizin und Anthropologie*, eds. Guido Naschert, and Gideon Stiening, 69–104. Hamburg: Meiners.

Nowitzki, Hans-Peter. 2018. "Die Akademisierung der Popularphilosophie. Johann Georg Heinrich Feders Lehrwerke in der universitären Lehre." In *Johann Georg Heinrich Feder (1740–1821): Empirismus und Popularphilosophie zwischen Wolff und Kant*, edited by Hans-Peter Nowitzki, Udo Roth, and Gideon Stiening, 363–386. Berlin, Boston: De Gruyter.

Nowitzki, Hans-Peter, Roth, Udo, and Stiening, Gideon. 2018a. "Zur Einführung: Johann Georg Heinrich Feder (1740–1821)." In *Johann Georg Heinrich Feder (1740–1821): Empirismus und Popularphilosophie zwischen Wolff und Kant*, edited by Hans-Peter Nowitzki, Udo Roth, and Gideon Stiening, 1–18. Berlin, Boston: De Gruyter.

Nowitzki, Hans-Peter, Roth, Udo, and Stiening, Gideon. 2018b. "'Mit dem Menschen hat es die Philosophie zu thun.' J. G. H. Feder – Von einer 'Physik des Herzens' zur praktischen Anthropologie." In *Johann Georg Heinrich Feder: Ausgewählte Schriften*, edited by Hans-Peter Nowitzki, Udo Roth, and Gideon Stiening, IX–XXXIV. Berlin, Boston: De Gruyter.

O'Neill, Onora. 2002. "Autonomy and the Fact of Reason in the Kritik der praktischen Vernunft." In *Immanuel Kant. Kritik der praktischen Vernunft*, edited by Otfried Höffe, 81–98. Berlin: Akademie.

Oberhausen, Martin, and Ricardo Pozzo. 1999. *Vorlesungsverzeichnisse der Universität Königsberg (1720–1804)*. Stuttgart-Bad Cannstatt: Frommann-Holzboog.

Palme, Anton. 1905. *J.G. Sulzers Psychologie und die Anfänge der Dreivermögenslehre*. Berlin: Fussinger.

Pasini, Enrico. 2005. "L'altra faccia dell'uomo della Luna. Leibniz e l'Erfindungskunst." In *La misura dell'uomo. Filosofia, teologia, scienza nel dibattito antropologico in Germania (1760–1915)*, edited by Massimo Mori, and Stefano Poggi, 49–70. Bologna: Il Mulino.

Paton, Herbert James. 1936. *Kant's Metaphysic of Experience. A Commentary on the First Half of the Kritik der reinen Vernunft*, 2 vols. London: Allen & Unwin.

Pauer-Studer, Herlinde. 2007. "Kommentar." In *David Hume: Über Moral*. Frankfurt am Main: Suhrkamp.

Pecere, Paolo. 2009. *La filosofia della natura in Kant*. Bari: Pagina.

Pecere, Paolo. 2015. "The Systematical Role of Kant's Opus postumum. "Exhibition" of Concepts and the Defense of Transcendental Philosophy." *Con-textos Kantianos* 1: 156–77.

Pecere, Paolo. 2016. "Monadology, Materialism and Newtonian Forces: The Turn in Kant's Theory of Matter." *Quaestio* 16: 167–189.

Petrus, Klaus. 1994. "'Beschrieene Dunkelheit' und 'Seichtigkeit.' Historisch-systematische Voraussetzungen der Auseinandersetzung zwischen Kant und Garve im Umfeld der Göttinger Rezension." *Kant-Studien* 85: 280–302.

Pietsch, Lutz-Henning. 2011. *Topik der Kritik. Die Auseinandersetzung um die Kantische Philosophie (1781–1788) und ihre Metaphern.* Berlin, New York: De Gruyter.

Pollok, Konstantin. 2001a. "Einleitung." In *Immanuel Kant: Prolegomena zu einer jeden künftigen Metaphysik, die als Wissenschaft auftreten wird können*, edited by Konstantin Pollok, IX–LXII. Hamburg: Meiner.

Pollok, Konstantin. 2001b. *Kants "Metaphysische Anfangsgründe der Naturwissenschaft." Ein kritischer Kommentar.* Hamburg: Meiner.

Pöschl, Viktor. 1989. *Der Begriff der Würde im antiken Rom und später.* Heidelberg: Winter.

Proß, Wolfgang. 1994. "'Meine einzige Absicht ist, etwas mehr Licht über die Physik der Seele zu verbreiten.' Johann Georg Sulzer (1720–1779)." In *Helvetien und Deutschland. Kulturelle Beziehungen zwischen der Schweiz und Deutschland in der Zeit von 1770 bis 1830*, edited by Hellmut Thomke, Martin Bircher, and Wolfgang Proß, 133–148. Amsterdam: Rodopi.

Prunea-Bretonnet, Tinca. 2015. "La méthode philosophique en question. L'Académie de Berlin et le concours pour l'année 1763." *Philosophiques* 42 (1): 107–130.

Prunea-Bretonnet, Tinca. 2022. "Eclectic Philosophy and 'Academic Spirit.' The Berlin Academy and the Thomasian Legacy." In *The Berlin Academy in the Reign of Frederick the Great: Philosophy and Science Oxford University Studies in the Enlightenment*, edited by Tinca Prunea-Bretonnet, and Peter Anstey 71–101. Liverpool: Liverpool University Press.

Rachold, Jan. 1999. *Die aufklärerische Vernunft im Spannungsfeld zwischen rationalistisch-metaphysischer und politisch-sozialer Deutung. Eine Studie zur Philosophie der deutschen Aufklärung (Wolff, Abbt, Feder, Meiners, Weishaupt).* Frankfurt am Main: Lang.

Reich, Klaus. 2001a. "Kant und die Ethik der Griechen." In *Klaus Reich: Gesammelte Schriften*, edited by Manfred Baum, Udo Rameil, Klaus Reisinger, and Gertrud Scholz, 129–146. Hamburg: Meiner.

Reich, Klaus. 2001b. "Einleitung in Immanuel Kants 'Einzig möglichem Beweisgrund zu einer Demonstration des Daseins Gottes.'" In *Klaus Reich: Gesammelte Schriften*, edited by Manfred Baum, Udo Rameil, Klaus Reisinger, and Gertrud Scholz, 287–305. Hamburg: Meiner.

Reinhard, Franz Volkmar. 1802. *System der christlichen Moral*, fourth edition. Wittenberg: Zimmermann.

Rescher, Nicholas. 2007. *Interpreting Philosophy. The Elements of Philosophical Hermeneutics.* Heusenstamm: Ontos.

Rickert, Heinrich. 1927/29. "Die Erkenntnis der intelligibeln Welt und das Problem der Metaphysik." *Logos* 16: 162–203, and *Logos* 18: 36–82.

Riedel, Manfred. 1989. "Historizismus und Kritizismus – Kants Streit mit G. Forster und J. G. Herder." In *Manfred Riedel: Urteilskraft und Vernunft. Kants ursprüngliche Fragestellung*, 148–170. Frankfurt am Main: Suhrkamp.

Riedel, Wolfgang. 1994. "Erkennen und Empfinden. Anthropologische Achsendrehung und Wende zur Ästhetik bei Johann Georg Sulzer." In *Der ganze Mensch. Anthropologie und Literatur im 18. Jahrhundert. DFG-Symposion 1992*, edited by Hans-Jürgen Schings, 410–439. Stuttgart, Weimar: Metzler.

Riedel, Wolfgang. 2004. "Erster Psychologismus. Umbau des Seelenbegriffs in der deutschen Spätaufklärung." In *Zwischen Empirisierung und Konstruktionsleistung: Anthropologie im 18. Jahrhundert*, edited by Jörn Garber, and Heinz Thoma, 1–17. Tübingen: Niemeyer.

Riehl, Alois. 1879. *Der philosophische Kriticismus und seine Bedeutung für die positive Wissenschaft. Zweiter Band, erster Theil: Die sinnlichen und logischen Grundlagen der Erkenntniss.* Leipzig: Engelmann.

Rischmüller, Marie. 1991. "Einleitung." In *Immanuel Kant: Bemerkungen in den "Beobachtungen über das Gefühl des Schönen und Erhabenen,"* edited by Marie Rischmüller. Hamburg: Meiner.

Rivero, Gabriel. 2014. *Zur Bedeutung des Begriffs Ontologie bei Kant. Eine entwicklungsgeschichtliche Untersuchung.* Berlin, Boston: De Gruyter.

Rivero, Gabriel. 2017. "Nötigung und Abhängigkeit. Zur Bestimmung des Begriffs der Verbindlichkeit bei Kant bis 1775." In *Das Verhältnis von Recht und Ethik in Kants praktischer Philosophie*, edited by Bernd Dörflinger, Dieter Hüning, and Günter Kruck, 45–70. Hildesheim: Olms.

Rivero, Gabriel. 2018. "Von der Abhängigkeit zur Notwendigkeit. Kants Perspektivwechsel in der Auffassung der Verbindlichkeit zwischen 1784 und 1797." In *Aufklärung, vol. 30: Pflicht und Verbindlichkeit bei Kant. Quellengeschichtliche, systematische und wirkungsgeschichtliche Beiträge*, edited by Gabriel Rivero, 217–236. Hamburg: Meiner.

Rosen, Fredrick. 2003. *Classical Utilitarianism from Hume to Mill.* London: Routledge.

Rosen, Michael. 2012. *Dignity: Its History and Meaning.* Cambridge: Harvard University Press.

Röttgers, Kurt. 1984. "J. G. H. Feder – Beitrag zu einer Verhinderungsgeschichte eines deutschen Empirismus." *Kant-Studien* 75: 420–441.

Rumore, Paola. 2007. *L'ordine delle idee. La genesi del concetto di rappresentazione in Kant attraverso le sue fonti wolffiane (1747–1787).* Firenze: La Lettere.

Saner, Hans. 1967. *Widerstreit und Einheit. Wege zu Kants politischem Denken.* München: Piper.

Sassen, Brigitte, ed. 2000. *Kant's Early Critics. The Empiricist Critique of the Theoretical Philosophy.* Cambridge: Cambridge University Press.

Schmitt, Arbogast. 2002. "Synästhesie im Urteil aristotelischer Philosophie." In *Synästhesie*, edited by H. Adler, and U. Zeuch, 109–147. Würzburg: Königshausen & Neumann, 2002.

Schmitz, Hermann. 1989. *Was wollte Kant?* Bonn: Bouvier.

Schmucker, Josef. 1961. *Die Ursprünge der Ethik Kants in seinen vorkritischen Schriften und Reflexionen.* Meisenheim am Glan: Hain.

Schneewind. Jerome B. 1998. *The Invention of Autonomy. A History of Modern Moral Philosophy.* Cambridge: Cambridge University Press.

Schönecker, Dieter, and Allen W. Wood, eds. 2002. *Kants "Grundlegung der Metaphysik der Sitten." Ein einführender Kommentar.* Paderborn: Schöningh.

Schönecker, Dieter. 2005. *Kants Begriff transzendentaler und praktischer Freiheit.* Berlin, New York: De Gruyter.

Schönecker, Dieter, ed. 2015. *Kants Begründung von Freiheit und Moral in Grundlegung III. Neue Interpretationen.* Münster: Mentis.

Schopenhauer, Arthur. 1819. *Die Welt als Wille und Vorstellung: vier Bücher, nebst einem Anhange, der die Kritik der Kantischen Philosophie enthält.* Leipzig: Brockhaus.

Schröer, Christian. 1988. *Naturbegriff und Moralbegründung. Die Grundlegung der Ethik bei Christian Wolff und deren Kritik durch Immanuel Kant.* Stuttgart: Kohlhammer.

Schröpfer, Horst. 1995. "Carl Christian Erhard Schmid – der 'bedeutendste Kantianer' an der Universität Jena im 18. Jahrhundert." In *Der Aufbruch in den Kantianismus. Der Frühkantianismus an der Universität Jena von 1785–1800 und seine Vorgeschichte*, edited by Norbert Hinske, Erhard Lange, and Horst Schröpfer, 37–83. Stuttgart-Bad Cannstatt: Frommann-Holzboog.

Schröpfer, Horst. 2003. *Kants Weg in die Öffentlichkeit. Christian Gottfried Schütz als Wegbereiter der kritischen Philosophie.* Stuttgart-Bad Cannstatt: Frommann-Holzboog.

Schwaiger, Clemens. 1995. *Das Problem des Glücks im Denken Christian Wolffs. Eine quellen-, begriffs- und entwicklungsgeschichtliche Studie zu Schlüsselbegriffen seiner Ethik*, Stuttgart-Bad Cannstatt: Frommann-Holzboog.

Schwaiger, Clemens. 1999. *Kategorische und andere Imperative. Zur Entwicklung von Kants praktischer Philosophie bis 1785.* Stuttgart-Bad Cannstatt: Frommann-Holzboog.

Schwaiger, Clemens. 2000. "Ein 'missing link' auf dem Weg der Ethik von Wolff zu Kant. Zur Quellen- und Wirkungsgeschichte der praktischen Philosophie von Alexander Gottlieb Baumgarten." *Annual Review of Law and Ethics* 8: 247–261.

Schwaiger, Clemens. 2011. *Alexander Gottlieb Baumgarten – Ein intellektuelles Porträt. Studien zur Metaphysik und Ethik von Kants Leitautor.* Stuttgart-Bad Cannstatt: Frommann-Holzboog.

Sensen, Oliver. 2011. *Kant on Human Dignity.* Berlin, New York: De Gruyter.

Springorum, Friedrich. 1929. "Über das Sittliche in der Ästhetik Johann Georg Sulzers." *Archiv für die gesamte Psychologie* 72: 1–42.

Stark, Werner. 1987. "Kant und Kraus. Eine übersehene Quelle zur Königsberger Aufklärung." In *Neue Autographen und Dokumente zu Kants Leben, Schriften und Vorlesungen*, edited by Reinhard Brandt, and Werner Stark, 165–200. Hamburg: Meiner.

Stern, Albert. 1884. *Über die Beziehungen Chr. Garve's zu Kant.* Leipzig: Denicke.

Stiening, Gideon. 2003/4. "'Aufseher seiner Selbst.' Bewußtsein und Selbstgefühl bei Wezel im Ausgang von John Locke." *Wezel-Jahrbuch* 6–7: 81–111.

Stiening, Gideon. 2004. "Ein 'Sistem' für den 'ganzen Menschen.' Die Suche nach einer 'anthropologischen Wende' der Aufklärung und das anthropologische Argument bei Johann Karl Wezel." In *Aufklärung durch Kritik. Festschrift für Manfred Baum zum 65. Geburtstag*, edited by Dieter Hüning, Gideon Stiening, and Ulrich Vogel, 113–139. Berlin: Duncker & Humblot.

Stiening, Gideon. 2009. "'Glücklicher Positivismus'? Michel Foucaults Beitrag zur Begründung der Kulturwissenschaften." http://www.germanistik.ch/publikation.php?id=Gluecklicher_Positivismus (09.04.2023)

Stiening, Gideon. 2012a. "'Ein jedes Ding muß seinen Grund haben?' Eberhards Version des Satzes vom zureichenden Grunde im Kontext der zeitgenössischen Kontroverse um das principium rationis sufficientis." In *Ein Antipode Kants? Johann August Eberhard im Spannungsfeld von spätaufklärerischer Philosophie und Theologie*, edited by Hans-Joachim Kertscher, and Ernst Stöckmann, 7–42. Berlin, Boston: De Gruyter.

Stiening, Gideon. 2012b. "'Es gibt gar keine verschiedenen Arten von Menschen.' Systematizität und historische Semantik am Beispiel der Kant-Forster-Kontroverse zum Begriff der Menschenrasse." In *Klopffechtereien – Missverständnisse – Widersprüche? Methodische und methodologische Perspektiven auf die Kant-Forster-Kontroverse*, edited by Rainer Godel, and Gideon Stiening, 19–53. München: Fink.

Stiening, Gideon. 2012c. "'Meine Begriffe von der menschlichen Natur.' Wielands Epistemologie und Anthropologie in *Was ist Wahrheit?* und in der *Geschichte des Agathon* (1766/67)." *Wieland-Studien* 7: 75–104.

Stiening, Gideon. 2014. "Dieser 'große Künstler von Blendwerken.' Kants Kritik an Herder." In *Philosophie nach Kant. Festschrift für Manfred Baum*, edited by Mario Egger, 473–498. Berlin, Boston: De Gruyter.

Stiening. Gideon. 2016. "Appetitus societatis seu libertas. Zu einem Dogma politischer Anthropologie zwischen Suárez, Grotius und Hobbes." In *Neue Diskurse der Gelehrtenkultur. Ein Handbuch*, edited by Herbert Jaumann, and Gideon Stiening, 389–436. Berlin, Boston: De Gruyter.

Stiening, Gideon. 2020. "'Womit aber hatten es die Kinder des Hauses verschuldet, daß er nur für die Knechte sorgte?' Schillers Auseinandersetzung mit Kants 'Rigorismus.'" *Kant-Studien* 111: 269–284.

Stöckmann, Ernst. 2009. *Anthropologische Ästhetik. Philosophie, Psychologie und ästhetische Theorie der Emotionen im Diskurs der Aufklärung.* Tübingen: Niemeyer.

Stolleis, Michael. 1972. *Staatsräson, Recht und Moral in philosophischen Texten des späten 18. Jahrhunderts.* Meisenheim am Glan: Hain.

Stolzenberg, Jürgen. 2004. "Was ist Freiheit? Jacobis Kritik der Moralphilosophie Kants." In *Friedrich Heinrich Jacobi. Ein Wendepunkt der geistigen Bildung der Zeit*, edited by Walter Jaeschke, and Birgit Sandkaulen, 19–36. Hamburg: Meiner.

Sturm, Thomas. 2009. *Kant und die Wissenschaften vom Menschen.* Paderborn: Mentis.

Tester, Steven. 2016. "Mental powers and the soul in Kant's Subjective Deduction and the Second Paralogism." *Canadian Journal of Philosophy* 46 (3): 426–452.

Thiel, Udo. 1997. "Varieties of Inner Sense: Two Pre-Kantian Theories." *Archiv für Geschichte der Philosophie* 79: 58–79.

Thiel, Udo. 2007. "Zum Verhältnis von Gegenstandsbewußtsein und Selbstbewußtsein bei Wolff und seinen Kritikern." In *Christian Wolff und die Europäische Aufklärung*, edited by Jürgen Stolzenberg, and Oliver-Pierre Rudolph, vol. 2, 377–390. Hildesheim: Olms.

Thiel, Udo. 2014. *The Early Modern Subject. Self-consciousness and Personal Identity from Descartes to Hume*, second edition. Oxford: Oxford University Press.

Thiel, Udo. 2018. "Tetens and Kant on the Unity of the Self." In *Kant and his German Contemporaries. Vol. 1: Logic, Mind, Epistemology, Science and Ethics*, edited by Corey W. Dyck, and Falk Wunderlich, 59–75. Cambridge: Cambridge University Press.

Thiel, Udo. 2019. "The Concept of a Person in Eighteenth-Century German Philosophy: Leibniz – Wolff – Kant." In *Persons. A History*, edited by A. Lolordo, 187–231. Oxford: Oxford University Press, 2019.

Thiel, Udo. 2021. "Experience and Inner Sense: Feder-Lossius-Kant." In *The Experiential Turn in Eighteenth-Century German Philosophy*, edited by Karin de Boer, and Tinca Prunea-Bretonnet, 98–118. New York, London: Routledge.

Thiel, Udo. 2022. "Locke in Göttingen." *Studi Lockiani. Ricerche sull'età moderna* 3: 151–177.

Thomas, Andreas. 2004. "Die Lehre von der moralischen Verbindlichkeit." In *Aufklärung durch Kritik. Festschrift für Manfred Baum zum 65. Geburtstag*, edited by Dieter Hüning, Karin Michel, and Andreas Thomas, 361–380. Berlin: Duncker & Humblot.

Tilliette, Xavier. 1995. *Recherches sur l'intuition intellectuelle, de Kant à Hegel.* Paris: Vrin.

Timmermann, Jens. 2007. *Kant's Groundwork of the Metaphysics of Morals: A Commentary*, Cambridge: Cambridge University Press.

Tonelli. Giorgio. 1959. "Der Streit über die mathematische Methode in der Philosophie in der ersten Hälfte des 18. Jahrhunderts und die Entstehung von Kants Schrift über die 'Deutlichkeit.'" In *Archiv für Philosophie* 9: 37–66.

Tonelli, Giorgio. 1964. "Das Wiederaufleben der deutsch-aristotelischen Terminologie bei Kant während der Entstehung der 'Kritik der reinen Vernunft.'" *Archiv für Begriffsgeschichte* 9: 233–242.

Tonelli, Giorgio. 1969. "Einleitung." In *Christian August Crusius: Die philosophischen Hauptwerke*, vol. 1, VII–LXV. Hildesheim: Olms.

Tonelli, Giorgio. 1976. "Analysis und Synthesis in the XVIIIth Century Philosophy Prior to Kant." In *Archiv für Begriffsgeschichte* 20: 178–213.

Torra-Mattenklott, Caroline. 2002. *Metaphorologie der Rührung. Ästhetische Theorie und Mechanik im 18. Jahrhundert.* München: Fink.

Tumarkin, Anna. 1933. *Der Ästhetiker Johann Georg Sulzer.* Frauenfeld, Leipzig: Huber.

Urban, Astrid. 2004. *Kunst der Kritik. Die Gattung Rezension in den Zeitschriften des späten 18. Jahrhunderts.* Heidelberg: Winter.

Vaihinger, Hans.1881. *Commentar zu Kants Kritik der reinen Vernunft. Zum hundertjährigen Jubiläum derselben*, vol. 1. Stuttgart: Spemann.

van Hoorn, Tanja. 2004. *Dem Leibe abgelesen. Georg Forster im Kontext der physischen Anthropologie des 18. Jahrhundert.* Tübingen: Niemeyer.

van der Zande, Johan. 1995. "In the Image of Cicero: German Philosophy Between Wolff and Kant." *Journal of the History of Ideas* 56: 419–442.

van der Zande, Johan. 1998. "The Microscope of Experience: Christian Garve's Translation of Cicero's De officiis." *Journal of the History of Ideas* 59: 75–94.

van Zantwijk, Temilo, and Paul Ziche. 2000. "Fundamentalphilosophie oder empirische Psychologie? Das Selbst und die Wissenschaften bei Fichte und C.C.E. Schmid." *Zeitschrift für philosophische Forschung* 54: 557–580.

Vesper, Achim. 2006. "Le plaisir de beau chez Leibniz, Wolff, Mendelssohn et Kant." *Revue germanique internationale* 4: 23–36.

Vesper, Achim. 2008. "Lust als 'cognitio intuitiva perfectionis.' Vollkommenheitsästhetik bei Wolff und ihre Kritik durch Kant." In *Christian Wolff und die Europäische Aufklärung*, edited by Jürgen Stolzenberg, and Oliver-Pierre Rudolph, vol. 4, 283–296. Hildesheim: Olms.

Vesper, Achim. 2018. "Durch Schönheit zur Freiheit? Schillers Auseinandersetzung mit Kant (Brief 1 und die Folgen)." In *Friedrich Schiller. Über die ästhetische Erziehung des Menschen in einer Reihe von Briefen*, edited by Gideon Stiening, 33–48. Berlin, Boston: De Gruyter.

Vogt, Wolfgang. 2005. *Moses Mendelssohns Beschreibung der Wirklichkeit menschlichen Erkennens.* Würzburg: Königshausen & Neumann.

Vollhardt, Friedrich. 2001. *Selbstliebe und Geselligkeit. Untersuchungen zum Verhältnis von naturrechtlichem Denken und moraldidaktischer Literatur im 17. und 18. Jahrhundert.* Tübingen: Niemeyer.

von Selle, Götz. 1937. *Die Georg-August-Universität zu Göttingen 1737–1937.* Göttingen: Vandenhoeck & Ruprecht.

Vorländer, Karl. 1992. *Immanuel Kant. Der Mann und das Werk.* Hamburg: Meiner.

Wagner, Hans. 1980. *Philosophie und Reflexion*, third edition. München, Basel: Reinhardt.

Waldron, Jeremy. 2012. *Dignity, Rank & Rights.* Oxford: Oxford University Press.

Waszek, Norbert. 1988. *The Scottish Enlightenment and Hegel's Account of Civil Society.* Dordrecht, Boston, London: Springer.

Watkins, Eric. 2005. *Kant and the Metaphysics of Causality*, Cambridge: Cambridge University Press.

Watkins, Eric, ed. 2009. *Kant's "Critique of Pure Reason" Background Source Materials*, Cambridge: Cambridge University Press.

Weldon, T. D. 1958. *Kant's Critique of Pure Reason*, second edition. Oxford: Clarendon Press.

Wölfel, Kurt. 1987. "Vorrede zu Garves Übersetzungen." In *Christian Garve: Gesammelte Werke*, vol. 9, I–XLIX. Hildesheim: Olms.

Wolff, Hans M. 1949. *Die Weltanschauung der deutschen Aufklärung in geschichtlicher Entwicklung.* München: Lehnen.

Wolters, Gereon. 1980. *Basis und Deduktion. Studien zur Entstehung und Bedeutung der Theorie der axiomatischen Methode bei J. H. Lambert.* Berlin, New York: De Gruyter.

Wreschner, Arthur. 1893. *Ernst Platner und Kant's Kritik der reinen Vernunft mit besonderer Berücksichtigung von Tetens und Aenesidemus.* Leipzig: Pfeffer.

Wunderlich, Falk. 2005. *Kant und die Bewußtseinstheorien des 18. Jahrhunderts*. Berlin, New York: De Gruyter.
Wunderlich, Falk. 2007. "Platners Auseinandersetzung mit David Hume." *Aufklärung, vol. 19: Ernst Platner. Konstellationen der Aufklärung zwischen Philosophie, Medizin und Anthropologie*, edited by Guido Naschert, and Gideon Stiening, 163–180. Hamburg: Meiner.
Wunderlich, Falk. 2012. "Empirismus und Materialismus an der Göttinger Georgia Augusta – Radikalaufklärung im Hörsaal?" In *Aufklärung, vol. 24: Radikale Spätaufklärung in Deutschland. Einzelschicksale – Konstellationen – Netzwerke*, edited by Martin Mulsow, and Guido Naschert, 65–90. Hamburg: Meiner.
Wunderlich, Falk. 2018. "Platner on Kant: From Scepticism to Dogmatic Critique." In *Kant and his German Contemporaries*, edited by Corey W. Dyck, and Falk Wunderlich, 155–171. Cambridge: Cambridge University Press.
Wundt, Max. 1945. *Die deutsche Schulphilosophie im Zeitalter der Aufklärung*. Tübingen: Mohr.
Zammito, John. 2002. *Kant, Herder, and the Birth of Anthropology*. Chicago: University of Chicago Press.
Zantop, Susanne. 1999. *Kolonialphantasien im vorkolonialen Deutschland (1770–1870)*. Berlin: Erich Schmidt.
Zelle, Carsten. 2010. "Encyclopédisme et esthétique. La dimension européenne de Sulzer." In *Ferments d'Ailleurs. Transferts culturels entre Lumières et romantisme*, edited by Denis Bonnecase, 187–212. Grenoble: Ellug.
Zimmerli, Walter Ch. 1983. "'Schwere Rüstung' des Dogmatismus und 'anwendbare Eklektik.' J. G. H. Feder und die Göttinger Philosophie im ausgehenden 18. Jahrhundert." *Studia Leibnitiana* 15: 58–71.
Zocher, Rudolf. 1959. *Kants Grundlehre. Ihr Sinn, ihre Problematik, ihre Aktualität*. Erlangen: Universitätsbund Erlangen e.V.

Index of Names

Albrecht, Michael 282, 306
Allais, Lucy 112
Allison, Henry E. 41, 103, 261, 344
Altmann, Alexander 173, 184
Anderson, R. Lanier 101
Arndt, Hans Werner 220
Aschenberg, Reinhold 105

Bachmann-Medick, Doris 252
Bacin, Stefano 141, 297
Baeumler, Alfred 166
Baier, Annette C. 121
Baillie, James 132
Barruel, Augustin 281
Barth, Roderich 174
Basedow, Johann Bernhard 57, 315, 325
Basso, Paola 147, 192
Batscha, Zwi 281f.
Baum, Manfred 167, 224, 269–271
Baumanns, Peter 1, 3
Baumgarten, Alexander Gottlieb 80, 87, 89, 165–170, 177–180, 182, 218, 220, 225
Beattie, James 315, 325
Beck, Lewis White 2, 239, 262
Beiser, Frederick C. 306f.
Berger, Andreas 95
Bieri, Peter 300
Blackwell, Richard J. 70
Böhr, Christoph 306
Bondeli, Martin 280, 292
Bonnet, Charles 14, 30, 33, 306, 315, 325
Bonnot de Condillac, Étienne 14, 306
Borchers, Stefan 303
Bouterwek, Friedrich 1
Brandes, Ernst 322
Brandhorst, Mario 300
Brandt, Reinhard 132, 136f., 167f., 283, 285, 297
Buchenau, Stefanie 2, 9, 237
Buhle, Johann Gottlieb 331

Campo, Mariano 156
Carboncini, Sonia 147, 221

Carl, Wolfgang 17, 95
Cassirer, Ernst 84, 152, 185, 196
Ciafardone, Raffaele 148
Cicero, Marcus Tullius 122, 237–248, 250–254, 261–263, 265f., 268, 272, 277, 325, 340
Cohen, Hermann 1, 82
Cramer, Konrad 104, 306, 321
Crusius, Christian August 8, 69–83, 85–87, 89–94, 145–163, 217–228, 230, 232f.
Cudworth, Ralph 321, 331–334, 340

Dahlstrom, Daniel O. 2
Darwall, Stephen L. 134
de Boer, Karin 2, 161
de Guiberts, Jacques-Antoine-Hippolyte 285
de Pauw, Cornelius 285
Décultot, Élisabeth 166
Dennett, Daniel C. 340
DeVleeschauwer, H. J. 39
Dörflinger, Bernd 299
Dubos, Jean-Baptiste 173
Dyck, Corey W. 2, 6

Ebbinghaus, Julius 307
Eberhard, Johann August 101f., 220, 262, 264, 284, 315
Edwards, Jeffrey 230
Engfer, Hans-Jürgen 160, 173
Erdmann, Benno 282f., 306
Euler, Leonhard 188, 191
Evans, Gareth 45

Fabianelli, Faustino 114
Feder, Johann Georg Heinrich 8, 57, 103, 119–141, 238f., 261f., 264, 279–303, 305–308, 315f., 321–323, 325, 344
Ferguson, Adam 237f., 241, 244f., 248, 252
Fichte, Johann Gottlieb 68, 82, 97–99, 105, 108, 114–117, 343
Flach, Werner 3, 97, 112
Förster, Eckart 3, 116
Forster, Georg 282, 284, 305f., 308
Frank, Manfred 47, 57, 114

Index of Names

Fricke, Christel 218, 231
Friebe, Cord 102
Friedman, Michael 162 f., 187 f., 192
Fugate, Courtney David 223
Fukuda, Kiichiro 311
Funke, Gerhard 3

Garber, Jörn 296, 303
Garve, Christian 3 f., 8, 103, 205, 215, 237–259, 261–266, 268, 271–280, 285, 299, 307, 321, 331, 340
Gava, Gabriele 99 f.
Gawlick, Günter 6, 121 f.
Gawlina, Manfred 284
Gentz, Friedrich 264, 281
Gerard, Alexander 315, 325
Glinka, Holger 292
Goethe, Johann Wolfgang 295
Goldenbaum, Ursula 306
Graubner, Hans 99, 104, 109
Grunert, Frank 8, 291
Gutiérrez-Xivillé, Ana-Carolina 229, 231
Guyer, Paul 82 f., 100 f., 184, 204, 289, 327

Haag, Johannes 99
Habel, Thomas 283
Hahmann, Andree 1 f., 8 f., 69, 79, 102, 280, 300
Hamann, Johann Georg 17, 101, 239, 262 f., 290
Hanna, Robert 99
Hausius, Karl Gottlob 306
Hegel, Georg Wilhelm Friedrich 2, 82, 101, 248, 289
Heidegger, Martin 1, 82–84, 93
Heidemann, Dietmar H. 101 f., 116
Heimsoeth, Heinz 75, 78
Heinz, Marion 9, 101, 165
Henrich, Dieter 69, 71, 78, 82–84, 86, 177, 217, 225
Heßbrüggen-Walter, Stefan 2, 69 f., 72, 78, 167, 175
Hiltscher, Reinhard 105, 114, 117
Hinske, Norbert 3, 105, 156, 306
Höffe, Otfried 3, 287
Horn, Christoph 211, 297, 342
Hruschka, Joachim 205

Hume, David 32 f., 43 f., 48, 59 f., 68, 119–123, 129–132, 134 f., 140 f., 166, 208–210, 289, 306, 310–312, 315, 324 f., 329, 332, 340 f.
Hüning, Dieter 9, 219, 261, 268, 290, 299
Husserl, Edmund 1

Ilbrig, Cornelia 293
Irrlitz, Gert 290
Irving, Karl Franz von 325

Jakob, Ludwig Heinrich 262, 282, 316, 318
John, Matthias 9, 114, 205, 217
Josifović, Saša 339

Kames, Henry Home, Lord 59
Kang, Ji-Young 290, 292
Karampatsou, Marialena 6
Keller, Pierre 99 f.
Kempe, Michael 293
Kitcher, Patricia 2, 8, 13
Klemme, Heiner F. 9, 203, 205, 208, 213, 216, 225
Klingner, Stefan 1, 8, 97, 99 f., 103, 113, 116 f., 290
Knoblauch, Hubert 282
König, Torsten 285
Kopper, Joachim 3
Kosenina, Alexander 68
Kreimendahl, Lothar 121 f., 229
Kruck, Günter 299
Kuehn, Manfred 2, 122, 126 f., 131, 306

Laermann, Klaus 303
Lambert, Johann Heinrich 8, 156, 165, 185–202, 315, 325
Lange, Joachim 221, 224, 227
Laywine, Alison 186
Lazzari, Alessandro 50, 68, 292
Leclerc de Sept-Chênes, Nicolas-Marie 322
Leibniz, Gottfried Wilhelm 2, 14–16, 25 f., 32, 35, 64, 71, 75, 79, 88 f., 91, 102, 113, 166, 170, 173, 177, 179, 205, 209 f., 300, 312 f., 315, 325, 332, 345
Leroy de Barincourt, Pierre-Paul 285
Levy, Heinrich 84
Lichtenberg, Georg Christoph 287

Locke, John   13–15, 17, 24f., 28, 35, 38, 44f., 47, 55, 66f., 87, 120, 123, 186, 188, 193f., 290, 306, 315, 325, 330, 332
Longo, Mario   306
Losurdo, Domenico   312
Ludwig, Bernd   157, 262, 268, 300, 316

Mackie, John Leslie   24
Maimon, Salomon   95, 240
Malter, Rudolf   306, 317
Marino, Luigi   280, 283, 306
Marti, Hanspeter   283
McDowell, John   97
Meier, Georg Friedrich   170, 176, 178f.
Meiners, Christoph   8, 55f., 279f., 282–289, 292–294, 296f., 299, 301–303, 305–319, 321–344
Melches Gilbert, Carlos   240
Mendelssohn, Moses   26, 146, 165, 170, 178f., 183f., 228, 240–242, 246, 264, 290, 315, 325
Menzer, Paul   217
Messer, August   1
Metzger, Johann Daniel   305f., 309
Meyer, Jürgen Bona   17
Mori, Massimo   209, 290
Motta, Giuseppe   307, 316

Nagl, Ludwig   3
Natterer, Paul   1
Newton, Isaac   159, 161, 188, 190f., 200, 268
Norton, David Fate   126f., 131
Nowitzki, Hans-Peter   49, 280, 284, 306f., 316

Oberhausen, Martin   147
O'Neill, Onora   296

Palme, Anton   166f., 170f.
Pasini, Enrico   192
Paton, Herbert James   1
Patzig, Günther   306, 321
Pauer-Studer, Herlinde   131
Pecere, Paolo   9, 185, 188, 196, 200
Petrus, Klaus   306, 310, 321
Pietsch, Lutz-Henning   282, 306, 308f., 312, 317
Pistorius, Hermann Andreas   305, 308

Platner, Ernst   8, 47–69, 82, 87–90, 94f., 284, 290
Pollok, Konstantin   188
Pöschl, Viktor   248
Pozzo, Ricardo   147
Proß, Wolfgang   166
Prunea-Bretonnet, Tinca   2, 9, 145f.

Rabaut Saint-Étienne, Jean-Paul   322
Rachold, Jan   283
Reich, Klaus   171, 212, 247, 269, 343
Reimarus, Hermann Samuel   64, 315, 325
Reinhard, Franz Volkmar   147, 342
Reinhold, Karl Leonhard   47–52, 56, 60–62, 64, 68, 82, 95, 167, 305, 307f., 316, 318
Rescher, Nicholas   4
Rickert, Heinrich   112
Riedel, Manfred   282
Riedel, Wolfgang   166, 296
Riehl, Alois   112
Riesbeck, Johann Kaspar   284
Rischmüller, Marie   171
Rivero, Gabriel   9, 217, 219, 229
Rosen, Fredrick   131
Rosen, Michael   238
Roth, Udo   280, 284, 307, 316
Röttgers, Kurt   141, 283, 306
Rousseau, Jean-Jacques   243, 248f.
Rüdiger, Andreas   71, 147f.
Rumore, Paola   229

Saint-Pierre, Jacques Henri Bernardin de   285
Saner, Hans   307
Sassen, Brigitte   6, 306
Schelling, Friedrich Wilhelm Joseph von   97–99, 114–117
Schiller, Friedrich   295, 299, 343
Schleiermacher, Friedrich   241
Schmid, Carl Christian Erhard   8, 69, 82, 90–95, 97–99, 105–118, 316
Schmitt, Arbogast   49
Schmitz, Hermann   3
Schmucker, Josef   181, 217f.
Schneewind, Jerome B.   101, 140, 182–184
Schönecker, Dieter   339, 342, 344
Schopenhauer, Arthur   1
Schröer, Christian   267

Index of Names

Schröpfer, Horst   98, 106, 280
Schulze, Gottlob Ernst   48, 103, 284f.
Schwaiger, Clemens   2, 170f., 205, 218, 225, 268
Search, Eduard   30, 315, 325
Selle, Christian Gottlieb   310
Sensen, Oliver   238
Smith, Adam   120, 122, 132, 209f., 332, 335, 340
Stark, Werner   167f., 211, 213–215, 231f., 317
Stern, Albert   240
Stiening, Gideon   8f., 57, 69, 166, 279f., 282, 284, 286, 289f., 293–295, 306f., 316f., 322
Stöckmann, Ernst   172f.
Stolleis, Michael   240
Stolzenberg, Jürgen   303
Sturm, Thomas   101
Sulzer, Johann Georg   8, 56, 146, 165–167, 170–177, 179, 183f., 203–216, 290, 315

Tennemann, Wilhelm Gottlieb   281f.
Tester, Steven   69f., 76, 82
Tetens, Johann Nicolaus   8, 13–45, 60, 82, 170, 264, 325
Thiel, Udo   2, 8, 13, 41, 44, 47, 49f., 54–57, 59, 306
Thoma, Heinz   303
Thomas, Andreas   173, 210, 266, 285
Thomasius, Christian   8, 299
Tiedemann, Dietrich   305, 308
Tilliette, Xavier   115
Timmermann, Jens   240, 265f., 269f., 273, 277, 328
Tittel, Gottlob August   284f., 305f., 308, 316
Tonelli, Giorgio   3, 146f., 152
Torra-Mattenklott, Caroline   173
Tumarkin, Anna   166

Urban, Astrid   286

Vaihinger, Hans   1
van der Zande, Johan   238, 306
van Hoorn, Tanja   303
van Zantwijk, Temilo   114
Vesper, Achim   8, 119, 166, 171, 295
Vogt, Wolfgang   178
Vollhardt, Friedrich   293
von Selle, Götz   283f.
Vorländer, Karl   283, 306

Wagner, Hans   112
Waldron, Jeremy   238
Waszek, Norbert   248
Watkins, Eric   2
Weldon, T. D.   36f., 39
Werdermann, J.G.K.   136
Wezel, Johann Karl   57, 293
Wölfel, Kurt   240
Wolff, Christian   6, 8, 14, 16, 18, 28, 47, 49f., 69–72, 74–77, 80–83, 85, 87f., 90, 92f., 95, 120, 141, 146–149, 152, 154, 162f., 166, 168–173, 175, 177, 179f., 182–184, 192, 205, 209, 212, 217–221, 224f., 227, 265–268, 314, 325
Wolff, Hans M.   267
Wolters, Gereon   185
Wood, Allen   82, 100f., 204, 289, 327, 344
Wreschner, Arthur   48, 60, 64, 67
Wunderlich, Falk   2, 6, 56, 60f., 284, 306, 309, 313
Wundt, Max   1, 283

Zammito, John   2
Zantop, Susanne   285
Zelle, Carsten   166
Ziche, Paul   114
Zimmerli, Walter Ch.   283, 306, 310
Zocher, Rudolf   3

Sources

Andreas Brandt's "Christoph Meiners's Critique of Kant" is the translation of his essay "Meiners' Kant-Kritik," which will be published in *Christoph Meiners (1747-1810): Anthropologie und Geschichtsphilosophie in der Spätaufklärung*, Werkprofile vol. 22, edited by Stefan Klingner, and Gideon Stiening. Berlin, Boston: De Gruyter, 2023 (forthcoming).

Andree Hahmann's "The Debate on the Fundamental Powers of the Soul: Crusius, Platner, Kant, and Schmid" is a revised and further developed version of the following essays: "Die Einbildungskraft eine 'General-Kraft'? Mit Crusius zu den letzten Kräften der Seele" in *Konzepte der Einbildungskraft in der Philosophie, den Wissenschaften und den Künsten des 18. Jahrhunderts*, edited by Rudolf Meer, Giuseppe Motta, and Gideon Stiening, 91–113. Berlin, Boston: De Gruyter, 2019; "Crusius on the Fundamental Powers of the Soul" in *Christian August Crusius (1715-1775): Philosophy between Reason and Revelation*, Werkprofile vol. 11, edited by Frank Grunert, Andree Hahmann, and Gideon Stiening, 89–113. Berlin, Boston: De Gruyter, 2021; and "Schmid über die Grundkräfte der Seele," which will be published in: *Carl Christian Erhard Schmid (1761-1812): Spätaufklärung im Spannungsfeld zwischen Leibniz und Kant*, Werkprofile vol. 24, edited by Marion Heinz, and Gideon Stiening. Berlin, Boston: De Gruyter (forthcoming).

Stefanie Buchenau's "Human Dignity. The Garve-Kant controversy" is the translation of her essay "Menschenwürde. Die Kontroverse zwischen Garve und Kant" in *Christian Garve (1742-1798): Philosoph und Philologe der Aufklärung*, Werkprofile vol. 14, edited by Udo Roth, and Gideon Stiening, Werkprofile vol. 14, 101–126. Berlin, Boston: De Gruyter, 2021.

Marion Heinz's "Johann Georg Sulzer and the Beginnings of Kant's Doctrine of Three Faculties" is the translation of her essay "Johann Georg Sulzer und die Anfänge der Dreivermögenslehre bei Kant" in *Johann Georg Sulzer (1720-1779): Aufklärung zwischen Christian Wolff und David Hume*, Werkprofile vol. 1, edited by Frank Grunert, and Gideon Stiening, 83–100. Berlin: Akademie Verlag, 2011.

Dieter Hüning's "'These Objections are therefore Nothing but Misunderstandings.' Kant's Critique of Garve in his Essay *On the Common Saying*" is the translation of his essay "'Diese Einwürfe sind also nichts als Mißverständnisse.' Kants Garve-Kritik im Gemeinspruchaufsatz" in *Christian Garve (1742-1798): Philosoph und Philologe der Aufklärung*, Werkprofile vol. 14, edited by Udo Roth, and Gideon Stiening, 207–224. Werkprofile vol. 14, Berlin, Boston: De Gruyter, 2021.

Patricia Kitcher's "Analyzing Apperception [*Gewahrnehmen*]" is a slightly modified version of her essay of the same title in *Johann Nikolaus Tetens (1736-1807): Philosophie in der Tradition des europäischen Empirismus*, Werkprofile vol. 6, edited by Gideon Stiening, and Udo Thiel, 103–132. Berlin, Boston: De Gruyter, 2014.

Heiner F. Klemme's "Johann Georg Sulzer's 'Mixed Doctrine of Morals': A Contribution to the History of the Development of Kant's Ethics Between 1770 and 1785" is a slightly modified version, translated by John Walsh, of his essay "Johann Georg Sulzers 'vermischte Sittenlehre.' Ein Beitrag zur Vorgeschichte und Problemstellung von Kants *Grundlegung zur Metaphysik der Sitten*" in *Johann Georg Sulzer (1720-1779): Aufklärung zwischen Christian Wolff und David Hume*, Werkprofile vol. 1, edited by Frank

Grunert, and Gideon Stiening, 309–322. Berlin: Akademie Verlag, 2011, and in *Metaphysik, Ethik, Ästhetik. Beiträge zur Interpretation der Philosophie Kants*, edited by Antonino Falduto, Karoline Kolisang, and Gabriel Rivero, 91–106. Würzburg: Königshausen & Neumann, 2012.

Stefan Klingner's "C. C. E. Schmid on Kant's Distinction between Sensibility and Understanding" is the translation of his essay "Kants Unterscheidung von Sinnlichkeit und Verstand bei C. C. E. Schmid," which will be published in *Carl Christian Erhard Schmid (1761–1812): Spätaufklärung im Spannungsfeld zwischen Leibniz und Kant*, Werkprofile vol. 24, edited by Marion Heinz, and Gideon Stiening. Berlin, Boston: De Gruyter (forthcoming).

Rudolf Meer's "'On this Occasion, I cannot but … speak a few words with Mr. Kant.' On the Meiners-Kant Controversy 1786" is the translation of his essay "'Bey dieser Gelegenheit kann ich nicht umhin […] einige Worte mit Herrn Kant zu reden.' Die Meiners-Kant-Kontroverse," which will be published in *Christoph Meiners (1747–1810): Anthropologie und Geschichtsphilosophie in der Spätaufklärung*, Werkprofile vol. 22, edited by Stefan Klingner, and Gideon Stiening. Berlin, Boston: De Gruyter, 2023 (forthcoming).

Paolo Pecere's "Lambert, Kant, and Solidity: a Matter of Method" was first published in *Johann Heinrich Lambert (1728–1777): Wege zur Mathematisierung der Aufklärung*, Werkprofile vol. 16, edited by Hans-Peter Nowitzki, Enrico Pasini, Paola Rumore, and Gideon Stiening, 211–230. Berlin, Boston: De Gruyter, 2022.

Tinca Prunea Bretonnet's "Crusius and Kant on Distinctness, Certainty, and Method in Philosophy" is the revised and translated version of her essay "Crusius et la certitude en 1763" in *Astérion* 9/2011 and was first published in *Christian August Crusius (1715–1775): Philosophy between Reason and Revelation*, Werkprofile vol. 11, edited by Frank Grunert, Andree Hahmann, and Gideon Stiening, 21–40. Berlin, Boston: De Gruyter, 2021.

Gabriel Rivero's "Dependence and Obedience. Crusius' Concept of Obligation and its Influence on Kant's Moral Philosophy" is a slightly modified version of his essay of the same title in *Christian August Crusius (1715–1775): Philosophy between Reason and Revelation*, Werkprofile vol. 11, edited by Frank Grunert, Andree Hahmann, and Gideon Stiening, 301–318. Berlin, Boston: De Gruyter, 2021.

Gideon Stiening's "The 'Entire Human Being' Rather Than 'Pure Reason.' Feder's *Philosophische Bibliothek* and His Review of the *Kritik der praktischen Vernunft*" is the translation of his essay "'Ganzer Mensch' statt 'reiner Vernunft.' Feders Zeitschriftenprojekt *Philosophische Bibliothek* und seine Rezension der *Kritik der praktischen Vernunft*" in *Johann Georg Heinrich Feder (1740–1821): Empirismus und Popularphilosophie zwischen Wolff und Kant*, edited by Hans-Peter Nowitzki, Udo Roth, and Gideon Stiening, 209–34. Berlin, Boston: De Gruyter.

Udo Thiel's "Between Empirical Psychology and Transcendental Philosophy: Ernst Platner on the Feeling of Self" is a revised version of his essay "Das 'Gefühl Ich.' Ernst Platner zwischen Empirischer Psychologie und Transzendentalphilosophie" in *Aufklärung, vol. 19: Ernst Platner. Konstellationen der Aufklärung zwischen Philosophie, Medizin und Anthropologie*, edited by Guido Naschert, and Gideon Stiening, 139–161. Hamburg: Meiners, 2007.

Achim Vesper's "Between Hume and Kant: The Foundation of Morality in Feder's *Inquiries on the Human Will*" is the translation of his essay "Zwischen Hume und Kant: Moralbegründung in Feders *Untersuchungen über den menschlichen Willen*" in *Johann Georg Heinrich Feder (1740–1821): Empirismus und Popularphilosophie zwischen Wolff und Kant*, edited by Hans-Peter Nowitzki, Udo Roth, and Gideon Stiening, 141–166. Berlin, Boston: De Gruyter, 2018.

www.ingramcontent.com/pod-product-compliance
Lightning Source LLC
Chambersburg PA
CBHW032055230426
43662CB00035B/365